BARBARIANS AND POLITICS
AT THE COURT OF ARCADIUS

The Transformation of the Classical Heritage
Peter Brown, General Editor

I   *Art and Ceremony in Late Antiquity*, by Sabine G. MacCormack

II   *Synesius of Cyrene: Philosopher-Bishop*, by Jay Alan Bregman

III *Theodosian Empresses: Women and Imperial Dominion in Late Antiquity*, by Kenneth G. Holum

IV   *John Chrysostom and the Jews: Rhetoric and Reality in the Late Fourth Century*, by Robert L. Wilken

V   *Biography in Late Antiquity: The Quest for the Holy Man*, by Patricia Cox

VI   *Pachomius: The Making of a Community in Fourth-Century Egypt*, by Philip Rousseau

VII *Change in Byzantine Culture in the Eleventh and Twelfth Centuries*, by A. P. Kazhdan and Ann Wharton Epstein

VIII *Leadership and Community in Late Antique Gaul*, by Raymond Van Dam

IX   *Homer the Theologian: Neoplatonist Allegorical Reading and the Growth of the Epic Tradition*, by Robert Lamberton

X   *Procopius and the Sixth Century*, by Averil Cameron

XI   *Guardians of Language: The Grammarian and Society in Late Antiquity*, by Robert A. Kaster

XII *Civic Coins and Civic Politics in the Roman East, A.D. 180–275*, by Kenneth Harl

XIII *Holy Women of the Syrian Orient*, introduced and translated by Sebastian P. Brock and Susan Ashbrook Harvey

XIV *Gregory the Great: Perfection in Imperfection*, by Carole Straw

XV   Apex Omnium: *Religion in the* Res gestae *of Ammianus*, by R. L. Rike

XVI *Dioscorus of Aphrodito: His Work and His World*, by Leslie S. B. MacCoull

XVII *On Roman Time: The Codex-Calendar of 354 and the Rhythms of Urban Life in Late Antiquity*, by Michele Renee Salzman

XVIII *Asceticism and Society in Crisis: John of Ephesus and the* Lives of the Eastern Saints, by Susan Ashbrook Harvey

XIX *Barbarians and Politics at the Court of Arcadius*, by Alan Cameron and Jacqueline Long

BARBARIANS AND POLITICS AT THE COURT OF ARCADIUS

ALAN CAMERON
JACQUELINE LONG
WITH A CONTRIBUTION BY LEE SHERRY

UNIVERSITY OF CALIFORNIA PRESS
Berkeley • Los Angeles • Oxford

University of California Press
Berkeley and Los Angeles, California

University of California Press, Ltd.
Oxford, England

Library of Congress Cataloging-in-Publication Data

Cameron, Alan.
 Barbarians and politics at the Court of Arcadius / Alan Cameron
and Jacqueline Long ; with a contribution by Lee Sherry.
     p.   cm. — (The Transformation of the classical heritage ; 19)
 Includes bibliographical references (p.   ) and index.
 ISBN 0-520-06550-6 (cloth : alk. paper)
     1. Synesius, of Cyrene, Bishop of Ptolemais.   2. Synesius, of
Cyrene, Bishop of Ptolemais.   De providentia.   3. Arcadius, Emperor
of the East, 377?–408, in fiction, drama, poetry, etc.   4. Byzantine
Empire—History—Arcadius, 395–408—Historiography.   5. Byzantine
Empire—Politics and government—To 527.   6. Byzantine Empire in
literature.   7. Authors, Greek—Biography.   8. Goths
—Historiography.   9. Goths in literature.   10. Allegory.   I. Long,
Jacqueline.   II. Sherry, Lee.   III. Title.   IV. Series.
PA4441.S9C36   1993
949.5'01'072—dc20   91-16486
                                                                              CIP

Printed in the United States of America
9 8 7 6 5 4 3 2 1

To the memory of our fathers

Allister Douglas Cameron
4 June 1908 – 4 December 1990

George Arnold Long
12 November 1920 – 3 June 1985

CONTENTS

Preface   ix
Chronological Table   xi

1 • Introduction   1

2 • Synesius of Cyrene   13

    I.   Family   13
    II.   Conversion?   19
    III. Baptism   28
    IV. Orthodoxy   35
    V.   Hypatia   39
    VI. The *Dion*   62

3 • Synesius in Constantinople   71

    I.   The Panhellenion   71
    II.   Paeonius   84
    III. The Date of the Embassy   91

4 • *De regno*   103

    I.   Summary   103
    II.   The Date of the Speech   107
    III. The Antibarbarian Tirade   109
    IV. Aurelian and the Barbarians   121
    V.   Publication   127
    VI. Synesius's Audience   134

5 • *De providentia* and the Ministers of Arcadius   143

    I.   Introduction   143
    II.   Summary   144
    III.   Collegiate Prefectures   149
    IV.   Aurelian's Consulate   161
    V.   Typhos   175
    VI.   The Restoration of Osiris   182
    VII. The Fall of Typhos   191

6 • *De providentia* and the Barbarians   199

    I.   The Massacre   199
    II.   Gaïnas and Tribigild   223
    III.   Aurelian's Return   233
    IV.   Fravitta   236

7 • Literary Sources of *De providentia*   253

    I.   Introduction   253
    II.   Egyptian Sources   254
    III.   Dio Chrysostom   265
    IV.   Panegyric and Invective   271
    V.   Neoplatonic Themes   281
    VI.   Oracles and Apocalypse   290

8 • Barbarians and Politics   301

    I.   Greeks and Romans   301
    II.   Political Exploitation of the Myth   311
    III.   Caesarius and the Exculpation of Gaïnas   316
    IV.   Anti-Germanism in Action   323
    V.   Conclusions   333

9 • Translation of *De providentia*   337

    Appendix I: Aurelian and Pulcheria   399
    Appendix II: Chrysostom's Movements
        in 400–402   405
    Appendix III: Synesius's Visit to Athens   409
    Bibliography   413
    Index   433

PREFACE

In my book on Claudian (Oxford 1970), I announced my intention of investigating Synesius's *Egyptian Tale*. This plan I soon abandoned, and it was not rekindled until 1983, when my friend Tim Barnes sent me the first draft of an article that eventually appeared in *Greek, Roman and Byzantine Studies* for 1986. I was moved to strong disagreement and sent him a list of comments longer than his manuscript. But for that stimulus (and the lively exchange of views that followed, each of us convincing the other on some key points), this book would never have been written.

Soon after, I gave a graduate seminar on the text, at which the regular members were Mark Hauser, Robert Lamberton, Jacqueline Long, Lee Sherry, and Glen Thompson. The original plan, soon superseded, was to publish an annotated translation with brief historical introduction. The translation and commentary were compiled by members of the seminar, and subsequently revised (and the commentary expanded) by Sherry, Long, and myself. The bulk of the narrative was written by myself, with Long contributing chapters 3.II, 4.VI, and all of 7 save the concluding section on apocalypse. Long also made many contributions to and criticisms of the rest of the manuscript. I took final responsibility for the narrative, and Long took responsibility for the translation.

Valuable criticisms by Peter Brown, Hal Drake, and Bob Kaster led to a better articulation of the argument. Wilbur Knorr kindly showed me a chapter of his then-unpublished book, *Studies in Ancient and Medieval Geometry* (Boston 1990). We are grateful to Wolf Liebeschuetz for an advance view of his *Barbarians and Bishops* (Oxford 1990), but though we have added a few references to the book, most of our references to his work on Synesius remain to the earlier articles on which the book is based. We would also like to acknowledge help or comments of various kinds from Maria Cesa, Garth Fowden, Karin Hult, Debra Nails, François Paschoud, and Alex Tulin.

A. C.
20. xi. 1991
New York City

CHRONOLOGICAL TABLE

ca. 370		Synesius born in Cyrene
390s		Synesius studies in Alexandria under Hypatia
391		destruction of the Serapeum of Alexandria
395	17 January	death of Theodosius I, leaving Roman Empire to Arcadius under Rufinus in the East and to Honorius under Stilicho in the West
	summer	Alaric and Goths ravage Thrace, threaten Constantinople; Stilicho and combined armies engage inconclusively
	27 November	Gaïnas and Eastern armies return to Constantinople, assassinate Rufinus; Caesarius appointed praetorian prefect; Eutropius emerges as power behind Arcadius's throne
396		Alaric and Goths ravage Greece
	summer	Stilicho campaigns inconclusively against Alaric in Greece; Goths continue to ravage Epirus[1]
397	19 January	Arcadius's third quinquennium begins

1. The redating of Stilicho's second expedition to Greece will be argued by Cameron in a forthcoming article.

	13 July– 4 September	Eutychian praetorian prefect
	September	Synesius arrives in Constantinople as Cyrene's ambassador, delivers *stephanotikos logos* (not extant)
397/98	winter	Synesius solicits interest of Paeonius with astrolabe and *De dono*
398	?	Alaric appointed MVM *per Illyricum*
398		Synesius delivers *De regno* (to restricted audience)
398/99		Fravitta appointed MVM *per Orientem*
399	summer	Tribigild and Greuthungi revolt in Phrygia; Eutropius sends armies under Leo against Tribigild and under Gaïnas to guard Hellespont; Leo defeated and killed
	ca. 1 August	Gaïnas has Eutropius deposed and exiled; Aurelian appointed praetorian prefect
	autumn	Eutropius recalled from exile, tried before Aurelian, and executed
400	1 January	Aurelian assumes consulate
	9 January	Eudoxia proclaimed Augusta
	early April	Aurelian, Saturninus, and John exiled by Gaïnas; Caesarius reappointed praetorian prefect
	12 July	Gaïnas leaves Constantinople; massacre of Goths remaining in city
	July	Gaïnas and troops remain near Constantinople; Synesius completes book 1 of *De providentia*
	summer	Gaïnas and troops withdraw into Thrace
	September/ October	Aurelian returns to Constantinople with fellow exiles, receives patriciate, renews consular festivities; Synesius composes book 2 of *De providentia*
	before mid- November	earthquake shakes Constantinople; Synesius escapes; sails to Alexandria
	autumn	Roman forces under Fravitta defeat Gaïnas in Chersonnese
400/1	December/ January	Huns under Uldin defeat and kill Gaïnas, send head to Constantinople

401	1 January	Fravitta assumes consulate
	spring	Synesius returns to Cyrene, baptized there; *Hymn* 1
	18 November	Alaric and Goths invade Italy
402–4		Synesius visits Alexandria, marries; *Hymn* 7
403–4	11 June– 3 February	Eutychian praetorian prefect
404/5		Synesius takes up residence in Cyrene
405	11 June– 10 July	Anthemius praetorian prefect
	?	Hierax secures death of Fravitta
410		Synesius elected bishop of Ptolemais, deliberates six months before accepting, meanwhile travels to Greece
411	after annual paschal letter	Synesius consecrated bishop
413	spring	Synesius dies
414	18 April– 10 May	Monaxius praetorian prefect
	4 July	Pulcheria proclaimed Augusta
	30 November/ 30 December	Aurelian reappointed praetorian prefect
415	March	Alexandrian Christians riot against Jews; Hypatia lynched
ca. 416		Aurelian installs bones of Isaac in martyrion dedicated to Stephen Protomartyr

ONE

INTRODUCTION

The purpose of this book is to reinterpret a famous episode in the reign of the emperor Arcadius—the Gothic rebellion and massacre of A.D. 399–400. The story has been told many times, always the same way. After all, one of our sources was written within months of the climactic events and by an eyewitness, the ambassador Synesius of Cyrene. He cast his story in the form of an edifying fiction, calling it *Egyptians; or, On Providence*. Scholars have always treated it as a thin disguise. They have translated Egyptian kings back into praetorian prefects and Egyptian Thebes back into Constantinople, and with relief passed over Neoplatonic sermonizing. With these adjustments they have credited all the details of Synesius's narrative, simply because he was a contemporary. But eyewitnesses do not always see clearly—or tell the truth.

The crisis was sprung by a combination of several tensions developing in the later Roman Empire. Arcadius's father, Theodosius I, had effected important transitions. In the wake of Valens's disastrous defeat by the Visigoths at Adrianople (378), Theodosius signed a treaty allowing Goths to settle in Roman territory under their own laws and chieftains. He outlawed both heresy (381) and paganism (391–92). Finally, on his unexpected death at Milan in January 395 the empire was divided between his two sons, never to be reunited.

Adrianople devastated the Eastern army that Theodosius inherited.

He could not expect to be able to challenge the Goths in open battle before rebuilding the Roman forces. Permitting the Goths to settle depopulated regions of the empire peacefully bought him much-needed time. Panegyrists like Themistius duly praised Theodosius's diplomatic clemency. Traditionalists deplored his "philobarbarism," though they were unable to propose workable alternatives for restoring Roman affairs.[1] Theodosius encouraged Gothic settlers to enter Roman service individually; Gaïnas and Fravitta, two major actors in the narrative that follows, were among these recruits. Even within the structure of the army, however, the Goths' Arianism prevented full assimilation. And dangerously large numbers of Goths remained grouped together in the Danubian region, free to recreate Gothia inside Romania. Unless supplied with regular subsidies they turned to pillage. Theodosius's military abilities might have been able to contain the situation, had he lived longer. In fact, the moment he was dead the young chieftain Alaric began a career of revolt. For fifteen years he remained a thorn in the Roman side. In 410 he finally sacked Rome itself.

Every emperor since Constantine had accepted the Christian faith, with only the exception of Julian, whose sole reign was brief (361–63). Theodosius's two predecessors as Eastern emperor, Constantius II (337–61) and Valens (364–78), conspicuously favored the Church.[2] Most Christian emperors discouraged but tolerated paganism. Theodosius broke off this tolerance. In 391–92 he issued a series of laws banning all forms of pagan worship. He forbade incense burning as well as animal sacrifice, in private as well as in public.[3] This must be borne in mind when assessing the widespread modern belief that the Eastern court at the turn of the fifth century was led by a band of intellectuals sympathetic to paganism.

Constantius and Valens both actively supported Arianism, giving it an edge over Catholicism in the competition for the devotion of the East. Theodosius reversed this trend. From as early as 380 he issued a series of ferocious edicts enforcing orthodoxy for all his subjects. The emperor's own words betray his attitude better than any summary of his actions:

> It is Our will that all the peoples who are ruled by the administration of Our Clemency shall practice that religion which the divine Peter the

1. Pavan 1964, with Matthews 1966, 245–46.
2. The best general account is Piganiol 1972.
3. King 1960, 71–86; Lippold 1980, 45–51.

Apostle transmitted to the Romans. . . . The rest, whom We adjudge demented and insane, shall sustain the infamy of heretical dogmas, their meeting places shall not receive the name of churches, and they shall be smitten first by divine vengeance and secondly by the retribution of Our own initiative.[4]

It was not a tolerant age.

Moderns always note 395 as the year in which the Roman Empire was irrevocably divided. Contemporaries could scarcely have noticed or anticipated the significance of this demarcation. The empire had been divided between at least two emperors almost continuously since Diocletian (284–305).[5] Valentinian and Valens ruled West and East respectively from 364. On Valentinian's death in 375 Gratian took over the West; Theodosius was appointed Valens's successor as emperor of the East in 379. It was only during the last four months of his life that Theodosius ruled as sole Augustus over a united empire.[6] There is something disturbingly paradoxical about dating the final division of the empire four months after its final unification.

Since Theodosius had two sons, it was inevitable that sooner or later one would rule the West and the other the East.[7] Nor was it simply the minority of Honorius or the incapacity of Arcadius that precipitated the crisis of the years following 395. With loyal and united ministers the empire had survived child emperors before. But when a pair of *rois fainéants* held separate courts, dividing the empire between them, the dynamics of the system changed.

In the West, the *magister militum* Stilicho claimed that with his dying breath Theodosius had appointed him regent of both his sons.[8] There were no legal provisions for the minority of an Augustus, but Honorius

4. *Cod. Theod.* 16.1.2 (28.ii.380), trans. C. Pharr; see Enßlin 1953; King 1960, 28f.; Lippold 1980, 21f.

5. The exceptions are the sole rules of Constantine (324–37) and Julian and Jovian (361–64).

6. That is to say, sole ruling Augustus; Arcadius and Honorius, though Augusti since 383 and 393 respectively, controlled no territory. For this distinction, see Palanque 1944, 48f., with Cameron in *CLRE* 13–16.

7. Indeed, Theodosius marked his decision between them as early as 389, when he proclaimed Honorius Caesar in Rome. In 394 he left Arcadius in Constantinople and even before his fatal illness summoned Honorius, now Augustus, to Milan, where he clearly intended to leave him as nominal ruler of specified western provinces under the guidance of Stilicho (Cameron 1968a, 265f.). As Mommsen saw (1903, 101), Ambrose referred to this disposition when he said in his funeral oration for Theodosius that his will "de filiis . . . non habebat novum quod conderet" (*De obitu Theod.* 5).

8. On the question of the regency, see Mommsen 1903, 101f. (= 1906, 516f.); Cameron 1968a, 276f., and 1970a, 39f.

was only ten and clearly in need of guidance. Stilicho was on the spot, in command of Theodosius's troops and related to the imperial family by his marriage to Theodosius's adopted daughter. The West had little option but to accept his claims. Not so the East. In civil law *tutela* ceased at the age of fourteen. Gratian had ruled the West at fifteen. Arcadius was eighteen. His ministers too had been installed by Theodosius and enjoyed his authority. It was not so much a question of belief in Stilicho's claims or their legitimacy: Arcadius's ministers, not unnaturally, wanted to play the role of regent themselves, in reality if not in name. The brother emperors were not in competition as the sons of Constantine had been, and their unity remained an ideal acclaimed by all. But the ministers of either emperor stood to lose their own authority if they accepted direction from their opposite numbers. Their rivalry parted the courts.

Among other consequences, this split prevented prompt or united action against Alaric, thereby exacerbating the Gothic danger. Other military crises were exploited by the opposing courts as weapons of rivalry. The Eastern court received the allegiance of Gildo when he led Africa in revolt from the West. Claudian's *In Eutropium* shows that Stilicho temporarily hoped to use the Gothic rebellion of 399 as an excuse to take over the East directly. Both groups of ministers took advantage of their emperors' inaction and doubtless encouraged it. Neither Arcadius nor Honorius ever attempted to exercise any personal control over affairs of state. Themes of late antique panegyric suggest that the two might have been redeemed before popular perception if they had ever led their own armies in the field, but this they also failed to do. Later generations remembered only the stories: that Arcadius could hardly keep his eyes open and Honorius thought of nothing but his chickens. The great Roman tradition of the soldier-emperor died with Theodosius. The political circumstances surrounding Theodosius's death marked out the lines along which power subsequently descended. In the West, Stilicho was the first in a long line of military dictators. In the East, power remained in the hands of civilians.

Contemporaries spoke of these ministers as all-powerful, and modern historians have tended to write of rule from behind the throne. It makes a convenient shorthand, but it oversimplifies the structures of power at the individual courts. No later Roman emperor or chief minister oversaw all the details of his administration, though of course some involved themselves more closely on individual issues (Arcadius and Honorius mark a low point of imperial involvement). The routine government of the empire was conducted by a large and stable bureaucracy divided into separate branches, each presided over by its own head. The heads normally held office for only a few years, but their staffs consisted of permanent civil servants. Policy decisions were reached in the emperor's consistory, at which the bureau heads and other high officials and court favorites presented their various recommendations and points of view. Even when an emperor was pressured into making decisions elsewhere, perhaps by his wife or a favorite eunuch, the decisions might still be challenged in the consistory: for example, by the counts of the sacred or private largesses, who would have to provide any funds required. Even the proposals of powerful prefects might be thwarted by other members of the consistory.[9]

When Theodosius marched against the Western usurper Eugenius in 394, he left his praetorian prefect Rufinus as "guardian" (*epitropos*)[10] of the inexperienced Arcadius. Given Arcadius's age, the relationship must have been intended purely informally, as a seal on Rufinus's authority. When Theodosius died, Rufinus took charge. The main basis of his power was undoubtedly his prefecture. The PPO had long been in effect vice-emperor:[11] though he no longer commanded troops, he had a treasury of his own, was paymaster general of all civil and military employees, and controlled conscription of troops; he appointed provincial governors, sat as a court of final appeal, and ruled with the force of law. Having been *magister officiorum* for nearly five years before reaching the prefecture,[12] Rufinus must have intimately understood the bureaucracy. He must also have picked many key officials on whose loyalty he could count.

Nevertheless, he did not enjoy power long. On 18 November he was lynched by the troops of the barbarian *comes* Gaïnas during a ceremonial reception at which it was later alleged Rufinus was planning to proclaim

9. Jones 1964a, 339–40. Jill Harries draws our attention to Theodosius II, *Nov.* 18, which shows a prefect circumventing financial objections to a proposal of his own prohibiting prostitution in Constantinople. But this is not to say that the members of the consistory ever "acquired sufficient *esprit de corps* to pursue a consistent and independent policy," as Jones rightly emphasized (340); that is to say, the consistory could hardly be described as a government.

10. Eunap. frags. 62, 63; John Ant. frags. 188, 190.

11. PPO is a convenient ancient acronym, P(raefectus) P(raetori)O. As regards the PPO's status as vice-emperor, *Cod. Theod.* 11.30.16 of 331 formally states that the PPO may hold court *vice sacra*, that is to say, in the emperor's stead. For a convenient summary tabulation of the various powers of the PPO, see Levy 1935, 12–14; for more detail, see Jones 1964a, 448–62.

12. On Rufinus's career see *PLRE* I.778–81; Clauss 1980, 197–99.

himself Arcadius's co-emperor. But immediately, as Claudian described it to his Western audience,

> Rufini castratus prosilit heres.
>
> Rufinus's castrated heir leaps forth.
> (*In Eutr.* 2.550)

That is to say, the man who succeeded to Rufinus's position as Arcadius's chief minister was the grand chamberlain Eutropius, a eunuch. Eutropius had been working against Rufinus for some time. Rufinus had planned to marry his own daughter to Arcadius, but Eutropius contrived to interest him in a candidate of his own, Eudoxia, daughter of the Frankish general Bauto. According to Zosimus (5.3), Rufinus had no idea his plans had been foiled until the imperial carriage drew up outside Eudoxia's house instead of his own. This is an early example of the intrigue for which the word Byzantine was to become proverbial. Once Rufinus was dead, Eutropius exercised his influence over Arcadius openly.

Contemporaries perceived Eutropius as wielding virtually absolute power between late 395 and mid-399. The basis of this power was the proximity to the emperor that his position gave him, combined with the ability to control the access of others.[13] But he cannot have found it as easy to control the imperial bureaucracy. He may always have been able to count on Arcadius's support when necessary, but Arcadius did not himself deal with the day-to-day details of administration. What Eutropius needed was allies among the actual administrators. It was the *magister officiorum* Hosius (allegedly a former cook) to whom he turned. The *magister officiorum* was only slightly less powerful than the PPO: he controlled the entire palace staff, including the state police, the palace guards, and embassies both internal and external, and was especially active in religious affairs.[14] Claudian describes the pair holding court:

> considunt apices gemini dicionis Eoae,
> hic coquus, hic leno.
>
> Here they sit, twin rulers of the East,
> he's a cook, he's a pander.
> (*In Eutr.* 2.350–51)

From the legal sources we know that two men held the praetorian prefecture during Eutropius's ascendancy, Caesarius (395–97) and Eu-

---

13. In general see Hopkins 1978, 172–96.
14. See Clauss 1980.

tychian (397–99), consuls respectively in 397 and 398. Were they, like Hosius, Eutropius's creatures? The fact that both returned to the prefecture soon after Eutropius's fall, Caesarius in 400–403, Eutychian in 404–5, does not suggest that either was seriously compromised by holding office under Eutropius. Perhaps Eutropius was able to rely on his personal ascendancy over Arcadius to override the informal influence a PPO could normally count on exercising. He had the *magister officiorum* in his pocket to help neutralize any opposition from the other ministers.[15]

There has been a tendency in recent studies (those of S. Mazzarino, E. Demougeot, and E. P. Gluschanin) to treat all legislation issued during, say, the ascendancy of Eutropius as directly reflecting his personal policies. But no favorite, however influential, could treat the consistory as a rubber stamp. We have to reckon with the likelihood that on particular issues even a Eutropius would find it prudent to acquiesce in being outvoted rather than spend his personal credit on appealing to the emperor. It is anachronistic in any case to suppose that any late Roman politician even attempted to impose a consistent social and economic policy on his administration, and much legislation that he supported in the consistory would have been initiated by others.

Eutropius's real Achilles' heel was in the military sphere, and he took drastic measures to protect it.[16] Of the two generals at court (*magistri militum praesentales*), Stilicho was now in the West, and the other, Timasius, Eutropius had exiled. He also exiled Abundantius, *magister militum* of Illyricum. None of the three were replaced. From 395 to 397 Illyricum was abandoned to the depredations of the renegade Goth Alaric. Eventually Eutropius solved that problem by appointing Alaric himself to the vacant post of MVM in Illyricum.[17]

In effect Eutropius took over the supreme command himself. In 398 he led a successful expedition against the Huns. But ambitious officers denied advancement by this policy naturally were resentful. Chief among these were Gaïnas, unrewarded for his role in the death of Rufinus, and another Goth, the *comes* Tribigild. In 399 Tribigild rebelled in Phrygia, and this time Eutropius decided against taking command himself. Gaïnas was at last given his chance, but with a colleague, Eutropius's protégé Leo. Leo was disastrously defeated; Gaïnas exploited the situation to his

15. The unfounded modern hypothesis that Eutropius divided the prefecture between two men to weaken its power will be discussed more fully in chapter 5.

16. Jones's claim (1964a, 177–78) that the scheme of five Eastern *magistri militum* attested by the *Notitia dignitatum* is the work of Eutropius is not borne out by the other evidence; see Demandt 1970, 726–39; and further below, p. 225 n. 122.

17. MVM = M(agister) V(triusqe) M(ilitiae).

own ends. He wrote to court saying that Tribigild was too strong for him and it would be better to come to terms, Tribigild's terms being that Eutropius be deposed. Unluckily for Eutropius these events coincided with a rift between himself and Eudoxia, who added her protests to those of Gaïnas. Arcadius finally gave way. Eutropius was deposed and sent in exile to Cyprus.

With Eutropius fell Hosius and the PPO Eutychian. No new *magister officiorum* is recorded, but the prefecture went to Aurelian, who had already held the prefecture of Constantinople in 393–94. A few weeks later he had Eutropius recalled from exile, and presided at a tribunal that condemned the eunuch to death. Aurelian's position in subsequent events confirms the obvious implication of Synesius's allegory in *De providentia*, that as praetorian prefect he was now the emperor's chief minister: thanks to its structural importance, the prefecture was able to recover its influence once Eutropius fell. Little else is known of Aurelian's short ministry, but he evidently failed to solve the problem of Gaïnas and Tribigild. Gaïnas wanted legitimation of his command and honors appropriate to his rank and services. In particular, he wanted to be consul, like so many of the great marshals of Theodosius before him.[18] Receiving no satisfaction, he decided to force Arcadius's hand once more. In April 400 he marched to Chalcedon at the head of his army and demanded to see Arcadius there in person. The terrified emperor complied. This time Gaïnas demanded the surrender of Aurelian, together with Saturninus, a veteran general, and John, a favorite of the empress. Arcadius yielded again.

Gaïnas was now master of the situation, but he did not know how to use it. Caesarius was reappointed to the prefecture; Arcadius agreed to designate Gaïnas as consul for the following January. But the presence of his Goths about the city roused apprehension and resentment. Gaïnas responded to the growing tensions by ordering his men to evacuate Constantinople on 12 July. Fear spread that he was planning to sack and burn the city. Panic erupted. In a wild riot, Roman civilians fell on the Goths still within the city walls, burning alive many thousands of Goths in a church where they had fled for asylum.

Once more, Gaïnas did not know what to do. After a few days of unsatisfactory negotiations, he withdrew to Thrace and was declared a public enemy. By this time the MVM *per Orientem*, Fravitta, another Goth, had arrived and was dispatched after him. A sea battle ensued in which Gaïnas was heavily defeated. He retreated to Thrace again, where

---

18. All these points will be justified in detail below.

he was cut off and killed by a band of Huns. Caesarius remained in the prefecture till 403, when he was succeeded briefly by Eutychian (404–5) before the long tenure of Anthemius, who held power till 414.

A dazzling series of poems by Stilicho's propagandist Claudian brilliantly illuminates the rivalry between the courts from the Western side.[19] On the intrigues of the Eastern court we are much less well informed. But it is possible to flesh out the bare bones of the narrative with the testimony of Synesius, a contemporary and participant in these events.[20] His *De regno*, formally an address to Arcadius attacking dependence on barbarians, and *De providentia*, an allegorized account of Gaïnas's coup in 400, have been held to document a bitter struggle between two parties that split the court after the fall of Eutropius. Caesarius is believed to have led a party of barbarophiles, committed to Theodosius's policy of filling the empty Roman legions with barbarians. Opposing them (it is held) were Caesarius's brother Aurelian and the nationalists, who were anxious to reduce this dangerous dependence on unreliable foreigners. Gaïnas's coup of April 400 is said to have been planned by Caesarius, as revenge on his brother for having been preferred to him for the prefecture. But the July massacre revealed the fiercely Roman sentiments of the populace. Thus vindicated, Aurelian was soon recalled to power, and a general purge of barbarians followed. The influential chapter in Otto Seeck's history (1913) is called "The Victory of Anti-Germanism."

This picture rests entirely on a misinterpretation and misdating of Synesius's two works. It was A. Güldenpenning (1885) who first put forward the theory of pro- and anti-German parties; four years later J. B. Bury described this as "perhaps the most valuable part of [Güldenpenning's] work."[21] But it was Seeck who worked the idea out in detail (1894, 1913, 1914), on the basis of a new, unhappily false chronology. Seeck considered that Synesius arrived at Constantinople in 399 and left in 402, that on the fall of Gaïnas in 400 Caesarius was disgraced, and that in 402–4 Aurelian was restored to power and the prefecture and completed the "de-Germanization" of the Eastern empire.

In 1931 K. Zakrzewski broadened the scope of these parties. For him it was not just the barbarian question that divided the court. He claimed that Aurelian was the leader of a nationalist movement that wanted to

19. Fully elucidated by Cameron 1970a; for a more recent attempt to cover the same ground, Döpp 1980.
20. He was not merely an eyewitness, as modern historians like to style him.
21. Bury 1889, 90 n. 1.

restore the empire of the Antonines in every sphere. He identified Synesius as the propagandist of this movement. He also argued that it had a
religious, as well as a political, dimension. The nationalists' creed was
Neoplatonism and, he believed, they were either actively pagan or
nominally Christian, but in any case sympathetic to Hellenism and the
old ways.

These views have dominated later research, notably the important
studies of Mazzarino (1942) and Demougeot (1951). K. Holum (1982)
was skeptical about the pro- and anti-German parties but succumbed to
the idea of a Hellenist party sympathetic to paganism. G. Albert (1984)
was skeptical of both antibarbarian and propagan movements; Gluschanin, reexamining Theodosius's Gothic policy, has also questioned the
antibarbarian thesis. But since neither made any attempt to reexamine
Seeck's chronology or to reconsider *De regno* or *De providentia*, neither
has come any nearer a satisfactory interpretation of Synesius or of the
political situation.

This book attempts to show that Seeck's chronology and interpretation are alike mistaken. The only fixed point in the chronology of Synesius's life and works is the earthquake during which he ended his three-
year stay in Constantinople. Seeck thought he could fix this date to 402,
and so great is his authority in such matters that everyone acquiesced.
But this is one of the rare occasions when Seeck erred. Contemporary
evidence he misunderstood shows that the relevant earthquake must in
fact be dated to 400. As a consequence, both *De regno* and *De providentia*
must be dated two years earlier. Inevitably the events to which they allude have to be differently identified and assessed. Even on the later
date, there is no evidence in *De regno* or elsewhere for pro- and antibarbarian parties. What *De regno* does document is hostility to Eutropius's
handling of the problem of Alaric and Illyricum in 397. *De providentia*
does not describe a "victory of anti-Germanism," since no such victory
was ever won, nor indeed was such a battle ever joined. The barbarian
crisis of these years took a different form. It is not that there was no antibarbarian sentiment; rather, since there was no *pro*-barbarian party,
there was no antibarbarian *party*. Aurelian was not restored to power on
Gaïnas's defeat at the end of 400. There was no purge of barbarians.

Chapters 5–7 provide the first attempt to analyze *De providentia* as a
whole on its own terms, revealing it to be a far more subtle, complex,
and deceitful work than has been appreciated hitherto. The self-con-
sciously enigmatic complexities with which Synesius has wrought it
have misled modern historians to mistake for facts the optimistic inter-

pretations he presented to his contemporaries. We have also included an annotated translation of *De providentia* in chapter 9. We hope thus to facilitate study of a complex work written in extraordinarily difficult Greek. In chapter 4 we discuss *De regno* and its true significance. Chapters 2–3 reassess the Hellenism of Synesius and Aurelian. For all Synesius's enthusiasm for Greek philosophy and culture, he was in fact an orthodox, if unconventional, Christian. Aurelian was the disciple of an ascetic monk and a stern persecutor of heretics.

In short, there emerges an entirely new picture of the crisis of the year 400.

TWO

SYNESIUS OF CYRENE

I. FAMILY

Synesius was born to an old and wealthy local family of Cyrene in the province of Pentapolis perhaps a year or two before A.D. 370.[1] He received his basic education at home, which he followed up in the 390s with several years of study at Alexandria under the celebrated mathematician and philosopher Hypatia, to whom he remained devoted throughout his life. His letters show his lifelong active involvement in the local affairs of Cyrenaica. In particular, he interrupted his philosophical studies for three years to go on an embassy to Constantinople, attempting to secure a reduction of taxes for Pentapolis. While there he became embroiled in national politics—the subject of this book.

---

1. The elaborate recent discussion by D. Roques (1989, 21–36, with full bibliography) reaches the improbably precise result of mid-370, by pressing Synesius's description of himself as πρεσβύτης in *Ep.* 117 after counting himself among the ἄνδρες in *Ep.* 47. Roques dates both letters to the same year, 412, insisting that Synesius must have passed his forty-second birthday between the two letters (see Cameron 1992)! But personal perceptions of old age have nothing to do with arbitrary categories varying from context to context (not that Roques produces any evidence for forty-two marking the onset of old age). For personal perceptions of old age in antiquity, see A. Cameron, *Callimachus and His Critics*, forthcoming, chap. 4. All of Roques's Synesian dates suffer from this exaggerated precision, fixing to weeks letters that others have been unable to fix to within a decade. In addition, his chronology of the early works rests on Seeck's mistaken date of 399–402 rather than 397–400 (justified below) for the embassy. It should be added that Synesius's dates are linked to the equally controversial chronology of Hypatia, on which see R. J. Penella, *Historia* 33 (1984): 126–28. The information on Synesius's family and estates is collected by Coster 1968, 150–52; Goodchild 1976, 239–54; Roques 1987, 136–38.

The two works he wrote during his embassy, the *De regno*, an essay on kingship cast into the form of an address to the emperor, and the *De providentia*, a political allegory in the form of the Egyptian myth of Typhos and Osiris, have long been regarded as our best evidence for the current politics of the Eastern capital. This evidence has traditionally been interpreted on the assumption that Synesius was a pagan at the time of his embassy and only converted to Christianity several years later. J. Bregman's recent study, for example, rests on two axioms—that the Cyrenean local aristocracy was necessarily pagan and that Synesius's great intellectual quest and achievement lay in reconciling Neoplatonism and Christianity.[2]

Yet while the aristocracies of Athens and Rome continued to be substantially pagan into the late fourth century,[3] we are not entitled to make the same assumption about Cyrene. This question has been treated at length in Denis Roques's recent book *Synésios de Cyrène et la Cyrénaïque du Bas-Empire* (Paris 1987)—unfortunately making the opposite assumption: that already by the age of Diocletian paganism had ceased to be an effective force at Pentapolis. Roques gives little indication of the extent to which his confident conclusions are based on the argument from silence—and usually the silence of the same writer, our only literary source for early fifth-century Cyrene: Synesius himself.[4]

For example, while it is true enough that Synesius was apparently more worried as bishop by heretics than by pagans,[5] this was an attitude shared by countless other fourth- and fifth-century Christians. To quote only one example, after his spectacular conversion in mid–fourth-century Rome, the former pagan professor Marius Victorinus devoted the rest of his life to attacking Arianism.[6] Anyone who inferred from his silence that paganism was a spent force in late fourth-century Rome would be making a grave error. The destruction of pagan temples in Cyrene vividly attested by their charred remains cannot (Roques claims) be dated as late as the Theodosian age because Synesius does not mention it. But before becoming a bishop he does not mention Christianity either. Nor is it because such things were a dead issue that he does not

2. Bregman 1982, chap. 1, gives a full account of earlier views on Synesius's alleged passage from paganism to Christianity. On Bregman, see particularly W. Liebeschuetz, *JHS* 104 (1984): 222–23; D. Roques, *REG* 95 (1982): 461–67; and G. Fowden, *CP* 80 (1985): 281–85.

3. For Rome see A. Cameron's forthcoming study *The Last Pagans of Rome;* for Athens, the assumption is based more on the argument from silence (the absence of Christian sources) than is usually recognized: see Fowden 1990, 496f.; Chuvin 1990, passim.

4. "Notre seule et unique source," as Roques himself concedes (1987, 18).

5. Roques 1987, 318.

6. P. Hadot, *Marius Victorinus: Recherches sur sa vie et ses oeuvres* (Paris 1971), passim.

mention them in *De regno*.[7] Why should he? They were not relevant to his purpose. Roques has it both ways here. In another context, he dismisses what Synesius does say in *De regno*, namely, that Cyrene was a city in decline. Or take another of Roques's confident assertions: "De l'histoire du paganisme au IIIe siècle ni les textes, ni les inscriptions, ni les monuments ne gardent le souvenir."[8] This claim may seem less significant when it is realized that the same is true of the history of Christianity in third-century Pentapolis. It is true that Pentapolis was already rich in bishoprics by the early fourth century;[9] on the other hand "the overwhelming majority of the known churches in . . . Cyrenaica are of the sixth century."[10] Roques naturally appeals to C. Lepelley's magisterial demonstration that the cities of late Roman North Africa were more prosperous than is usually thought. But it is the incomparably richer documentation from the North African cities—literary, epigraphic, and archaeological—that allows such a picture to be drawn. And even so it is not a simple picture. We now know that Christianity made early strides in North Africa and that there were a great many churches and bishoprics by the fourth century.[11] Lepelley has been able to document a sharp decline in public works on pagan temples, statues, and the like.[12] But we also know that there was a vigorous pagan resistance well into the fifth century.[13]

Roques may be right. There may have been very few pagans left in late fourth-century Pentapolis. But the evidence he cites comes nowhere near establishing even a probability. "Rien n'indique" gets us nowhere when there is no evidence either way. It would be satisfying to be able to set Synesius in the context of the Cyrenean society of his age. In the absence of evidence all we can do is treat him as representative of that society, while remaining uncomfortably aware that so eccentric a figure cannot be anything of the sort.

But if we cannot locate Synesius's peers, perhaps we can at least find

7. Roques 1987, 321.

8. Roques's dismissal of the facts about Cyrene stated in *De regno*: "Ces déclarations, tenues dans un discours officiel, sont exagérées. . . . La 'ruine' de la Cyrénaïque du IVe siècle s'avère ainsi, à bien comprendre Synésios, non matérielle, mais exclusivement spirituelle" (1987, 31–32); for his confident assertion, quoted, 1987, 318.

9. A. H. M. Jones, *Cities of the Eastern Roman Provinces*, 2d ed. (Oxford 1971), 498 n. 17; Roques 1987, 317–41.

10. J. B. Ward-Perkins, "Recent Work and Problems in Libya," *Actas del VIII Congreso Internacional de Arqueologia Cristiana, Barcelona, 4–11 Octubre 1969* 1 (Barcelona and Rome 1972), 232–33.

11. W. H. C. Frend, *The Donatist Church*, 3d ed. (Oxford 1985).

12. *Les cités de l'Afrique romaine au Bas-Empire*, vol. 1 (Paris 1979), 345f.

13. "La suppression autoritaire de l'exercise public du paganisme n'empêchait nullement de nombreux Africains du lui rester fidèles" (Lepelley 1979, 355f.).

his house. An elegant townhouse has been excavated in the center of Cyrene, with a central peristyle surrounded by columns.[14] No coins later than Constantius II (337–61) have been found there, suggesting that it was destroyed in the earthquake that ravaged Cyrene in 365.[15] Yet a series of mosaic inscriptions makes it clear that the owners were Christian.[16]

One of these inscriptions mentions a certain Hesychius, a Libyarch. Another inscription from the area commemorates the same man as a *ktistes*, that is to say, a major civic benefactor. R. G. Goodchild and Joyce Reynolds identified him with a correspondent of Synesius who was governor of Libya early in the fifth century,[17] but this prominence comes much too late for him to have been the owner of a house destroyed in 365.[18] It might be added that in *Ep.* 93 Synesius says that he and his friend Hesychius were brought together by "holy geometry," that is to say, in the lecture room of Hypatia.[19] If Synesius first met Hesychius as a student in Alexandria, this implies that he had not met him earlier; namely, that he was *not* (as often assumed) a native Cyrenean.[20] A much more attractive identification has recently been suggested by W. Liebeschuetz: Synesius's own father Hesychius.[21]

Synesius's seventh hymn (= 8), a prayer for his whole family, commends himself, his brother, his two sisters, and, as he sums up, "the entire house of the Hesychidai to the protection of the deity" (31). It follows that their father was called Hesychius.[22] The inference is strengthened by the fact that Synesius called his own firstborn Hesychius.[23] It is clear that Synesius came from one of the few local families with the wealth to hold the expensive honor of the Libyarchy and own such a

14. R. G. Goodchild, *Kyrene und Apollonia* (Zurich 1971), 89–90, with plates 31–32.
15. Goodchild 1971, 44–45, 89.
16. For the inscriptions, see Joyce Reynolds, *JRS* 49 (1959): 100–101; *JTS* 11 (1960): 286–87 (= *SEG* XVII, 745–46).
17. Synesius says that his office was "new in both name and function" (*Ep.* 93), whence Roques argues that he was a *defensor civitatis*, and so probably Cyrenean. But the *defensor* was *not* new in the early fifth century (Jones 1964a, 144–45), and *PLRE* II.553 offers a much more satisfactory explanation.
18. So already *PLRE* II.553.
19. τῆς ἱερᾶς γεωμετρίας ἀλλήλοις ἡμᾶς μνηστευσάσης. p. 155.5 Garzya; the metaphor clearly implies that this was their first meeting.
20. Although Lacombrade describes Hesychius as "issu comme Synésios d'une des plus nobles familles de la Pentapole" (1951a, 50–51; so too Roques 1987, 206), nothing in the only letter to mention him justifies the assumption.
21. Liebeschuetz 1985b, 159. This identification is still possible even if, as some believe (S. Stucchi, *L'architettura cirenaica* [Rome 1975], 490; Roques 1987, 211), the Hesychius inscriptions date from after, rather than before, the quake of 365.
22. So first P. Maas, *Philologus* 72 (1913): 451 (= *Kleine Schriften* [Munich 1973], 175).
23. *PLRE* II.553, no. 4.

house. We may doubt whether there were two men called Hesychius answering to this description in impoverished mid–fourth-century Cyrene.[24] Very probably the house was Synesius's father's, and he abandoned it after the destruction of the earthquake in favor of an estate more in the country. The dates would fit nicely: Synesius could just have been born in the house.

Synesius's seventh hymn begins with ten lines on his beloved younger brother Evoptius,[25] recently and unexpectedly recovered from a serious illness. The next two lines have been seriously misinterpreted in the past. The MSS present

$$\gamma\nu\omega\tau\grave{\alpha}\nu \ \tau\epsilon \ \sigma\upsilon\nu\omega\rho\acute{\iota}\delta\alpha$$
$$\tau\epsilon\kappa\acute{\epsilon}\omega\nu \ \tau\epsilon \ \phi\upsilon\lambda\acute{\alpha}\sigma\sigma\omega\iota\varsigma.$$

This text appears to mean "And may you keep safe my sister and the [her?, my?] pair of children." It poses several problems. First, Synesius had two sisters. No one since 1907 has hesitated to print Wilamowitz's correction $\gamma\nu\omega\tau\hat{\alpha}\nu$ (Doric genitive plural), giving a pair of sisters. But that creates another problem: how do we interpret $\tau\epsilon\kappa\acute{\epsilon}\omega\nu$? The traditional assumption is that $\sigma\upsilon\nu\omega\rho\acute{\iota}\delta\alpha$ governs both $\gamma\nu\omega\tau\hat{\alpha}\nu$ and $\tau\epsilon\kappa\acute{\epsilon}\omega\nu$: two sisters *and* two children. That gives rise to yet another question: whose children? For the early editors and biographers, Synesius's children and the poem dated from 411/12, when he was already a bishop. But this assumption creates yet more problems. For Synesius had three children, first one son and then twin sons.[26] To be sure they died in succession, so that there was a moment when he had only two. But *Ep.* 70 implies that all three died within the space of a year, and *Ep.* 89 that the first two died in quick succession.[27] Synesius says nothing about the cause of these deaths, but it is difficult to doubt that they were connected: perhaps some infectious disease. When he describes his brother's recovery from illness in such detail (19–28), it is difficult to believe that he would have disposed so briefly and casually of his two remaining sons after the recent death of his firstborn. Even if the first did not die of an infection that threatened his brothers, we should certainly expect a father who had just lost his firstborn to address a more heartfelt and anx-

24. Roques (1987, passim and esp. 15–52), with considerable exaggeration, attempts to expose as a "myth" the traditional picture of Synesius's Cyrene as a city in decline.

25. Not his older brother, as sometimes supposed: rightly Roques 1987, 131.

26. Roques (1989, 37–45) reaches his usual overly precise dates for the births of Synesius's three children (mid-November 404; early September 405).

27. Cf. too Lacombrade 1951a, 269–70.

ious prayer to the deity on behalf of those that remained to him. Instead
he links them with two sisters who were evidently less close to him than
his brother. Furthermore, he continues with a prayer for his wife that
deserves quotation:

> Beneath your hand protect also[28] the partner of my marriage bed, free
> of illness and harm, faithful, of one mind with me. Keep my wife in
> ignorance of clandestine associations. May she keep my bed holy, un-
> sullied, pious, inaccessible to unlawful desires.

This is a decidedly curious prayer for a man to make on behalf of a woman
married to him for ten years and the mother of three sons. It seems rather
the prayer one would make (if at all) at the beginning of a marriage. Most
men set great store on having a son, especially men like Synesius who
are very conscious of a family line stretching back over the centuries. It is
hard to believe that Synesius devoted ten lines to his brother, nine to his
wife, and only one to his two surviving sons, without even a word for
his poor dead firstborn. Nor is there any obvious reason for him to link
his sons to his two sisters rather than to his own wife.

Ch. Lacombrade suggested that the children are those of Synesius's
sisters. One, whose name is unknown, was married to a certain Amelius
and had a daughter; the other, Stratonice, was at any rate married.[29] For
Lacombrade, they had a pair of children between them: "Mes deux
soeurs et leurs deux enfants, protège-les." But even supposing that Synesius's sisters did have two children between them, the expression is
curiously artificial. Moreover, it raises the question of why Synesius
should have mentioned his sister's children but not Evoptius's son
Dioscurius,[30] who actually lived with Synesius ca. 405 and of whom he
was very fond (*Ep.* 53 = 55 Garzya [hereafter G]).

A simple repunctuation solves all problems. Remove the stops at the
end of lines 30 and 32; add stops at the end of lines 31 and 36:

$$\begin{aligned}
&\gamma\nu\omega\tau\hat{\alpha}\nu \ \tau\epsilon \ \sigma\upsilon\nu\omega\rho\acute{\iota}\delta\alpha \\
&\tau\epsilon\kappa\acute{\epsilon}\omega\nu \ \tau\epsilon \ \phi\upsilon\lambda\acute{\alpha}\sigma\sigma\omicron\iota\varsigma \qquad\qquad 30 \\
&\acute{\omicron}\lambda\omicron\nu \ \ \dot{\rm H}\sigma\upsilon\chi\iota\delta\hat{\alpha}\nu \ \delta\acute{\omicron}\mu\omicron\nu. \\
&\dot{\upsilon}\pi\grave{\omicron} \ \sigma\hat{\alpha} \ \chi\epsilon\rho\grave{\iota} \ \kappa\rho\acute{\upsilon}\pi\tau\omicron\iota\varsigma \\
&\kappa\alpha\acute{\iota}^{31} \ \mu\omicron\iota \ \zeta\upsilon\gamma\acute{\iota}\omega\nu, \ \ \acute{\alpha}\nu\alpha\xi,
\end{aligned}$$

---

28. This translation presupposes the new punctuation of the entire passage proposed below.

29. Lacombrade 1956, 67–72; 1978a, 91 n. 2.

30. Given wrongly as Dioscorus in *PLRE* II.367, no. 1.

31. This καί will now have to be translated as *etiam* rather than as *et*, a particularly
common usage in Synesius, as illustrated by the helpful *indices verborum* to the editions of
Terzaghi, dell'Era, and Lacombrade.

ξυνήονα δεμνίων,
ἀπόνουσον, ἀπήμονα,   35
ἐρίηρον, ὁμόφρονα.
κρυφίων ἀδαήμονα
ὀάρων ἄλοχον σάου·
ὅσιον δ᾽ ἐφέποι λέχος
πανακήρατον, εὐαγές,   40
ἀδίκοις ἄβατον πόθοις.

Guard my two sisters, and the whole house of the children of Hesychius. Beneath your hand protect also the partner of my marriage bed, free of illness and harm, faithful, of one mind with me. Keep my wife in ignorance of clandestine associations. May she keep my bed holy, unsullied, pious, inaccessible to unlawful desires.

Those problematic children have now vanished. Or rather, it is Synesius himself and his three siblings who together make up the children of Hesychius. Having disposed of the house of Hesychius, Synesius then moves on to his own house, which at this stage consists only of himself and his wife. In fact the poem was surely written for the occasion of his marriage. Synesius presumably married during his second long stay in Alexandria, for he notes that the patriarch Theophilus presided at the ceremony (*Ep.* 105). The assumption that Synesius did not leave Constantinople till late 402, during an earthquake hitherto assigned to that year, would date the marriage to 403/4. But both the quake and Synesius's departure must be moved back to the autumn of 400, so that 402 or even 401 is equally possible.[32]

Modern readers have always stressed the strong Neoplatonic coloring of all Synesius's hymns as evidence of his pagan leanings.[33] In this connection, and especially given the early date for *Hymn* 7, it is noteworthy that though it lacks any specifically Christian language or doctrine, the poem is unmistakably Christian (cf. line 5, "illustrious scion of a virgin").

II. CONVERSION?

From 404/5 on, Synesius seems to have lived more or less continuously on his beloved estates, devoting his leisure to philosophy but when necessary taking an active role in repelling the barbarians whose attacks were to plague Cyrenaica almost every year. In 410 he was sud-

32. Cameron 1987, 346–47.
33. See section III below.

denly offered the bishopric of Ptolemais.[34] After deliberating for six months, he eventually agreed, and as he had feared, he was at once overwhelmed with the responsibilities of his new office. The man who preferred to spend his days in philosophic contemplation was obliged to end them fighting corrupt governors, barbarians, and heresy. These various struggles lost him many of his former friends, and he seems to have died, in or soon after 412, a sad and lonely man.[35]

The evidence discussed so far suggests that Synesius was born a Christian. But it has never commanded the same attention as the famous *Ep.* 105 in which he airs the three problems that caused him to hesitate about the bishopric: the origin of the soul, the eventual destruction (but not the creation) of the world, and the resurrection. To Bregman, as to most scholars before him, these doubts have suggested that Synesius did not accept fundamental Christian doctrine: therefore he was a pagan. His close association with the pagan philosopher Hypatia has also weighed heavily in this reckoning. But in the words of H.-I. Marrou, Synesius's concerns are "precisely the problems to which the Christian thinkers who followed Synesius in the Alexandrian tradition of Neoplatonism were to devote their most important works."[36] Synesius did not positively disbelieve in the resurrection: rather, he remarked, "As for the resurrection *such as common belief admits it*, I see here an ineffable mystery, and I am far from sharing the views of the vulgar crowd on the subject." Synesius would not be the last good Christian to have qualms about literal belief in the resurrection. And as a serious academic philosopher, he feared that in a public airing the untrained intellects of the common people could only confuse ineffable mysteries.

But the point at issue is not whether Synesius was a *good* Christian before he became a bishop, but whether he was ever a pagan. It is important not to let his theological doubts obscure the important evidence of what the letter does *not* say. For example, there is no suggestion that Synesius's doubts might disqualify him from being considered a Chris-

34. For the controversy about the date, see Liebeschuetz 1986b, 180–83; and Barnes 1986b, 33 (supporting 407); for a further argument in favor of 410, see appendix 3. The latest study, Roques 1989 (26; cf. 47–64), dates Synesius's election to the beginning of Lent in 411 because *Ep.* 14 refers to Lent and displays new "Christian charity" toward the horse thief Synesius arraigned in *Ep.* 6. Roques thus violates his own principles (cf. 14) by subjectively assessing "Christian" language as a basis for chronology, and quite ignores the more important change in Synesius's circumstances: in *Ep.* 6 he was frustrated by attempts to catch a thief, and in *Ep.* 14 the thief was in his control and crying penitently for mercy.

35. Roques 1989, 247.

36. Marrou 1963, 147–48.

tian, just from being a bishop. It is also significant, as Marrou pointed out, that he does not raise the objection that he had not been baptized.[37]

Synesius was very close to his brother, to whom he addressed more of his letters than to anyone else. It is in these if anywhere that we might have expected to find some hint of the "conversion" that is so much discussed in the modern literature; "yet there is no trace in his very personal works of any crisis or change in his faith; he did not go through the spiritual turmoils of his contemporary, Augustine of Hippo."[38] It is not surprising that it should have been to his brother that Synesius addressed the fullest statement of his doubts. But it is also significant in a different way that it was to his brother that he addressed what was obviously intended to be an open letter to the entire Christian community. Evoptius must have been a respected member of that community. Indeed, he may well be the Evoptius who was bishop of Ptolemais in 431, having succeeded to the see on his brother's untimely death.[39] The brothers would have been raised as Christians together.[40]

Synesius's theological objections have always attracted attention, but it is important not to overlook the rest of the letter. To start with, it is above all things as frank a statement of Synesius's doubts as could well be imagined. He lays down the terms on which he will accept the see. He will not preach on dogmas he does not believe. He refuses once and for all to separate from his wife.[41] He would rather not give up his hunt-

37. Marrou 1952, 477; on the question of Synesius's baptism, see below, section III.
38. Young 1983, 170.
39. Lacombrade 1951a, 19–20; *PLRE* II.422.
40. Synesius in *Ep.* 8 to Evoptius emphasizes that they were "born of the same parents, brought up together and have had our education in common. Everything has combined to unite us in every way." Seeck (1894, 465), followed by Lacombrade (1951a, 17 n. 32) disputes the address of *Ep.* 8 "to his brother" because Synesius describes their common parentage in a negative conditional clause. But the sentence permits reading it as contrary to fact ("even if we had not been born of the same parents . . .") as easily as the simple condition Seeck presumes ("even if we were not born . . ."), and no other individual to whom Synesius is so closely bound appears in the letters. Roques (1989, 164) rightly accepts it.
41. Oddly enough, it is commonly assumed (e.g., Grützmacher 1913, 137–38; Lacombrade 1951a, 225; Tinnefeld 1975, 167; Roques 1987, 315, "sans aucune doute") that Synesius must have had to yield on this point. Yet in the Eastern church it was quite normal for bishops to continue to live with their wives, though opinion differed about whether they might decently still procreate children: J. Bingham, *Antiquities of the Christian Church*, bk. 4, chap. 5; Jones 1964a, 927–29; cf. too P. Brown, *The Body and Society* (New York 1988), 292–93. According to Socrates (*HE* 5.22), writing in 450, celibacy among the episcopate of the Eastern church in his day, though common, was entirely voluntary. Certainly, "no eastern council enjoined continence on the clergy" (Jones 1964a, 928). Socrates noted: "There have been many bishops who have had children by their lawful wives dur-

ing either, but this he will do if it is the will of God. He repeats, "I will never conceal my beliefs." Having stated these terms, he concludes that the patriarch must either now "leave me to lead my own life and phi-losophize" or else "leave himself no grounds on which hereafter to sit in judgment over me." The episcopate would mean a profound and perma-nent change in Synesius's life; it was a role for which he knew he was ill qualified and had little enthusiasm. It was essential to make the electors absolutely clear just how ill qualified he was. Nothing could have been worse than to accept first and have his qualifications called into question afterwards.

If Synesius had only recently abandoned paganism or was still un-baptized, this was the moment to say so, either in this letter or in his hardly less important but less quoted letter of acceptance to the elders of Ptolemais (*Ep.* 11). It deserves to be quoted in full:

> I was unable, for all my strength, to prevail against you and to decline the bishopric, and this in spite of all my machinations; nor is it to your will that I have now yielded. Rather was it a divine force that brought about the delay then, as it has caused my acceptance now. I would rather have died many deaths than have taken over this religious office, for I did not consider my powers equal to the burden. But now that God has accomplished, not what I asked, but what he willed,[42] I pray that he who has been the shepherd of my life[43] may also become the defender of his charge. How shall I, who have devoted my youth to philosophic leisure and to the idle contemplation of abstract being, and have only mingled as much in the cares of the world as to be able to acquit myself of the duties to the life of the body and to show myself a citizen—how, I say, shall I ever be equal to a life of daily routine? Again, if I deliver myself over to a host of practical matters, shall I ever be able to apply myself to the fair things of the mind that may be gathered in happy lei-sure only? Without all this, would life be worth living to me, and to all those who resemble me? I, for one, know not, but to God they say all things are possible, even impossible things [Matt. 19.26]. Do you there-fore lift up your hands in prayer to God on my behalf, and give orders both to the people in the town and to as many as inhabit the fields or frequent the village churches to offer prayers for us alike in private and

ing their episcopate," remarking with surprise on his discovery that in Thessaly a cleric was liable to be degraded if he slept with his wife—an innovation, he adds, of the novelist Heliodorus when bishop of Tricca. Of course, the mere fact that Synesius made this stipu-lation reveals him well aware of the moral pressure; but it also reveals him determined to defy it. If Theophilus wanted Synesius to accept his offer, he had to accept Synesius's terms. It is true, as Grützmacher observes, that Synesius does not mention his wife after becoming bishop; but with the exception of *Hymn* 7 neither does he mention her before.

42. Perhaps meant to suggest Jesus' prayer in Gethsemane: Matt. 26.39; Mark 14.36; Luke 22.42.

43. A common biblical and homiletic image.

in the congregation. If I am not forsaken by God, I shall then know that this office of priesthood is not a decline from the realms of philosophy, but on the contrary, a step upwards to them.

Here too Synesius makes no attempt to conceal his doubts and openly admits that his past has been devoted to philosophy. On the traditional interpretation of his intellectual development, philosophy was first a barrier and finally a bridge to Christianity: it was a stage through which he passed. His spiritual history has generally been cast into the mold of the conversion to, and then from, philosophy that Augustine so fully describes for himself. Synesius's prayer that "He who has been the shepherd of my life may become also the defender of his charge" could have been the perfect opening to thank God for guiding his steps even when they were following the paths of unrighteousness. Yet neither of these two letters gives any such impression. In *Ep.* 105 he tells Theophilus that if not appointed he will return to his philosophy, and *Ep.* 11 concludes with the hope that the priesthood will not be a descent from philosophy but an ascent to it. That this was more than a literary flourish is proved by the fact that he repeats the idea in an evidently slightly earlier letter to his old friend Olympius, a fellow student of Hypatia:

I call to witness that divinity whom both philosophy and friendship honor, that I should have preferred many deaths to the priesthood. But God has imposed upon me not what I desired but what He wished. I pray Him, therefore, who has been the giver of my life, to be its protector also, so that this office may not seem to me a descent from the realm of philosophy, but rather a step upwards to it.[44]

The only difference is that here he actually prays to God to make his bishopric an ascent to philosophy. In conclusion he tells Olympius:

If possible, I shall perform my duties[45] with the aid of philosophy; but if they cannot be reconciled with my convictions and way of life, what else can I do but set sail straightaway for glorious Greece?

It was not so much the conflict for his soul between Christianity and philosophy that worried Synesius as the demands of episcopal duties on his time and energy.[46] Numerous passages in the letters and elsewhere show how much he valued the leisure required to pursue philosophy.[47]

44. *Ep.* 96; on Olympius see *PLRE* II.800–801. It is clear from the way Synesius describes his acceptance of the bishopric that Olympius is a Christian, a point not made in the *PLRE* entry. Synesius was not Hypatia's only Christian pupil.

45. Perhaps an allusion to Soph. *Ant.* 267.

46. On the reference to Greece, see p. 56 and appendix 3.

47. See Runia 1976, 193–208.

As Liebeschuetz has recently put it,

> beneath the formulated objections we can recognize a deep unwilling-
> ness to take on the full-time, life-consuming professionalism of the
> bishop's office. Men of the highest social rank were not accustomed to
> full-time, life-long careers. . . . The fabric of Synesius's life was woven
> out of study and recreation, the latter provided by sociability and hunt-
> ing. Study of philosophy to raise his soul from defilement to purity
> through knowledge and understanding was the real centre of his life.[48]

Synesius makes the point quite explicitly in a public address read before
his congregation in 412, his famous denunciation of the rascally governor Andronicus: "A philosophical priest needs leisure.[49] I do not condemn bishops who are occupied with practical matters, but, knowing that
I am barely capable of one, I admire those who can do both" (Ep. 57 =
41G). Later on in the same speech he says that he will not attempt to
court popularity as a bishop just as he never used to court popularity
when a philosopher.[50] In another of the letters from his episcopate he
proudly styles himself a "philosopher-priest" (Ep. 62). He was even to
go down in Christian legend as "Synesius the philosopher."[51]

In short, it seems clear that Synesius made no attempt to abandon
either his philosophy or his pose as a philosopher when he became
bishop. It is in this context that we must interpret the passage that has
often been held to prove that he was brought up a pagan:[52]

> Above all, pray for me, for you will be praying for a man abandoned by
> all, deserted, and in need of such support. I shrink from asking of God
> anything for myself. All things are turning out quite contrary to my de-
> sires, on account of my rash presumption. A sinful man, *brought up out-
> side the Church* (ἀπότροφος ἐκκλησίας), following a different way of life
> (ἀγωγὴν ἐτέραν ἠγμένος), I grasped at the altars of God.[53]

Taken by themselves, the italicized words might indeed suggest that
Synesius was brought up a pagan. But in the context another meaning is
not only possible but virtually certain. This, the longest and most passionate of all Synesius's letters, is addressed to Theophilus and is concerned with a disputed election to a minor episcopate within his juris-

---

48. Liebeschuetz 1986b, 185.

49. σχολῆς δεῖ τὸ μετὰ φιλοσοφίας ἱερατεύοντι, p. 66.13 Garzya.

50. ὥσπερ οὐδὲ φιλόσοφος ἐγενόμην δημόσιος . . . οὕτως οὐδὲ ἱερεὺς δημόσιος εἶναι
βούλομαι, p. 68.13–16 Garzya.

51. John Moschus Prat. spir. 195 (PG 66.1043f.).

52. According to Nicolosi (1959, 13), who cites this passage, "è certo che Sinesio fu
educato nel paganesimo"; cf. Bayless (1977, 149): "It is quite clear that he was raised as a
pagan"; Bayless cites Ep. 66 (= 67G), discussed below.

53. Ep. 67 fin. (= 66G, p. 121.1ff.).

diction that was not only absorbing all his energies during a period of illness but also bringing him considerable unpopularity. It would have been entirely irrelevant for him to close this very detailed report with a lament for his pagan past. ἀγωγήν has usually been translated "training" and has been taken to refer to Synesius's allegedly pagan education in the classroom of Hypatia, but "way of life" is surely preferable.[54] It was not the formal education of his student days that left Synesius so ill qualified to deal with the practical problems of church discipline (many, perhaps most, bishops of the age had enjoyed much the same education),[55] but the fact that, unlike most bishops, he had never been a priest or played any part in church affairs before his consecration.[56] The "rash presumption" to which he refers is that of accepting the episcopate despite his lack of experience in ecclesiastical administration.

This interpretation is strongly supported by the parallel protest in the preceding letter, also addressed to Theophilus and also concerned with a controversial episcopal election: "For my part (μέν), I have not in the past been nurtured in the holy laws, nor has it fallen to my lot to learn much lately, since last year I was not yet even on the list of bishops" (*Ep.* 66 = 67G, p. 123.1f.). Once more, taken by themselves, the words "nurtured in the holy laws" could be taken to imply that Synesius was brought up a pagan.[57] But the next clause, explaining that he had not yet had time to learn much in the few months of his episcopate, shows that the "holy laws" are *not* Christianity itself, but the practical details of ecclesiastical discipline. Once again, it would have been irrelevant to his subject to say that he had not yet had time to learn much about doctrine, whereas it made perfect sense for him to remind Theophilus how little experience he had had in handling delicate situations such as the one in which he now found himself. But it is also suggestive that he contrasts his present state with merely not having been a bishop a year ago, rather than indicating some more drastic change. That only discipline is at issue here is put beyond doubt by the immediately fol-

54. For "way of life" see LSJ, s.v. II.4.

55. The three Cappadocian Fathers are a well-documented example of the education of bishops in the period; see the useful summary in Young 1983, 92–122. "The great majority of the higher clergy, the urban deacons and priests and the bishops, were drawn from the middle classes, professional men, officials, and above all *curiales*" (Jones 1964a, 923–24). Most will have followed the traditional rhetorical training, often under pagan teachers, even if few went on to the schools of philosophy. Gregory Nazianzen attests that he and Basil once made a pact to share a "life of philosophy" together (*Ep.* 1).

56. Roques (1987, 302) independently reached the same interpretation of this passage, appositely citing the following remark by Ambrose, made in similar circumstances: "non in ecclesia nutritus sum, non edomitus e puero" (*De paen.* 2.72 [PL 16.514]).

57. So, for example, Bayless 1977.

lowing sentence (which opens with a δέ, picking up the μέν): "So too I
see old men not even pretending to understand the situation clearly, but
terrified in case they should offend against some canon of the Church."
These men are clearly elders of the church, and Synesius's point is that
despite their experience they appear to be no better informed about the
same "holy laws" than himself. In *Ep.* 66 as in *Ep.* 67, Synesius's point is
simply that ecclesiastical affairs have played no part in the life he led before his episcopate.

When recapitulating the antecedents of the schism in the second letter, Synesius makes a revealing admission. The people of Palaebisca
deposed their bishop Orion on the grounds of senility, arguing that his
feebleness "was a reproach in the eyes of those who consider that the
episcopate should be activist, a champion in human affairs." [58] When the
people of Ptolemais asked Synesius to be their bishop, they knew that
he was more at home with Plato than the Gospels. But they remembered his services as ambassador and his connections at court. They
knew they would not be getting a theologian or canon lawyer for their
new bishop; what they wanted, in Synesius's own words, was an "energetic champion."

Other passages that have been thought to betray pagan sympathies
may also be explained quite otherwise. For example, an early letter, *Ep.*
143 to Herculian, has sometimes been cited as proof that Synesius was
afraid of prosecution for magic practices: "You have not kept your promise, my dear friend, the promise that you made to me that you would not
reveal those things that ought to remain hidden. I have just listened to
people who have come from you. They remembered some expressions
and begged me to reveal the meaning to them." Then comes the key passage, which for the moment we may leave in the original: ἀλλ᾽ ἡμεῖς τὸν
ἡμέτερον τρόπον καὶ πρὸς αὐτοὺς οὔτε μετεποιήθημεν τῶν συγγραμά-
των, οὔτ᾽ ἐπιγινώσκειν αὐτὰ ἔφαμεν. Lacombrade paraphrased somewhat as follows: "Synesius did not recognize the books, insisting that he
did not know them," concluding that "there was no clearer way he could
indicate that the philosophical secrets betrayed by his friend were contained in one of these exceedingly rare volumes, possession of which
rendered a man liable to prosecution for magic." [59] But he has completely
misunderstood the Greek, like Augustine Fitzgerald before him, who
translated: "According to my custom I did not pretend to them that I
understood the writings in question, nor did I say that I knew them." [60]

58. προστάτιν εἶναι τὰ εἰς ἀνθρώπους καὶ πολυπράγμονα, p. 108.2 Garzya.
59. Lacombrade 1951a, 62.
60. Fitzgerald 1930, 237.

μεταποιοῦμαι does not mean "understand," but "lay claim to";[61] ἐπιγινώσκειν not "to know," but "to recognize." It is not dangerous secrets
from the Chaldaean Oracles that Herculian has been divulging, but
phrases from something written by Synesius himself! The sentence
means "But in my usual way I did not assert my ownership [or lay claim]
to the book in front of them, nor did I admit that I recognized it." The
whole thing is a joke.

We have only to read on to see that it is not forbidden secrets that are
at issue, but merely Synesius's disapproval of talking about philosophy
in front of laymen. He goes on to quote Lysis the Pythagorean:

> "To explain philosophy to the mob," as Lysis says in his somewhat Dor-
> ian dialect, "is only to awaken amongst men a great contempt for things
> divine." How often have I met, time and time again, people who, be-
> cause they had rashly listened to some stately little phrases, refused to
> believe themselves the laymen that they really were! Full of vanity, they
> sullied sacred dogmas by pretending to teach what they had never suc-
> ceeded in learning.[62]

It might be added that if Synesius were really afraid of prosecution for
magic, he would not have confided his fears to a letter in the first place.
Letters often went astray, and those of a celebrity like Synesius were
particularly likely to be intercepted and passed around for all to enjoy.[63]

According to Bregman, Synesius never "finally underwent a total
conversion to orthodox Christianity through Christ."[64] At heart he always remained a Neoplatonist. It is a conventional, but false, antithesis.
Christian Neoplatonists certainly existed. Besides such spectacular cases
as Pseudo-Dionysius the Areopagite, several fifth- and sixth-century
professors of philosophy at Alexandria were Christians.[65] Whether they
were orthodox Christians is an entirely different matter. Even when he
was a bishop, the classics tripped off Synesius's tongue more readily
than the scriptures, and it is hard to believe that he ever read much theology. It is probably true, as Bregman neatly put it, that "he accepted
Christian dogma to the extent that it was compatible with philosophy.
He did not attempt to use philosophy in order to prove the rational va-

61. See Lampe, s.v. B.1, in addition to LSJ.
62. *Ep.* 143, p. 250.10–17 Garzya; for quotation of Lysis, cf. Diogenes Laertius 8.42;
R. Hercher, *Epistolographi Graeci*, 601; cf. Diels-Kranz, *Vorsokr.* I⁷, 421.
63. For examples from Synesius's own experience alone see Pando 1940, 65.
64. Bregman 1982, 178.
65. Westerink 1962, xii–xxv.

lidity of Christian doctrine."[66] But it is nonetheless a fundamental error
to confuse belief with orthodox belief. In the fifth century, as in many
later ages, there were many who knew little of scripture and less of theology but believed fervently in the message of Christ crucified. Had not
Jesus himself said, "Only believe"? It would be fascinating if we could
trace the conversion of an intellectual like Synesius, an Eastern counterpart to the well-documented spiritual odyssey of Augustine. Historians
of philosophy and dogma will find interesting matter in Bregman's analysis of Synesius's thought. But to the social historian it is more interesting and perhaps more important to discover that a man of Synesius's
background, education, and attitudes was in fact born and raised a
Christian.

III. BAPTISM

Synesius's writings include eight poems composed at various points
over the course of his life, cast in the form of hymns. In ancient generic
terms the hymn was simply a personal meditation addressing God. It
need not be designed for use in public worship like Ambrose's, nor need
it even be metrical: the emperor Julian, for example, wrote hymns in
prose. Synesius's hymns testify that the Neoplatonism of his youthful
education remained fundamental to his thought throughout his life.
Nicolaus Terzaghi assumed that they should reflect an increasing commitment to Christianity and concomitant turning away from philosophy. He deduced their order of composition accordingly and so arranged them in his edition: 1–2 still pagan; 3–5 Christian; 6–8 explicitly
Christian work composed by Synesius as bishop.[67] Bregman too took it
for granted that Synesius's shifting religious convictions could be read
directly from the successive poems in this sequence. The validity of the
sequence itself he never argued or examined. But even if the long and
philosophical 1–2 are earlier than the short and Christian 6–8, it by no
means follows that Synesius did not believe in Christianity when he
wrote 1–2 or that he had abandoned philosophy when he wrote 6–8.
And we have already seen that the Christian 7 is in any case early (see
section I above). As A. J. Festugière has observed, "on ne constate dans
les hymnes aucune évolution profonde, comme il serait naturel de la
part d'un païen devenu, à un certain moment, chrétien."[68] It is true that

66. Bregman 1982, 161.
67. See his edition, xvii–xix.
68. *REG* 58 (1945): 269, a long review (268–77) of Terzaghi's first edition of the hymns
(1939), apparently unknown to Bregman. Compare too Ch. Vellay's conclusion (*Etudes sur
les Hymnes de Synésius de Cyrène* [Grenoble 1904], 30–31): "La pensée n'a point de variation

Christ is not named in 1–2. But then he is only named once in all the acknowledged Christian hymns (3.5). The name Jesus also appears only once (6.4). The third person of the Trinity, as Festugière notes, is always designated *pnoia*, never by the proper Christian term *pneuma*. *Hymn* 8 deals not merely with the incarnation, crucifixion, and resurrection, but also with Christ's noncanonical descent to Hell. And yet there is not a single technical or familiar Christian term in the poem. The Savior is addressed by none of his familiar names or epithets, but as "son of the Virgin of Solyma" (γόνε παρθένου Σολυμηΐδος), Solyma being Synesius's classicizing name for Jerusalem. It is Hades to which Christ descends, and he meets Cerberus there. The poem is full of predicates and motifs from that bizarre text so beloved of the Neoplatonists, the Chaldaean Oracles.[69] The stars are referred to as the "gods of the night" (48), and the poem concludes with a description of that stock figure of late pagan poetry, Aion,[70] "steward of the eternal resting place of the gods" (70–71). As for *Hymn* 6, while it is true, as Lacombrade observes, that "toute considération philosophique . . . est banni du récit,"[71] Christian themes do not take its place. There is no theology either; it is free from philosophy because it is a short, simple poem, with style and diction that are as "pagan" as ever.

If this is what the "Christian" hymns are like, how pagan are the "pagan" hymns? The most important is *Hymn* 1, a long, complex poem full of motifs from the Chaldaean Oracles. The fact that it begins with an apostrophe to the "king of the gods" (8) should no longer seem too significant in the light of references to a plurality of gods in the otherwise manifestly Christian 8. The truth is that for all its Neoplatonic language *Hymn* 1 is a deeply Christian poem, more deeply than has hitherto been realized. It was written on Synesius's return to Cyrene after his long stay in Constantinople. But the widely held view that he was continually revising and expanding the poem has made it hard to exploit its biographical data with any confidence.[72] But this revision is an unnecessary and implausible hypothesis.

It has been universally agreed since Wilamowitz that two passages

---

sensible ni de développement marqué; la forme et les idées n'accusent point de long intervalles de composition; tout est un, dans l'inspiration et l'expression." There are of course *differences* between one hymn and another, but only prejudice finds it necessary to diagnose them all as conscious development, "intellectual bridges" carefully constructed between Neoplatonism and Christianity.

69. H. Lewy, *Chaldaean Oracles and Theurgy: Mysticism, Magic and Platonism in the Later Roman Empire*, ed. M. Tardieu, 2d ed. (Paris 1978).

70. Cameron 1970a, 205–7.

71. Lacombrade 1978a, 84.

72. So already Wilamowitz 1907, 282 ("durch zahlreiche Zusätze erweitert") and 293–94.

date from Synesius's episcopate, 44ff. and 359ff. After an opening address to the deity, Synesius states:

> I have come to your dwelling place, to your bosom.[73] Now to your august rites (ἐπὶ σεμνὰς τελετηφορίας), to your holy shrines have I come as a suppliant. Now to the summit of high mountains have I come as a suppliant, now to the great ravine of desert Libya have I come, to her southern border that no godless blast of wind sullies.

According to Fitzgerald and Terzaghi, followed by Bregman (among others), the rites here mentioned are pagan mysteries. So too, they claim, in the reference to Synesius's stay in Constantinople at 449ff.:

> As many temples (νηοί) as were built for your holy rites (ἐπὶ σαῖς ἀγίαις τελετηφορίαις), O King, to all these I went, prostrate, a suppliant, wetting the ground with the dew of my eyes, for fear that my journey might be in vain, praying to the gods.

But they allow themselves to be misled by Synesius's classicizing terminology. Not only is it highly improbable that there were numerous pagan temples at Constantinople in the fifth century; it should also be noted that pagans did not need to go to their temples to pray or to be initiated into mystery rites. Nor, if Synesius really did undergo pagan initiations in Constantinople, would he have referred to them so openly. By this time such rituals were unquestionably illegal. It is particularly unlikely that he would have referred to pagan initiations so positively, not to say emotionally, if he had been a Christian at the time he wrote the poem. That question aside, however, the repeated word *teletephoria*, in an equivalent metrical formula, must bear the same sense in both passages—as Festugière rightly insisted, a Christian sense.

What now of the allegation that 44ff. is a later addition? Festugière remarks:

> Comment, dans ce mouvement de joie qu'éprouve le poète à être revenu, loin de la grande ville bruyante, à son beau domaine cyrénéen, comment peut-il dire, tout aussitôt: "Maintenant, me voici arrivé, suppliant, aux temples sacrés de tes saints rites"? En quoi cela le changeait-il de Constantinople où se trouvaient, partout, des νηοί bâtis ἐπὶ σαῖς ἀγίαις τελετηφορίαις du Dieu chrétien? Comme l'a marqué Wilamowitz,[74] Synésius ne peut parler ainsi que s'il a une raison particulière de mentionner les mystères chrétiens de Cyrène, c'est-à-dire s'il est déjà membre officiel de l'Église cyrénéenne, s'il est évêque de cette Église.[75]

73. κόλποι, a Chaldaean term: see E. Des Places, *Oracles Chaldaïques* (Paris 1971), 38–39.

74. "So konnte erst der Bischof reden" (Wilamowitz 1907, 293).

75. Festugière 1945, 273.

But Synesius has *not* in fact previously spoken of the Libyan countryside, nor is any contrast implied with the noise of Constantinople.
Nor is there any reason why the vague term *teletephoria* should imply an
official connection with the Cyrenean church. The same word cannot
imply any such connection to the Constantinopolitan church at 449ff.,
the one passage in the poem that cannot possibly be a later interpolation. Wilamowitz and Festugière made the same objection to 359ff.:

> Behold now my soul, feeble and exhausted in your Libya, at your holy
> rituals (ἐπὶ σᾶς σεπτᾶς ἱερηπολίας), singing to you in holy prayer.

Festugière claimed that since *hierapolos* is a ritual term that "designates a
priest of superior rank," these lines must have been added after Synesius himself became a bishop. But why should Synesius be using a technical term of paganism to refer to a technical term of Christianity?[76] The
phrase as a whole is just a variation on the metrically equivalent νῦν ἐπὶ
σεμνᾶς τελετηφορίας and ἐπὶ σαῖς ἁγίαις τελετηφορίαις of 44–45 and
452–53. All three bear the same meaning, a general reference to Christian worship.

Taking 44ff. and 359ff. together, one might ask *why* should Synesius
have interpolated these two references to his episcopate? If the critics are
right to find these passages so glaringly intrusive and inconsistent with
the "original" context, why did Synesius put them there? Why did he
spoil his poem with such crude and irrelevant additions? Since, alone
among Synesius's hymns, 1 is clearly anchored to a precise date and context, his return from Constantinople to Cyrene, pointers to a quite different date and context would be especially misleading and disruptive.

What then are the "holy rites" to which Synesius so pointedly refers? The key is provided by two further passages, first 536–43:

> To help me on the holy path that leads to you, give me as a token your
> seal, and chase from my life and my prayers the deadly demons of
> matter.[77]

And next 619–35:

> Now at last let my suppliant soul bear the seal of the father (σφραγῖδα
> πατρός), a terror to hostile demons, who dart aloft from deep lurking
> places of the earth to breathe godless impulses upon mortals; and let
> this be a sign (σύνθημα) to your pure ministers, who throughout the
> depths of the glorious universe are key-bearers to the fiery ascents.

76. The more so since Synesius "professe l'horreur du terme exacte" (Lacombrade
1951a, 33).
77. σύνθημα δίδου σφραγῖδα τεάν, κηριτρεφέας δαίμονας ὕλας σεύων ζωᾶς εὐχᾶς τ'
ἀπ' ἐμᾶς.

By the year 400 the word *sphragis*, "seal," had become the standard term for Christian baptism.[78] Yet students of Synesius have been curiously reluctant to admit this sense in these two passages. According to Lacombrade, for instance, the first *sphragis* is merely a synonym for *synthema*, a Chaldaean term for the password the soul has to remember in order to return to its source in heaven.[79] Bregman found the Christian reference a "minor mystery of the hymns" and likewise chose to look for Chaldaean or Orphic sources.[80] In particular, he identified the repeated *synthemata* with occult symbols used by theurgists. But this takes us a long way from the word *sphragis*, and none of these pagan associations give any real point to the *context* in either Synesius passage.

On the other side stands the host of passages listed in Lampe's *Patristic Lexicon* under the rubric "seal given to Christians in baptism, considered as distinguishing mark of Christ's flock, *and also as protection against evil, demonic powers*." Lampe also lists another host of passages under the less specialized rubric "sign of cross as distinguishing mark of Christians *and safeguard against demons*." In both passages from Synesius the *sphragis* is specifically and emphatically stated to frighten evil demons. It may well be that there is some Chaldaean influence too. For example, the first set of demons is associated with matter, and the passage goes on to pray that Synesius's spirit may be kept ἀμόλυντον, "undefiled," a classic term of the Chaldaean Oracles.[81] The second passage also talks, in language as much Chaldaean as Christian, of the soul's ascent from earth to the fiery realms. Nonetheless, the word *sphragis* itself is foreign to the Oracles, and given the double emphasis on frightening demons, no contemporary Christian reader could have been in the slightest doubt that Synesius was referring to Christian baptism.

Baptism is a very specific and special element in the Christian experience, something that happens only once. Not only does Synesius mention it twice in quick succession; the very next stanza announces the poet's repentance (μετά μοι μέλεται):

> I repent of this life of clay. Away, eyesores of godless mortals, dominations of cities. Away, sweet infatuations, grace that is no grace, by which the beguiled soul is held fast in bondage to earth.

78. See F. J. Dölger, *Sphragis, eine altchristliche Taufbezeichnung in ihren Beziehung zur profanen und religiösen Kultur des Altertums* (Paderborn 1911); and the wealth of passages cited in Lampe, s.vv. σφραγίς and σφραγίζω.

79. Lacombrade 1978a, 58 n. 2. Cf. *Oracles Chaldaïques* frags. 2 and 108–9 Des Places.

80. Bregman 1982, 91. It is in fact neither mysterious nor minor. Compare too Terzaghi's (1939) note ad loc.: "sphragis, potius gnostica quam Christiana."

81. Des Places 1971, 39.

He is paraphrasing the rite of baptism: he renounces worldly pomp and the temptations of the flesh. And what follows, for all its Chaldaean coloring, can likewise be interpreted as the Christian soul yearning for cleansing through baptism:

> Kindle, O King, the lights that lead aloft, giving to me light wings. Cut the knot, loose the grip of the twin desires by which artful Nature bends down souls to the earth. Grant me to escape the destiny of the body and to spring swiftly even to your courts, to your bosom, whence flows forth the fountain of the soul.

Just because Chaldaean doctrine was important to the pagan Neoplatonists of Athens, it does not follow that the doctrine itself was irredeemably pagan. There was no reason why a philosophical Christian should find any serious problem in adapting the Chaldaean account of the descent and return of the soul to his faith.

The stanzas preceding the first mention of *sphragis* describe Synesius's long stay in Constantinople. This passage has often been exploited for the poet's biography, but less attention has been paid to its role in the structure of the poem. It is not at all a casual reminiscence. It begins:

> This debt (χρέος), O Lord of the mighty universe, I came to pay (τίσων, future participle) from Thrace, where I spent three years.

What "debt" did he come from Constantinople to Cyrene to pay? Not the tax remissions he had already won for Cyrene in Constantinople. At 496f. he begged the deity to preserve these benefits for the Libyans during the long stretch of time. He might expect gratitude when he got home, but there was no *financial* debt that he himself had yet to pay there. At 70–71 Synesius pictures his soul "rendering the hymn that is your due" (τὸν ὀφειλόμενον ὕμνον ἀποίσει), but the debt itself should be something over and above the hymn that describes it.

We venture to suggest a new solution. Synesius had earlier vowed that if, with God's help, he accomplished his mission in Constantinople and got safely back to Cyrene, he would be baptized there. This would explain the joy with which he returned to those problematic Libyan *teletephoriai* and *hierepoliai*. It was not just the beloved countryside of home to which he was returning, but to baptism in a beloved church in that countryside. Such a hypothesis would at once make sense of the poem as a whole, rendering unnecessary all the supposed additions and expansions. Though repetitious and rambling, the poem has a simple basic structure: the poet has returned home to fulfill the vow he made in Constantinople.[82]

The only possible objection is that, according to the *Ecclesiastical History* of Evagrius (1.15), published in 594, Synesius was not yet baptized when offered the episcopate. This is one of a series of capsule biographies of literary men inserted into the opening chapters of Evagrius's *History*, all superficial and full of errors, none detectably based on independent biographical information.[83] For example, his reference to "Claudian and Cyrus the poets" (1.19) treats them as Christian writers even though both, if not actually pagans, wrote purely secular work. Claudian is even dated to the wrong reign.[84] Synesius too is dated to the wrong reign: the *De regno* is said to have been addressed to Theodosius.[85] It is also alleged that he was offered the episcopate despite his refusal to believe in the resurrection, in the confidence that belief could not fail to follow in so virtuous a man; "and they were not deceived in their hope." There is of course no evidence that Synesius changed his mind in the short period left to him, and it is intrinsically most improbable.

We cannot have much confidence in Evagrius's otherwise unsupported claim that Synesius had not been baptized. On the other hand, as already noted, the three letters that describe Synesius's hesitations in such detail say nothing of baptism. Synesius's reluctant elevation is often compared to the reluctant elevation of the unbaptized Ambrose to the see of Milan. Yet Ambrose's baptism plays a well-documented and central role in his consecration.[86] Baptism was more than a mere formality. Synesius's failure even to mention so fundamental a point surely suggests that he had in fact been baptized; if he fulfilled the intention announced in *Hymn* 1, he presumably undertook the rite on his return to Cyrene in the spring of 401.[87] The poem suggests a serious decision, only made after long and solemn reflection during his lonely and unhappy years at Constantinople:

$$\text{ἤδη φερέτω}$$
$$\text{σφραγῖδα πατρὸς}$$
$$\text{ἱκέτις ψυχά.}$$

---

82. According to Roques (1987, 306), "rien ne s'oppose" the idea that he was baptized in Alexandria by Theophilus. Nothing except the only evidence we have.

83. See Allen 1981, 72, 86–90.

84. Cameron 1970a, 11–12.

85. Possibly Theodosius II, Arcadius's son, rather than his father; but even so the error is patent.

86. F. Homes Dudden, *The Life and Times of St. Ambrose*, vol. 1 (Oxford 1935), 66–68.

87. See below and Cameron 1987, 348–49.

Now at last let my suppliant soul
bear the seal of the father.

IV. ORTHODOXY

Given the lack of evidence that Synesius was ever a pagan, in particular the conspicuous absence of any reference in Synesius's own writings to anything resembling a conversion, there is no reason to resist the
natural implication of all these texts: that Synesius had always been
a Christian, however conventional and uninterested in doctrine or
theology.

None other than the patriarch Theophilus married him (*Ep.* 105). It
has often been claimed that this fact need prove no more than that his
wife came from a Christian family. Yet it is not easy to believe that the
patriarch of Alexandria would marry a pagan, even if the bride was a
Christian. As Marrou has pointed out, Synesius's remark, made before
he became bishop, that the wedding was solemnized by the "sacred
hand" of Theophilus suggests that he himself viewed it as a religious
occasion, that is to say that he was a Christian at the time.[88]

Several other texts also, on the most natural interpretation, betray
an unself-consciously Christian viewpoint. Perhaps the most telling is
De providentia 90C, describing how the wicked Typhos [= Caesarius]
"wholeheartedly despised all wisdom, both Egyptian wisdom and
such foreign (ὑπερόριος) wisdom as the king was having his son Osiris
[= Aurelian] taught."[89] This distinction between native and "foreign"
wisdom, though presented in Egyptian terms, makes no sense in an
Egyptian context: no people was less sympathetic to foreign culture than
the ancient Egyptians. The phrase must refer to the world of A.D. 400.
And there its reference is clear. There are countless references in Christian writers of the age to "outside," "external," or "foreign wisdom,"
ἡ ἔξω(θεν) or ἡ θύραθεν (φιλο)σοφία, οἱ ἔξω(θεν) (φιλό)σοφοι.[90] They

88. Marrou 1952, 477.
89. These identifications with Caesarius and Aurelian will be justified in detail later.
90. οἱ or τὰ ἔξω(θεν) denoting people or things "outside the Church" is a usage that
goes back to St. Paul: 1 Cor. 5.12 and 13; 1 Tim. 3.7; Mark 4.11 (cf. Bauer, s.v. ἔξωθεν
1.b.β). But the earliest example of this formula qualifying (φιλο)σοφία in the sense "pagan
learning" seems to be Gregory Thaumaturgus *Pan. or.* 10 (PG 10.1081A), τοὺς ἔξω φιλο-
σόφους. Some of the innumerable fourth- and fifth-century examples are collected by
Lampe, s.v. ἔξω, ἔξωθεν, and Anne-Marie Malingrey, *Philosophia*, Etudes et commentaires
40 (Paris 1961), 212–13. Here is a more varied selection: ἡ ἐ. (φιλο)σοφία. Euseb. *HE*
6.18.2; Ps.-Athanasius *V.Antonii* 93 (PG 26.973B); Greg. Naz. *In laud.Heron.*, PG 35.1204A;
Greg. Nyss. *C. Eunom.* 12, PG 45.1101B; *In Hexaem.*, PG 44.65B and 80D; *De vita Moys.* 2.10

mean secular, as opposed to Christian, learning. The usage is particularly common in the Cappadocian Fathers and John Chrysostom and is bound to have been familiar to Synesius's audience. Though often used defiantly or slightingly, the formula could also be applied neutrally or even as a compliment: Christians could be praised for their mastery of secular culture. It was perhaps instinctively as much as appropriately that Valesius translated τῆς ἔξωθεν παιδείας in Eusebius (*HE* 2.4.2) as *humanioribus litteris*, reflecting the Renaissance distinction of all learning between *divinae* and *humanae litterae*.

As usual in *De providentia*, Egyptian stands for Roman, but with an additional nuance: as was to become standard usage in the Byzantine period, Roman is in effect identified with Christian.[91] While it is only Osiris who is credited with studying "foreign wisdom," Typhos despises *both* pagan and Christian learning alike. So the passage serves two purposes. Not only is Typhos denounced as a boor, but the stage is set for the later allegation that he was also a heretic, too sympathetic to Arianism (121B). This is why it is made clear that Osiris studied only as much "foreign wisdom" as his father thought fit.[92] It is significant that a man like Synesius, whose own commitment to Hellenic culture was unqualified, was so careful to qualify the culture of his patron Aurelian. The explanation is obvious: it would not have been appropriate to praise so pious a Christian for unqualified devotion to pagan culture. Under

---

and 2.41; *De an. et resurr.*, *PG* 46.49B; Chrysostom *Adv.opp.mon.vitae*, *PG* 49.362. οἱ ἐ. (φιλό)σοφοι: Euseb., *Comm. in Ps.*, *PG* 23.117A; Basil *Ep.* 135; Greg. Naz. *In laud.Basil.* 66.3; Chrysostom *De Lazaro*, *PG* 48.994; *Ad pop.ant.* 17.2 and 19.1, *PG* 49.173 and 189. τὰ ἔξωθεν μαθήματα: Euseb. *HE* 8.10.1; Basil *Ad adulesc.* 4.1. οἱ ἐ. συγγραφεῖς: Chrysostom *Hom. 1 Cor.* 1, *PG* 61.9C; Theodoret *Comm. Dan.* 2.37 (2.1089). τῆς ἐ. παιδείας: Euseb. *HE* 2.4.2; Marc. Diac. *V.Porph.* 8; Basil *Ad adulesc.* 10.3. οἱ ἔξω: Greg. Nyss. *Or. cat.* 1, *PG* 45.13A; *De vita Greg. Thaum.*, *PG* 46.901; Basil *In Hex.* 1, *PG* 29.5C; C. *Eunom.* 1, *PG* 29.516B; Didymus *De trin.* 3.21, *PG* 39.904B. Note particularly ἡ ἔξω φιλοσοφία, divided into ἡ Ἑλληνική and ἡ βάρβαρος φιλοσοφία in Greg. Nyss. *De vita Greg. Thaum.*, *PG* 46.901. ἡ θύραθεν παιδεία (the standard formula for secular learning in Byzantine Greek: cf. Lemerle 1971, 123): Theodoret *HE* 4.30.2; ἡ θ. σοφία: Basil *Ad adulesc.* 3.9; Theodoret *HE* 1.23.2; cf. Evagrius *HE* 5.24. The preceding examples were collected in the old-fashioned way, with much labor. Use of the *TLG* through an Ibycus computer turned up in minutes more than a hundred examples of the formula ἡ ἐ. (φιλο)σοφία (vel sim.) in Chrysostom alone, with several score more in Basil and the two Gregories. There seems no point in reproducing even a selection of this material; it was obviously a common formula, familiar to all. On the other hand, Synesius's distinction between "Greek and Egyptian lore" at 127D (where the idea that human events recur cyclically is said to agree with both) seems to be the traditional one of Greek philosophy, between its own investigations and the revealed wisdom of other cultures.

91. On the use of "Roman" to designate the Byzantine state (though without stressing the religious aspect), see J. Jüthner, *Hellenen und Barbaren* (Leipzig 1923), 108f.

92. The passage has nothing to do with Aurelian's actual father, Taurus, who was in fact an Arian; Synesius uses the philosopher-king of his myth as a validating stamp on the activities he endorses.

the circumstances, the best way to handle the motif was to praise him for his proficiency in both cultures—making it clear which was secondary. This was to become standard practice in the Byzantine age. To quote only one example, Theodoret praised a bishop for "possessing both sorts of knowledge, secular and divine" (γνῶσιν ἑκατέραν ἔχων, καὶ τὴν θύραθεν καὶ τὴν θείαν).[93] Another common antithesis in Byzantine texts is "theirs" and "ours" (ἡ ἐφ᾽ ἡμῖν, ἡμετέρα). Opinions might differ about the degree of approval accorded to "outside" learning, but the perspective itself was possible only for a Christian. And clearly Synesius shared it.

There are also a couple of other passages that may now be given a more comfortable Christian interpretation.[94] First, there is this exclamation in *De regno* 29A of (probably) 398: "There is nothing more striking to watch or hear than an emperor raising his hands before his people, worshipping his and their common father. It is only proper for the deity to delight in the praises of a pious ruler devoted to his service and to have an ineffable relationship with him." Lacombrade will not allow that these are the words of a Christian, on the grounds that Christian and pagan ruler theory were indistinguishable. But when the speaker is addressing Christians on the subject of a Christian emperor praying to the God of the Christians, Synesius must at any rate have expected his words to be taken in a Christian sense. To be sure they are cloaked in Neoplatonic turns of phrase,[95] but even as a bishop Synesius never renounced his Neoplatonism.

It is a grave error to judge the tone and language of Synesius's writings by the yardstick of a John Chrysostom or a Gregory Nazianzen. It is not an error that contemporaries made—or the Christian generations that followed. It was precisely for their style and philosophy that the Byzantines who preserved Synesius's writings admired them. The great fourteenth-century statesman Theodore Metochites wrote an essay on Synesius, admiring him as a philosopher with a sense of style.[96] His pupil Nicephorus Gregoras produced an elaborate commentary on the *De insomniis*,[97] as well as a work on the construction of an astrolabe in imitation of Synesius. Even the essay on baldness inspired a Byzantine

---

93. *Haeret. fab. compendium*, PG 83.396A.

94. For one or two less certain such passages, see Roques 1987, 309–10.

95. The "ineffable" (ἄρρητος) is certainly a word with Neoplatonic associations that flows often from Synesius's pen; but it is also frequently found of the "ineffable mysteries" of Christ in Christian writers, as a glance at Lampe, s.v., will illustrate. And οἰκειοῦσθαι, translated "relationship" above, is also a word widely used by Christians of the relationship of God to man (Lampe, s.v.).

96. N. G. Wilson, *Scholars of Byzantium* (London 1983), 262.

97. PG 149.521–642; Lacombrade 1951a, 31; Hunger 1978, 1:463.

reply.[98] Synesius's letters were much admired as stylistic models in the favorite Byzantine genre of epistolography.[99] Antonio Garzya enumerated no fewer than 260 manuscripts of Synesius's letters, almost all of the fourteenth century and later.[100] Many have explanatory scholia, some by the greatest scholars of the age—Manuel Moschopulos, Thomas Magister, and Maximus Planudes. The De providentia is described in the tenth-century Suda lexicon as "an amazing book in Hellenic style." Synesius himself was remembered in Byzantine hagiography as "Synesius the philosopher."[101] That age at least saw nothing incongruous in Synesius's intellectual leanings—and certainly nothing hostile to Christianity.

Lay Christians were under no obligation to write on Christian subjects in Christian language. Even De providentia and De insomniis could easily have been written by a Christian; they were certainly read and admired by the Christian Byzantines. In fact, for all its bizarre Egyptian and Neoplatonic coloring, De providentia shows itself not only Christian, but orthodox. According to 121B Typhos "scythianized in his belief about God": that is to say, he sympathized with Arians. At 114D a god foretells to the character who represents Synesius himself that Typhos will fall "when those who are now in power attempt to tamper with our religious rituals." The sequel makes it clear that this is an allusion to Gaïnas's demand for an Arian church inside Constantinople, probably supported by the prefect Caesarius: "Not long afterwards there arose a false piece of religious observance, a counterfeit ritual like a counterfeit coin—something ancient law bars from the cities, shutting the impiety outside the gates, beyond the walls" (115B).[102] It might be objected that even a pagan would have appreciated the significance and importance of Gaïnas's demand, but why should a pagan have gone so far as to retroject an "ancient law" against heresy into Pharaonic Egypt? In reality, the current law to which he alludes dated from as recently as 381.[103] It is not as if this were the only evidence for Synesius's attitude to Arianism. J. C. Pando has drawn attention to "the bitter tone in which Synesius speaks of heretics and the strenuous action he took against them" when bishop.[104] Ep. 5 (= 4G) is a passionate denunciation of "those who have

98. Fitzgerald 1930, 2:436–37, 394–96.

99. See the preface to A. Garzya's edition and his numerous preliminary studies, collected in his Storia e interpretazione di testi bizantini (London 1974), chaps. 21–28; Hunger 1978, 2:215f.; G. Karlsson, Idéologie et cérémonial dans l'épistolographie byzantine (Uppsala 1962), 23f., 114f.

100. Reprinted in Garzya 1974; and see too his edition of the letters (1979).

101. John Moschus Prat.spir. 195.

102. See further below, p. 327.

103. Socr. HE 5.10.

104. Pando 1940, 150.

taken up the godless heresy of Eunomius"; they are trying to "sully the Church," and "false teachers are spreading their nets for the souls of weaker brethren." *Ep.* 67 (= 66G) to Theophilus likewise refers with horror to the "godless days of the Arians" and to the bad old days of Valens "when the influence of heresy was powerful."[105] Pando found this hostility so surprising, so different from Synesius's usual "attitude toward religious belief," that he was confident that it sprang "not so much from doctrinal zeal, as from a hatred of social unrest."[106] Bregman rejects out of hand the possibility that Synesius had "become orthodox," and takes it for granted that his persecution of heretics was insincere, undertaken purely for political reasons.[107] It may be that we should not attach too much personal significance to Synesius's public policies as bishop. On the other hand, it is also possible that he imbibed such attitudes from an orthodox Christian upbringing and took them perfectly seriously.

According to one recent account, "not warped by religion or partisanship like so many others . . . , Synesius just sailed along in his well-adjusted, even-tempered way."[108] There is a false syllogism here: paganism was tolerant; Synesius was a Hellene (and therefore a pagan at heart, a subsidiary invalid deduction); therefore Synesius was tolerant. But tolerance was a scarce commodity by the second half of the fourth century, conspicuously lacking, for example, in that genuinely religious Hellene Julian. Synesius's letters reveal a generally attractive and humane personality, but *De regno* is a paradigm of racial bigotry, and *De providentia* a classic of political partisanship woven out of lies, half-truths, and personal abuse. Synesius was not simply a latter-day Xenophon who somehow ended his days as a bishop. Such a freak would indeed baffle explanation. If we are actually to understand Synesius as he was, we must not blind ourselves to his darker side.

V. HYPATIA

What then is the basis for the widespread modern conviction that Synesius was born and raised a pagan? To be sure, this is what Photius says ("a former Hellene devoted to philosophy"), but what was his evidence? As it happens, we can make an educated guess: nothing more than the passage of Evagrius already discussed. Synesius is Cod. 26 in Photius's *Bibliotheca*, Evagrius Cod. 29, both very brief notices (pp. 5–6

105. Respectively, p. 112.19G and p. 108.7–10G, cf. too *Ep.* 45 (= 44G), with Pando 1940, 150–52; and Bettini 1938, 33–35.
106. Pando 1940, 150.
107. Bregman 1982, 171–74.
108. T. B. Jones 1978, 96.

Bekker). That is to say, almost certainly Photius had both books on his table at the same time as he wrote.[109] It is significant that Evagrius makes no such explicit statement. He says merely that Synesius was a man of letters (*logios*), so distinguished a philosopher "that he was admired by such Christians as judge what they see impartially"; they persuaded him to submit to baptism and become a bishop, although he had not yet accepted the doctrine of the resurrection. Anyone who compares the two notices carefully will at once see that Photius makes all the same points as Evagrius, merely embellishing a little on the question of the resurrection from his own reading, as he notes, of Synesius's letter to Theophilus. His claim that Synesius was a "former Hellene" is no more than a misunderstanding of Evagrius's portentous periphrasis for baptism (σωτηριώδους παλιγγενεσίας).[110]

In fact, modern opinions rest on little more than Synesius's dedication to Neoplatonism, coupled with the fact that he studied in the school of the pagan Hypatia. Her grisly end (lynched by monks) inevitably casts her in the role of pagan martyr, suggesting in turn a powerful pagan influence on the impressionable youth of Alexandria.[111] Since Synesius continued to speak of Hypatia in the warmest terms throughout his life, we are justified in assuming that she exercised a considerable influence on his development. It will therefore be worth discovering what we can about this remarkable woman, whose real achievements have unfortunately been overshadowed by her savage end.

Our biographical knowledge of Hypatia comes in the main from just three sources: the *Ecclesiastical History* of Socrates, written ca. 450; the *Life* of his predecessor Isidore, written early in the sixth century by Damascius, the last scholarch of the Academy in Athens; and the *Chronicle* of the seventh-century Coptic bishop John of Nikiu. The first two form the basis of all modern accounts, but John of Nikiu has hitherto been almost entirely ignored.[112] Yet he preserves important details other-

109. Or at any rate his notes from both books. We are not entitled to assume that Photius actually owned all the books he describes or that he had access to them all at any one time.

110. Photius's account of Evagrius is similarly based on no more than superficial inference from the text: W. T. Treadgold, *The Nature of the Bibliotheca of Photius* (Washington, D.C. 1980), 59.

111. So, for example, Kingsley's Hypatia, "a Greek philosopher who looks, and, alas, behaves, as if she had stepped off a Greek vase" (Susan Chitty, *The Beast and the Monk: A Life of Charles Kingsley* [New York 1975], 152). Mary Ellen Waithe's chapter on Hypatia in her *History of Women Philosophers*, vol. 1, *Ancient Women Philosophers, 600 B.C.–500 A.D.* (1987), 169–95, is a careless compilation, full of errors and exaggerated claims. Maria Dzielska will soon be publishing a comprehensive study of Hypatia's life and influence.

112. Not quoted at all, for example, in the standard account by Rist (1965) or Chuvin (1990, 85–90).

wise unattested and, above all, is the only source to tell the story from the point of view of the patriarch Cyril.[113]

Socrates and Damascius pose a rather curious problem. We might expect to find the ecclesiastical historian and the pagan philosopher disagreeing in their assessment of Hypatia. And so they do. But it is Socrates who is favorable, and Damascius, fellow pagan and fellow philosopher, who is hostile. Indeed, the extent and source of his hostility have not been appreciated, and as a consequence some details in his account of Hypatia have been misunderstood.

We may begin with a simple illustration. According to Damascius, the Athenian scholarch Isidore, his own teacher, excelled Hypatia "not only as a man excels a woman, but also as a real philosopher excels a mere geometrician."[114] In the light of this remark, we may turn a little more cautiously to Damascius's claim that she "taught *publicly* (δημοσίᾳ) as she paraded through the city to anyone who wanted to hear, Plato or Aristotle or any other philosopher you care to name."[115] This has usually been interpreted to mean that Hypatia held a public chair of philosophy.[116] But the contemptuous tone and the context suggest that it is the location, rather than the financing, of Hypatia's teaching that is at issue.[117] Damascius is subtly (and, as we shall see, falsely) denigrating her for teaching philosophy in public, to large classes rather than to a small and exclusive circle of initiates, as in the School of Athens.

He also describes her as wearing the *tribon*, the "rough cloak which was virtually the uniform of the Cynic preachers and their monastic successors." On this basis scholars have not hesitated to classify Hypatia's philosophical teaching (about which we know absolutely nothing) as "the Platonism of the Cynic preacher."[118] A recent monograph on Alex-

113. Properly emphasized in a forthcoming monograph on late Roman Alexandria by Christopher Haas, to which I am much indebted. For a good account of John and his sources, see A. Carile, "Giovanni di Nikius, cronista bizantino-copto del vii secolo," *Felix Ravenna* 4, ser. 1 (1981): 103–55. John seems to have written a little before 700 and to have drawn on all three of the early Byzantine chronicle sources known to us (Malalas, John of Antioch, Paschal Chronicler), though in earlier and fuller redactions. He also used Coptic sources now lost (particularly evident in his account of Hypatia). Unfortunately the only text we have is a seventeenth-century Ethiopic translation made from an Arabic translation; the standard edition (English only) is that of R. H. Charles (London 1916), though the commentary (Ethiopic and French) in Zotenberg (Paris 1883) remains useful.

114. C. Zintzen, *Damascii vitae Isidori reliquiae* (Hildesheim 1967), 218 (*Epit. Phot.* 164).

115. Zintzen 1967, 70 (frag. 102).

116. Lacombrade 1951a, 44; Marrou 1963, 134; Rist 1965, 220; Shanzer 1985, 65; Chuvin 1990, 85.

117. E. Évrard, *REG* 90 (1977): 69–74; M.-O. Goulet-Cazé, in L. Brisson, M.-O. Goulet-Cazé, R. Goulet, and D. O'Brien, *Porphyre: La vie de Plotin*, vol. 1 (Paris 1982), 245–46.

118. Rist 1965, 220–21 (both quotes); on the Cynic "uniform," M.-O. Goulet-Cazé, *ANRW* II.36.4 (1990): 2738–39.

andrian Neoplatonism pigeonholes her as "stoico-cynic."[119] But how seriously is this remark to be taken? If Hypatia really wore the *tribon*, it is remarkable that her adoring pupil Synesius, in a letter to none other than Hypatia herself (*Ep.* 154), refers slightingly to criticisms of his own work by those who wear the *tribon*.

One more example. The most famous (if not the most attractive) story told of Hypatia is how she discouraged unwelcome attentions from a student by throwing a used sanitary napkin at him, saying: "This is what you are in love with, young man, nothing that is beautiful." The poor youth was shocked out of his infatuation. It has often been observed that this story "shows the Neoplatonist philosopher acting in a way that would far better have befitted the Cynic."[120] A recent paper, after assembling parallels in the behavior of Cynic females, nonetheless goes on to accept the story as true, although told by a hostile source who goes on to refer to what he calls an "ignorant" alternative version, according to which Hypatia cured the student of his passion through music.[121] Because of the "ignorant," R. Asmus and C. Zintzen thought the music version a "Christian calumny,"[122] but, far from being a calumny, it shows Hypatia in a far more sympathetic light. Damascius dismissed it on the strange ground that "knowledge of music had by then long disappeared." Presumably this is to be explained in the light of his account of the musical researches of Isidore's teacher Asclepiodotus,[123] according to whom the first of the three types of musical harmony (enharmonic, chromatic, and diatonic) had fallen out of use entirely.[124] But the

119. Aujoulat 1986, 6; see too Chuvin 1990, 86.

120. D. Shanzer, "Merely a Cynic Gesture?" *Riv. di fil.* 113 (1985): 62; R. Asmus, "Hypatia in Tradition und Dichtung," *Studien zur Vergleichenden Literaturgeschichte* 7 (1907): 16.

121. C. Zintzen, *Damascii vitae Isidori reliquiae* (Hildesheim 1967), 76–79; cf. R. Asmus, *Das Leben des Philosophen Isidoros von Damaskios aus Damaskos* (Leipzig 1911), 31–32. Shanzer (1985) shows no interest in the source of the story and does not mention Damascius.

122. Asmus 1911, 14, followed by Zintzen 1967 ad loc. John Toland, author of an inflammatory pamphlet entitled *Hypatia, or the History of a most beautiful, most vertuous, most learned and every way accomplished Lady, who was torn to pieces by the Clergy of Alexandria to gratify the Pride, Emulation and Cruelty of their Archbishop commonly but undeservedly stiled St. Cyril*, part 3 of *Tetradymus* (London 1720), dismissed this version on the grounds that music was "rather an incentive to Love, than an antidote against it" (123). Toland gives a most moving, and not unscholarly, account of "poor Hypatia's tragedy," but it is obvious that he picked the theme to attack the established church of his day. This is sufficiently proved by the publication of a reply the following year by one Thomas Lewis, under the no less provocative title *The History of Hypatia, a most impudent School-Mistress of Alexandria: In defence of Saint Cyril and the Alexandrian Clergy from the Aspersions of Mr. Toland.* Hypatia's name is blackened to save the good name of the clergy of eighteenth-century London.

123. *Epit. Phot.* 127 (p. 170.13f. Zintzen).

124. So too Macrobius *Comm. in Cic. somn. Scip.* 2.4.13; for the three types see too Proclus *In Tim.* 2.168.14f.

others had not, and this version finds strong support in the remark of an independent Egyptian source, John of Nikiu, that Hypatia devoted much of her time to music.[125] It also presents her behaving in a way better befitting a Platonist.[126] Plato himself was keenly interested in music,[127] and Iamblichus had stressed its therapeutic value in his *Life of Pythagoras*.[128]

One recent account noted that as "a philosopher himself, Damascius accurately characterized the teaching of Hypatia."[129] On the contrary, I would suggest that the similarities between Hypatia and what another scholar has called "her Cynic sisters" were invented, rather than simply reported, by Damascius.[130] A critical reading of Damascius's account of Hypatia suggests that he systematically represented her as no more than a street-corner philosophical huckster, a latter-day Cynic. He draws a vivid and coherent picture. But is it true? Modern historians of philosophy classify her *teaching* as Cynic, either not noticing or not thinking it relevant that Damascius was referring to her *behavior*. At least one of his claims can be shown from an earlier and more reliable source to be distinctly misleading. His remark that Hypatia paraded through the city teaching philosophy to all comers implies an old-fashioned Cynic haranguing passersby. But according to Socrates, it was from her carriage that the monks grabbed her. Street philosophers do not drive around town in their carriages.[131]

Cynic techniques would be uncharacteristic in a late antique Platonist. Cynics had never got on with Platonists.[132] It should be enough to refer to the one genuine Cynic mentioned by Damascius, Salustius of Emesa, who mocked everyone, walked the streets barefoot, and tried to

125. Quoted in full below, pp. 59–60.

126. Shanzer argues that Hypatia was in fact quoting Plotinus on noetic beauty "in order to bring [the student] to his senses." She claims: "For Plotinus the menstrual flow is seen not as an object of horror or disgust, but neutrally (*Enn.* 2, 9) as a metaphor for the generative substrate, and almost positively (*Enn.* 5, 8) as something that by giving life might impart beauty" (1985, 66). But how can any of this be related to the throwing of the sanitary napkin, which must have been intended, as it was construed by both the student and the Neoplatonist Damascius, who tells the story, as a disgusting, deterrent gesture?

127. D. H. Fowler, *The Mathematics of Plato's Academy* (Oxford 1987), 130–57.

128. τὴν διὰ μουσικῆς παιδείαν πρώτην κατεστήσατο [Pythagoras], διά τε μελῶν τινῶν καὶ ῥυθμῶν, ἀφ᾽ ὧν τρόπων τε καὶ παθῶν ἀνθρωπίνων ἰάσεις ἐγίγνοντο (*Vita Pyth.* 15).

129. Chuvin 1990, 167 n. 34.

130. "It has long been noted that the freedom of Hypatia's bold and outrageous gesture has much in common with such behaviour as the κυνογαμία attested for the famous Hipparchia" (Shanzer 1985, 62–63, repeating the usual references ancient and modern).

131. Nor do they usually teach mathematics and astronomy, Hypatia's specialities.

132. See M.-O. Goulet-Cazé, "Le cynisme à l'époque impériale," *ANRW* II.36.4 (1990): 2720–2833, who observes, "Tout comme dans le cynisme ancien, Cyniques et Platoniciens sous l'Empire ne faisaient pas bon ménage" (2814).

dissuade young men from devoting their lives to philosophy, thereby earning the hostility of Proclus.[133] Damascius's attempt to tar Hypatia with the same brush is not only improbable in itself: more important, nothing could be more unlike the conception of philosophy entertained by her pupil Synesius.

Our other sources for Hypatia's teaching—Synesius and what can be reconstructed of her published work—tell a very different story. First, what we can glean about her publications. It has long been customary to lament the disappearance of Hypatia's writings, but such regret may be premature, in more senses than one. She is credited by her entry in the Suda with "a commentary on Diophantus, the *Astronomical Canon,* and a commentary on the *Conica* of Apollonius":[134] commentaries, that is, on the *Arithmetica* of Diophantus of Alexandria (second or third century A.D.) and the *Conic Sections* of Apollonius of Perge (third century B.C.).[135] The central item on the list is more of a puzzle. Following Paul Tannery, most critics have inserted an εἰς, "on," construing "<a commentary on> the Astronomical Canon."[136] The work in question looks like Ptolemy's *Handy Tables* (πρόχειροι κανόνες τῆς ἀστρονομίας), a revised and expanded edition of astronomical tables originally included in his *Almagest.* All the relevant Suda entries relating to this work give the word "Canon" in the singular.[137]

Hypatia's father, Theon, is credited with not one but two commentaries on the *Handy Tables* in addition to his thirteen-book commentary on the *Almagest* itself. Tannery suggested that one of the commentaries was in fact by Hypatia.[138] We now have critical editions of one and part of the other, and it is established by their prefaces and by cross-references between them that Theon did indeed write both himself, first the "large commentary" in five books, and then the much-simplified

133. *PLRE* II.972–73; Goulet-Cazé 1990, 2814–16.

134. ἔγραψεν ὑπόμνημα εἰς Διόφαντον, τὸν ἀστρονομικὸν κανόνα, εἰς τὰ κωνικὰ Ἀπολλωνίου ὑπόμνημα.

135. Waithe's claim (1987, 176f.) that the commentary on Diophantus survives is based on a misunderstanding of Tannery.

136. *Mémoires scientifiques,* vol. 2 (Paris 1912), 77.

137. Suda, s.v. Πάππος: ὁ γράψας εἰς τὸν Πτολεμαίου κανόνα; s.v. Θέων: εἰς τὸν τοῦ Πτολεμαίου κανόνα; s.v. Πτολεμαῖος: κανόνα πρόχειρον. The Arabic writer Yaʿqubi (A.D. 875) refers to Theon's smaller commentary on the *Handy Tables* simply as "the Canon" (Neugebauer 1949, 242–43). According to a scholion in an imperial list published by H. Usener in Mommsen, *Chron. Min.* III (1898), 451, it was in the reign of Marcus that τὸν κανόνα ἔγραψεν Πτολεμαῖος. A late Latin version goes under the name *Preceptum canonis Ptolomaei* [sic] (Neugebauer 1975, 970). On the *Handy Tables* themselves, Neugebauer 1975, 969–1028.

138. *Diophanti Alexandrini opera,* vol. 2 (Leipzig 1895), viii.

"small commentary" in one book.[139] It is impossible to believe that
Hypatia added a third. Furthermore, the word order is against Tannery's
insertion. In the text as transmitted the word "commentary" appears at
both beginning and end of the list, implying that it is only the first and
last items on which Hypatia wrote commentaries. If it had been all three,
we might have expected to find "commentaries" (in the plural) once
only, whether at the beginning or end of the list: "commentaries on A,
B, and C." The middle item is surely just the title of her book: *Astronomical Canon.*

The *Handy Tables* themselves do not survive in Ptolemy's original
edition, but in a version in modern times widely attributed to Theon.
But the attribution is not attested by any MS,[140] nor does Theon himself
refer to any such edition or redaction in either of his commentaries. On
the contrary, the improbable way he explains some of Ptolemy's calculations in those commentaries proves conclusively that he cannot have
checked the figures.[141] On the basis of the unemended Suda entry, we
are surely entitled to infer that it was Hypatia who actually edited the
text, no doubt under Theon's guidance and encouragement.[142]

In support, we may turn to the much-discussed subtitle to book 3 of
Theon's commentary on the *Almagest:*

Commentary by Theon of Alexandria on Book III of Ptolemy's *Almagest,*
edition revised by my daughter Hypatia, the philosopher.

Θέωνος Ἀλεξανδρέως εἰς τὸ τρίτον τῆς μαθηματικῆς Πτολεμαίου Συν-
τάξεως ὑπόμνημα, ἐκδόσεως παραναγνωσθείσης τῇ φιλοσόφῳ θυγατρί
μου Ὑπατίᾳ.

It has always been assumed that it was Theon's *commentary* that Hypatia
revised. Theon's editor A. Rome looked, in vain, for linguistic differences between book 3 and the other books.[143] A speculative recent study
by W. Knorr claims to detect contradictions between book 3 and other

---

139. J. Mogenet and A. Tihon, *Le 'Grand Commentaire' de Théon d'Alexandrie aux Tables
Faciles de Ptolémée,* vol. 1, Studi e testi 315 (Rome 1985), 69 and 220.

140. Neugebauer 1975, 968; cf. 977; there exists only the unsatisfactory edition by
N. Halma in three volumes (1822–25). For a list of MSS, J. L. Heiberg, *Ptolemaei opera astronomica minora,* vol. 2 (1907), cxci–cciii.

141. A. Tihon, "Théon d'Alexandrie et les Tables Faciles de Ptolémée," *Archives internationales d'histoire des sciences* 35 (1985): 119.

142. So already Usener, in Mommsen, *Chron.Min.* III (1898), 362: "patre auctore ac
duce Hypatiam tabulas manuales retractasse . . . inutile est quaerere et semper intra do-
mesticos Theonis parietes abditum erit, quae fuerint filiae in tabulis retractandis partes."

143. A. Rome, *Commentaires de Pappus et de Théon d'Alexandrie sur l'Almageste,* vol. 3,
Studi e testi 106 (Rome 1943), cxvi–cxxi.

books, implying additions of substance by Hypatia.[144] But the solution is provided by the headings to books 1 and 2 that do *not* mention Hypatia:

> Commentary by Theon of Alexandria on Book I (II) of Ptolemy's *Almagest*, his own edition.
>
> Θέωνος Ἀλεξανδρέως τῆς παρ' αὐτοῦ γεγενημένης ἐκδόσεως εἰς τὸ πρῶτον (δεύτερον) τῆς Συντάξεως Πτολεμαίου ὑπόμνημα.

According to Rome, this is "the original edition, in contrast to Hypatia's."[145] But we might naturally assume that when writing books 1–2 Theon had not yet written book 3, much less seen it revised by Hypatia. And while it at least makes sense to speak of a commentary of Theon in an edition revised by Hypatia, it is nonsense to speak of a commentary of Theon in his own edition.[146] In the ordinary way, one's own books are always in one's own edition. It is too self-evident to be worth stating at all. There is an exact parallel in the headings to the works of an early sixth-century commentator on the same sort of texts, Eutocius of Ascalon. First, in the headings to the two books of his commentary on Archimedes, *De sphaera et cylindro*, Eutocius refers in exactly the same terms to an "edition checked by my teacher, Isidore of Miletus the engineer" (ἐκδόσεως παραναγνωσθείσης τῷ Μιλησίῳ μηχανικῷ Ἰσιδώρῳ ἡμετέρῳ διδασκάλῳ).[147] This Isidore is the architect of St. Sophia, and the heading has always been interpreted to mean that Eutocius's commentary was revised by Isidore. But there are fatal objections to this hypothesis. In the first place the verb παραναγιγνώσκειν does not mean "revise" in the sense "correct" or "modify." It means, invariably, "check for exact verbal accuracy."[148] In the second, there can be no doubt that Isidore was a generation older than Eutocius. It would be odd for the teacher to revise the commentary of the student. Once again, we may compare the headings to another of Eutocius's commentaries, on all four books of the *Conica* of Apollonius of Perge, where again the "edition" is said to be Eutocius's own (τῆς κατ' αὐτὸν ἐκδόσεως).[149] As with books 1 and 2 of Theon, Eutocius cannot be saying that this is his own edition of his own commentary. Who else's edition could it be? Obviously he is referring to his own commentary *and* his own edition of the text of Apollonius. In this case we can be certain, since in the course of his com-

---

144. Wilbur R. Knorr, *Textual Studies in Ancient and Medieval Geometry* (Boston 1989), 753–803.

145. Rome 1936, 317 n. 1.

146. Both these points are argued at greater length in Cameron 1990.

147. F in Heiberg's first edition of 1888, A in his second of 1915 (III^2.48.26; cf. 224.7, 260.10).

148. Cameron 1990, 103–27.

149. II^2.168, 290, 314, 354 Heiberg.

mentary Eutocius refers to his edition of the text quite explicitly. In the preface to book 4 he distinguishes between his ἔκδοσις and the σχόλια with which he has equipped it.

This provides the key to the identical distinction between ὑπόμνημα and ἔκδοσις in the headings to Theon's *Almagest* commentary. In the lexicon of the scholar, ἔκδοσις and ὑπόμνημα denote two quite different sorts of book, the edition *of* and the commentary *on* the text in question. Certainly this is how Theon himself elsewhere used the terms. For example, in the course of book 1 of his *Almagest* commentary, he remarks: "That sectors of equal circles are to one another as the angles on which they stand, I have proved in my *edition* of [Euclid's] *Elements* (δέδεικται ἡμῖν ἐν τῇ ἐκδόσει τῶν Στοιχείων) at the end of the sixth book."[150] Now Theon did not write a commentary on Euclid, but he did edit the text. And just such a proposition appears in almost all extant MSS of the *Elements* at the end of 6.33. Indeed, some of these MSS are explicitly stated to be "from Theon's edition" (ἐκ τῆς Θέωνος ἐκδόσεως). It is now well known that the original text of Euclid's *Elements* was almost entirely supplanted by a simplified and edited version by Theon, designed to make Euclid "easier for his students to use."[151] Theon also produced similar "editions" of two other works of Euclid, the *Data* and *Optics*.[152]

The possibility that he might have produced an edition of the *Almagest* to accompany his commentary was aired long ago by his latest modern editor, J. L. Heiberg, on the basis of alleged interpolations in one family of MSS.[153] The headings to books 1–3 contain explicit allusions to such an edition, hitherto overlooked. But it was only the first two books that Theon himself edited. At that point in the long task that lay ahead of him he enlisted his daughter's assistance, and they divided the labor between them, Theon compiling the commentary and Hypatia editing the text. Theon went on to compile the large and small commentaries on the *Handy Tables*, and during his labors he may well have come to feel the need for a new edition of the text. If so, to whom is he more likely to have entrusted the task than Hypatia? She would already have covered much of the ground when editing the *Almagest*. Such editions would not,

150. Rome 1936, 492.6–8 (translation by T. L. Heath).

151. G. J. Toomer, *Dictionary of Scientific Biography* 13 (1976): 322; cf. K. Ziegler, "Theon 15," *RE* 5.A.2 (1934): 2078–79; for the details, J. L. Heiberg, *Euclidis opera*, vol. 5 (Leipzig 1888), xxivf., li–lxxvi; T. Heath, *The Thirteen Books of Euclid's Elements*, vol. 1, 2d ed. (London 1926), 46–63.

152. Toomer 1976, 322–23; Ziegler 1934, 2078–79; H. Menge, *Euclidis opera*, 6: xxxii–xlix; 7:xlix–l; J. L. Heiberg, *Literargeschichtliche Studien über Euclid* (Leipzig 1882), 129–48.

153. *Ptolemaei opera astronomica minora*, vol. 2 (Leipzig 1907), cxxvi. But D, in Heiberg's eyes the most interpolated MS, has been substantially rehabilitated by G. J. Toomer (1984, 3).

of course, have been based on systematic collation of MSS; their purpose, like Theon's Euclid, was largely pedagogical. Far from Hypatia's works being entirely lost, we may have more than 1,000 pages of Greek edited by her. The "large number of interpolations" recently detected in the *Almagest* by G. J. Toomer may in the main be Hypatia's work.[154]

In fact we can go farther still. Of the thirteen original books of Diophantus's *Arithmetica,* only six survive in Greek. Tannery suggested that this was because Hypatia's commentary stopped with book 6 and that the rest was found too difficult to read without such assistance.[155] But we now know that at least another four books survived to be translated into Arabic ca. 860. An Arabic MS has recently been found containing books numbered 4–7, which seem to follow the Greek books numbered 1–3. More interesting still, the Arabic text is an expanded version of Diophantus's text, incorporating verifications of his demonstrations, alternative resolutions, and interpolated problems.[156] Clearly the purpose was to make a difficult text easier to follow. Either the translator incorporated into his text material from an elementary exegetical commentary or the text he translated had already been amplified in this way. Either way, the obvious candidate for this amplified Greek original, as J. Sesiano, the first editor of the text, was quick to point out, is Hypatia, Diophantus's only known ancient commentator. Knorr raised what he engagingly conceded to be the "sentimental" objection that identifying Hypatia "via stylistic comparisons of the Arabic and Greek texts would thus isolate an essentially trivial mind. This is in direct conflict with ancient testimonies of Hypatia's high caliber as a philosopher and mathematician."[157] Nonetheless, it may be that Hypatia's work on Diophantus was, if not trivial, elementary, exegetical rather than critical, designed for the use of elementary students. Theon's *Almagest* commentary was, as its preface concedes, no more than a redaction of his lecture notes.[158]

The same may have been true of Hypatia's commentary on Apollonius. A century later Eutocius of Ascalon produced another com-

154. *Ptolemy's Almagest* (London 1984), 5, 683.

155. *Mémoires scientifiques,* vol. 2 (Paris 1912), 73–90. As he pointed out, much the same happened with the *Conica* of Apollonius, where only the four books edited and commented on in the sixth century by Eutocius survive. On Eutocius's editorial method, see Cameron 1990.

156. J. Sesiano, *Books IV to VII of Diophantus's* Arithmetica *in the Arabic Translation Attributed to Qusta ibn Luqa* (New York 1982), 48–57; 68–73; R. Rashed, *Diophante: Les Arithmétiques III–IV* (Paris 1984).

157. *American Mathematical Monthly* 92 (1985): 152. Rashed's contemptuous dismissal of the suggestion (*Diophante III* [1984], lxii, note) is simply part of a personal attack on Sesiano: see G. J. Toomer, *Revue des questions scientifiques* 156 (1985): 237–41.

158. G. J. Toomer, *Dictionary of Scientific Biography* 13 (1976): 321; Neugebauer (1975, 968) refers to the "dullness and pomposity of these school treatises," quoting A. Rome's verdict that "nous plaignons les étudiants."

mentary on Apollonius's *Conica*, "mostly of a trivial nature, and, unlike his commentary on Archimedes, providing almost nothing of historical value."[159] Working as he was so soon after Hypatia and, like her, in Alexandria, Eutocius must have known and read her work. The presumption is that, like her work on Diophantus, Hypatia's commentary on Apollonius mainly consisted of simple exegesis.

It may be, then, that so far from having to lament the loss of Hypatia's published writings, we are in fact in a position to form a rather accurate impression of them. The more extravagant expectations are certainly dashed. It seems clear that, like her father, she spent much of her time teaching mathematics and astronomy. There is no record of any philosophical publications of any kind. But we do not need to leave it there. We might bear in mind that even today academic publications do not tell us all we might like to know about a professor's teaching. Hypatia's publications certainly do not explain her reputation, beginning with the veneration in which she was held by her student Synesius.

So let us see what we can learn from Synesius. John Rist has argued that Hypatia was a very old-fashioned Platonist, "not an exponent of the philosophy of either Plotinus or Iamblichus,"[160] mainly on the grounds that Synesius quotes Plotinus and Porphyry less often than he does Plato and Aristotle.[161] But this is a highly misleading inference. All Neoplatonists quote Plato more often than Plotinus and Porphyry. After all, they claimed to be Platonists. The recent book by N. Aujoulat takes a similar position, underlining Hypatia's concentration on the exact sciences.[162]

This view squares nicely with the traditional view of the nature of Alexandrian Neoplatonism during Synesius's lifetime. It used to be assumed that the Alexandrians taught a rather old-fashioned Platonism in the early fifth century.[163] Hierocles, a generation younger than Synesius,

159. G. J. Toomer, *Apollonius, Conics Books V to VII: The Arabic Translation of the Lost Greek Original in the Version of the Banu Musa*, vol. 1 (New York 1990), xvi. For a list of the earlier texts read and cited by Eutocius, see J. L. Heiberg, "Über Eutokios," *Jahrbücher für classische Philologie*, Suppl. 11 (1880): 363–71; Heiberg concludes that he was "ein sehr fleißiger Sammler von weit ausgedehnter Belesenheit" (363); see also Bulmer-Thomas 1971, 489–91.

160. J. M. Rist, "Hypatia," *Phoenix* 19 (1965): 219; so too E. Évrard, *REG* 90 (1977): 69 ("professait un néoplatonisme primitif"); Chuvin 1990, 85. More cautiously, Lacombrade argued only that Iamblichus played a smaller part in her teaching than Porphyry (1951a, 49).

161. Rist 1965, 276–77, relying on the statistics assembled rather amateurishly long ago by Fitzgerald (1926, 16): 126 quotations from Plato, 20 from Aristotle, 9 from Plotinus, and 3 from Porphyry.

162. Aujoulat 1986, 6.

163. From K. Praechter, "Christlich-neuplatonische Beziehungen," *BZ* 21 (1912): 1–27 (cf. *RE* 8.2.1481) to T. Kobusch, *Studien zur Philosophie des Hierokles von Alexandrien: Untersuchungen zum christlichen Neuplatonismus* (Munich 1976).

is held to have been closer to Middle Platonism than to Plotinus, Porphyry, and Iamblichus. But I. Hadot has recently challenged this long-established view, at least in the case of Hierocles, arguing that there was no real difference between the teachings of Alexandria and Athens.[164] Hierocles was just as indebted to Iamblichus and the Chaldaean Oracles as to the school of Plutarch.[165]

Perhaps Hypatia was not so old-fashioned either. If Rist had looked at Synesius a little more carefully, he would have found evidence hard to reconcile with this view. The defining feature of Synesius's Neoplatonism (as we have already seen) is his enthusiasm for the so-called Chaldaean Oracles, a collection purporting to be divine revelations in hexameter verse composed or edited by an otherwise unknown Julian the Chaldaean in the reign of Marcus Aurelius.[166] They were rediscovered and given a Platonizing interpretation by Porphyry, followed by Iamblichus and further elaborated by Plutarch, Syrianus, and Proclus at Athens. It was the theurgy that was based on the Oracles that formed the most esoteric part of Athenian Neoplatonism.[167] Synesius directly quotes them by name four times in his work on dream divination, and there are countless echoes in his hymns.[168] Who initiated Synesius into these secrets? Who can it have been but his only known guru, Hypatia?

Where and with whom did Hypatia study philosophy? The usual assumption that she studied mathematics and astronomy with her father seems reasonable enough. But Theon was no philosopher. We are fortunate in having a fairly detailed account of the successors to Iamblichus in Eunapius's *Lives of the Philosophers and Sophists*. As Robert J. Penella's useful recent study has underlined, the only philosophers active in his own lifetime that Eunapius included are those who carried on the Iamblichan tradition, with its emphasis on theurgy and the Chaldaean Oracles.[169] This is surely the principal reason he ignores Themistius; not just because he was perceived as a collaborator with Christian emperors, but because he stood outside the Iamblichan tradition—indeed was perhaps openly contemptuous of it.[170] Perhaps the strangest name on Eu-

164. *Le problème du Néoplatonisme alexandrin: Hieroclès et Simplicius* (Paris 1978); and see too now Noël Aujoulat, *Le Néoplatonisme alexandrin: Hieroclès d' Alexandrie*, Philosophia antiqua 45 (Leiden 1986).

165. I. Hadot 1978, 70–71.

166. Even his date is uncertain: see G. Fowden, *Historia* 36 (1987): 90–95.

167. The standard work is H. Lewy, *The Chaldaean Oracles and Theurgy*, 2d ed. (Paris 1978), with the edition of E. Des Places, *Oracles Chaldaïques* (Paris 1971).

168. As first shown in detail by W. Theiler (1942).

169. R. J. Penella, *Greek Philosophers and Sophists in the Fourth Century A.D.: Studies in Eunapius of Sardis* (Liverpool 1990), 39–78, 134–37.

170. *Or.* 23, 295B (ii.90.10f. Downey-Norman); cf. Dagron 1968, 43–44; Cracco Ruggini 1972, 63, 72.

napius's list is Sosipatra of Pergamum, who is said to have been taught by two mysterious strangers. Since they are expressly described as being "initiates of the Chaldaean wisdom,"[171] it seems clear that Sosipatra stood in this tradition. Her son Antoninus, who inherited his mother's gift of clairvoyance, traveled to Alexandria and then taught Platonic philosophy at the Canopic mouth of the Nile, dying shortly before the destruction of the Serapeum in 391, which he had foretold.[172] Penella has made an interesting suggestion about this part of Eunapius's book:

> Did the Sardian Eunapius have Hypatia in mind in writing his full and flattering sketch of Sosipatra, intending her to be understood as an Asianic answer to Alexandria's female sage? The admirer of the theurgic Sosipatra will not have been well disposed towards the strongly rational bent in Hypatia's philosophy. And he will not have failed to appreciate the irony in the fact that Sosipatra's son Antoninus throve as a teacher of philosophy in Egypt . . . during Hypatia's own lifetime.[173]

But "rational bent" apart, Antoninus and Hypatia can hardly have been teaching in Egypt at the same time. The conventional date of ca. 370 assigned for Hypatia's birth is probably too early,[174] but she must surely have still been a student when Antoninus died ca. 390. Eunapius does not mention her because he had not yet heard of her when writing his book in the mid-390s.[175] Indeed, it is tempting to conjecture that it was precisely with Antoninus that she studied. He is certainly the only representative of the Iamblichan tradition known to have taught in the neighborhood of Alexandria in Hypatia's lifetime. It is extraordinary that Antoninus is not so much as mentioned in any of the three recent books on early fifth-century Alexandrian Neoplatonism.[176] It is true that Hypatia's younger contemporary Hierocles (born ca. 390)[177] expressly ascribes his initiation in the Iamblichan tradition to Plutarch of Athens.[178] But al-

171. Eunap. *VS* 468, with Pack 1952, 203.
172. Eunap. *VS* 471–73.
173. Penella 1990, 61–62.
174. Penella 1984, 126–28.
175. T. M. Banchich (*GRBS* 25 [1984]: 183–92) tries to date the *Vitae Sophistarum* to 399, arguing that the θόρυβος referred to in 479 is the revolt of Tribigild. But it is difficult to see why Tribigild's revolt should lead to the subordination of the proconsul of Asia to the praetorian prefect. And of all politicians of the age, Eutropius is the least likely to have increased the power of the praetorian prefect; the prefect was a far more dangerous rival to his own power than was the proconsul of Asia. It must have been a prefect who was responsible for this reform, at a time of now unidentifiable θόρυβος. If Paschoud (*Cinq études sur Zosime* [1976], 171) were right to date the book as late as 413, we should certainly have expected a reference to Hypatia.
176. Namely, Kobusch 1976; I. Hadot 1978; Aujoulat 1986.
177. Aujoulat 1986, 6.
178. ὡς . . . καὶ Πορφύριος καὶ Ἰάμβλιχος καὶ οἱ ἐφεξῆς. ὅσοι τῆς ἱερᾶς (ὡς αὐτός φησι) γενεᾶς ἔτυχον φύντες. ἕως Πλουτάρχου τοῦ Ἀθηναίου. ὃν καὶ καθηγητὴν αὐτοῦ τῶν

though he later taught at Alexandria, there is no evidence where he was born or brought up, and consequently no basis for claiming that such an initiation was not available at Alexandria during Hypatia's lifetime. Indeed, it evidently was, since it is Hypatia whom Synesius credits with his own initiation.

Synesius undoubtedly took an interest in what would now be called the occult. Hypatia's father, Theon, wrote books "on signs and the examination of birds and the croaking of ravens,"[179] and "commentaries on the books of Hermes Trismegistus and Orpheus," in addition to a substantial body of unexotic mathematical and astronomical work.[180] The standard work on Theon assumes that these items have been transferred by error from the bibliography of some other Theon.[181] A sober commentator like Hypatia's father could not have wasted his time on such nonsense. But there is in fact a link with Synesius here. Synesius wrote a book on dream divination, which drew heavily on the Chaldaean Oracles. When in the course of that work he had occasion to comment on the superiority of dream divination over bird divination, he revealed himself remarkably well informed about the technicalities of the latter.[182] Synesius also shows knowledge of Hermetic writings.[183]

Did he dabble in yet murkier arts? Several manuscripts ascribe to him a brief alchemical text,[184] in the form of a commentary on the *Physica et mystica* of Ps.-Democritus (in fact, Bolus of Mendes), the basic text of Greek alchemy.[185] Some have ruled out even the possibility that one so devoted to Hellenism and the exact sciences could stoop to a barbarian pseudoscience,[186] but these are anachronistic categories: this distinction

τοιούτων ἀναγράφει δογμάτων, in Photius's summary of Hierocles, Περὶ Προνοίας, *Bibl.* cod. 214, p. 173a, 37–39 Bekker.

179. Suda, s.v. Θέων.

180. Malalas, p. 343B = p. 186 Aus.

181. G. J. Toomer, *Dictionary of Scientific Biography* 13 (1976): 323, who does not cite the commentaries on the Hermetica.

182. οἱ δὲ ἐν ὀρνίθων κλαγγαῖς καὶ καθέδραις καὶ πτήσεσι [ὁρῶσι τὸ μέλλον] (*De insomniis* 132B). "Les Grecs, plus subtils, subdivisèrent la matière en trois ou même quatre points; le *vol* (πτῆσις), le *cri* (φωνή, κλαγγαί), l'assiette ou *siège* (ἕδρα, κάθεδρα), l'attitude ou *opération* (ἐνεργεία)" (Bouché-Leclercq 1879, 136). Aelian mentions those ἕδρας ὀρνίθων καὶ πτήσεις παραφυλάττοντες (*De nat. anim.* 3.9), but only Synesius names as many as three of the things to look for at once.

183. As shown in detail below, chapter 7, section 6.

184. *Collection des anciens alchimistes grecs*, vol. 2, ed. M. Berthelot and C.-E. Ruelle (Paris 1888), 56–69.

185. On this mysterious figure, see P. M. Fraser, *Ptolemaic Alexandria* (Oxford 1972), 440–43; Festugière 1950, 224–38.

186. Lacombrade 1951a, 69–79: alchemists are said to reject "la tradition grecque pour lui préférer la tradition barbare" while "nul n'est plus soucieux que Synésios des νόμιμα de l'Hellade"; Synesius, "le disciple de la 'géomètre' [Hypatia] voit dans les mathématiques la règle infaillible de vérité."

was not made by late antique Hellenism. Synesius's *De insomniis* is extant. Theon's occult interests are securely enough attested. At least two other Alexandrian philosophers also are credited with alchemical writings, Olympiodorus and Stephanus.[187]

The commentary ascribed to Synesius is no better. It is not really a commentary, since it explains none of the arcane notions or terms with which its text abounds; it is simply a dialogue, addressed to "Dioscoros the priest of Great Sarapis in Alexandria," in which the master communicates arcane lore to his pupil. Synesius is represented saying things like "Have you not heard the saying of Hermes that 'wax is white and wax is yellow?'"[188] Dioscoros thanks him effusively for every such pearl. Neither Synesius nor Olympiodorus wrote these absurd productions, but we should not, with Lacombrade, for example, suppose that Synesius the alchemist was an earlier homonym, innocently confused with the Cyrenean.[189] He is given Synesius's own regular style "Synesius the philosopher,"[190] and the dedication to Dioscoros situates him in Alexandria some time before the destruction of the Serapeum in (probably) 391.[191]

187. On both see Fowden 1986, 178–79; Wolska-Conus 1989, 15. The commentary on Zosimus of Panopolis ascribed to Olympiodorus (II.69–106 Berthelot-Ruelle) can hardly be genuine. As Westerink has observed, it is hard to believe that a man who devoted his life to explaining texts could have brought himself to write a work that "explains nothing at all" (*The Greek Commentaries on Plato's Phaedo* [Amsterdam 1976], 22–23).

188. II.62.4 Berthelot-Ruelle.

189. Lacombrade 1951a, 64–71; against, Fowden 1986, 178.

190. Just as Olympiodorus the alchemist is styled Ὀλυμπιοδώρου φιλοσόφου Ἀλεξανδρέως, the regular style of the philosopher.

191. Fowden 1978, 69–71; Schwartz 1966, 110; King 1960, 104–5; Seeck 1913, 534–35. The extant antipagan law of 16 June 391 (*Cod. Theod.* 16.10.11) is addressed, exceptionally (Seeck 1919, 7.16), to both Evagrius the Augustal prefect and Romanus the count of Egypt, both named in connection with the destruction of the Serapeum by Sozomen (*HE* 7.15.5) and Eunapius (*VS* 472: Euetius and Romanus). If this law is in fact the imperial command mentioned in Sozomen's account, then the destruction of the Serapeum must have taken place soon after its arrival. Since it was issued in Aquileia, we should allow up to a month for transit. The early fifth-century illustrated chronicle from Alexandria *P. Goleniscev* (A. Bauer and J. Strzygowski, *Eine Alexandrinische Weltchronik*, Denkschrift der k. Akad. der Wiss. in Wien, Phil.-hist. Kl. 51.2 [1905], 69–73) dates the destruction to 392, apparently its final entry. But although its date and provenance might seem to invest this chronicle with formidable authority, of the eight events it dates between 384 and 392 (the extant fragment), only two are correct. There are even problems with its prefects of Egypt, apparently due to the chronicler's inability to harmonize his three dating systems: consuls, prefects of Egypt, and era of Diocletian (see the full discussion in C. Vandersleyen, *Chronologie des préfets d'Egypte de 284 à 395* [Brussels 1962], 169–81). If the destruction took place as late as September 391, it may be that the chronicler simply confused the new indiction with the new consuls of 392. None of the studies cited above have exploited the evidence of Palladas, despite Ch. Lacombrade, *Pallas* 1 (1953): 23; R. Keydell, *BZ* 50 (1957): 1; A. Cameron, *JRS* 55 (1965): 21–28. According to Jones 1964a, 168 n. 77 (III.32), the date of the law has no bearing on the destruction "and might be earlier or later than it."

A further significant detail is that in section 6 Synesius the alchemist gives an uncharacteristically clear and precise description of an apparatus for distilling mercury. The description is illustrated by equally clear line drawings preserved in at least three MSS.[192] According to M. Berthelot, writing in 1888, "c'est un appareil qui est encore en usage aujourd'hui." Zosimus of Panopolis, who seems to have lived at the beginning of the fourth century, wrote a work *On Furnaces* which is unfortunately lost, but confessed in the surviving introduction that he could do no better than "the ancients."[193] It is generally accepted that the alembic described by Synesius the alchemist was a new development of his age, a natural consequence of the growing interest in chemical experiment that was the essence of alchemy. Significantly, Synesius of Cyrene stands out among his contemporaries for his interest in scientific apparatus. His *De dono* describes how he himself, following Hypatia's instructions, designed the astrolabe of which he gives so detailed a description.[194] And another letter begs Hypatia, as a matter of urgency, to send him a "hydroscope."[195] The remarkably precise description he appends shows that he means what is now called a hydrometer, an instrument for measuring the specific gravity of liquids. The man who ascribed the commentary on Ps.-Democritus to "Synesius the philosopher" knew what he was doing; it is a deliberate forgery.[196] Whether or not the real Synesius concerned himself with alchemy in any way, he was a man well known for his interest in scientific apparatus, here, as in his Neoplatonism, a true pupil of Hypatia.

The interest in Hermetica and bird divination might seem to point to Theon rather than Hypatia. Is it possible that Synesius actually studied with Theon? Surely not. Since Synesius nowhere mentions Theon, we may reasonably assume that he was dead by the time Synesius knew

192. I.164–65 Berthelot-Ruelle; see too the discussion in H. Kopp, *Beiträge zur Geschichte der Chemie* (Braunschweig 1869), 217–39.

193. By which he may have meant the Καμινογραφία of Maria the Jewess referred to by Olympiodorus the alchemist (II.90.19 Berthelot-Ruelle): see Festugière 1950, 273–74; and H. M. Jackson, *Zosimus of Panopolis on the Letter Omega* (Missoula, Mont. 1978), 42 n.10.

194. On the various problems in Synesius's description, see Neugebauer 1949, 248–51.

195. Οὕτω πάνυ πέπραγα πονήρως ὥστε ὑδροσκοπίου μοι δεῖ (*Ep.* 15). The tone may suggest that he needed it for some medical purpose.

196. In which case "Dioscoros the priest of great Serapis in Alexandria" may also be a forgery, a piece of local color designed to fix the writer at the right place and time (Zosimus of Panopolis claims that various arcane records were kept in the temples, "especially the Serapeum" [*On the Letter Omega* 10 Ruelle = 8 Jackson]). It may after all turn out for the best that he was left out of *PLRE* I. It follows that the commentary of Ps.-Synesius may be of much later date than hitherto supposed. It is quoted by Ps.-Olympiodorus (II.90.20; 102.10 Berthelot-Ruelle), but what does that prove?

Hypatia. The latest datable reference in Theon's commentaries is to 377, and Synesius can hardly have entered Hypatia's classroom before ca. 390. The most natural explanation is that Hypatia, here as elsewhere, followed in her father's footsteps, teaching the same subjects, recommending her father's books to her own pupils. A fascinating hint of this has recently been published in the form of a marginal note in a MS of Theon's large commentary on the *Handy Tables:* "of Synesius the philosopher." [197] Presumably the MS in question derives from a copy that once belonged to Synesius. Unfortunately there are no scholia of any substance that can be attributed to Synesius.

Another nice illustration is Synesius's letter about the astrolabe. It was Hypatia, he claims, who taught him how to make it (*De dono* 311A). No doubt it was. But here too she was following in Theon's footsteps, for it was Theon who wrote the basic work in the field, his treatise *On the Small Astrolabe.*[198]

Synesius and Theon make an interesting pair; both devoted to the exact sciences and yet also curious about divination and the occult. And yet they probably never met. In the case of the exact sciences we can be confident that the missing link was Hypatia. It is surely natural to assume that she played the same role in the case of divination and the Hermetica. Theon also commented on Orphic writings. What more natural than that his daughter, with her more philosophical bent, should have been drawn to the Chaldaean Oracles?

Listen to the way Synesius speaks of Hypatia's philosophical teaching. In a letter to a fellow student he says: "We have seen with our own eyes, we have heard with our own ears the lady who rightfully presides over the mysteries (ὀργία) of philosophy" (*Ep.* 137). In *Ep.* 4 (= 5 G) he asks his brother to "salute for me the most holy and revered philosopher, and give my homage also to the blessed company that delights in her oracular utterance (θεσπεσίας αὐδῆς)." On his deathbed, he writes to her as "mother, sister, teacher, benefactress in all things" (*Ep.* 16).

---

197. J. Mogenet and A. Tihon, *L'antiquité classique* 50 (1981): 530–34, and (incorporating a suggestion by Neugebauer) in the *'Grand Commentaire' de Théon*, vol. 1 (1985), 75–77. Another scholion places the MS in Apamea by 462 (1985, 73). By a curious coincidence the main text in the MS is none other than the pre-Theonic version of Euclid's *Elements*.

198. Lost, but in its main lines reconstructed from Philoponus and two Arabic works by Neugebauer 1949, 240–56; cf. too Neugebauer 1975, 872–79 and G. J. Toomer, *Dictionary of Scientific Biography* 13 (1976), 323. Because Theon's treatise "contained a systematic discussion of the theory of the astrolabe and its application, far superior to the disorganized and utterly insufficient presentation we find in Synesius" (Neugebauer 1975, 873), Neugebauer suggests that Synesius wrote before Theon. But Synesius's very incompetence may be sufficient explanation, and whenever Theon actually wrote his treatise, it is hard to believe that he learned from his daughter and her pupils.

This might be Eunapius singing the praises of Sosipatra. It would not be surprising if it was from the teacher he describes in such terms that Synesius had derived both his knowledge of the Chaldaean Oracles and more generally his conception of philosophy as an esoteric mystery, not to be discussed with uninitiates or mentioned in a letter that might fall into their hands (*Ep.* 137, 143).

When he refers to her instruction in the exact sciences, it is in the same ecstatic terms, "holy geometry" or "divine geometry" (*Ep.* 93), treating it, not as a basic skill, but as a propaideutic to philosophy.[199] As he put it elsewhere, "astronomy itself is a venerable science and might become a stepping-stone to something more august, a science that I think is a convenient passage to mystic theology, for the happy body of heaven has matter underneath it, and its motion has seemed to the leaders in philosophy to be an imitation of mind" (*De dono* 310C–311A). But it was above all as a philosopher that he revered Hypatia. His letters to her are headed either "Hypatia the philosopher" or just τῇ φιλοσόφῳ, "the philosopher" (fem.). And it is as "the philosopher" that her father proudly styled her in the heading to book 3 of his *Almagest* commentary.

So some at least of Hypatia's classes must have been just as esoteric as those of Plutarch and Syrianus at Athens. Why then did Damascius so misrepresent her? He may simply have been misled by her lack of metaphysical publications. On the other hand, he may have been responding polemically to the famous letter Synesius wrote to his brother from Athens in 410,[200] lamenting its sad decline:

> Athens no longer has anything sublime except the country's famous names. . . . Today Egypt has received and cherishes the fruitful wisdom of Hypatia. Athens was formerly the home of wise men: today the beekeepers alone bring it honor. Such is the case with that pair of Plutarchean *sophists* who draw the young to their lecture room not by the fame of their eloquence, but by pots of honey from Hymettus.[201]

The "pair of Plutarcheans" he mentions in *Ep.* 136 must be Plutarch son of Nestorius (d. 431/34), the Athenian who reestablished Athens as the center of philosophical study in the early decades of the fifth century,[202] and his disciple and successor Syrianus. Garzya's edition prints

199. This was a well-established view: H.-I. Marrou, *Histoire de l'éducation dans l'antiquité*, 6th ed. (Paris 1965), 276–77. Proclus lectured regularly on Euclid, and his successor Marinus on both Euclid and Ptolemy, and the tradition was no less firmly maintained among the philosophers of Alexandria in the school of Ammonius: Neugebauer 1975, 1036–45.

200. On the date see appendix 3.

201. *Ep.* 136.

202. *PLRE* I.708 and II.1051; see too H. D. Saffrey and L. G. Westerink, *Proclus: Théologie platonicienne*, vol. 1 (Paris 1968), xxvif.

σοφῶν, "wise men," with only one MS, but most offer σοφιστῶν, "sophists," printed by R. Hercher (1873) and surely what Synesius wrote. In itself the term "sophist" simply designates a teacher of rhetoric. But in the context, coming from a man who considered himself a philosopher and despised teachers of rhetoric, it is hard to doubt that we are meant to detect something of a sneer. The two terms are repeatedly contrasted in *De dono:* in section 1, to do everything for show "is the mark of sophistry, not philosophy" (οὐ σοφίας ἀλλὰ σοφιστείας ἐστίν); section 3 draws an even sharper distinction between "the tribe of sophists" (τὸ σοφιστικὸν φῦλον) and the "true sons of philosophy" (ἀληθεῖς φιλοσοφίας συντρόφους).[203] It is also relevant to add that Syrianus evidently once earned his living teaching rhetoric. We have two commentaries on Hermogenes by him, both headed in the MSS "Syrianus the Sophist."[204] On several occasions in these works Syrianus is careful to distinguish sophists from philosophers.[205] Plutarch himself may also have been a sophist by profession, if (as often thought) he is to be identified with the sophist Plutarch who put up a statue in Athens to Herculius, prefect of Illyricum in 408–10, and was himself honored with a statue there for three times defraying the cost of the sacred ship of Athena at the Panathenaea.[206] Synesius is not likely to have had much respect for philosophers who earned their living teaching rhetoric.

203. There is another example a few sentences later, and compare the attacks on professional teachers in the *Dion* (see section VI below).

204. H. Rabe, ed., *Syriani in Hermogenem commentaria,* 2 vols. (Leipzig 1913).

205. φιλοσόφων ἢ σοφιστῶν, 2:15.3; φιλοσόφων τε καὶ σοφιστῶν, 2:1.6; πολλοὶ καὶ ἄλλοι σοφιστῶν τε καὶ τῶν Πλατωνικῶν φιλοσόφων, 1:1.8; cf. 2:48.24; 18.1; 1:28.25; Rabe, 2:v–vi.

206. *IG* II², 4224 (Πλούταρχοσ μύθων ταμίης ἔστησε σοφιστής) and 3818 (βασιλῆα λόγων), with Robert 1948, 73, 95–96; *PLRE* II.893–94; for the identification, Frantz 1988, 63–64 (with earlier bibliography); and Fowden 1990, 499, with n. 30, emphasizing σοφιστῶν in Synesius. It is true that Eunapius included philosophers and sophists in the same book (Penella 1990, esp. 4–5), but doubts remain. While it is entirely possible that the philosopher Plutarch was also a sophist, we might expect at least one of the epigrams to allude to his philosophical attainments as late as 410 (if φιλοσοφία is metrically intractable, σοφία and σοφός are not). As it is, the Herculius epigram not only characterizes its Plutarch straightforwardly as σοφιστης, but adds μύθων ταμίης as well, and (pace Frantz) μύθων suggests words rather than myths. If the man had been a famous philosopher, why not use the space for a more specific allusion (σοφίης ταμίης, σοφίῃ προέχων, or some such phrase)? And despite the importance of the concept λόγον διδόναι in Plato, βασιλεὺς λόγων certainly implies sophist rather than philosopher. As Robert (95–96) has shown, it was a stock formula for sophists from the second century on: from Philostr. *VS* 2.17, 598 (βασιλέα λόγων, of Herodes Atticus; cf. Lucian *Rhet. praec.* 11) to Greg. Naz. *Ep.* 24 (βασιλεὺς . . . λόγων, of Themistius) and the inscription to the statue of the sophist Prohaeresius in Rome: ἡ βασιλεύουσα Ῥώμη τὸν βασιλεύοντα τῶν λόγων (Eunap. *VS* 492). And the moral emphasis of σταθερῆς ἕρμα σαοφροσύνης (*IG* II², 3818.2) suggests restraint rather than wisdom, implying perhaps a governorship (for the evocation of such virtues in epigrams on governors, see Robert 1948, passim).

Rist inferred that "Synesius . . . had come to feel some distaste for philosophy which differed from that traditionally taught at Alexandria." But this is to take Synesius's jocular tone altogether too seriously—and if Hadot's argument about Hierocles extends to the previous generation, the teaching of the two schools may not have differed greatly in any case. From Synesius's point of view, we need read no more into the letter than the partisanship of the loyal disciple of Hypatia. But if Damascius came across the letter during his research for the *Life of Isidore,* he is bound to have been scandalized at Synesius's flippant exaltation of Hypatia over his own revered predecessors, and it would not be surprising if he had avenged the insult.[207]

For all their inevitable differences of style and emphasis, Hypatia and Plutarch may in fact have taught much the same form of Neoplatonism, emphasizing Iamblichus and the Chaldaean Oracles. They were also both pagans. And yet this is surely where the atmosphere of the two schools differed most. Hypatia's paganism has always seemed the strongest argument for assuming that Synesius too was a pagan in his younger days. But when he became a bishop he neither turned against her nor tried to convert her; he continued to treat her with the same awe and affection as before. There were many pagan teachers in the largely Christian cities of the late fourth- and early fifth-century Greek world. Libanius and Themistius are only the most famous such names; many more are chronicled in Eunapius's *Lives of the Philosophers and Sophists.*

In Athens it was different. The school of Plutarch and Proclus and Damascius was to remain one of the last bastions of paganism in the Roman world. The philosophers themselves were strict observers of the ancient cults, and their teaching was often bitterly anti-Christian.[208] Clearly there was no such aggressively pagan atmosphere in Hypatia's classroom.[209] Indeed, every identifiable student of Hypatia was a Christian. There is no sign that her paganism worried Synesius at all. This may seem an improbable claim when we reflect on her murder at the hands of a Christian mob, but that was many years later, in a situation deliberately exacerbated by an unscrupulous patriarch. We have already seen

207. It may be significant that (on our admittedly fragmentary evidence) Damascius did not include Synesius in his book; Photius might have been expected to quote an excerpt relating to Synesius. Not only did Synesius insult the Athenian school. As we shall see, he prided himself on being a more genuine philosopher than the professional pedants, and in addition was a Christian who ended his days as a bishop. One way to deal with such an upstart would have been polemic, something in which Damascius certainly excelled. Instead he opted for a contemptuous silence.

208. Cameron 1969; Chuvin 1990, 102f., 135f.

209. "Her coterie should not be mistaken for a hotbed of pagan agitators" (Chuvin 1990, 85).

that Synesius never took the slightest steps to conceal his devotion to philosophy, even as a bishop.

Hypatia's murder in 415 is more of a problem than is generally appreciated. There is no suggestion that her paganism played a role in the detailed and circumstantial account of Socrates.[210] Socrates sets the murder in its political context and suggests a purely political motive. The question of how to handle a long series of riots between Jews and Christians in Alexandria brought the prefect Orestes into conflict with the patriarch Cyril. A band of Nitrian monks came into the city to support Cyril and on one occasion wounded Orestes with a rock. The man who did it was arrested and tortured to death, which was perceived as a setback for Cyril, who nonetheless treated the death as a martyrdom. On another occasion monks killed Hypatia, believing that she was influencing Orestes to persist in his feud with Cyril. For Rist, this was sufficient explanation; there was no evidence that Hypatia "exploited her power to forward the political position of neoplatonism," and accordingly no reason to believe that her paganism played any part in her killing.[211]

But the first proposition does not imply the second. However circumspect Hypatia's pagan activities, they may still have been noticed and found objectionable by the Christian community, or at any rate by a vocal minority thereof. That this was indeed the case is shown by John of Nikiu. John's account does not so much contradict Socrates' as complement it, revealing what Socrates (perhaps deliberately) left out. For Socrates had his own axe to grind. Cyril was the great enemy of the church of Constantinople, where Socrates lived. The killing of Hypatia was a stick to beat Cyril with; better to portray her as the innocent victim of a savage murder than as a dangerous pagan who might be held to deserve such a fate. John gives us a glimpse of the other point of view.

According to John, Hypatia was a sorceress, who "beguiled many people through her satanic wiles." Socrates merely reports that the monks accused Orestes of being a pagan, which he denied. We might be tempted to guess that it was his association with Hypatia that had prompted the accusation, but Socrates does not make any such connection. Compare now the very different emphasis in John's account: "The governor of the city honored her exceedingly; for she had beguiled him through her magic. And he ceased attending church as had been his custom. . . . And he not only did this, but he drew many believers to her,

---

210. *HE* 7.13–15, in essentials followed in the full recent account of Chuvin (1990, 86–90).

211. Rist 1965, 223.

and he himself received the unbelievers at his house."[212] We do not need
to believe all of this to see that Orestes was indeed compromised by his
relationship with Hypatia.

It is fascinating to see how the most innocent interests were turned
against her. John complains that "she was devoted at all times to magic,
astrolabes, and instruments of music." Now the astrolabe was a scientific instrument, not even associated with what we would now call as-
trology rather than astronomy. Nonetheless, there are facts behind these
silly slanders. Like her father, Hypatia *was* interested in astrolabes; it
was she who taught Synesius how to make one. And the reference to
musical instruments recalls (and supports) the alternative version of
how she cured her lovesick student. Given her mathematical expertise,
we might guess that she experimented with harmonics and that her activities were interpreted as some sort of magic ritual.

Hypatia was a highly visible pagan, very active in Alexandrian public life. According to Damascius, all Alexandria "doted on her and wor-
shipped her";[213] the new governor would always make Hypatia's house
his first port of call. When Archbishop Cyril was passing one day, he
caught sight of "the gorgeous train of horses and slaves who crowded
the door of her academy," and on asking whose house occasioned such
a stir, was told, to his indignation (envy, claimed Damascius): "That is
the house of the philosopher Hypatia."[214] This influence she exercised in
the traditional way. A concrete example may be given, in the form of a
letter from Synesius written only two years before her death. After lamenting his own declining influence, Synesius continues as follows:

> You are still powerful (δύνῃ) and long may you continue to make use of
> that power (δύναιο). See that all those who honor you, both private in-
> dividuals and magistrates (καὶ ἰδιώταις καὶ ἄρχουσι), do what they can
> so that Nicaeus and Philolaus, excellent young men and kinsmen of
> mine, recover their property.[215]

Socrates confirms her connections among the governing class. In order
to explain how her "frequent meetings" with Orestes were misunderstood by "the people of the Church," he makes clear that she met regularly with magistrates (τοῖς ἄρχουσι) and "was not embarrassed to be in
the company of men." It was no doubt (as Socrates implies) in search of

212. *Chronicle* 87, pp. 100–101 Charles; the sentence omitted is corrupt, apparently
mentioning one visit to church.
213. ἥ τε ἄλλη πόλις ἠσπάζετό τε καὶ προσεκύνει διαφερόντως, p. 79.13f. Zintzen.
214. Frag. 102, p. 79.14–23 Zintzen.
215. *Ep.* 81, p. 147 G.

mundane political favors, rather than to undermine his faith, that she met with Orestes. If Orestes missed church a couple of times and entertained the odd pagan at his home, we may be sure that this had little to do with Hypatia. But it is easy to see how the Nitrian monks could have been persuaded otherwise.

There is also a more obvious factor, one so obvious that it is easy to overlook: her sex. The rising tide of Christian asceticism had brought about some drastic changes in the public position of women during Hypatia's lifetime. On the one hand, Christianity allowed women new scope and new status. On the other, the insistence on submissiveness increasingly circumscribed their public activity.[216] The much-traveled grandes dames of the age, like the two Melanias, were always accompanied by large bands of fellow virgins.[217] Another Egyptian of the age, Isidore of Pelusium, reports the drastic steps a virtuous Christian girl took to discourage a would-be lover. She shaved her head completely, wiped a mixture of ashes and water all over her face, and then addressed him in much the same terms as Hypatia had her admirer: "Is this the ugliness you are in love with?"[218]

It was not just that Hypatia was a conspicuous pagan who liked to play an active role in Alexandrian public life. She was a woman, and (by all accounts) an attractive woman, who was often to be seen walking or driving around the streets of Alexandria and conversing with men as equals. When Orestes called at *her* house, there could be only one explanation. He was bewitched—or worse.

Cyril was probably not much concerned with the fact that all she taught most of her students was elementary mathematics. It was not right that a pagan, a single woman at that, should be so popular and influential. The fact that she had well-known Christian pupils like Synesius could be turned against her. This was a sorceress, casting her spell on good Christians, even bishops. It was a disgrace that prominent pagans should continue to enjoy such respectability twenty-five years after Cyril's predecessor Theophilus had destroyed the great Serapeum of Alexandria. It was with this event that an illustrated Alexandrian chronicle concludes: on its final page we see the portrait of Theophilus

216. On this paradox, Elizabeth Clark, *Ascetic Piety and Women's Faith* (Lewiston 1986), 175–208; Susan Ashbrook Harvey, *Asceticism and Society in Crisis: John of Ephesus and the Lives of the Eastern Saints* (Berkeley 1990), 108–33.

217. Palladius *Lausiac History* 41.2, 46.1 and 5, 61.6.

218. ταύτης τῆς ἀκοσμίας ἐρᾶς (Isidore Pel. *Ep.* 2.53 [*PG* 78.497A]). John Moschus (*Prat. spir.* 205 [*PG* 87.3.3096B]) tells of a woman who in similar circumstances used a less flamboyant version of Hypatia's artifice: she simply pleaded her period, warning him of the smell.

triumphant, with another scene representing dark-robed monks destroying the Serapeum.[219] Having only recently stepped into Theophilus's shoes, Cyril badly needed a spectacular success of his own to establish him as undisputed champion of the Egyptian church. In quick succession he had turned his violent hands on heretics (Novatians) and Jews. Orestes had thwarted his attack on the Jews, but with Hypatia Cyril hit the jackpot. On Hypatia's death, according to John of Nikiu, "all the people surrounded the patriarch Cyril and named him 'the new Theophilus'; for he had destroyed the last remains of idolatry in the city."[220]

Hypatia's murder was the consequence of a complex of factors that had little to do with her religious beliefs, teaching, or standing in the Alexandrian community during the quarter-century of her friendship with Synesius.

VI. THE *DION*

For all his enthusiasm for the Chaldaean Oracles and his talk of "ineffable mysteries," Synesius's was essentially a cultural rather than a religious Hellenism. The focus of his interest is amply demonstrated by his *Dion; or, On Living by His Example*. The importance of this essay is still insufficiently appreciated, even after the excellent commentary by K. Treu.[221] The introduction lays down the lines on which study of Dio has proceeded to this day. Synesius claims against Philostratus that Dio's career fell into two stages: he was simply a sophist till his exile, and then converted to philosophy. Most students of Dio now reject this claim,[222] perhaps wrongly.[223] Synesius had read works of Dio we do not have.[224] It is true, as C. P. Jones says, that Synesius's "main concern was with himself rather than Dio,"[225] but since he did not himself undergo either a midlife conversion to philosophy or any sort of conversion to Christianity, Dio's conversion is no part of the personal parallel. Synesius's own works do not fall into two periods. As *Ep.* 154 reveals, he laid himself open to accusations of triviality, from contemporary as from modern

219. A. Bauer and J. Strzygowski, *Eine Alexandrinische Weltchronik*, Denkschrift Wien 51.2 (1905), 66–73; Tafel VI verso.

220. *Chronicle* 84.103.

221. Treu 1958; cf. Garzya 1973; Tinnefeld 1975.

222. E.g., J. L. Moles, *JHS* 98 (1978): 79–100; C. P. Jones, *The Roman World of Dio Chrysostom* (1978), 11–12 and passim.

223. See a forthcoming paper by Oswyn Murray.

224. In addition, there is internal evidence that the corpus of Dio's works as it has come down to us is severely mutilated: Highet 1983, 74–99.

225. Cf. A. Momigliano, *Quinto contributo* (1975), 966; and C. P. Jones 1978, 12.

critics,[226] with works like *On Baldness*, a reply to a sophistic trifle by Dio called *On Hair*, and the book on hunting that eventually led him to write the *Dion*. But he does not suggest that they were works of his youth, still less written before his eyes were opened to philosophy. On the contrary, his object, as Jones rightly put it, was to show "that rhetorical and liter-ary gifts are not incompatible with philosophy." For this end, there was no real objection to the view of Philostratus he rejects, namely that Dio was "a sophist and philosopher in one."[227] There is thus no need to be-lieve that he twisted the facts to support his thesis. In any case, his his-torical approach, his criticism of Philostratus, and his insistence that Dio's oeuvre cannot be understood unless read in chronological sequence all deserve a mention in any history of ancient literary criticism.[228]

The body of the *Dion* is not further concerned with Dio, except inso-far as he serves Synesius as the supreme model of a serious philosopher with an elegant, graceful style. It is in the main a polemic against phi-losophers and, apparently, monks. Its occasion is clarified by a letter to Hypatia (*Ep.* 154) that supplies more explicit details. According to the letter, Synesius is defending himself against criticisms from two groups, those in white *tribones* and those in black. Libanius and Eunapius regu-larly single out black robes in their invectives on monks,[229] and Synesius himself wrote a letter to a philosophical friend who had become a monk, suggesting that a white *tribonion* might have been more appropriate than the black one he has heard that John is wearing (*Ep.* 147). Since *Dion* 13–15 is an attack on professional teachers, it looks as if Synesius's two groups of critics are, respectively, professional philosophers and Chris-tian monks.

Synesius tells Hypatia he had written a book on hunting that was much admired by "certain young men who cared for Hellenism and grace" (οἷς ἑλληνισμοῦ τε καὶ χάριτος ἔμελε),[230] who also said that some of his poems reproduced the "antique touch" (τι τῆς ἀρχαίας χειρός).[231]

226. "Not so much a philosopher . . . as a rhetorician" (Marrou 1963, 130).

227. C. P. Jones 1978, 11.

228. Yet there is not a word, for example, in the standard works of J. F. D'Alton, *Ro-man Literary Theory and Criticism: A Study in Tendencies* (London 1931) or G. M. A. Grube (1965).

229. Lib. *Or.* 30.8; Eunap. *VS* 6.11.7, p. 39.18 Giangrande; frag. 55 Mueller = 48.2.17 Blockley.

230. Synesius modestly claims that the book on hunting "escaped from my house without my knowledge" (*Ep.* 154); whether or not he had formally published it, the work was clearly going round the literary circles of Alexandria. For the date and place, Treu 1958, 3–4. The date may now be advanced by up to two years (402/3 rather than 404/5), following the advancement of Synesius's stay in Constantinople, for which see below, chapter 3, section III.

231. As Treu (1958, 64) observes, "antique" does not here imply archaic style in the modern sense, but "as good as the ancients."

One group of critics maintained that he was

> sinning against philosophy by my knowledge of fine phrases and
> rhythm, and because I ventured an opinion on Homer and the figures
> of the rhetoricians. . . . In the eyes of such persons, one must hate
> literature in order to be a philosopher (τὸν φιλόσοφον μισόλογον εἶναι
> προσήκει) and concern oneself exclusively with heavenly things. They
> contemplate the intelligible, but for me it is not allowed, because I take
> time off to purify my tongue and sweeten my wit.

There is something strange about this criticism. Why should anyone object to style? The real objection must have been that he was nothing but
a stylist, not a real philosopher at all. However this may be, Synesius
naturally has little trouble in lecturing such imperceptive critics on the
importance of style.

More interesting are the objections of what the letter describes as the
"dark-robed" critics, or "barbarians," as they are called in the *Dion*. The
fairly detailed description of basket-weaving fanatics in *Dion* 45C–46D
certainly seems to fit the desert communities of Nitria and Scetis, as
Treu argues. They are styled barbarians, not because Synesius is hostile
to them (the chapter is in fact remarkably sympathetic) but partly because they were Copts and partly because, by their rejection of all literary culture, they were so clearly not Hellenes.[232]

Synesius does not by any means condemn their dedication to man-
ual labor but finds it excessive; he concludes that the barbarian is more
determined than the Hellene, for he will never give up any enterprise
once begun (46D). The Hellene, by contrast, is refined and has more
moderation in his makeup, and so is more likely to yield. The study of
literature and even the sciences, he continues, is an excellent preparation for the mind:

> They brighten the eye within us and clear away the rheum and thor-
> oughly arouse it and accustom it by degrees to the objects of vision so
> that it may some day take courage to face a more august spectacle still
> and not blink at once when facing the sun. Thus the Hellene trains his
> perceptions by his pleasures and even out of sport derives advantage
> for his most important objective.

It would be hard to imagine a more eloquent account of the use of classical culture for the Christian. "But," he goes on, "those who tread the
path deemed to be of adamant [i.e., the monks], though some certainly
reach the goal, they seem to me scarcely to have traveled a path at all, for

---

232. On Synesius's definition of Hellene, see below, pp. 66–68.

how is a path possible where there is no gradual progress, where there is no first step and second step—in fact no order at all" (47D). Once more, Synesius does not claim that the rigorism of the monks is futile. What he objects to is its lack of rational method. They simply leap, like a man possessed (48A). He concludes this section with the remarkable claim that monks and philosophers are really striving for the same goal, the only difference being that philosophers fortify themselves with years of careful preparation. The monks fortify their virtues by habit rather than reason (49D). For example, they abstain from sexual intercourse for its own sake, "thus making the smallest thing of the greatest importance, for they imagine that the preparation is the goal." Synesius does not, of course, mean that abstinence is unimportant, but that it is merely a means to the end of self-discipline. The monks confuse means and end.

The letter gives a less sympathetic account of the dark-robed critics, whose boldness is only excelled by their ignorance and who are readier than anyone to deliver a harangue on God. Whenever you meet them, he observes, you have to listen to their "unsyllogistic syllogisms": presumably Synesius means that their theological discourse does not follow the rules of logic. They want Synesius to be their pupil, claiming that in no time he will be bolder than anyone on the subject of God, able to hold forth night and day without stopping. But Copts who spent their days making baskets (46B) are not likely to have wanted Synesius to be their pupil; nor would they have been distressed by his excursion into belles lettres. For the attitude of Nitrian monks to philosophers it is enough to think of the fate of Hypatia. The answer is perhaps that the letter attempts to dramatize the very different pressures that Synesius, as a would-be philosopher, was experiencing in Alexandria. These pressures somehow came to a head in the publication of his belles lettres. His serious-minded friends in both camps felt that he was frittering away his talents and training. The Christians who were trying to capture his talents for the faith cannot have been illiterate Coptic basket makers. They were men like Theophilus, who eventually succeeded.

By the same token we must not look for too much precision on the other side either. Marrou, for example, argues that Synesius's philosophical critics represent "Neoplatonism corrupted by the superstitious pagan belief in theurgy, . . . an Alexandrian criticism of contemporary Athens." But if the *Dion* really were a debate between theurgy and monasticism, why is it, as Marrou himself emphasized, that "the discussion is never conducted in religious terms"?[233] It is on very different grounds

233. Marrou 1963, 145.

that Synesius criticizes at least some of these people; "some philosophical writers," he notes, "might be called grammarians, men who combine and separate syllables well enough but never succeed in bringing to birth anything of their own" (56B–C). This description does not suggest theurgists. And in his conclusion he positively boasts that he never bothered to correct the text of the books in the library of which he was so proud: the man of letters attacks textual critics as a philosopher (59D–60A). Just as the men in black robes are not just monks, so too the men in white are not just philosophers but professional pedants of every sort. It was simply to obtain a sharper antithesis that the letter to Hypatia focuses on the contrasting colors.

As for Synesius's Hellenism, it is common knowledge that by the second half of the fourth century the word "Hellene" had come to be the standard Greek word for "pagan." To start with, it was an exclusively Christian usage, but by the time of Julian more aggressive pagans began defiantly to call themselves Hellenes. It is unnecessary to cite examples, since the usage of almost any Christian writer will suffice.[234] One important consequence to which contemporaries were more alert than moderns, who tend to see everything in terms of Christian-pagan conflict, is that the centuries-old cultural connotations of the word were thus effectively rendered unusable.[235] Some pagans were quite happy with this narrowing connotation of the word. For instance, more than half the examples in Julian clearly refer to pagans or paganism,[236] and perhaps only two to Hellenism in the cultural sense.[237] Indeed, by his infamous edict banning Christians from teaching the pagan classics, Julian did much to accelerate the identification of pagan culture and cult.

Many contemporaries regretted this identification, Christians and pagans alike. Particularly striking is the bitter invective of Gregory Nazianzen, who was particularly outraged by Julian's ban on Christian teachers: "First of all, he dishonestly changed the meaning of the word to belief, as though to speak Greek was a religious, rather than a linguistic,

234. See in general, J. Jüthner, *Hellenen und Barbaren* (1923), 98, with 146–47; Lampe, under all the ἑλλην- words.

235. See, however, Jüthner 1923, 98; and for some fascinating new perspectives, G. W. Bowersock, *Hellenism in Late Antiquity* (Ann Arbor 1990). Naturally even Christians continued to use ἑλλην- roots with linguistic or ethnic reference (Greek language; Greeks and barbarians, Celts, etc.).

236. See the index to J. Bidez and F. Cumont, *Iuliani epistulae leges poematia* (Paris 1922), 302 (hereafter Bidez-Cumont).

237. At *Ep.* 97 (p.153.7 Bidez-Cumont) he claims that Libanius's speeches are admired by οἱ ἀληθῶς Ἕλληνες; at *Misop.* 367C he describes himself as γένος . . . Θρᾴκιον, Ἕλληνα τοῖς ἐπιτηδεύμασι.

affair. This was his excuse for banning us from literature, as though we were stealing the goods of another."[238] Later on he waxed more indignant still: "Do you own Hellenism (σὸν τὸ ἑλληνίζειν)? Tell me, how can this be? Does the alphabet not belong to the Phoenicians? . . . Do you own Atticism? . . . Do you own poetry?"[239]

We do not know Libanius's reaction to Julian's edict, but it is possible to trace a significant shift in his concept of Hellenism. In his earlier letters, cultural connotations still predominate. Festugière has drawn attention to a number of passages where Libanius uses ἑλληνικόν to mean, in effect, "civilized." For example, it is "Hellenic" to write to one's friends or to assist a friend.[240] It is not Hellenic to poach students from one's colleagues.[241] Forgiveness is more Hellenic than revenge.[242] All these texts presuppose that certain ideals of conduct were shared by those who had enjoyed the traditional *paideia*. But in his later works Libanius is clearly aware of the growing link between religion and literature (ἱερά and λόγοι, to use his own terms).[243]

Themistius by contrast never uses "Hellene" in the sense "pagan." For Themistius, the word continued to have cultural, rather than religious, connotations.[244] He is always speaking of the value of philosophy, which for him seems to boil down, as G. Downey well put it, to "an eclectic synthesis of the classical tradition."[245]

Synesius was heavily influenced by Themistius, and it is clear from the *Dion* that his definition was likewise cultural rather than religious. Writing as he was a generation later than Themistius, Synesius could not have failed to be familiar with the now-standard sense of Hellene/ pagan, so it is the more significant that he so conspicuously sidesteps it. The key passage (42B) states:

ἀξιῶ γὰρ ἐγὼ τὸν φιλόσοφον μηδ᾽ ἄλλο τι κακὸν μηδ᾽ ἄγροικον εἶναι, ἀλλὰ καὶ τὰ ἐκ Χαρίτων μυεῖσθαι, καὶ ἀκριβῶς Ἕλληνα εἶναι, τοῦτ᾽ ἔστι δύνασθαι τοῖς ἀνθρωποῖς ἐξομιλῆσαι, τῷ μηδενὸς ἀπείρως ἔχειν ἐλλογίμου συγγράμματος.

238. *Or.* 4.5, p. 92, ed. J. Bernardi, Sources Chrétiennes 309 (Paris 1983) (*PG* 35.536A). Though, as R. R. Ruether (1969, 164) justly observes, he "never develops at length an unequivocal justification for Christian acculturation in the classical milieu."

239. *Or.* 4.107, p. 258 Bernardi (*PG* 35.643C).

240. *Ep.* 347.2, 411.4, 357.1.

241. *Or.* 43.18.

242. *Ep.* 75.4, 1120.2; Festugière 1959, 222.

243. *Or.* 42.8; cf. Festugière 1959, 229f.

244. The *index nominum* to volume 3 of the Downey-Norman edition (p. 149) gives a convenient list of ἑλλην- words in Themistius.

245. Downey 1955a, 306.

In my opinion the philosopher must not be of bad character in any way,[246] or uncultivated,[247] but initiated into the secrets of the Graces[248] and a Hellene in the full sense of the word, that is to say, able to associate with men on the basis of a knowledge of all worthwhile literature.

"Pagan" was only one sense of the word, a sense in which Synesius clearly has no interest here. This emphasis on civilized behavior corresponds exactly to the use of "Hellenic" in Libanius just discussed. Synesius roundly condemns its opposite a few pages later: the philosopher who despises literature will "associate with men in a vulgar way (φορ-τικῶς), which no gentleman (ἐλεύθερος)[249] would do" (34D).[250] One of the things he does not like about the monks is that they "take no part in public life or intercourse" (ἀπολιτεύτους τε καὶ ἀκοινωνήτους, 45D).

In his correspondence Synesius uses the word a number of times, always in a cultural rather than a religious sense. For example, Ep. 1 asks his Constantinopolitan friend Nicander to "share" his On Baldness "with the Hellenes," undoubtedly people in Constantinople "who appreciate and cultivate the classical culture of the Hellenic paideia."[251] There is nothing significantly pagan about the book, and Synesius himself regretfully confesses to Nicander that he cannot really count it as a work of philosophy but likes it just the same. He writes to the poet Theotimus that Anthemius's fame will live in Theotimus's works "so long as Hellenes exist" (Ep. 49 = 51G). When he receives a letter from Pylaemenes, he summons a "gathering of the Hellenes in Libya" (Ep. 101, p. 169.7G).[252] When asking Hypatia's opinion about the Dion, he undertakes to suppress it if she judges it not "worthy of Hellenic ears" (τῆς τῶν Ἑλλήνων ἀκοῆς ἄξιον) (Ep. 154, p. 276.5G). To be sure Hypatia was a pagan, but the Dion could not be described as a book aimed at pagans. It is as a connoisseur of literature that Synesius appeals to her.

More important still, whereas Themistius's rather similarly defined Hellenism had in effect ignored Christianity, the Dion is a work that explicitly sets out to weigh pagan and Christian criticisms of Synesius's

246. Compare Cato's famous definition of the orator as "vir bonus dicendi peritus."
247. Not merely "rude" (Fitzgerald), but "nicht vertraut mit der griechischen Bildung, unbelesen" (Treu); cf. ἀγροικία at 52C.
248. Not merely "gracious conduct" (Fitzgerald).
249. This use of ἐλεύθερος is not given in LSJ or Lampe, though LSJ does list the allied use of ἐλευθέριος (opposed to βάναυσος) applied to words like τέχνη and παιδεία, where it is normally translated "liberal." Sophocles lists only John Moschus, PG 87.3093A, translating "gentleman."
250. Cf. 44D and 54A.
251. Runia 1976, 165 n. 67.
252. But much the same phrase in Ep. 148 init. seems to have an ethnic rather than a cultural connotation.

work. Themistius too speaks often of critics, both philosophers and sophists.[253] Like Synesius, Themistius firmly and proudly sat on the fence in this age-old battle. But Synesius explicitly took a third set of criticisms into account, the attempts of the Christians to bring him into their camp. Synesius declined the invitation, no less politely and no less firmly than he rejected the criticisms of the philosophers and sophists and grammarians. Synesius had no intention of serving any masters but the Muses.

An important corollary seems to follow. The criticisms of the Christian community are less clearly defined than the others, but they are presented as if essentially similar in kind. There is, for example, no suggestion that they involved pressure to convert from paganism first. Synesius criticizes them for their dogmatism on the subject of God, but not for being mistaken. He does not suggest that he must resist their overtures because he does not share their religion. As for the philosophers, sophists, and grammarians, nothing is said of their religious views, but this need not imply that he approves of them as fellow pagans; after all, by 400 by no means all sophists and grammarians were pagans. Synesius is at least as critical of their narrowness in their own field as he is of the Christians. To all appearances he considers and rejects the criticisms of both sides on the same basis. Yet if he had been a pagan at the time, how could he have considered Christian objections in the same way as those of philosophers, sophists, and grammarians? And why should Christians have been as disturbed as pagans by a pagan's preoccupation with belles lettres? How could they have expected him to write on Christian topics? The implication is that Synesius was a Christian when he wrote the *Dion*.

One other passage in the *Dion* points to the same conclusion. At 39B Synesius describes how Dio mentions the Essenes somewhere, adding that they lived by the Dead Sea in the middle of Palestine "not far from Sodom itself." The Essenes are represented as a happy, self-sufficient community, and the point of the emphatic "itself" is obviously the juxtaposition of the virtuous Essenes and the archetypally wicked Sodomites. Sodom is occasionally mentioned by pagan authors,[254] but simply as a spectacular natural disaster, not as an example of sin duly punished. Only a Jew or a Christian would have been struck by the paradoxical juxtaposition of Essenes and Sodomites. Dio may have mentioned Sodom, but the emphasis can have been added only by the Christian Synesius.

253. Dagron 1968, 42f.
254. Tac. *Hist*. 5.7 (unnamed); Strabo 16.44.

· THREE ·

SYNESIUS IN CONSTANTINOPLE

I. THE PANHELLENION

It was during his embassy to Constantinople that Synesius wrote both *De regno* and *De providentia*, the principal subjects of the following chapters. But there are two important preliminary questions. What is the date of the embassy? And once it had brought him to the capital, in what circles did he move?

The most important of Synesius's Constantinopolitan connections was undoubtedly Aurelian, one of the protagonists of the crisis of 400. It was he who, as PPO, finally granted Synesius's request for a reduction in the taxes of Pentapolis. In gratitude, Synesius took his new patron's side in the troubles of 400 and drew a flattering portrait of him under the guise of Osiris in *De providentia.* But it is not only politics that have been thought to bind Synesius to Aurelian. They are also supposed to have shared a passion for Hellenic culture. It has been widely believed that in Constantinople Synesius joined a sizable literary circle gathered around the great man. Bury characterizes Aurelian as "a man of considerable intellectual attainments . . . surrounded by men of letters."[1] This itself is doubtful enough. Moreover, added to this claim is the belief that the members of this circle were all either pagans or pagan sympathizers.

According to Demougeot, for example, while Theodosius was still

---

1. Bury (1923) 1958, 1:132.

alive, Aurelian "took care to conceal his sympathy for paganism, even going so far as to build a church in Constantinople." But in later years "his literary tastes, inherited from his father, brought him close to rhetors and pagans. . . . All those who dreamed of a pagan reaction and government by philosophers, as in the days of Julian, gathered around him and begged him to be their guide."[2] This passionate Hellenism is linked in turn with the passionate nationalism that is thought to have inspired the hostility of this group to barbarian encroachments on Greco-Roman ideals and privileges. This vivid page from a usually sober history is but a pale reflection of the thesis of Zakrzewski's book *Le parti théodosien et son antithèse* (Lvov, 1931). According to Zakrzewski, the politicians of Arcadius's court fell into two groups: those who continued the policies of Theodosius and were prepared to trust and work with barbarians (Rufinus, Eutropius, Caesarius), and the nationalists, the party of Aurelian whose spokesman was Synesius, specially invited for that purpose on the strength of his recent triumphs in the Neoplatonist circles of Alexandria. Their aim was to restore the empire of the Antonines, and their political activities were pursued under the cover of literary and scientific studies, with branches in the provinces but headquarters at Constantinople, in a circle called the Panhellenion. The "soul" of the movement was Neoplatonist philosophers, "agitators of the pagan party," as in the days of Julian.[3] Thus crudely stated, this "Neoplatonic freemasonry" (Zakrzewski's own phrase) may seem merely absurd, but in a more muted and insidious form it still exercises considerable influence.[4] Synesius's own enthusiasm for Greek literature and philosophy is beyond question. But even in his case culture is not at all the same thing as cult.

We may begin with the church Aurelian is supposed to have built as a young man to disguise his pagan sympathies. Aurelian was one of a number of Constantinopolitan magnates, including also the generals Victor and Saturninus, who were ardent followers of the Syrian monk Isaac. According to his *Life*, when Isaac died, his followers were carrying the body to its intended final resting place in their own monastery when a troop of men stationed outside by Aurelian, "one of the dignitaries of the emperor," seized it and carried it off to Aurelian's church of St. Stephen, which happened to be directly opposite, and placed it in the sanctuary to the right of the altar.[5]

2. Demougeot 1951, 236.
3. Zakrzewski 1931, 65f.
4. For example, Holum, while rejecting Zakrzewski's nationalist party (1982, 68 n. 80), nonetheless works with the same simplistic identification of Hellenism and paganism.
5. *Vita Isaaci* 4.18 (*Acta Sanctorum* May VII 258). We are here following up a suggestion made to us in conversation by Cyril Mango.

The *Life of Isaac* gives a precise consular date for Isaac's death: Merobaudes II and Saturninus. Thus Aurelian would have built his well-documented church of the protomartyr no later than 383.[6] Most historians have accepted this seemingly precise date for the church without question,[7] but the truth is not so simple. Isaac went down in history as the founder of Byzantine monasticism.[8] But there was one major difficulty in his biography: as contemporary sources show, Isaac had also been one of the most vigorous opponents of John Chrysostom. John tried to break Isaac's power over the monks of Constantinople, and Isaac naturally took steps to defend himself.[9] But after being hounded into exile and an early death, Chrysostom was soon rehabilitated and canonized. It then became an embarrassment that the saintly Isaac had led the dogs in what now seemed a shabby and spiteful vendetta. His biographers eventually solved the problem by a neat, if drastic, artifice: they antedated his death. If, as the *Life* alleges, Isaac died in 383, how could he have had anything to do with a persecution that did not begin until twenty years later? The truth is that Isaac undoubtedly outlived Chrysostom; all we know for certain is that he was succeeded by Dalmatios some time between 406 and 425.[10]

The *Life of Isaac* in its present form was compiled no earlier than the sixth century,[11] and it is by no means a reliable text. Yet it was a fact that Isaac's body was laid to rest in the wrong church, much to the evident embarrassment and regret of his followers. There seems no reason to doubt that Aurelian was responsible for securing it for his own church. But he would have been very young in 383. More importantly, it is odd that Aurelian should have built a church to Stephen of all the saints and martyrs as early as 383. The great explosion of interest in St. Stephen came with the discovery of his bones in a village near Jerusalem on 3 December 415.[12] Thereafter churches and martyria sprang up all over the empire, mainly to accommodate one or more of his rapidly circulating bones.

We cannot exclude the possibility that Aurelian simply chanced to

6. Theodore Lector, pp. 132.11, 134.13; see Janin 1969, 472–73. It was destroyed in the earthquake of 869: Downey, 1955b, 599.

7. To name only the most recent, von Haehling 1978, 79 ("im Jahre 383"); Clauss 1980, 148.

8. Dagron 1970, 229–76.

9. Dagron 1970, 245; Liebeschuetz 1984a, 90f.

10. Dagron 1970, 245.

11. Dagron 1970, 231f.; Rochelle Snee, *GRBS* 26 (1985): 405f.

12. Lucian, *Epistola ad omnem ecclesiam de revelatione corporis Stephani martyris*, ed. S. Vanderlinden, *REB* 4 (1946): 178–217; see too E. D. Hunt, *Holy Land Pilgrimage in the Later Roman Empire, A.D. 312–450* (Oxford 1982), 211–18.

pick on Stephen before 415, but it is incomparably more likely that his church, which is explicitly described as a martyrion,[13] dates from after then. It was not till 439 that the first relics reached Constantinople, brought by the empress Eudocia and subsequently housed in Pulcheria's church of St. Lawrence.[14] But it may be that Aurelian had hopes of obtaining some much earlier. Indeed, there is good reason to believe that this is precisely what happened. In 1906 F. Nau published an extract from an unpublished Paris MS of the *Life of Isaac* that includes an extra clause. Here we read that Aurelian "built in front of and to the south of the monastery of Isaac a martyrion under the name of the holy protomartyr Stephen [to place there his holy body brought from Jerusalem; then, having failed in this, *for by the will of god it was placed in the Constantianai*, he formed the plan of getting the body of Isaac in its place, which came to pass]."[15] Nau argued that the entire bracketed clause is an interpolation. The phrase printed in italics is certainly interpolated, since it refers to a much later story concerning relics deposited in her own church in the Constantianai by Anicia Juliana in the early sixth century.[16] But there seems no reason to exclude the rest of the clause. After years of eclipse during the ascendancy of Anthemius, Aurelian was finally restored to power and the prefecture in 414–16. It is entirely plausible that he should have wished to secure for himself the glory of bringing the first relic of the newly found bones of Stephen to Constantinople. We may imagine his embarrassment when, having built a martyrion specifically to house and display the holy relic, he learned that the authorities at Jerusalem were not going to deliver, and we may understand, if we cannot condone, the measures he took to make good the

13. That is to say, a building (of whatever architectural form) that was intended to display "an object of Christian testimony" (C. Mango, *Byzantine Architecture* [New York 1975], 10, 73–75), in this case obviously a martyr's relics. For a sample of the literary evidence, Lampe, s.v. III.

14. See the recent discussions by K. Holum and G. Vikan, *DOP* 33 (1979): 115–33; J. Wortley, *GRBS* 21 (1980): 381–94; and E. A. Clark, *Church History* 51 (1982): 141–56. Holum and Vikan argued for 421, but contemporary and even near-contemporary sources are silent (most notably Sozomen: see Wortley 1980, 383). The earliest and really the only evidence is Theophanes, A.M. 5920 (p. 86.26f. de Boor), which Holum and Vikan redate to 421. Holum (1982, 103f.) reiterated his reliance on a pseudonymous encomium of Stephen (*PG* 63.933), but even if this is the work of Proclus of Constantinople (as asserted without evidence or argument by F. J. Leroy, *L'homilétique de Proclus de Constantinople*, Studi e testi 247 [Vatican City 1967], 158), that would still not prove that it refers to 421 rather than 439. Indeed since Proclus was at Constantinople from 426 to 446, it is more likely that he is referring to Eudocia's relics of 439. That might explain why he says of Pulcheria only that she "housed" the relics (ἐθαλάμευσε γὰρ αὐτὸν ἡ βασιλὶς καὶ παρθένος, *PG* 63.933).

15. *Revue de l'orient chrétien* 11 (1906): 199f.

16. Janin 1969, 474–76, with Wortley 1980, 385–86.

deficiency. Isaac was not the protomartyr, but he was at any rate a bona fide holy man—the best substitute that could be obtained at short notice.

On this scenario, Isaac died in or soon after 416.[17] Such a date harmonizes perfectly with the known limits for his death (406–25), the discovery of the bones of Stephen, and Aurelian's restoration to the prefecture.[18] But there can be little doubt that Aurelian's devotion to Isaac dates back at least to 400. His associate Saturninus, who is also recorded as a follower of Isaac,[19] did not long survive 400.

It is hardly likely that the disciple of a Syrian monk also cultivated pagan Neoplatonists. And yet some scholars have been prepared to take all too literally the following report in *De providentia* of Osiris's exile: "It might be added that to a man who is blessed in all things even exile may be not without profit. During that time he was initiated into the most perfect rites and mysteries of the gods above. Letting go the reins of government, he lifted up his mind to contemplation."[20] Since the Osiris of Synesius's myth represents Aurelian, Lacombrade inferred that Aurelian really was initiated into the mysteries during his exile.[21] But (as we shall see in more detail in the following chapters) nothing is more dangerous than simplistic translation from the mythical to the historical plane. The dramatic date of Synesius's tale is many centuries before Christ. Obviously Osiris could not be shown going into a Christian church. If Synesius wanted to draw attention to Aurelian's piety, he had to do so in pre-Christian terms. Furthermore, it is a grave error to suppose that the mystery terms he uses were restricted to pagan mysteries. All of them—τελετή, τελεῖσθαι, ἐποπτεύειν, θεωρία, and, above all, μυστήριον (which he happens not to use here)—were used routinely by Christians of the age for a variety of Christian rites, notably baptism and the eucharist.[22] Synesius mentions θεωρία as emphatically in letters from his episcopate as earlier. It is his particular term for union with God, the ultimate goal of the contemplative life. The activity is open to Christian and pagan alike. In *Ep.* 57 he underlines the importance of θεωρία as the

17. The dedication of Aurelian's church may have taken place after he laid down his prefecture in May 416, which would be less than six months after the discovery of the relics.

18. The fact that the biographer changed his consular date but retained the circumstantial details that point so clearly to another date is strong corroboration that the main lines of the story about Aurelian are true.

19. *Vita Isaaci* 4.14.

20. τὰς τελεωτάτας τῶν ἄνω θεῶν τελετὰς ἐτελέσθη τε καὶ ἐπώπτευσε καὶ θεωρίᾳ προσανέσχε τὸν νοῦν (123D). Book 2 is full of such references to mysteries.

21. Lacombrade 1951b, 106.

22. It is enough to refer to the entries for all these words, especially the last, in Lampe.

goal of the priesthood itself, regretting that it cannot be reconciled with the life of action.[23] It is attainable only through the intensive study of literature and philosophy, for which the prerequisite was leisure.[24] The essential point of *De providentia* 123D is simply that now Osiris has "let go the reins of government" he has the leisure necessary for θεωρία. We have already seen that the similar terms τελετηφορίαι and ἱερηπολίαι in Synesius's hymns only make sense when interpreted as Christian references, and the same is true of the present passage. Whatever Aurelian may have done in the privacy of his exile, it is inconceivable that Synesius should have represented a Roman consul of the year 400 undergoing initiation into forbidden pagan mystery cults. Whether or not Synesius had anything precise in mind, we may be sure that he intended and his readers understood Christian rites. If he did intend a precise rite, the obvious guess is baptism.

G. R. Sievers made this very suggestion long ago.[25] But he went on to connect the passage with the heading to *Ep.* 1.54 of Nilus of Ancyra, Αὐρηλιανῷ ἰλλουστρίῳ ἀπὸ Ἑλλήνων, "to Aurelian, *vir illustris*, the former Hellene"—a text that would have delighted Zakrzewski and his followers if they had known it, since here at least "Hellene" must mean "pagan."[26] Nilus's dates are uncertain, but the only other correspondents who can be identified do fall in the early fifth century: the emperor Arcadius, Gaïnas, and a general called Candidianus, perhaps to be identified with a general of that name attested in 424.[27] Since, moreover, there were only a handful of high offices that carried the rank of *vir illustris* at this date, and Aurelian held no fewer than three of them, it might seem that there was a strong case for identifying Nilus's correspondent with Synesius's patron, who would then be attested by someone who knew him as a converted pagan.

Nonetheless, it is precisely the title that calls the identification into doubt. For Nilus's correspondence is beset by a major problem of authenticity. It is not the letters themselves that come into question so much as their headings:[28] the names of Nilus's correspondents are equipped with numerous titles that did not exist in his lifetime.[29] There can be little doubt that these titles were added by a sixth-century redactor, perhaps anxious to enhance Nilus's reputation by enhancing the im-

---

23. On θεωρία and πρᾶξις in Synesius, see Tinnefeld 1975, 165; Runia 1976, 203f.

24. The importance and interdependence of these two concepts, θεωρία and leisure, is well brought out by Tinnefeld (1975, 155f.).

25. Sievers 1870, 367: "Ist damit angedeutet, daß er damals getauft wurde?"

26. On the various meanings of "Hellene" in writers of the age, see above, pp. 66–68.

27. Cameron 1976b, 181–96.

28. Though the letters do have many puzzling features: Cameron 1976b, 181–82.

29. For a list, Cameron 1976b, 182–85.

portance of his correspondents. At the beginning of the fifth century, the illustrate, as it came to be called, was a rank restricted to present and past holders of fewer than a dozen offices. Such men were normally styled by office *and* rank, not rank alone. A man as distinguished as Aurelian, who had held the two highest offices within this category (the urban and praetorian prefectures), would have been addressed as prefect or ex-prefect (ἔπαρχος or ἀπὸ ἐπάρχων) rather than just as *vir illustris* (ἰλλούστριος in Greek). But by the sixth century the illustrate was enormously debased. It was bestowed freely as an honorary title on men who had held no office of any sort.[30] It was men such as these who proudly styled themselves just *illustris*. The heading to *Ep.* 1.54 automatically falls under suspicion. There are many other headings that specify former occupations, most (e.g., *Ep.* 1.67, "to the monk who used to be a soldier") obviously inferred from the letter in question.[31] *Ep.* 1.54 is one of perhaps only two (with *Ep.* 3.4, "to Martin the elderly, rich whorelover") where there is nothing in the letter that could have suggested the heading. K. Heussi argued that they must therefore derive from an editor who knew the men personally.[32] But if the titles are no earlier than the sixth century, it is difficult to feel any confidence in the descriptions, neither of which can have stood on the letters as Nilus originally wrote them.

Nothing can be built on such a shaky foundation. It is best to forget about Nilus's "former pagan." It might be added that a pagan who later converted is not at all the same as the philhellene Christian of Zakrzewski and his followers. And while *De providentia* 123D might be a classicizing description of the baptism of one who, like Synesius himself, left it to mature years, it could not refer to the conversion of a pagan. The reference need not be to anything so specific as baptism. The word *theoria* might be held to suggest retreat to a monastery. In any case, for contemporaries, familiar with the linguistic conventions of contemporary Christian literature, there is nothing in *De providentia* that would for one moment have suggested that Aurelian was a pagan.

Further evidence of Aurelian's religious outlook can be obtained if we look forward to his restoration to power under the regency of Pulcheria in 414–16.[33] The year 415 saw an outburst of religious activity

30. The fullest account is by Stein 1949, 429–31; to the examples he cites add the Justinianic poets Ablabius illustris (*AP* 7.762) and Eutolmius scholasticus illustris (*AP* 6.86, 7.611, 9.587); but *not* the poet formerly known as Tiberius illustris, since Denys Page (1981, 546) has shown that the title is a misreading of the Palatine MS.

31. Cameron 1976b, 185–86.

32. *Untersuchungen zu Nilus dem Asketen* (Leipzig 1917), 68.

33. For Aurelian's role in Pulcheria's proclamation as Augusta see appendix 1.

on all fronts.[34] On 2 October the relics of Joseph, the son of Jacob, and Zechariah, the father of John the Baptist, were escorted into Constantinople and deposited in St. Sophia.[35] St. Sophia itself was re-dedicated on 10 October after being rebuilt following the fire of 404.[36] And it now appears that it was in 416 that Aurelian built his church of the protomartyr Stephen to house the relics recently found near Jerusalem.

December saw Theodosius II's first law against paganism, banning pagans from all public offices.[37] In October and November very stringent laws were issued against heretics;[38] *Cod. Theod.* 16.5.58 expressly withdrew from Eunomians the privilege of making wills, which had been restored to them by Aurelian's brother Caesarius in 395.[39] Another law of October 415 degraded the Jewish patriarch Gamaliel VI, a move described by M. Simon as "the culmination of an underground campaign against the patriarchate."[40] All these laws were addressed to and some at least must have been prompted by Aurelian. This was also the year that saw the terrible anti-Jewish riots in Alexandria that led eventually to the murder of Hypatia.

It has long been customary to ascribe the initiative in this illiberal campaign to the young Augusta Pulcheria.[41] As Sozomen put it in the fulsome panegyric he prefixed to book 9 of his *Ecclesiastical History*, she "provided zealously and wisely that religion might not be endangered by the innovation of spurious dogmas." But the emphasis here falls on *new* dogmas, as the following sentence makes clear: "That new heresies have not prevailed in our times we shall find to be especially due to her, *as we shall see*." He is clearly referring forward to his discussion of Nestorianism (which does not in fact survive). We are hardly justified in as-

34. A. Lippold, *RE*, Suppl. 13 (1972): 967; cf. 1015–16.

35. *Chron.Pasch.*, p. 572.15f. = *Chron. Min.* II.72, giving a.d. 6 Non., where presumably we correct to a.d. 6 Id.

36. *Chron.Pasch.* p. 572.15f.

37. *Cod.Theod.* 16.10.21; MSS 416, but by 26 August 416 Aurelian had been succeeded by Monaxius, and 415 is the generally accepted correction (Seeck 1919, 88.7).

38. *Cod.Theod.* 16.5.57–58.

39. The privilege was first withdrawn from them by Theodosius in 389 (*Cod.Theod.* 16.5.17), restored in 394 (16.5.23), revoked by Rufinus in 395 (16.5.25), restored by Caesarius the same year (16.5.27), confirmed by Eutychian in 399 (16.5.36), revoked again by Anthemius in 410 (16.5.49) and by Aurelian in 415 (16.5.58). It might seem surprising that the compilers of the Code (438) should record all these vacillations, but it was only by an examination of the whole series that it could be determined whether a given will was valid or not; it would depend on exactly when it was made (cf. Honoré 1986, 171).

40. *Cod. Theod.* 16.8.22; cf. M. Simon, *Verus Israel*, trans. H. McKeating (Oxford 1986), 130f., for the details and consequences.

41. So, for example, von Haehling 1978, 83; Holum 1977, 161; 1982, 100.

suming that she was as aggressive in the fight against heresy in 415, when she was only sixteen.

It is worth underlining that all three of the patrons under whose auspices Aurelian's career flourished—Rufinus,[42] Eudoxia, and Pulcheria—were figures of conspicuous Christian piety.[43] Rufinus and Pulcheria were, in addition, well known for their orthodoxy. The man who wormed himself into the favor of all three is hardly likely to have been an enthusiastic patron of the Neoplatonist underground, longing for the restoration of paganism.

Synesius sharply attacked Arian sympathies on the part of the Typhos of his *De providentia;* as a bishop he vigorously denounced heresy himself. He was evidently confident that Aurelian would never deal weakly with heretics. Quite possibly it was because of his impeccable orthodoxy that Synesius, as later Pulcheria, turned to Aurelian. There is no evidence that Aurelian had any sympathy for paganism.

When Lacombrade claimed that Aurelian "delighted in pagan philosophers," it is obvious that, first and foremost, it was Synesius he had in mind. He is the only member of Aurelian's alleged circle whose writings survive. If Synesius had indeed been the pagan philosopher of Zakrzewski's romance, there would at least have been some basis of comparison for the rest. But not only has the pagan character of Synesius's writings been much exaggerated; he proves on inspection to have been an orthodox Christian.

The only evidence for the existence of any literary circle in Constantinople ca. A.D. 400 comes in Synesius's *Ep.* 101 to his Constantinopolitan friend Pylaemenes. Synesius claims to be afraid to write to "the venerable Marcian" in case he "exposed himself to correction from the pedants who polish every syllable." "There is no small danger," he adds, "that the letter would be read in the Panhellenion. This is what I call the place in which many a time I thought deep thoughts, where the famous from all parts meet to hear the sacred voice of the old gentleman whose researches comprehend tales both past and present."

It seems reasonable to infer that this Marcian held some sort of salon, which both Synesius and Pylaemenes had attended. In another letter Synesius asks his friend Tryphon to "salute Marcian the philosopher for me," adding that he had once been governor of Paphlagonia (*Ep.*

42. For Aurelian's connection with Rufinus, see pp. 180–81.

43. Thanks to her unfortunate feud with an unbalanced patriarch, Eudoxia has come in for much unfair criticism: Teetgen's book (1907) is full of phrases like "impetuous caprice," "vain and passionate," "steeped in the flattery and luxury of the corruptest city in the Empire" (14). For the truth, Holum 1982, 57f.

119). But it should be clear from the way Synesius expresses himself that "Panhellenion" was just a name of his own that he did not expect even Pylaemenes to recognize, a private joke.[44] There is in any case no evidence that Marcian was either a pagan or sympathetic to pagan ideas. People simply liked to talk literature and philosophy at his house.

No evidence suggests that Aurelian ever attended such a gathering. Only three of Synesius's letters are addressed to Aurelian (*Ep.* 31, 34, 38). *Ep.* 31 praises him fulsomely for his conduct while praetorian prefect. It does so in semiphilosophical terms, but is nonetheless very much a letter to an Important Person, not a philosopher. *Ep.* 34 opens with a discreet allusion to *De providentia*, but only to give a personal touch to an otherwise routine letter of recommendation. *Ep.* 38 also begins in philosophical style, again neatly recalling a panegyrical theme developed in *De providentia*. But once more, the body of the letter is a routine recommendation.[45] The only other reference to Aurelian in Synesius's letters is to his "dear friend Aurelian the consul" in *Ep.* 61, emphatically underlining the fact that he actually knew such an Important Person. There are no letters on personal or literary themes—and no sign that he ever received a reply from Aurelian.

The traditional picture of Aurelian as a philosopher and patron of letters is drawn entirely from the portrait of Osiris in *De providentia*. It would be naive enough to make such an inference from a panegyric directly addressed to Aurelian under his own name. But *De providentia* is a fable. The fact that select contemporary persons and events are evoked in the fable does not mean that we may substitute Aurelian and Caesarius for Osiris and Typhos and treat it as history.[46] If Synesius had

44. Albert (1984, 28–33) independently came to a similarly skeptical conclusion about Synesius's Panhellenion. The "real" Panhellenion was a creation of Hadrian centering on Athens, with representatives from the older Greek cities (Spawforth and Walker 1985, 78–104; 1986, 88–105). Cyrene was a member, as we know from a monument found there, which must have been familiar to Synesius (reedited with new fragments by J. Reynolds, *JRS* 68 [1978]: 111–21). Fraser and Oliver were probably wrong to see a reference to the heroes Achaeus and Dorus in line 10 (Reynolds 1978, 116–17), but there is emphatic evocation of the Cyreneans' Spartan pedigree and "pure descent" (ἰθαγενεῖς) (Spawforth and Walker 1986, 97). We cannot but recall Synesius's claim to direct descent from Eurysthenes the Dorian, a claim recorded, he states, on public monuments in Cyrene (*Ep.* 57 = 41, p. 63.15f.G). Under the circumstances, it is not surprising that he should have thought playfully of Marcian's salon as reviving this noble assembly, with himself representing Cyrene.

45. "It is not because the young Herodes is my relative that I recommend him to your notice, but because he is seeking his rights."

46. For a particularly glaring example of this fallacy see Holum 1982, 86 n. 30 ("on Aurelian's religion [see] Syn. *De providentia* I.18").

wanted to write a history, he could easily have done so. It was not to protect himself that he fictionalized his story,[47] but so that he could make use of the greater license fiction allowed him.

For example, Demougeot's claim that Aurelian inherited his literary tastes from his father rests on the simplistic assumption that the picture of the old philosopher-king in book 1 of *De providentia* is an accurate biography of the real-life father of his hero, Fl. Taurus cos. 361.[48] This "king, priest, and sage" is not even an idealized version of the long-dead former notary who became Constantius II's lieutenant.[49] He is not a real person at all. He is merely the appropriate paternal mouthpiece for traditional advice to a son who is about to succeed him; as, for example, in *De IV consulatu Honorii* Claudian imagines how Theodosius once advised the new emperor Honorius on kingship. The parallels between this speech and Synesius's *De regno* are so close that actual derivation of one from the other has often been suspected—unnecessarily and implausibly: both Claudian and Synesius wrote in the same well-established tradition.[50] The old king comes straight from that tradition, a composite, emblematic stock character with little or nothing in common with the historical Taurus, just as the Theodosius who delivers Claudian's learned and philosophical discourse has little in common with the soldier-emperor Theodosius.

It is this idealized philosopher-king who discourses on encosmic and hypercosmic gods, not the father of Aurelian. As for the idea that Aurelian himself was a philosopher, there is no basis for it even in Synesius. Quite the contrary: Osiris is nowhere praised for either his eloquence or his wisdom. The most that Synesius claims for him is patronage of education in general and the "rustic philosopher" in particular. Least of all are there any grounds for associating him with Hellenism; as we have seen, he studied only as much "foreign culture" as his father thought fit (*De providentia* 90C).

Anyone familiar with the imperial panegyrics of Themistius and

47. As supposed by Zakrzewski, who misinterprets in this sense Synesius's love of mystification. We may well doubt whether he actually published either book during the crisis, though he took steps to ensure that *De providentia* 1 at least did not antagonize Gaïnas. In any case, the contemporary allusions were so transparent that mere denial would hardly have sufficed.

48. Demougeot also takes for granted Seeck's extraordinary claim (1894, 445–46) that Taurus (presumably a native Greek speaker) is to be identified with the (Latin-speaking) agrarian writer Palladius Rutilius Taurus Aemilianus, rightly rejected by von Haehling (1978, 293–94). See too A. Cameron, *JRS* 75 (1985): 173.

49. According to *De providentia*, "Egyptian tales say that he was also a god." Constantius II's lieutenant had been dead since at least 367: see below, p. 317 and n. 53.

50. Cameron 1970a, 21–23; Barnes 1986a, 107.

Julian will at once recognize the tendency of Greek panegyrists to represent Roman emperors as philosopher-kings who patronized philosophy and letters.[51] For Constantius II, there is Themistius *Or.* 2 and Julian *Or.* 1 and 3. In Themistius *Or.* 5 it is Jovian who has recalled philosophy to the palace ("recalled," after Julian!). In Themistius *Or.* 6, 7, 8, and 11 all the same claims are made for Valens; *Or.* 8 extols his love of philosophy in extraordinary detail. *Or.* 9 dilates on how his love of eloquence and philosophy affects the education of his young son (then three years old). In *Or.* 10 and *Or.* 15 Theodosius is praised for not barring philosophers from the palace, in *Or.* 13 Gratian; in *Or.* 18 it is the young prince Arcadius who studies philosophy.

Not one of these emperors took any personal interest in philosophy, and the only philosopher they all invited to the palace was, of course, Themistius. For Constantius it is instructive to contrast the verdict of Libanius, the leading sophist of the age, a man who no less than Themistius had the opportunity of observing the emperor's treatment of intellectuals at close quarters: "Philosophers and sophists and those who were initiates of Hermes or the Muses, these he never invited to the palace, never saw, never praised, never spoke to, never heard speak" (*Or.* 62.9). In fact Libanius evidently saw Constantius as an enemy of classical culture.[52] Add to this Ammianus's succinct assessment of the cultural attainments of Valens, subject of no fewer than five of Themistius's philosopher-king panegyrics: "subagrestis ingenii, nec bellicis nec liberalibus studiis eruditus" (31.14.5). He did not even know Greek. Themistius's speeches have considerable interest and importance for the history of Greek political ideas under the Roman Empire.[53] But they tell us nothing about the private culture of the emperors and little enough about their public patronage. There is no reason to believe that Synesius's idealized picture of Aurelian is any more accurate.

We may briefly review the other names listed as members of Aurelian's supposed cultural circle. First Troïlus of Side, a celebrated sophist influential with the prefect Anthemius.[54] Troïlus was already claimed as a pagan by Bury and E. Stein before Zakrzewski dubbed him a "grand agitateur païen et nationaliste."[55] According to Holum, Anthemius's "association with Troïlus confirms [his] receptiveness to the claims of the

---

51. On the importance of imperial patronage of literature and philosophy down the centuries, see F. Millar, *The Emperor in the Roman World* (London 1977), 496f.

52. Festugière 1959, 229f., 239.

53. See G. Dagron's useful study of Themistius under the title *L'empire romain d'orient au IVe siècle et les traditions politiques de l'hellénisme* (1968).

54. *PLRE* II.1128.

55. Bury (1923) 1958, 213; Stein 1959, 246; Zakrzewski 1931, 122.

Hellenes."[56] The truth is that nothing whatever is known of Troïlus's religious beliefs. Holum's apparently more restrained formulation is more insidiously false than the crude error of his predecessors; for it makes it impossible to understand the combined devotion to rhetoric and Christianity that is the hallmark of Byzantine culture. Anthemius may well have been a cultivated man who patronized men of letters, but Holum implies something more sinister: an organized party of Hellenes who have claims on him. He will allow no more than that "like . . . Aurelian, [Anthemius] must have professed Christianity," and elsewhere expresses doubts about even this.[57] Against these wider suspicions it is enough to point out that Troïlus's pupils included two bishops and an ecclesiastical historian.[58]

Lacombrade claimed Troïlus as "un partisan chaleureux d'Aurélien" on the grounds that his pupil Eusebius Scholasticus "compose, comme Synésios, sur le soulèvement des Goths, un écrit d'actualité."[59] But since, to judge from Socrates' reference to Eusebius's *Gaïnias,*[60] it covered the war itself rather than, like *De providentia,* the antecedents alone, it is difficult to see how it could possibly have had the exiled Aurelian as its hero. Indeed, the heroes must have been Fravitta and Caesarius.[61] Though a modest literary circle might be allowed to his successor Anthemius, for Aurelian there is no evidence whatever.

Many of the same considerations apply to the Hellenism of the other alleged members of the "Panhellenion"—for example, the successful poet Theotimus,[62] another friend of the prefect Anthemius; Nicander, a man of literary interests and influence unspecified;[63] Pylaemenes, one of Synesius's closest Constantinopolitan friends, an advocate with literary and philosophical interests;[64] Anastasius, tutor of Arcadius's children and a friend of Troïlus;[65] Simplicius, a *magister militum* and native of the Pentapolis who according to Synesius had asked for a copy of his poems

56. Holum 1982, 87; cf. Zakrzewski's paper in *Eos* 31 (1928), at p. 422 ("membre du parti national formé en 399"), 423 ("une ancienne famille sénatorienne, animée par l'esprit païen," "personnellement chrétien, mais . . .").

57. Holum 1977, 169f.; against, see Cameron 1982, 272. Holum (1982, 86 n. 30) replies that he finds his own view "amply attested in the sources and more plausible than that of Cameron," yet provides no new evidence or arguments.

58. Socr. *HE* 7.12.10 (Ablabius, Novatian bishop of Nicaea), 7.37.1 (Silvanus, bishop of Troas); the ecclesiastical historian is Socrates himself.

59. Lacombrade 1951a, 8.

60. *HE* 6.6 *fin.,* our only source.

61. This conclusion will become clearer after the discussion of *De providentia* in chapter 6.

62. *PLRE* II.1111, with D. T. Runia, *Historia* 28 (1979): 254–56.

63. *PLRE* II.781.

64. *PLRE* II.931.

65. *PLRE* II.77–78.

(*Ep.* 130 *fin.*). Once again, Synesius's three letters to this important man are all concerned with business rather than literature.

According to Holum, "Synesius of Cyrene associates [Aurelian] with a circle of poets, philosophers and politicians who called themselves 'Hellenes.'" [66] The truth is that not a single one of them is associated with Aurelian in any way. Nor do they call themselves Hellenes. It is Synesius who (three times) applies the term to correspondents, never with any religious connotations, and certainly not as the name of an organized group or circle. It is simply a compliment to the literary taste of his friends.

II. PAEONIUS

Another of Synesius's Constantinopolitan patrons deserves more extended discussion. Soon after his arrival Synesius presented a military man called Paeonius with a silver astrolabe that he had had made in Alexandria. In the modern literature this man is always styled Count Paeonius, but the one source that identifies him by name, the letter that accompanied the gift (generally known as *De dono*), never indicates his rank. This letter is one of a group of essays Synesius later sent to Hypatia, noting, "And so the reckoning will be complete, I have added my *On the Gift*, an old piece from the time of my embassy, to a man with great influence over the emperor. And Pentapolis had some profit from the essay and from the gift" (*Ep.* 154).

Though he has not known Paeonius for long (*De dono* 310C), Synesius takes the opportunity of writing to him because, he explains, "I heard you recently expressing indignation on behalf of philosophy" (307B). Moreover, Synesius claims, "it was largely on my account that you were so incensed at the present state of philosophy" (308A). On the face of it, a man of philosophical interests. Indeed, we might even infer some familiarity with the Alexandrian school, since Synesius writes as though Paeonius will recognize his reference to "my most revered teacher" (311A, unnamed but feminine), namely, Hypatia. On the other hand Synesius presents the astronomy and metaphysics introduced by the gift as unfamiliar subjects.[67]

66. Holum 1977, 159, citing thirteen letters of Synesius as though they supported his assertion.

67. Synesius's own expertise wins severe criticism from Neugebauer 1975, 876–77: "Synesius was not competent as a scientist, but he was rich and well-educated. . . . [The astronomical content of the *De dono* is] badly organized and obscured by philosophical verbosity and boasting; . . . [parts are] obviously nonsense."

According to Synesius, what had been vexing Paeonius is the fact that false philosophers "enjoy a good reputation with rulers and people alike, while no one pays any attention to true philosophers" (307A). While states should be governed by philosophers, the truth is that

> the tribe of sophists lay their snares for the ignorance of the multitude, and that as a result of this the legitimate sons of philosophy come to have less repute than the supposititious and fraudulent. But when those who hold the reins of government and have the affairs of the cities in their grasp are not of the people, but possess intellectual culture, they will quickly make the distinction between the legitimate and illegitimate philosopher, and no longer will the common people have any problem learning what sort of deception has been practiced upon them.[68]

Zakrzewski was in no doubt that this is all to be taken quite seriously.[69] The true philosophers he easily identified as Neoplatonists. But the false philosophers seemed to him more than just sophists, and the "deception" they practice on the people nothing else but Christianity: "Le parti des vrais philosophes est celui des néoplatoniciens qui livre secrètement combat à la nouvelle société triomphante. Cependant le parti des philosophes cherche un homme qui saurait unir la sagesse à la puissance, afin d'assurer à la philosophie sur la société l'influence qui lui est due."[70] This seductive hypothesis does no great violence to what Synesius actually says. But, criteria of probability aside, it runs into serious problems. To start with, Zakrzewski was embarrassed that Synesius's addressee who unites temporal power with philosophy—in effect, a Platonic philosopher-king—should be an obscure count not otherwise on record. Such a key figure in the Neoplatonic freemasonry should at the very least be someone identifiable.[71] This problem he solved by assuming that the name, though common enough at the time,[72] was in fact a pseudonym.

His first thought was the MVM Simplicius, who, though not actually called a philosopher, was at any rate interested in poetry. But not even Simplicius was really important enough for Zakrzewski's interpretation of the *De dono*, and he finally settled on the veteran general Saturninus who was exiled together with Aurelian in April 400. This ingenious suggestion does at least yield a known associate of Aurelian. But quite apart from the improbability of this career soldier being a Neoplatonist, by 400 he had not held a command for nearly twenty years.

68. *De dono* 309B–D.

69. Zakrzewski 1931, 67–71.

70. Zakrzewski 1931, 69.

71. "C'est parmi les personnages que nous connaissons par ailleurs qu'il faut chercher aussi bien Paionios que Typhos" (Zakrzewski 1931, 68).

72. Three, if not four, other examples in *PLRE* (I.657, II.817).

Synesius's words make it clear that his Paeonius was in office at the time of writing.[73]

To turn to more traditional tools, according to *PLRE* "Paeonius is certainly identical with an unnamed count at Alexandria mentioned as an acquaintance and correspondent of Synesius there in three letters." But is he? It is worth subjecting the evidence to a detailed examination, if only to illustrate the machinery of connections through which favors were won and influence peddled in late antiquity.

Synesius's letters are arranged haphazardly for the most part.[74] Atypically, however, his letters to his school friend Herculian are at least segregated by addressee. I. Hermelin dated the whole group after Synesius's first period of study in Alexandria but before his embassy to Constantinople.[75] The letters' tone is generally consonant with a recent separation and fresh enthusiasm for studies recently shared, but the evidence is too lacunose to link up into a firm absolute chronology. In the letters where he gives a clear indication, Synesius writes from home in Cyrene to Alexandria.

Ep. 144 and 146 appear to be a pair. Though the actual business concerned is obscure, *Ep.* 146 (p. 257.12–20G) formulates principles of decorum fairly clearly:

> Your brother Cyrus should have brought back writings from you concerning what you disclosed because of the count from Pentapolis. I was grateful to the motive of the introducer, but you forgot that I am trying to be a philosopher. And I rate at little all honor unless it comes on account of philosophy; so, thanks to God, I require nothing, for we neither do nor suffer wrong. It was fitting that he should do such a thing on our behalf, but not suitable that we should make the request; for if there was a need to seek letters, they should have been sent to me (for then I would have been honored), not on my behalf to the count.

Apparently Herculian made some overtures on Synesius's behalf to "the count from Pentapolis." Synesius protests, first because he is not interested, and second because his own position should have led the count to seek him out. His interest might properly have been solicited. Having solicitations made on his behalf puts him in a dependent position that is not appropriate.

Ep. 144 (p. 254 G) recants just such a proud refusal, apparently this one. Hermelin accordingly dated it later.

73. αὐτὸς ἄρξων . . . τά τε γὰρ κοινὰ πράττειν πιστεύῃ, 309C. Aware of the contradiction, and ignoring this passage, Zakrzewski (1931, 68) simply asserts that "il ne suit pas du discours de Synésius que Paionios fut général en activité à l'époque dont nous parlons."
74. Seeck 1894.
75. *Ep.* 137–46. Hermelin 1934, 19–25; cf. Lacombrade 1951a, 52–53; Theiler 1953, 195–97 (review of Lacombrade); Runia 1976, 27–30. On Herculian, *PLRE* II.545.

You have written to me through Ursicinus about the count (I mean the one who holds command over the soldiers in this country),[76] and you asked me to give the word, and there would be writings from your friends able to do it, both to him and to the ordinary commander. Even then I accepted the motive. But I refused the deed as superfluous, as I was stripping myself to grapple with philosophy. But now wronged friends, both private citizens and soldiers, force me to want to take part in politics, for which I know I wasn't born, and they themselves share that knowledge with me. But for their own sakes, they force even an unwilling man to do something. So now if you think it good to do this, I leave it to you. . . . My whole household greets you. Ision is now added to it, whom you longed for because of his stories. He has caused me to make that ignoble and unphilosophic request for writings to those in power, in some things required personally on behalf of many, and in others by the letters he brought. So he waits for you till the twentieth, as I said.[77]

Ep. 144 fills in Ep. 146's picture of the interplay of power and etiquette in recommendation letters. Synesius heavily stresses his personal lack of interest in the favors to be sought. He acts only on behalf of others. Even this indirect need is demeaning: his mere recantation is an "ignoble and unphilosophic request" for which he has to apologize.[78] Ision took the same tack, "on behalf of many." Beyond the lowest level, requests were conveyed by third parties. The letter writer distanced himself from the need as much as possible so as not to weaken his own position; he might then voice the request more compellingly.

Ep. 99 to another school friend, Olympius, also mentions both "your Ision," living at Synesius's house, and an unnamed count, to whom Olympius shall judge "whether or not to give what I have written" (p. 167.21 G). On the most economical interpretation, Synesius means the letter itself, an elegant recommendation of the poet Theotimus.[79] Synesius assists the poet by sending him to Alexandria, not to one patron alone, but to someone who can also smooth his approach toward a further target. The coincidence of Ision and *comes* seemed to Hermelin to date this letter to the same period as the letters to Herculian.

76. Since the description of Ep. 146, τὸν ἐκ Πενταπόλεως κόμητα, suggests personal origin in Pentapolis, τοῦ κόμητος . . . τοῦ τυχόντος ἀρχῆς τῶν ἐν τῇ πατρίδι στρατιωτῶν here seems to stress the fact that the count holds command over soldiers in his own native district. Roques (1989, 78–79) implausibly interprets the former to mean that the count "a rapidement quitté le province" after holding a temporary command there.

77. Cf. Ep. 143: Synesius planned to wait for Herculian till the twentieth of Mesore, but then he had to travel himself.

78. All his remarks on Ision sound like afterthoughts, so the slight distancing of his description does not imply that he had made some other, grosser prostration.

79. On whom see generally D. T. Runia, *Historia* 28 (1979): 254–56. Ep. 61 (p. 102.10–11 G) explicitly tells Pylaemenes to show that letter to Asterius.

Ep. 98, again to Olympius, followed, for it too mentions an unnamed count, to whom Synesius says he has written often but sends another letter through his brother, since Olympius accuses him of not having written. This letter explicitly locates Olympius in Alexandria, whither Synesius will depart as soon as he is well enough. *Ep.* 143 and 144 also refer to a journey, but the plans are spoken of in very different terms. The corpus of Synesius's letters reflects a great deal of travel and visiting among his friends, so it is reasonable to assume that Ision could have stayed with Synesius more than once. If he did, nothing in these letters need date them with the group to Herculian. Moreover, as David Runia points out, Olympius's count is in Alexandria, whereas Herculian's is "in command over the soldiers in this country" and "from Pentapolis." Probably therefore he was *dux Libyarum*.[80] With him it is a matter of writing letters, whereas Olympius evidently sees his count in Alexandria. A possible candidate for either count might be Simplicius, MVM *per Orientem*, who did serve in Pentapolis and hunted often with Synesius and who was also interested in poetry.[81]

It is important to note this complicated multiplicity of counts, as well as the ways Synesius deals with them, because a third letter to Herculian contains another, who has always been identified with Paeonius.[82] In *Ep.* 142 (p. 249 G), Synesius asks Herculian to

> speak to the admirable count (τὸν θαυμάσιον κόμητα), toward whom I did not initiate an address in my own person. There is poetry's tag "begin, for you are younger in age" [*Il.* 21.439]. War and contention he thinks it right that the young man begin, but friendliness the elder. And yet with me the man is honored and deserving of all, who alone of the men of our time brought together education and military ability, which have been barricaded apart by great walls, discovering in these pursuits some ancient kinship (ὃς παιδείαν καὶ στρατείαν διατετειχισμένας θριγκοῖς μεγάλοις τῶν ἐφ' ἡμῶν μόνος εἰς ταὐτὸν ἤγαγε, παλαιάν τινα ἐξευρὼν ἐν τοῖς ἐπιτηδεύμασι τούτοις συγγένειαν). Being noble as no soldier yet, "from neighbors" he escapes the arrogance that dwells next to nobility. Him as such a one then, even if I do not write, I love, and if I do not serve, I honor.

The discussion of the Iliadic tag makes plain that Synesius has not written to the count directly because he does not yet possess his acquain-

---

80. Runia 1979, n. 15.

81. *Ep.* 130, esp. pp. 223.4–7, 224.10–14 G; cf. *Ep.* 24, 28, 134, p. 233.11–14 G; *PLRE* II.1013–14. Roques (1989, 80–82) conflates the unnamed counts and identifies the composite as Simplicius. Another possible *dux Libyarum* in Synesius's letters is Uranius (*Ep.* 40 = 37 G), though there is too little evidence to be certain of anything: *PLRE* II.1186.

82. E.g., *PLRE* II.816–17: "certainly identical"; Barnes 1986a, 110: "clearly Paeonius."

tance. He wants Herculian to break the ice for him. The compliments are for Herculian to use in doing so. He is to pass them on, perhaps even handing the letter over for the count to read, like Olympius *Ep.* 99 on Theotimus to that count. Synesius echoes himself almost exactly in *De dono:*

> How then shall I not assign the middle place in my soul to the admirable Paeonius, who discovered how to bring back and unite philosophy and military ability, long barricaded apart by great walls, seeing in these pursuits some ancient kinship?

> πῶς οὖν οὐ μέλλω τὴν μέσην ἐν τῇ ψυχῇ χώραν τῷ θαυμαστῷ Παιονίῳ νέμειν, ὃς ἐκ πολλοῦ διατετειχισμένας θριγκοῖς μεγάλοις φιλοσοφίαν καὶ στρατείαν ἐξεῦρεν ἐπαναγαγεῖν καὶ συνάψαι, παλαιάν τινα ἐνιδὼν τοῖς ἐπιτηδεύμασι τούτοις συγγένειαν;[83]

Indeed the parallel is striking. But though it is clear that Paeonius holds a military post, he is nowhere explicitly styled count. And it must be remembered that while the count of *Ep.* 142 was evidently in Alexandria for Herculian to "speak to" him, Paeonius is now in Constantinople. Of course, a military man of significant rank is likely enough to have been a count, and since some time must have intervened between *Ep.* 142 and *De dono* for Synesius to get from Cyrene to Constantinople, Paeonius might have been transferred to the capital during the same interval. *PLRE* suggests a rise from *comes Aegypti* to *comes rei militaris.* But far too much weight has been placed on the veracity and specificity of Synesius's compliment.[84]

More importantly, praise for erudition is Synesius's great war-horse. He trots it out whenever he wants a favor, evidently believing it the most flattering tribute a potential patron could wish to hear. His later *Ep.* 73, to Troïlus, for example, asking him to solicit the praetorian prefect Anthemius on Pentapolis's behalf, begins: "You are both a philosopher and a philanthrope, so I must lament before you the troubles of the land that bore me. You will honor her because of her citizen the philosopher and you will pity her because of the gentleness of your nature, and because of both things you will try to lift again her who has fallen" (p. 130 G). *Ep.* 118 enlists Troïlus again to approach Anthemius, now on behalf of Synesius's cousin Diogenes. Synesius notes Diogenes' connections, but, clinchingly, "Troïlus the philosopher will see the young man's inner qualities and esteem him on that basis." Synesius recommends Di-

---

83. *De dono* 308B–C.
84. The fact that he puts it into the third person in *Ep.* 142 has no independent significance, for Herculian is to convey it to the count on Synesius's behalf.

ogenes to Pylaemenes principally on the grounds of friendship but does not neglect to note that he respects his "kinship with a philosopher" (*Ep.* 131, p. 226.5 G). *Ep.* 26 salutes Troïlus in thanks for some intercession with Anastasius as "best of philosophers, for so I delight to call you, as your deeds proclaim." The last passage is particularly instructive. For Troïlus was not in fact a philosopher. His pupil and admirer Socrates refers to Troïlus no fewer than five times, invariably styling him "the sophist" and several times referring to his pupils.[85] More explicitly still, he is known as the author of a commentary on the *Staseis* of Hermogenes.[86] However learned and prudent a man he may have been, there can be no question that by profession he was a teacher of rhetoric, a tribe elsewhere openly despised by Synesius and directly opposed to true philosophers in the *De dono*. But when he has a favor to ask, Synesius "delights to call him a philosopher."

In *Ep.* 119 he asks Trypho to "greet Marcian the philosopher, the former governor of Paphlagonia, for me," so that he too may assist Diogenes (p. 205 G). This must be the Marcian of Synesius's "Panhellenion" (*Ep.* 101), and the fact that Synesius cannot sufficiently identify him by referring to it here reinforces the argument that the salon did not dominate the Constantinopolitan scene. If so, Marcian's influence will have rested more in his political than his literary position; thus Synesius calls him "philosopher" here as a conciliating compliment. Marcian more than some others may have found it apposite and welcome, of course. The final conclusion to be drawn is that the reluctance Synesius expresses in *Ep.* 101 to write to Marcian directly reflects not the modesty over his style he asserts, but as with the count of *Ep.* 142, his inability to claim sufficiently close acquaintance to take the initiative.

As for his major works, the peroration of *De regno* begins: "May you fall in love, my king, with philosophy and true education" (31C). Synesius dwells on the theme for a while, applying to philosophy the same Iliadic tag he had applied to Paeonius and himself in the *De dono*,[87] and he finally concludes that if Arcadius realizes his image of the philosopher-king, "I would have the right to be the first to rejoice at the shoot from my seeds, how I shaped you as king, experiencing such a thing, whenever I offer and receive speech about the things the cities request" (32C). He claims that Cyrene sent him as ambassador to convey two things, its

---

85. *HE* 6.6.36, 7.1.3, 12.10, 27.1, 37.1; cf. in general *PLRE* II.1128.

86. H. Rabe, ed., *Rhetores Graeci* (Leipzig 1895), 6:28–92; Kennedy 1983, 120.

87. "I have no need of this honor. I understand that I am honored by the decree of Zeus." *Il.* 9.608f.; *De dono* 308B; *De regno* 32A.

crown gold and philosophy (2C): thus all the philosophy of the speech reflects on his mission. Still more in *De providentia* is Osiris praised for achieving a golden age through due respect for education (102D–104B). In particular the exemplary rustic philosopher is granted by Osiris that "he himself was not obliged to perform public service, and his country's obligations had been made less burdensome" (113A–B). Synesius takes care to make it everywhere obvious that education and concrete favors ought to go together. Nothing in *Ep.* 142 indicates why Synesius esteemed this count so highly. But in view of the ease with which he dispensed such compliments, we can hardly exclude the possibility that at different times he found more than one man who "alone of our time" united philosophy or education with temporal power. In the age that produced Themistius's implausible series of philosopher-emperors, it is not strange that Synesius chose a kindred ploy.

To sum up, we cannot safely identify Paeonius with any of these counts. So there is no firm basis for the view that Synesius was exploiting a connection originally made in Alexandria. On the contrary, the opening of *De dono* suggests that he had only just met Paeonius. But perhaps we have reached a positive conclusion nonetheless. It is that the motif of the philosopher-king did not need to be restricted to kings. In the debased and trivialized rhetorical lexicon of the early Byzantine world it could be applied to any prospective patron, however implausibly, even to a career soldier.

III. THE DATE OF THE EMBASSY

Before we can reach a satisfactory interpretation of either *De regno* or *De providentia*, we must identify the three wretched years Synesius spent in Constantinople,[88] the three years during which he wrote both works.

He had come as an ambassador (*De regno* 1A), seeking alleviation of the taxes imposed on "the cities" (32C), that is to say, the cities of Pentapolis.[89] Our only evidence for the specific occasion of his visit is what he proclaims in *De regno*: he had come to "crown [the emperor's] head with gold" (2C). That is, he had come to present him with *aurum coronarium*, "crown gold," on behalf of the Pentapolis.

Emperors were normally presented with crown gold on the occasion of their accession and on the successive quinquennial celebrations of

88. *De insomniis* 14; *Hymn* 1.431f.
89. Liebeschuetz 1985b, 154–55.

their reign.[90] Additional "presentations" might be required on the occasion of an imperial victory, as, for example, in celebration of the defeat of the usurper Maximus in 388.[91] There being no obvious occasion for an extraordinary presentation during Synesius's years at Constantinople,[92] we are left with one of Arcadius's quinquennial anniversaries.

The truth was seen long ago by Sievers and at once forgotten.[93] Since then no one but T. D. Barnes has made any serious attempt to identify this occasion, the one and only precise clue *De regno* provides. Seeck tried instead to pin the date down by working backwards from Synesius's departure. In *Ep.* 61 Synesius describes how he left Constantinople during an earthquake, which Seeck identified with the quake placed in 402 by Marcellinus. Departure in 402 at once became canonical as the one secure date, it was thought, in Synesian chronology. Thus, if Synesius spent three years in Constantinople, he could not have arrived earlier than the autumn of 399, and *De regno* would have to have been delivered in 399 or even 400. To the question of this earthquake we shall be returning. But if it was in 399 that he arrived, which quinquennial anniversary was the crown gold designed to commemorate?

Lacombrade, taking Seeck's departure date of 402 as axiomatic, was reduced to the desperate expedient of assuming that Cyrene was four years late honoring Arcadius's "accession," by which he meant the beginning of his effective reign on the death of Theodosius in January 395.[94] But as Barnes rightly observed, "a Roman emperor began to rule from his *dies imperii*, not from the death of one of his imperial colleagues, even if that colleague was his father."[95] Since Arcadius was proclaimed Augustus on 19 January 383,[96] his quinquennial celebrations should on the usual inclusive reckoning have fallen on 19 January 387,

---

90. Klauser 1944, 129–53 (= 1974, 292–309); Millar 1977, 140–42; Barnes 1986a, 105–6; R. Delmaire, *Largesses sacrées et res privata* (Rome 1989), 387–400.

91. McCormick 1986, 44; cf. Lib. *Ep.* 846, 878. Another might have been expected in 395 after the victory over Eugenius (McCormick 45–46), though Theodosius's death early in the year may have caused a change of plan. But that would have been too early for Synesius anyway. To judge from several scenes of men bearing crowns on the reliefs of Arcadius's column, there was another in 401 to celebrate the defeat of Gaïnas (T. Klauser, *Ges. Arbeiten* [1974], 303). That would have been too late.

92. Barnes (1986a, 105) suggests and rightly rejects the possibility of the birth of Arcadius's daughter Pulcheria on 19-i-399. There is no parallel for requiring crown gold to commemorate imperial births.

93. Sievers 1870, 378.

94. Lacombrade 1949, 58.

95. Barnes 1986a, 105–6.

96. *Chron.Min.* I.244.

392, 397, 402, and 407.[97] The only year that would suit Synesius's visit is 397.[98]

The quinquennial year would have begun on 19 January 397 and ended on the same day in 398. The crown gold presumably was expected some time between these two dates. If the city chose to send it in the custody of an ambassador charged with a mission at court, as in Synesius's case, it would not have been tactful for him to arrive late. Given the limitations on sea travel during the winter months, we can exclude the possibility that Synesius arrived as late as January 398. A letter from Cyrene to his old friend Herculian (*Ep.* 144) lamenting his co-option on the embassy and implying departure in the near future is dated 20 Mesore, that is to say, 13 August. From Cyrene to Alexandria could be done in five days;[99] from Alexandria to Constantinople in nine.[100] So the trip could be done in two weeks, though we do not know whether or how long Synesius stopped over on the way. We may probably assume that he arrived early in September 397.

In ideal circumstances, the ambassador would present the gold crown and his address together shortly after arrival. Synesius's extant *De regno,* which betrays clear signs of frustration at dealing with an unresponsive emperor and court, cannot, for a variety of reasons, have been the speech Synesius delivered on that occasion. It is the wrong sort of speech—and far too long. But the fact that it begins with a reference to the crown gold (2C) suggests a date not too far removed from his arrival.

Synesius described his departure from Constantinople in *Ep.* 61, to his friend Pylaemenes:

> God shook the earth repeatedly during the day, and most people were on their faces in prayer; for the ground was shaking. At the time, considering the sea to be safer than the land, I rushed to the harbor, speak-

97. There is a tendency for emperors to take the consulate in quinquennial years (somewhat overstated in Richard Burgess's useful paper, "Quinquennial Vota and Imperial Consulship, 337–511," *Numismatic Chronicle* 148 (1988): 77–96; cf. Cameron, *CLRE* 23–24). J. P. C. Kent suggests to us that Arcadius celebrated his third quinquennalia in 396, when he was consul, rather than in 397, when he was not. But this would be impossibly early for Synesius. It is not easy to believe that he arrived a year late when he had a favor to ask.

98. According to Barnes 1986a, 106, Arcadius "celebrated the fifteenth anniversary of his accession on 19 January 398" (a slip of the pen, as he admits); correctly, Sievers 1870, 378.

99. *Ep.* 51, with Casson 1971, 284–85.

100. Theoph. Simocatta 8.13.14 (Casson 1971, 281–96, cites no examples).

ing no word to anyone except Photius of blessed memory—and I only shouted to him from afar and signaled with my hand that I was about to leave. He who left Aurelian, his dear friend and consul (ὕπατον), without a farewell has given an adequate apology for the same behavior toward Asterius the clerk.[101]

Seeck referred this earthquake to one recorded by Marcellinus under 402, and emended ὕπατον ("consul") to ὕπαρχον ("prefect") to harmonize Aurelian's office with the prefecture that he had invented for him in 402. But if Synesius arrived in the autumn of 397 and remained for three years, he would indeed have left in the autumn of 400, Aurelian's consular year. Barnes remarks that "to suppose an earthquake in the city in 400 as well as in 402 presents no difficulty."[102] Fortunately we need not merely suppose one.

Though omitted from all four modern lists of earthquakes in Constantinople,[103] one in 400 with exactly the consequences Synesius describes is in fact securely attested by a contemporary source. In his *Homily* 41 on Acts (*PG* 60.201) Chrysostom says: "Did not God last year (πέρυσιν) shake our whole city? Did not all run to baptism? Did not fornicators and homosexuals and abandoned men leave their homes and their haunts and change and become religious? But after three days they returned to their own particular sort of wickedness. And why? From sheer laziness!" And again in *Hom.* 7 of the same series (*PG* 60.66): "If you remember how it was when God shook our city with an earthquake, how subdued all men were? . . . No knavery, no villainy then; such is the effect of fear and affliction!" From the days of Tillemont and Montfaucon, it has been a fixed point in Chrysostomian chronology that the fifty-five homilies on Acts were delivered at Constantinople during 400/1.[104] Seeck was of course well aware of these texts, but he dismissed them entirely from the reckoning by alleging that they were delivered

101. This section is abbreviated from Cameron 1987, 332–50.

102. Barnes 1986a, 104.

103. W. Capelle, "Erdbebenforschung," *RE* Suppl. 4 (1924): 347; G. Downey, "Earthquakes at Constantinople and Vicinity, A.D. 342–1454," *Speculum* 30 (1955): 597; V. Grumel, *La Chronologie* (Paris 1958), 477; A. Hermann, "Erdbeben," *RAC* 5 (1962): 1104–12. All but Grumel, who does not cite him at all, cite Synesius without comment for 402. It is time for a new, critical list, by someone familiar with the problems of transmission. For some that do not arise in the present case see Brian Croke, "Two Early Byzantine Earthquakes and Their Liturgical Commemoration," *Byzantion* 51 (1981): 122–47. On Byzantine attitudes to earthquakes, see G. Dagron, "Quand la terre tremble . . . ," *Travaux et mémoires* 8 (1981): 87–103.

104. See the summary account in Quasten 1960, 440–41 (though he omits the important work of Bonsdorff discussed below).

thirty years earlier in Antioch (to be precise, in 373).[105] Though his arguments were justly described by his only critic as "light as a feather,"[106] Seeck won a decisive victory: neither Chrysostom passage has ever been discussed since in this connection.[107] Since Max von Bonsdorff's valuable work seems to have had no impact beyond the study of Chrysostom and the point is central to Synesian chronology, the main points must be briefly recapitulated.

First, a number of passages unmistakably describe the preacher as a bishop. For example, the last four columns of *Hom.* 3 (*PG* 60.39–42) are entirely devoted to an account of the responsibilities of a bishop, and at one point Chrysostom insists that he is "simply speaking as I find it in my own actual experience" (col. 39). *Hom.* 8 (*PG* 60.74) refers emphatically to the power of excommunication he enjoyed as bishop, even over the emperor ("as long as I sit on this throne," col. 60). At the end of *Hom.* 9 an imaginary interlocutor is represented as saying to Chrysostom: "Yes, but you are the leader and bishop" (col. 84). Many other passages refer to the power and responsibility he enjoyed to legislate for his flock.[108] None of this suits Chrysostom's status in Antioch. While already celebrated for the brilliance of his preaching, he was no more than a simple priest in rank and had always behaved with the utmost tact toward his bishop, the patriarch Flavian.[109]

Second, another series of passages alludes to the emperor and his palace as conspicuous fixtures in the world of his listeners. For example, *Hom.* 21 (*PG* 60.168) alludes to the possibility of an invitation to the palace from the emperor himself; *Hom.* 3 (col. 39) refers to both the palace and the bishop's throne; *Hom.* 8 (col. 99) and *Hom.* 11 (col. 170) refer to the emperor's *adventus* and victories; the last passage also to the need for petitioners to approach the emperor while seated, since when he rises the audience is at an end; *Hom.* 32 (col. 170) refers to the emperor and his council deliberating on military and domestic issues, in particular (appropriately enough for 400/1) "overcoming those who make war on them." It is hardly worth discussing Seeck's positive arguments in favor

105. Seeck 1894, 460 n. 44.

106. Max von Bonsdorff, *Zur Predigttätigkeit des Johannes Chrysostomus* (Helsinki 1922), 90.

107. Grützmacher referred to Seeck's treatment of the homilies in a footnote (1913, 72 n. 3); Lacombrade in passing (1951a, 100–101); after that, silence.

108. Collected by Bonsdorff 1922, 87–88.

109. Baur 1959, 1:390–95. With the passages quoted above, contrast the beginning of *Hom.* 3 *De statuis:* "When I look on that throne, deserted and bereft of our teacher" (alluding to the absence of Flavian).

of Antioch. The account of Theodorus's conspiracy there in 372 to which he attributed so much importance (*Hom.* 38, cols. 274–75) is recounted as a reminiscence of Chrysostom's distant youth in another city.

It was undoubtedly at Constantinople that Chrysostom preached his homilies on Acts. Therefore the following passage in *Hom.* 44 (*PG* 60.66) becomes vital: "By the grace of God I too have now spent three years (τριετία), not indeed exhorting you night and day, but often every three or seven days." The formulation is imprecise, since naturally his regular listeners could be counted on to know exactly what he had in mind. But there can be little doubt that what he meant was three years preaching as bishop of Constantinople. Since he was consecrated on 26 February 398, his third year would have ended on 26 February 401. We cannot be sure that he meant three full years,[110] but on the simplest interpretation he delivered *Hom.* 44 and in all probability *Hom.* 41, too, early in 401. πέρυσι can mean "twelve months ago," but also no more than "last year," that is to say, 400 if spoken in early 401.

When did Chrysostom begin the series? He is known to have thought that Pentecost was an appropriate time to study Acts (cf. his homily *Cur in Pentecoste Acta legantur*),[111] and early editors inferred from a passage in *Hom.* 1 (*PG* 60.22) that he began at or near Easter. But he goes on in the same homily to ask his listeners whether they are waiting for Lent to be baptized, telling them that this is wrong; any time of the year will do. Obviously he cannot have been speaking at Easter. *Hom.* 4 on the account of Pentecost in Acts 2.1 does not at all suggest that the festival was at hand when he spoke. And a passage in *Hom.* 29 clearly states that Easter has come and gone (col. 218); indeed it continues "summer is past, winter is here" (col. 219). There is nothing in the context to suggest a metaphorical winter rather than the real thing. The end of *Hom.* 26 (col. 204) vividly evokes cold weather.

There is also one fairly clear allusion at the end of *Hom.* 37 (*PG* 60.267) to the expulsion and massacre of the Goths of 12 July 400. After denouncing the war between the soul and the body, virtue and vice, anger and gentleness (and so forth), Chrysostom continues:

110. This passage is not to be pressed too hard, since as in his preceding paragraph Chrysostom is clearly and deliberately alluding to the passage of Acts that forms his text: "for three years [the same word, τριετία] night and day I did not cease" (Acts 20.31). Thus he says "I too." But there seems no reason to doubt that he had indeed been bishop for three years; this was why he thought of exploiting the text in this way.

111. For a full collection of references to this practice see Joseph Bingham, *Antiquities of the Christian Church* (1708–22; reprint, London 1875), bk. 14, chap. 3, and bk. 20, chap. 6.

Let us make an end of this war, let us overthrow these enemies, let us set up these trophies, let us establish peace in our own city. We have within us a city and a civil polity, with citizens and many aliens (ξένοι); but let us drive out the aliens (ξενηλασίαν ποιώμεθα), that our own people may not be ruined. Let no foreign or spurious doctrine enter in, nor carnal desire. Do we not see that if an enemy is caught in a city, he is judged as a spy? Then let us drive out the aliens. Indeed let us not merely drive out aliens; let us send our enemies packing too. If we catch sight of a wicked thought,[112] let us hand it over to the ruler, our mind, the thought that is a barbarian tricked out in the garb of a citizen. For there are within us many thoughts of this kind, by nature enemies, though clad in sheep's skins. Just like Persians when they take off the tiara and trousers and barbarian shoes and put on the clothing that is usual with us, and shave themselves close and converse in our own tongue, but still conceal war under their outer garb; just apply the tests and you bring to light what is hidden.

Bonsdorff seems to have taken the second sentence literally.[113] Chrysostomus Baur justly objected that Chrysostom "spoke of the expulsion of moral enemies (vices), which dwell side by side with the citizens (virtues) in the city of the soul."[114] No careful reader could doubt that Chrysostom's language is indeed metaphorical. But why did he choose these metaphors? The idea of a battle between virtues and vices for man's soul is a commonplace, but there seems to be no other example of the virtues and vices being represented as citizens and aliens. On the other hand there is a striking parallel here with a passage from the antibarbarian tirade in *De regno*: "Many parts of the empire are aflame, as though it were a human body in which alien elements are incapable of mingling in a healthy state of harmony. Then in the case of cities as in that of the body, we must remove the alien elements" (22B–C). Synesius speaks of the body and Chrysostom of the soul, but both compare barbarians in the state to alien elements in man.

The xenelasia Chrysostom recommends was hardly the traditional way of dealing with racial conflicts in Greco-Roman society. A number of classical texts explicitly repudiate it as a harsh Spartan practice, altogether out of keeping with Athenian ways.[115] Yet this is just what Syne-

112. λογισμός; for the sense "evil thoughts or desires" see Lampe, s.v. 2c.; A. J. Festugière, *Les moines d'Orient*, vol. 4.1 (Paris 1964), 23 n. 337.

113. "Es gibt der Fremdlinge und der Bürger in der Stadt viele, sagt Chrysostom, und er ermahnt seine Zuhörer, den Frieden wieder herzustellen und die Vertreibung der Fremdlinge zu veranstalten, damit die eigene Landsleute nicht verdorben werden" (Bonsdorff 1922, 94).

114. *Chrysostom*, vol. 2 (1960), 96 n. 31.

115. H. Volkmann, *Kleine Pauly* 5 (1975): 1406.

sius urges in *De regno* (21, 26A; 24C–D, "purge the army"; cf. *De providentia* 108D). Did Chrysostom share these extremist views? Could he, like Synesius, have uttered these words *before* the violent expulsion of the Goths in July 400? Surely not.

For Chrysostom had till then pursued an entirely different policy concerning the Gothic presence in Constantinople, one aiming at assimilation rather than expulsion.[116] It is best described in the words of Theodoret:

> Appointing presbyters and deacons and readers of the holy scriptures who spoke the Scythian tongue, he assigned a church to them and with their help won many from their error [i.e., Arianism]. He used frequently to go there and preach himself, using an interpreter who was skilled in both languages, and he got other good speakers to do the same. This was his constant practice in the city.[117]

One of the sermons he preached in this Gothic church survives (*PG* 63.499–510): were not Abraham and Moses barbarians? he asked them; who were the baby Jesus' first visitors but barbarians? He also sent missionaries to Goths still living on the Danube. Theodoret quotes a letter from Chrysostom to Leontius, bishop of Ancyra, asking him to recommend suitably qualified men (*HE* 5.31). It is true that he opposed allowing the Goths an Arian church inside the city, but that was a religious, not a racial, question. His goal was to draw the Goths away from Arianism into the true faith. Nor did he stand alone in the attempt: there survive eight letters from the ascetic writer Nilus of Ancyra purporting to be addressed to Gaïnas himself, attacking Arianism and urging him to convert.[118] It is hard to believe that Chrysostom would have uttered such words even in metaphor before July 400. After then, of course, it was a different matter. Not only would such liberal views have been unpopular in the immediate aftermath of Gaïnas's defeat; the mere fact of his coup may have disillusioned many who had till then favored a policy of assimilation.

Granted that Chrysostom was speaking at some time in late 400 or early 401, the fate of the Goths of Constantinople is bound to have been on his mind. Despite the fact that the only aliens he names are Persians

---

116. It was thus an oversimplification when A. Momigliano claimed that "St. John Chrysostom supported the anti-German party in Constantinople" (*Conflict between Paganism and Christianity in the Fourth Century* [Oxford 1963], 14); so too S. Mazzarino, *End of the Ancient World* (London 1966), 63.

117. *HE* 5.30.

118. *Ep.* 1.70, 79, 114–16, 205–6, 286 in *PG* 79.

and (later) Jews,[119] the allusion to "sheep's clothing" was hardly less transparent. There is a close, though more explicit, parallel in the homily on the exile of Saturninus and Aurelian, delivered some time in the early summer of 400, apparently before the massacre.[120] Chrysostom is here talking about the "civil" war of 400, a war that is concealed, not open: "On every side there are a thousand disguises. There are many sheep's skins and countless wolves everywhere concealed in them" (*PG* 52.415). He goes on to denounce those who "flattered and kissed your hand yesterday, but now reveal themselves openly as enemies and cast off their disguises." While these allusions might seem to suggest nothing more than the ill-fated wolf who so disguised himself in the fable,[121] the Goths were notorious for dressing in skins, a fashion that caught on in the capital and was widely denounced by conservatives. In *De regno* 22A the Goths in Constantinople are compared to wolves among dogs, the guardian dogs of Plato's Republic.[122] In *De regno* 23C Synesius waxed indignant at the shame of

> a man in skins leading warriors who wear the chlamys, exchanging his sheepskins for the toga to debate with Roman magistrates and perhaps even sit next to a consul, while law-abiding men sit behind. Then these same men, once they have gone a little way from the senate house, put on their sheepskins again, and when they have rejoined their fellows they mock the toga, saying that they cannot comfortably draw their swords in it.

Here we have the same idea of barbarians hypocritically and temporarily exchanging their skins for Roman dress. The word σκυθίζουσιν, "behave in Scythian fashion," in *De providentia* 118B may also refer to clothing. In the West at least, laws were passed forbidding the wearing of trousers and skins.[123] To discredit him, Claudian alleged that the prefect Rufinus wore skins.[124] The word *pellitus* became the standing epithet in Latin poets of the age for Goth.[125]

"Foreign doctrine" in *Hom.* 37 was no less clear an allusion to the ancestral Arianism of the Goths. Synesius, too, refers to "Scythianizing"

119. It will be remembered that there was a short-lived threat of war with Persia in mid-399: Demougeot 1951, 225.
120. See below, p. 174.
121. B. Perry, *Aesopica* (Urbana, Ill. 1952), 500, no. 451.
122. Pl. *Rep.* 375Ef.
123. *Cod.Theod.* 14.10.2 (399?; cf. Seeck 1919, 77); 3 (399); 4 (416).
124. *In Ruf.* 2.79f.
125. Claud. *IV Cons. Hon.* 466, *Bell. Get.* 481; Rut. Namat. *Red.* 2.49.

in religion (*De providentia* 121B). There can be no question that this passage was written when the memory of the Gothic massacre was still
fresh in the minds of all, no earlier than the autumn of 400.

How frequently did Chrysostom preach? During Lent and the festival days of Easter, often every day: for example, *Hom.* 5, 7, 12, 13, and
14 *De statuis* open with the word "yesterday." [126] In *Hom.* 32 on Acts (*PG*
60.238) there is one "yesterday" referring to *Hom.* 31, but other evidence
suggests a more relaxed tempo for this series, which as we have seen
was not preached during Lent or Easter. In the passage already cited
from *Hom.* 44, he says that he has been preaching "not every day and
night, but often every third or seventh day": either once or twice a week.
A passage in *Hom.* 29 (*PG* 60.217) refers to "so many prophets twice in
every week discoursing to you, so many apostles and evangelists." This
implies that twice a week was the norm. If so, it must have taken at least
six and perhaps as many as eight or nine months to deliver all fifty-five
homilies. If he began later in the year than Easter/Pentecost 400 and had
reached winter by *Hom.* 29, he could not have finished before 401. And
we have already seen that there are grounds for placing *Hom.* 44, at any
rate, later than 26 February 401.

There is no way of guessing when Chrysostom began, but he cannot
have preached continuously through the summer of 400. Already in
April or May he was persuaded to postpone a trip to Asia Minor because
of the "expectation of trouble," and our informant goes on to explain
that "it was the barbarian Gaïnas who was the expected trouble." [127] Before long, Chrysostom became very involved in the political crisis. In his
homily on the exile of Saturninus and Aurelian he begins by apologizing
for not addressing his flock for so long. [128] Theodoret describes how he
went to Thrace on an embassy to Gaïnas (*HE* 5.33), and in his lost *Life of
Chrysostom*, summarized by Photius (cod. 273, p. 507b Bekker), he evidently gave more details about these negotiations. The trip to Thrace fell
after the massacre (12 July), when Gaïnas retreated from Constantinople
to Thrace in late July or August.

The homilies on Acts could have been delivered in unbroken sequence starting in the late summer or early autumn of 400. That scarcely

126. For other examples, see J. Bingham, *Antiquities of the Christian Church*, bk. 14,
chap. 4; Baur 1959, 1:222.
127. Palladius, *Dialogus de vita S. Iohannis Chrysostomi* 49, ed. P. R. Coleman-Norton
(Cambridge 1928), 87.2; cf. Albert 1980, 506–8.
128. *PG* 52.413f.

leaves long enough for all fifty-five before the end of 400. We can either divide them between 400 and 401 with Bonsdorff or put them all in 401. For our present purposes, all that matters is that a substantial number of the homilies must in any case be assigned to 401. If so, then the earthquake referred to in *Hom.* 41 as having taken place "last year" must have fallen in 400.

It is one of the curiosities of scholarship that, having so ably countered Seeck's attempt to transfer the homilies on Acts to Antioch in the 370s, Bonsdorff accepted Seeck's transference of Synesius's departure to 402. He therefore knew of no evidence for an earthquake in 400 and weakly concluded that Chrysostom, who was very vague ("ungenau") about chronology, was referring to a supposed earthquake of 398.

Yet would even the vaguest of writers say "last year" when he meant "three years ago," especially when it was only three years since he had arrived in Constantinople himself? It is only three homilies later in the series (*Hom.* 44) that Chrysostom stressed those three years he had now spent in Constantinople.

More important, there was no quake in 398. A careful analysis of the sources has shown that all of them refer to 396—before Synesius even arrived in Constantinople.[129] In the light of the true chronology of Chrysostom's homilies, his reference to "last year" and the fact that Synesius's letter refers to Aurelian as consul, we can no longer doubt that both writers are describing one and the same earthquake, in 400.[130] It should be noted that Synesius's "repeatedly during the day" clearly implies a one-day quake, whereas the earthquake of 396 continued for a week.[131] Chrysostom is less precise, but his remark that three days later his quake was forgotten hardly suggests a series lasting seven days.

There may well have been another earthquake in 402. But in the absence of other documentation, can we have any confidence that Marcellinus did not simply misdate the quake of 400? Alternatively, Theodoret records a providential quake that is said to have changed the empress Eudoxia's mind about the first banishment of Chrysostom in

129. Cameron 1987, 340–44.

130. As taken for granted by scholars before Seeck: e.g., Clausen 1831, 16 n. 2; Montfaucon's preface to Chrysostom reprinted in *PG* 60.9–10. Oddly enough Sievers (1870, 378) also argued for a visit lasting from 397/8 to the autumn of 400, though without discussing the earthquake at all.

131. Marcellinus, s.a. 396 = *Chron.Min.* II.64 ("per dies plurimos"); Glycas, p.478.20 Bonn = *PG* 158.484C (seven days).

September 403.[132] If this quake happened at all,[133] it happened in 403. No one can exclude the possibility that there were quakes at Constantinople in 400, 402, and 403,[134] but we should at least consider the possibility that Marcellinus's quake is in fact the same as Theodoret's, in which case it would have to be transferred to 403.[135] If so, that would remove any possibility of linking it to Synesius's departure, since he cannot possibly still have been in Constantinople as late as September 403. In all probability only one earthquake took place during Synesius's three years at Constantinople, in the autumn of 400. This fits perfectly with our earlier calculation that he must have arrived with the crown gold in the autumn of 397.

Since Synesius returned home by sea, he is not likely to have found a passenger boat ready to leave after the end of the sailing season, 10 November at the latest.[136] His three-year embassy will have kept him in Constantinople from some time in the autumn of 397 to late autumn of 400.

132. *HE* 5.34; Theodoret's quake is repeated with further embellishments in two worthless later *Lives* of Chrysostom: see Baur 1960, 2:271 n. 11.

133. The better-informed Palladius (p. 51.17 Coleman-Norton) says that there was a "calamity in the bedchamber," which has usually been taken to imply a miscarriage. Of course an earthquake might bring on a miscarriage; the emperor Leo VI describes an earthquake *in* the imperial bedchamber (Baur 1960, 2:271 n. 11.)!

134. *Ep.* 2.265 of Nilus of Ancyra (*PG* 79.265) purports to reply to a letter of Arcadius asking why the city is being so troubled with earthquakes. Nilus replies that it is a judgment for exiling Chrysostom, which implies that he is writing after the quake of 407 (cf. Cameron 1976b, 187). However they are counted, there were a lot of earthquakes during the reign of Arcadius.

135. Marcellinus is in general one of the more reliable chroniclers, but he does misdate the earthquake of 478 to 480: Stein 1949, 787, with B. Croke, *Byzantion* 51 (1981): 131. Nearer in time he misdates the destruction of the Serapeum (391; see p. 53 n. 191) to 389.

136. See Cameron 1987, 344f.; J. Rougé, "La navigation hivernale sous l'empire romain," *REA* 54 (1952): 316–25.

FOUR

DE REGNO

I. SUMMARY

In form, the *De regno* is an address to the emperor Arcadius about the virtues and duties of the ideal king. Much of the speech is concerned with topics far beyond the scope of this book. Lacombrade's annotated translation usefully illustrates some aspects of the speech,[1] though there is still room for a study that will set it firmly in the long history of Greco-Roman kingship literature. Our purpose is more limited: first, to discover when and in what circumstances the speech was composed and delivered; second, to investigate the nature and reference of its famous tirade against barbarians in Roman service; and third, to consider its immediate purpose and approach. But so that readers may be able to form some idea of the contents, character, and, above all, the tone of the speech as a whole, we begin with a full summary.

1 Though I come on embassy, I will not flatter or speak merely pleasing rhetoric. Rather I will exhort the emperor as a philoso-
2 pher. My speech will be virile; it may sound harsh, but it is intended to do good.
   I bring crown gold from Cyrene. My city's ancient glory has
3 fallen and it requires the king's hand to raise it again. The prosperity of his realm, the number of citizens he benefits, directly reflects

1. Lacombrade 1951b; see too A. Garzya's translation of 1989.

the virtue of the ruler's soul. Therefore this instruction will benefit the whole empire. Do not balk at reproof, but accept correction.

4   The resources of empire are boundless good fortune; but this exterior gift can only be maintained by inner virtue. Virtue may even excite Fortune's reward, as it did for your father. You have in-
5   herited what he labored to win. Now you must labor to preserve it, with God's help. The good king is always diligent. He bears all his
6   subjects' dangers for them. Only a tyrant expects his subjects to
7   support his luxury. Both king and tyrant have power, but prudence is required to use power well; prudence is the most kingly virtue. It is realized in action, just as an evil and ignorant nature will do less
8   harm if it has fewer resources. You who have so much must use it well. Thus the king imitates God. The universally recognized es-
9   sence of God is His beneficence; follow this model and you will de- serve praise.

     Wisdom accumulated from antiquity to today establishes this ideal image of the king: first, his piety is the foundation of every-
10   thing. Next, with God's direction, he must rule himself. Even a commoner who governs the baser elements of his soul is king over himself, and godly; but a king is especially godly, for his virtue will affect whole nations. The calm he achieves in himself will encour- age his friends, the good, and defeat his wicked enemies with ter-
11   ror. Only he who controls his separate impulses can be constant and at one with himself.

     The good king benefits his friends and benefits from their ad-
12   vice and information, for only God is truly self-sufficient. The ty- rant's treachery toward his friends, conversely, isolates him. Flat- tery must not be allowed to beguile. True love of his friends is a king's virtue and strength.

     The second rank of the king's friends are his soldiers. He should make himself truly their comrade-in-arms by sharing all their labors. Such open exercise is not really toilsome; moreover, all
13   eyes will turn upon him and the goodwill he wins will fortify him. As Plato observed, the military is like a dog, who fights loyally for the master he knows. Addressing soldiers of all ranks by name es- pecially inspires them. Homer voices this excellent advice through
14   Agamemnon. Finally, war is the king's craft and his soldiers his tools. He must know them to use them well.

     The barbarian pomp that has grown up about the Roman em- peror is the greatest impediment to this useful knowledge. Your

15 isolation reduces you to a life of sensuous fatuity. Your favorites are petty clowns who injure you by befogging your mind. You reject serious thought. But consider the many examples of history: it is the austere warrior peoples who conquer and maintain dominion.

16 The Roman emperor should uphold the noblest Roman traditions: not the obscene luxury that fetters you, but the simple manliness

17 that won the empire. Proper aggression once held off the barbarians. Now they terrorize you.

A story from the not very distant past will instruct and inspire

18 you. The emperor Carinus,[2] on campaign against the Parthians, did nothing to impress their embassy but stayed sitting on the ground, eating pea soup. He punched his threat against their king with a joke about his own baldness, invited the ambassadors to join him at chow, and cut short the audience. The ambassador's report

19 of this remarkable behavior so terrified the enemy that their king surrendered on the spot. And he was not the last good emperor.

From hatred of tyranny, Romans have avoided the title of "king" since they expelled the Tarquins; instead you call yourself

20 emperor, which means a military leader with absolute power. Such an attitude vindicates kingship. A tyrant on the other hand avoids the public eye to protect his majesty. This ridiculous attitude is contradicted by history, whose great kings were not ashamed of their

21 frugality. Moderation and wisdom bring all things into order. True kingship abhors arrogance and extravagance.

Return us to kingship that serves its people, for we face great

22 danger. God will aid the good. Again, the king is properly understood to be a military leader who associates freely with his soldiery. Naturally, his own people best provide this soldiery. Arming peoples who have been raised under different laws, of whose loyalty you lack that guarantee, is like mixing in wolves with your sheep dogs. By such very wolves are we now threatened, as anyone can see: outbreaks have already begun. Our present course is suicidal. The Scythians must be excluded; all Romans must be

23 pressed into service. The military must be kin with them it defends, or it will prey upon them.

The first step will be to ban these skin-wearing foreigners from

24 the Roman civic honors they insult. It is absurd to let the same race

2. The wrong emperor for the story. Probably Carus (so Gibbon 1909, chap. 12 n. 79), though Probus too has been suggested (by Petau and Tillemont: discussion in Krabinger 1825, 261–62).

govern us as provides our meanest slaves. As they did under Spartacus and Crixus, the slaves will rise up to murder their masters. We now face an even greater threat, whole armies we have supinely allowed to penetrate us. The foreign infection must be purged
25 from the army, before it spreads. The Scythians are an effeminate race the Romans conquered of old; they have come to us as suppliants driven from their own land. Theodosius raised them up, but now they repay his compassion with insolence. Hordes of for-
26 eigners extort subsidies from us on their example. We must recover our military strength and drive them forth. The task will not be too hard for soldier-citizens led and inspired by their own king; and the king is first a warrior.

His warlike strength will protect his peace. After attending to
27 his soldiers, the king should turn to the rest of his realm. Again, personal knowledge serves him best, supplemented by embassies. They give him godlike omniscience, so that his beneficence can answer all his people's needs. The soldiers must be reminded that they fight to protect the civilians; their billeting should not oppress them.

The good king will not exhaust his cities with taxes. He does not need to wage war constantly, for as I have shown he cannot be
28 overcome. He is not luxurious. He uses prudently what he has, and can even forgive shortfalls. Greed in a king is even more despicable than it is in a merchant; though there too it subjects the ruling intelligence to base appetites, and the good king should help his citizens to drive it forth from themselves by his virtuous example.
29 Virtue should be honored above all things. The king should lead his people to it. He does so especially in public worship of God, Who is his own and their King. So he shows them due honor to his own model, and God Himself must rejoice in it.

Like God, the king should be tireless in beneficence toward his people. He should make his closest associates echo him in kingly
30 adornment of soul. Governors extend his reach, just as Nature extends God's benevolence to all; the king too must choose just administrators. Virtue, not wealth, should be his criterion. By his judgment will all be influenced.
31   Finally, I pray that you may embrace Philosophy, for she dwells with God and will guide you in kingship. Bring to life my image of
32 the ideal king, and I will rejoice whenever I have to speak on behalf of cities.

II. THE DATE OF THE SPEECH

The fact that it was from 397 to 400, rather than from 399 to 402, that Synesius was in Constantinople has major consequences for the interpretation of *De regno*—and indeed of the politics of the Eastern court as a whole. The year 399, to which the speech has hitherto generally been assigned, saw the revolt of Tribigild and the fall of Eutropius. With few exceptions,[3] it has always been taken for granted that *De regno* was not delivered till after Eutropius's fall. If Synesius did not arrive till 399, it was a reasonable assumption that it was the end of the year before he delivered a speech that already betrays his frustration with Arcadius's court. And if that speech embodied what Bury called "the anti-German manifesto of the party of Aurelian,"[4] how could it be otherwise? But now we know that Synesius arrived two years earlier, it is by no means self-evident that he would wait till this late date.

One passage in particular proves that he did not—15A–B, addressed to Arcadius:

> Those you associate with at table and elsewhere, those who have easier access to the palace than generals and captains, those you treat as your favorites, men with small heads and petty minds . . . people able to laugh and cry incessantly at the same time, playing the buffoon with gestures, noises, and all means possible, these are the folk who help you to waste your time, to dissipate with an even greater evil the fogginess of mind you have from not living in accordance with nature. The half-witted thoughts and words of these men suit your ears better than a philosophical concept clearly and tersely expressed. And the result of this astonishing seclusion is this: you despise and disdain sensible people, while admitting the senseless *and stripping in front of them*.[5]

Most of this diatribe against the emperor's unworthy favorites consists of fairly commonplace abuse. But the allegation that he strips in front of senseless people is both extraordinary and precise. What courtiers might watch the emperor undress, and why, when, and where would he do such a thing? There is, as Barnes acutely observed,[6] only one imperial favorite who might without impropriety be present when his mas-

3. Sievers 1870, 384 ("gewiß bevor Eutropius gestürzt war"); Bury (1923) 1958, 129 (before Eutropius's fall but after the outbreak of Tribigild's revolt).

4. Bury (1923) 1958, 129. So too Grützmacher 1913, 38; Stein 1959, 235; Coster 1968, 165 at p. 167 calling Synesius "the mouthpiece of Aurelian."

5. πρὸς ἐκείνους ἀπογυμνούμενοι, evasively translated "vous vous montrez à elle [sc. la sottise] à visage découvert" by Lacombrade (1951b, 52).

6. Barnes 1986a, 108.

ter removed his clothes: the grand chamberlain. The chamberlain often acquired wide-ranging power, but as his title indicates, his proper function was to be *praepositus sacri cubiculi*, in charge of the sacred bedchamber. A poem by Theaetetus Scholasticus on a statue or painting of Justinian's chamberlain Callinicus describes how he

> ever lulls the emperor to sleep in his bedchamber,
> sowing all gentleness in his ears.
>
> *(Anth. Plan.* 33.3–4)

Callinicus was a powerful man who played a key role in the succession to Justinian,[7] but even he might be represented in art performing his original humble role in the imperial bedchamber. The difference between the two passages is of course that Theaetetus writes in praise and Synesius in disgust. There can be no question about the object of this disgust, the unworthy chamberlain who is Arcadius's confidant: Eutropius.

It can be added more generally that the principal subject of this section, the seclusion of the emperor, is a motif often associated with the excessive power wielded by eunuchs, who received most of the blame for keeping the emperor shut up in his court, ignorant of what was happening outside.[8] Sensing this suggestion of "eunuch-rule" in the passage but never doubting that it was written after the fall of Eutropius,[9] Albert makes the unhappy and paradoxical suggestion that Synesius is warning Arcadius against certain supporters of Eutropius who were still either in office or powerful at court. In particular, he claims that Hosius the *magister officiorum* is meant. The alleged allusion to Hosius is entirely unconvincing,[10] and if Hosius was a lowborn creature of Eutropius, as Claudian alleges, he probably fell with his patron. So at least Claudian believed:

> dissimulant socii coniuratique recedunt;
> procumbit pariter cum duce tota cohors.
>
> *(In Eutr.* 2pr.15–16)

> His associates deny him, his accomplices abandon him;
> the whole band perishes together with their leader.

7. Averil Cameron 1976, 132.

8. It is eunuchs "qui soli principes perdunt . . . claudentes principem suum et agentes ante omnia ne quid sciat" (*HA Alex. Sev.* 66.3); it is because of eunuchs and courtiers that "imperator, qui domi clausus est, vera non novit" (*HA Aurel.* 43.4). See K. F. Stroheker, "Princeps clausus," *Bonner Historia-Augusta-Colloquium 1968/69,* Antiquitas 4.7 (Bonn 1970), 273–83; Guyot 1980, 160; Albert 1984, 53.

9. Lacombrade too saw that "une critique voilée semble viser Eutrope" (1951b, 110).

10. See Albert 1984, 45: ἅπασι τοῖς ἐν ταῖς αὐλαῖς ὅπλοις (12A) in a different context could refer to the *scholae palatinae,* under the command of the *magister officiorum*—but here

Hosius is not recorded in office after 15 December 398, and although no new incumbent is attested before 404, it is likely that he was replaced at once by the future regent Anthemius.[11] In any case, the motifs of an attack on a eunuch do not fit an attack on a bureaucrat. Even supposing Hosius had survived Eutropius's fall and continued to exercise what was felt to be an unhealthy influence on Arcadius, it was no part of his office to keep him shut up in the palace.

Albert constantly recurs to this thesis that one of Aurelian's chief worries in the early days of his ascendancy was a comeback by Eutropius. But of all imperial favorites, it was the eunuch whose fall was most sudden and final. With no kin and no friends, he had no resources to stage a comeback. Eutropius's one hold on power had been his personal access to Arcadius; once deprived of that, where could he turn?[12] According to Zosimus, it was because of Gaïnas's vindictiveness that he was soon after recalled from exile and executed.[13] There seems no reason to substitute modern conjecture for ancient testimony here, especially since Zosimus's version is indirectly supported by Synesius.

III. THE ANTIBARBARIAN TIRADE

The most strikingly concrete part of the *De regno,* and the most important to the historian, is the long section (22A–26C) criticizing the dependence of the Roman state on "Scythians," by which are meant Goths. Unfortunately it has in the past been misinterpreted on every level. The Goths in question have been identified as those led by Tribigild in the rebellion of 399–400; Synesius's tirade against them has been supposed to reflect the policy of the new prefect Aurelian, the leader of the nationalist party, whose avowed aim is believed to have been to rid the Eastern empire of barbarians; many have thought that the entire passage was directed against Gaïnas.[14] All the assumptions embraced by

they are to be "used to keep flattery from slipping in wearing the mask of friendship," so the connection Albert draws makes no sense. The expression is merely a colorful version of "all the resources available," with perhaps the additional implication that the emperor ought to be especially well defended.

11. Though not attested as *magister officiorum* until January 404 (*PLRE* II.94), Anthemius clearly exercised considerable influence before winning the prefecture itself in June/July 405, since he was ordinary consul in January 405. To receive such an honor, he must have been holding high office for several years. That of *magister officiorum* is an obvious vacancy; no other name is attested after Hosius in December 398.

12. K. Hopkins, *Conquerors and Slaves* (1978), 189f.

13. See too Eunap. frag. 75.6 Mueller = 67.10 Blockley.

14. E.g., Albert 1984, 54–63.

these contentions are false. Gaïnas could only have been a target, for example, if Synesius had been writing as late as the fall of Eutropius, at the end of July 399. But the *De regno* cannot be that late; in fact it cannot be later than the first half of 398. Not only does the passage make perfectly satisfactory sense in terms of the new date, but its details strongly support an earlier date in their own terms.

In the first place, a number of passages make it clear that Synesius was warning of a disaster that at the time of writing was yet to come. It is a "rock of Tantalus suspended over the state by fragile cords" (22B). The Scythians "*will* fall upon us the first moment they think the attempt will succeed" (22B). The shepherd must not mix wolves with his dogs, "for the moment they notice any weakness or slackness in the dogs, they *will* attack them, flock, shepherd, and all" (22A). The oblique comment that "only a fool or a prophet" would not be apprehensive of the Gothic danger (22B) means either someone too obtuse to appreciate these threats or someone who has foreknowledge that they will come to nothing. Then there is 24D: "You must remove the foreign body causing the disease *before* the abscess festering beneath the surface erupts, *before* the hostility of these dwellers in our land is exposed. For evils may be overcome *when they are just beginning* (ἀρχόμενα), but as they progress they gain the upper hand." Most striking of all: "Consider too that in addition to their existing forces, they may, *whenever they wish*, have our slaves as soldiers" (24C).

That makes eight separate warnings looking to barbarian trouble *in the future*. Goths in Roman territory are an abscess festering beneath the skin; their hostility is not yet exposed; they will attack when they see a weakness, when they think they will succeed. One of two conclusions must follow. Either Synesius really was writing before there was any serious barbarian trouble or he was writing afterwards and pretending to have foreseen the trouble. That would make the entire speech a dramatic fiction and the antibarbarian section a *post eventum* prophecy. To be sure, Synesius did employ this technique in book 1 of *De providentia*, where a god lists as the signs that will presage the expulsion of the barbarians portents that had already happened at the time of writing in the middle of A.D. 400. The beauty of *post eventum* prophecy is precisely the advantage of detail that hindsight affords. Specificity reinforces the thesis. Moreover, *De providentia* is set in the distant past, purporting to prove that history repeats itself. But there could be little point in pretending that Synesius had delivered *De regno* a mere twelve months earlier, especially since any contemporary would see through the pretence. Synesius's antibarbarian invective is in any case so general that he could not have claimed to foresee anything so precise as Tribigild's revolt and Gaïnas's disloyalty. Indeed, if anything, his warnings suggest a revolt by Alaric that never happened. This very inconclusiveness argues against the hypothesis of retrospective exploitation of knowledge of 400.

Synesius wrote at a time when he felt that his contemporaries were underestimating the dangers of current policies simply because no serious consequences had yet been identified. He could not possibly have taken this tone or stance as late as the autumn of 399, when Tribigild's rebellion was six months old and Gaïnas's collusion plain to all. As for the prophecy that slaves would join any barbarian rebellion (24C), though hindsight reminds us that slaves did join Tribigild's rebellion in Phrygia,[15] Synesius does not describe anything so distant. He is in fact concerned with the danger literally at his own doorstep. As he had said only a page earlier, "every house, however humble, has a Scythian slave. The butler, the cook, the water-carrier, all are Scythians, and the servants who carry through the streets on their shoulders the litters on which their masters sit, these are all Scythians" (23D). Synesius even had a Scythian slave of his own.[16] His fear was that even though the expected Gothic rebellion might take place in the provinces, the slaves of Constantinople would rise up and join. This did *not* happen in 400.

After the reference to the rock of Tantalus, Synesius adds: "The first skirmishes are already taking place, and many parts of the empire are aflame." There has long been general agreement that he refers here to the outbreak of Tribigild's revolt. But ἀκροβολισμοί implies minor hostilities—that Synesius claims nonetheless augur worse to come. What could possibly have been worse than a major rebellion that was devastating three provinces, with slaves and malcontents joining on all sides, one Roman army defeated with its general killed and the other colluding with the enemy? All that remained, as by late 399 many no doubt already feared, was for Gaïnas and Tribigild to march on Constantinople itself. And Alaric could easily have joined in from Illyricum. Hardly "skirmishes." It would have been fatuous to warn against Gothic unreliability in such portentous terms after Gaïnas and Tribigild together had brought Eutropius down. In so doing they had shouted aloud the threat Synesius could only deduce from hints and generalities. Then everyone's worst fears were confirmed. On the traditional date and interpretation, Synesius would be guilty of one of the most spectacular

15. Zos. 5.13.4; cf. Claud. *In Eutr.* 2.222, "bella dabunt socios." Claudian uses the future tense because he is describing in retrospect advice given to Tribigild before the revolt.

16. *Calv. Enc.* 77B.

cases in history of warning about the stable door after the horse has bolted.

In the second place, as Peter Heather has recently shown in an important paper,[17] Synesius's detailed account of the history of the Goths (25A–D) fits Alaric in Illyricum, not Tribigild in Phrygia. For Synesius, the Goths are a people "always fleeing their own country," driven out by one invader after another. Finally they came as suppliants to the Romans (the treaty of 376), but then became insolent (the battle of Adrianople in 378), and paid the penalty to Theodosius (various engagements between 379 and 381). Theodosius then took pity on them, gave them offices (i.e., Roman commands) and even Roman land (the treaty of 382). Unfortunately, "the barbarian does not know the meaning of goodness: from then right up to the present moment," Synesius remarks, "they have treated us with derision."

This is a fairly accurate summary of the history of the Tervingi, the main body of Visigothic immigrants, from 376 to the 390s.[18] Those who were given Roman commands included Modares, Munderic, Fravitta, Gaïnas, and probably Tribigild.[19] Most conspicuous among those who remained with the federates in the lands granted by the treaty of 382 and who according to Synesius "treated us with derision" was the young chieftain Alaric. Alaric led a rebellion in 391, and though he served under Theodosius in the campaign against Eugenius in 394, he rebelled again almost immediately. In 395 he briefly laid siege to Constantinople and left only after receiving from Rufinus some sort of promise of high command. It was never fulfilled. From 395 to 397 Alaric devastated the Balkans continuously until Eutropius finally saved the situation by appointing him *magister militum per Illyricum*.[20]

Alaric's repeated treachery over many years matches Synesius's description perfectly. But it does not at all match the Greuthungi led to rebellion by Tribigild in 399.[21] The Greuthungi crossed the Danube in 386 under their chief Odothaeus, not as suppliants but as invaders.[22] They

17. Heather 1988, 152–72.

18. The fullest recent narrative account is E. Demougeot, *La formation de l'Europe et les invasions barbares*, vol. 2.1 (Paris 1979), 134–69.

19. Roman commands—that is to say, regular commands in the Roman army as opposed to irregular service as federates, like Alaric. See E. A. Thompson, *Romans and Barbarians* (1982), 41–42.

20. Demandt 1970, 730.

21. As Albert seems to be uncomfortably aware. He acknowledges that Synesius's account fits "vor allem der terwingischen Goten," but argues that "in diese kompromittierende Nachbarschaft wird also Gaïnas gesetzt, ungeachtet der Differenzen, die ihn und seine Gefolgsleute von Alarich und seinem Volk trennten, und ohne auf den völlig unterschiedlichen Lebensweg des Gaïnas einzugehen" (1984, 59).

22. For the sources, Seeck 1913, 208 and 519; Paschoud 1979, 426–29.

were defeated by Theodosius's general Promotus and settled en bloc in Phrygia.[23] Once there they are not known to have caused any trouble till 399.

These Greuthungi, being in effect prisoners of war, and so understandably called *captivi* by Claudian (*In Eutr.* 2.582), will not have been given the favorable terms accorded to the Tervingi. Compare here another passage of *De regno:* "Only a foolhardy man or a prophet would look without fear on this mass of differently bred youth living according to their customs and practicing the art of war in this country" (22A). In the preceding sentence Synesius had warned against giving arms to those "not born and brought up under Roman law." Once again, the remark suits the Tervingi in Illyricum,[24] not the Greuthungi in Phrygia; for the Tervingi were indeed allowed to live in Roman territory under their own customs and laws. Although they were liable to military service if the emperor should call on them, they served in their own units under their own tribal commanders.[25] The old tribal organization and loyalties therefore remained intact. It was not Synesius alone who found this the most disturbing aspect of the Gothic settlement in the Balkans.[26]

But Odothaeus's Greuthungi will have been treated like other *dediticii*,[27] segregated into a number of small units settled in different places precisely so as to break up old tribal organization and loyalties as far as possible. They were then known (in Gaul at least) as *laeti* and were expected to furnish recruits.[28] That is to say, they would normally serve in regular army units under Roman discipline and officers. Whereas the optimates at any rate among the Tervingi were presumably given land in freehold, the Greuthungi will have become *coloni,* tenants who at this date were little more than serfs.[29] Claudian draws precisely this distinction between them:

> concessoque cupit vixisse *colonus*
> quam *dominus* rapto.
>
> (*In Eutr.* 2.205–6)

23. Zos. 4.35, 4.38, 5.13; Claud. *In Eutr.* 2.174f.; Seeck 1913, 306–7; so already Güldenpenning 1885, 100.

24. So, for example, Jones 1964a, 157 n. 46.

25. On the terms of the treaty of 382 see Lippold 1980, 31–32, with Demougeot 1974, 143–60.

26. Amm. Marc. 31.16.8; cf. Straub 1943, 255f.; Pavan 1964, 41f.

27. The technical term for those who surrendered unconditionally to Rome and accepted whatever terms were imposed: A. Momigliano, *Ricerche sull'organizzazione della Giudea sotto il dominio romano* (1934), 2–5; Jones (1960) 1968, 130f.

28. *Laeti:* Jones 1964a, 620; Hoffmann 1969, 139 and passim (see the index in Hoffman 1970, 252); Liebeschuetz 1990, 12–13, 100–101. The name *laeti* is not found in the East.

29. G. E. M. de Ste. Croix, *The Class Struggle in the Ancient Greek World* (Ithaca, N.Y. 1981), 158–60, 247, 249–53.

> He is happy to live as a tenant on sufferance
> rather than a master on plunder.

According to Zosimus (5.13.2), Tribigild was the commander "of the barbarian, not the Roman troops in Phrygia." This has often been taken to imply that he was the leader of a band of federates, and it may well be what Zosimus himself thought. For example, at 5.16.1 he says Tribigild marched into Pamphylia "with his barbarians." But he also repeatedly refers to Gaïnas and "his barbarians." Zosimus may have believed that both, like Alaric, led barbarian hordes. But he was certainly wrong about Gaïnas, who led a regular field army, whatever its ethnic composition.

According to Philostorgius, Tribigild had the rank of *comes,* and his troops were stationed at Nacoleia.[30] F. Paschoud doubted whether "this Gothic federate" really held a Roman rank,[31] but Socrates and Sozomen claim that Tribigild was a kinsman of Gaïnas.[32] There seems no obvious reason why this detail should have been invented: the probability is that Tribigild was not a Greuthung at all,[33] but a Tervingian who had enlisted in the Roman army with Gaïnas and Fravitta long ago under Theodosius.[34] Indeed this would explain why he was so disgruntled and why he made common cause with Gaïnas. Both were men who after twenty years' loyal service had gradually risen through the ranks to the modest rank of *comes.* Alaric won himself a mastership of the soldiers at one stroke simply by burning and looting.

One possibility is that Tribigild was a regular officer in command of barbarian federates. This is the post Gaïnas had held on Theodosius's western expedition of 394, likewise with the rank of *comes.*[35] But federates were only enlisted for the duration of specific campaigns and then dismissed.[36] According to Socrates, Tribigild was "tribune of the troops

30. *HE* 11.8, p. 138.17 Bidez-Winkelmann.
31. Paschoud 1986, 126.
32. Socr. *HE* 6.6; Soz. *HE* 8.4.2.
33. As often assumed, and explicitly stated in *PLRE* II.1125.
34. If Tribigild was related to Gaïnas by marriage, the possibility that he was a Greuthung would be left open. But it is unlikely that an ambitious man would have contracted so disadvantageous a match—or one outside his tribe.
35. Zos. 4.57.2, 4.58.2; cf. Demandt 1970, 733.
36. Indeed this is doubtless the cause of much of what our sources dismiss as barbarian treachery. When federates were dismissed their subsidies were discontinued. Of course, the Romans had always used barbarian federates this way, paying them *ad hoc.* When such federates returned to their usual way of life beyond the frontiers, that caused no problems. The problems started when discarded federates were forced to turn to a life of plunder within the frontiers. The Germans who served Rome so loyally during most of the fourth century were trained to follow experienced officers and received pay, equipment, and bonuses until they retired with a pension. Before we condemn Gothic federates too readily for their treachery, we should take into account the fact that they enjoyed none of these advantages.

stationed in Phrygia."[37] "Tribune" was the normal title for commanders of regular units,[38] and the phrase as a whole implies that both Tribigild and his unit were regular army. Tribunes were often given the rank of *comes*.[39] An unusually precise passage of Claudian corroborates this inference:

> legio pridem Romana Gruthungi,
> iura quibus victis dedimus, quibus arva domusque praebuimus.
>
> > (*In Eutr.* 2.576–78)
>
> The Greuthungi were once a Roman legion;
> we conquered them and gave them laws, we let them have fields and homes.

If the Greuthungi were a Roman legion that obeyed Roman laws before their rebellion, they cannot have been federates.[40] It was common for even elite units to be recruited from *laeti* and barbarians.[41] A regular military base for elite Roman units in the neighborhood of Nacoleia happens to be well documented, from at any rate the mid-fourth century down to the reign of Justinian.[42] It was no doubt to supply recruits for these units that Theodosius had settled the defeated Greuthungi there in 386.

The fact that it was in 399 that they revolted suggests a connection with the expedition against the Huns the year before. We learn from Claudian that Eutropius's army consisted largely of Goths,[43] among them presumably the Greuthungi from Nacoleia, and perhaps a contingent of Alaric's Tervingi as well. According to Zosimus (5.15.3), Tribigild had only just arrived from Constantinople when the revolt began, which accords well enough with Claudian's account of his return from

37. Τριβιγίλδου . . . χιλιαρχοῦντος τῶν ἱδρυμένων ἐν τῇ Φρυγίᾳ στρατιωτῶν, HE 6.6. χιλίαρχος is standard classicizing Greek for a military tribune: H. J. Mason, *Greek Terms for Roman Institutions* (Toronto 1974), 99–100.

38. Jones 1964a, 372, with note 16.

39. Jones 1964a, 372.

40. *In Eutr.* 2.176 describes Tribigild more vaguely as "Geticae dux improbus alae." But even here *ala* may be used in its technical sense of a cavalry unit (G. Webster, *The Roman Imperial Army*, 3d ed. [1985], 145–48); Tribigild certainly had cavalry (Zos. 5.15.5, 5.16.3).

41. Jones 1964a, 621.

42. See particularly the epitaph of a *ducenarius* in the crack regiment of the *Cornuti seniores* from Nacoleia dated to 356, published with valuable commentary by Thomas Drew-Bear, *HSCP* 81 (1977): 257–74. A *senator* is attested at the nearby city of Dorylaion (Drew-Bear, *Glotta* 50 [1972]: 220), as also is the *schola gentilium iuniorum* (Drew-Bear and W. Eck, *Chiron* 6 [1976]: 305–7). See also Theophanes, p. 236.16f. In 562 Justinian transferred units of the *scholae* stationed in various bases in Asia Minor (including Dorylaion) to Thrace.

43. "adloquiturque Getas," *In Eutr.* 1.242; Seeck 1913, 564; Demougeot 1951, 224; Albert 1979, 630.

court *vacuus donis*, indignant at the haughty eunuch's insults.[44] He had evidently been trying to get better terms of some sort.

Though he shares the affectation common at the period of designating all Goths as "Scythians,"[45] it is difficult to believe that Synesius was unaware of the different origin, location, treatment, and behavior of Alaric's Goths and Tribigild's Goths. Claudian, though living in the West since 395, draws a sharp distinction between the two groups in book 2 of his *In Eutropium* (174–229), written at Milan late in 399. Bellona comes upon Tribigild trudging home with empty hands from the meeting with Eutropius. Taking on the form of his wife, she urges him to imitate the boldness of Alaric's Goths, who have conquered Greece: "The Greuthungians will make good farmers. . . . Happy those other women whose glory is seen in the towns their husbands have conquered . . . whose servants are fair captives of Argos or Thessaly." She reproaches him for timidly sticking to treaties while "the man who lately ravaged Achaea and devastated defenseless Epirus is master of Illyricum; he now enters as a friend within the walls that he once besieged, and administers justice to those whose wives he has raped and whose children he has murdered." Here there is an interesting parallel with Synesius. At *De regno* 23C he draws a vivid picture of a skin-clad warrior briefly changing into a toga and sitting in the senate, right at the front by the consul.[46] To have enjoyed the precedence (προεδρία) Synesius describes, this Goth must presumably have been a *magister militum*, who, like prefects and consuls, had the rank and precedence of *vir illustris*. The only candidates who come into the reckoning are Alaric, Gaïnas, and Fravitta. Fravitta was certainly MVM *per Orientem* by 399, but another man, Simplicius, held the command between December 396 and March 398.[47] It is quite possible that Fravitta was not yet MVM when Synesius wrote.[48] In any case, Fravitta remained conspicuously loyal throughout the period.

Synesius's arrogant Goth who mocks the toga must be either Alaric or Gaïnas. It was Gaïnas, according to Albert,[49] because Alaric was not a central figure in the crisis of 399–400. Again, this argument relies solely on the presupposition of a later date for the speech. It was not till the

44. *In Eutr.* 2.178, 192.
45. See, for example, the indexes to Julian and Themistius. Huns, on the other hand, usually appear as "Massagetae" (see Maenchen-Helfen 1973, 3–7).
46. The passage is quoted in full above.
47. *PLRE* II.1013–14; Demandt 1970, 728.
48. *PLRE* I.372 mistakenly allows the possibility that Fravitta was MVM as early as 395; see rather Demandt 1970, 728.
49. Albert 1984, 56.

outbreak of Tribigild's rebellion in the spring of 399 that Gaïnas was even promoted to the rank of MVM,[50] and not till late summer that any suspicion of his own disloyalty can have arisen. Our sources, writing after the event, not unnaturally assumed that he was in league with Tribigild from the start,[51] but obviously no one can have suspected this at the time or he would never have been appointed to the command against Tribigild in the first place. Since Synesius certainly wrote well before Eutropius's fall in August 399, this consideration seems to rule out Gaïnas too. For Albert, the Goth had to be Gaïnas going to and fro between Phrygia and Constantinople in the summer of 399, not Alaric far away in Illyricum. But Gaïnas was not some skin-clad ruffian out of place in the big city. Even the hostile Zosimus refers to Gaïnas as one of the senators distressed at Eutropius's maladministration.[52] As a Roman officer of some twenty years' standing, he must have spoken fluent Latin, and perhaps Greek too; at any rate, the Ancyrene monk Nilus addressed him a series of letters in Greek.[53] He lived in a grand palace in Constantinople.[54] We can hardly doubt that he normally wore Roman dress. But Alaric was an authentic prince of the Gothic royal house. As for the likelihood of his paying visits to Constantinople, we may compare Claudian's picture, written in the summer of 399, of Alaric striding impudently into cities he had once besieged. It is immaterial whether or not Alaric really did pay official visits as MVM either to Constantinople or to cities he had once besieged. The point is that the Romans would do nothing to stop this arrogance if he wanted to. Both Synesius and Claudian use their images to reinforce the sense of affront and shock: it was a disgrace that a barbarian chieftain with Roman blood on his hands should be honorably received as a Roman magistrate.

Since the Gothic villain of *De providentia* is so clearly Gaïnas, it might be thought implausible to identify the Gothic villain of *De regno* differently. Synesius did much to confuse the issue by reusing several points from the antibarbarian tirade of *De regno* in the old beggarwoman's outburst against Gaïnas's Goths in *De providentia* (118A–B). Nevertheless,

50. See the full discussion by Demandt 1970, 733–36.

51. So Synesius *De prov.* 108C; Zos. 5.13.2, 5.14.3 and 5: see chapter 6, section II for full discussion.

52. 5.13.1; "L'expression maladroite de Zosime pourrait laisser croire que Gaïnas faisait partie du Sénat de Constantinople, ce qui est évidemment exclu pour ce Barbare peu assimilé" (Paschoud, comm. p. 122). Cf. too, for what it is worth, Malalas, p. 348.18 Γαïνὰς ὁ συγκλητικός.

53. *Ep.* 1.70, 79, 114–16, 205–6, 286, in *PG* 79; it must be added that there are some doubts about the authenticity of this correspondence, though the letters to Gaïnas are among the least suspicious items (Cameron 1976b, 187).

54. T. Preger, ed., *Scriptores originum Constantinopolitanarum* (Leipzig 1907), 2:252.5.

the lapse of time and the rapid succession of events between the two works must not be overlooked. In 398, when Synesius composed *De regno*, there cannot have seemed any reason to single out one small settlement of Greuthungi in Phrygia; nor in fact did Synesius do so. Gaïnas was still merely an unemployed count cooling his heels at court. No one could have identified him as a future public enemy. When he had been promoted against Tribigild and used his position to topple two successive ministries, however, all the stakes were changed. In the heat of crisis, persuasion and the careful marshaling of facts were no longer needed.[55] But some two years earlier, it was Alaric who must have seemed the real danger, the man who had rebelled so often in the past. There was no telling how long he would honor the agreement recently concluded with Eutropius. Its terms were a fresh, humiliating insult for the Romans, on top of the threat Alaric continued to represent in the Balkans. How much longer would he be satisfied with the plunder of Greece? How much more Roman gold would it take to keep him away from Constantinople?

Stilicho had twice attempted a military solution, in 395 and 396. On both occasions he failed.[56] Since he did fail, his propagandist Claudian is understandably vague about both campaigns, and Zosimus, here as elsewhere, is curiously ill informed about Alaric between 394 and 402. Stilicho's expedition of 396 put Eutropius on the horns of a dilemma. On the one hand his position would be threatened if Stilicho defeated Alaric when he had failed; yet at the same time he could not allow Alaric's depredations to continue indefinitely. At some point he declared Stilicho a public enemy; whether before or after his ignominious withdrawal is unfortunately uncertain.[57] If Stilicho had failed twice, how could Eutropius expect one of his own armies to face Alaric?

In the modern accounts that see everything in terms of a struggle for power between pro- and antibarbarian parties, Eutropius has always been classified as pro-barbarian.[58] Not by his choice. In fact, he kept Alaric waiting nearly three years for the command he had perhaps been promised by Rufinus. The cost to the Balkans was terrible. Gaïnas too seems to have been given no command between Rufinus's murder in November 395 and his appointment against Tribigild. And Claudian depicts Tribigild leaving an audience with Eutropius empty-handed:

---

55. For the charge that Gaïnas was being ungrateful, compare Theod. *HE* 5.32.

56. Cameron 1970a, 156–88.

57. Paschoud 1986, 113–15. He would have had a better pretext afterward, if he had accused Stilicho of collusion; but there is no way of deciding. For the mystery about Stilicho's failure, see Cameron 1970a, 168–76.

58. So first Güldenpenning 1885, 93.

viso tum forte redibat
Eutropio vacuus donis.
(*In Eutr.* 2.177–78)

The poem goes on to blame Tribigild's rebellion on Eutropius's folly and mismanagement. Indeed, it can hardly be doubted that it was precisely because he did not treat Gaïnas and Tribigild as he had treated Alaric that they resorted to Alaric's tactics. But by appointing Alaric to the Illyrican command he laid himself wide open to the charge of philobarbarism at its most shameful.

Much of the advice Synesius offers in *De regno* is conventional: Arcadius cannot be the master of men until he is master of himself. Much is also utopian: the good king will not need to impose high taxes to pay an army because he will not make enemies (27D)! The two points that stand out for their emphasis and actuality are the attack on Eutropius and the attack on barbarians. The two themes must be connected. Synesius is attacking Eutropius for his barbarian policy.

Synesius draws the connection with surprising delicacy, however— a point to whose implications we shall be returning. The passage that identifies Eutropius most clearly does so to illustrate how far Arcadius goes in preferring a crew of asinine boobs to "sensible men" who can "express a philosophical concept clearly and tersely" (15A–B). In itself the accusation is fairly vague and exclusively moral. But as Synesius repeatedly emphasizes, philosophy's demands on Arcadius are the whole substance of his speech. He equates listening to his speech with "allowing philosophy to dwell with you" in the proem (1B), and he closes with the thought that in the single word *philosophy* he has summed up all his thoughts on kingship (32A). He even speaks of philosophy as a separate entity that controls the speech (4D, 26A, 32B–C). Synesius intends the moral argument to carry weight in its own right. It is part of the same radical approach that makes piety the "pedestal" for Synesius's "statue" of the ideal king (9D). But the speech as a whole amounts to practical, if unrealistic, advice on how Arcadius is to live up to his role as philosophy requires him to: αὐτοκράτωρ for Latin *imperator,* a military leader with absolute power (19C). Specifically,

> philosophy demanded of the king that he should often mix with the military and not keep to his palace, for it taught us that goodwill toward him, his only real safeguard, was fortified by this daily intercourse. This once admitted, in the company of what race of soldiers should a philosopher devoted to his king desire that he should train his body and dwell in the camps?

This passage (21C–D) introduces the whole antibarbarian tirade. Synesius does not try to claim that Eutropius directly prevents Arcadius from acting as a warrior-king, personally involved with a native army whose loyalty blood and nurture alike guarantee,[59] but that the isolation and irresponsibility eunuch-rule fosters prevent him from the proper understanding of his role, which in turn requires him to act. Again, it is a radical, intellectual approach; but the antibarbarian tirade works out its practical consequences: policies Arcadius himself is not taking the trouble to direct have brought the empire into danger.

Synesius has come in for a good deal of admiration over the years for his sagacity in diagnosing in the East a key factor in the fall of the West: Lacombrade comments: "Aussi n'est-il pas inutile, pour apprécier à sa juste valeur la clairvoyance politique de Synésios et des milieux byzantins cultivés de cette fin du IVe siècle, de lui opposer l'aveuglement fatal dont la Rome occidentale est victime à la même date."[60] Elsewhere Lacombrade writes of "l'honnête clairvoyance d'un patriote vigilant," going so far as to compare *De regno* to Demosthenes' *First Philippic*.[61] Does Synesius really deserve such credit? Not, at any rate, on the traditional date and interpretation of *De regno*. If writing in the autumn of 399, he was forecasting that the Goths would attack when they had already attacked. And what was his solution? "Let them be excluded from magistracies and deprived of the privilege of sitting in the senate" (23B); and let us raise a native army with the spirit to drive them out or make them till the soil (26B).[62] The bland recommendation to raise a national army would have raised a smile in any Roman court: emperors had been trying and failing to raise a national army for centuries.

How could Synesius have made such feeble and irrelevant recommendations as late as the autumn of 399? At that moment all three Eastern *magistri militum* were Goths: Alaric, of proven disloyalty; Gaïnas, suspected of collusion with the rebellious Tribigild; and Fravitta, in command of all remaining Eastern troops, on whom everything depended. It was the most serious crisis that had faced the Eastern court since its establishment at Constantinople. This was not the moment to debate

59. One may contrast the panegyrical approach Claudian applies to Honorius at *III Cons. Hon.* 73–87, where although too young to be allowed to do it, he desires to march out with his father against Arbogast and Eugenius; or Synesius to Osiris at *De providentia* 91D–92A: "While still a youth Osiris shared in the generalship with the men appointed to that office: the law did not permit arms to someone so young, but he ruled their will as if he were their mind, and used the generals as his hands."

60. Lacombrade 1951b, 26.

61. Lacombrade 1951b, 86; Cracco Ruggini (1972, 285) also writes of Synesius's "courageous" speech—or rather speeches, since she apparently thought that he delivered *De providentia*, as well as *De regno*, before Arcadius.

62. αὐξηθέντων ἡμῖν τῶν καταλόγων . . . καὶ γενομένων οἰκείων τῶν συνταγμάτων. Note that there should be a comma after καταλόγων, not a colon as in Terzaghi's text.

long-term options like new methods of recruitment or turning the Goths into farmers. But if he was writing in 398, these recommendations, if still utopian,[63] were at any rate not superfluous. Alaric was then a problem for the future.

Not only is it intrinsically implausible to identify the objects of Synesius's antibarbarian tirade as the revolt of Tribigild and treachery of Gaïnas, but its main section clearly alludes to Eutropius's agreement with Alaric in 396 or 397.[64] To resentment at this humiliating treaty would have been added apprehension at the large number of Goths present in Eutropius's expeditionary force against the Huns in early 398. As for the "first skirmishes" (ἀκροβολισμοί), so casual a reference must be to some isolated act of plunder after the treaty, which Synesius is holding up as a warning of worse to come.

IV. AURELIAN AND THE BARBARIANS

On the old chronology, which put *De regno* in 399, it was generally assumed that the antibarbarian tirade reflected the policy of the new praetorian prefect Aurelian. But if *De regno* was written at least a year before Aurelian reached the prefecture, under the ascendancy of Eutropius, the antibarbarian sections cannot represent what Stein called "le programme du nouveau gouvernement."[65] Do they even represent the views of "Aurelian and his party"? Curiously enough, despite his advocacy of the earlier date, even Barnes continued to cling to this unnecessary and now implausible assumption.[66]

To be sure, *De providentia* is full of similar antibarbarian sentiments, associated in a very general way with the figure of Osiris. And since Osiris stands for Aurelian in Synesius's allegory, it has come to be taken for

63. There is also a distinctly racist element in Synesius's thought. At 22B he compares the empire to a human body "in which alien elements are incapable of mingling in a healthy state of harmony." Not only are Goths servile by nature: they are tainted, as Herodotus pointed out "and as we see ourselves," by a "feminine malady" (Hdt. 1.105.4; a parallel reference in the Hippocratic corpus, *Aër.* 22, makes clear that the malady is impotence; see further G. E. R. Lloyd, *Magic, Reason and Experience* [Cambridge 1979], 31). It is a curious coincidence that Charles Kingsley, in the preface to his *Hypatia* (1853), describes the Goths as "untainted by hereditary effeminacy"!

64. This treaty must follow the failure of Stilicho's second campaign against Alaric in the spring of 396 and precede Eutropius's expedition against the Huns in the spring of 398 (Albert 1979, 630). Eutropius would hardly have left Constantinople if he had not secured the situation in Illyricum.

65. Stein 1959, 235.

66. Barnes 1986a, 108.

granted (*a*) that this was indeed the policy of Aurelian and (*b*) that in *De regno* Synesius was articulating these policies on Aurelian's behalf.

But if Synesius were really Aurelian's propagandist, why present Aurelian's program as if it were his own? To make the obvious comparison, we are never in any doubt whose program Claudian is articulating. But not only is there no reference, direct or indirect, to Aurelian throughout *De regno*, there is no suggestion that there is even one sane counsel at court. Synesius is a voice in the wilderness. Throughout the speech he ostentatiously strikes the pose of the philosopher, the only man who has the courage to say what needs to be said ("only listen to me"). But if he really hoped that his speech would influence people, why so emphasize his isolation? If he was in fact merely acting as a "mouthpiece" (C. H. Coster) for the views of a rich and powerful senator with a party behind him, why so carefully conceal the fact? If such views were dangerous, Aurelian could surely have expressed them himself with less risk than Synesius.

The truth is that the modern picture of Aurelian as a fanatical barbarophobe rests entirely on a misinterpretation of *De providentia* and a misreading of *De regno* in the light of this misinterpretation. Since the antibarbarian sentiments of *De providentia* appear to be associated with its hero, Osiris/Aurelian, it has been assumed that when we encounter similar antibarbarian sentiments elsewhere in Synesius, we may see Aurelian there too.

Yet the anti-Germanism of *De providentia* is much more muted and its association with Osiris/Aurelian much more oblique than has so far been appreciated.[67] At no point in the work is Osiris himself directly credited with any antibarbarian sentiments. In the early chapters of book 1 Synesius in his own person pours scorn on the foreigners who support Osiris's wicked brother Typhos, men rightly deprived of a vote. But Osiris himself neither says nor does anything about them. In the second half of book 1 Typhos's wife, plotting a coup for her husband with the aid of these foreigners, tells their general's wife that Osiris is planning to depose him and rid the kingdom of foreign mercenaries.

Now this is essentially the advice Synesius had given in *De regno*, and to that extent we may be sure that he himself considered it both wise and honorable. Yet the plans outlined by Typhos's wife in *De providentia* are certainly not presented as wise and honorable. "Osiris has decided," she claims (108C), "to bring [your husband] back with all the compulsion and trickery he can manage. As soon as he is away from his troops,

---

67. Though see the brief but sensible remarks of Liebeschuetz (1983, 42–43).

he will take away his command and cruelly destroy him and you and your children. These fine children, these beautiful babies, he has decided to cut their throats before they grow up!" The general's wife gullibly swallows these allegations, which, as here presented, we are manifestly not meant to consider genuine plans of the upright and plain-dealing Osiris.

Typhos's wife goes on to "add horror after horror every day, announcing supposed secret plans against them: the Scythian race was to be completely eliminated from the country and Osiris was daily working toward this end, infiltrating the military rolls [i.e., with nonbarbarians] and making other provisions, so that the Egyptians might be independent. The barbarians they would either kill or drive out" (108D). From what we have been previously told of Osiris's conduct and policies as king, these are clearly meant to be understood as calumnies, the only way resentment could be created against a virtuous ruler.

The gods warn Osiris that his brother will bring destruction on the state, but he ignores their advice and "weakly" (their word, 102D) allows Typhos to remain. It is because of this weakness that Typhos is able to stage the coup that deposes Osiris and hand the state over to the barbarians. In book 2 Osiris returns just as Typhos is about to be condemned to death for his treachery. True to character, he "interceded with an enraged populace" and spares Typhos a second time, acting "with more clemency than justice" (124A). As a result, Typhos remains in power (122A–B).

Not only is Osiris not depicted by Synesius in the colors of the ruthless and energetic barbarophobe Aurelian of modern textbooks, but Synesius clearly implies that but for Osiris's weakness, the barbarian coup would never have happened. He takes every opportunity to praise Osiris's virtue and culture; the economy flourished under his rule, education prospered, all were happy, everyone sounded his praises. Synesius does his best to palliate his hero's one weakness by representing it as clemency and to minimize barbarian responsibility for the coup by representing them as the reluctant tools of Typhos's ambition. Was it not praiseworthy and noble in a man to see only the best in his brother?

Nonetheless, the fact is that Synesius portrays Osiris as failing to foresee or forestall the uprising. And while his fictionalized version neatly transfers the responsibility to Typhos's deceit, in real life innocence and ignorance are no excuse. So far from Osiris putting into effect the policies advocated in *De regno*, the truth is that *De providentia* provides a casebook demonstration of the disasters that happened when they were *not* followed.

The antibarbarian sentiments in both *De regno* and *De providentia* are Synesius's own. He proclaimed them loud and clear in his own person in *De regno*. But in *De providentia* they are more muffled because they do not really fit the story he is trying to tell. The purpose of this curious work was to present an apologetic version of Gaïnas's coup, a version that would minimize the responsibility of both Aurelian (now Synesius's patron) and Gaïnas (at the time of writing still master of Constantinople and so best not offended).[68] This is why the lion's share of the blame is laid on a character nowhere so much as mentioned in our other sources for these events, Osiris/Aurelian's brother, Typhos/Caesarius.

Modern accounts, claiming to follow Synesius, tell of a bitter *political* struggle between Aurelian and Caesarius. Aurelian was the spokesman for the nationalists, the antibarbarians; while Caesarius was the leader of the Theodosian party, the pro-barbarians. But this picture of a dramatic struggle between pro- and antibarbarian factions is entirely imaginary. Puzzlement has sometimes been expressed that no one but Synesius so much as mentions it. The truth is that Synesius does not mention it either.

For Synesius the struggle between Typhos and Osiris is purely personal. In the election described in 1.5–7 Osiris wins easily because everyone loves and votes for him. Typhos loses because the only people who support him are the "senseless and numerous category of swineherds and foreigners" who do not have a vote (94A–B). They like Typhos because they are "senseless," and we are never specifically told that Typhos liked them. As for the rebellion, it is made clear that Typhos only turned to the barbarians because he, or rather his wife, could think of no other way to get rid of Osiris. In return for their support he offers to allow them to sack Thebes (i.e., Constantinople), an offer they themselves nobly turn down (110C)! In short, the rivalry between Typhos and Osiris is both personal and one-sided. Osiris is not represented as harboring a single hostile thought about barbarians and is gentle and forgiving toward his brother.[69] Typhos is motivated throughout by hatred and envy of his brother and turns to the barbarians only as a last resort. If Caesarius and Aurelian had been the leaders of pro- and antibarbarian parties respectively, why did Synesius not exploit this in *De providentia*?

It follows that there is no reason for identifying the antibarbarian sentiments of *De regno* as Aurelianic propaganda. In fact Synesius as

68. For more detail, see below, p. 320.
69. The hostile plans attributed to him in the speech of Typhos's wife (108C–110A) are clearly represented as calumnies: see pp. 122–23 above.

good as says so himself. The rustic philosopher is represented as "rejecting the idea of addressing Osiris on the subject of himself, because he considered words an unequal recompense for deeds and was ashamed lest he acquire a reputation for flattery because of the rusticity of his background" (113C). It was not till after Osiris's exile that he "began to publish. . . . In speech and in writing he called down the direst curses on Typhos. . . . Osiris was everywhere in his discourse" (113D). The second part of this claim undoubtedly corresponds to Synesius's activity in 400: *De providentia*, praising Aurelian and attacking his brother, was not written till after Aurelian's exile.

This being so, there seems no reason to doubt that the first part of the claim also corresponds to real life; namely that Synesius did not publish anything about Aurelian before his exile. But this is a curious claim to make. Boldly denouncing "Typhos" obviously reflected well on Synesius. But why insist that he had *not* published anything about Aurelian? The motive given—reluctance to appear a flatterer—is hardly satisfactory. What of the gross flattery in *De providentia*? It looks as if Synesius is obliquely defending himself against the charge of not rallying to Aurelian's support till it was too late. The more so in view of the very precise (and anachronistic) claim that the stranger had indeed *written* both verse and prose on Osiris before the exile but had not *published* it (οὐ μὴν ἐξέφερεν εἰς τὸ πλῆθος, 113B). This feeble defense surely implies that Synesius had at any rate not published a speech glorifying Aurelian's solution to the ills of the age: namely, a work such as *De regno* on the traditional interpretation.

This would explain why the speech nowhere even hints at either of the real-life counterparts of Typhos and Osiris. If *De regno* had been written as usually supposed, after Eutropius's fall but before Aurelian's exile, we should expect to find (*a*) praise of Aurelian and (*b*) warning against Caesarius. But the criticism of Arcadius's ministers, forthright though it is, focuses on their buffoonery, not the wickedness of a Typhos. This fits Eutropius, with his servile origins, despised status, and low tastes, but not Caesarius as Synesius chose to portray him in *De providentia*. It is relevant to observe that Claudian used the same sort of weapons against Eutropius: he is clown, pander, pervert, an object of disgust and shame rather than fear. Chrysostom too dwelled on Eutropius's gluttony, drinking parties, and love of the games.[70] Rufinus, in sharp contrast, Claudian depicted (like Typhos) as the personification of

70. *PG* 52.391–92.

evil, a nursling of the Furies, sent to earth to destroy the felicity bequeathed to mankind by Theodosius. To be sure, Synesius does in passing accuse Typhos of gluttony and orgies, but from start to finish he is
presented (like Rufinus) as the ally of evil demons.

So *De regno* cannot be one of the invectives on Typhos or panegyrics
on Osiris mentioned in *De providentia*. It was written earlier, in a different political situation. Nor is there any reason for postponing the
speech, with Barnes, till Synesius had won Aurelian's favor. We have already seen that there is nothing in the antibarbarian tirade that points to
Aurelian, and (once more) the lack of any suggestion that Arcadius had
at least one prudent counselor strongly suggests that as yet Synesius
owed nothing to Aurelian.

Barnes further suggests that Synesius may have been promised his
tax concessions in advance of Aurelian's elevation to the prefecture in
recompense for his services as propagandist. But if Synesius had really
established such a connection as early as 398, why did he not leave for
Cyrene the moment Aurelian was elevated to the prefecture? Aurelian is
attested in office by 27 August 399,[71] in comfortable time for Synesius to
get a boat from the Constantinople he had grown to detest before the
closure of the seas. But instead he stayed another whole year. Could it
be that he had *not* secured Aurelian's favor before August 399; that he
had to start his lobbying afresh with the new administration?

Once we abandon the traditional Synesian chronology, *De regno* and
De providentia actually turn out to have less in common than usually supposed. Synesius came to Constantinople in the autumn of 397 and delivered *De regno* a few months later in 398. Not surprisingly, it reflects
hostility to Eutropius, still in power, and anxiety about his recent legal-
ization of Alaric's depredations in the Balkans. It was not till after Aurelian came to power in August 399 that Synesius won the tax concessions he had been seeking (*De providentia* 113B), perhaps not till early
400. Unfortunately, before he could leave for Cyrene with the opening of
the seas, Aurelian fell from power in (probably) April 400, and the new
prefect reduced or abolished them (112C). Synesius was obliged to stay
on till the autumn of 400 in the hope of obtaining some redress. He
wrote *De providentia* in the late summer of 400, naturally turning now to
the new development of Gaïnas's coup. Book 1 he did not complete till
after the massacre of 12 July, to which the closing chapter clearly alludes.
Book 2 he wrote "after the return of the best men" (88B) but before his
own departure in probably October 400.

71. *Cod. Theod.* 2.8.23.

V. PUBLICATION

Thus far it has been convenient to speak of the *De regno* as an oration on kingship addressing Arcadius. That is ostensibly its form. Not only is Synesius's second-person addressee the emperor in a contemporary setting, but he is described in terms that clearly identify Arcadius: he is a young ruler who inherited the realm his father won, his father having defeated two usurpers and died a natural death (5A–B).[72] But scholars have always felt some uneasiness at Synesius's tone. Could he really have delivered his blistering criticisms of Arcadius and his court before—Arcadius and his court? Is this credible?[73] Predictably, the verdicts divide. For example, on the one side Demougeot simply asserted: "Il est probable que ces paroles hardies ne furent jamais prononcées," citing the distant and scarcely parallel precedent of Cicero's *Pro Milone*.[74] On the other, for Coster "Synesius was a man of rare honesty and courage; we must believe, with Gibbon and with Seeck, that he did deliver the address in substantially the form in which it was published . . . one of the frankest addresses that a monarch has ever been called upon to listen to."[75] According to Lacombrade, *De regno* not only was delivered in its present form but further "a transmis sans apprêt, sans retouches, l'image exacte des préoccupations patriotiques qui, en 399, animaient l'élite intellectuelle de Byzance."[76]

Fortunately we are not limited to the purely subjective. On the matter of boldness and sincerity we have another work by Synesius for comparison. A considerable part of *De providentia* consists of obsequious flattery of Aurelian, thinly disguised as Osiris—from whom Synesius was hoping for benefits. Hitherto critics have satisfied themselves that Aurelian was indeed a man of superlative moral character, warmly deserving such praises. A closer look at the evidence suggests that he was no better, and perhaps rather worse, than his brother Caesarius,[77] on whose head (disguised as Typhos) Synesius heaps malicious and scurrilous abuse. In short, *De providentia* reveals a Synesius as adept as Claudian himself at shifting effortlessly from ferocious invective to fulsome

---

72. The usurpers were Maximus (387–88) and Eugenius (392–94).

73. For a recent anthology of views see the (inconclusive) discussion in Albert 1984, 63–66.

74. Demougeot 1951, 238.

75. Coster 1968, 155.

76. Lacombrade 1951b, 87; cf. Young 1983, 174: "There was a time when scholars believed it could not be the actual words he spoke in the presence of the emperor, a view successfully demolished by Lacombrade."

77. See pp. 177–81.

panegyric—a typical courtier of the age. Is this really the man who on a different occasion delivered the boldest, most honest speech ever pronounced before a Roman emperor?

There are also other grounds for doubting that the speech as extant was ever delivered in court. Since it purports to accompany the presentation of crown gold, Lacombrade naturally compared the formula for the relevant speech (*stephanotikos logos*) in the late third- or early fourth-century treatise ascribed to Menander.[78] But he dismissed without argument the formula's one purely objective requirement, that of length. The *stephanotikos* ought not to exceed 150–200 lines. The *De regno* runs to nearly 1,200. This excess alone makes it hard to believe that the speech was delivered in court.[79] Granted, Menander's prescriptions were guidelines rather than rules; one good example of the *stephanotikos*, a speech by Themistius dated to 357 (*Or.* 3), presents a crown to Constantius on behalf of Constantinople in about 300 lines. But a 600 to 800 percent overrun cannot be reconciled with the setting. Even an ambassador like Synesius, possessing the highest opinion of his own and his city's merits, cannot have expected to do their cause any good by so flagrantly defying protocol. No reader of panegyrics doubts that late antique tolerance for ceremonial elaboration was high. But there were limits. The crown gold was an anniversary tax, and the number of cities having requests to present along with it must have been considerable; the court cannot have wished to see any one presentation unduly prolonged. We can hardly doubt that it was with just such considerations in mind that Menander prescribed a short speech.[80]

As to content, Menander directs that the *stephanotikos* should be almost entirely devoted to praise of the emperor and should close with a reading of the honorific decree of the city sending the crown. Lacombrade could discern praise of Arcadius by allowing it to be "anticipatory";[81] the question of the decree he ignores. "Cyrene sends me, to crown your head with gold and your soul with philosophy" (2C) is a fleeting hint of it but goes no farther. Synesius then begins to lament his

---

78. Lacombrade 1951b, 83–85; cf. *Menander Rhetor*, ed. D. A. Russell and N. G. Wilson (Oxford 1981): on the date, xxxix–xl; on the *stephanotikos*, 178–81, with notes on 336–37.

79. And is rightly adduced by Barnes 1986a, 106. Strangely, Russell and Wilson (1981, 336) cite *De regno* as a "good instance" of the *stephanotikos*. Klauser too cites it as a typical example of a "Kranzrede" (*Ges. Arbeiten* [1974], 301).

80. His remarks on the similarly concise *kateunastikos*, dispatching a newlywed couple to the bedroom, illustrate his sensitivity to the patience inherent in an occasion (Russell and Wilson 1981, 146–59, with 317–23).

81. Lacombrade 1951b, 85.

city's fallen glory (2D), suggesting the subgenre of the *presbeutikos logos*.[82] Besides the city's need, Menander recommends that the ambassador dwell on the emperor's humanity and generous beneficence. But for Synesius this theme is merely a springboard for an elaborate *peri basileias*. Indeed this very title in the manuscripts (whether original or not) recognizes its true nature. The designation is thematic rather than formal, a "semi-philosophical discussion with no set rules on the merits and duties of the ideal king."[83] It is an established topic; but again, impossibly overgrown for the oration's ostensible setting.

It has often been asserted that Synesius himself claims to have delivered the speech before Arcadius. He says in the *De insomniis* that dream divination made him "bolder than any Greek has ever been when addressing the emperor" (ἐς τὴν βασιλέως ὁμιλίαν, 148C). *Homilia* in Christian usage was the normal term for "sermon."[84] In the strict sense it denoted an informal exegesis of a passage from scripture, but "in later antiquity . . . [it] was often extended to include all kinds of Christian sermons except panegyric."[85] It might thus seem to describe the rambling *De regno* better than a formal *stephanotikos*. But even this extended sense is still technical: it refers to the sermon of a priest in a church, not discourse in general, still less the presentation speech of an ambassador in court. Even in the Christian period *homilia* retained its broader classical sense "association" or "intercourse"—which could embrace any kind of speech while Synesius was in the emperor's presence. The argument that *De insomniis* refers specifically to *De regno* has to exploit both senses of *homilia* simultaneously: a sermon (loosely conceived) about the emperor, delivered in the emperor's company. Such double duty overworks the term. Synesius may well have spoken boldly to Arcadius in the brief audience at which he presented Cyrene's crown gold soon after his arrival. But it does not follow that the speech he delivered on that occasion was the surviving version of *De regno*.[86]

If Synesius revised for publication the *presbeutikos* he did deliver, he could easily have added or elaborated points that did not fit the real occasion. Pliny rewrote his *Panegyric* endlessly before releasing it to the world. But *De regno* does not just include a few outspoken but detach-

82. Russell and Wilson 1981, 180–81, with 337–38.

83. Cameron 1970a, 322.

84. See the relevant entries in the lexica (LSJ, Bauer, and Lampe).

85. G. A. Kennedy, *Greek Rhetoric Under Christian Emperors* (Princeton 1983), 182; cf. his *Classical Rhetoric and Its Christian and Secular Tradition from Ancient to Modern Times* (Chapel Hill, N.C. 1980), 136–38.

86. Contrast Lacombrade: "La hardiesse de cette pièce d'éloquence avait surpris ses contemporains comme elle déconcerte la posterité" (1951b, 81).

able passages. As the composition stands, it is an organically conceived whole. Synesius introduces it by repeatedly proclaiming (2A–B) that it will not be light and witty but solemn and stern,

> words that refuse to court the bounty of the great by servile adulation . . . ready to wound if opportunity arises, threatening to bite into the heart, not just on the surface but to the very core, if anyone may be helped by suffering. . . . Freedom of speech should be of great price in the ears of a monarch. Praise at every step is seductive but harmful. . . . A frank speech saves the mind of a young emperor from such paths as the license of power might open to him. Endure then this unusual speech.

Synesius deliberately strikes the Cynic pose of a philosopher rebuking the king.

The last chapter of *De providentia* includes a transparent self-portrait of Synesius, introducing a stranger "nurtured by philosophy in a rather rustic manner" who, "like all mankind, had met with innumerable benefits from Osiris. He himself was not obliged to perform public services, and his country's obligations had been made less burdensome." This man was as grateful as any, "even more so, being better endowed. For he wrote both poems and speeches and sang to the lyre in the Dorian mode" (113A–C). The "Dorian mode" is a flagrant anachronism in the Egyptian context, and the reference to the philosopher-poet-essayist winning tax remissions for himself and his native city inescapably evokes Synesius's own errand at court. This is not Hitchcock making a walk-on appearance in his own film. The self-portrait is so precise and detailed that Synesius's select audience was obviously meant to look for further correspondences. Nor would they have looked in vain. This rustic philosopher strikes the same Cynic pose in an address before the tyrant Typhos (114A):

> He paid no attention to older men and friends who admonished him. Fear did not shake him from his impetuosity; he was like a man raving with unrestrained madness. He did not stop until he stood as close as possible to Typhos himself, at a time when distinguished men from all the world were gathered around him, and gave a long speech in favor of Typhos's brother.

Though never losing its obvious risks, such boldness was an established convention. The emperor was expected to endure the criticism, as Typhos manages to do here.[87] Julian, the one authentic philosopher-

---

87. "But from his face one could picture what was going on in his mind" (114B). Cf. D. R. Dudley, *A History of Cynicism* (London 1937), 125f.; R. Höistad, *Cynic Hero and Cynic*

emperor of the age, satisfied himself with answering Cynics in kind.[88] Sometimes the philosopher even won a fair hearing. For example, the unfavorable report of the philosopher Iphicles provoked Valentinian to investigate the conduct of his praetorian prefect.[89] But Iphicles presented Valentinian with a verifiable complaint about an absent minister. Synesius in contrast purports to be criticizing Arcadius himself to his face in the harshest possible terms. The adulation the emperor receives is "barbarian" (14C). The isolation that reinforces the impression of his exalted status is a "disease" (14D). In consequence Arcadius is ignorant and "lives the life of a jellyfish" (14D). His jeweled robes recall Homer's phrase "stony cloak," a degraded death by stoning (16A; *Il.* 3.57). He is fettered in gold, and it is every bit as confining as the basest stocks (16C). He skulks in his lair like a lizard (16D). Synesius warns him at 3B–C:

> If in the course of this address some act of yours appears among those we know to be wrong and which you so recognize yourself, in that case you should show your anger with yourself and blush because something not worthy of you has come to light. Assuredly this color promises the virtue that comes from a change of mind, for this shame is divine and so seems to Hesiod.[90]

On the model of diatribe, the oration satirizes its addressee's acts in order to inspire him with revulsion and thus drive him to correction. It is a unity.

Tradition has indelibly labeled Arcadius a sluggard; but Synesius's harshly exaggerated images strain even that slack tolerance. Pace Coster, they go well beyond a question of frankness or courage. Still more so the accusation that Arcadius's closest associates are "small-headed men with little understanding, whom nature deceitfully misstrikes, just as money changers criminally do to coins, and the witless man becomes a gift to the king, and a greater gift the more witless he is," who will sink to any depth in their buffoonery.[91] Even if imperial forbearance or colossal dullness prevented Arcadius from responding to the attacks on himself, no tradition or incapacity restrained his ministers. Least of all could a eunuch, "the senseless element you strip in front of," tolerate being denounced in front of the only protector he had. Eutropius had exiled

---

King (Uppsala 1948), 150f.; H. A. Musurillo, *The Acts of the Pagan Martyrs* (Oxford 1954), 236f., 267f.; Festugière 1959, 274–76; R. MacMullen, *Enemies of the Roman Order* (Cambridge, Mass. 1966), 53f.; J. Hahn, *Der Philosoph und die Gesellschaft* (Stuttgart 1989), 182f.; on popular outbursts at the theater and hippodrome, Cameron 1976a, 157–83.

88. *Or.* 6 and 7.
89. Amm.Marc. 30.5.8–10; cf. *PLRE* I.464.
90. Referring to Hes. *Op.* 197ff.
91. 15A–B; the part paraphrased here is quoted in full above, p. 107.

Abundantius and Timasius, military men actually serving the imperial administration, as merely potential threats.[92] If Synesius had dared to speak 15B in open court, he could at the very least abandon all thought of tax remissions.

Why then did Synesius write the *De regno* in its present form? What could be done with a speech too dangerously offensive to be delivered? The well-documented circumstances attending the publication of many speeches of Libanius provide instructive examples. His funeral speech on his uncle Phasganius Libanius divided into three sections. The last, because he was afraid it would offend Julian, he recited to a select group of friends behind closed doors, insisting that they refrain even from applauding (*Ep.* 33, 282). His monodies on Nicomedia and Aristaenetus were declaimed before an audience of only four (*Ep.* 33). A closer parallel to *De regno* is *Or.* 15, the proem to which represents Libanius as leading an embassy to Julian in Mesopotamia in order to reconcile him to Antioch. Libanius begs the emperor not to interrupt him (*Or.* 15.14), apostrophizing him throughout and speculating at the end as to how he will dare return to Antioch if unsuccessful. Yet the truth is that there was no embassy, Libanius never left Antioch, and the speech was never delivered to Julian, who was dead before it was even finished. Both it and *Or.* 14, which also purports to have been delivered before Julian, were in fact recited in private before a few friends Libanius could trust.[93]

Or. 3 of Themistius, purporting to have been delivered before Constantius at Rome in 357, may be another such case. The orator begins, like Synesius, by offering the emperor crown gold on behalf of Constantinople to commemorate his thirty-fifth anniversary.[94] But many scholars have doubted whether Themistius actually went to Rome on this occasion. A careful study by G. Dagron attempts to dispel these doubts,[95] and he may be right; but if he is wrong, a fictitious setting would be an obvious and acceptable explanation. *Or.* 13 was certainly delivered in Rome, but not in the presence of Gratian, as sometimes inferred from a few second-person invocations.[96] It would be easy to multiply earlier ex-

92. *PLRE* I.4–5, 914–15.

93. Liebeschuetz 1972, 25–26; P. Petit, "Recherches sur la publication et la diffusion des discours de Libanius," *Historia* 5 (1956): 479–509 (= *Libanios*, Wege der Forschung 621, ed. G. Fatouros and T. Krischer [Darmstadt 1983], 84–128, here 95).

94. Not vicennalia, as in the chroniclers' notices (*Chron. Min.* I.239): Long 1988, 115; Themistius *Or.* 3.40C = I.58 Downey.

95. Dagron 1968, 20–21, 205–12.

96. E.g., O. Seeck, *Briefe des Libanius* (1906), 303; *PLRE* I.891; correctly, Dagron 1968, 22–23; T. D. Barnes, *HSCP* 79 (1975): 329.

amples: the *legatio* of Athenagoras purports to have been addressed to Marcus and Commodus, apparently in September 176,[97] but we must agree with R. Lane Fox that "the setting is a literary fiction."[98]

Less clear-cut cases are Libanius's many speeches of social criticism from the Theodosian age. Undoubtedly he took his role as social critic seriously, and on occasion he took risks. But he was never rash. A letter describes how, on the advice of friends more current with court politics than himself, he kept his speech against a certain law unpublished until the law was rescinded—when as a call for reform it had been completely neutralized.[99] It is hard to believe that Libanius was imprudent enough to publish some of the extant speeches while the men he attacked in them were still in power.[100] A notable case is the *Pro templis* (*Or.* 30), an impassioned demand for religious toleration addressed to Theodosius himself, for all the world as if Libanius were standing before him ("Now too I come on the same errand," *Or.* 30.1). So forthrightly did Libanius attack the fanatical praetorian prefect Cynegius, it is most unlikely that the speech was made public at all, much less presented at court, as long as he was still in office. Libanius doubtless sent it to one or two reliable friends at court.

As A. F. Norman put it, "such restricted circulation was utilitarian in purpose, since it directed propaganda to the right quarters at court in safety and with effectiveness, the orator's friends there acting as intermediaries (cf. *Or.* 2.70f.). Hence the unexpected combination of social criticism and violent personal abuse."[101] Synesius was in a similar position. A similar presentation would solve the problems of delivering *De regno* publicly. A further point in confirmation is the fact that Synesius's self-portrait, the rustic philosopher of *De providentia*, "entrusted" his works only to discerning and serious audiences (113B–C). His reticence is mentioned merely to excuse his not returning a *gratiarum actio* for Osiris's favors, but if modesty compelled silence then, all the more did the real dangers to his mission that *De regno* courted, had it come to Eutropius's ears. The tone and emphases of the speech conform to what Barnes termed opposition-literature.[102] It does not, however, as Barnes himself thought, put forward the policies of an opposition party. Rather it is an appeal by Synesius *to* such a party, whose sympathy he hoped to enlist for his own cause—the embassy.

97. T. D. Barnes, *JTS* 26 (1975): 111–14.
98. *Pagans and Christians* (New York 1987), 306.
99. *Ep.* 916; cf. Petit 1983, 97–98.
100. For examples, see Liebeschuetz 1972, 30; Petit 1983, 107f.
101. *Libanius: Selected Works*, vol. 2 (Cambridge, Mass. 1977), 94.
102. Barnes 1986a, 112.

VI. SYNESIUS'S AUDIENCE

Since *De dono*, the first document from Synesius's embassy, complains to Paeonius that others have disregarded him (308A), it may be presumed that the *presbeutikos logos* with which he presented the Cyreneans' crown gold bore no fruit. *De regno* displays further frustration at court inaction. Paeonius, though currently holding office (309C), was apparently not implicated in this unresponsive policy: perhaps then a disaffected official. Since Synesius had brought his silver astrolabe from home, he doubtless bestowed it on a suitable target soon after his arrival, perhaps in early 398. It was certainly more a political than a scientific instrument; Synesius took care to link respect for philosophy with the advantage of cities (309B–C). We do not know how Paeonius reacted to the solicitation. In *Ep.* 154 Synesius credits him with some benefaction to Pentapolis; on the other hand, the tax concessions he wanted could only be granted from the very top. *De providentia* confirms that it was Aurelian, prefect on Eutropius's fall, who actually granted them (113A–B). The next prefect revoked them (114B), and *Ep.* 61 shows that Synesius faced further exertions, "sleeping before the Great Archives," right up until he fled Constantinople during the earthquake. The rug he promised Asterius the shorthand writer represents his politicking at the lowest level. Paeonius obviously required more subtle handling. He surely played the all-important intermediary role so well documented in Synesius's correspondence. Not himself in a position to give Synesius what he wanted, he could nonetheless introduce him to others from whom better things might be hoped. This group corresponds to the select audience of Synesius's rustic philosopher in *De providentia* (113B–C).

The portrait of Arcadius's favorites in *De regno* can have done nothing to conciliate the officeholders of the day. But by the time the speech was written, Eutropius's relations with Alaric and the disturbances to which Synesius alludes may have suggested to many that he could not maintain his position long. Clearly Synesius had abandoned hope of success with the current administration. Nothing remained but to burn this unprofitable bridge behind him. Sensibly, he did not burn it openly; and resourcefully, he burnt it in a way that might engage the sympathies of men who shared his hostility toward Eutropius, those who might be expected to succeed him in influence.

Interpreted in this light, *De regno* represents a fresh start for Synesius's embassy. In it he says what he would have liked to say in his real *presbeutikos*. The setting gave him the advantages presupposed in a real embassy presenting crown gold: if his city sent the emperor a gift, it deserved something in return. At the same time, complicit knowledge of "true facts" too dangerous for publication helps engage the audience's sympathy.

On the other hand, since Synesius no longer faced the real occasion of the speech, he could disregard its formal requirements. He took time to do full justice to his themes: the enlightened conduct of public affairs, with particular regard to choice of favorites and advisers, conduct of military and barbarian affairs, and protection of cities. There is no reason to doubt that he was attracted by the idea of writing a *peri basileias* for its own sake. His emphasis on the value of education, repeated in *De dono*, *De regno*, *De providentia*, and *Dion*, was certainly sincere. The reason he expected prospective patrons to honor philosophy in him and to receive compliments of it as the highest praise was that he himself so prized it. And the use of philosophy to mold the highest ruling power must provide a speaker with his highest subject. The great influence of the beloved Dio's four orations on kingship (*Or.* 1–4) will also have been a factor.[103] Dio's censorious Rhodian, Alexandrian, and Tarsian orations showed even the harshest criticism made acceptable by rhetorical polish.[104] Synesius's verdict is that Dio "showed virility of mind beyond any of his contemporaries; he set himself to admonish mankind whether kings or private citizens, speaking to both individuals and the masses" (*Dion* 38A). Synesius admired this stance. It is no coincidence that he uses the same word, "virile," to characterize both *De regno* and the outspoken words of the rustic philosopher who represents him in *De providentia* (113B).[105] The moral courage the Cynic pose implicitly asserts adds extrarational persuasive force to the speaker's arguments. It is a further resource of Synesius's setting.

The three points of his hidden agenda significantly affect the way he

103. Asmus 1900, 85–151. Synesius's *Dion* is of course the greatest testimony of the importance Dio held for him; but for motifs borrowed specifically from Dio's kingship orations for the *De providentia* see below, chapter 7, section III.

104. *Or.* 31–33. It is currently fashionable to date the Rhodian and Alexandrian orations early (see the summary in C. P. Jones 1978, 133–34), but see a forthcoming paper by O. Murray.

105. Of *De regno*: λόγους . . . ἀρρενωποὺς καὶ σεμνούς, 1C; cf. Dio Chrys. *Or.* 4, p. 74.4 von Arnim, ἀρρενωπόν τε καὶ σεμνόν. Common though the metaphor is in the rhetorical lexicon, it is tempting to suspect that here Synesius intended a barbed, if glancing, allusion to the eunuch Eutropius. There are more than sixty separate allusions, some extended, to Eutropius's physical condition in the two books of Claudian's *In Eutropium*, most stressing his lack of virility: 1.8, 10, 29 (*virum*), 39, 45–57, 110f., 145, 152, 171 (*semivir*), 187, 190, 193, 214, 231, 234, 240, 243, 252, 255, 261f., 277f., 281, 296, 298, 315, 319, 324, 326, 337, 364, 419, 425, 438, 461–62, 467, 494, 497; 2pr. 21, 26, 33, 43, 45–46, 51, 74, 75; 2.22 (*semivir*), 49 (*castrati consulis*), 55, 62, 67, 74, 80, 90, 112 (*mollitia*), 122, 138 (*virilis*), 157, 192, 223–24 (*viris . . . alter sexus . . . eunuchis*), 415, 550, 552, 555, 563.

presents his general theme. His *peri basileias* addresses not Arcadius but a group of men excluded from and hostile to Eutropius's administration, men sufficiently prominent to be likely successors when it fell. Synesius plays on their ambitions by stressing the power and prestige of the emperor's friends.[106] Unremarkably, perhaps, the properly chosen circle of the good king's friends will be good men (10C), who will match him in their "kingly adornment of soul" (29C). It is more significant that Synesius identifies those who actually enjoy sight of the king as the true wielders of power (16B).[107] The extended discussion of 11B–12B elaborates the point. The king's near and dear league about him, and he will confer with them about everything. They are a "kingly possession," sweet for him to share good fortune with, loyal in bad, trustworthy in praise, and able to admonish without causing pain. By making them enviable the king gives sure general proof of his goodwill. The king relies on his friends to bring him to the omnicompetence of God, "for thus he will see with the eyes of all, he will hear with the hearing of all, and he will take counsel with the opinions of all resolving on a single decision." This perfect relationship can be perverted on either side, by the capriciousness of the tyrant or by the imposture of flattery. Synesius concludes that "love toward his friends is not the least virtue of the king." The vital role of advisers, their power, and the favors a munificent ruler will return them are dangled alluringly before Synesius's audience. He does not explicitly evoke their natural conviction that they themselves deserve to be enjoying these things, but he implicitly flatters them with his scathing portrait of the vile buffoons who presently do. This is one line by which he binds his listeners to him.

A second is his criticism of current barbarian policy. It is worth emphasizing that the theme of the barbarian threat is absent from *De dono*. Synesius did not arrive in the capital burning with antibarbarian fervor. Nor (as we have seen) is there any reason to believe that the antibarbarian sentiments of the speech were specially tailored to Aurelian. Aurelian was doubtless one of the main contenders for the prefecture on Eutropius's fall, but it cannot have been certain that he would get it. In 399, the only thing that mattered was Pentapolis.

The barbarian danger was a serious issue that aroused legitimate anxieties. In this respect the moderns who applaud Synesius for shrewdly identifying a crucial political problem of his age show sound instincts. But Synesius develops the theme with emotive rhetoric, not serious political suggestions. His audience shared the mortification of Themis and

106. For a survey of their position and privileges, see Millar 1977, 110–22.
107. Synesius probably uses βουλευταί here in the more etymological sense "counselors" rather than, as Fitzgerald translates, "senators."

the god of the battle line when a skin-clad foreigner took precedence over native generals or, briefly changed into a toga, over native aristocrats in the senate.[108] They were the very "legitimate men" the upstart outranked (23B–C). Synesius stresses the prevalence of Scythian slaves not merely to alarm his audience at how close the danger had come, but to feed their sense of injury. Even the threat of being mastered by "the kin of our own slaves" is an insult (23D–24C). Similarly the effeminacy and abjection of the often-defeated Scythians not only offer reassurance that they will not be too hard to subject again, but reinforce a sense of humiliation at submitting to them now (24D–26B).

The vagueness of Synesius's proposals likewise reflects his real purpose. He wrote *De regno* in ignorance of the impending dangers from Tribigild and Gaïnas. He wrote without attention to the West, under the thumb of the half-Vandal Stilicho—still less to its future when less Romanized barbarians inherited his loyal ascendancy. Had Synesius been enunciating the program of an antibarbarian party, more specific and realistic proposals might have been expected. In the event he was simply rousing feeling against the current regime. His limited purpose was to show that current policies were disastrous. There was no need to suggest alternatives in realistic detail. Such vagueness suited the situation perfectly. Synesius knew his audience perceived a barbarian problem—but he had no idea how they would cope with it. Needing their favor, he did not want to risk supplying perhaps unwelcome detail. A bare demand for change would demonstrate his common cause without running risks. Conventional appeals to pristine Roman militarism were a fine note to sound, lending weight and emotive force but no substantive content. If his new patrons wanted a spokesman, they could supply the content later.

De regno is actually very different from superficially similar works of the age, and it employs correspondingly different tactics. Much traditional material is shared, for example, by *De regno* and the miniature *peri basileias* Claudian set within his panegyric for the fourth consulate of Honorius. Arcadius in the one and Honorius in the other are both instructed to share the life of their armies—to ride with the cavalry, march with the infantry, address individual soldiers by name, and so forth.[109] The advice corresponds to no known intention of either unwarlike em-

108. The native generals are emblematized by their *chlamydes,* the *vox propria* for the military cloak. From the imperial purple on down, garment iconography was a voluble language of late antique thought.

109. *De regno* 12B–14B; *IV Cons. Hon.* 320–52. Th. Birt (*De moribus Christianis quantum Stilichonis aetate in aula imperatoria occidentali valuerint disputatio* [Marburg 1885], xvi–xxii) and Lacombrade (1956) collect ideas common to the two works; but they are all commonplaces and do not indicate that either was derived from the other.

peror. But where Claudian puts it into Theodosius's mouth as affection-
ate advice from father to son, Synesius hurls bitter rebukes at the hapless
Arcadius in his own person. Claudian's purpose was to present the military ideal as a dynastic tradition still vested in Honorius, Synesius's to
lament its absence in the current degenerate regime. He explicitly assigns the ideal to philosophy: its authority is intellectual and imper-
sonal. The only emotional ties evoked are the ones the king will form
with his soldiers. Eutropius having been a trusted minister of Theodosius,[110] dynastic sentiment would not help Synesius here. Moreover, he
puts Arcadius's failure to live up to the ideal in a light that reflects badly
on Eutropius. If Arcadius associated with sensible men instead of this
"senseless element," he would be exposed to the philosophical principles by which he could rule well (15A–B). Synesius does not draw the
connection any tighter, because (of course) it was not in his hearers' interest to turn Arcadius into a warrior-king, or even a strong ruler in less
anachronistic style. They wanted to enjoy the power behind the throne
themselves. The practical implication of the ideal is merely that Arcadius
would receive better advice from different advisers.

Again, protest at the emperor's seclusion is commonplace and often,
as in the *Historia Augusta*, blamed on the influence of eunuchs. It is normally implicit, disguised as criticism of the current emperor's predecessors. Synesius does just this: "Do not be angry, for the fault is not yours;
it is the fault rather of those who first created this mischief and transmitted to Time's heritage an evil now zealously maintained" (14D). Pacatus's
panegyric on Theodosius (389) provides a good parallel: "Some emperors (you know who I mean) consider the imperial majesty dimin-
ished and vulgarized unless they lock themselves away in some corner
of the palace as if in some Vestal shrine" (21). Pacatus was probably influenced by a similar development in Pliny's panegyric on Trajan. According to Pliny, previous emperors had been "afraid of being brought
down to our level" (24.5).[111] For Synesius too it was "fear of becoming
like other mortals" that led to seclusion. The difference is that Pacatus,
like Pliny, was careful to imply throughout that his emperor repudiated
this vicious practice of safely dead predecessors. Ostensibly pure praise
incorporates a warning against less praiseworthy behavior. Synesius, in
contrast, after conceding that Arcadius did not begin this isolation, goes
on to rebuke him for maintaining it. He describes Arcadius's seclusion

110. Ca. 393, Theodosius sent him to Egypt to consult a holy man about the war
against Eugenius: Claud. *In Eutr.* 1.312–13; Soz. *HE* 7.22.7–8.

111. In Pliny's case, clearly Domitian, but it is hardly likely that it is also Domitian to
whom Pacatus alludes, as E. Galletier thought (*Pan. Lat.*, vol. 3 [Paris 1955], 88 n. 2). Perhaps rather Theodosius's junior colleague Valentinian II.

brutally, saying that it reduces him to the enjoyment of only the meanest bodily pleasures, living the life of a jellyfish (14D).[112] The deliberate offensiveness of the exaggeration, inconceivable in a real address to an emperor, bears the moral force of Synesius's real argument. Eutropius's influence debases Arcadius.

If a speaker wanted to reform the emperor, there were time-honored ways to try it. The various indirect devices were known collectively as ὑπόθεσις ἐσχηματισμένη, "simulated argument." Rhetoricians deployed them when, as Philostratus put it, "one needs to curb what one actually says, but to apply the spur to what one leaves unsaid."[113] Philostratus singles out Scopelianus, Rufus of Perinthus, and Hermocrates as specialists in this delicate art.[114] He also describes with incredulity how Herodes Atticus, frantic with grief,

> launched into invectives against the emperor and did not even use simulated arguments (οὐδὲ σχηματίσας τὸν λόγον), though it might have been expected that a man who had been trained in this kind of oratory would have had his own anger under control. But with an aggressive and unguarded tongue he persisted in his attack.[115]

Thanks to his long-standing friendship with Marcus, who must have known why he was so distraught, Herodes came to no harm.[116] Less securely placed, most speakers reasonably preferred caution.

Themistius is the fourth century's best-known practitioner. As Dagron put it, his technique was "to congratulate emperors for the qualities they most conspicuously lacked: Constantius for his gentleness, Valens for his love of literature and capacity for forgiveness."[117] For example, Themistius praises Valens for his statesmanlike and merciful treatment of the followers of the usurper Procopius (*Or.* 7). Our other sources document a ruthless persecution. By speaking directly against fact, Themistius offered advice, suggesting to Valens how he could be effec-

---

112. The image of the jellyfish is taken from Pl. *Phlb.* 21C.

113. Philostr. *VS* 597 (trans. W. C. Wright, Loeb edition). See the convenient summary in the glossary of rhetorical terms in W. C. Wright's Loeb edition, p. 570; cf. too de Blois 1986, 282–83.

114. *VS* 519, 597, 609.

115. *VS* 561.

116. On the circumstances of Herodes' speech, see G. W. Bowersock, *Greek Sophists in the Roman Empire* (Oxford 1969), 92–100.

117. Dagron 1968, 84 n. 2. It is interesting to note that at least one contemporary appreciated the element of criticism wrapped up in Themistius's flattery (Socr. *HE* 4.32), though unfortunately he chose an example that does not survive (Dagron 1968, 186–89). Socrates describes how the orator reproached Valens at Antioch for persecuting fellow Christians. The extant *Or.* 12 *ad Valentem de religionibus* (vol. iii, pp. 137–41, Downey-Norman) is acknowledged to be a modern forgery.

tive and win respect.[118] There is no reason to doubt that Pacatus was praising Theodosius in the passage just cited. But if he had been addressing, say, the young Valentinian II, it would have been legitimate to suspect discreet criticism.[119]

Synesius knew Themistius intimately, not to mention countless lesser panegyrists now forgotten. He was thoroughly familiar with all these devices. In *De providentia*, for example, he palliates the sting of the discreet warnings Osiris ignores to his cost, by detaching the advice from the events and setting it within the metaphysical discourse of his father. The eventual disaster is foreshadowed; but at the same time Osiris's overall moral superiority is affirmed through a friendly voice. It was not through either incompetence or boldness that Synesius neglected these obvious devices in *De regno*. It was because Arcadius was not really his addressee at all. He uses the form of an imperial address simply as a device to address a different audience, appealing to their common hostility to Arcadius's current ministers.

The only straightforward appeal in the speech is that on behalf of cities. Its one complexity is that listeners are meant to understand themselves in Arcadius's place. It is they who are meant to carry through Synesius's principles of good government, they who can expect his gratitude when they do. As in Synesius's appeal to Paeonius, kingship motifs are applied to lesser magnates.

Synesius does not introduce Cyrene, her crown, and her needs (the central themes of an ordinary *presbeutikos logos*) until after the groundwork of his Cynic pose has been laid. Her need must make her bold of speech. This privilege he had already claimed for philosophy; if Arcadius takes to heart the philosophy with which Cyrene sends Synesius to crown his soul, he will restore her to her ancient glory, and Synesius will gladly "bring a second crown from my great and then happy city" (2C–3B). The thought that philosophy encourages Arcadius to support cities underlies Synesius's whole theoretical *peri basileias*. He should follow the perfect model of God in his beneficence, "flooding the cities with all good things and pouring as much happiness as possible on every subject" (9C). The great hint of the *De dono*, "no greater misfortune could possibly befall cities than that the powerful be senseless and the wise without power" (309B–C), is recalled verbally in the interplay of compounds of $\phi\rho\dot{\eta}\nu$ and $\nuο\hat{\upsilon}\varsigma$, $\dot{\iota}\sigma\chi\dot{\upsilon}\varsigma$ and other expressions of capacity, in Synesius's ecphrasis of the Egyptian Hermes and Sphinx at *De*

118. Cameron 1985b, chap. 9, p. 12.
119. See Ambrose *Ep.* 20.28 for the arrogance of Valentinian's chamberlain Calligonus.

regno 7B–C: he claims that both figures were designed to symbolize the need to unite judgment and power. Similarly, the *De dono*'s "greatest misfortune" is realized in Synesius's description of Arcadius's life under Eutropius's domination at *De regno* 15A–B. Neither of these passages expressly relates its ideas to cities, but the connection must have been present in Synesius's mind and would have occurred to anyone who had also seen *De dono*. Similar situations in the letters make it a fair inference that Paeonius would have shown the essay around when he began to introduce Synesius to a new circle of patrons in Constantinople.[120]

Embassies are of great value to the king, Synesius insists, because they extend his knowledge over the whole of his realm. He should therefore be especially gracious toward embassies and their requests (27A–B). He had already assigned the same function to the king's friends (11D–12A), and the fact that he does not identify ambassadors and the king's friends is further confirmation that he is addressing this group rather than Arcadius himself. The ambassador should be favored but remains deferential to those he waits upon.

As ambassador, Synesius urges several points in general terms without explaining their specific relevance to Cyrene; he did not want to banalize his speech with tedious specifics he could give later if his audience had any questions. First, the provisioning of soldiers should not overburden the cities they are supposed to be protecting (27B–D).[121] Second, cities should not be heavily taxed and indeed should be released from unavoidable shortfalls (27D–28A). The benefits received by the rustic philosopher in *De providentia* confirm Synesius's interest specifically here (113B). Third, since in so large an empire the king cannot rule all directly, he must take particular care to select governors who will administer the provinces justly. In general, honor should be paid to virtue rather than to wealth (29D–31C). Synesius's later troubles as bishop with the unjust governor Andronicus confirm at least the general relevance of this point.[122]

In conclusion, Synesius calls his audience to the love of philosophy once more and promises his gratitude when he has occasion to speak again on behalf of cities. This combination of themes has overarched the

120. E.g., *Ep.* 1, 74, 154 involving Synesius's own works; 99 on Theotimus; 101 on Pylaemenes' letters and the "Panhellenion."

121. *Ep.* 95 shows an ongoing concern with related troubles: see Liebeschuetz 1985b. He argues persuasively that the letter was written while Synesius was trying to avoid consecration as bishop, rather than concerning Synesius's own embassy, its traditional association.

122. *Ep.* 57 (= 41 G), 58 (= 42 G), 72, 73, 79; *PLRE* II.89–90; cf. also *De providentia* 111D.

whole speech. The needs of the city form its fundamental theme, and the dictates of philosophy Synesius's basic model for addressing them. He attacks the court and Eutropius's barbarian policy to engage his audience's sympathy. The attacks contain much important material for the historian; and it is no less important that for Synesius they were like the astrological protreptics of *De dono*, edifying in themselves but principally deployed to serve a practical end. His search for the patronage he required brought him into contact with men who soon became the highest officials of the day. Synesius himself never lost sight of his basic goal.[123]

123. We are thus in sharp disagreement with Roques, who claims that "dans l'ensemble du *Discours* Synésios se présente comme le porte-parole de la philosophie. De soucis matériels il n'est nullement question; . . . il s'agit d'un traité sur la *Royauté*, non d'un plaidoyer pour Cyrène" (1987, 30).

FIVE

DE PROVIDENTIA AND THE MINISTERS OF ARCADIUS

I. INTRODUCTION

The two books of *De providentia* were originally published separately. But Synesius later republished them together, with a brief preface explaining the history of composition and announcing that the story also incorporates a "history of contemporary events" (88B). Some events can be recognized easily: for example, the massacre of "Scythians" by the citizens of "Thebes" that opens book 2 must be the massacre of the Goths in Constantinople on 12 July 400. The unsuccessful war the Egyptians are fighting against a rebel represents Tribigild's revolt in Phrygia. The return of the good brother from exile during his "eponymous year" (124A) unmistakably identifies him as Aurelian, cos. 400, who did indeed return from exile before the year was over.

Nonetheless, it is far too optimistic to declare with Dagron that "ce récit à clés se laisse aisèment traduire; il est une source excellente pour l'histoire des événements."[1] For as Synesius also announces, the tale has been elaborated throughout with a view to philosophical and ethical edification. It pauses often for disquisition. Characters are illustrated by much that is pure fantasy. The basic myth is adapted freely. Characters for whom Synesius found no historical correspondent he dropped, most strikingly Isis, in Greco-Roman tradition really the central figure of the

1. Dagron 1969, 30.

myth. On the other hand he added characters like the old king in book 1 and the great priest in book 2, who have no foundation in the myth but serve his contemporary purposes. Historical events were subject to editing too. For example, Synesius makes no suggestion that the administration and fall of Eutropius were background to his central events, which he approaches not even from the myth but from an entirely fictional setting. And the history he does include is distorted by prejudice and wishful thinking.

The generic designation Synesius originally applied to the work is *mythos*, fictional narrative (89A).[2] This label sets up expectations much vaguer than, say, those of a formal invective like Claudian's *In Rufinum*. Historians have a clear warning at least to question the enormities Claudian heaps on Rufinus's head, in particular (to take only one example highly relevant to Synesius) his constantly reiterated charge that Rufinus was forever plotting to betray the empire to barbarians.[3] Still less do we believe that Stilicho possessed all the virtues with which Claudian credits him. But, in fact, the scope of distortion available to fiction is no less broad and, since its intent is not as plainly marked, far more seductive. Synesius is generally believed when he accuses Typhos of the same vices and credits Osiris with the same virtues. Nor do the incidents with which he supports his ethical judgments receive due scrutiny. For example, although the royal election in book 1 is too fantastic to win credence, no one has doubted the historicity of the only marginally less fantastic trial of Typhos in book 2. In both cases Synesius's purpose was to illustrate what he wanted to imply was popular opinion. Such inventions go well beyond the simple operation of bias that leads Synesius to downplay or ignore good qualities in his Typhos and bad in his Osiris and to overemphasize, respectively, their crimes and virtues.

In short, *De providentia* produces a far more distorted picture of Arcadian court politics than has so far been appreciated. More surprisingly, Synesius has even managed to persuade his modern readers, though scarcely his contemporaries, that the wrong man won! We must not let his conviction that Osiris *ought* to have won blind us to the clear evidence that he lost.

II. SUMMARY

Historians only interested in the politics of the year 400 are frustrated and puzzled by the long stretches of fantasy and philosophy in *De*

2. Cf. p. 81.
3. See Demougeot 1950, 185f.; Cameron 1970a, 71f.

providentia. But ignoring them leads to unfortunate results. For example, those who praise Synesius for his sober reporting may be surprised and disturbed to see how large a role gods and demons play in the passages they skip. Chapter 9 provides a complete annotated translation. But it may be helpful at this stage, as with *De regno,* to offer a fairly close summary. It shows at once how little of the work comes even close to being a straightforward roman à clef. To be sure, Synesius was not writing a serious speculative treatise on Providence. But neither was he a reporter. His primary purpose was not to record the crisis of 400, which he could naturally assume to be only too familiar to his readers, but to offer a philosophical interpretation of it that would support a particular partisan view. He exploited only such events as suited his thesis. Similarly it was not out of mere perversity or self-protection that he gave his protagonists mythical names. Rather, in using the outline of the myth of Osiris to give a tendentious view of contemporary politics, Synesius also ended up creating an imaginative reinterpretation of the myth. It in turn circumscribed his treatment of historical facts.

Book I

89   This is an Egyptian story, which means it may also be something more profound.

90   Typhos and Osiris were brothers, but their souls were wholly unrelated. Osiris, the younger, was a divine soul, as he showed from earliest childhood in his eagerness to learn, good manners, modesty, and generosity. The elder, Typhos, despised all learning,

91   rejected all discipline, and enjoyed petty delinquency. He felt no affection for anything but only hated his brother.

92   As they grew, Osiris showed precocious military ability while still too young to serve. He rose through successive high offices, adding honor to each by his tenure. Typhos's character was tested in a few minor posts: he disgraced himself criminally at every turn. He was depraved in his private life and in his public administration

93   ferocious, insane, and abruptly derelict.

94   When the time came for their father to join the greater gods, all Egypt gathered according to law to elect his successor as king. Only swineherds and foreigners were banned, as unfit; they were also the only people in Egypt who would support Typhos. The Egyp-

95   tian election is carefully elaborated to give the greatest authority to the priests and a lesser to the native soldiery. It also accommodates divine intervention in ambiguous contests. But now every vote and every god was on Osiris's side immediately. Typhos tried

to corrupt the election but succeeded only in humiliating himself.

96   The people received Osiris with joy. His father and the gods initiated him into the mysteries of kingship and warned him
97   against Typhos, who lived only to bring disaster upon Osiris and all Egypt. Osiris affirmed that the gods could protect all things and set all things right. His father explained that though they could, it
98   is not proper for them to be so involved with the demon-infested world of perishable matter. They impart a first motion to the world but then return to contemplation until the impulse runs down.
99   Their Providence operates through divine souls sent into the world. Such souls must protect themselves against the demons of
100   matter. First the demons will attack the heavenly soul through the
101   passions; but if they cannot conquer it, they will fight to uproot it lest its survival in their dominion mock them. Therefore the ruling power must be both wise and strong. It has the power to preserve
102   itself and should not trouble the gods.

Osiris's father repeated the gods' warning and departed with
103   them. Osiris inaugurated a reign of peace and prosperity. He honored virtue and for its sake, education, and gave to every commu-
104   nity and individual what he needed. Everyone was happy. But Osiris could not bring himself to eliminate Typhos. He vainly hoped that his own excess of virtue would transform him.

105   Typhos was miserable in defeat and miserable in the happiness of the kingdom. His wife, a whorish virago with whom he was infatuated, was disappointed in her hope of prostituting the government on a larger scale than before. Osiris's wife in contrast was so good and modest that only the rare sight of their son Horus proved
106   to the world that she existed. For Osiris realized that happiness depends on inner virtue, not on the outward panoply of Fortune.

107   Typhos sank into childish despair, even making himself sick for many months—and aroused no sympathy. Finally his wife rescued him through baser passions, distracting him with orgies. The
108   demons of matter fastened on them and showed their way to a coup that would destroy the good order Egypt was enjoying, the ruin of the demons' plans.

The Egyptians employed foreign mercenaries, who were fighting a sham war on the Egyptians' behalf against a part of their own people that had rebelled. Typhos's wife persuaded the wife of the
109   foreign general that Osiris was planning to depose the general, murder their children, and eliminate the Scythians from Egypt. If the Scythians would support Typhos in a coup, he would let them

110   exploit all Egypt as they chose. The women sowed suspicions in the general and finally arranged a meeting where Typhos repeated his wife's promises, even offering up Thebes for destruction. The general refused, however, and insisted he acted only to defend himself against Osiris. Everything else must be harmed as little as possible.

111   Osiris surrendered to avert universal destruction. Typhos demanded that he be killed at once, but the barbarians respected his virtue and chose only to exile him. Osiris thus was removed from the country in its darkest hour. Typhos sought the misery of the people by every administrative abuse possible, multiplying taxes
112   and encouraging extortionate governors, reversing all Osiris's just judgments and revoking his benefactions. Relief could only be obtained by pandering to Typhos's wife, toadying to his friends, or slandering Osiris.

113   A certain rustic philosopher, also an orator and poet, was among those whom Osiris had benefited. Modesty and fear of seeming to flatter had kept him from publicly thanking Osiris
114   while he reigned, but now nothing could prevent him from venting his outrage against Typhos. Typhos in response behaved worse. But a god appeared to the philosopher and told him that only months of misery and tyranny remained. The barbarians would soon be driven out, and though Typhos would remain for a while, then water and fire would purify the air of the breath of the god-
115   less, Typhos would be deposed, and a new reign would follow. The philosopher marveled. But soon he recognized one of the god's signs in an impiety Typhos proposed, and he turned to hope for better days.

116   *Book II*

117   Then the gods' attention began to make itself known. The barbarians held the city at their mercy, in human terms, but began to be frenzied at some irrational fear. They stole away from the city with their families and valued possessions. The Egyptians despaired all the more. But the gods restored their spirits and brought them to save themselves.

118   An elderly beggarwoman by the city gates alone had courage to rebuke the escaping Scythians for their ingratitude and warn that the gods would avenge the destruction they obviously intended. A Scythian sprang to cut her down but was met by a god.

119 General fighting broke out. The Scythians were separated inside
120 and outside the gates, and the Egyptians determined at least to die
with glory. Only at the gates was it apparent how weak they really
were; but before the Scythians could regroup, the Egyptians triumphed. Truly, the will of god is invincible!

121 The Egyptians triumphed at the gates, then turned to smoke
out the aliens still within the city. Typhos wanted to negotiate with
the enemy and readmit their army, but the leaderless people with-
stood him by the power of god. His tyranny was virtually broken.

The people met in the presence of the great priest. They
122 offered thanks and prayers and demanded the return of Osiris. Typhos they resolved to beguile for the present. He behaved even
more abominably in his now hollow tyranny, still trying to woo
back the retreating barbarians.

At last he destroyed all his support, and the gods and elders
123 sat in judgment over him. His own partisans brought evidence
of his treachery. The human jurors voted for his arrest and a second trial to sentence him; the gods commended their verdict and
damned him in the afterlife.

Osiris had profited from exile, spending it in contemplation.
124 He returned to joyful festivals and a year named after him. He
spared his brother again, as ever more merciful than just.

So much may be said about Osiris; it would be profanation to
disclose more. We can just hint that his glory increased with his
years, that the gods vindicated him in the face of human injury,
and that he restored and improved the prosperity he had earlier
given the Egyptians, and which Typhos had destroyed. It was a
125 golden age, as when Justice dwelt with men. If the gods did not
restore his rule at once, it was only because good cannot be
wrought instantly, like evil. It must be prepared for. And there
was much Osiris needed to see and hear before kingship preoccu-
pied him.

But we must not stray onto ineffable mysteries. It remains to
be investigated how good and evil appear in such close proximity.
126 Philosophy would answer that the god must balance good and evil
in a family, so if one child is purely good or evil, the next will be the
opposite.

127 Another remarkable thing is the way patterns of events recur in
different times and places. The cosmos is interconnected and inter-
dependent in all its parts: thus the blessed body that moves in a
circle causes the events of this world. As its movements recur, so

128 do the events. And so men will seek through ancient stories for
hints of what will be. But it is not for me to unravel these mysteries

129 prematurely. That would be impious. All will be made plain in the
fullness of time.

III. COLLEGIATE PREFECTURES

In the first half of book 1 Typhos and Osiris are rival candidates for
the kingship of Egypt. Osiris wins, legitimated by an elaborate and
purely fictional voting system. Typhos schemes with the "leader of the
foreign troops" in Egypt, manifestly corresponding to Gaïnas, to overthrow his brother. He at once becomes king of Egypt in turn. Aurelian,
who was exiled and then returned from exile in the year of his own consulate, must be Osiris. The kingship of Egypt evidently represents an
office that changed hands during the troubles of 399–400, being held
first by Aurelian. Sievers correctly identified it over a hundred years ago
as the praetorian prefecture of the East, or at any rate the prefecture of
the East after the fall of Eutropius had restored it to its former power.[4]
Accordingly, since Synesius makes it clear that Typhos succeeded Osiris,
the prefect who succeeded Aurelian must be Typhos. All we need to do
is establish the sequence of prefects of the East from the fall of Rufinus
in 395 to the appointment of Anthemius in 405.

Unfortunately, this is "one of the most intricate chronological and
prosopographical conundrums that the compilers of the *Theodosian Code*
have bequeathed to modern scholarship."[5] Two names come into question, Caesarius and Eutychian, both of whom held the prefecture of
Oriens at least twice during this period. The evidence is almost exclusively limited to the dates of laws addressed to them in the Code, and
the problem centers on how to deal with the unusually large number of
conflicts and overlaps between these dates.

Seeck's solution was to accept the overlaps by positing a collegiate
prefecture, with Eutychian in office continuously from 396–405, and
Caesarius (395–98 and 400–401) and Aurelian (399–400 and 402–5?) as
his colleagues in turn.[6] A characteristically trenchant article of A. H. M.
Jones showed that collegiate prefectures were an entirely unnecessary
postulate.[7] But Jones simply set out the sources that supported his con-

---

4. Sievers 1870, 388. Of course the election bears no relationship to the direct appointment of prefects by the emperor.

5. Barnes 1986a, 97.

6. This thesis was more fully developed in his 1914 article, pp. 1–12.

7. Jones 1964b, 78–89 (= 1974, 375–95).

clusion, without discussing the views of Seeck and his followers. As a consequence, R. von Haehling, M. Clauss, and G. Albert have recently revived Seeck's thesis, albeit in a somewhat modified form.[8] All three reject the incredible ten-year prefecture Seeck assigned to Eutychian, but still keep Caesarius and Eutychian as joint prefects from at least 396–98, and Eutychian and Aurelian as joint prefects at the end of 399. For all three, the noncollegiate prefecture started in 400.

Since the postulate of collegiate prefectures allows even the soberest scholars to play fast and loose with the evidence, it is essential to preface any discussion of the complex and controversial issue of the Eastern prefecture between 395 and 416 with a discussion of collegiate prefectures.

Believers in collegiate prefectures have always been curiously intolerant toward unbelievers. For example, in the course of a polemic against T. Mommsen, who had vigorously repudiated collegiate prefectures, Seeck wrote scornfully of Mommsen's "theory of a unified prefecture."[9] Clauss too wrote of the case against as a "thesis," repeating E. Stein's criticism of J.-R. Palanque's "phobia" concerning collegiate prefectures.[10] For Albert, a collegiate prefecture at least up to the fall of Eutropius was "certain."[11]

The truth is that the *onus probandi* lies on the believers. The one and only documented collegiate prefecture is the one shared by Ausonius and his son Hesperius in 378–79. This was obviously an exceptional case, the purpose presumably being to honor the father but let the son do the work.[12] It cannot provide a model or parallel for any of the other collegiate prefectures postulated in modern times. For there is a fundamental respect in which it differs from them. According to Seeck, the point of dividing the prefecture was to divide its power; the two prefects were intended as checks on each other. But this was clearly not why Gratian shared power between Ausonius and his son. Collegiate prefectures as Seeck conceived them are an entirely modern creation, with no ancient support or analogy. They are no more than one of several different ways of dealing with that most tiresome of prosopographical problems, conflict of date and office in the subscriptions to imperial laws. The normal way of dealing with such conflicts is to identify the element

8. Von Haehling 1978, 74–78; Clauss 1980, 133–36; Albert 1984, 183–95.
9. Mommsen 1910, 284–302; Seeck 1914, 9. When discussing a particular case later in the article, Seeck dismisses Mommsen's solution (accepted now by Jones 1974, 380) as contrived, "seine Theorie zu Liebe" (21).
10. Clauss 1980, 134; cf. E. Stein, *Byzantion* 9 (1934): 340.
11. Albert 1984, 186.
12. Jones 1974, 375.

of the date that is in error and attempt to correct it.[13] But there are so many more such conflicts in the case of PPOs that an additional explanation was felt necessary: hence Seeck's collegiate prefectures.[14]

There are indeed more clashes in the case of PPOs, but there are simple and obvious reasons. In the first place, there survive far more laws addressed to PPOs than to any other officials. For this in turn there are a variety of reasons. The great majority of imperial laws are addressed to praetorian prefects.[15] At any given moment there were at least three, and often four, separate PPOs. And individual PPOs tended to stay in office longer than most other officials. As a consequence, prefects like Caesarius and Eutychian who held office for many years on at least two separate occasions were the recipients of large numbers of laws spanning many years.

Anyone who has worked at all closely with the subscriptions to imperial laws (as distinct from merely checking in cases of conflict) knows that the percentage of error is very high in all three elements—day, month, and especially year.[16] Conservative critics insist that a date should be corrected only as a last resort, when it is demonstrably false. Correction to another specific date is admittedly a speculative procedure. But it is perfectly legitimate to call a transmitted date into question without proposing a specific correction. All who work in this area depend on the massive and subtle classification of errors that makes up the greater part of the preface to Seeck's *Regesten* (1919). But invaluable though it remains, his work has fostered the notion that there are relatively few, easily identified sources of error. To many false dates none of his solutions can plausibly be applied: yet there is manifestly an error somewhere.

The great majority of officeholders addressed in imperial laws are attested by only one or two laws. And in most cases we know the names of so few holders of individual offices that we cannot begin to draw up *fasti*. So in most cases the question of conflict and overlap never arises. But this does not mean that most laws are dated correctly, merely that

13. The different sorts of error were catalogued and illustrated at length in the preface to Seeck 1919. For one that he systematically misused (postulating false postconsulates), see *CLRE*, chap. 7.

14. But he did not invent them. The credit apparently belongs to Tillemont: Mommsen 1910, 290 n. 1.

15. As Seeck observed (1919, 141).

16. For a recent survey, see *CLRE*, chap. 7. Seeck argued that the incidence of error was less nearer the date of the Code itself (438); though the presumption is reasonable and no doubt generally valid, the conclusion was in part based on his recourse to collegiate prefectures for the later period rather than emendation.

there is no way of checking them. For example, the date of the only law in more than two centuries addressed to a *corrector* of Paphlagonia is registered in all the handbooks without any note of query or doubt.[17] It may indeed be correct. But we should not be surprised if a new inscription or papyrus were to prove one (or all) of its three elements wrong. With no other evidence to confute or confirm, perforce we take it on trust.

In the case of the Eastern prefecture between 395 and 405, by contrast, we have many scores of laws and know the name of every prefect. It is not surprising that there are more conflicts here than in almost any other time or place.

There is also another factor to be taken into account. All the prefects in office at any given moment (the prefects of Oriens, Italy, the Gauls, and Illyricum) formed a college. In that sense the regional prefecture had always been a collegiate office. Whenever any individual member of the college issued an edict, it bore the names of the entire college.[18] During the fourth and early fifth centuries prefects were listed in order of seniority; after ca. 420 the local prefect was named first.[19] Even dedications by prefects were made in the names of the entire college: a recently published statue base from Antioch bearing the names of all five prefects in office in 336 is a pair to a similar, but mutilated, base from Tubernuc in Africa proconsularis.[20] Another Constantinian edict from the college of prefects found at Delphi awaits publication. Evidently each base was dedicated by a different member of the college in the absence of the rest. A few extant imperial edicts are addressed to all current prefects as a college,[21] though normally the Codes only preserve the copies received

17. *Cod. Theod.* 8.2.22, to Heraclianus, dated to 3 July 395; cf. Seeck 1919, 287; *PLRE* I.417.

18. T. Mommsen, *Ges. Schriften* 6 (1910): 285; W. Enßlin, *RE* 22.2 (1954): 2430; A. H. M. Jones, *LRE*, vol. 3 (1964): 61 n. 10; A. Chastagnol, *REA* 70 (1968), 323f.; D. Feissel, *Travaux et mémoires* 9 (1985): 427–33; and 11 (1991): 437–64.

19. See Feissel 1991 for the change. We infer the date from the fact that it was in 421 that a similar change took place in the listing of the consuls. Up till then the first named consul was senior to his colleague throughout Roman territory; from 421 the Eastern consul was named first in the East and the Western in the West (*CLRE* 22). The earliest dated example of the new sequence for a prefectorial edict is 439–42.

20. Feissel 1985, 421–34. The African stone (*ILT* 814) was recently discussed by T. D. Barnes (*The New Empire of Diocletian and Constantine* [1982], 134–36), unfortunately in ignorance of the parallel but undamaged dedication from Antioch. Ch. Vogler (*Constance II et l'administration impériale* [Strasbourg 1979], 130–32) had the quaint idea that these joint dedications were the outcome of periodical "summit conferences" of the college of prefects. See too A. Chastagnol, *L'Africa romana: Atti del III convegno di studio, Sassari, 13–15 dicembre 1985*, ed. A. Mastino (1987), 263–73.

21. See *Cod.Theod.* 6.27.1 and the nine other fragments of the same law quoted in Mommsen's note ad loc.; cf. too Seeck 1919, 177; and P. Maas, *Kl.Schriften* (1973), 621–22.

by individual prefects.[22] We may probably assume that this was standard practice. Right down to the sixth century, when Italy was an Ostrogothic kingdom, Eastern prefects continued to include the name of the prefect of Italy in the headings of their edicts.[23] More surprisingly, individual prefects are often referred to in plural terminology (e.g., οἱ ἔπαρχοι) in documents where only one of the college can be meant.[24]

What Seeck and his followers ask us to believe is that each individual member of the college might himself be a college. But the prefecture of the East was the highest office of state, the top of the administrative pyramid; the prefect has often been compared to a grand vizier or prime minister. How could such an office be divided? And why? Even Seeck never attempted to offer any overall explanation of this remarkable and surely unworkable division of powers. But he did suggest a reason in the case that concerns us here, the Eastern prefecture after the fall of Rufinus:[25] Eutropius divided what he saw as the excessive power accumulated by Rufinus in order to weaken possible rivals. It should be noted at once that this explanation cannot plausibly be alleged in any of the other cases where Seeck postulated collegiate prefectures. Nor does it really work even here.

The notion might seem superficially attractive in the light of the frequent division of the prefecture in the first three centuries. But that was an entirely different matter. The commander of the praetorian guard was as well placed to eliminate as to protect his master, and from the days of Sejanus on, many an emperor found reason to fear his PPO. Under these circumstances it made sense to divide the command.[26] But the situation was different once the prefect lost his military powers. It is hardly coincidental that in the four centuries between Diocletian and the disappearance of the prefecture in 680, there is not a single case of a PPO rebelling against his emperor. In fact it is doubtful if it was ever even tried.[27]

Seeck's theory makes some sort of sense as an attempt to deal with

22. Normally for information only, since imperial laws were not automatically valid in all parts of the empire. But occasionally a prefect of, say, Italy might wish to issue a law of his Eastern colleague in his own domains. This would explain why we find copies of laws of the Eastern prefects of 384 and 396 displayed at Rhegium (*Cod.Theod.* 3.1.5, 15.1.35).

23. E.g., *ACO* I.i.iii, p. 69 = I.iii, p. 38 (435); *Ann. Epigr.* 1961, n. 190 (ca. 440, from Ephesus); Just. *Nov.* 166.

24. For examples, see below, p. 155 and notes.

25. Seeck 1914, 13.

26. In addition, often one of the prefects was a lawyer and the other a soldier, a division of expertise that could not arise in the late empire.

27. There is only the dubious claim that Rufinus had been planning to seize power when he was murdered: see Cameron 1970a, 90.

the evidence of the Code. But it makes none at all when applied to Synesius. For if Seeck were right, then the kingship of Egypt should have been collegiate. Typhos and Osiris could both have been king simultaneously. Naturally this would make nonsense of the fierce rivalry depicted in the myth. It would also be odd for Philostorgius to have described Caesarius at an earlier date as "succeeding to the office of Rufinus" if he had been only one of two successors.[28]

Seeck attempted to get round these problems by alleging that the kingship of Egypt denoted not simply the prefecture, but the prefecture combined with the regency. A more recent study reverses the emphasis: the kingship represents the regency combined with the prefecture.[29] The other prefect—for Seeck, Eutychian—was "politically speaking altogether colorless."[30] But the Romans made no provisions for a formal regency.[31] And while there may have been some justification for Stilicho claiming to exercise an informal regency for the ten-year-old Honorius in 395 or Anthemius for the seven-year-old Theodosius in 408, there cannot have been any such formal arrangement attached to a specific office,[32] as Seeck suggested for the twenty-two-year-old Arcadius in 399. The kingship of Egypt represents the prefecture of the East plain and simple.

It is amusing to trace the parroting of Seeck's unhappy characterization of Eutychian down the decades: "un technicien de l'administration sans couleur politique"; "a colorless personality"; "inoffensive."[33] But if Eutychian really had been a colorless collaborator with Eutropius, how did he survive Eutropius's fall? On the other hand, how could a man who, if Seeck were right, held the highest office of state for an entire decade while colleagues came and went have been politically unimportant?

Mommsen reasonably observed that if, as Seeck argued, collegiate prefectures had been a regular occurrence, with all their potential for conflict we should have expected some indication somewhere in our sources. In his later article Seeck tried to show that there was in fact literary evidence for collegiate prefects, citing two texts referring to prefects of Oriens in the plural.[34]

There are in fact dozens of such texts, but they have nothing to do with collegiate prefects. They are simply collective references to the college. For example, papyri of 368 and 388 refer to "the most splendid pre-

28. *HE* 11.5.
29. Clauss 1980, 134.
30. "Politisch ganz farblos" (Seeck 1894, 452).
31. Mommsen 1906, 516f.
32. Any such formal attachment is rendered less likely still by the fact that Aurelian's predecessor as "regent" was a eunuch chamberlain, Honorius's "regent" a *magister militum*.
33. Stein 1959, 230; von Haehling 1978, 78; Demougeot 1951, 244.
34. Seeck 1914, 13–14.

fects" where the reference has to be to the prefect of the East alone.[35] An inscription from Beroia in Macedonia refers again to "the most splendid prefects" where only the prefect of Illyricum must be meant.[36] An inscription from Jerusalem describes a man as kinsman of "Areobindus the prefects (τῶν ὑπάρχων),"[37] a phrase strikingly paralleled by a passage in the *Miracula S. Demetrii*, ἀνήρ . . . τῶν τηνικαῦτα τοῦ Ἰλλυρικοῦ ἐπάρχων συγγενής.[38] Honorific epigrams refer to *vicarii* sitting on "the judgment seats of prefects."[39] Cassiodorus too refers to a vicar as "functus . . . vicibus praefectorum,"[40] and the *Miracula S. Demetrii* provide a parallel again.[41] Justinian's *Novel* 8 is addressed to John the Cappadocian, undoubtedly sole prefect of the East in 535. Yet a *notitia* appended to this law describes it as "lex quam ad gloriosissimos nostros praefectos scripsimus,"[42] and the *notitia* itself refers several dozen times to "the office of the most glorious prefects" (τῇ τάξει τῶν ἐνδοξοτάτων ἐπάρχων), a formula that occurs often elsewhere.[43] A particularly illuminating example is to be found in a description of an imperial procession of 559 preserved in the *Book of Ceremonies*,[44] recording the participation of "the office of the prefects [i.e., PPO] and the prefect [i.e., PVC]" (τάξις τῶν ἐπάρχων καὶ τοῦ ἐπάρχου). Since the procession took place in Constantinople, the reference must be to the staff of the Eastern prefect alone.

Most of these texts come from times (the sixth century) and places (Illyricum) where not even Seeck ventured to suggest the possibility of collegiate prefectures. The two texts he quoted from ca. 400 cannot bear much weight, especially since the first comes from Mark the Deacon's *Life of St. Porphyrius of Gaza* (54), which is now recognized to be a forgery of the sixth century or later.[45]

The second text is a passage in Palladius's *Dialogus de vita S. Iohannis Chrysostomi* where the followers of Chrysostom petition that some followers of Theophilus be investigated "before the prefects" in 403 (p. 43.12

---

35. *P.Lips.* 63.10, 64.11.

36. D. Feissel, *Receuil des inscriptions chrétiennes de Macédoine du IIIe au VIe siècle* (Paris 1983), no. 56; cf. no. 85, p. 85.

37. P. Thomsen, "Die lateinischen und griechischen Inschriften der Stadt Jerusalem und ihrer nächsten Umgebung," *Zeitschrift des Deutschen Palästina-Vereins* 44 (1921, rpt. 1972): 1–61, 90–169, with E. Stein, *Bas-Empire*, vol. 2 (1949), 215 n. 1 (from 214).

38. *PG* 116.1265A = p. 114.18 Lemerle (Paris 1979).

39. L. Robert, *Hellenica* 4 (1948): 46f.

40. Cassiod. *Var.* 9.7.2; cf. 6.15.1.

41. τοὺς τῶν ὑπάρχων θρόνους τοὺς κατὰ τὸ Ἰλλυριῶν ἔθνος, 1204A = p. 57.6–7 Lemerle.

42. *Nov.* 8, p. 80.15 Schoell-Kroll.

43. E.g., *Nov.* 22 *fin.*, 24 *fin.*, 25 *fin.*, 26 *fin.*, 27 *fin.*

44. *De caer.* 1.497.13–498.13 Bonn; for the date, Stein 1949, 818–19.

45. P. Peeters, *Analecta Bollandiana* 59 (1941): 65–100; R. MacMullen, *Christianizing the Roman Empire* (New Haven 1984), 86–89.

Coleman-Norton). It could be merely one more example of the collective plural referring to the college as a whole. But in this case there is another possibility. Palladius may have in mind the praetorian and the city prefects, who both held courts in Constantinople. Indeed, a law of the following year (*Cod. Theod.* 16.2.37) reveals the city prefect Studius presiding over an investigation into another accusation in the campaign against Chrysostom. But Palladius then describes how John was escorted to Cucusus by "soldiers of the prefect" (p. 63.19), where he presumably now means the PPO,[46] since three pages later he describes "soldiers of the praetorian prefect" escorting him from Cucusus to Pityus (p. 66.28). It seems clear that both the city and praetorian prefects were called on to play a part in the ecclesiastical battles of 403–4. Indeed Palladius elsewhere gives a list of the senior dignitaries in the city that begins with both: "Studius the prefect of the city, Eutychian of the praetorium" (p. 19.17). It is worth emphasizing that he does not repeat the word "prefect" before "praetorium"; there was clearly only one of each. According to Seeck, Eutychian held office continuously from February 396 to June 405 *with a colleague.*[47] When put together, these passages of Palladius prove beyond doubt that in 403–4 at any rate he was sole praetorian prefect.

The simplest and clearest way to present the legal evidence for the prefects of 395–405 is by means of a table. Dates that on any hypothesis must be false are bracketed (thus); dates that must be false if collegiate prefectures are excluded are bracketed [thus].

YEAR	EUTYCHIAN	AURELIAN	CAESARIUS
395			(24 June: 16.5.27)
			30 Nov.: 10.6.1
			29 Dec.: 12.1.150
396	[24 Feb.: 3.30.5]		13 Feb.: 9.42.14
			14 Feb.: 6.25.7
			27 Feb.: 6.27.10
			23 Mar.: 16.7.6
			24 Mar.: 15.1.34
			17 Apr.: 7.4.21
			21 Apr.: 16.5.31–2
			25 Apr.: 15.6.1

---

46. Though H. Moore (1921) 89 n. 3 assumes that it is Optatus, Studius's successor as PVC and a known persecutor of the Johannites. But the authority of the PVC was limited to the city and environs.

47. Seeck 1914, 13–14; 1919, 475.

YEAR	EUTYCHIAN	AURELIAN	CAESARIUS
396 (*continued*)			
			9 May: 8.17.1
			3 Aug.: 9.1.18
			+9.42.15
			12 Aug.: 6.3.2
		(6 Oct.: 4.2.1	31 Aug.: 9.38.9
	[8 Dec.: 3.12.3]	5.1.5)	7 Dec.: 16.10.4
	[15 Dec.: 12.18.2]		
	[31 Dec.: 6.4.30]		
397	[19 Feb.: 13.2.1]		16 Feb.: 9.26.1
	[1 Apr.: 16.5.33]		6 Mar.: 11.18.1
			8 Apr.: 6.26.9
			29 Apr.: 6.2.19
			23 June: 6.26.10
			1 July: 16.8.13
			13 July: 8.15.8
	4 Sept.: 6.3.4		
	+9.14.3		
	8 Nov.: 9.6.3		
	23 Nov.: 2.33.3		
	3 Feb.: 2.1.10		
398	4 Mar.: 16.5.34		
	7 Mar.: 13.11.9		
	23 May: 7.4.25		
	3 July: 15.1.38		
	6 July: *CJ* 11.62.9		
	27 July: 9.40.16		
	+9.45.3		[26 July: 16.2.32]
	+11.30.57		
	+16.2.33		
	+*CJ* 1.4.7		
	25 Oct.: 12.1.159		
	6 Dec.: 1.2.11		
	13 Dec.: 15.1.4		
399	10 Mar.: 11.24.4	(17 Jan.: 9.40.17)	
	14 Mar.: 13.7.1		
	10 Apr.: *CJ* 11.62.10		
	25 May: 11.24.5		
	6 July: 16.5.36		
	10 July: 16.10.16		

YEAR	EUTYCHIAN	AURELIAN	CAESARIUS
399 (*continued*)			
	25 July: 9.40.18		
		27 Aug.: 2.8.23	
		2 Oct.: 15.6.2	
	[11 Dec.: 12.1.163]		
	[28 Dec.: 12.1.164]		
	[30 Dec.: 12.1.165]		
400			8 Dec.: 1.34.1
401			3 Feb.: 8.5.62
402			
403			11 June: *CJ* 7.41.2
	3 Feb.: 16.8.15		
404	14 July: 15.1.42		
	18 Nov.: 16.4.6		
	11 June: *CJ* 5.4.19		
405			

If Caesarius and Eutychian were really prefects jointly from 396 to 399, why do almost all Caesarius's laws fall between November 395 and July 397 and Eutychian's between September 397 and July 399? Why did each get only one in 396 and 398 and Caesarius none at all in 399?[48] And if Eutychian was really prefect all the time from 395 to 405, why did he have no laws in 400–403? The distribution obviously supports the commonsense inference that they were prefects *successively* in 395–99. Contrary to Seeck's claim that there are very few erroneous dates in the Code as late as this, there are at least four in this table that even he admitted to be false. Caesarius cannot have been prefect as early as June 395 because his predecessor Rufinus did not die till 27 November; the two laws to Aurelian as prefect in October 396 must be in error (we cannot have three prefects in office!); as too Aurelian's law of January 399, since he did not assume office till Eutropius's fall in August (the law actually concerns Eutropius's *damnatio memoriae*).

It might seem drastic to postulate another seven or ten errors, but it is no less drastic to postulate a collegiate prefecture.[49] There are innum-

48. Caesarius's law of 398 seems to be an extract from the law addressed to Eutychian the following day.

49. So already Bury: "There are many errors in the dates of the laws . . . from 395–400. The solution certainly does not lie in Seeck's theory that Caesarius and Eutychian held the Pr. Prefecture conjointly in 396 and 397" ([1923] 1958, 132 n. 1).

erable other certain errors in the Code and many more we cannot check, but no other evidence of collegiate prefectures. Even Albert conceded that in general Jones had substantiated his claim that they were an "invention of modern scholars."[50] But he apparently did not realize how fatally this weakened the case for making the assumption here alone. If collegiate prefectures were an established phenomenon, this is a case where one might at any rate be considered. But the circumstances do not justify postulating an isolated instance.

In any case, less drastic measures may suffice. Jones proposed that Eutychian's six laws from February 396 to April 397 were addressed to him as prefect of Illyricum.[51] Another man is attested as prefect of Illyricum from June 397 to November 399, so there is plenty of room before then.[52] Yet though accepted by Barnes and Liebeschuetz,[53] this thesis cannot be accepted as formulated, since one at least, and perhaps two, of the laws in question concerns Constantinople. *Cod. Theod.* 6.4.30 of 31 December 396 deals with praetors assigned to the Theodosian aqueduct, and cannot therefore have been sent to the prefect of Illyricum.[54] And 16.5.33 of 1 April 397 commands "the teachers of the Apollinarians to withdraw with all haste from the habitations of Our Dear City." Coming from Arcadius, who had spent most of his life in Constantinople, these words must refer to Constantinople and so have been addressed to the prefect of Oriens. The dates of these two laws at any rate must be in error. But *P.Vindob.lat.* 31, evidently a prefectorial edict,[55] is contemporary evidence that the prefecture of 397–99 was Eutychian's second. All that survives of the heading is the following:

]anus II Fl. Vincentius Fl.[
]praesidi provinciae Arcadiae[

The name of the province Arcadia points to a date in or after 386 and the only fully preserved name is undoubtedly that of Vincentius, prefect of the Gauls from 18 December 397 to 9 December 400. Since at this period prefects were listed strictly according to the date of their appointment,[56] -anus II must have been appointed before 18 December 397. He cannot

50. Albert 1984, 184: "Das mag ihm in den meisten Fällen gelungen sein"; Jones 1974, 375.
51. Jones 1974, 380.
52. *PLRE* II.83, Anatolius 1.
53. Barnes 1986a, 98; Liebeschuetz 1987.
54. As a defense of last resort it might be argued that this is the *copy* sent to the prefect of Illyricum of a law addressed to the prefect of Oriens; see above for the practice of sending copies of laws to prefects to all members of the college.
55. As Feissel (1991) has confirmed.
56. See Feissel 1989.

therefore have been Aurelianus, not appointed till August 399. The name must be restored [Eutychi]anus (September 397–July 399), in which case the iteration number proves that he had already held a prefecture, doubtless the prefecture of Illyricum hypothesized by Jones.

The identity of the incumbents of the prefecture before Eutropius's fall might not seem very relevant to an investigation of *De providentia*. It was not till after his fall that the prefecture became, in Synesius's allegory, the kingship of Egypt. But there is one flaw in the postulate of a collegiate prefecture that is central to this inquiry. According to Seeck and now Clauss,[57] Caesarius was prefect jointly with Eutychian right up to the moment of Eutropius's fall. Then Aurelian took over, until Caesarius became prefect again (as Typhos) on Aurelian's fall in April 400.

But how can this be squared with *De providentia*? Admittedly, Synesius deliberately ignores the antecedents of Osiris/Aurelian's rule. There is no suggestion, for example, that he came to power at a moment of crisis. And if the prefecture did not become the kingship of Egypt till after Eutropius's fall, it was arguably irrelevant who had held it before then. But even so, if Caesarius had in fact been Aurelian's predecessor,[58] Synesius would surely have described the rivalry between the brothers in different terms.

Plutarch, his main source for the myth, told only of a plot concerted by Typhos (for Plutarch the younger, not the older brother) against an Osiris who was already king.[59] Synesius instead begins with the throne empty at the old king's death (in effect, the fall of Eutropius). He delineates an elaborate election system, which is rendered unnecessary by Osiris's manifest excellence and universal popularity. Typhos canvasses desperately for votes (95C–D) and is devastated by his failure (104C–105A). Synesius fabricated the whole thing. Since none of it makes sense at the mythical level, it should imply a genuine rivalry for power in historical reality. If the historical truth had been that Aurelian ousted Cae-

57. Clauss 1980, 150.

58. Following Mommsen, Bury ([1923] 1958, 128 n. 2) objects to the identification with Caesarius: "If Typhos is Caesarius, it ought to have been stated that he had already held the office of king [referring to his tenure of 395–97]." But an allegory is not to be pressed in this way; as noted above, it ignores the historical antecedents of Aurelian's prefecture of 399. And yet by what is presumably an oversight induced by the desire to make a point, at 105B, a passage obviously missed by Mommsen and Bury, Synesius lets slip that Typhos *had* previously been king: "Her husband's fall from the kingship (βασιλείας ἐκπεπτωκέναι) distressed [Typhos's wife] even more, because she had been planning to prostitute the government on a larger scale." Both ἐκπεπτωκέναι and the "larger scale" point to a previous tenure of the kingship rather than to his failure to win it in the election just described. But this is not an argument for Caesarius rather than Eutychian, since both had held the prefecture before Eutropius's fall.

59. *De Is. et Os.* 356Af.

sarius from the prefecture, Synesius could easily have adjusted his mythical version accordingly. Having made Typhos the older brother, presumably because Caesarius really was older than Aurelian, he had a ready-made explanation why Typhos might have become king first. He could then have presented the noble Osiris pitying the sufferings of the Egyptians under his wicked brother's rule and driving him from the throne. The rest could have followed much as it is now, Typhos being mercifully spared to plot his coup with the aid of the barbarians.

It is a delicate task to discern historical facts behind Synesius's often distorted allegory, but the consideration here adduced supports the natural implication of the table of prefects: that Eutychian alone was prefect up to the moment of Eutropius's fall. It was he whom Aurelian replaced.

IV. AURELIAN'S CONSULATE

Though few laws survive from the second half of 399, the table of prefects shows clearly enough Aurelian's assumption of power in August. Much less clear is the identity of his successor, Synesius's Typhos.

To anticipate our conclusion, we believe that Typhos is Caesarius. But according to the transmitted dates, Eutychian was prefect in December 399. For Seeck, Eutychian was merely Aurelian's colleague, as he had previously been Caesarius's colleague. But for nonbelievers the consequences are problematic. Jones boldly embraced them all. Not only did he make Eutychian Typhos. He moved both Gaïnas's coup and Aurelian's fall from April 400 to, at latest, the beginning of December 399. And his position has now been firmly restated by Liebeschuetz and R. Delmaire.[60]

If Gaïnas's coup did not take place till April 400, the new prefect cannot have been in office longer than three or four months by the time of the massacre on 11 July. According to Liebeschuetz, this is not long enough for all the wickedness Synesius attributes to Typhos up to that point. For example, referring to Typhos's unpopular new taxes (mentioned at 111C), Liebeschuetz suggests that "in view of the slowness of communication in the Roman Empire it would take something like three months at least for a new fiscal policy to be put into effect and to provide a response from the taxpayer." As if Synesius would wait to sound public opinion for a point of invective! New taxes are axiomatically un-

60. Liebeschuetz 1987, 419–31, and 1990, 253–72; Delmaire 1989, 115–18.

popular. They are a harsh imposition of a tyrant on his suffering people; and Synesius's purpose was to portray Typhos as a stock tyrant. And in any case, since Synesius specifies that the taxes are imposed on *cities*, there can be no doubt that once again it is the tax burden of Cyrene that principally concerns him. Liebeschuetz relies heavily on a very dubious combination of Synesius and Sozomen. In Synesius, the demand for an Arian church in Constantinople is made when Typhos had already been in power for some time. Since Sozomen places the comet of mid-March to mid-May after the affair of the church,[61] Liebeschuetz infers that Gaïnas had been in power for some time by mid-March. But Socrates, undoubtedly Sozomen's main source here, places the comet shortly before the massacre, as indeed does Synesius himself.

If (as argued below) the coup fell at the beginning of April 400, that allows Typhos more than three months before the massacre, ample time to do all that Synesius describes. On the other hand, if the coup fell as early as the beginning of December, that only leaves four months for Aurelian, an impossibly short tenure. It is true that the achievements credited to his administration by Synesius belong to the realm of panegyric rather than history and cannot be pinned down in real time. But he does happen to remark that Typhos fell ill for "several months" and nearly died—a source, he nastily adds, more of mirth than pity (107B). Since this illness has no point as a fiction, it is presumably fact. So we must reckon with a long and serious illness distracting Typhos from his wicked schemes during "several months" of Aurelian's prefecture.

More important is the series of long journeys that have to be fitted into the period between the fall of Eutropius and the fall of Aurelian. Eutropius was deposed ca. 1 August 399, following an ultimatum sent by Gaïnas from Phrygia: so Zosimus says explicitly (5.17.5). Eutropius was then sent in exile to Cyprus, a journey of some 800 miles. Before long he was recalled from Cyprus and executed under pressure from Gaïnas, presumably again through correspondence; which in turn implies an exchange of messengers between Constantinople and Phrygia. Then Gaïnas apparently returned to Constantinople in person, where he concluded an agreement with Arcadius in Tribigild's name. The fact that an exchange of oaths is mentioned implies a face-to-face meeting. Liebeschuetz alleges that Gaïnas concluded this treaty while in Constantinople for Eutropius's execution, which would obviate messengers to and from Phrygia, but this is neither stated nor permitted by our only narrative source, Zosimus (5.18). After the agreement with Arcadius Gaïnas went back to Phrygia again, presumably via Dorylaion,[62] accord-

---

61. For this comet, see below, p. 168.
62. W. M. Ramsay, *The Historical Geography of Asia Minor* (London 1890), 168.

ing to Zosimus joining forces with Tribigild at Thyatira to sack Sardis. We shall later see reason to doubt this concerted attack on Sardis,[63] allegedly thwarted by heavy rainfall that rendered "the rivers" impassable.[64] But the rain at least must be fact, though unfortunately it does not help to pin down the season. Most of the rain in western Anatolia falls between October and March, with the heaviest falls in December or January.[65] The floods mentioned by Zosimus could be made to fit either chronology. Gaïnas then marched again through the province of Asia to Constantinople, where he demanded the deposition of Aurelian. On Liebeschuetz's chronology, this could not have been later than 11 December, when Eutychian (for Liebeschuetz, Aurelian's successor) is attested as PPO.

If Zosimus's narrative is to be relied on, between the beginning of August and the beginning of December we have to fit the following substantial journeys, in sequence:

1. Eutropius's voyage to Cyprus
2. Message from Constantinople to Gaïnas in Phrygia
3. Message from Phrygia to Constantinople
4. Message to Cyprus
5. Eutropius returns from Cyprus to Constantinople
6. Gaïnas comes to Constantinople in person
7. Gaïnas returns to Thyatira
8. Gaïnas comes again to Constantinople

Is it credible that all these journeys took place between August and December? For Liebeschuetz, who glossed over (2) and (3), it is possible. Perhaps it is possible—just. But possible is not the same as probable.

Even accepting Liebeschuetz's claim that Eutropius's execution fell no later than 1 October, the rest of his calculations still barely add up. He claims that the journey from Constantinople to Thyatira and back, some 780 miles, could have been done, at an average of 12 miles per day, in the course of October and November. He concedes that "the schedule would . . . have been tight, and could have been maintained only if Gaïnas hurried deliberately." But he offers no satisfactory explanation why Gaïnas should have been in such a hurry to return to Constanti-

63. See below, p. 229.
64. Zos. 5.18.5; evidently the Hermus and its feeders. The Sardian Eunapius no doubt gave extensive local color that Zosimus as usual suppressed. Compare Herodotus's account of Cyrus's famous winter surprise attack on Sardis, "watered by the Hyllus and other streams that join another and larger one called the Hermus" (1.80.1).
65. *Turkey*, vol. 1, British Naval Intelligence: Geographical Handbook Series, B.R. 507 (April 1942), 220 and 223, with figs. 61 and 62 and tables 12 and 13 on pp. 414–16.

nople—in winter—when he had only just left it.[66] Certainly there is no hint of haste in Zosimus. Quite the contrary. According to his very detailed account, the only one we have, after leaving Constantinople Gaïnas marched through Phrygia and Lydia till he reached Thyatira. There he joined Tribigild and marched due south. After the botched attempt on Sardis, they separated, Tribigild making for the Hellespont, Gaïnas for Bithynia, both pillaging as they went. We have already seen that the failure of the attack on Sardis is put down to sudden floods, not urgent news from Constantinople. The implication is that several weeks, if not months,[67] passed before Gaïnas decided to return to Constantinople. Indeed, the natural assumption, as we shall argue later, is that Gaïnas's return belongs to the following spring.

But it is the evidence of Aurelian's consulate that is decisive. If Aurelian was exiled before the end of 399, he could not appear as ordinary consul for 400. Liebeschuetz attempted the same way out as Bury, pressing Synesius's reference to Osiris's "eponymous year" in the context of his return from exile (124A). According to Bury, Aurelian "had been designated for the consulate of the year 400," but because of his exile was naturally "unable to enter upon it in January."[68] It was not till after his return from exile at the end of the year that he was finally invested with his consulate "and the name of whatever person had been chosen to fill it by Typhos and Gaïnas was struck from the fasti."

Unfortunately, this hypothesis cannot be reconciled with the rest of our fairly abundant consular documentation for the year. It is true that we do not have a papyrus dated to the early months of 400 by the name of Aurelian. And though we do have several laws so dated, that proves nothing, since the dating formulas of laws preserved in the Code were retroactively harmonized with the official Eastern *fasti* by the Theodosian compilers.[69]

But no fewer than four histories of the period refer to Aurelian's consulate at the time of his exile: Socrates, Sozomen, Zosimus, and John of Antioch. It is true that three of them refer incorrectly to Aurelian and Saturninus, who was consul in 383, in the same terms: Socrates to both

66. See the alternative account of the alleged collusion between Gaïnas and Tribigild below, pp. 229–31.

67. Compare Paschoud's note ad loc. (p. 145): "Gaïnas et Tribigild durent rester assez longtemps en Phrygie, je pense tout l'automne et l'hiver 399–400."

68. Bury (1923) 1958, 134; this theory was already adumbrated by Sievers (1870).

69. For example, Eastern laws from the first half of 399 must originally have been dated *Eutropio et Theodoro consulibus;* but all extant laws are dated *Theodoro consule,* reflecting Eutropius's *damnatio memoriae* of August. For fuller discussion of this point, see *CLRE,* chap. 7.

as "ex-consuls" (*HE* 6.6); Sozomen to both as "consulars" (*HE* 8.45); and John to both as "consuls" (*FHG* 4.611b). But nothing could be more precise than Zosimus, who distinguishes them as "Aurelian, who held the office of consul that year" and "Saturninus, formerly numbered among the consuls" (5.17.8). And even if it were to be suggested, as a last resort, that all four derived from a common source (itself an improbable hypothesis, given the differences between their accounts) that was misled by the official *fasti* into concluding that Aurelian was consul at the moment of his exile, the fact remains that this source must, like all four surviving historians, have dated Aurelian's exile to 400 rather than 399.

Furthermore, if the allegedly pro-barbarian government of Typhos/Caesarius and Gaïnas had, as Bury supposed, appointed another man consul in January 400,[70] we should have known about it, for he would have been acknowledged by the Western government in the ordinary way, and his name would still appear in such consular dates, at any rate, as were not liable to subsequent correction: namely, those carved on inscriptions. We have at least seventeen, and perhaps as many as twenty-five,[71] inscriptions with consular dates of 400 from the city of Rome, together with four more from Italy and Dalmatia; the earliest date from 8 and 12 January, the latest from 13 and 19 November. Every one gives the name of just one consul, Stilicho himself.

Seeck long ago saw the explanation: the West did not recognize Aurelian's consulate.[72] According to Liebeschuetz, it is "at least as likely" that his name was omitted from the Western formula because, being in exile at the time, "he had not been inaugurated." But if this had happened, a quite different formula would have been used. As was often to happen in the fifth century, if the year opened in the West [East] with no information about the new Eastern [Western] consul, the new Western [Eastern] formula would be *X consule et qui de Oriente [Occidente] nuntiatus fuerit*. If the name of the second consul arrived in the course of the year, this provisional formula would be superseded by a new one giving both names. On the Bury-Liebeschuetz hypothesis we should expect to find a new Western formula in the last quarter of the year, after Aurelian's alleged belated inauguration. But we do not. All year long the West dated by the consulate of Stilicho alone—and in Africa by the post-consulate of Stilicho alone until June 401. It seems clear that no new for-

70. If they had, there can be little doubt (for reasons given below, p. 327) that he would have been none other than Gaïnas.

71. That is to say, eight more dated by Stilicho as sole consul where for one reason or another it is possible that an iteration number has been omitted and the reference is to 405: *CLRE*, s.a. 400, pp. 334–35; add *Ann. Epigr.* 1985, no. 57.

72. Seeck 1919, 300.

mula including Aurelian's name was sent out to the West at any time during the course of 400.

The fact that this formula was in use in Rome as early as the first week of January allows only one conclusion. The Western court knew who the Eastern consul was in time for the usual proclamation on 1 January but refused to include his name. The reason we can be so positive is that the same thing happened the year before when the news of Eutropius's consulate arrived. This time, in addition to the omission of Eutropius's name from all Western inscriptions and consular lists, we have the express testimony of Claudian that Stilicho refused to recognize Eutropius's consulate.[73]

The state of cold war that existed between East and West at this period is well documented by Eunapius, Zosimus, and, above all, the poems of Claudian. Those who had been hoping that Eutropius's fall would restore good relations were to be disappointed. As Claudian bitterly observed at the beginning of book 2 of *In Eutropium* late in 399:

> at vos egregie purgatam creditis aulam,
> Eutropium si Cyprus habet.

> You think you have done a marvelous job of cleaning up the court because Eutropius is exiled in Cyprus.

The removal of Eutropius did not result in an Eastern government Stilicho could recognize.[74] This is why his propagandist Claudian is at such pains, when celebrating Stilicho's own consulate in January 400, to distinguish between Arcadius, to whom Stilicho's loyalty was unshaken, and the "feeble and wicked cabal" of his ministers:

> fratrem levior nec cura tuetur
> Arcadium; nec, si quid iners atque impia turba
> praetendens proprio nomen regale furori
> audeat, ascribis iuveni.
>
> (*Stil.* 2.79–82)

> No lighter care [in you, Stilicho] watches over [Honorius's] brother Arcadius; and you do not ascribe to the young man [Arcadius] the audacities of the feeble and wicked cabal that hides its own madness behind the imperial name.

Since Claudian names no names, in theory it could be Eutychian who was the head of this cabal. But since it was undoubtedly Aurelian Stilicho so insulted as not to recognize as his fellow consul for 400, it seems

---

73. *In Eutr.* 1.319, 488f.; 2.127.
74. Cameron 1970a, 138.

perverse not to recognize behind this continued hostility that Aurelian continued to hold power at the Eastern court.

The only way out would be to postulate a gradual decline in Aurelian's power: he might have been deposed from the prefecture in December 399, but allowed to be consul for 400 and not exiled till six months later. Yet Zosimus, Socrates, and Sozomen all imply a sudden coup, with Gaïnas dictating to Arcadius terms that were immediately put into effect. Most of all does such a hypothesis conflict with Synesius, for whom Typhos was helpless until he could mobilize the (as he claims) reluctant Gaïnas to help him. The unmistakable implication of all our sources is that Osiris remained in, and Typhos out of, office right up to the moment of Gaïnas's coup.

Nor could it be argued that the consulate for 400 was a face-saving compensation for Aurelian in return for stepping down from the praetorian prefecture in 399. It is true that the consulate was a title without powers, but there is nonetheless one crucial respect in which it differed from, say, an English peerage conferred on a retiring politician. The consul was required to provide lavish games at his own expense on his inauguration and, if he chose, on other occasions during the year. It was an opportunity to win popularity—too dangerous an opportunity to give a political rival. All the great ministers of this period, Tatianus, Rufinus, Caesarius, Eutychian, and Anthemius, became consul *during* their tenure of the prefecture. So too did Eutropius during the last year of his more informal ascendancy. Aurelian's consulate was the culmination of his career, not compensation for its premature termination.

How then do we explain Synesius's reference to the "eponymous year"? Liebeschuetz was reading too much into the passage when he made an argument of the fact that "the honour to have the year named after him is listed among the distinctions conferred on Osiris/Aurelian *after* he had returned from exile." Synesius does no more than include the phrase in a list of events that followed Osiris's return: "night-long festivals, torch-lit processions, distributions of gifts, the eponymous year, and the second sparing of his hostile brother" (124A). We shall shortly argue that Aurelian was not, as is usually supposed, restored to the prefecture on his return. But he remained consul until the end of the year, and it would have been a shrewd stroke to draw the maximum publicity and popularity from his restoration by giving splendid new consular games. Synesius could not be more explicit within the Egyptian context of his narrative. Nor had he any wish to be so. His purpose in the closing sections of book 2 was to imply that Aurelian had been restored to as much of his former glory as he desired. So he makes as much of Aurelian's consulate as he can.

A different possibility is suggested by Barnes: in the course of 400 Aurelian "lost and later regained his consulate."[75] It is barely conceivable that, like Eutropius, Aurelian was stripped of his consulate on his exile and then reinstated on his return. Synesius might then have been referring to this reinstatement. But Aurelian was not, as far as we know, accused of treason, the normal justification for *damnatio memoriae*. Nor is there any parallel for reinstatement after *damnatio memoriae*. Nor yet is there any hint of either in our sources.

Whatever the explanation of this passage of Synesius, there is no reason to doubt that Aurelian was inaugurated as consul in the ordinary way on 1 January, and so that he was still in office as prefect at the beginning of 400.

Another argument clearly points to the same conclusion. On 6 January 400, Epiphany, Asterius of Amasea delivered a homily attacking the pagan festival of the Kalends, wrongly preferred by some, he protests, to the ensuing Christian festival of Epiphany.[76] By way of conclusion he attacks the consulate too, first with a diatribe against the folly, expense, and ambition of those who pursue it, and then with a list of recent consuls who have come to grief. His list includes Rufinus cos. 392, Timasius cos. 389, Abundantius cos. 393, Tatianus cos. 391, and, by way of climax, Eutropius cos. 399, the preceding year. He describes their exiles and executions in full and harrowing detail as clear proof of the danger of ambition. If Aurelian had already been exiled by the time he wrote, in company with another former consul, the veteran general Saturninus, Asterius could scarcely have omitted their names. All the narrative sources that mention the exile of Aurelian and Saturninus draw attention to their consulates.

Immediately after describing the surrender of Saturninus and Aurelian to Gaïnas, Socrates (*HE* 6.6) and Sozomen (*HE* 8.4) both describe a "comet of prodigious magnitude" that presaged Gaïnas's entry into Constantinople. Chinese sources describe a large comet that would have been visible at Constantinople from mid-March to mid-May 400.[77] Gaï-

---

75. Barnes 1983, 255. A similar suggestion was made long ago by Sievers: "Wahrscheinlich aber war bei seinem Sturze decretirt werden, daß sein Name aus den Fasten gestrichen werden sollte, und dieses Decret wird jetzt aufgehoben" (1870, 367–68).

76. *PG* 40.223–25; C. Datema, *Asterius of Amasea: Homilies I–XIV* (Leiden 1970), 39–43, with notes on pp. 228–31.

77. Ho Peng Yoke, "Ancient and Medieval Observations of Comets and Novae in Chinese Sources," in *Vistas in Astronomy* 5, ed. A. Beer, 161, no. 183; and *The Astronomical Chapters of the Chin Shu* (Paris and The Hague 1966), 243; W. Gundel, *RE* 11 (1922): 1190.

nas's coup must have fallen later than the appearance of this comet in mid-March.

Synesius himself makes a slightly different use of the portent of this comet. The last chapter of book 1 lists a series of obviously *post eventum* prophecies that are supposed to presage the downfall of Typhos and his barbarians. At the end of the list the god who is making these predictions says that better things will come "when with water and fire we purify the air about the earth," adding by way of explanation that the gods drive out such monsters "with fire and thunderbolts" (115A). This conclusion to the list of portents would be very lame if it did not refer to some conspicuous recent meteorological phenomenon. In the context, it can only mean the comet. How could Synesius have passed up this most dramatic, but rarest, of all traditional portents when it was shining in the sky above him? Where Socrates and Sozomen had seen it as presaging the evil of Gaïnas's coup, he sees it as presaging the good of his fall. Since the comet was still visible in mid-May and the pogrom took place only two months later, it was a plausible and attractive association.

Then there is Palladius's very precise account of the suit between Eusebius of Valentinopolis and Antonius of Ephesus. Early in 400 Eusebius accused Antonius of simony before Chrysostom in Constantinople. It was in the "thirteenth indiction" that they arrived,[78] that is to say, at some time between 1 September 399 and 31 August 400. Whether coming by land or sea (more probably the latter), the bishops are not likely to have traveled during the winter. The outside limits of the sailing season were 10 March to 10 November.[79] Chrysostom decided to go to Ephesus in person to interrogate witnesses, but before he could leave, a message came from the palace warning him not to go away when "trouble was expected." "The expected trouble was Gaïnas the barbarian," Palladius obligingly explains.[80] Chrysostom appointed Palladius and two other bishops to go in his place, and the synod laid down that both litigants were to appear at Hypaipa with witnesses within two months or be excommunicated. Soon after this Eusebius and Antonius came to terms, and so did not keep their meeting with Palladius and his associates at Hypaipa, expecting that they would not wait long "since it was the hottest period of summer."[81] We need not follow this sordid story any far-

78. *Dialogus*, p. 83.9 Coleman-Norton, with his preface, p. xvii; and Albert 1980, 506–7.
79. L. Casson, *Ships and Seamanship in the Ancient World* (Princeton 1971), 270.
80. *Dialogus*, p. 87.2.
81. *Dialogus*, p. 87.29.

ther. It is enough for our purposes that the "hottest period of summer" in this part of Anatolia falls around mid-June.[82] Two months back from then takes us to mid-April 400. If we weigh this consideration together with the limitations of the sailing season and the dates of the comet, we can hardly date Gaïnas's coup earlier than the beginning of April.

Another pointer is the proclamation of Eudoxia as Augusta, dated by the *Paschal Chronicle* to 9 January 400. Dates in the *Paschal Chronicle* are by no means to be taken on trust, and this one in particular would make Eudoxia's coronation surprisingly early. It was by no means routine for the emperor's consort to be proclaimed Augusta. The title had always been something of an anomaly. During the first three centuries it was conferred on wives, mothers, daughters, and even nieces of emperors—though never systematically.[83] Sometimes wives were given the title immediately, sometimes not until they had produced an heir, sometimes not at all. For unknown reasons it was conferred very sparingly in the second half of the fourth century:[84] not, for example, on the wives of Constantius II, Julian, and Valens; not on either wife of Valentinian I or on the second wife of Theodosius I.[85] In fact Theodosius I's first wife, Flaccilla, was the first Augusta since Constantine's wife Fausta, and Flaccilla was not proclaimed till after the coronation of her son Arcadius in 383.[86] It might have been expected that Arcadius too would wait till after the coronation of his son, the future Theodosius II (born 10 April 401, crowned 10 January 402).

The date in the *Paschal Chronicle* is one of a group of anniversaries in the family of Arcadius that have generally been treated as authoritative. Six are plausible in themselves and agree with the dates given in the *Chronicle* of Marcellinus,[87] and so may be presumed to go back to their

82. According to Albert 1980, 507.

83. T. Mommsen, *Römisches Staatsrecht*, vol. 2.2, 3d ed., 821–22.

84. One might hazard the guess that the debacle of Fausta, who was executed so soon after her elevation, played a part. The rarity of conferral is not noted in the rather oversimplified discussion in Bury (1923) 1958, 9–10. Holum (1982) has useful material but no systematic discussion.

85. Of course in every case the argument is from silence, but the silence of the coinage must be held decisive. Surprisingly enough, in the face of the precedent of Eudoxia, Honorius did not give the title to either of his wives. He issued a formal protest at the "unprecedented" circulation of Eudoxia's images around the provinces "to universal disapproval" (*Epistulae imperatorum pontificum aliorum*, in *CSEL* 35, ed. O. Guenther [Vienna 1895], no. 38.1). Presumably Stilicho did not want to risk his daughters' showing any of the independence of the Eastern Augustae.

86. J. W. E. Pearce, *RIC*, vol. 9 (London 1953), 153, 183, 194, 222, 245, 256, 282, 301.

87. Birth of Flaccilla: 17 June 397; birth of Pulcheria: 19 January 399; birth of Theodosius II: 10 April 401; coronation of Theodosius II: 10 January 402; birth of Marina: 10 February 403; death of Eudoxia: 6 October 404.

common source, a local chronicle of Constantinople maintained on a year-by-year basis.[88] For two others, the birth of Arcadia and the coronation of Eudoxia, we have only the *Paschal Chronicle*. Arcadia's birth is assigned to 3 April 400: plausibly enough, since the sequence of sisters in Sozomen's *Historia ecclesiastica* (9.1.1) places her between Pulcheria and Marina. There is no way of obtaining positive confirmation of the date of Eudoxia's coronation, but a recently found coin hoard has revealed bronze issues of Eudoxia Augusta from the mint of Antioch with no corresponding issues for Theodosius II.[89] That is to say, we now know that she received the imperial title before him. Since the priority of Eudoxia's coronation was the only real problem with the date in the *Paschal Chronicle*, there is no longer any reason to question it.

In January 400 Eudoxia was six months pregnant. The fact that Arcadius did not wait until she gave birth (in the event to a third daughter) suggests unusual circumstances. The obvious conjecture, long since made, is that the title was a reward for the role she had played in the fall of Eutropius and the appointment of his successor as Arcadius's chief minister, the new prefect Aurelian.[90] If so, it is another indication that Aurelian was still in power at the time. If he were already in exile by December 399, Eudoxia would have to have been proclaimed during Gaïnas's regime.

A Eudoxia-Gaïnas axis would be hard to credit. The traditional view of court politics has usually placed Eudoxia at the center of an antibarbarian coalition. We have already seen reason to doubt whether such a coalition existed, but there are other issues that link Eudoxia to the men Gaïnas had exiled—Aurelian, Saturninus, and John. Neither Saturninus nor John held office at the time, but both were influential at court.[91] John was actually rumored to be the father of the baby Theodosius the following year.[92] Whether true or (more probably) false, the rumor was evidently contemporary and suffices to place John among Eudoxia's intimates. The principal factor was perhaps hostility to the patriarch John Chrysostom. Eudoxia's feud with Chrysostom was to pass into legend.[93] Prominent among her anti-Johannite allies were Marsa, the wife of Pro-

88. Cameron, in *CLRE* 54–56.

89. Information from J. P. C. Kent, who is preparing *RIC*, vol. 10. Most of this hoard seems to have come from the Antioch mint.

90. "Als Geste der Anerkennung des Aurelianus für die Mitwirkung Eudoxias bei der Entmachtung des Eutropius" (Albert 1984, 68). So already, for example, Seeck 1913, 317.

91. For Saturninus's influence at court, see Zos. 5.9.3 and p. 334 below.

92. See p. 241 below.

93. Both exaggerated and minimized already by contemporaries, its origin and successive stages are not easy to determine: Holum 1982, 70f.; Liebeschuetz 1984a, 85f.; Ommeslaeghe, *Anal.Boll.* 97 (1979): 131–59; and see too below, pp. 234–35.

motus, in whose house Eudoxia had been brought up after her father's death,[94] and Castricia, the widow of Saturninus.[95] Saturninus himself was linked to Aurelian by their common devotion to the Constantino-politan monk Isaac, one of the leaders of the anti-Johannite movement. John too was a bitter enemy of Chrysostom.[96]

Gaïnas had lived for many years on the fringes of the Byzantine court. He must have realized that the three men he singled out as his deadliest enemies were bound by a variety of ties to Eudoxia. It is hard to believe that it was Gaïnas who went out of his way to encourage her independence by rushing through her proclamation as Augusta while she was still pregnant. On the other hand, it is easy to see why Aurelian, unable to count on Arcadius as Eutropius had, would be anxious to in-crease the authority of his ally in the palace. More specifically, it may have been a well-founded apprehension of Gaïnas's intentions that was responsible for the haste.

It was a long-standing tradition that the suggestion to elevate an Au-gusta should come from the senate.[97] For example, this had been the procedure when the title was conferred on Trajan's sister Marciana and on Marcus's wife Faustina.[98] There is no reason to believe that the cus-tom died out. Emperors continued to foster the fiction (which was some-times more than a fiction) that they were elected by the senate and people of Constantinople,[99] and on two occasions imperial consorts with unsuitable names were publicly renamed by the people before being crowned Augusta.[100] The fullest description we have of the ceremony is John of Ephesus's account of the proclamation of the wife of Tiberius II in 578: the empress was invested with the robes and insignia of royalty at the palace in the presence of the emperor, patriarch, "and the whole senate" before proceeding to the cathedral, where she was crowned under the new name chosen by the Blue faction.[101]

94. At the time of her marriage to Arcadius (395) she was residing with one of Pro-motus's sons after Promotus's own death in 391: cf. Zos. 5.3.2, with Paschoud, comm. p. 81.

95. Palladius *Dialogus*, p. 25 Coleman-Norton. There is apparently a vague allusion to the "dames de cour" among Chrysostom's enemies in the contemporary panegyric by Ps.-Martyrius to be published by F. van Ommeslaeghe (see 1979, 150).

96. See below, pp. 234–35.

97. Mommsen 1887–88, 822 n. 4. See pp. 223–24 n. 115 for some other examples of the senate playing a role in issues one might have expected to be decided by the emperor alone.

98. Pliny *Pan.* 84.6; *HA Vita Pii* 5.2.

99. H. G. Beck, *Senat und Volk von Konstantinopel*, Sitzber. München (1966); Cameron 1976a, 261f.

100. Justin I's wife Euphemia, formerly Lupicina, and Tiberius II's wife Anastasia, formerly Ino: Cameron 1976a, 145–46, 255.

101. John of Ephesus *HE* 3.9, p. 182 Payne Smith; on the other accounts, see Payne Smith's note ad loc. and Averil Cameron, *Byzantion* 45 (1975): 16–18.

Naturally, the whole affair would normally be a prearranged formality, and the emperor could always refuse the senate's request, as Pertinax did for his wife in 193.[102] But it is significant that there was an established mechanism for initiating the proposal independently and bringing pressure to bear from outside. Such a mechanism bore obvious possibilities for exploitation by an ambitious empress—as it was, it seems, by Eudoxia. It is by no means irrelevant to observe that during his second prefecture of 414–16 Aurelian was to play a similar role in the proclamation of Eudoxia's daughter Pulcheria.[103]

There is also one other text that has often been thought relevant to the chronology of these months, a homily of Chrysostom entitled *When Saturninus and Aurelian Were Exiled and Gaïnas Left the City: On Avarice* (*PG* 52.413–20). On the face of it, the title might seem to suggest that Gaïnas departed from Constantinople shortly after the exiles; in other words, that Gaïnas seized power only shortly before the massacre.

But what is the authority of the title? What is its manuscript attestation? Does the text of the homily itself bear out this linking of the exile of Saturninus and Aurelian to Gaïnas's departure from Constantinople? Thanks to the expert guidance of Père M. Aubineau, the second question at least can be answered more confidently now than hitherto. The latest edition remains Migne's reprint of Montfaucon's text (Paris 1721), based on only one manuscript, Par. gr. 764, of the eleventh century. The published volumes of the *Codices Chrysostomici Graeci*, still far from complete, list only three witnesses. Père Aubineau knows of another twelve, all of the eleventh, tenth, and even ninth centuries. A few manuscripts lack the subtitle *On Avarice*, but in other respects the title clearly rests on a wide and solid manuscript base.

Chrysostom begins with an apology for not addressing his flock for so long because of his involvement in the political crisis. The sermon itself alludes to the crisis only obliquely. Chrysostom tells his flock that he has not been spending his time in idleness but "settling troubles, lulling waves, calming the storm, raising the shipwrecked, hastening to help the drowning into the calm of a harbor," for he is the father "of those in danger as well as those in safety." This is why he has been away "approaching, begging, beseeching, entreating that our lords (τοῖς κυρίοις) be spared from disaster." These "lords" must be Aurelian and Saturninus; apparently Chrysostom is claiming that he successfully begged for their lives. Having done that, he continues, "I have come back to you

102. Dio Cass. 74.7.2.
103. See appendix 1.

who are safe, sailing in the calm; I went to them to stop a storm, I have returned to you to prevent one arising." This contrast between the danger in which Aurelian and Saturninus stood and the present safety, with only the threat of danger, of his congregation in Constantinople suggests that he spoke before the massacre. "Everywhere," he says, "there is tumult and chaos, everywhere rocks and precipices . . . fear, danger, suspicion; . . . no one trusts anyone," adding the image already discussed of wolves in sheep's clothing,[104] a clear reference to the Goths. But when he goes on to claim that "everything is in the grip of civil war," he does not mean that fighting has yet broken out, for he at once qualifies his words, adding, "civil, and yet not open, but concealed." This is presumably why he was able to devote the bulk of the rest of the sermon (cols. 416–20) to the "love of money, the mad desire for wealth," meaning that greed was the source of all their troubles to Aurelian and Saturninus.[105]

Furthermore, what is meant by Gaïnas's "leaving the city"? In theory, this could be a reference to his personal departure on pretext of sickness immediately before the massacre.[106] But even so it would be odd to single out Gaïnas's departure rather than the massacre as the key event. More probably the reference is to the departure of Gaïnas's entire army from the area as a whole a week or two later. The massacre of such Goths as happened to be inside Constantinople, mostly civilians, was a major psychological blow to Gaïnas, but he still had enough soldiers in his main encampment outside the walls to take equally terrible revenge if he had wished. It was not till the Gothic army retreated from Constantinople to Thrace that the city could truly celebrate Gaïnas's departure. We may compare Eunapius: "Gaïnas departed from the city, which he left behind a populous and magnificent tomb, the occupants of which had not yet been buried."[107] Unfortunately this is a stray fragment quoted without context in the Suda, but since the city is described as a tomb, it is clear that the massacre had already taken place at the time of the departure described. It must be Gaïnas's departure for Thrace that is meant, here as in the title of Chrysostom's sermon.

So the sermon refers to a period between Gaïnas's demand that Saturninus and Aurelian be surrendered to him and his final departure from Constantinople after the massacre in July. What then of the link between their exile and Gaïnas's "departure" in the title? The answer is

104. Above, pp. 97–99.
105. On this, see below, p. 179.
106. Discussed in detail on p. 216.
107. Frag. 79 = 67.13 Blockley.

that it is not a genuine title at all. The sermon itself refers only to the sparing of Saturninus and Aurelian, not even to their exile. And there is nothing in it about Gaïnas leaving the city. It is simply a chronological label attached by a secretary,[108] as, for example, *When He Returned from Asia.*[109] The title was attached early enough for someone to be able to identify the "lords" who were in danger as Saturninus and Aurelian and to associate the "civil war" with Gaïnas's coup—but not a contemporary, who would not have made the blunder of identifying the "civil war" Chrysostom referred to with the pogrom of some two months later.

Liebeschuetz argues the converse, namely, that the homily dates from after the massacre in July and that Chrysostom had just returned from his embassy to Gaïnas in Thrace.[110] But Chrysostom makes it clear at the very beginning that the immediate reason for his absence was his recent efforts to save Aurelian and Saturninus. And we know from Synesius that the sparing of Aurelian and his subsequent exile, described in book 1 of *De providentia*, took place well before the massacre,[111] described in book 2. The god who predicts the end of Typhos's tyranny shortly after the massacre assigns it "months not years" (114C). The interval corresponds closely to the time Synesius wrote, for the rustic philosopher soon recognizes some of the god's signs (115B), and he and Synesius both look forward to Typhos's speedy demise. Book 2 shows Synesius's confidence eroded; the preface states explicitly that book 2 was added later.

The close link between exiles and massacre at first suggested by the title of the homily cannot be substantiated. Nonetheless, the three-month interval allowed by a date in April for Gaïnas's coup seems easier for a reasonably well-informed error to span than the nine months given by Jones's date in December.

V. TYPHOS

So what do we do about the apparent legal evidence for Eutychian as prefect in December 399? Three laws with separate dates (11, 28, and

108. Chrysostom himself scarcely had time to do any such editorial work on his countless sermons in the hectic last few years of his life.

109. *PG* 52.421, now published in the original Greek version by A. Wenger (1961, 110–23).

110. Liebeschuetz 1986a, 158.

111. Though book 1 was not finished till shortly after the massacre.

30 December) might seem fairly solid evidence.[112] But these laws appear consecutively in the Code (12.1.163–65), so that if the first was in error, the other two were virtually certain to follow suit. Moreover, the last two,[113] and perhaps all three, may actually be fragments of the same law. Variation in day is surprisingly common among extracts from the same law,[114] and it is unlikely that as many as three separate laws on the subject of curial obligations were issued within such a short space of time.

Four numbers earlier in the same title of the Code (12.1.159) we find an exactly similar law on decurions addressed to Eutychian as prefect and dated to 25 October 398. The obvious guess is that all four reflect Eutychian's continuing preoccupation with the problem of decurions in the autumn of 398, but that the last three somehow got separated from their fellow and assigned to the wrong year. Alternatively perhaps only the month is in error: they may come from earlier in 399.

Since Eutychian definitely was prefect from September 397 to July 399 and again from February 404 to June 405, any cautious student of the Code would feel bound to allow the possibility that this little batch had strayed from one or other of those tenures. The moment we disallow collegiate prefectures, the table quoted above (pp. 156–58) provides a number of illustrations for both Eutychian and Caesarius.

Cavalier though it might seem to reject the MSS date of these laws, in order to obtain a plausible sequence of prefects some dates *must* be rejected. Naturally the fewer the better, but, as in textual criticism, we must not feel obliged to put up with the improbable just because it is possible; in this case barely possible. The immediate context in this title is not entirely sound. *Cod. Theod.* 12.1.160, three numbers earlier, is addressed to Optatus as prefect of Constantinople and dated 22 November 398 (*Honor. IV et Eutychiano*). But someone else was prefect of Constantinople from July 398 to September 399,[115] and Optatus is otherwise

112. For example, according to Liebeschuetz, "altering three separate dates . . . would be arbitrary" (1987, 420).

113. So Seeck 1919, 301.

114. There is evidence that day dates are often just guesses. Laws in the Code could not be valid *sine die et consule* (1.1.1). For one startling case where nine separate extracts from the same law all appear with different day dates, see Maas, 1973, 621–22; as he rightly observes, the only possible conclusion is that "das Original hatte überhaupt kein Datum" and the nine different dates transmitted were all "aus freier Phantasie ergänzt." Another illuminating case (omitted from the recent discussion in *CLRE*) is *Mosaicarum et Romanarum legum collatio* 6.6, where the compiler notes that he has found a law of Diocletian in both the contemporary Codes (Gregorian and Hermogenian), each with a different date (15 March 291 and 9 June 287).

115. *PLRE* I.831, Severinus 3.

securely attested in this office in 405.[116] There can be little doubt that Seeck was right to correct the year to 404. In this case we can easily posit a confusion between the fourth and sixth consulates of Honorius, while in the case of Eutychian's three laws (12.1.163–65), no such neat confusion can be invoked. It is always more satisfying when the textual critic can produce a paleographical basis for his emendation, but sometimes there is none, however necessary and compelling the emendation. For example, the consular formula of the misdated law of Caesarius in 398 could not easily have been confused with the formula for any one of the seven years to which it must be transferred, but it is none the less wrong for that. In the case of Eutychian's three laws dated *Theodoro consule* (399), it can at least be observed that the two preceding laws are both dated *Theodoro consule*. Though it is seldom possible to prove it, many a law must have mistakenly picked up the consular formula of a neighboring item when they were lying in the form of undated extracts on the compiler's table. For a parallel multiple error slightly earlier in the same title, see 12.1.131–32 and 138, where the confusion between Aurelian's praetorian and urban prefectures has infected the whole group.

When these considerations are added to the problems already raised about ending Aurelian's prefecture as early as December 399, there must be serious doubt whether these three laws are sufficient basis for postulating a second prefecture for Eutychian at this time. Moreover, since it seems clear that Eutychian's first tenure terminated abruptly with the fall of Eutropius, it would be surprising to find him restored to favor and power this soon.

If so, then (as Seeck saw) Aurelian's successor—and of course Typhos—must be Caesarius after all. He will have succeeded in April 400 on Aurelian's exile, though he happens not to be attested in office till December. It is worth noting that the laws for this period are relatively sparse.

On other counts too Caesarius makes a more likely Typhos. He is known to have been devoted to his wife (Soz. *HE* 9.2.4), as Synesius says Typhos was (105B); and there is some evidence that he was at least tolerant of Arianism, which would explain Synesius's allegation of "Scythian," that is, Arian, sympathies in Typhos.

Jones argued against Caesarius that the posts Synesius records for Typhos's earlier career do not match the earlier career of Caesarius. But

116. *PLRE* I.649–50.

his identifications of these posts are open to question. ταμίας χρημάτων
(92A) Jones translated *comes sacrarum largitionum*, a post not attested for
Caesarius.[117] But Synesius at once adds after this title the parenthesis
"for his father thought it best to make trial of his sons' characters *in lesser
posts*." The *comitiva sacrarum largitionum* was unquestionably a major
post. Synesius alleges that Typhos disgraced himself by accepting bribes
and behaved even worse in his next post, during which "the province of
the noble kingdom over which he presided had one unspeakably bad
year" (92B). Jones identifies this tenure with the praetorian prefecture,
but quite apart from the fact that both Caesarius and Eutychian held the
prefecture, neither held it for so short a spell as one year. Synesius is
much more likely to be referring to some provincial governorship, perhaps a proconsulate, posts traditionally held for one year.[118] Jones also
objected that Synesius's words do not correspond with the post of *magister officiorum* that Caesarius held in 386–87. This is true enough, but
while he took obvious pleasure in giving an imposing list of the high
positions held with distinction by Osiris/Aurelian, *magister officiorum*
and city prefect, Synesius had no reason to give Caesarius's complete
cursus honorum. After all, Caesarius had reached all the highest offices,
including the consulate, before his younger brother. Instead Synesius
singled out a couple of minor early posts in which he could allege mis-
conduct with less fear of rebuttal.

In his major offices Caesarius had acquitted himself with great distinction. In an honorific inscription from Tralles he is described as savior
(*soter*) and benefactor (*euergetes*), apparently the last known example of
these terms being applied to a private citizen.[119] In 387 Theodosius dispatched him to Antioch while *magister officiorum* to investigate a serious
riot against taxes. He evidently handled the situation with great skill and
tact, as we learn from a speech by Libanius that thanks him for pleading
the city's case with the emperor and forecasts his future consulate (*Or.*
21.29). Liebeschuetz describes the speech as a panegyric and emphasizes that there is no suggestion in it that Caesarius's father had been

117. Not that this proves that he did not hold it; no eastern *comes sacrarum largitionum*
is attested between 386 and 391, and there are other gaps in the *fasti* (*PLRE* I.1065; Delmaire 1989, 301–2). Delmaire's identification of Eutychian as CSL "vers 388–389" (115–18)
depends entirely on the assumption that Synesius's ταμίας χρημάτων means CSL; *quaestor
sacrarum largitionum* in Barnes 1986a, 101, is a *lapsus calami*, as his note 30 makes clear.

118. Barnes (1986a, 102) suggests the proconsulate of Achaea.

119. P. LeBas and W. H. Waddington, *Inscriptions Grecques et Latines recueillies en Asie
mineure*, 2 vols. (Paris 1870; reprint Meisenheim/Glan 1972), 1652d, with A. D. Nock, *Essays on Religion and the Ancient World*, vol. 2 (Oxford 1972), 731–32.

prefect and consul under Constantius II.[120] Had it been a formal panegyric, the absence of a section on distinguished ancestors might well
deserve to be seen as proof that he had none. In fact it is a panegyric in
neither form nor content. Like the companion piece (*Or.* 22) addressed
to Ellebich the *magister militum,* it is almost entirely concerned with the
riot, the investigation by Caesarius and Ellebich, and Caesarius's journey to Constantinople to plead with Theodosius for clemency. Of its
thirty-three chapters, thirty-two are devoted to the riot. The one that is
not (chap. 4) is a *praeteritio:* if Libanius were to touch on Caesarius's
other achievements, "we would give the impression of disparaging the
present theme." In such a context there was neither room nor place for
the traditional panegyrical themes of birth and upbringing. It makes
a fascinating contrast with Synesius's picture of a thieving, corrupt,
lecherous, treacherous monster to listen to the topics Libanius was
obliged to put on one side: "his good behavior as a child, and then,
childhood left behind him, his courage, whenever courage was needed,
his resolution, his general affability, the manner in which, despite his
capacity to inspire fear in others, he personally remained beyond the
reach of criticism . . . praised by all [emperors] alike."

Modern readers of *De providentia* tend to swallow uncritically Synesius's picture of a struggle between the powers of light and darkness and
to believe that Aurelian was a noble patriot and Caesarius an unprin-
cipled traitor. But it did not seem that way to everybody at the time.
Nothing could be more instructive than Chrysostom's sermon on the
exile of Aurelian and Saturninus. It comes as a surprise to discover that
the theme of the sermon is avarice. Wealth is a runaway; it never stays
with a man for long. Indeed it not only abandons him, it often ruins him
too. Chrysostom had used exactly the same series of metaphors in his
homily on Eutropius:[121] Eutropius's fall had also been the inevitable consequence of his greed for wealth and power. Of course, this is the simplistic perspective of the moralist. Eutropius may or may not have been
more avaricious than the average imperial favorite, but that certainly
was not why he fell at the moment he did. Nor did avarice have anything
to do with the exile of Aurelian and Saturninus. Chrysostom is simply
using them as texts on the perils of worldly ambition. But what is so il-

120. Similarly, Delmaire assumes that ταμίας χρημάτων implies that Typhos was at
one stage CSL and objects to the identification with Caesarius that Libanius's *Or.* 21 "ne
souffle mot d'une charge financière qui était pourtant l'occasion rêvée pour exalter ses ver-
tus" (1989, 116).

121. As pointed out by Albert 1984, 163–65.

luminating is precisely that he does not distinguish between Eutropius and Aurelian: he treats both indifferently as types of the man driven by ambition to ruin. There is no suggestion in this contemporary work by a man not afraid to stand up to Gaïnas that he saw Aurelian and Saturninus as heroes, martyrs to the cause of righteousness. Indeed, there is good reason to believe that it was Caesarius, not Aurelian, who was really the hero of the hour.

There is one earlier occasion on which it is possible to make a direct comparison between the behavior of the two brothers. In 392 the unscrupulous Rufinus engineered the ruin of the then praetorian prefect Tatianus and his son Proculus, prefect of Constantinople. Rufinus could no longer tolerate the rivalry of these flamboyant Lycians and was not content with their dismissal. He inveigled Proculus, who had gone into hiding, back to Constantinople with false conciliatory messages and then had both men tried and condemned. Tatianus was exiled and Proculus executed. In addition, not only were all their *acta* revoked: a decree was issued excluding all Lycians from all public offices.[122]

Rufinus succeeded to the praetorian prefecture himself and naturally saw to the appointment of loyal supporters to the urban prefecture. The first was Aristaenetus (later consul in 404),[123] and soon after (from, at any rate, February 393) Aurelian. Of the five extant laws that nullify *acta* of Tatianus and Proculus, two bear the name of Rufinus,[124] and two Aurelian.[125] On Rufinus's fall in November 395 Caesarius became prefect and saw to the repeal of Rufinus's law banning Lycians from public service.[126] And he repealed a particularly harsh law of Rufinus withdrawing from the Arian Eunomians the right to make wills.[127] But he also issued a law excluding the widow of a proscribed man from forfeiture of goods and property that were legally hers,[128] and we know from Zosimus (5.8) that Rufinus's widow and children were allowed to retire in safety to Jerusalem. The generosity of Caesarius contrasts sharply with the vindictiveness of Aurelian and his master Rufinus.

---

122. Known from the law that repealed it (*Cod.Theod.* 9.38.9) and from Claudian (*In Ruf.* 1.230–34); for the context, Cameron 1970a, 81–82 and 490.

123. *PLRE* I.105; he is expressly attested as an adherent of Rufinus by Lib. *Ep.* 1110, of 393.

124. *Cod.Theod.* 9.42.12 (12 June 393), 11.1.23 (12 June 393).

125. *Cod.Theod.* 12.1.131 (27 February 393), 14.17.12 (20 November 393); the other is to Drepanius the *comes rerum privatarum: Cod.Theod.* 9.42.13 (12 January 393).

126. *Cod.Theod.* 9.38.9 (31 August 396).

127. *Cod.Theod.* 16.5.27.

128. *Cod.Theod.* 9.42.15 (3 August 396); this law seems not to have been associated with Rufinus's widow before, but the date and context in the Code immediately following the law repealing the ban on Lycians, leave little room for doubt.

Indeed, this glance back to the antecedents of Synesius's story goes a long way toward explaining the rivalry between the brothers. In the ordinary way Caesarius might have expected his successful tenure as *magister officiorum* in 386–88 to lead shortly to the praetorian prefecture.[129] But he had counted without Rufinus. During the entire period of Rufinus's ascendancy (388–95) Caesarius was excluded from office. Perhaps he was thought too soft on heretics for the passionately orthodox Rufinus. But on Rufinus's fall he at once became the new prefect. Aurelian took care to court Rufinus as he rose, and was duly rewarded: he succeeded Rufinus as *magister officiorum* in 392 and then rose rapidly to the prefecture of Constantinople (393–94).[130] Not surprisingly, it was Aurelian who was excluded from office during the ascendancy of Eutropius. He was naturally anxious to resume his career when Eutropius fell in his turn. Put in its historical context, the rivalry between the brothers takes on a different complexion: each cast in his lot with different factions at court; and each both prospered and suffered accordingly.

But we might well wonder whether in real life the brothers were such deadly enemies as Synesius portrays them. Doubt has indeed sometimes been expressed whether in real life they were brothers at all, but a couple of passages in *De providentia* seem to put it beyond doubt. First, the statement in the preface that this book tells the story of "the sons of Taurus" is clearly meant to identify the protagonists outside the myth. Second, against the myth, Synesius makes Typhos, rather than Osiris, the older brother. Their respective careers make it clear that Caesarius was indeed the older.

Moreover, Severian of Gabala writes at Constantinople in 402: "The best painters often try to illustrate unanimity of spirit by placing behind emperors *or brothers who are also magistrates* (ἐπὶ βασιλέων ἢ ἀδελφῶν καὶ ἀρχόντων) a Concordia in female form who embraces with both arms

129. The laws do not attest him in office after 387, but it does not look as if his successor Rufinus was in office before 388: *PLRE* I.778; Clauss 1980, 187.

130. According to *PLRE* I.128 ἐπιστάτης δορυφόρων in *De providentia* 92A implies *magister officiorum* and τὰς ἀκοὰς πιστευθεὶς *quaestor sacri palatii*. It is more natural to refer both phrases to the same office, with Barnes 1986a, 101: "The *magister officiorum* both commanded the *scholae* and had certain functions relating to imperial audiences and petitions" (referring to Clauss 1980, 15f. and 60f.). In the same way Synesius goes on to characterize Aurelian's urban prefecture in two phrases: πολιαρχήσας καὶ βουλῆς ἄρξας. It is a mistake to interpret the last phrase as implying the separate office of *princeps senatus* (so Terzaghi ad loc.; cf. Dagron 1974, 205), not in any case attested for Constantinople. Synesius's words may be construed as an additional description of the duties of the city prefect, who acted as the senate's representative in all dealings with the emperor (A. Chastagnol, *La préfecture urbaine à Rome sous le Bas-Empire* [Paris 1960], 69–72). If we make the natural assumption that Synesius is listing the posts in sequence, there is no room for Aurelian to have held the quaestorship as well between 392 and his urban prefecture in 393.

those she unifies."[131] The obvious way to make this point, especially in 402 when the joint consulate of Arcadius and Honorius was being widely publicized as the restoration of brotherly concord, was simply to cite paintings of the two emperors. Why then does Severian cloud the issue by adding "brothers who are also magistrates"? Civilian brothers did not share office in the way brother emperors did, and advertisement of concord suggests its reverse, seldom appropriate for civilian magistrates. The author of an early Latin translation was evidently puzzled, for he omits the "magistrates," writing only *ubi regum vel fratrum tabulae pinguntur.*[132] But he still preserves the alternatives: emperors *or* brothers, not, as we might have expected, emperors *who are* brothers. In the context there is one obvious explanation. In the three years before Severian wrote, the two most important magistrates in the Eastern empire had indeed been both brothers and conspicuous long-standing political rivals. It was normal for high officials to be represented in all their insignia of office in a variety of media: statues, paintings, ivory diptychs, and even pottery.[133] Female personifications are common on the diptychs, as they are in Claudian's panegyrics, even for civilian consuls. For Stilicho, Roma and her sister provinces do the honors; for the more literary Theodorus (cos. 399), it is the Muses. A painting in a church at Ephesus shows the archangel Michael presenting another Theodorus with the insignia of the mastership of the offices.[134] Is it not possible that there came a moment when Caesarius and Aurelian decided it was time for a restoration of their brotherly concord too?[135] Pictorial representations would naturally have followed the established imperial pattern.

VI. THE RESTORATION OF OSIRIS

According to Synesius's allegory, it was by plotting with the "foreigners" (Gaïnas's Goths) that Typhos became king of Egypt, whereupon he sent his brother into exile. But since he ruled as a tyrant, everyone was

131. Ed. A. Papadopulos-Kerameus, in Ἀνάλεκτα Ἱεροσολυμιτικῆς Σταχυολογίας 1 (1891), 17, discussed in more detail below, in chapter 6, section IV, and appendix 2.

132. *PL* 52.598–99; the text is also given in parallel columns with the Greek by Papadopulos-Kerameus, p. 17.

133. For diptychs, the standard corpus is W. F. Volbach, *Elfenbeinarbeiten der Spätantike und des frühen Mittelalters*, 3d ed. (Mainz 1976); for pottery, there is a useful collection by J. W. Salomonson, *Bulletin Antieke Beschaving* 48 (1973): 5–82.

134. *Anth.Pal.* 1.36. But see Cameron, *Greek Anthology* (Oxford 1993), 153.

135. Presumably after Aurelian's return from exile, at the same time as the restoration of imperial concord: see below, p. 248.

unhappy and eventually the resentment against his "darling barbarians" (122B) burst forth in a massacre, which Synesius describes in book 2. Everyone clamored for Osiris's return, and at this juncture Aurelian did in fact return. Synesius's narrative becomes very vague and imprecise from now on, but he appears to say that Typhos was deposed and condemned and Osiris/Aurelian restored to power, thus inaugurating another golden age. It is during this second tenure of the prefecture, dated by Seeck to 402–5, that Aurelian is supposed to have put into effect the ruthless "de-Germanization" of the state for which he has been so much admired over the past century.

Absolutely central to this interpretation is Seeck's assumption that Aurelian was restored to power after the fall of Typhos. It rests on two passages of Synesius: *De providentia* 124C (which Seeck misdated and misinterpreted) and *Ep.* 61 (which he emended), and two laws (which he also emended). It also rests on his assumption (based on the wrong earthquake) that Synesius did not leave Constantinople till the autumn of 402.

It will be best to begin with the legal evidence, two laws (*Cod. Theod.* 4.2.1 and 5.1.5) addressed to Aurelian as praetorian prefect and dated 6 October 396, that is to say, *Arcadio IV (IIII) et Honorio III consulibus.* Since Caesarius was certainly prefect on that day, in fact from November 395 to July 397, either the year or the office or both must be wrong. Relying on the common confusion between imperial consulates, Seeck, followed by von Haehling, redated to *Arcad. V et Hon. IV (IIII)*, i.e., 402. On precisely the same basis Jones backdated the two laws to 394, *Arcad. III et Hon. II.* In terms of intrinsic plausibility there is nothing to choose between the two solutions; but in terms of economy Jones's is clearly preferable, since it creates no otherwise unattested office for Aurelian. We may even point to three laws of 393 (*Cod. Theod.* 12.1.131, 132, and 134) that, while clearly belonging to Aurelian's city prefecture, nonetheless incorrectly style him praetorian prefect.

Von Haehling relied heavily on Seeck's correction of ὕπατον to ὕπαρχον ("consul" to "prefect") in Synesius *Ep.* 61, assuming a reference to the earthquake of 402 and claiming that it "expressly attests" a prefecture for Aurelian in 402. But with the quake of 400 now securely reinstated, there is no call to tamper with the text. Aurelian was still consul when the quake occurred.

There is in fact decisive evidence that Aurelian did not return to the prefecture in 402 or indeed at any time before 414. Between December 414 and May 416 the prefecture was again held by a man called Aurelian.[136] According to no fewer than seven out of the thirteen laws addressed to him, this was his second tenure of the prefecture (PPO II). Furthermore, there are two separate entries in the *Paschal Chronicle* under 414 and 416 that describe him even more precisely as "for the second time prefect of the sacred praetorium and patrician." Naturally Seeck and von Haehling could not identify this man with an Aurelian who for them was already PPO II in 402.[137] Von Haehling argued from the reference to Osiris's old age in *De providentia* 124C that Aurelian would have been dead by 414.[138] But that is to misunderstand the purpose of the passage. There is no reason to believe that Aurelian was much more than sixty in 414.[139] The fact that there are no extant letters to him from Synesius later than ca. 401–2 proves nothing. He was less a personal friend than a useful patron so long as he was in power. And after 400 he was no longer in power.[140]

If the PPO II of 414–16 were another man, we would have to accept that in the course of fifteen years there were two different men called Aurelian, both of whom held at least two prefectures and won the patriciate. But when did this second Aurelian hold his first prefecture? The *fasti* of the Eastern prefecture are completely full between 381 and 414.[141] In view of the long and certainly unbroken tenure of Anthemius, it would be impossible to insert anyone else between the two appearances of Aurelian (namely, 399–400 and 414–16).[142] The decisive text is the epigram to a gold statue of Aurelian erected in the senate house:

οὗτος ὁ κοσμήσας ὑπάτων θρόνον, ὃν τρισέπαρχον
καὶ πατέρα βασιλῆες ἑὸν καλέσαντο μέγιστοι,

136. For the sources, *PLRE* I.129.

137. Seeck 1894, 449; von Haehling 1978, 82–83.

138. Demougeot (1951, 338) also assumed that Aurelian died or retired soon after 404; so too B. Malcus, *Opusc. Athen.* 7 (1967): 123 n. 5.

139. His first high office was the mastership of offices, presumably held from September 392, when Rufinus moved up to the praetorian prefecture. Even if he was as old as forty at the time, he would have been no more than sixty-two in 414. The mistaken belief that he built his church of St. Stephen in 383 has contributed to the assumption that he was much older.

140. For Seeck and von Haehling, of course, Aurelian was at the height of his power between 402–5, but this is precisely the point at issue.

141. Florus (381–83), Postumianus (383), Cynegius (384–88), Tatianus (388–92), Rufinus (392–95), Caesarius I (395–97), Eutychian I (397–99), Aurelian I (399–400), Caesarius II (400–403), Eutychian II (404–5), Anthemius (405–14), Monaxius I (414), Aurelian II (414–16), Monaxius II (416–20). For the details, see *PLRE* I–II.

142. Not even Seeck suggested extending the collegiate prefecture into the fifth century. A prefecture of Illyricum might be a possibility.

χρύσεος ἔστηκεν Αὐρηλιανός· τὸ δὲ ἔργον
τῆς βουλῆς, ἧς αὐτὸς ἑκὼν κατέπαυσεν ἀνίας.[143]

(Anth. Plan. 73)

This is the man who adorned the seat of the consuls,
who held the prefecture three times,
whom the mighty emperors called father [i.e., patrician]:
Aurelian stands in gold. It is the doing
of the senate, whose woes he willingly eased.

Since there can be no question of either the suffect or honorary consulate at this time and place,[144] this must be Aurelian cos. 400, who did indeed hold the patriciate and, as we reconstruct his career, three prefectures, in 393–94, 399–400, and 414–16.

Demougeot, convinced that Aurelian was at the height of his popularity and power between 402 and 404, argued that the prefect of 414–16 was another man; identified the prefectures of the epigram as 393–94, 399–400, and 402–4; dated the statue to 404; and claimed that the epigram described Aurelian as "delivering the senate from its enemies."[145] But the epigram refers only to Aurelian "easing the woes" of the senate. There is no need to see any allusion here to the wider political scene; Aurelian may simply have secured a reduction in the senatorial tax. He was apparently out of office from 401 to 414. So far from willingly "turning over the direction of affairs to his friend Anthemius" in 405,[146] Aurelian was Anthemius's rival. Only after Anthemius's long tenure of 405–14 was Aurelian able to return to power. Nor was it only Aurelian who was excluded from office throughout this period. It is suggestive that his son Taurus is not attested in any public office till June 416. After that, consulate, prefectures, and the patriciate followed thick and fast. He made a very late start for the scion of so distinguished a family.[147] Father and son alike were kept out of office during the ascendancy of Anthemius.

Mazzarino identified the prefects of 399–400 and 414–16 but used

143. It may be stated for the record that the text has been collated against the only MS, Marcianus gr. 481.

144. Cameron 1976c, 183.

145. Demougeot 1951, 338 n. 660.

146. Demougeot 1951, 338.

147. The fact that he was named after his grandfather in the traditional way suggests the firstborn of a first marriage, in which case, given the known dates of his father's career, he can hardly have been less than forty in 416. He was made patrician between 433 and 434 (by which time he must have been in his fifties: see the place of the patriciate in the careers listed by Barnes 1975b, 167–68) and died in 449: *PLRE* II.1056–57.

the epigram to support Seeck's prefecture in 402, arguing that the word τρισέπαρχος implied three tenures of the *same* prefecture and therefore did not include his city prefecture of 393–94.[148] But the usage of the time does not support this hypothesis. For example, the two urban and two praetorian prefectures of Petronius Maximus cos. 433 and 443 are summed up on *CIL* 6.1197 as *IIII praefectus*. Florentius cos. 429, with one urban and two praetorian prefectures documented, is several times styled "former urban and praetorian prefect six times" in the Acta of the Council of Chalcedon.[149] Closest of all in time is the predecessor and successor of Aurelian in his tenure of 414–16, Monaxius, who with one urban and two praetorian prefectures is also described as τρὶς ἔπαρχος.[150]

We may forget about the second Aurelian: there was only one, who held the praetorian prefecture twice, in 399–400 and 414–16. Thus armed, we may turn to Synesius.

Seeck found confirmation of his hypothesis in *De providentia* 124C: "[Osiris] grew more glorious in old age than youth and received from the gods the reward of presiding over the state with a higher title. . . . And the prosperity that he had given to the Egyptians and found extinguished during Typhos's supremacy, he restored and actually increased." But over and above the legal and historical objections to a second prefecture in 402, we now know that Synesius left Constantinople in the autumn of 400. *De providentia* cannot allude to any office held by Aurelian later than that year.[151] On the legal evidence Caesarius was still prefect when book 2 was being written. Furthermore, *De providentia* 124C reads rather differently in its context. The entire section that deals with Osiris's return from exile (123C–125C) has a curiously evasive and apologetic tone that must be taken into account.

It begins with the claim that while there is no problem with telling Typhos's story, because of its earthly nature, "the affairs of Osiris are a sacred tale, of divine inspiration, so that it is dangerous to risk a narrative" (123C). The rest of the section, indeed the whole of the rest of

148. Mazzarino 1942, 350.

149. *PLRE* II.478–79; all eight passages are cited in full in the prosopographical index to *ACO* IV.3.2, p. 201.

150. Callinicus *Vita Hypatii* 21.11, p. 138 Bartelink (who wrongly translates "trois fois il avait rempli la fonction de préfet du prétoire"). For Monaxius's three prefectures, see appendix 1, p. 400. It is of course merely a question of orthography whether we write one word or two. *AP* 9.697.4 uses τρισέπαρχος where *AP* 1.97.2 uses τρὶς ὕπαρχος of the same man on the same occasion, Theodorus three times urban prefect under Justinian: cf. Cameron 1976c, 269–86.

151. For Liebeschuetz's theory that book 2 was completed or interpolated after 414, see pp. 186, 315.

book 2, keeps recurring to this motif: "We must take care not to divulge any of the ineffable mysteries" (125D); "It is no act of piety to attempt to unearth what should be buried for the present" (128B); "Once [the actor] has learned his part, he must keep silent before rushing to make it public" (128D); "Men hate babblers" (129A). This unending praise of reticence is directly linked to Osiris's return. The statement that his affairs are a "sacred tale"[152] is followed by the concession that it is permitted to tell of "his birth and upbringing, his schooling, his education, his high offices," and so on as far as the conspiracy: that is to say, a recapitulation of book 1. "Let his holy return be told also," he adds, describing it in half a dozen lines (124A). But the next section begins: "This much we may venture to say about Osiris; let holy silence cloak the rest. So says one who touches on holy discourse cautiously. It would take a rash mind and tongue to attempt what lies beyond; let it remain in holy silence, undisturbed by writing, lest someone 'cast his eyes on things unpermitted.'" Then after several more lines of the same: "Perhaps this is the one thing we may and do say, cloaking the inviolable as we are able: the glory of Osiris's youth increased with his years, and the gods granted him the reward of presiding over the state with a higher title, to show that he was above the injuries inflicted by men." Read in its context, this extract does not at all make the straightforward statement of fact that it is tempting to deduce from it in isolation. In the first place, Osiris is not simply reappointed to the kingship of Egypt. Synesius's terminology is much less precise: "preside over the state ($\dot{\epsilon}\pi\iota\sigma\tau\alpha\tau\hat{\eta}\sigma\alpha\iota\ \tau\hat{\eta}\ \pi\sigma\lambda\iota\tau\epsilon\dot{\iota}\alpha$) with a higher title ($\sigma\dot{\nu}\nu\theta\eta\mu\alpha$)." And unlike the kingship, which he had originally won "on the vote of gods and godly men," this "higher title" is given him by the gods alone as a consolation for "the injuries inflicted by men." And why is this the only thing Synesius dare say about Osiris's return? If he had been restored to the throne of which he had been robbed by the wicked Typhos, why not proclaim it joyfully from the rooftops?

Doubts about the reality of Osiris's restoration are reinforced by the elaborate piece of apologetic with which the section closes at 125C:

> But if the gods, having brought him back from exile, did not immediately put everything into his hands at the same time ($\ddot{\alpha}\mu\alpha$), let us make no more of it than this: the nature of the body politic does not admit of wholesale change for the better as it does for the worse. For evil is an instinctive thing, whereas virtue is acquired by toil. Someone

---

152. The phrase "sacred tale" Synesius had used twice in book 1, at 89B and 115B, in the latter case (the riddle of the wolf) again, *more Herodoteo*, of a matter he refused to discuss further.

must intervene to clear the way (ἔδει δὲ μεσεῦσαι τοὺς προκαθαίρον-
τας); the divine must proceed in a leisurely and orderly fashion (σχολῇ
καὶ τάξει). It was necessary for Osiris, before engaging in affairs (πρὶν
ἄσχολον εἶναι),[153] to see and hear many things. A king's ears are often
deceived.

Synesius concedes that Osiris was *not* restored to power on his return,
or at any rate not to all his powers all at once.

The reference to delay might still be explained on Seeck's hypothesis, as for him several months passed between Gaïnas's defeat in December 400 and Aurelian's restoration in the winter of 401/2.[154] More recently, Liebeschuetz saw an allusion to the delay of fourteen years
before Aurelian's eventual restoration in 414. There are various problems
with this hypothesis, not least the fact that Synesius died in 412.[155] But
the main objection to both is that Synesius is not describing delay, either
brief or long, terminated by restoration. The restoration, such as it is,
comes first. Nothing in the text gives any reason to believe that Osiris
had "seen and heard" enough things to become king again at the time
Synesius wrote. If he had, Synesius would have done better to eliminate
all those lame excuses about the advantages of waiting.

There is another pointer in the summary of Osiris's career at 123D,
translated as follows by Fitzgerald: "how the plot was formed against
him, to what extent it succeeded and how it ultimately failed."[156] Here, if

153. σχολή is a word of many meanings; elsewhere Synesius draws a contrast between σχολή and political activity (*Ep.* 100). When picked up in the next sentence by
ἄσχολος there can be little doubt: at the time of writing Osiris was not engaged in affairs;
he had not yet been reappointed to public office.

154. So at least his latest thoughts: Seeck 1913, 326.

155. Lacombrade 1951a, 273; Coster 1968, 262–63. Liebeschuetz (1983, 40) argues that
"in view of the rather chaotic survival of only part of Synesius's correspondence" the absence of any reference to the patriarchate of Cyril (November 412) or the death of Hypatia
(415) cannot be pressed. But all we can be reasonably sure of is that Synesius did not publish his letters himself (see Garzya 1979, xlviii–li). There is no evidence that large numbers
have perished. No fewer than 44 of the 156 surviving letters date from his episcopate,
covering a period of barely two years. Since they were not arranged chronologically (indeed, most of the episcopal letters appear in the first half of the collection), we cannot
simply hypothesize the loss of a later block. The fact that even in the collection's "chaotic"
state Synesius's last years are best represented suggests that the argument from silence is
trustworthy.

156. καὶ ὡς ἐπ᾽ αὐτὸν ἡ συνωμοσία συνέστη, καὶ εἰς ὅσον ἐκράτησε καὶ ὡς οὐκ εἰς
ἅπαν ἐξίκετο. There is also the preface (88A), presumably the latest part of the work,
which explains that book 2 was added "after the return of the best men, at their request, so
that the book should not be left incomplete with their misfortunes." There is no suggestion
of any major new development beyond the mere fact of the return of Aurelian and his
associates from exile.

anywhere, we should expect a resounding reference to the failure of Ty-phos's plot—if Osiris really had been restored. In fact, the final clause makes a much more modest claim: "and how it did not succeed in every respect" (ὡς οὐκ εἰς ἅπαν ἐξίκετο). The "plot" as Synesius had described it in book 1 could be said to have suffered a couple of setbacks with Gaïnas's defeat and Aurelian's return from exile, but so long as Caesarius remained in office and Aurelian out of office, it had not entirely failed.

Osiris/Aurelian's "higher title" is evidently some new honor, and so not the consulate, which Aurelian had held since January 400, and not the prefecture, which he had held before his exile. The only alternative is the patriciate, which was not an office conferring power but a personal title.[157] It is worth exploring the standing of the patriciate. By a law of 382 (*Cod. Theod.* 6.6.1) it was established (1) that the consulate took prece-dence over all other offices, (2) that the consulate and either the prae-torian prefecture or the mastership of soldiers took precedence over the consulate alone, and (3) that the consulate and one of these offices com-bined with the patriciate should outrank any other combination. As pre-fect, consul, and patrician Aurelian could reach no higher. But even so it is doubtful whether he outranked his brother. Caesarius had won both consulate and prefecture first and is attested as patrician by an inscrip-tion from Tralles that dates at latest from his second prefecture.[158] Even if Aurelian's patriciate came first, it is significant that Synesius lays such weight on a detail of (thinly disguised) Roman protocol. On the mythical plane, nothing could be "higher" than the kingship of Egypt; yet this he conspicuously fails to mention.

In other circumstances one might have assumed that Aurelian simply retired from public life. In the late Roman world, as in eighteenth- or nineteenth-century England, aristocrats often felt that they had done their duty by state and family if they held high office for a year or two. But in Aurelian's case we cannot make this assumption, for Synesius's lame excuses make it clear that his supporters had hoped and still hoped that he would return to power. Book 2 closes by exhorting readers to wait patiently: "It makes no sense for a man who will soon attain his just deserts to distress himself." He ends with a tag from Pindar: "The re-maining days are the wisest witnesses" (*Ol.* 1.33–34).

There should no longer be any mystery about all this mystification and evasiveness. Synesius is trying to make the best of the fact that

157. On other evidence Aurelian is not attested as patrician until 414/15 (*PLRE* I.129), but then there is no evidence at all for his career between 399 and 414.
158. LeBas-Waddington 1652d, with Mazzarino 1942, addenda to p. 349; *PLRE* I.171.

while no doubt welcomed warmly enough on his return, especially by his supporters, Aurelian was *not* restored to office. He had to be content with the trappings rather than the realities of power.

The evidence of the letters bears out the reluctant admission of the *Egyptian Tale*. First, *Ep.* 34 (= 47G), a letter written after Synesius's return to Cyrene to request patronage:

> Not yet does Providence care for the Romans, but she will one day, and those who have the power to save the commonwealth (οἱ τὰ κοινὰ σῴζειν δυνάμενοι) will not skulk in their houses (οἰκουρήσουσιν) for ever. As to our friend the rhetor, *the power you possess at the present* (ἡ παροῦσά σοι δύναμις) suffices for his current request. May he alone profit from your power for the moment, though later may all mankind profit.

It is usually assumed that this letter dates from before one or another of Aurelian's praetorian prefectures, whether the real one of 399 or Seeck's of 402. But the reference to Providence suggests *On Providence*, the subtitle of Synesius's *Egyptian Tale*. And it is difficult not to recognize in "those with the power to save the commonwealth" the citizens of Constantinople who once did just that, in Synesius's eyes, by massacring the Goths in the city. No one could have foreseen this remarkable and apparently spontaneous uprising, vividly described in the *Egyptian Tale*, and the unfair description of these people as now "skulking in their houses" (the word is usually used of women, or of men avoiding military service)[159] puts the allusion beyond doubt. The letter must have been written soon after Aurelian's return from exile, and the reference to his "present power sufficing" to help Synesius's rhetor makes it clear that Aurelian no longer held high office.

One other letter to Aurelian from Cyrene (*Ep.* 31, p. 45G) opens as follows: "If cities have souls, as they must, divine guardians and spirits, you may be sure that they are grateful to you and *remember* (ἀπομεμνῆσ-θαι) your good works, those which you brought about for all nations during your great administration (ἐπὶ τῆς μεγαλῆς ἀρχῆς [perhaps rather "during your tenure of the supreme office"])." Garzya assigns this letter to Aurelian's supposed prefecture of 402, but Synesius here must be alluding to the tax remissions that he had asked for in his *De regno* (27D) and for granting which during his first prefecture he had praised Aurelian in the *Egyptian Tale* (103D). The reference to "remembering" only confirms that Synesius is referring back to Aurelian's first tenure—and suggests that he was no longer in office when Synesius wrote.

159. Cf. LSJ, s.v. II.

VII. THE FALL OF TYPHOS

If so, then there is a consequence that has not so far been explored. If Aurelian did not return to the prefecture after his exile, who did become prefect then? It has hitherto been taken for granted, even by Jones, that both the sequence of prefects and Synesius indicate a change of prefect after the defeat of Gaïnas.

For Jones, one of the attractions in having Eutychian as Typhos was that on the legal evidence he was replaced by Caesarius before the end of 400. That harmonized nicely with a date of 23 December for the defeat of Gaïnas.[160] For Seeck, things were not quite so straightforward. He could not place Aurelian's restoration (inferred from *De providentia*) later than Synesius's departure in (for him) the fall of 402. He was therefore compelled to emend the law that kept Caesarius, his Typhos, in office as late as 11 June 403.[161]

But if on a closer reading Synesius does not after all say that Osiris was restored to office, does he in fact say that Typhos fell from office? Once again, he *appears* to say this, but it is a matter that requires a closer look.

Synesius is at such pains throughout the *Egyptian Tale* to link Typhos with the barbarians that it might seem inevitable that in due course he would share Gaïnas's ruin. After the massacre, claims Synesius, people called for Osiris, "seeing no other salvation for their affairs" (121C). This they did at what is called an "assembly" (ἐκκλησία), presided over by a "great priest." Who does this priest represent? Older scholars took him for John Chrysostom, the patriarch.[162] But since Seeck he has been generally seen as Arcadius.[163] Neither identification really works.

160. *Chron.Min.* II.66. In *PLRE* I.171 Eutychian's deposition is dated "after July 12," implying that he fell immediately after the massacre.

161. *Cod.Just.* 7.41.2, with Seeck 1919, 77.

162. E.g., Volkman 1869, 177, note; Sievers 1870, 366; Crawford 1901, 456 ("can be no other than").

163. E.g. (as though it were self-evident), Clauss 1980, 134: "Arcadius wird in dem Mythos nur zweimal unter der Bezeichnung ἱερεὺς μέγας kurz erwähnt." So too Bury in his edition of Gibbon (Gibbon 1909, 3:533): "The insignificance of Arcadius is reflected in the myth by the fact that he is never mentioned except in one passage where he appears as the high priest." McCormick (1986, 109 n. 126), while apparently accepting the identification with Arcadius, infers that the "assembly" is a "thanksgiving service" to commemorate the expulsion of the Goths. But this *ekklesia* is held immediately after the massacre, when the main body of Gaïnas's army was still encamped outside the city, poised to take terrible revenge if Gaïnas so ordered. It was during this period of uncertainty that Synesius wrote book 1 of *De providentia* (see below), which explains its astonishingly conciliatory attitude to Gaïnas. This was hardly yet the moment for a thanksgiving service. In any case, such a hypothesis is excluded by the context. The *ekklesia* is clearly an (anachronistic) public assembly.

The fact that the word used for "assembly" is *ekklesia*, by Synesius's day the normal term for a church, might be thought to point to Chrysostom. And Chrysostom did play an important part in the events of 399–400: pleading for the lives of first Eutropius and then the exiles, standing up to Gaïnas over the question of the Arian church, and leading an embassy to Gaïnas in Thrace.[164] But if Synesius had thought to introduce Chrysostom into his allegory, he might have portrayed him doing the things he actually did. Yet Synesius's priest holds a public meeting at which he promises that the exiles will return and the people decide to "string Typhos along for a while."[165] No patriarch could make promises like this. The priest's power has been thought to point to Arcadius,[166] but there is no obvious reason to give him priestly functions Arcadius did not possess. On his only other appearance, Typhos tries to "get around the priest with flattery and bribes" (122A), an absurd tactic for a prefect to employ on his emperor.

There is a further alternative: the priest has *no* counterpart in the real world. Like the old king in book 1, he is simply a stock character. With the old king dead and Osiris in exile, Synesius needed a force for good to oppose to Typhos, and within his Egyptian framework a high priest was the only character who could be depicted as exercising influence over even a king.[167] It should be proof enough that he appears in such an obviously fictitious context. The fate of praetorian prefects was not debated in popular assemblies in the year A.D. 400. And the alleged outcry for the recall of Osiris is itself almost certainly an invention of Synesius, presupposing Aurelian's actual return soon afterwards and Synesius's own allegation in book 1 that it was Caesarius, rather than Gaïnas, who was responsible for his exile.[168] Since the hostages were actually prisoners of Gaïnas,[169] no one in Constantinople had the power to recall them. Nor is there any reason to believe that many wanted to; after all it was Aurelian's policies that had led to Gaïnas's coup, and there was no reason to believe that he would cope with the aftermath of the massacre any better than Caesarius.

Just as Aurelian was not immediately restored to power, so "Typhos did not immediately suffer his due penalty" (121D). In fact, "as he was

164. Albert 1984, 151–79.
165. βουκολῆσαι, 121C; the general sense is clearly that they will let him continue as king for a while.
166. E.g., Grützmacher 1913, 55.
167. The contemporary parallel here is perhaps less close than it might seem. No bishop of Constantinople had yet attempted to stand up to an emperor.
168. See below, pp. 319–23.
169. See chapter 6, section III.

still in the outward panoply of despotic power, he began levying taxes more keenly and shamefully than ever." A little later we read that "he was glad that he would not live to see Osiris return and take part in politics" (122B). But eventually, although late in the day, there was a meeting of "gods and elders" concerning Typhos, and

> the men condemn Typhos to imprisonment (φρουράν) and decide to hold a second trial to determine what punishment he should suffer or what fine he should pay; the gods praised the assessors (σύνεδροι) who took part for having condemned him according to his deserts, and they themselves voted that when he had left this life he should be given up to the avenging deities and should dwell in Cocytus.[170]

Both the status and the actions of this fantastic tribunal are unclear, to say the least. Yet without a word of qualification or justification, Bury translated it into sober record: "The conduct of Typhos was judicially investigated, his treasonable collusion with Gaïnas was abundantly exposed, and he was condemned provisionally to imprisonment."[171] Stein went farther still, insisting that the "synod of gods and elders" at 122D "can only represent the consistory and senate combined," allegedly the first example of a new judicial procedure in which senators were allowed to participate in the trials of their peers.[172] It is merely a detail that, as Stein himself conceded, all the other political trials of the age (those of Tatianus, Timasius, and Eutropius) were held in the old way before the emperor or his nominees.[173] More important, he does not justify his assumption that "gods" here alone in Synesius refers to imperial officials rather than to gods pure and simple, who of course do play a large part in *De providentia*. In fact Synesius makes it quite clear that he means what he says by referring to the two categories of jurors again on the next page (123A–B) as gods and "humans" (ἄνθρωποι).

The presence of divine jurors should suffice to warn us that these proceedings cannot be translated straightforwardly into fifth-century realities. The gods' punishment sounds frightful enough, but of course it will be posthumous. The imprisonment threatened by the human jurors sounds more realistic, yet they postpone to a later occasion the specifics of the sentence, and nothing is ever said of the promised second trial.

---

170. 123B.

171. Bury (1923) 1958, 134, repeating almost exactly what he wrote in his first edition (1889, 89). Even the normally sensible Liebeschuetz took this preposterous trial seriously (1990, 122).

172. Stein 1949, 73 n. 3 ("ne peuvent signifier que").

173. Stein 1949, 72 n. 1.

Once again, it does not translate into historical terms. From time to time imperial ministers or generals were prosecuted: the last few years had seen the trials of Tatianus, Timasius, Abundantius, and Eutropius.[174] But in each case the trial was merely a device to give a veneer of legality to condemnation. Not one of these marked men was ever acquitted, still less restored to office. And yet on a literal translation of the present case we are asked to believe that Caesarius was actually tried for betraying Constantinople to the barbarians, with witnesses producing "damaging evidence that he had surrendered key positions and all but arranged the siege himself" (123A), and then was neither deposed nor executed.

We cannot even take refuge in the supposition that he was acquitted. The next section describes Osiris's return from exile, which culminated in his "sparing his hostile brother for the second time, begging off the anger of an infuriated people, and beseeching the gods to save him, acting more generously than justly" (124A). If clemency was required to save Typhos, it follows that he was found guilty. Aurelian's clemency is taken quite literally in most modern accounts, which represent Caesarius escaping the execution that awaited his associate Fravitta only thanks to the magnanimity of his brother.[175] But once again, it does not translate. The penalty of a praetorian prefect found guilty of treason was not determined by popular vote, nor was Aurelian, who at this point held no office at all, in any position to exercise such clemency. The one fact that underlies this whole fantastic rigmarole is that nothing at all happened to Caesarius. Indeed the evidence of the laws shows he continued as prefect.

Since there can have been no such trial and no such act of clemency in the real world of Constantinople in A.D. 400, why invent them? If his purpose was to depict Caesarius's power crumbling while he still remained in the prefecture, Synesius could have devised more plausible stratagems: perhaps something Roman like popular protests in the circus, or spectacular celestial manifestations from the gods. Why something so precise and yet so feeble as a nonexistent trial followed by nonexistent clemency to explain the inconclusiveness of the trial? The answer is simple. Both trial and clemency are data of the myth.

According to Plutarch, "Typhos formally accused Horus of being an illegitimate child, but with the help of Hermes to plead his cause it was

174. For the sources, see their entries in PLRE I.
175. E.g., Demougeot 1951, 265: "Caesarius et Fravitta furent naturellement condamnés à mort, mais Aurelianus se donna l'élégance de gracier son frère, qui ne pouvait plus être son rival politique." On the execution of Fravitta see below, chapter 6, section IV.

decided *by the gods* that he was legitimate."[176] Egyptian sources imply that the lawsuit concerned not Horus's legal entitlement to his father's kingdom, but rather its apportionment between Typhos and Horus. Nonetheless, they do bear out the story of a formal trial before the gods. Since he has not made Horus an actor in the allegory, Synesius had to alter the details: he made Typhos the defendant rather than the plaintiff. Similarly, the former conspirators who bring evidence against Typhos at the trial (123A) are a transposed echo of the "many" partisans who desert Typhos's side for Horus's before their battle. In the myth, as in Synesius, the deserters were Typhos's closest intimates, including "his concubine Thoueris."[177]

Furthermore, Plutarch also records that after Typhos had been captured by Horus and delivered in chains to Isis, she "did not cause him to be put to death but released him and let him go." This unexpected release of the mythical Typhos was a godsend to Synesius, desperate to explain why Caesarius had still not paid the penalty for his crimes. The two incidents are not connected in Plutarch, but they are related in successive chapters, and it is not surprising that Synesius was moved to combine them. Since no room had been found for Isis, obviously someone else had to do the sparing, and since Osiris had spared Typhos once already in book 1,[178] he was the obvious choice.

In general, book 2 owes little to the myth, for obvious reasons: the return of Osiris and the absence of both Isis and Horus made it impossible to round the story off in the usual way. But being obliged to continue the story he had begun, it was only natural for Synesius to incorporate whatever mythical detail he could.

Contemporary readers would not have misread the passage, partly because whether or not they knew the myth, they at least knew the facts. And partly because they would not have been expecting Synesius to tell the truth in the first place. Moderns have made the colossal error of supposing that Synesius was celebrating the victory of Aurelian and gloating over the defeat of Caesarius. The truth was the exact reverse. He was trying to make the best of the fact that Caesarius won and Aurelian lost. There would have been no point in simply relating the facts to contemporaries who knew them already. When he finished book 1,

176. *De Is. et Os.* 358D, restated in more symbolic terms at 373B: see Griffiths 1970 ad loc.

177. Plut. *De Is. et Os.* 358D.

178. 104B; cf. 97A–B, where Osiris rejects the gods' repeated warning that he should banish his brother.

Synesius could hope to see Caesarius fall soon. He invoked the mythical
paradigm of Osiris's eventual vindication at the hands of Horus (115B).
By the time he wrote book 2, this hope had dimmed. Now the best he
could do was to suggest that although Aurelian was not actually restored to power, he had won a moral victory; and that although Caesarius remained in power, he was universally despised as a traitor.
Again, he turned to the myth. Contemporaries were never in danger of
misunderstanding this purpose, since naturally they knew which of the
two was prefect. The problem arises only for us unfortunate historians
of the twentieth century, who are forced to use Synesius to discover
such elementary facts.

At 114C the god prophesies that Typhos's reign will last "not years,
but months." Many a scholar has fallen into the trap of taking this as a
statement of fact, certifying a very short tenure of the prefecture for Caesarius (or in Jones's case, Eutychian).[179] But on any hypothesis Typhos
was still in power when Synesius wrote book 1. The "months, not
years" is an encouraging prophecy *for the future.* Synesius may well have
believed that Caesarius could not hang on much longer, but his belief is
worth nothing as evidence.

It is instructive to compare the very limited claim made in the preface. Synesius took the story up again in book 2, he alleges, "since those
things that were foretold according to God [i.e., the fall of Typhos]
seemed to be in the course of fulfillment (ἐδόκει περαίνεσθαι)" (88B). The
present infinitive is to be compared with the present participle in the following sentence, "the tyrant's overthrow being already set in motion"
(πραττομένης οὖν ἤδη τῆς τυραννικῆς καθαιρέσεως). Both sentences
stop significantly short of asserting that Typhos has actually fallen.

While certainly suggesting, and perhaps even believing, that Caesarius's credit was irretrievably ruined and his fall from power imminent, Synesius nowhere says that Typhos was actually deposed from
office.

So there is no reason to tamper with the date of *CJ* 7.41.2. Caesarius
remained in office till at least 11 June 403 and perhaps till the end of the
year. By February 404 Eutychian was briefly back in office before the
long tenure (405–14) of Anthemius. This second tenure of Caesarius will
have lasted from April 400 to perhaps the end of 403, three and a half
years. What with his earlier spells as both prefect and *magister officiorum,*

179. E.g., Bury (1923) 1958, 134 n. 3: "From Synesius we know that his tenure of the
office was less than a year."

that was long enough for any man to devote to such responsible offices. There is no need to suppose that his crimes finally caught up with him. He may simply have resigned—or even died. At all events, we can forget the idea that he was disgraced and condemned on Aurelian's return. He did not go down in history as a traitor, but as "one of the great men of the age, promoted to the rank of consul and prefect."[180]

For the sake of clarity, here is our own reconstruction of the *fasti* of the Eastern prefecture from 395 to 416, except in the case of Aurelian's first prefecture observing the limits supplied by dated laws:

30 November 395–13 July 397	Caesarius (24 laws)
4 September 397–25 July 399	Eutychian (25 laws)
27 September 399–April 400	Aurelian (2 laws)
8 December 400–11 June 403	Caesarius II (3 laws)
3 February 404–11 June 405	Eutychian II (4 laws)
10 July 405–18 April 414	Anthemius (59 laws)
10 May 414–30 November 414	Monaxius (2 laws)[181]
30 December 414–10 May 416	Aurelian II (12 laws)

180. Sozomen (*HE* 9.2.4), writing half a century later.
181. On the significance of the brief prefecture of Monaxius between Anthemius and Aurelian II, see appendix 1.

SIX

DE PROVIDENTIA
AND THE BARBARIANS

I. THE MASSACRE

We possess numerous accounts of the massacre of the Goths in Constantinople: Synesius, Socrates, Sozomen, and Zosimus; and less full but still important notices in Philostorgius and Marcellinus.[1] But only one is ever taken seriously.

Generations of scholars have congratulated themselves on possessing in Synesius a well-informed eyewitness, whom they follow unreservedly as their prime source for the events of 400. So, for example, Demougeot, who explained in revealing detail why Synesius's account is always to be preferred:[2] Zosimus is suspect because he drew on Eunapius, who was born in Sardis, one of the cities menaced by Tribigild and Gaïnas. Yet it is easy enough to discount this rather minor bias, and Sardian chauvinism can hardly explain (to give an example discussed in detail below) the conflict between Synesius and Zosimus about the presence of palace guards in Constantinople.

Socrates and Sozomen Demougeot considered inferior to Synesius

---

1. Syn. *De providentia* 2.1–3; Socr. *HE* 6.6; Soz. *HE* 8.4 (clearly based on Socrates, but with a number of independent details); Zos. 5.18.10–19.1–5; Philostorg. *HE* 11.8, p. 139 Bidez-Winkelmann; Marcellin. s.a. 399 = *Chron.Min.* II.66.
2. Demougeot 1951, 248 n. 74.

because they drew on Eusebius Scholasticus's lost epic poem *Gaïnias*,[3] which she characterizes as an "oeuvre de circonstance" written after the event, flawed by its weakness for the miraculous.[4] But *De providentia* was no less an "oeuvre de circonstance," and while the laws of nature are never suspended in its narrative portions, nonetheless gods and demons frequently join in the action. Eusebius's alleged weakness for the miraculous rests on the assumption that it was from him that Socrates got his story of angels in the form of gigantic soldiers foiling repeated attempts by Gaïnas's men to burn down the imperial palace. But it is for what he twice calls "the war" that Socrates cites Eusebius, and it may be that the poem, as we might expect of an epic, was largely concerned with Fravitta's campaign and the sea battle off the Chersonnese.[5] If so, it should be noted that this is the most straightforward and factual part of Socrates' account. At the very least, Eusebius's poem would have made a fascinating comparison with the contemporary epics Claudian was composing for Western audiences during this period. And inevitably it would have reflected a different point of view from *De providentia*. A poem on Gaïnas's defeat could not have had Aurelian as its hero.

It is worth observing before we proceed how tendentiously the word "eyewitness" is applied to *De providentia*.[6] An eyewitness is someone who "has seen an occurrence or an object with his own eyes and so is able to give a firsthand report on it."[7] Synesius did indeed live in Constantinople during Gaïnas's coup, but he was not alone among our sources in doing so. Socrates was a native,[8] and Eusebius at least resided

3. It is only Socrates who cites Eusebius, and the similarities between them are best explained by the assumption that Sozomen copied Socrates rather than a source common to both. Sozomen did not share Socrates' enthusiasm for classicizing literature: Cameron 1982, 282.

4. Garzya too praises Synesius as "un testimone oculare dei fatti, più fededegno sia di un Eunapio . . . dislocato nella lontana Sardi, sia di un Socrate, influenzato dalla Gainiade di Eusebio Scolastico" (*Hommage à André N. Stratos* 2 [Athens 1986]: 440), and Becatti (1959, 167) underlines the difference between all other sources and "un testimone oculare sensibile e appassionato come Sinesio."

5. Clover (1979, 67–68), approved by Paschoud (comm. p. 163), detects a metrical sequence in Eunapius frag. 81 Mueller—$\pi\eta\xi\acute{\alpha}\mu\epsilon\nu\text{o}\varsigma$ $\delta\rho\text{o}\mu\acute{\alpha}\delta\alpha\varsigma$ $\tau\rho\iota\alpha\kappa\text{o}\nu\tau\acute{\eta}\rho\epsilon\iota\varsigma$ $\Lambda\iota\beta\epsilon\rho\nu\acute{\iota}\delta\omega\nu$ $\tau\acute{\upsilon}\pi\omega$—and suggests that it is a brief quotation from Eusebius's poem, concerned with the sea battle.

6. It appears in every modern account, from Seeck ("so frisch und anschaulich dargestellt, wie nur ein Augenzeuge es vermag," 1894, 442) to Barnes ("a patent eyewitness account," 1986a, 96).

7. *Webster's Third New International Dictionary*, ed., s.v. "eyewitness."

8. Born (ca. 380) and educated in Constantinople, where he seems to have spent most of his life: Chestnut 1977, 168f. It has often been alleged on the basis of an "as they say" when discussing Chrysostom (*HE* 6.3) that Socrates was absent during the period

there at this period. Possibly Philostorgius did too;[9] he gives what is undoubtedly an eyewitness description of the short, swarthy, lethargic Arcadius standing by the side of the tall, handsome, alert Rufinus.[10] When Socrates calls Eusebius an "eyewitness (αὐτόπτης) of the war," he uses the word in its strict sense: Eusebius had actually watched the destruction of Gaïnas's fleet, perhaps off the coast at Lampsacus.[11] Very little of *De providentia* even purports to give an account of things Synesius had actually seen. The story of the rustic philosopher in book 1 appears to be a fancifully embroidered autobiographical account, and we follow earlier historians in extracting from it details applicable to Synesius's embassy.[12] On the other hand, it is not the sort of tight narrative the phrase "eyewitness account" generally implies. Similarly, Synesius doubtless saw the festivities associated with Aurelian's return from exile but alludes to them summarily rather than describing them.[13] The part that comes closest to an "eyewitness narrative," the description of the massacre, is just as distorted by fiction and interpretation as the rest of the work. Without Socrates, Sozomen, and Zosimus we should not have been able to supplement and correct Synesius's tendentious account. To praise him as an eyewitness is to misplace the emphasis. As with Claudian, it is his bias rather than his accuracy that gives his testimony its unique value.

Unfortunately, the only detail on which all sources agree is that Gaïnas was planning to burn and loot the city—where his own house stood. A drastic plan, but most modern accounts treat it as both true and uncontroversial. For example, F. M. Clover explains it as follows:

> He had then crossed the straits and entered Constantinople. Immediately[14] he tried to occupy the capital with barbarian forces under his command. After the attempt failed, he withdrew from the city, intending to have his troops seize it on a signal. The plan miscarried. The angry inhabitants massacred those of his men who were in the capital.[15]

398–404, but the reference is to Chrysostom's *temperament*, and we need only conclude that the young layman never met the patriarch. Nor need the reference to Eusebius as an eyewitness imply that Socrates was absent himself, since it is to Eusebius's qualifications to write on the war as an eyewitness that he is alluding.

9. See the evidence assembled in Bidez's edition, pp. cvii–ix.

10. *HE* 11.3, p. 134.24f. Bidez-Winkelmann.

11. It was Lampsacus that Gaïnas was aiming for, according to Socrates.

12. *De insomniis* 148C–D, also in supernatural terms, at least confirms the sense of danger and unpleasantness Synesius carried away from this period.

13. 124A; cf. 88B.

14. In fact after nearly three months' delay, from April to 12 July.

15. Clover 1979, 65.

That is to say, the failure of the plan to seize Constantinople is held to explain the massacre. But if Gaïnas's aims had been so straightforward, he had no need to negotiate at length with Tribigild and Arcadius. He had for a long time given every indication that all he wanted was a government at Constantinople willing to bestow on him the command and honors to which he felt entitled.[16] There can be no question that he exploited Tribigild's revolt to his own advantage, but Zosimus concedes that at a stage when "everyone" understood his true goals Gaïnas himself continued to play the loyal Roman officer.

Why revert to barbarism when he had finally come so far within the Roman system? He had been appointed *magister militum praesentalis*. He had successfully demanded the exile of the PPO. Politically he was already master of Constantinople. As *praesentalis*, stationed at the capital, he had free access to the city. Indeed, he and his family had lived there for many years, in a grand mansion still known as the House of Gaïnas half a millenium later.[17] Even Synesius states matter of factly that "the general of the foreign troops had his home in the royal city" (108B).

If it was cash he needed to pay his men, extortion would have been simpler and more satisfactory than violence. As Socrates put it, the malleable Arcadius "was ready to conciliate Gaïnas in every way, in both word and deed." It is significant that the only specific instance of looting mentioned is Socrates' claim that Gaïnas had been *intending* to rob the banks, but the bankers, "forewarned of his intention," hid their cash. A truly ruthless pillager would hardly have been deterred by so simple a stratagem. The only specific allegation of burning is another and even less plausible unfulfilled intention:[18] a plan to burn the imperial palace, foiled by angels. What could the Goths possibly have achieved that was worth the opprobrium of burning the palace?[19]

With the sole exception of Synesius, all surviving accounts of Gaïnas's coup were written after Alaric's sack of Rome in 410. They all make the implicit assumption that as a Goth Gaïnas intended to sack New Rome in the same way. In fact the comparison suggests precisely the opposite conclusion. It was not, as Romans flattered themselves, because

16. For full discussion of Gaïnas's successive demands and bargains, see below, pp. 324–28.

17. Preger, *Script. orig. Cpol.*, 2:252.5–7.

18. "All of a sudden the imperial palace went up in flames": so H. Wolfram, *Die Geburt Mitteleuropas* (Vienna and Berlin 1987), 149, not noticing that, like the planned bank robberies, this too was an unfulfilled intention.

19. Demougeot (1951, 255), anxious at all costs to salvage an ancient source, suggests: "Peut-être eut-il l'intention de s'emparer du palais, non pour le détruire, mais pour s'assurer de la personne de l'empereur et se débarrasser de la cour restée nationaliste."

Alaric was obsessed with Rome that he laid siege to the city three times. He was trying to extort from the Western government a position for himself and his people within the empire. It was only because all his attempts failed that, in frustration, he finally sacked the city for its gold and valuables:

> For Alaric, the sack of Rome was an irrelevance, forced upon him by the failure of his other policies; and his aim now, as he marched south to attempt a crossing to Africa, was the same as it had always been—to win security for his people, and a place for them to settle in peace. This, it is clear, had been his objective throughout his negotiations with the court of Ravenna during the two years of his occupation of Italy. During this time, he had used the threat to march on Rome as merely the most valuable diplomatic counter which he possessed in his attempts to achieve a negotiated settlement with Honorius.[20]

There is an obvious parallel in tactics. Both Gaïnas and Alaric used extortion as a means to an end. But their aims were different and Gaïnas (briefly) *succeeded* where Alaric was to fail. Far from being a frustrated barbarian chieftain, unable to satisfy the following on which his power depended except by plunder, in April 400 Gaïnas had reached the summit of his ambitions. Arcadius had granted his every demand.[21] He was supreme commander of the Eastern army and consul designate for 401.[22]

His aims were simpler, of course; unlike Alaric, he had no people to provide for. This point has been obscured by the tendency of our sources to depict him as the leader of a barbarian horde. A modern version of this position has recently been embraced by Liebeschuetz, for whom Gaïnas commanded only barbarian federates, unlike his colleague Leo, who is held to have led Roman troops.[23] This is paradoxical to start with, since Liebeschuetz does not dispute that Leo was Gaïnas's second in command (ὑποστράτηγος). But why should the second in command be given Roman troops while the commander in chief led only federates? In addition, both Liebeschuetz and Albert have argued that Gaïnas had a *personal* barbarian retinue anticipating the *bucellarii* of later times.[24] For a true understanding of Gaïnas's intentions it is important to disprove these assumptions.

20. Matthews 1975, 301.
21. Demougeot 1951, 251: "Arcadius consentit à tout."
22. See p. 327.
23. Liebeschuetz 1990, 101–2.
24. Albert 1984, 112f. ("Gefolgschaft"); Liebeschuetz 1986c. Against this suggestion Gluschanin (1989, 246–47) makes the excellent objection that Gaïnas had been unemployed since 395 and was hardly in a position to pay for a private army.

In order to maintain that Gaïnas was appointed to a federate command in 399, Liebeschuetz was obliged to maintain that he was still a
count (*comes foederatorum*) at the time,[25] as he had been on the Frigidus
campaign in 394. On that occasion Zosimus lists Timasius and Stilicho as
magistri militum in command "of the Roman troops," and Gaïnas (with
Saul and Bacurius) as *comites* in charge of barbarian federates.[26] By 400
Gaïnas was certainly *praesentalis*. But when was he promoted? Liebeschuetz disposes of this vital point in a footnote, with no systematic discussion of the relatively abundant sources, remarking that only Socrates
"implies" that Gaïnas held a lesser rank, but is "probably careless and
wrong."[27]

The facts are as follows. Socrates states explicitly at the beginning of
his account of the rebellion that Gaïnas "was appointed general (στρατηλάτης) of the Roman horse and foot."[28] John of Antioch, who seems
otherwise to be following Socrates very closely here, adds that he "had
only recently been promoted to general." Since there seems no reason
why he should have thought to add such a detail, it may be that this
phrase has fallen out of the text of Socrates.[29] Philostorgius refers to
Gaïnas twice as "general" (στρατηγός) directly after referring to Tribigild "having the rank of count."[30] Theodoret, again at the beginning of
his account, says that "Gaïnas was a general at that time," and (more
important) describes his troops as consisting of "many of his fellow-
tribesmen, but also a Roman army of cavalry and infantry."[31] Zosimus
too twice styles Gaïnas "general" (στρατηγός) at the beginning of his account. It is only Sozomen who might be held to "imply" otherwise, by
postponing reference to Gaïnas's promotion to "command of infantry
and foot" until his meeting with Arcadius at Chalcedon.[32] But since even
Sozomen begins his account by describing how Gaïnas "rose from common soldier to the rank of general" (ἐς τὴν τῶν στρατηγῶν τάξιν), he
cannot be used to support the hypothesis that Gaïnas was only a count
when he marched against Tribigild. Liebeschuetz rests his case on Marcellinus and Jordanes, both of whom style Gaïnas *comes*. But (*a*) the title

25. Following *PLRE* I.379–80.
26. Zos. 4.57.2–3, with Paschoud's comm. pp. 463–65.
27. Liebeschuetz 1990, 101 n. 62.
28. *HE* 6.6.
29. ὑπὸ Ῥωμαίων κατ᾽ ὀλίγου ἐπὶ στρατηγίδα προελθών, frag. 190, *FHG* IV, pp.
610b–611a; Müller's notes (p. 611) point out another passage where Socrates is perhaps to
be corrected from John. It seems less likely that both drew on a common source; the parallels are otherwise of such a nature as to suggest that John copied Socrates directly.
30. *HE* 11.8, p. 138 Bidez-Winkelmann.
31. *HE* 5.32.1.
32. πεζῶν καὶ ἱππέων ἡγεμονίαν, *HE* 8.4.1.

comes is often found in combination with higher ranks,[33] and (*b*) Marcellinus merely repeats under 399 and 400 the style he had first used under 395 (*Gaïna comes*)—just as he continues to use the formula *Stilicho comes* as late as 408. As for Jordanes, anyone who looks up the relevant passages will see at once that his source was Marcellinus.[34]

Since all Greek sources are united in styling Gaïnas στρατηγός or στρατηλάτης in 399, the standard Greek equivalents for *magister militum*,[35] there is no justification for doubting that Gaïnas was indeed promoted to *magister militum* in 399.[36] If an explanation is required for Sozomen's late mention of the promotion, the simplest is to suppose with Paschoud that Gaïnas was *further* promoted from *magister militum per Thracias* to *praesentalis*. And if Gaïnas was already *magister militum* when he marched against Tribigild, then his army must have contained, not just barbarian federates, but the usual proportion of regular units—a "Roman army of cavalry and infantry," as Theodoret put it. It is inconceivable that a Goth was sent to quell a rebellious Goth with an army that consisted only of Gothic federates.

According to Liebeschuetz, "Gaïnas's forces are consistently described as barbarians and contrasted with the Roman forces of Leo," citing half a dozen passages of Zosimus.[37] This is certainly what Zosimus says, but can we really have any confidence that this notoriously careless and imprecise historian began (and ended) with Gaïnas so precise and systematic a distinction between the different elements in a late Roman army? Liebeschuetz is no doubt correct to claim that Roman armies at this period consisted not only of regular units, which might themselves be largely barbarian in composition (though trained and commanded by Roman officers), but also of barbarian irregulars not represented in the *Notitia*—not to mention the possibility of *bucellarii*. But these references in Zosimus imply something quite different and much simpler: that Gaïnas's entire army consisted of nothing but barbarians.

The explanation is surely that, writing as he was long after 410, Zosimus had Alaric in mind and simply assumed that Gaïnas was the leader of a barbarian horde.[38] Hence his frequent references to Gaïnas

33. E.g., κόμης καὶ μάγιστρος τῶν στρατιωτῶν, *BGU* IV.1092; *PLRE* I.855 cites a number of inscriptions that accord Stilicho the title *comes et magister utriusque militiae*.

34. *Romana* 319, *Getica* 176 (Mommsen, ed., *MGH: AA* 5 [1882]).

35. W. Enßlin, *Klio* 23 (1930): 323–24; examples are cited on p. 225 n. 127 below.

36. So Demandt 1970, 733–34; and Paschoud 1986, 122–23.

37. Liebeschuetz 1986c, 466: Zos. 5.14.3, 17.1, 18.6, 18.10, 19.2, 21.9.

38. Zakrzewski argues that Gaïnas had long been preparing the army for revolt "en la pénétrant d'éléments germaniques" (1931, 47), but does not explain how he could have done this while apparently out of office between 395 and 399.

and "his barbarians." Socrates too implies that Gaïnas's forces were all barbarians,[39] and a late source like Jordanes writes straightforwardly of *Gothorum foederatorum manus*. But Zosimus contradicts himself in his own last reference to Gaïnas's forces. After the final defeat by Fravitta, Gaïnas

> was afraid that another Roman army might follow and attack the few barbarians that remained with him; he was also suspicious of the Romans who still followed him. So he killed them all before they suspected his intentions and crossed the Danube with his barbarians, planning to return to his native land and spend the rest of his days there.[40]

Zosimus can hardly have invented a detail in such sharp conflict with his own picture of a barbarian horde. Even at the lowest point in his fortunes, there were still some nonbarbarians in Gaïnas's army.[41]

That more is involved here than the simplification or ignorance of later writers is shown by a whole series of references in Synesius. For example, that the barbarians "were conducting a campaign against a contingent of their own[42] people who had rebelled" (*De providentia* 108B), unmistakably and falsely implies that the forces of both Gaïnas and Tribigild were wholly barbarian. Osiris's plan to reduce the barbarian element in the army is amusingly described as "infiltrating the military rolls" (108D), that is to say, surreptitiously adding nonbarbarians. Nevertheless, though Synesius had introduced a native soldiery participating in the royal election (94C–D), throughout the rest of the allegory soldiers are simply equated with barbarians. References are particularly frequent in the first half of book 2.

Such simplifications on Synesius's part are not to be accorded the authority of a "well informed eyewitness."[43] His aim was not to describe

---

39. Liebeschuetz (1986c) seems to take seriously Socrates' claim (*HE* 6.6) that Gaïnas "sent for the entire Gothic race from his own land and gave his kinsmen commands in the army" (cf. Soz. *HE* 8.4.1: "He summoned his Gothic fellow tribesmen from their own ways"). See Liebeschuetz's own claim that "Gaïnas's Goths appear to have been recruited from the East of the Danube outside the Empire" (466). But Socrates' only illustration of kinsmen given commands is Tribigild, who of course was not appointed by Gaïnas; and surely there were no Tervingians (Gaïnas's "fellow tribesmen") left in their homelands. Socrates' claim may be no more than a way of emphasizing the barbarian danger by presenting Gaïnas as a proto-Alaric. Note too his exaggerated remark that Gaïnas's arrival in Constantinople meant that the city was "inundated with barbarians."

40. Zos. 5.21.9.

41. Gaïnas did not in fact "return to his native land" beyond the Danube: see below, p. 331.

42. For the text "of their own" see notes ad loc., p. 367.

43. Demougeot 1951, 249 n. 74.

the composition of Gaïnas's army, but to provide a pseudomythical paradigm of what happens when a mighty kingdom entrusts its defense to foreigners. He thought of himself as a philosopher, not a historian; not the particular, but the general was his prime concern.[44]

In Synesius's judgment the Eastern empire had surrendered its defense to barbarians. The modern historian rightly draws a sharp distinction between regular units trained and commanded by regular officers, even when recruited from barbarians, and bands of federates led by hereditary chieftains. But not Synesius. Two years earlier in *De regno* he wrote as though the Romans relied exclusively on barbarians, lamenting the fact that they had no force to "counterbalance" the Goths,[45] protesting that there was no reason why the Romans should not have an army of their own (21D). At 18A he had referred disapprovingly to the tall, blond, long-haired guards who accompanied the emperor wherever he went.[46] The imperial guards, the *scholae palatinae*, were indeed, as Synesius's description implies, recruited almost entirely from barbarians.[47] There is no evidence that they were ever disloyal, but Synesius feared all wolves the unwise shepherd might mix with his dogs (22A). That is why he goes on to warn that it makes no difference whether they are caught as cubs and appear to have been tamed, since "the moment they notice any weakness in the dogs they will pounce on them, flock, shepherds, and all." These "wolf cubs" must be barbarian recruits in regular units, naturally including the *scholae*.[48] It follows that we cannot make any precise inferences from Synesius's use of the term "barbarian."

It seems to be generally accepted that Gaïnas's army occupied Constantinople. According to Demougeot, for example, Gaïnas "couronna cette revanche spectaculaire par une entrée solennelle dans la capitale qui ne s'était jamais vue occupée par des barbares. Ses troupes nombreuses, 35,000 hommes sans doute, eurent quelque mal à se loger, terrorisèrent les habitants et les exaspérèrent."[49] Albert makes much of

44. See above, p. 145 for a fuller statement of this point, and chapter 7 on literary aspects of *De providentia*.

45. τὸ δὲ μήτε ἀντίπαλον αὐτοῖς κατασκευάζεσθαι δύναμιν, 21C.

46. On this passage see Frank 1969, 133, 149; Hoffmann 1969, 300.

47. Frank 1969, 59f.; Hoffmann 1969, 299f. Frank (59) refers to palace guards in the passage on the danger of having Gothic "guards" at 21D, but in the context the reference is clearly to the guard dogs of Pl. *Rep.* 375E; cf. Syn. *Ep.* 131, p. 225.15f. G.

48. Perhaps *laeti*, barbarians settled by the government on Roman soil with a view specifically to their breeding recruits for the army: Jones 1964a, 620.

49. Demougeot 1951, 252. She assumes that Gaïnas's troops were all barbarians. Cf. Dagron 1974, 111 ("[Gaïnas] . . . pénètre dans la ville, par un véritable coup d'état, avec ses 35 000 Goths"): Wolfram 1988, 149 ("Gaïnas marched to Constantinople and occupied the city"); Albert 1984, 130f. On the size of Gaïnas's army, see p. 383 n. 247.

the problem of provisioning and disciplining this horde inside the city.[50] If Gaïnas really did quarter 35,000 Gothic soldiers in Constantinople, it is easy to see why the situation got out of control. But did he?

According to the transmitted text of Zosimus 5.18.10,

> once established in Constantinople, [Gaïnas] dispersed the soldiers under his command in all directions, *so that the city was deprived of even the palace guards*, and he secretly ordered his barbarians that when they saw *him*[51] secretly leaving the city, they should immediately attack it, bereft as it was of military protection, and hand the supreme power over to him.

There are various problems with this passage. First, Gaïnas is said to have replaced palace guards (the *scholae*) with barbarians,[52] so that he could seize the city when it was left defenseless. But a few lines later the same Zosimus tells us that Gaïnas "left enough barbarians in the city greatly to outnumber the palace guards" (5.19.2), and a few lines later again (5.19.3) he mentions the palace guards twice in his account of the actual massacre. They are also mentioned by Philostorgius, and twice each in the accounts of both Socrates and Sozomen.

Clearly Gaïnas did *not* replace the *scholae* with his own men. He would have been going far beyond his authority if he had. The *scholae* were commanded by tribunes answerable only to the emperor, and it is hard to believe that Arcadius would have consented to be deprived of his own bodyguards. There were seven regiments of the *scholae*, elite units consisting of 500 men each.[53] Gaïnas can hardly have contemplated a pitched battle with the emperor's guards in the streets of Constantinople. Moreover, his own men, regular units rather than a personal following, were not likely to attack the emperor's guards even if he had given the order. Nor could such a show of force have brought him any advantage.

50. Albert 1984, 131; cf. Demougeot 1951, 252.

51. According to the Vatican MS, it is Gaïnas whose secret departure (ἐξελθόντα λάθρᾳ) is to be the signal to sack the city. Since Gaïnas leaves the city in the very next sentence and nothing of the sort happens, it may be that (with most editors) we should read ἐξελθόντας and translate "when they saw *them* [that is to say, the palace guards] leave the city." If so, then the second λάθρᾳ will have to be deleted or emended. But since this plan too remained unfulfilled, it is not obvious that emendation brings any real gain.

52. Paschoud implausibly argues that the "soldiers under his command" are not the army Gaïnas arrived with, but Roman soldiers stationed in the capital who now fell under his command as *magister militum praesentalis* (comm. p. 152). But these could only have been the *scholae*, who were commanded directly by the emperor (and administratively by the *magister officiorum*: Jones 1964a, 613), never by the *praesentalis*.

53. Frank 1969, 52 n. 20; Hoffmann 1969, 280. That this was more than a paper figure is proved by a passage of Palladius indicating one regiment with an active strength of 400 in 404 (*Dialogus de vita S. Iohannis Chrysostomi*, p. 57.18 Coleman-Norton).

Zosimus 5.18.10 does not prove that Gaïnas formally stationed troops inside the city. The army of the *praesentalis* was normally dispersed in a variety of camps or barracks in the neighborhood of Constantinople.[54] Zosimus need not imply any more than that Gaïnas quite properly dispatched his army to these various legitimate destinations. Albert confesses that he cannot find any satisfactory motive for the occupation of the city but concludes that Gaïnas acted to strengthen his position in Constantinople, where, though commander in chief, he was "powerless" because he could not bring his troops inside the city.[55] But this is to confuse power with military strength. In the ordinary way no imperial commander in chief had anything to fear inside a city, nor did his political authority rest on the exercise of military power. And even if he felt that it did, even 5,000, let alone 35,000, troops would be more hindrance than help in such a confined space.[56] They would be more useful if stationed in the usual barracks a mile or two outside the city.

Book 2 of *De providentia* admittedly implies a substantial Gothic presence inside the city. For example, according to 116B, "the barbarians were using the city like a camp." According to 117A, "cavalrymen rode about the marketplace in file, moving in squadrons to the sound of the trumpet. If any of them needed a shopkeeper or shoemaker or someone to polish his sword, all the rest stood guard over his need, so that the phalanx would not be broken even in the streets." Even within the obvious hyperbole, Synesius does not describe soldiers carrying out a for-

54. Dagron 1974, 108 ("sur les deux rives du Bosphore, et sans doute aussi à l'Hebdomon").

55. Albert 1984, 130 ("da . . . innerhalb der Stadt keine Truppen lagen"). The argument is confused and incorrect as stated. The evidence to which he refers (cited below, p. 211 and notes) forbids *civilians* to bear arms *anywhere*, not soldiers to bear arms inside cities. The purpose of this constantly reiterated ban was to prevent civilian, not military, disorder and ambition: "those who have entered into a conspiracy to raise a mob or a sedition or who keep either slaves or free men under arms" (*Digest* 48.6.3). In the city the emperor was attended everywhere by the *scholae*, like earlier emperors by their praetorians in Rome (J. B. Campbell, *The Emperor and the Roman Army, 31 B.C.–A.D. 235* [Oxford 1984], 113f.). No further troops were required. It is often claimed (e.g., by Dagron 1974, 110) that when the emperor was absent, troops were not allowed in the city even to defend it against invasion. But the only evidence cited is Socrates *HE* 4.38, where the people of Constantinople are alleged to have clamored in the hippodrome: "Give us arms and we ourselves will fight." But this is an *ironic* protest addressed to Valens when present and (they claimed) himself too scared to face the Goths. There is no question here of a garrison to defend the city in the emperor's absence. On the other hand, when the Goths actually attacked Constantinople after defeating Valens at Adrianople shortly afterwards, there was in fact a garrison in the city, a contingent of Saracens "recently summoned thither . . . who rushed forth boldly from the city" (Amm. Marc. 31.16.5).

56. While conceding this point, Albert implausibly supposes that Gaïnas himself did not discover it till too late: "Vor allem aber blieb ihm *jetzt* weiterhin die effektive Kontrolle seiner Leute durch die räumlichen Verhältnisse der Großstadt erschwert" (1984, 133).

mal occupation, but off-duty soldiers throwing their weight about the marketplace intimidating civilians. No doubt many of Gaïnas's officers, like himself, were now living in Constantinople. Even without a formal occupation, the city must have been full of swaggering soldiers, creating noise and nuisance at all hours. And Synesius's jaundiced eye exaggerated the Gothic presence in every quarter. In *De regno* he had complained that the city was full of Scythians—for even the humblest houses had Scythian slaves (23D).[57] He warned that when the next Gothic attack came, the Gothic slaves of Constantinople would rise up and join them, "reckless and valiant soldiers who will perform the unholiest deeds to win their liberty" (24C). *De providentia* shows nothing that bore out these fears.

More tellingly, if Gaïnas had held Constantinople by force, we should expect the myth to describe a corresponding enslavement of Egyptian Thebes. Yet at the end of book 1 the Scythian general emphatically refuses Typhos's invitation to enslave Thebes:

> "Your soldiers can make themselves rich by enslaving a prosperous city," [said Typhos]. . . . But the Scythian refused. For he held in high esteem the sacred senate and the decent citizens and the prerogatives of the city. He said that he marched against Osiris not as a volunteer but under a compulsion that Osiris himself had created. And if he succeeded in overcoming him, *with the city safe* and the countryside unravaged, he said, he would reckon it a gain that no greater evil proved necessary.[58]

Of course this tendentious exchange does not reflect the realities of A.D. 400.[59] It is one of a series of attempts in book 1 to shift responsibility from Gaïnas to Caesarius. Synesius was evidently reluctant to antagonize Gaïnas, still a threat to Constantinople at the time of writing. As in the case of his similar displacement of the responsibility for Osiris's deposition and exile in 111A–B,[60] Synesius reversed their true roles. But the crucial fact behind this transparent artifice is that Thebes was *not* enslaved. Whether the initiative comes from Typhos or the Scythian, enslavement is represented as an unfulfilled intention. Like everyone else, Synesius expected Gaïnas to enslave and plunder Constantinople. But at the time of writing the disaster had not yet happened.

Compare too a neglected passage at the end of book 1, the rustic

57. The passage is quoted in full above, p. 111.
58. 110C–D.
59. Contra Paschoud (comm. p. 152) on the usual grounds that Synesius was a "témoin oculaire."
60. See chapter 8, section III, for a fuller discussion of this point.

philosopher's reflection on the god's prediction that the Goths would soon be driven out: "For it was beyond human prediction to guess that a vast armed force—the barbarians had the legal right to carry arms even in peacetime—would be defeated with no force to resist them" (115A).[61] If Gaïnas had occupied the city by force, it would have been an act of war; and if the barbarians mentioned here had been soldiers on active duty, they would not have needed any special dispensation to carry arms. It was *civilians* who were strictly forbidden to bear or manufacture arms, partly in the interests of public order but more importantly to prevent private citizens usurping power with the aid of personal militias.[62] Half a century later the historian Priscus makes a Roman deserter living among the Huns complain that Romans cannot protect themselves against barbarians because they are not allowed to bear arms "through <fear of> usurpers."[63] Synesius himself was well aware of the ban and its rationale when he himself later had arms manufactured to defend Cyrene: "Are you going to tell me," he writes to his brother, who had evidently reminded him of the ban, "that private individuals are not allowed to bear arms but are allowed to die? Apparently the government doesn't like people trying to save their own lives!"[64] It is clearly this well-known ban from which the barbarians of Synesius's myth are being exempted. It would have been absurd to suggest that soldiers on active duty needed such an exemption. It follows that the barbarians he has in mind here are civilians or off-duty soldiers and that the massacre took place in peacetime.

The massacre is beginning to take on an entirely different complexion. There were no doubt a certain number of Gaïnas's soldiers in the city at the time on one errand or another. But we no longer need to believe that unarmed civilians spontaneously rose up against and defeated an army of several thousand Gothic warriors.[65]

61. καὶ γὰρ οὐδὲ ἀνθρώπινον ἦν εἰκάσαι δύναμιν ἀθρόαν. ἐν ὅπλοις οὖσαν καὶ ἐν εἰρήνῃ σιδηροφορεῖν νόμον ἔχουσαν. ἐξ οὐδεμίας ἀντιστασέως ἡττῆσθαι.

62. Under the provisions of the *Lex Julia de vi publica*, constantly reiterated: see the extracts in *Digest* 48.6.1 and the detailed restatement in Just. *Nov.* 85 of 539. See too Jones 1964a, 671, and chap. 25, n. 54; Dagron 1974, 108–15; Cameron 1976a, 123–24; the same ban applied already for the republican period, when it was a capital offense for a civilian to bear arms: see P. A. Brunt, *Past and Present* 35 (1966): 10–11; and see especially Brunt's *Roman Imperial Themes* (Oxford 1990), 255–66.

63. Frag. 8 Müller = 11.2 Blockley (p. 268, line 440).

64. *Ep.* 107; cf. 108.

65. Not that such a feat would be incredible in itself; Dio (80.2.3) and Herodian (7.11) record two spectacular battles between the people of Rome and the praetorian guard in 222/23 and 238. The so-called moneyers' revolt under Aurelian, in which 7,000 are alleged

To be sure Synesius tries to suggest that this is precisely what happened. He follows his vignette of Gothic cavalrymen quoted above with the claim that it was these same warriors who "fled in rout from naked, unarmed, disheartened men who had not even a prayer of victory." He insists that there was "not a weapon in the city nor anyone to use it" (116C); that "the Egyptians had no spearman, no spear; no javelinthrower, no javelin" (120A); that "anything that came to hand was a weapon in time of need" (119A). In short, our eyewitness assures us that superbly trained and equipped cavalry were routed by completely unarmed civilians.[66]

Once more, we simply cannot believe him. No fewer than four other sources—Philostorgius, Socrates, Sozomen, and Zosimus—expressly state that the palace guards played a part. According to Zosimus, for example, it was the guards who raised the alarm and "everyone . . . together with the guards" who drove Gaïnas's men from the walls (5.19.3). Some of these guardsmen may have cut a better figure on the parade ground than on the battlefield, and Palladius claims that the 400 *scholae* who killed a number of catechumens in 404 were hotheaded recruits.[67] Nonetheless, they made up a force of some 3,500 well-armed elite troops accustomed to operating (as in 404) on the streets of Constantinople.

One significant but overlooked detail in the accounts of Socrates and Sozomen strongly supports their versions against Synesius's on this point. According to Socrates, when Gaïnas left the city on the fateful day, "together with him went barbarians secretly carrying out arms, some concealing them in earthenware pots, some in other ways. And when the soldiers who guarded the city gates detected the stratagem, they would not allow them to take out the arms, whereupon the barbarians drew their swords and killed the guards." Sozomen adds a few details: "Some of the barbarians remained in Constantinople, and others accompanied Gaïnas, secretly carrying arms in ladies' carriages and pots containing daggers. When they were discovered, they killed the guards at the gates when they tried to stop them taking out the weapons."[68] Philostorgius's briefer narrative says nothing about concealed weapons but confirms that Gaïnas's party broke through guards posted at the gates. These concealed weapons are too circumstantial to reject. Why should anyone have invented such a curious detail? The barbarians who

to have perished, is a much more dubious proposition: cf. M. Peachin, *Studies in Latin Literature and Roman History*, vol. 3, ed. C. Deroux (Brussels 1983), 325–35.

66. Not to mention earlier believers, note Dagron 1974, 111: "Ce dénouement ne fait intervenir aucune force armée, aucune milice, seulement une population insurgé."

67. Demougeot 1951, 329.

68. Socr. *HE* 6.6, Soz. *HE* 8.4.15.

accompanied Gaïnas on this occasion cannot, as usually supposed,[69] have been his bodyguard alone, for naturally they would have carried weapons openly. They must have been mainly civilians, as the reference to ladies' carriages confirms. Gaïnas's party was obliged to submit to inspection by guards manifestly not answerable to Gaïnas himself. On discovering the forbidden weapons, the guards correctly tried to confiscate them.[70] It follows that Gaïnas's army cannot possibly have been in military occupation of Constantinople at the time.

We have already seen that Synesius himself explicitly alludes to barbarians receiving a special dispensation to carry arms (115A). Why did he go out of his way to import this puzzling anachronism into his Egyptian myth? He cannot have had Gaïnas's army in mind, since it would go without saying that soldiers carried arms. It was civilians who were forbidden to bear arms, and yet it is hardly credible that Gothic civilians resident in Constantinople really were given special permission. What would have been the point? On Synesius's own earlier testimony, many of them were slaves, and many more women and children. How would it benefit even Gaïnas to arm untrained civilians when he already had a trained army?

Synesius's reference to this special dispensation comes at the end of book 1 among the obviously *post eventum* prophecies of the coming massacre, immediately following the veiled allusions to the request for an Arian church inside Constantinople and the comet of the spring of 400 (114D–115B). Contemporary readers would therefore have been prompted to interpret the allusion to Goths bearing arms in terms of the antecedents of the massacre. They would have been reminded of the incident Socrates and Sozomen describe. It was after all the discovery that Gothic civilians were carrying weapons that led to the first bloodshed. Synesius makes the wicked Typhos allow the barbarians to carry, openly, the arms that had to be concealed in A.D. 400, to transfer the initiative to Typhos and exaggerate his tyranny. His illegitimate power rested on "his darling barbarians" (122B); he armed his supporters by an illegitimate concession, exempting them from the general ban. Common to both myth and reality are the barbarians' weapons; the difference is simply a question of responsibility. Clearly Synesius meant to suggest that in real life Caesarius had connived at the hidden weapons, as part of the modern Typhos's plot to hand Constantinople over to the barbarians. This is characteristic of the way Synesius adapts and improves on contemporary events in his myth.

69. E.g., Albert 1984, 135.
70. See the provisions of Just. *Nov.* 85, *De armis*.

Despite the rumors they themselves preserve that the Goths were planning to sack the city, both Socrates and Sozomen make it clear that it was only when the Goths started to *leave* the city, and to leave *secretly*, that violence erupted. Here Synesius is in complete agreement with them: "[The barbarians] withdrew from the city at a signal, stealing away with their children, their wives, and their most valued possessions" (117A–B). For Synesius too the killing began at the city gates, though he says nothing of guards and concealed weapons. Imperial guards could not be admitted to a myth where there was no emperor and the only soldiers were disloyal barbarians. For Synesius, it was an old beggarwoman who "saw in the distance what the Scythians were doing, since it was fully daylight and they kept running in and out like burglars, all packing their goods and carrying them away" (117D). The beggarwoman denounces the Scythians, and one of them "sprang upon her, cutlass drawn to chop the head off the wretched creature who, he surmised, was reviling them and had made their night's work public" (118B). The blow is warded off by "either a god or someone like a god," and the fighting begins. Firmly in the grip of the "eyewitness" fallacy and undeterred by the fact that the old woman's speech is a reprise of the antibarbarian tirade from Synesius's own *De regno*, Bury incautiously assumed that Synesius was, as usual, simply reporting the facts: "It happened that a beggar-woman was standing at one of the western gates."[71]

Synesius places the incident of the beggarwoman first thing in the morning (117D). Philostorgius placed Gaïnas's departure just before nightfall; and according to Socrates the massacre did not begin till one day after the incident of the concealed weapons. All Synesius did was to omit the earlier incident and concentrate on the outbreak of the actual massacre the following morning. It is likely enough that Goths were still trying to get out of the city on the next day. Mutual fear would have been at its height, Romans seeing the concealed weapons as part of some such Gothic plot to sack the city, as all our sources report in one form or another, and Goths fearing reprisals from the Romans. It only needed a spark to set off the conflagration. The spark might even have been some old beggarwoman, though doubtless without Synesius's color and drama, let alone the deus ex machina who saves her.

In its essentials Synesius's version agrees well enough with Socrates and Sozomen here: the barbarians were trying to leave the city in secret when they were found out. At the very beginning of his account Synesius adds a detail that helps to explain this furtive departure: "The gen-

71. Bury (1923) 1958, 133; as portrayed, she is a literary creature, owing much to the prophetess in Dio Chrys. *Or.* 1.53f.: see the notes to the translation, pp. 381–82, and p. 271.

eral suffered from terrors in the night—Corybantes, I think, assaulted him—and outbreaks of panic seized the army by day. The recurrent alarm rendered them witless and unable to control their thoughts. They wandered around alone or together, all of them like men possessed" (116B–C). What were the barbarians afraid of? Central though this fear is to his account of the evacuation, Synesius offers no reasonable explanation. He insists that it was sent by God, completely at odds with the apparent probabilities of the situation, in vindication of divine Providence. Synesius's verbiage in the passage just quoted is emphatic: the barbarians' distress is ascribed to Corybantes and Pans,[72] and their final state is, literally, "like men stolen by nymphs" (ἅπαντες ἐοικότες τοῖς νυμφολήπτοις). On the other side, "no human remedy (ἀνθρώπινον ἀλέξημα) was anywhere to be found; . . . there was not a weapon in the place nor anyone to use it, and the populace was an easy prey delivered up by Typhos . . . naked, unarmed, disheartened men who had not even a prayer of victory" (116B–117A). The massacre is introduced precisely as an instance of what happens "if no one intervenes to produce the result, and the invisible alone is the cause of victory—an unimpeachable refutation of those who do not believe that the gods care for mankind" (116D).

Synesius makes no concessions to the historian who wants to understand events in terms of human motivations. Though unexplained, the portrait of mutual paranoia he offers is itself reasonably plausible. Before positive divine inspiration, "when the populace saw them packing up, they did not yet understand what was happening, but despaired for themselves all the more." Some flee and some prepare for death (117B). Synesius explicitly declares their attitude to be mistaken, but its correction waits on the gods (117C). The old beggarwoman shows more spirit, but she too interprets all Scythian action exclusively in terms of threat: they were moving out all their families and valuables "so that the city would no longer contain anything of theirs as security. As soon as they had moved camp, they would strike the first blow without fear that they might share in the consequences, as would have happened if criminals and victims had been living together" (118A). Her judgment is meant to be plausible, from the citizens' limited perspective, but that perspective is expressly vitiated in favor of the gods' intervention.

Zosimus offers an opposite unfulfilled intention: "Leaving enough barbarians in the city greatly to outnumber the palace guards, [Gaïnas] retired to a suburb forty stades away, whence he intended to make his

---

72. πανικοὶ θόρυβοι; possibly Synesius intended an allusion to Plut. *De Is. et Os.* 356D, where the adjective is derived from the behavior of the Pans and Satyrs dwelling near Khemmis, when they learned of the death of Osiris.

own attack *after the barbarians in the city had begun the attack in accordance with their orders"* (5.19.2). This plan, Zosimus continues, was spoiled by Gaïnas's barbarian rashness: "Instead of waiting for the signal, he approached the wall and the guards were startled and raised the alarm." Marcellinus more simply claims that Gaïnas "secretly ordered his barbarians to prepare civil war," without details.[73] Synesius did not require his explanation to bear much weight, and the other does no better.

The detail that rings truest in Synesius's account is the fear that drives the barbarians to leave the city. It operates as divine machinery to help unman the ferocious, well-trained soldiers to a point where they can be routed by unarmed civilians. But for the gods this mechanism would not have been necessary; that is to say, Synesius had no motive to invent Gothic fear for the sake of his version. If anything, it detracts from the glory of the Constantinopolitans. For Synesius's purposes they could as well have fallen on the Goths in the marketplace. Since, moreover, the furtive flight of the Goths from the city is corroborated with such circumstantial detail by Socrates and Sozomen, we must accept it as fact and dispense with intrinsically improbable unfulfilled intentions.

It is also relevant to compare the various accounts of Gaïnas's own departure from the city, evidently a key event in the sequence that led up to the massacre. According to Socrates and Sozomen, he left for the church of St. John the Evangelist seven miles distant, feigning demonic possession. According to Zosimus, he claimed that he was weary and needed to free his mind from cares. According to Marcellinus he feigned illness.[74] The differences are perhaps less striking than the general agreement that he made some pretext or other. For in the ordinary way a Roman commander in chief did not need to make excuses to leave Constantinople. The implication is that Gaïnas left at a time and in a manner that was thought to require some justification. Philostorgius gives no pretext but connects his fear with the decision to leave the city "immediately, although night was falling."[75] A hasty nighttime departure by the commander in chief and his entourage was liable to inspire alarm among both Romans and barbarians.

Whatever it was that so terrified the civilian Gothic population of Constantinople, it is difficult to believe that they would have fled the city in such panic if it had been occupied by 35,000 Gothic soldiers. It was the

73. *Chron.Min.* II.66: "ad praeparandum civile bellum barbaros suos occulte ammonet."

74. Blockley (1983, 147 n. 150) rightly dissociates Eunap. frag. 75.2 (= 67.1 Blockley), which refers to illness, from Zos. 5.19.1.

75. ὁ δὲ Γαινᾶς εἰς τοσοῦτον κατέστη δέους, ὡς αὐτίκα νυκτὸς ἐπεχούσης μεθ' ὅσων ἠδύνατο, τοὺς ἐπὶ τῶν πυλῶν βιασάμενος, ἐξελαύνει τῆς πόλεως, HE 11.8, p. 139.5–7 Bidez-Winkelmann.

non-Gothic population of Constantinople they were afraid of—a fear that was to prove only too justified. Both Synesius (121A) and Zosimus (5.19.3) place *before* the massacre a rather confused account of Romans locking the city gates against barbarians attacking from outside. For Zosimus, this was part of Gaïnas's botched plan to seize the city, but more probably it was a desperate attempt by such of Gaïnas's men as were near enough to prevent the massacre.

It has hitherto been assumed that it was Gaïnas's military occupation of Constantinople that drove its people to massacre their oppressors. But we do not need to postulate anything so drastic as full-scale military occupation. Gaïnas's blatant blackmail of the emperor, the execution of Eutropius, the exile of Aurelian and his associates, against the background of the large number of Gothic civilians and off-duty soldiers in the city can only have created an atmosphere of extreme mutual fear and hostility toward Goths. Leaving aside divine participation, this is exactly the picture Synesius draws. The hyperbole of panic-mongers like him raised tensions still higher. Gothic residents fearing for their safety inside the city started to leave, secretly, so as not to provoke attack while they were encumbered and least able to fight back. Gaïnas himself, observing the rapid deterioration of the situation inside Constantinople, escorted one such group; the "ladies' carriages" presumably carried the families of some Gothic notables. His actions were felt to be suspicious, whence the excuses, which were perceived as such. The discovery of concealed weapons only made matters worse. The apprehensions of both Gothic and Roman residents were sharpened even further. Synesius states that "each side had long feared attack from the other" (119B). The Romans may genuinely have feared that the Goths were removing their women and children so that they could set fire to the city, and accordingly refused to allow them to leave. The Goths did their best to defend themselves but with few Gothic soldiers inside the city to protect them were no match for the enraged populace, especially once the several thousand troops of the *scholae* joined the fray. Synesius admits that some of the Goths left behind in the city "were still in their houses" (119D). Many, if not most, of the Goths killed were burned alive in what Socrates describes as the "church of the Goths." Since there were no Arian churches in the city, this was presumably the one Gothic church within the city walls, the Catholic church "beside the church of Paul."[76] Many of these must have been the resident Catholic Goths to whom we know John Chrysostom preached.

---

76. That the church was Catholic: Marcellinus, s.a. 399, "fugientes ecclesiae *nostrae* succedunt." That it was located "beside the church of Paul": Chrysostom, *PG* 53.499; for detailed discussion, see the commentary to the translation of 121A.

One other text, a fragment of Eunapius, may allude to the massacre; it has been much discussed in recent years but still not satisfactorily explained:

> Perses [a Persian?], prefect in [New?] Rome, reduced the success of the Romans to mockery and laughter. Wishing to offer a representation of what had happened, he put together many small panels in the middle of the hippodrome. But the subject matter of these paintings was laughable, and he unwittingly mocked his subject by the representation. For nowhere did the paintings show or even hint at the bravery of the emperor or the strength of the soldiers or any obvious, regular war. But there was a hand extending as if from the clouds, and this inscription by the hand: "the hand of God driving off the barbarians." (It is shameful but necessary to record this.) And in another place: "the barbarians fleeing God," and other things more fatuous and distasteful still, the ravings of drunken painters.[77]

The paintings here described evidently embodied a Christian interpretation of a recent imperial victory over barbarians. But there are problems.

First, was Perses prefect of Rome or Constantinople? Rome, according to most recent discussions.[78] Reasonable though this might seem at first glance, there is in fact a series of objections.

In the first place, there is no room for another prefect of Rome in the already full *fasti* of the relevant period, 399–402:[79] Nicomachus Flavianus (6 June 399–8 November 400), Protadius (400–401), Longinianus (401–2), and Albinus (6 December 402). None of them could by any stretch of the imagination be described as Persians, nor, pace Baldwin, is it easy to see how any of them could have come by the nickname Perses. Second, this part of Eunapius's narrative betrays so little interest in or knowledge of the West that it would be surprising to find such a Western reference. Third, the Western court normally celebrated Eastern victories at the Western capital, Milan, not in Rome.[80]

According to R. C. Blockley, this fragment is a digression that refers "to an event in the West, perhaps the defeat of Gildo [July 398], in which

---

77. Eunap. frag. 78 = 68 Blockley.

78. Cracco Ruggini 1972, 101–2; Baldwin 1976, 7–8; *PLRE* II.1222; Blockley 1981, 161 n. 64; Paschoud 1986, 156; McCormick 1986, 118.

79. Chastagnol 1962, 251–60; *PLRE* II.1252. *PLRE* does in fact try to squeeze Perses in between Protadius and Longinianus.

80. As, for example, in 421 at Ravenna, discussed by McCormick 1986, 119. On the preceding page McCormick makes much of the statues dedicated by the city prefect Albinus in 389 to commemorate Theodosius's victory over Maximus the preceding year, but it makes all the difference here that Theodosius was himself present in Rome at the time. Nor are statues erected by Roman officials quite the same as victory games given by the emperor.

the power of God was stressed in the official version."[81] But Gildo was a rebellious Roman official, not a barbarian enemy, nor was there any such official version.[82] Lellia Cracco Ruggini sees a reference to expeditions of Stilicho. But it is not likely that Stilicho would have allowed himself to be robbed of his credit by God in this way. The evidence of both Claudian and contemporary monuments suggests on the contrary that he was anxious to make the most of all his successes during these years.[83] According to Michael McCormick, Eunapius was describing a celebration held at Rome to commemorate Fravitta's victory over Gaïnas in 401. But the sequence of the fragments points to a slightly earlier context. Frag. 68 is no. 72 in the *Excerpta de sententiis*. No. 70 (frag. 67.10Blockley [hereafter B]) describes Gaïnas's destruction of Eutropius and dealings with Tribigild; no. 71 (frag. 67.11B) Gaïnas in league with Tribigild; no. 72 (frag. 69.1B) Fravitta's appointment to a command despite poor health, evidently the command against Gaïnas; no. 74 (frag. 69.4B) Fravitta's defeat of Gaïnas and designation to the consulship for 401.

Wherever the sequence of the *Excerpta* can be checked, they are in chronological order, and there seems no reason to doubt that the present sequence is too. So Perses' pictures in the circus were mentioned between the account of Gaïnas's collusion with Tribigild and Fravitta's appointment to the command against Gaïnas. If the passage came in Eunapius's main narrative, the "barbarians fleeing God" should be the barbarians killed in the massacre. If in a digression, the digression must at any rate have been hung on the account of the massacre; it is therefore unlikely to be a reference forward to Fravitta's victory.[84] If the reference is to the massacre rather than to Fravitta's victory, the circus games can hardly have been Western. Such victory celebrations were held only on receipt of official victory bulletins circulated around all the principal cities of the empire.[85] No such bulletin would have been issued to commemorate the burning alive of civilians in a Catholic church in Constantinople, especially since it caused, rather than terminated, a civil war.

But in Constantinople itself there was doubtless a good deal of unofficial celebrating, and it is entirely possible that the city prefect had

81. Blockley 1981, 161.

82. Orosius 7.36.5f., to which Blockley refers (1981, 161 n. 64 *fin.*), can hardly be so described when the poems of Claudian tell such a different story.

83. Cameron 1970a, passim.

84. The possibility cannot be excluded, of course; but if Eunapius had wanted to refer to pictures celebrating the victory of his hero Fravitta, why not discuss them when referring to that victory rather than another, less glorious and less honorable?

85. McCormick 1986, 192–95 (and index, p. 425) gives a full account of these victory bulletins.

some such pictures made to decorate the hippodrome. Rome here could well be New Rome. Already in the lifetime of Constantine, Constantinople is styled New or Second Rome,[86] and where there was no likelihood of confusion, it eventually became normal to write Rome alone. Most of the datable examples are of the sixth century,[87] the earliest securely dated being an inscription from the base of a statue to the great Constantinopolitan charioteer Porphyrius of ca. 500.[88] *AP* 9.799 on a certain Muselius who had a building called the Museion repaired and extended may be nearly a century earlier if it refers to the Musellius who was *praepositus sacri cubiculi* in 414.[89]

More specifically, "Rome" alone was undoubtedly a feature of the titulature of the prefect of Constantinople. There are a number of weights, in glass, lead, and bronze, that bear the names of prefects of Constantinople, evidently the authority who issued or guaranteed the correctness of the weights. The word "Constantinople" itself never appears, just "eparch,"[90] sometimes with the word ΡΩΜΗΣ in the central field.[91] Since the provenance of these weights is Asiatic or Egyptian where known, several of them found at Istanbul itself, and since the legends are invariably in Greek, there can be no doubt that here at least Rome does mean New Rome. Some of them, moreover, bear relatively uncommon names borne by known prefects of Constantinople. For example, Zemarchus, in office in 565,[92] documented by one glass,[93] and three bronze,[94] weights; and Gerontius, prefect in 560. There is also an inscription from Constantinople supplemented (in the only available edition):

86. For a fairly comprehensive list of texts, see Dölger 1964, 70–115; and Cameron, *Constantinople: Birth of A New Rome* (forthcoming).

87. *APl* 62.2 of 531 (cf. Cameron 1977, 42f.); *AP* 1.10.43 of 524–27 (Mango and Sevcenko 1961, 243–47); *AP* 9.697.3 of 524–26 (Cameron 1976c, 269f.); *APl* 32b.1.

88. *AP* 15.47.1 (τοῦτον Πορφύριον Λιβύη τέκε, θρέψε δὲ 'Ρώμη); cf. Cameron 1973, 150f.

89. Line 3 of *AP* 9.799: Μουσεῖον 'Ρώμη δ' ἐχαρίσσατο; on the Musellius who was *praepositus sacri cubilici*: PLRE II.768, with C. Mango, *The Art of the Byzantine Empire: 312–1453* (1972), 46–47.

90. In the form ΕΠΙ ΙΩΑΝΝΟΥ ΕΠΑΡΧΟΥ, for example.

91. G. Schlumberger, *REG* 8 (1895): 59f., nos. 5, 8, 12, 13; more were published by H. Grégoire, *BCH* 31 (1907): 321–27. Others await publication: for example, in the Menil Foundation Collection in Houston, Texas (G. Vikan and J. Nesbitt, *Security in Byzantium: Locking, Sealing, Weighing*, Dumbarton Oaks Publications 2 [1980], 37), and in the British Museum (personal communication from Chris Entwhistle).

92. Stein 1949, 779 n. 4; D. Feissel, *Rev.Num.* 6 sér. 28 (1986), 132–42.

93. G. Schlumberger, *REG* 8 (1895): 63, no. 3: (ἐπὶ) ΖΙΜΑΧΟΥ ΕΝΔΟΞ(οτάτου).

94. G. Schlumberger, *Gazette archéologique* 8 (1883): 298: ΕΠΙ ΖΙΜΑΡΧΟΥ ΤΟΥ ΕΝΔΟΞΟΤΑ(του) κ(αὶ) ΕΠΑΡΧΟΥ ΡΩΜΗΣ (18 nomismata, or 79.50 gr., from Beirut); and ΕΠΙ ΖΗΜΑΡΧΟΥ ΤΟΥ ΕΝΔΟΞ(οτάτου) κ(αὶ) ΕΠΑΡΧΟΥ ΡΩΜΗΣ κ(αὶ) ΑΠ⁰ΥΠΑΤ(ων) (62 nomismata, or 309.50 gr.). Simon Bendall showed Cameron a magnificent unpublished specimen at a bus stop in Houston.

A[πὸ ὑπ]ΑΤΩΝ ΠΑΤΡΙΚΙΟΥ Κ(αὶ) ΕΠΑΡΧΟΥ ΡΩ[μης τῆς νέας].[95] The supplement ΝΕΑΣ is out of place here; it was standard, perhaps invariable, usage to place "New" before, not after, "Rome." Since the anonymous prefect held his consulate before his prefecture, it must have been honorary rather than ordinary, in which case the inscription cannot be earlier than the late fifth century.[96] There is also another Constantinopolitan inscription with ΕΠΙ ΔΙΟΜΗΔΟΥΣ ΕΠΑΡΧΟΥ in a circular legend and ΡΩΜ(Η)Σ in the form of a cruciform monogram.[97] According to E. Cuq, this is the Diomedes who was prefect of the East in 576.[98]

In the headings to laws as preserved in the *Theodosian Code* and *Novels* of Justinian, the standard formula was *praefectus urbi* (with *Constantinopolitanae* understood, but normally omitted where there was no likelihood of confusion); or in Greek ἔπαρχος πόλεως. But when the author of the *Paschal Chronicle* recorded the appointment of the first prefect of Constantinople in 359, he used the formula ἔπαρχος Ῥώμης.[99] We may well doubt whether this reflects current usage in 359, but the evidence of the weights and inscriptions shows that it was an official title by the sixth century at any rate.[100] Official titles normally follow informal usage, and we cannot exclude the possibility of an informal example as early as 400. It should be noted that the text as given in the *Excerpta* cannot in any case reflect Eunapius's *ipsissima verba* as transmitted. "Prefect *in* Rome" (ἦν ἐν Ῥώμῃ ἔπαρχος) would be an odd way to refer to the prefect of either Rome or Constantinople, and the construction is abrupt and improbable.[101] It seems clear that the excerptor has at the very least abridged an originally fuller sentence, as often happens at the beginning of an excerpt, possibly substituting something closer to the style of his own day. At all events, we cannot exclude the possibility that Perses was prefect of Constantinople.[102]

According to the standard manuals, a certain Clearchus was prefect of Constantinople between 8 May 400 and 22 March 402. It has often been assumed that "Perses" was a nickname of some sort borne by

95. *CIG* 4.8611.
96. Cameron, in *CLRE* 9–10.
97. Sorlin-Dorigny 1876, 90.
98. *Revue archéologique,* 3d ser., vol. 31 (1897): 109.
99. *Chron.Pasch.,* p. 543.9 = *Chron.Min.* I.239.
100. Compare too "the illustrious prefects of each Rome" from Just. *Nov.* 79.2, οἱ ἐνδοξότατοι ἔπαρχοι τῆς ἑκατέρας Ῥώμης.
101. ἦν . . . παραφέρων = "there was a man who reduced," the entire sentence introduced by the excerptor's ὅτι.
102. McCormick objects that "elsewhere Eunapius calls Rome and Constantinople by their proper names" (1986, 118 n. 167), but that does not mean that he never used any other formula, and it could be, for example, that he was parodying the fact that Perses himself had used this rather pretentious style.

Clearchus.[103] But though Eunapius was fond of making puns on proper names,[104] there is no parallel for a nickname *substituted* for the true name, except for the rather different case of a brigand to whom he gives the name Cercio (frag. 18.4) after the brigand killed by Theseus. If Clearchus is, as usually assumed, the son of the Clearchus who held the prefecture of Constantinople in 372–73 and 382–84 and was consul in 384, he came from a well-to-do Greek family.[105] Why then "Persian"?

There is another possibility. Clearchus is not securely attested in the prefecture before 21 September 401.[106] The law usually cited as evidence for 8 May 400 is dated by the MSS to 8 May 399 (*Theodoro consule*).[107] Since another man, Severinus, was still in office on 25 September 399,[108] this date must be in error. But there is no good reason to change the year to 400 rather than 401, 402, or even 403 (the first consulate of Theodosius II, perhaps confused with Theodorus). That would leave two years between the last attestation of Severinus (September 399) and the first secure attestation of Clearchus (September 401). Obviously another man might have held the post in the summer of 400, during and after the massacre of 12 July.

In the circumstances, one might propose Hormisdas the Persian, son of the Hormisdas who deserted to Rome in 324, son in his turn of the Persian king Hormisdas II. The youngest Hormisdas was proconsul of Asia in 365–66 and commanded troops for Theodosius I in 379.[109] He is the only Eastern dignitary of the age who *was* regularly styled "the Persian."[110] An even simpler alternative is that the prefect of the summer of 400 was actually called Perses, a name not otherwise known from this period, but not to be rejected on principle.

With Eunapius frag. 68 referred to the massacre, we have in the ascription of the destruction of the Goths to the "hand of God" a telling parallel to the explanation of Socrates and Sozomen in terms of angels and Synesius's invocation of Providence. The pagan Eunapius was angry to see the god of the Christians given credit for the deeds of the emperor and his brave troops.[111] But if the "deeds" in question were *not* in fact

103. Mazzarino 1942, 362; Matthews, *CR* 22 (1974): 102; Baldwin 1976, 5.

104. On Leo in frags. 67.6 and 67.7; on Hierax in frags. 71.2, 71.3, 72 *ad fin.*; on Arbazakios in frag. 71.

105. *PLRE* I.211–12.

106. *Cod. Theod.* 6.26.12.

107. *Cod. Theod.* 13.1.16.

108. *Cod. Theod.* 6.12.1.

109. *PLRE* I.444.

110. So Eunapius himself, frag. 34.8; and Zos. 4.30.5.

111. Is this Eunapius's own purely idiosyncratic reaction to Perses' pictures (in which case we should probably have to suppose that he had seen them himself)? Or is he reflect-

a regular imperial victory, but the massacre of civilians in a Catholic church,[112] there was a more pressing reason for official commemoration of the event to be as imprecise as possible. The usual victory iconography would hardly do. But who could quarrel with a pictorial representation of barbarians fleeing before the wrath of God? Who could quarrel with divine Providence?[113]

II. GAÏNAS AND TRIBIGILD

The new prefect Caesarius did his best to salvage the situation. Synesius describes, with real or affected outrage, how even after the massacre Typhos "asked for negotiations with the barbarians, scheming again to admit the enemy army on the grounds that no irremediable evil had occurred" (121B). Synesius professes astonishment that even this manifest treachery did not bring immediate retribution down on Typhos's head, but Gaïnas himself had played no part in the massacre, and it was the Goths, for the most part unarmed civilians, who had been the victims. Synesius's evident anxiety not to offend Gaïnas in book 1, written in the days immediately after the massacre,[114] is enough to show that there was a short-lived fear that he would take revenge. Such fear tells against Socrates' claim that Arcadius declared Gaïnas a public enemy *before* the massacre.[115] There may have been several days of negotiations

---

ing a more widely held distaste for such radical new victory iconography, not necessarily confined to pagans (as MacCormack 1981, 11, seems to imply)?

112. Socrates mentions the burning of the church but does not actually say that Goths were inside it at the time; Synesius refers callously to the Egyptians "smoking them out like wasps, together with their temples and priests" (121A). But according to Zosimus, "the more devout Christians considered that a grave defilement had been perpetrated in the midst of their city" (5.19.5).

113. Cf. McCormick 1986, 195, on the standard use of scriptural quotation to introduce later Byzantine victory proclamations.

114. See chapter 8, section III.

115. φανερὸν πολέμιον κηρύξας. According to Zosimus (5.11.1), Eutropius used the senate of Constantinople to declare Stilicho a *hostis publicus* in 397, just as Stilicho had used the senate of Rome to declare Gildo a *hostis publicus*. See Paschoud (comm. pp. 113–15) for a discussion of the two occasions, concluding that it was the Roman senate that acted first. At 5.20.1 Zosimus claims that it was the senate (of Constantinople) that chose Fravitta for the command against Gaïnas κοινῷ ψήφῳ (both Ridley 1982 and Paschoud translate "unanimously," though at 5.11.1 they translate κοινῷ δόγματι, respectively, "by imperial decree" and "par un décret officiel"; surely both phrases represent the same formula, perhaps best rendered "by official decree"). Paschoud (comm. p. 160) suggests that the reference to the senate at 5.20.1 is a doublet of 5.11.1, but perhaps this is the occasion to which Socrates refers; it makes sense that the declaration of Gaïnas as *hostis publicus* would be combined with the appointment of the general sent after him. If Arcadius asked the

before Gaïnas finally made the irrevocable decision to follow the same path as Tribigild and Alaric.

Who was responsible for the declaration of war on Gaïnas and the dispatch of Fravitta? According to Demougeot, it was Caesarius, "looking for a compromise with the antibarbarian party."[116] They were happy with Fravitta because, though a Goth, he was "one of those rare foreigners converted to Greek paganism."[117] There is not a word about nationalists or compromise in any of our sources.[118] Which nationalists, anyway? Aurelian, Saturninus, and John were still in exile. This explanation inadequately and unnecessarily attempts to palliate the unwelcome, but obvious, fact that it was the supposedly pro-barbarian Caesarius who took prompt and decisive action against Gaïnas. In reality there is neither problem nor paradox. There was no pro-barbarian party. Caesarius had already enjoyed and still held the highest honors the Roman state could offer. Why should he have wished to collaborate with an incompetent and unpopular barbarian? As soon as the situation allowed, he did what he could to eliminate the problem.

Where did Fravitta and his army come from? Demougeot assumed that the army consisted of citizen soldiers and deserters from Gaïnas's army, an improvised force hastily trained by Fravitta.[119] There may well have been a certain number of deserters, and there were also the 3,500 guardsmen. But the core of the army must have been some portion of the troops already under Fravitta's command in his capacity as *magister militum per Orientem*.

It is hard to believe that in a matter of weeks Fravitta could have improvised and trained from deserters and raw recruits an army capable of defeating the army of the *magister militum praesentalis*.[120] On the other hand the Eastern army must have been somewhere. The *Notitia dignitatum* gives a complete list of the thirty-five units "sub dispositione viri

senate to declare Stilicho *hostis publicus* in 397, he could as well have followed the same procedure for Gaïnas in 400. We do not need to accept all that Dagron has written on the role of the senate in politics at this period (1974, 201f.) to detect senatorial influence on a weak emperor.

116. Demougeot 1951, 259–60.

117. Ἕλλην τὴν θρησκείαν, Eunap. frag. 80 = 69.2 Blockley. According to frag. 82, Fravitta's only request to Arcadius after his victory was to be allowed to worship god κατὰ τὸν πάτριον νόμον, which might seem to imply *Gothic* paganism. H. Wolfram, *History of the Goths* (Berkeley 1988), 110, argues for a "Gothico-classical syncretism." For what is known of Gothic paganism, see Wolfram, pp. 106–12. There is no known example of a high-ranking Goth clinging to Gothic gods after twenty years in Roman service.

118. Against the strange notion that these (nonexistent) nationalists were sympathetic to paganism, see above, chapter 3, section I.

119. Demougeot 1951, 260.

120. Indeed Gaïnas had probably absorbed in addition what remained of the forces of his late fellow *praesentalis*, Leo.

illustris magistri militum per Orientem."[121] It is true that the Eastern part of the *Notitia* as we have it dates from no later than ca. 394.[122] But when raising the army he took west with him, Theodosius will not have disturbed the troops on the eastern frontier,[123] essential to its protection against the very real threat of a Persian invasion. Just such a threat had in fact suddenly arisen in the course of 399.[124] Even if false, the alarm betrays an instinctive apprehension that Persia would exploit any deflection of the Roman war effort in the East, such as Tribigild's rebellion. Whatever the differences between Rufinus, Eutropius, Aurelian, and Caesarius, it is not easy to believe that any of the four would have dared to weaken the defense of the eastern frontier.

The civilian ministers of Arcadius may have feared the ambitions of the *magistri militum praesentales*, who were stationed at court: Eutropius seems not to have appointed one at all between ca. 395 (the dismissal of Timasius) and 399 (the appointment of Leo and Gaïnas). But there is solid evidence for *magistri militum per Orientem* continuously from 393 to 398: Addaeus from 393 to 396 and Simplicius from December 396 to March 398.[125] Zosimus does not give Fravitta's rank at the time of his appointment to the command against Gaïnas in the summer of 400 but reports that he had "freed the entire East from Cilicia to Phoenice and Palestine from bandits" (5.20.1). To have campaigned over so wide an area he must have been *magister militum per Orientem*. In confirmation, a fragment that is clearly extracted from the passage of Eunapius on which Zosimus here depends describes Fravitta specifically as "general of the East" (στρατηγὸς τῆς ἀνατολῆς) at the time.[126] This is standard Greek usage of the age for *magister militum per Orientem*.[127] The achievements

121. *ND Or. 7*, as reconstructed by Hoffmann 1969 (Beilage, pp. 4–5).

122. Indeed it has been plausibly suggested that our text descends from a copy of the official Eastern *Notitia* in the possession of an Eastern bureaucrat in Theodosius's army when he marched west against Eugenius in 394. This copy then remained in the West, where Western lists were added and maintained to a somewhat later date: Hoffmann 1969, 52–53, 516–19; Barnes 1978, 82.

123. Indeed there is good reason to believe that the defense of the eastern frontier had remained unchanged in its essentials since Diocletian: Jones 1964a, 3:357.

124. Cameron 1970a, 140.

125. *PLRE* I.13, II.1013–14; Demandt 1970, 728.

126. For example, it is here that Zosimus describes Fravitta as a pagan in his θρησκεία, using the same terminology as Eunapius (frag. 88 = 69.2 Blockley). There is a closely similar formulation in Philostorgius (*HE* 11.8, p. 139.12 Bidez-Winkelmann), whose account of Fravitta likewise derives, like much other secular information in Philostorgius, from Eunapius: see L. Jeep, *Jahrb.f.class.philol.*, Suppl. 14 (1885): 56–64, with Bidez's edition, pp. cxxxviii–ix.

127. στρατηγὸς or στρατηλάτης (standard official Greek for *magister militum*: Enßlin 1930, 323) followed by (in the genitive) either ἕω or ἀνατολῆς; for the latter, the following list will suffice: Callinicus *V.Hyp.* 2.1; *V. Dan. Styl.* 55; Malalas, pp. 360, 364, 411, 423B; Theophanes A.M. 6011, 6021; *Chron.Pasch.*, p. 612.13; Preger, *Script. orig. Cpol.*, 2:220.8.

with which Zosimus credits him suggest at least one campaigning season, and there is no reason to doubt that he was the direct successor of Simplicius, in office possibly from late 398, but certainly by 399.[128] The normal peacetime headquarters of the *MVM per Orientem* was Antioch; he is bound to have followed the movements of Tribigild and Gaïnas throughout 399–400, poised to take appropriate action.

One source actually refers to the existence of the eastern frontier army before the massacre. According to Socrates, one night Gaïnas sent his barbarians to burn down the palace.[129] They were repulsed by a band of angels in the form of gigantic warriors and reported the presence of this "large and noble army" to their leader. Gaïnas did not believe them, "for he knew that the bulk of the Roman army was some way away, stationed among the cities."[130] Of course, the context is not reassuring. Not to mention the angels disguised as soldiers, it is most unlikely that the barbarians attempted to burn the palace in the first place. Nonetheless, the army at the disposal of the *magister militum per Orientem* was indeed "some way away," dispersed among the various eastern frontier provinces.[131]

It is worth exploring why Fravitta did not act earlier. If Gaïnas had really seized Constantinople in April 400 and held it by force till 12 July, Fravitta could not have stood idly by. If Gaïnas had really joined forces with Tribigild the previous summer and helped him plunder Asia, as Zosimus alleges, Fravitta could hardly have ignored that either.[132] A simple and revealing explanation of such protracted inaction suggests itself.

Historians have always taken it for granted that Gaïnas really did join forces with Tribigild in the summer of 399, openly revealing himself as a rebel long before he "seized" Constantinople in April 400. Certainly contemporaries believed that the two were in league. It was natural, perhaps inevitable, that in retrospect Gaïnas should be thought to have planned every stage of his coup in advance. According to Zosimus, he

---

The former is the preferred usage of Procopius: *BP* 1.8.1, 1.11.24, 1.13.9, 2.24.13; *Anecd.* 4.13. Enßlin oddly claimed of Eunapius's formula that it "nur heißen soll, daß er der östlichen Reichshälfte angehörte" (324, followed by Mazzarino 1942, 392). But in a context where there was no likelihood of any reference to a Western *magister militum*, there was no reason for Eunapius to supply so superfluous a detail.

128. So Demandt 1970, 728.

129. *HE* 6.6.

130. ἠπίστατο γὰρ μὴ παρεῖναι τὸ πολὺ τῶν Ῥωμαίων ὁπλιτικὸν, κατὰ τὰς πόλεις γὰρ ἐνίδρυτο.

131. See map 4 in Jones 1964a and map 3 ("Kleinasien und Orient") in Hoffmann 1970.

132. Though if there really was a Persian threat, it is possible that part at least of the eastern frontier army was being mobilized in case of invasion.

and Tribigild planned the whole thing in Constantinople early in 399 before Tribigild went out to Phrygia. The fullest and most recent modern discussion, by Paschoud, sees no reason to doubt this version.[133] But apart from serious internal improbabilities in Zosimus's account, analyzed below, both Claudian and Synesius tell against it.

In his narrative Synesius says only that the barbarian general and his troops "were waging an unsuccessful war against a rebellious contingent of their own people" (108B). But a few lines later Typhos's wife alleges that Osiris was planning to accuse the general of treason on the grounds "that he was fighting a collusive war, the barbarians pursuing a common policy with divided armies" (108C). This is another neat illustration of the way book 1 avoids accusing Gaïnas outright: the narrative is neutral, with the accusation coming in a speech by a character presumed to be lying. If called, the author can disavow it.[134] The status of the allegation is therefore unclear. Synesius no doubt believed it. He had freely predicted barbarian treachery in *De regno*. But his very evasiveness here suggests that it was less than established fact.

Early though the testimony of Synesius is, even book 1 was not written till after the massacre. Book 2 of Claudian's *In Eutropium* seems to have been written before Eutropius's fall. It is true that the elegiac preface and proem (lines 1–23) allude to his exile (August 399), but the rest of the book (24–602) presupposes that he was still in power. In particular, responsibility for the outbreak and success of Trigibild's rebellion is laid squarely on Eutropius. An elaborate section (376–461) describes how Leo's incompetence allowed Tribigild to destroy the Roman army and rampage unchecked through Pamphylia and Pisidia. The book closes with a denunciation of Eutropius that merges into an appeal to Stilicho for rescue (550–90). Lines 562–83 review Tribigild's revolt, claiming that Eutropius ignored it and thought only of dancing and feasting; to compensate for the revenue from the lost provinces he simply divides those that remain in half! The concluding appeal to Stilicho begs:

> eripe me tandem servilibus eripe regnis.
> (*In Eutr.* II.593)

> Save me, save me at last from the servile kingdom.

---

133. Paschoud 1986, 124f., quoting earlier bibliography.

134. This crucial distinction between narrative and speech is fatally blurred in Seeck's paraphrase: "Der Hauptmann der fremden Söldner führt Krieg gegen einem abgefallenen Theil seiner eigenen Genossen, und es regt sich der Verdacht, daß er mit dem Feinde im Einverständnis sei" (1894, 443).

The two leitmotifs of the poem are eunuch and slave. There are twenty-nine references to Eutropius's one-time servile status, some extended.[135] There can be no doubt that the "servile kingdom" means the East under the rule of Eutropius. In line 517, the Easterners are alleged to admit that they deserve punishment for "entrusting themselves to the governance of slaves" (*qui se tradiderint famulis*). At 535 a suppliant Aurora, addressing Stilicho, refers to herself as "a plaything of slaves" (*ludibrium famulis*). Usage and context put it beyond doubt that Stilicho is being asked to rescue the East from Eutropius because he is both unable and unwilling to stop Tribigild. It follows that the appeal was written *before* Eutropius's fall, when it could still be alleged that only Stilicho could stop Tribigild.[136]

Of course it did not happen this way. Gaïnas intervened instead, using the threat of Tribigild's superior strength to persuade Arcadius to depose Eutropius. Six months later he seized power himself. Claudian evidently had no idea of these developments when he wrote book 2 of *In Eutropium*.[137] Paschoud claims that Claudian's account is "not irreconcilable with the version of an early agreement between the two Gothic generals."[138] But the motive Claudian assigns for Tribigild's revolt is his own indignation at being treated worse than Alaric. It is true, as Paschoud observes, that Gaïnas had the same grievance, but the key fact is that Claudian applies it only to Tribigild. Moreover, Leo's defeat is attributed entirely to his own incompetence, which is used as another stick with which to beat Eutropius. Seeck argued that Claudian did not mention Gaïnas because he was Stilicho's secret agent in the East;[139] but it was for himself, not Stilicho, that Gaïnas seized power a few months later. And in any case it is not true that Gaïnas's part in the story is entirely suppressed. At 578f. Claudian describes how the Greuthungi lay waste Lydia and Asia, "relying not on their own valor or their numbers,"

> sed inertia nutrit
> proditioque ducum, quorum per crimina miles
> captivis dat terga suis.

135. 1.26, 30–44, 58–77, 83, 100–109, 122, 125, 142, 148–50, 176–77, 184–86, 212, 252, 276, 310–11, 478–81, 507–13; 2pr.3, 29–30, 62; 2.56, 69, 81, 132, 319, 351–53, 517, 535, 593. For the motif of the eunuch, see above, p. 135 n. 105.

136. Cameron 1970a, 136f., unconvincingly disputed by Döpp 1978, 187f.; 1980, 161f.

137. As observed long ago by Gibbon: "The conspiracy of Gainas and Tribigild, which is attested by the Greek historians, had not reached the ears of Claudian, who attributes the revolt of the Ostrogoth to his own martial spirit and the advice of his wife" (1909, 389 n. 27).

138. Paschoud 1986, 125.

139. Against this notion see Cameron 1970a, 148; Döpp 1980, 164.

> But the treachery and feebleness of our leaders helps them;
> it is through their crimes that our soldiers flee before their own slaves.

The feebleness obviously points to Leo, but the treachery can refer only to Gaïnas. Clearly for Claudian Gaïnas's treachery became an element in the story only after Leo's defeat. As even Zosimus's account makes clear (5.14.1–2), the two Roman generals divided their task; Leo marched into Phrygia, where Tribigild had been last reported, while Gaïnas stayed by the Hellespont, in case Tribigild marched north to cross into Europe. In the event he marched south, pursued by Leo, and Gaïnas did not march south until Leo had met with disaster. It cannot have been until then that the first suspicions arose of Gaïnas's collusion, prompted by his evident (and understandable) reluctance to engage the victorious Tribigild.

It is worth taking a closer look at Zosimus's account. At first sight, the sheer number of treacherous acts he details might seem to leave little room for doubt. In fact what we find is one after another of those all too familiar unfulfilled intentions—not surprisingly, seeing how little the early movements of Gaïnas and Tribigild suit the hypothesis of collusion. Instead of joining forces as soon as possible, Gaïnas waited by the Hellespont while Tribigild marched off in the opposite direction. At 5.14.3 Zosimus claims to know that Gaïnas began by ordering Tribigild to march north to the Hellespont, but Tribigild "was afraid of the troops stationed there" (Gaïnas's army?) and so marched south into Pisidia. If the plan had been carried through, "all Asia would have been taken." At 5.15.4 we are told once more that if Tribigild had marched east into Lydia instead of west into Pamphylia, all Ionia would have fallen, followed by the whole East as far as Egypt. Why then did he march west? The unfulfilled intentions even continue after the two Goths had allegedly joined forces: for example, he claims that they planned to take Sardis together but were foiled by unexpected spring rains (5.18.5).

The disproportionate detail in Zosimus's narrative of Tribigild's revolt derives from local information;[140] much of the action took place not far from the native city of his source, Eunapius of Sardis. Most of the incidents related are doubtless true enough, but the motives inevitably are all guesswork. We gain a lively insight into the fears and conjectures of people who suffered from "those aimless and destructive marches and countermarches,"[141] people who knew only that two Roman *magistri*

---

140. 5.13–19 (nine pages in Paschoud's edition), "a copious and circumstantial narrative (which he might have reserved for more important events)," according to Gibbon, ed. Bury (1909), 7:387 n. 21.

141. E. A. Thompson 1982, 42.

militum had failed to stop one rebel, and who suspected the worst. It was easy for such people to believe that even while far away by the Hellespont Gaïnas "secretly sent forces to assist Tribigild" (5.15.3) or sent "his barbarians" to corrupt and harass the various Roman units that were threatening Tribigild from all sides (5.17.1).[142]

Like the Tacitean Tiberius, even when Gaïnas does the right thing, it is from the wrong motive. For example, at one point Tribigild appeals to him in desperation; Gaïnas is distressed but, not wishing to reveal his hand, dispatches Leo *against* Tribigild (5.16.5)! In the event Tribigild inflicted a surprise defeat on Leo, allegedly with Gaïnas's secret help, but if Gaïnas had really wanted to protect Tribigild, he might better have sent Leo on some other errand and temporized.

Not only are all these secret acts and plans hard to believe; they would have been harder still to execute and involved Gaïnas himself in considerable risk.[143] Tribigild had only a very small force to begin with, and Gaïnas could not have counted on the revolt spreading in the way it did.[144] Nor was it a foregone conclusion that Eutropius would select Gaïnas, whom Zosimus admits he treated badly, to send against Tribigild. Furthermore, how far could Gaïnas trust Tribigild? Suppose that, having defeated Leo, Tribigild had turned on Gaïnas too? Suppose Alaric had intervened?[145] How could Gaïnas possibly have calculated on being able to manipulate to his own advantage so many imponderables?

Zosimus describes a meeting between Arcadius and Gaïnas in probably the fall of 399 at which "it was obvious to everyone that he was moving toward revolution." Once again, unfulfilled intentions, and Zosimus adds that Gaïnas himself behaved as though his intentions were still undetected (5.18.4). There is in fact no secure evidence that he ever joined forces with Tribigild. According to Zosimus (5.18.9), after reaching Chalcedon Gaïnas "ordered Tribigild to follow him." On the conspiracy theory, we should certainly expect to find Tribigild sharing in Gaïnas's triumph, but in fact Zosimus never mentions him again. Indeed, according to Philostorgius, who also drew on Eunapius, "after

142. A claim incredibly taken quite seriously by Paschoud, comm. pp. 136–37.

143. Ridley (1982) comments laconically on 5.15.3: "It is difficult to see how Gaïnas could have managed this."

144. Zos. 5.13.4, 15.2. As Bellona assures Tribigild:

> cunctaris adhuc, numerumque tuorum
> respicis exiguumque manum? tu rumpe quietem;
> bella dabunt socios.
>
> (Claud. *In Eutr.* 2.220–22)

145. See below, pp. 328–33.

suffering many losses, [Tribigild] escaped to the Hellespont and, crossing thence into Thrace, was killed soon afterwards."[146]

It was not till he marched into Thrace a few days after the massacre
that Gaïnas first stepped outside the law. Up till then he had done nothing to warrant interference by Fravitta without instructions from Arcadius. To be sure he had exploited Tribigild's victories to his own advantage; he had prevaricated and bullied and blackmailed, but each time
Arcadius had been intimidated and had acquiesced. It was Arcadius, not
Gaïnas, who had dismissed first Eutropius and then Aurelian. When refused his Arian church within the walls, Gaïnas had meekly accepted
defeat. And even when the people of Constantinople had risen up and
massacred 7,000 of his fellow countrymen,[147] he did not take the immediate revenge the city expected.

It must have been an unbearably tense interval, through which Caesarius successfully stalled. To Synesius's highly tendentious representation of this period it is instructive to compare Claudian's account of
Rufinus's behavior during Alaric's brief siege of Constantinople in 395:

> Rufinus rejoices in the beleaguered city and exults in its misfor-
> tunes. . . . From time to time he laughs. He has only one regret: it is not
> his hand that strikes the blows. He watches the whole countryside
> ablaze *by his own orders.*[148] . . . He boasts that to him alone the enemy
> camp opens its gates and that he is allowed to parley with them. When-
> ever he goes forth to arrange some marvelous truce his companions
> throng around him, and . . . Rufinus himself in their midst drapes
> tawny skins about his breast.[149]

Since Alaric did leave, it is apparent that Rufinus arranged a satisfactory
truce. Yet Claudian does not flinch from alleging that it was he who had
arranged the siege in the first place. Synesius similarly makes Typhos's
former allies testify "that Typhos had surrendered key positions and all
but arranged the siege himself, so that the holy city might be gripped by
a reign of terror" (123A). He is no more to be believed than Claudian,
especially since this testimony is given at the wholly imaginary trial.

As to Caesarius's conduct when Constantinople was effectively "besieged"—that is, in the immediate aftermath of the massacre, when
Gaïnas had withdrawn "a little distance away" (119C–D) from Constan-

---

146. *HE* 11.8, p. 138.25–27 Bidez-Winkelmann; Eunap. frag. 75.7 (= 67.11 Blockley)
may allude to Tribigild's death.

147. For the figure 7,000, Zos. 5.19.4.

148. *praeceptis incensa suis, In Ruf.* 1.71; for the text here, see Cameron 1968b, 392,
accepted in the new text of J. B. Hall (1985).

149. *In Ruf.* 2.61–85.

tinople, but before he retreated further into Thrace—Synesius charges
that "he demanded that they negotiate with the barbarians, and was
again working to admit the enemy army, claiming that no irreparable
damage had been done" (121B). But the people stoutly and righteously
resisted him, Synesius continues, "and in general his tyranny was as
good as dead, since the force that sustained it had been driven from the
city." Thus he implies that Caesarius's excuses were presented to the
people of Constantinople—to whom indeed they might sound pretty
feeble. But the claim "that no irreparable damage had been done" makes
much better sense as palliation extended to Gaïnas. It was his fellow
Goths who suffered what damage had been done, and he who, with an
army encamped not far away, might be expected to seek revenge. Synesius himself, writing book 1 at just that time, took great pains to transfer
all responsibility for his hero's fall from the Scythian general to Typhos:
clearly he too feared to offend Gaïnas. It was Caesarius's responsibility
as PPO to conciliate Gaïnas. He will have wanted to "readmit the enemy
army" to Roman service, to prevent it from attacking the city as an enemy in deed. Naturally he had to minimize the effects of the riot and
offer to repair what he could.[150]

In the event, these negotiations came to nothing. Gaïnas was not
reconciled, but neither did he attack Constantinople. Even before the ex-
tension and reinforcement of the walls under Theodosius II, it would not
have been easy for him to take the city by force. Alaric did not even
try.[151] Nor is it likely that Gaïnas could have counted on the loyalty of his
men if he had made the attempt. What finally drove him to turn his back
on all his hopes and march off into Thrace was perhaps the news that
Fravitta was on his way. It was not till then, surely, that Arcadius finally
dared to pronounce him a public enemy.

It is significant that Synesius's narrative leaps straight from the massacre of July to Aurelian's return in September.[152] To be sure, he was writing before Fravitta's victory and Gaïnas's death at the hand of Uldin the
Hun. But the campaign must have been under way by the time Aurelian

150. It may be significant that Synesius mentions Typhos's negotiations immediately
after his "indignant protest" over the burning of the church and "Scythianizing religious
beliefs." Caesarius could hardly have conceded anything to Gothic Arianism (cf. below,
p. 328), but Synesius is only concerned to represent his sympathy in the most unattractive
light possible. It would not be unreasonable if his offers to repair damage had included
something like a new Gothic Catholic church.

151. Nor did the Goths who attacked the city in 378 immediately after their defeat of
Valens at Adrianople: Amm. Marc. 31.16.4–7.

152. On the date, see below, section III.

returned. He makes no attempt to assign Aurelian any credit even for his own return. The technique is reminiscent of Claudian. Naturally Synesius did not want to report that it was another Goth who had rescued the situation. Least of all did he want to allow Typhos any credit. But in all plausibility he could not allow Aurelian any either. So he said nothing. Aurelian's return is simply recorded, without explanation.

Yet it must have been Caesarius who claimed the political credit for suppressing the rebellion—and for bringing back the exiles. However much Synesius might muddy the waters with talk of treachery and malice, the fact remains that it was Aurelian's policies that provoked Gaïnas's revolt and Caesarius's that brought it to a rapid and successful conclusion. It was not Aurelian, but the brother Synesius caricatured as a barbarian-lover who sent the barbarian packing. The man who allows his opponent to play his only card does not deserve to get back into the game. It is not surprising that Caesarius remained in office for another two and a half years.

III. AURELIAN'S RETURN

Seeck was in no hurry to bring Aurelian back from exile, since he was not planning to make him prefect again till late in 401. That way he could reconcile established facts with his own theories: the fact that Arcadius rewarded Fravitta with the consulate for 401 for his victory over Gaïnas with his theory that Aurelian immediately had him tried for treason and executed. His explanation of the paradox is that Arcadius's honors fell in December 400, while Aurelian did not return till early in 401.[153] But Aurelian was back before Synesius left Constantinople, since book 2 describes his return (124A). And the exigencies of the sailing season mean that Synesius left no later than early November 400.

The case for postponing the return till the spring of 401 rests mainly on Zosimus 5.22.3,[154] which describes the death of Gaïnas at the hand of Uldin the Hun, the sending of Gaïnas's head to Constantinople, and Fravitta's subsequent mopping up of deserters in Thrace. Gaïnas's head did not reach Constantinople till January or February 401.[155] It is clear that this chapter of Zosimus refers to 401.

The account of Fravitta's expedition breaks off abruptly, thanks to

153. Seeck 1913, 326.
154. Following Seeck 1913, 326: e.g., Mazzarino 1942, 224.
155. See below, section IV.

the loss of a leaf in the Vatican codex. The text resumes halfway through what is apparently the return of the exiles:

> . . . decided [singular] to cross, and they, fearing they would be harshly treated if they fell in with him, disembarked near Epirus. Thinking of their own safety, which the gravity of their offenses made very precarious, they gave their prisoners a chance to escape; others, however, say they bought their release. Whatever the manner of their escape, they unexpectedly returned to Constantinople and appeared before the emperor, the senate, and everyone else.

The sequence of the chapters implies a date well into 401. But it is never safe to place much trust in Zosimus's chronology, and this part of his narrative may be more confused than most. The next sentence begins: "Henceforth the empress's hatred for John, the Christian bishop, increased." And the very next sentence after that claims that "after the return of John and the others, she became his open enemy." Why, Paschoud has recently asked, does Zosimus link Eudoxia's feud with Chrysostom so closely to the return of the exiles?[156] His own answer is that Zosimus has confused Count John the exile with John Chrysostom the bishop.

The suggestion is not absurd; Zosimus is certainly very careless, and such a confusion would neatly explain the emphatic link here between the two Johns. But it is not the only possible explanation. All three exiles were hostile to Chrysostom. Both Aurelian and Saturninus were followers of the monk Isaac,[157] who took a prominent part in the attack on Chrysostom.[158] According to Palladius, Saturninus's widow, Castricia, was one of a band of fanatical anti-Johannites who carried on the fight after her husband's death.[159] As for John, the eleventh charge against Chrysostom at the Synod of the Oak was "informing against the Count John during the mutiny of the soldiers."[160] No other mutiny took place at Constantinople at this period, and it is difficult to imagine what this could refer to except the coup of Gaïnas.[161] The obvious guess is that Chrysostom had refused John sanctuary in a church.[162] The accusation

156. Paschoud 1985a, 43–61.
157. *Vita Isaaci* 4.14 and 4.18.
158. Liebeschuetz 1984a, 90f.
159. Palladius *Dialogus de vita S. Iohannis Chrysostomi* 16, p. 25.13 Coleman-Norton.
160. Photius *Bibl.* cod. 59, p. 18a.19.
161. So, for example, Liebeschuetz 1984a, 98; Albert 1984, 155. There is nothing to be said for the interpretation offered in *PLRE* (II.593, Ioannes 1) that John was "accused by John Chrysostom . . . of inciting a mutiny in the army." Count John was a civilian, and why should the bishop John have taken it upon himself to interfere in a military matter?
162. A. Moulard, *Saint Jean Chrysostome: Sa vie, son oeuvre* (Paris 1949), 300.

may, like many of the others, have been unfair or unfounded.[163] But it certainly suggests that Chrysostom was felt by contemporaries to have played an equivocal role in the confrontation with Gaïnas.

After 400 his Gothic missionary activities must have looked less innocent than they did at the time. And the very fact that he was selected to lead the embassy to Gaïnas in Thrace shows that he was felt to be a man Gaïnas might listen to. The ecclesiastical historians all praise the courage with which he stood up to Gaïnas's demand for an Arian church inside Constantinople. But they wrote after his rehabilitation and the defeat of his enemies, and even if this is not to be interpreted as "an attempt to counter John's reputation of having been excessively pro-Gaïnas,"[164] it was an issue on which, as patriarch, he simply could not give way. It is significant that the unpublished contemporary *Life* of Chrysostom, whose value has recently been recognized by F. van Ommeslaeghe, reveals that despite his opposition to Gaïnas on this issue, his enemies alleged that "he had wanted to sacrifice to [Gaïnas] the interests of Church and Empire alike."[165]

Count John may then have had personal, as well as political and religious, grounds for his hostility to Chrysostom, and since he was in addition closely enough associated with the empress to be reputed her lover, it is not surprising that the return of these three anti-Johannites should have changed Eudoxia's attitude. There is a perfectly reasonable alternative to Paschoud's explanation. Whether Zosimus confused the two Johns or simply knew the connection between the exiles, the empress, and Chrysostom, either cause could have led him to link the return of the exiles with the campaign against Chrysostom. If so, he need not have mentioned their return at its correct point in the strict chronological sequence of his narrative. It was not, after all, a detail of any importance in itself. Its importance lay rather in the impetus it gave to the campaign against Chrysostom.

Several passages of Synesius strongly suggest that the exiles returned in the fall of 400. First there is the reference to Osiris's "eponymous year." This flagrant anachronism in the Egyptian context only makes sense if it was intended to evoke Aurelian's consulate. It would have been an obvious and unnecessary lie if Aurelian did not return till 401. Second, there is *Ep.* 61, where Synesius's regret that he did not say good-bye to Aurelian, his "dear friend and consul," clearly implies that

163. If true, Chrysostom's refusal of sanctuary to John would naturally have been compared unfavorably with his granting of sanctuary to Eutropius the previous year.

164. Liebeschuetz 1984a, 99.

165. Ommeslaeghe 1979, 152.

he was present in Constantinople before Synesius left. If so, then he was back before the *mare clausum*, mid-November at latest—perhaps a little earlier than that, since Synesius also claims that book 2 of *De providentia* was written "after the return of the best men" and at their invitation. We also have to allow a couple of weeks at least for the preparations for the consular games, which Synesius apparently witnessed before finishing book 2 and leaving himself.

All in all the exiles must have been back by late September or October. It is easy to believe that their guards saw no need to keep a close watch the moment things started to go badly with Gaïnas. After the massacre in Constantinople on 12 July and Gaïnas's retreat to Thrace soon after, it must have been obvious that he had lost control of the situation. Zosimus's fragmentary narrative does not make it clear where the hostages were sent originally, but at the moment of their escape the party had just "disembarked near Epirus." This was a long way from the now-doubtful protection of Gaïnas. It is not surprising that the guards should have begun "to think of their own safety" and let their prisoners go free. They will not have waited till Gaïnas was actually defeated by Fravitta at the end of the year.

It is instructive to contrast the quite different explanation offered by Synesius for the return of the exiles: "The people demanded Osiris, seeing no other salvation for their affairs" (121C). Evidently he was anxious to play up the importance of Aurelian's return, but the formulation of his narrative, still theoretically set in Egyptian Thebes, is hardly appropriate to the circumstances of Constantinople in 400. It was not up to the people or even to Caesarius to recall Aurelian and his fellows. It was Gaïnas who had exiled them. Zosimus makes it clear that their return, though welcome, was unexpected, perhaps even the result of bribery. That was not good enough for Synesius; he does his best to suggest, quite falsely, that Aurelian's return was a consequence of the waning influence of Caesarius.

IV. FRAVITTA

Hitherto the execution of Fravitta in (it has been assumed) 401 has been seen as the culmination of Aurelian's anti-Germanism, an inevitable part of his purge of Caesarius's administration. But now that we have eliminated both Caesarius's fall from and Aurelian's return to the prefecture, how are we to interpret Fravitta's death? Did he indeed die in 401? Was he executed? Were Caesarius and his supposed pro-German administration responsible, unexpectedly and ungratefully turning on the architect of Caesarius's own success? Or was Aurelian working his will behind the scenes, perhaps exploiting John's influence on the empress Eudoxia?

In fact, the sources give clear answers. Four writers describe Fravitta's victory over Gaïnas: Socrates, Sozomen, Eunapius (a fragment), and (abridging Eunapius) Zosimus. Of the four, the fairly detailed narratives of Socrates (*HE* 6.6), Sozomen (*HE* 9.4), and Zosimus (5.21) do not even mention Fravitta's death. On the contrary, each of them reports that the emperor honored him with the consulate for the following year, 401. We have three fragments from what was evidently a full account by Eunapius (frags. 82, 85–86 = *FGrH* 4.49–51). Fravitta's death is mentioned only in the two later fragments (frags. 85–86), which have no connection with the ample account of his reception in Constantinople after the victory (frag. 82). Arcadius asked him what reward he wanted; Fravitta replied only that he be allowed to worship god in his ancestral fashion, which Arcadius graciously granted, adding the consulate as well. Eunapius took this opening to describe Fravitta's paganism, and this much survives in Zosimus's abridgment. They also both report that some people accused Fravitta of not pushing home his advantage after the battle and deliberately letting Gaïnas escape. Yet the one thing they do not do is what modern historians find so self-evident: link Fravitta's death with this accusation of treachery.

The ecclesiastical historians do not even mention the accusation of treachery; their account of Fravitta, if less detailed, is as favorable as that of the two pagan writers. Yet if Fravitta was really executed for treason soon after his victory, as modern writers assume, we should expect at least one of the four to have mentioned so striking and relevant a fact. We should certainly have expected Eunapius or Zosimus, for whom Fravitta was the incarnation of virtue and military expertise, to accuse Arcadius, whom both despised, of ingratitude. It might be added that the entry "Fravithos" in the Suda lexicon (= frag. 80), clearly compiled from Eunapius and purporting to give a summary of his career, again praises him for his virtue and military skill, without a word about execution deserved or undeserved. In short, there is nothing in our relatively abundant documentation to suggest that Fravitta was executed either for treason or soon after the victory that brought him the consulate for 401.

Quite the contrary. He made a triumphal entry into Constantinople,[166] an honor granted to few private citizens. And his victory was

---

166. μάλα φαιδρῶς καὶ <λαμπρῶς ἐπανῄει> ἐπὶ τὴν Κωνσταντίνου πόλιν (Eunap. frag. 82 = 69.4, line 18 Blockley, with Boissevain's supplement of a gap in the MS). McCormick (1986, 49 n. 58) compares Philostorgius's account of a triumphal entry of Theodosius I: λαμπρῶς ἐπὶ τὴν Κωνσταντίνου πόλιν ἄνεισιν (*HE* 9.19, p. 125 Bidez-Winkelmann).

commemorated by two monuments. First, on the narrative reliefs of the triumphal column erected by Arcadius on the Xerolophos hill in 402.[167] The column itself was pulled down ca. 1716,[168] but a number of sketches of the reliefs survive. There can be little doubt that one at least of these drawings depicts a general making a triumphal entry into the city on horseback, followed by a group of barbarian captives.[169] It must be Fravitta's triumphal entry described above. Then there is the "marble liburna" in the heart of the city, not far from the Milion and the Augusteon.[170] Fravitta made devastating use of the light galley known as *liburna* when Gaïnas's army tried to cross the Hellespont on rafts. Both Zosimus (5.20.3–4) and a fragment attributed to Eunapius single out his liburnas for special comment.[171] There had been no imperial sea victory since that of Constantine over Licinius in 324, and given the prominent role played by the liburna in the battle of 400, there can be no doubt that the marble liburna commemorated Fravitta's victory. The immense amount of workmanship required by the spiral reliefs of the column must have taken some time; the colossal statue of Arcadius on its top was not dedicated till 421.[172] One of the reliefs on the base,[173] obviously the first stage in the project, already shows Arcadius and Honorius as consuls. Clearly the design alone, not to mention the execution, must postdate their joint consulate in January 402. If Fravitta really is portrayed in any of the reliefs on the column itself, he can hardly have suffered rapid disgrace. Moreover, if he had been tried for treason and executed in his consular

167. Janin 1964, 82–84, 439–40. The date is given by Theophanes, p. 77.24 de Boor.

168. *The Complete Letters of Lady Mary Wortley Montague*, vol. 1: *1708–1720*, ed. R. Halsband (Oxford 1965), 402 ("about 2 year befor I came," 10 April 1718).

169. The fullest discussion, with bibliography, is that of Becatti 1960, 151–264; see too McCormick 1986, 49–50, and figs. 2–5 on pp. 52–55. Some have identified the horseman as Arcadius, but if the drawing can be depended on, he wears no diadem. It has also been suggested that some of the reliefs may commemorate victories by Theodosius I, but Theodosius erected his own column in 386, and he won no further victories over barbarians after that date. All Theodosius's victories would have been commemorated already on his own column, and it would be strange if they had been repeated on Arcadius's. The precedent of earlier triumphal monuments, colossal arches as well as columns, lends support to the assumption that only Arcadius's victories would have been depicted (in general, see R. Brilliant, *Visual Narratives* [Ithaca, N.Y. 1984], chap. 3). Arcadius's only other victory over barbarians was Eutropius's campaign against the Huns, which is not likely to have been very prominently featured in a monument erected after his disgrace.

170. "liburnam marmoream, navalis victoriae monumentum," in *Notitia urbis Constantinopolitanae* 5.11, p. 232 Seeck, with Janin 1964, 59.

171. Eunap. frag. 81 Müller (Suda Λ.490, s.v. Λίβερνα), omitted from Blockley's collection (cf. Blockley 1981, 162 n. 65: "assigned to Eunapius . . . on no good grounds"). See now the thorough and judicious discussion in Paschoud's commentary (pp. 161–65).

172. Marcellinus and *Chron. Pasch.*, s.a.; *Chron. Min.* II.75. The column of Marcus Aurelius was dedicated in 180 and not completed till 193.

173. Becatti 1960, 257; R. Grigg, *Art Bulletin* 59 (1977): 469 n. 3.

year, he would surely, like Eutropius, have suffered *damnatio memoriae*. The fact that our fairly abundant documentation for his consulate shows no such sign effectively excludes this possibility.[174]

How then did Fravitta die—and when? The evidence all comes from three fragments of Eunapius, where the story is not told in connection with the victory over Gaïnas, but as part of what looks like a long digression on a personal bête noire of Eunapius's called Hierax (frags. 85–87 Müller). First, the date. Historians from Seeck to Mazzarino and Demougeot have stated, as though there could be no question or doubt, that he was executed in 401.[175] For Seeck, he was attacked by the "anti-German party" the moment the exiles were back; for Mazzarino, it was Alaric's invasion of Italy in the fall of 401 that provided the pretext. Fravitta was removed from his command and tried for high treason together with Caesarius, who had been deposed from his prefecture following the return of the exiles. The "trial" is inferred from the entirely fictitious trial jointly conducted by the gods and the people of Constantinople in *De providentia* 122D–123B. Both Fravitta and Caesarius are imagined to have been found guilty and condemned to death,[176] though Caesarius was spared through his brother's intercession. Yet unless we emend a law, he is still attested as prefect in 403.[177] And why did Synesius say nothing about Fravitta's share in this trial? According to Demougeot, it was to cover up this "injustice" that Eunapius blamed Fravitta's death on the private intrigues of Hierax. But why should he have covered up an injustice done to one of his heroes by one of his villains? Why not rather proclaim it loud and clear? And that still leaves Synesius's silence to be explained.

Synesius's silence is easy to explain. He was writing book 2 of *De providentia* by September 400, well before the end of Fravitta's campaign against Gaïnas. And even if the trial he describes at 122D–123C were not, as it is, wholly imaginary, it is quite clearly placed *before* Osiris's return. Indeed, the alleged clamor for Typhos's punishment is linked to

174. Aurelian's consulate was not canceled, but then he was neither accused of treason nor executed, merely exiled; Abundantius was also exiled without suffering retroactive loss of his consulate. Liebeschuetz (1990, 124 n. 75) attempts to exploit the mutilated and incoherent Eunap. frag. 72.4 Blockley, where there is vague talk of killing "the consul himself out of lust for power ($\delta\iota\grave{\alpha}$ $\phi\iota\lambda\alpha\rho\chi\acute{\iota}\alpha\nu$)." But since Fravitta's death is a thing of the past already in frag. 72.1, and Stilicho is named in both 72.3 and 72.4, the presumption is that Eunapius is here writing of the West at a later date. In fact it looks as if Stilicho is the consul in question (though he was not in fact consul in the year of his murder). Liebeschuetz's further argument from the dates of Arbazacius is circular, since it only works if Hierax's governorship fell after Fravitta's death.

175. Seeck 1913, 326; Mazzarino 1942, 224; Demougeot 1951, 265.

176. So even Albert (1984, 78).

177. *CJ* 7.41.2 (11 June).

the clamor for Osiris's return, twin demands of the same alleged popular movement. This is the only evidence there is for a trial associated with the revolt of Gaïnas.

It is obvious from frags. 85–87 that Eunapius gave copious detailed information about the circumstances surrounding Fravitta's death. The fact that it is not mentioned by Zosimus is no problem in itself, since Zosimus abridged Eunapius fairly drastically. The question is, To what point in Zosimus's narrative do the Eunapian fragments correspond?

According to Blockley, the relevant part of Zosimus's narrative has fallen out of the surviving text in a lacuna between 5.25 and 5.26.[178] Such a lacuna is marked in Mendelssohn's text and Ridley's translation—but incorrectly. There is indeed an abrupt break in the narrative at this point, reflecting Zosimus's change in sources. A certain abruptness was to be expected, since Eunapius's history stopped in 404 and Olympiodorus's, on which the remainder of Zosimus's work is based, did not begin until 407.[179] But there is no sign in the Vatican MS of physical damage or loss, as Paschoud has recently confirmed.[180] Paschoud himself suggests that the story of Fravitta's end is lost in the undoubted lacuna between 5.22 and 5.23 already mentioned. One page has been torn out of the Vatican MS here. It would have contained around fifty-two lines in Mendelssohn's edition. The text breaks off in the middle of Fravitta's mopping-up operations of 401 and resumes with the return of the exiles. If it was on this missing page that Zosimus told the story of Fravitta's death, the order of narration would support the traditional date.

Yet there is a fatal objection to this hypothesis. According to Eunapius frag. 85 (quoted in full below), a major role in the plot that brought Fravitta down was played by Count John.[181] But according to Zosimus's own text John was in exile between 5.18.8 and the end of the lacuna. Paschoud implausibly argues that Zosimus erred here; that Count John was *not* exiled with Saturninus and Aurelian. It is true that Zosimus is the only source to record John's name among the exiles, but that can be easily explained by his youth and relative unimportance at the time.[182] Even if Paschoud is right in his suggestion that Zosimus confused Count John and John Chrysostom (which is more than doubtful), the main basis for such a confusion must have been the fact that both

178. Blockley 1980, 173–74.
179. Paschoud 1971, lviii.
180. Paschoud 1985a, 46–47. Paschoud has also shown Cameron a photo of the relevant page of Vat. gr. 156.
181. John is not actually attested as count before 404 (*PLRE* II.593, Ioannes 1), but we so style him to avoid confusion with John Chrysostom in the present context.
182. Note that at 121C Synesius refers to a plurality of unnamed fellow exiles expelled together with Osiris.

Johns went into and returned from exile in quick succession. If *no* John went into exile in 400, how can Zosimus have thought that the John who returned was Chrysostom? In any case, the accusation at the Synod of the Oak that Chrysostom informed against Count John "during the mutiny of the soldiers" makes it virtually certain that John suffered during Gaïnas's seizure of Constantinople.[183] And a long-misattributed homily of Chrysostom has now revealed the occasion on which Chrysostom "informed" on John, at a moment when soldiers were threatening the emperor.[184]

Paschoud further points out that if Count John had been in exile during the summer of 400, he could not have been the father of the baby Theodosius II, born on 10 April 401.[185] But he goes too far in concluding that the rumor could not have started unless John were known to have spent the summer of 400 in Constantinople. Rumors notoriously disregard unwelcome facts. Furthermore, on the chronology here proposed for the return of the exiles, they could in fact have been back in time for it to be theoretically possible for John to be the father.

There is no serious reason to doubt that John was one of the exiles. So Fravitta's death, in which he played a part, cannot have been described in the missing page of Zosimus. The alternative is that Zosimus simply omitted the story of Fravitta's death, as he omitted so many other details in the much fuller narrative of Eunapius. It would be rash to make far-reaching inferences from the silences of so incompetent a historian, but the relevant fragments of Eunapius do suggest a reason: his detailed account belonged in the category of biographical anecdote rather than political history. Zosimus naturally tended to omit much of the more scurrilous biographical material that so enlivens the pages of Eunapius.

Nonetheless, the Eunapian fragments must correlate somehow with Zosimus's narrative. The only safe guide to follow for Eunapius here is the sequence of fragments in the Constantinian *Excerpta de sententiis*.[186] No study of the chronology of fragments preserved in any of the Constantinian *Excerpta* has yet found any clear case of an individual fragment out of sequence.[187] The relevant fragments are

183. See above, p. 234, for the accusation that Chrysostom informed against John "during the mutiny of the soldiers."
184. Cameron 1988a.
185. Paschoud 1985a, 54–55.
186. That is to say, we are omitting from consideration in this context fragments preserved in the Suda and similar sources, since their place in the sequence can only be conjectural.
187. See, for example, J. M. Moore, *The Manuscript Tradition of Polybius* (Cambridge 1965), 125; Brunt 1980, 477–94; Croke 1983, 297–308; the undoubtedly misplaced fragments of Malchus given as nos. 18 and 19 by Müller are almost certainly "a case of simple

82M = 69.4B   Fravitta defeats Gaïnas and wins the consulate
                for 401

83M = 71.2B   Character study of Hierax the Alexandrian

85M = 71.3B   Fravitta destroyed by John, the patron of Hierax

86M = 71.4B   Hierax governs Pamphylia after the Isaurian in-
                vasions of 404; reference to the death of Fravitta

87M = 72.1B   Reference (anticipatory?) to the punishment of
                Hierax, apparently under Pulcheria Augusta
                (i.e., no earlier than 414)

We may begin with frag. 86M = 71.4B:

> While being ravaged by the Isaurian war, Pamphylia found the blows of
> the Isaurians pure gold. Just as in a thunderstorm a thunderbolt is more
> to be feared than a flash of lightning (the latter only frightens whereas
> the former kills), so too our noble Hierax from Alexandria made the
> Isaurians, in truth most dreadful to see and hear, look like a dainty little
> flower on a green spring day, as he investigated and gathered together
> everything he needed to kill Fravitta ($\pi\acute{a}\nu\tau a\ \delta\iota\epsilon\rho\epsilon\upsilon\nu\eta\sigma\acute{a}\mu\epsilon\nu o\varsigma\ \kappa a\grave{\iota}\ \sigma\upsilon\nu$-
> $a\rho\pi\acute{a}\sigma a\varsigma\ \grave{\epsilon}\pi\grave{\iota}\ \tau\hat{\omega}\ \Phi\rho a\beta\acute{\iota}\theta o\upsilon\ \phi\acute{o}\nu\omega$). And having made off with it in se-
> cret, he tried to escape.

The Isaurian invasions mentioned here can be dated with certainty to
404.[188] So Hierax's activity in Pamphylia, presumably as governor,[189] cannot be dated before then. But what was he investigating? And what did
it have to do with Fravitta? It has so far been taken for granted that $\grave{\epsilon}\pi\grave{\iota}$
$\tau\hat{\omega}\ \Phi\rho a\beta\acute{\iota}\theta o\upsilon\ \phi\acute{o}\nu\omega$ means "after the murder of Fravitta."[190] But $\grave{\epsilon}\pi\acute{\iota}$ plus
the dative cannot mean this, in Greek of any age.[191] In a temporal sense
$\grave{\epsilon}\pi\acute{\iota}$ plus the dative can mean only "at," "for," or "during." The only ex-

---

misplacement of a page" (Blockley 1981, 124 and 1984, 152–53, arguing against R. M. Errington 1983, 82–110).

188. On the strength of Zos. 5.25, Soz. *HE* 9.25, and Chrysostom *Ep*. 14.4 (*PG* 52.617);
see Maenchen-Helfen 1973, 62–63; Paschoud's n. 52 on Zos. 5.25.

189. He is listed as *consularis* of Pamphylia in 404 by *PLRE* II.556.

190. So, for example, Blockley and Müller ("post Fravittae caedem").

191. See the entries in LSJ, Bauer, and Lampe, s.v.; Kühner-Gerth, *Ausführliche
Grammatik der griechischen Sprache*, II.1, 3d ed. (Hannover 1898), 499–503; Blass-Debrunner-
Funk, *A Greek Grammar of the New Testament*, 10th ed. (Chicago 1961), 123. W. Fritz (*Die
Briefe des Bischofs Synesius von Kyrene* [Leipzig 1898], 157–59) surveys the use of $\grave{\epsilon}\pi\acute{\iota}$ in Synesius's letters (101 examples): the majority fall into the category "zur Bezeichnung des
Grundes . . . Zweck, Absicht und Bestimmung." Least of all could $\grave{\epsilon}\pi\acute{\iota}$ plus the dative =
post plus the accusative be explained as a "late" usage, since in general $\grave{\epsilon}\pi\acute{\iota}$ plus the dative
simply disappears from the vulgar speech: for the few usages that survive see, for ex-
ample, K. Mitsakis, *The Language of Romanos the Melodist*, Byz. Archiv 11 (Munich 1967),
112–13. It is certainly not a usage one would expect to find in an educated writer: for example, see Keydell's *index graecitatis* to his edition of Agathias's *Historiae* ([Berlin 1967], 225).

ception is a restricted usage implying immediate or inevitable succession of one thing or person to another, in either a spatial or a temporal sense. Since the usage is amply documented in the grammars and lexica, it will be enough to cite one famous example from Xenophon (*Mem.* 3.14.2): ἐσθίουσι μὲν γὰρ δὴ πάντες ἐπὶ τῷ σίτῳ ὄψον, "everybody eats dessert after dinner." The relationship of dessert to dinner is not casual temporal sequence. It is this sense that is involved in another passage of Eunapius to which Paschoud referred as a parallel: καὶ ἐτελεύτα . . . γηραιός, Ἰάμβλιχός τε ἐπ᾽ αὐτῷ (*VS* 461, p. 17.3 Giangrande). This could be translated "he died an old man, and after him Iamblichus," but in the context it is clearly implied that the two men died in quick succession. Add οἱ περὶ Γάλβαν, Βιτέλλιον, Ὄθωνα· Οὐεσπασιανὸς δὲ ἐπὶ τούτοις καὶ Τίτος, "for example, Galba, Vitellius, Otho, and after them Vespasian and Titus" (*VS* 455, p. 5.9). Here the context is quite explicitly the rapid succession of short-lived emperors. This usage cannot be extended to the fragment about Hierax and Fravitta.

Moreover, even supposing such a temporal meaning there, what would the point be? On the traditional chronology Fravitta was condemned for treason in 401. Why are Hierax's depredations in far-off Pamphylia being linked to Fravitta's death in Constantinople three years earlier? *PLRE* assumes that he was made governor of Pamphylia "as a reward" for his part in Fravitta's death.[192] ἐπί certainly could not bear *that* meaning. In any case, why so long a wait for the reward? And there is yet another problem. It is not Hierax's governorship that is being linked to the death of Fravitta, but his "investigating and gathering" (διερευνη-σάμενος καὶ συναρπάσας). It has been assumed hitherto that this refers to no more than theft and extortion, undertaken purely from motives of avarice. συναρπάσας certainly implies that, and we need not doubt that Hierax did indeed fleece his province unmercifully. But why should extortion require investigation, the natural meaning of διερευνησάμενος?[193]

In this, as in many other examples of ἐπί plus the dative with an abstract noun in Eunapius, there can be no serious doubt that we are faced with a *final* expression, a standard classical usage still common in Greek writers of the fifth century A.D.[194] Since the point is crucial for the

---

192. So too by implication Paschoud 1985b, 280: "[Hierax] joua un rôle dans la mise à mort de Fravitta et fut ensuite gouverneur."

193. It might perhaps be suggested that Hierax had left no stone unturned in his search for booty, but in that case διερευνησάμενος would be a rather colorless word for a writer like Eunapius.

194. Kühner-Gerth, II.1³, 502f.; and above all Karin Hult, *Syntactic Variation in Greek of the Fifth Century A.D.*, Studia latina et graeca Gothoburgensia 52 (Göteborg 1990), 74, 89, 102, 115; note especially p. 225: "Eunapius has a rather high frequency of prepositional final expressions." We are grateful to Dr. Hult for fruitful correspondence on this point.

date of Fravitta's death it seems worth setting out every example in Eunapius. In the first five cases, all from the *Vitae Sophistarum*, the version
given is that of W. C. Wright, the Loeb translator, always sensitive to
this idiom:

1. *VS* 478, p. 51.16: καὶ ἀνεπέμφθη γε εἰς τὴν Ἀσίαν ἐπὶ κατα-
   βολῇ τῶν χρημάτων, "he was sent into Asia to make payment of
   the money"
2. *VS* 488, p. 70.11: ὁ δὲ ἀνθύπατος αὐτοὺς τὸ δεύτερον ὡς ἐπὶ τι-
   μαῖς συγκαλέσας, "the proconsul called them together a second
   time as though to award them honors"
3. *VS* 492, p. 78.2: τὴν Δήμητρος ἐπιδημίαν ἐπὶ τῇ τοῦ σίτου δω-
   ρεᾷ, "how Demeter sojourned among men that she might bestow on them the gift of corn"
4. *VS* 498, p. 88.5: Ἰουλιανὸς . . . αὐτὸν συνήρπασεν ἐπὶ τῇ τέχνῃ,
   "Julian . . . carried [Oribasius] away with him to practice his art
   [i.e., to be Julian's doctor]"
5. *VS* 504, p. 100.22: Ἑλλησπόντιος . . . παρὰ τὸν Χρυσάνθιον
   ἧξων ἐπὶ μαθήσει, "Hellespontius came to Chrysanthius to
   learn"
6. Frag. 74M = 66.2.21B: οὐδὲν διαφέρειν δοκεῖ μοι τοῦ πιεῖν τι
   τῶν δριμέων καὶ πικρῶν ἐπὶ σωτηρίᾳ, "it seems to me just like
   drinking something bitter or pungent to cure oneself"
7. Frag. 87M = 72.1.29B: men robbed by a thieving governor: τὰς
   ὕβρεις οὐκ ἐνεγκόντες ἐπὶ κατηγορίᾳ τῆς λῃστείας ὥρμησαν
   ἐπὶ τὸν τῆς αὐλῆς ἔπαρχον, "refusing to endure the abuses,
   went to the praetorian prefect to lay charges of robbery"
8. Frag. 1.67B (*FHG* IV, p. 13a): Lycurgus the Spartan lawgiver:
   ἐς ὃν καὶ ἡ τοῦ θεοῦ μαρτυρία διὰ στόματος ἅπασι θεὸν ἀντι-
   κρυς ἀνακαλοῦντος ἐπὶ τῷ θεῖναι τοὺς νόμους, "everyone knows
   about the testimony of the god to him, declaring him divine
   on account of his work in legislation" (Blockley, again following
   Müller: ("dei . . . diserte deum vocitantis ob ferendarum legum
   sapientiam"). If correctly so construed, this would be the closest
   parallel to the Fravitta example. But it cannot be correct. Eunapius is evidently alluding to the famous oracle (much quoted
   in late antiquity)[195] Lycurgus is said to have received when he
   went to Delphi to ask for a new constitution for Sparta. After

195. Testimonia are cited in H. W. Parke and D. E. W. Wormell, *The Delphic Oracle*
(Oxford 1956), 2:89, no. 216; and J. Fontenrose, *The Delphic Oracle* (Berkeley 1978), 270, Q 7.

greeting him as a god, Apollo granted his request for a constitution. That is to say, his legislation was still in the future at the time he was greeted as a god. Presumably once again final: "calling him a god to establish his laws."

To return to frag. 86M = 71.4B, Hierax was turning his province upside down "to kill Fravitta," that is to say, he was searching for *evidence* "for the purpose of killing Fravitta." Such an interpretation is strongly supported by the word order. Given its position at the end of the clause, the prepositional phrase ἐπὶ τῷ Φραβίθου φόνῳ is clearly controlled by the two verbs and πάντα. If Eunapius's purpose had really been to date Hierax's activity after Fravitta's death, we should have expected the prepositional phrase to come at the beginning of the clause, before the verbs.[196] It will be noticed that in almost all the other cases of final ἐπί plus the dative listed above, the ἐπί clause comes, as here, at the end of the sentence.

On this interpretation, a plausible and intelligible scenario can be reconstructed. Before being appointed to the command against Gaïnas, Fravitta had successfully "freed the entire East, from Cilicia to Phoenice and Palestine, from the plague of brigands" in his capacity as *magister militum per Orientem*.[197] Since Cilicia adjoins Isauria, the obvious inference is that the "brigands" in question were Isaurians, who made regular incursions into the neighboring provinces of Cilicia and Pamphylia, and sometimes even farther afield.[198] It is surely no coincidence that it was during his governorship of Pamphylia that Hierax gathered this evidence against Fravitta, who had perhaps taken the opportunity to do a little plundering of his own while pursuing Isaurians—or had at any rate been accused of so doing. Hierax would be in a position to gather evidence at first hand in Pamphylia.

Frag. 87 describes how the *vicarius* Herennianus subsequently arrested Hierax and "made him pay more to escape than he had stolen and thus inflicted upon him a fitting penalty for the murder of Fravitta," in

---

196. Apparently accepting the argument (seen in an earlier draft) here made that ἐπί plus the dative cannot mean "after," in the text of frag. 86 appended to his *Zosime* (3:334–35), Paschoud marks a lacuna after φόνῳ ("quaedam omisse videtur excerptor") and translates "fouilla et pilla systématiquement tout, outre l'assasinat de Fravithos." But in his commentary he continues to refer to Hierax being "récompensé pour son rôle dans la mise à mort de Fravitta" (190). Liebeschuetz, after translating "after" in his text, adds the following qualification, presumably intended to meet our objection: "'after' or 'in connection with' or 'with a view to,' but in any case *close in time* to" (1990, 124 n. 78).

197. Zos. 5.20.1; Eunap. frag. 69.2B = 80M.

198. J. Rougé, *REA* 68 (1966): 282f.; R. Syme, *Ammianus and the Historia Augusta* (Oxford 1968), 43f.

fact 4,000 solidi (frag. 86). As an illustration Eunapius compares the sale of provincial governorships under the empress Pulcheria,[199] when prosecution of offending governors would result in confiscation of ill-gotten gains by the prefect in return for acquittal. He describes a man buying himself whichever governorship he wanted, "wherever he craved to commit his crimes *or had enemies.*" Clearly this is what Hierax had done, secured himself Pamphylia both to make his fortune and to dig up whatever he could against a personal enemy, Fravitta. On this hypothesis everything falls into place—but only if we date Fravitta's death *after* Hierax's return from Pamphylia. If so, it could not be earlier than 405.

Eunapius evidently disliked Hierax (cf. frag. 83) as much as he admired Fravitta, and we should beware of accepting without qualification his picture of a purely personal vendetta. Eunapius frag. 85, which is important enough to quote in full, touches on wider political issues:

> He directed his words at John: "But it is you who are responsible for all these troubles, you who break up the concord between our emperors, undermining, dissolving, and destroying this most heavenly and divine arrangement with your plots. It is a most blessed thing, an invincible and adamantine bulwark, when emperors in two separate bodies hold a single empire." Those present when these things were said fearfully shook their heads in silent disagreement; for he seemed to be speaking good sense to them. But they were afraid of John, and each was preoccupied with the thought of his own gain (for licentiousness lavishes honor even on the wicked, as it is said), and so, heedless of the public weal, they made John their leader, the crafty hirer of Hierax, and took Fravitta's life.

There seems no reason to doubt that this is Count John, and in favor of the later date here proposed for Fravitta's death it should be noted that it is not till 404 that John is first attested in a major office, *comes sacrarum largitionum.* The reference to the destruction of concord between Arcadius and Honorius also has chronological implications. It has so far been assumed that with the supposed restoration in 402 of the Aurelian whose consulate Stilicho had refused to recognize in 400 relations between East and West sunk to a new low and stayed there for several years. This a priori assumption is not borne out by facts long accessible but still unexploited.

Stilicho did not recognize the Eastern consuls of 399 and 400, but

---

199. We agree with Paschoud (1985b, 280–81) that Eunapius is citing an illustration from his own day, a decade after the actual cutoff point of his history. Blockley improbably suggests emending Pulcheria to Eudoxia (1980, 175–76).

he did recognize Fravitta's consulate in 401,[200] and in 402 Arcadius and Honorius assumed the consulate together. Solidi of Eudoxia proclaiming SALVS ORIENTIS FELICITAS OCCIDENTIS[201] must refer to an occasion later than Eudoxia's proclamation (9.i.400) but earlier than her death (6.x.404) when the East was "saved," and this can only have been the defeat of Gaïnas. And while coin legends might be dismissed as clichés, not to be pressed too closely, we can hardly sidestep the column of Arcadius.

Despite the loss of the monument itself, a number of detailed drawings give a fairly accurate picture of the base. Its

> three carved sides, in the manner of a panegyric, celebrated the mutual triumph and concord of [Arcadius and Honorius]. . . . On all three sides the emperors were shown standing side by side in order to display their concord, neither one being exalted over the other.[202]

Roma and Constantinopolis stand beneath arches on each side of the second register on the eastern face, flanking representatives from the senates of both cities, bearing crown gold.[203] On the third register Arcadius and Honorius stand in the center, each holding aloft in his right hand the consular *mappa*. Next to Arcadius, as G. Becatti rightly saw,[204] stands his chief minister, the praetorian prefect: Caesarius. Next to Honorius stands a figure in a *chlamys*: Stilicho.

More suggestive still, in the top register two winged victories or angels support a rectangular frame in which are shown two diminutive figures who flank and support a large cross. Apparently these figures are Arcadius and Honorius again.[205] As Robert Grigg has shown, the best commentary comes from the coinage. First, the reverse of a solidus with

200. Fravitta's name does not appear on Roman inscriptions at the beginning of the year, whence it was inferred in *CLRE* (p. 337) either that he was not recognized at once or that there was a delay in proclamation. The latter is more likely. Fravitta must have been designated very late in the year, and it would not be surprising if the news was late reaching Rome.

201. J. Sabatier, *Description générale des monnaies byzantines*, vol. 1 (Paris 1862), s.v. Eudoxia I, pl. IV.25; Demougeot 1951, 264; A. A. Boyce, *Festal and Dated Coins of the Roman Empire: Four Notes*, ANS Num. Notes and Mon. 153 (New York 1965), 86; R. Grigg, *Art Bulletin* 59 (1977): 478. Eastern coins with the legend CONCORDIA AVGVSTORVM (R. A. G. Carson, *Principal Coins of the Romans* [London 1981], no. 1574) might as easily refer to 396 as 402.

202. Grigg 1977, 469.

203. A. Grabar, *L'empereur dans l'art byzantin* (Strasbourg 1936), 229; Becatti 1960, 256.

204. Becatti 1960, 257. But we differ from him in identifying the emperor on the left, flanked by a *chlamydatus*, as Honorius, flanked by Stilicho.

205. Becatti 1960, 258; Grigg 1977, 472.

the legend SALVS REIPVBLICAE minted at Rome (467/72) that shows
Anthemius and Leo facing each other in military attire, holding a tall
cross between them.[206] Anthemius, an Easterner who had just become
emperor of the West, was anxious to stress that despite recent hostility
he could count on the support of his Eastern colleague. We may compare
Sidonius's panegyric of Anthemius, congratulating the East on sharing
in Rome's triumphs: *valeat divisio regni*, "farewell, division of empire!"[207]
Then there is a bronze coin minted at Thessalonica under Theodosius
(II?) bearing the legend CONCORDIA AVGVSTORVM on an almost
identical reverse.[208] Presumably this issue commemorated some occasion
when the East rendered military assistance to the West.[209] The original
motif, of course, was two emperors jointly holding a victorious standard; it was Christianized by the transformation of the standard into a
cross. It is therefore a symbol of peace and concord. Here too we may
compare a striking literary parallel, the following words from a homily
on peace delivered in the autumn of 402 by Eudoxia's ecclesiastical favorite, Severian of Gabala, and intended to symbolize his (short-lived) rec-
onciliation with Chrysostom:

> Just as the best painters often try to illustrate unanimity of spirit by
> placing behind emperors or brothers who are also magistrates[210] a Con-
> cordia in female form who embraces with both arms those she unifies in
> order to show that the divided bodies are one in mind, so the Peace of
> Christ unifies by embracing those who are divided.[211]

Writing as he was in 402, we can hardly doubt that what Severian had in
mind was pictorial representations of the concord of Arcadius and Honorius. The preceding sentence illustrates how his thoughts were preoc-
cupied by imperial imagery at the time:

> Just as in the case of an imperial *adventus* the streets are swept and the
> colonnades decorated with all sorts of beautiful objects so that there
> should be nothing unworthy of the emperor's gaze.

206. J. P. C. Kent, *Roman Coins* (New York 1978), 762; Grigg 1977, 474.
207. *Pan. Anthem.* 66. For more detail, W. E. Kaegi, *Byzantium and the Decline of Rome*
(Princeton 1968), 35f.
208. Sabatier 1862, 1: pl. V.11; Grigg 1977, 474–75.
209. See Grigg 1977, 475, for the various possibilities.
210. Perhaps a reference to paintings of Aurelian and Caesarius: see above, pp.
181–82.
211. The text is only available in the *editio princeps* of Papadopulos-Kerameus,
Ἀνάλεκτα Ἱεροσολυμιτικῆς Σταχυολογίας I, 15–26 (quotation from p. 17; this passage is
also quoted in the original by C. Weyman, *Hermes* 29 [1894]: 626–27). The date is not 401,
as hitherto supposed (Aubineau 1983, 13): see appendix 2.

Compare too the following from another homily of Severian from about the same date:[212]

> I am singing the praises of the pair of brothers and the harmony of the empire (συμφωνίαν . . . τῆς βασιλείας), as Holy Scripture verifies: "Brother being helped by brother is like a strong city and a fortified palace."[213] "These are the two anointed sons who stand near the Lord of the whole world."[214]

It is fascinating to see how aptly Severian can illustrate the theme with biblical quotations; fascinating too to see how similarly it is expressed by both Christian preacher and pagan sophist. With Eunapius's "invincible and adamantine bulwark" we may compare Severian's quotation from Zechariah, "a strong city and a fortified palace." Both also stress the divine origin of this dual earthly kingship and its unity despite division between the brothers. But there is an important difference: whereas the speaker in Eunapius frag. 85, presumably Fravitta, accuses John of trying to undermine the concord, according to Severian it had only just been reestablished: "The truth has shone forth and falsehood runs away; concord has shone forth and discord has fled."[215] When Severian wrote in the autumn of 402 this emphasis on the restoration of concord between East and West was something new; this is why his attention was caught by its pictorial representation. But by the period of which Eunapius was writing, the situation had changed.

The accusation that John was undermining the new imperial concord implies the previous existence of concord. This would make little sense in 401–2, which saw the much vaunted restoration of concord after six years of almost open war. In 403 Stilicho recognized the first consulate of Arcadius's infant son Theodosius. But for the next two years he returned to his earlier policy of not recognizing Eastern consuls, repudiating Aristaenetus (404) and Anthemius (405).[216] In 404–5 Fravitta's accusation would make sense. By now relations were clearly deteriorating.[217]

We are fortunate enough to possess an official letter of protest from

212. The passage goes on to describe the "blessed (μακάριος) emperor shining amidst his sons, for his glory has not died": so, evidently written after the death of Theodosius.

213. Prov. 18.19; the only MS (Sinait. gr. 491; text published by Wenger 1952, 48) omits a few words ("like a strong, tall city, and is mighty like a fortified palace," Septuagint).

214. Zech. 4.14, with Grigg 1977, 479.

215. On the text of this passage, see below, appendix 2.

216. The evidence is all assembled in *CLRE* under these years.

217. It was in 405 that Anthemius became consul and took over the prefecture.

ca. June 404 in which Honorius lists a series of recent *iniuriae* he has suffered at the hand of his brother.[218] It will be noted that this period of concord coincides exactly with Caesarius's tenure of the praetorian prefecture, from mid-400 to late 403.

It would be an oversimplification to see Caesarius and Fravitta as
favoring Stilicho. They did not invite Stilicho to return to the East and
exercise the regency over Arcadius to which he laid claim. Nor is it likely
that Stilicho's half-German blood had been the main source of Aurelian's
hostility. As self-proclaimed regent of both Arcadius and Honorius, if
Stilicho had returned to the East, he would no more have tolerated Caesarius as a rival than Aurelian. The difference between the Western policies of Aurelian and Caesarius was probably more a question of style
than of substance. Aurelian continued Eutropius's unrealistic policy of
confrontation, whereas Caesarius, while no more acceding to Stilicho's
demands than Aurelian or Eutropius, was prepared at any rate to recognize him as Honorius's chief minister.

Support of entente between East and West may have been one
source of the hostility that eventually brought Fravitta down, though all
the passage of Eunapius tells us is that in his own defense Fravitta accused his accusers of subverting the ideal *concordia Augustorum* to which
all paid lip service, implying that such as John were not fit to accuse a
patriot like himself. There is certainly no hint of antibarbarian sentiment. Indeed, Eunapius claims that most even of John's followers agreed
in their hearts with Fravitta. It need not be true, but it would have been
an absurd thing to say if the accusers had, as popularly supposed, been
a baying pack of barbarophobes. Nor is it likely, four years after the
event, that the main basis of the accusation was collusion with Gaïnas.
Fravitta's fall might perhaps be connected rather with the departure of
the moderate Caesarius from the prefecture, Hierax providing timely
ammunition.

The main consequence of this redating of Fravitta's death is that it
can no longer be seen as the logical culmination of a successful process
of de-Germanization of the state, requiring no other explanation. According to Jones (following Seeck and the *communis opinio*) there was "a
revulsion against the employment of Germans in high military commands" after the fall of Gaïnas, though Jones does go on to remark that

218. *Epistulae imperatorum pontificum aliorum, CSEL* 35, ed. Guenther, 85, no. 38: Eudoxia's proclamation as Augusta; concealment of Alaric's devastation of Illyricum in 403–4
(in case Stilicho intervened in eastern territory again, as in 395 and 396); the treatment of
Chrysostom. Honorius protests: "haec ego quamvis crebris iniuriis lacessitus tacere de-
buerim nec coniunctissimum fratrem . . . tam fideliter admonere."

"our information is admittedly very incomplete" and adds that "by the 420s the feeling against German *magistri militum* had evidently waned."[219] When it is pointed out that in the period between 400 and Arcadius's death in 408 we know the name of only one *magister militum* besides Fravitta, and that an Armenian, Arbazacius, the weakness of the argument from silence stands out more clearly still.

The year after Arcadius's death we find as *magister militum* a man whose name suggests that he was of Persian origin: Varanes, cos. 410. The next Gothic general of note is Plinta, significantly enough an Arian, first attested as *magister militum* in his consular year 419. But to have won so high an honor (the first Gothic consul since Fravitta), his career must have begun under Arcadius. Then there is Ardabur (cos. 427), not attested as *magister militum* before 424, but whose son Aspar (cos. 434) may have held the same rank in the same year, and in any case by 431. Clearly Ardabur too must have been winning his spurs as early as the reign of Arcadius.

If Fravitta's disgrace and death fell as late as 405, the traditional picture of barbarians being feverishly replaced by native stock in the immediate aftermath of Gaïnas's rebellion has to be abandoned. The only two *magistri militum* on record between Gaïnas's fall and Arcadius's death were non-Romans. The ranking general during most of this period was Fravitta, a former consul who had saved the state.

It is also instructive to find a cultivated Greek intellectual like Eunapius, who shared Synesius's enthusiasm for Neoplatonism, taking Fravitta's part so warmly. The main reason is no doubt their shared paganism. Yet Eunapius's admiration was surely based on something more than the bare fact that Fravitta was not a Christian. According to Zosimus (here closely following Eunapius), Fravitta "was a Hellene, not just by habit (τρόπῳ), but also in his way of life (προαιρέσει) and religious observance (θρησκείᾳ)" (5.20.1). Some twenty years earlier, when he first entered Roman service, he had married a "Roman" wife (Eunap. frag. 60M = 59B), which, since he served in the East, presumably means a Greek wife. The same fragment of Eunapius gives a fascinating glimpse of a party thrown by Theodosius himself in celebration of the wedding. The Goths, says Eunapius, were divided into two factions, those who were determined to abide by the oath they had sworn a few years before to destroy Rome, and those who rejoiced in their present good fortune. One of the extremists, a fanatic called Eriulph, reproached Fravitta publicly for forsaking his oath. Fravitta did not want to be reminded; he

219. Jones 1964a, 1:181.

drew his sword and ran his comrade through on the spot. Here was a man who had made an irrevocable choice. Fl. Fravitta,[220] as he was henceforth to be known, learned Greek and by 400 could no doubt boast an acceptable veneer of Greek culture. His paganism was probably less of a handicap in society than the Arianism of Gaïnas and most other Goths in Roman service. Pagans were lost souls ripe for conversion, whereas heretics were damned forever. Fravitta was not an uncouth soldier out of his element in the drawing rooms of Constantinople. His children were doubtless as Hellenized, and perhaps as Christian, as Eudoxia, daughter of the Frankish general Bauto, selected to be the wife and mother of Roman emperors. While we need not believe that Fravitta actually spoke the flowery words Eunapius puts in his mouth in frag. 85, the picture of Fravitta holding his own in the cut and thrust of Byzantine politics may not be so far from the mark. This was why he made enemies, not just because he was a Goth.

Nothing certain is known of his posterity, but it is difficult to doubt that he was related to Fravitta, presbyter of the church of St. Thecla, mentioned in the Acta of the Council of Chalcedon in 450,[221] and later briefly patriarch of Constantinople in 489.[222] Since presbyters had to be at least thirty, he must have been very old by the time he became patriarch, an honor he was to enjoy for only three months and seventeen days. Patriarch Fravitta may actually have been the son (or at any rate grandson) of the conqueror of Gaïnas.[223]

220. On the use of the praenomen, see *CLRE*, pp. 36–40; Cameron 1988b, 26–33.
221. *ACO* II.5.132.4.
222. Nicephorus *Opusc. hist.*, p. 116.26 de Boor (specifying that he had formerly been presbyter of St. Thecla).
223. Fravitta is described as a young man in the early 380s (Eunap. frag. 60M = 59B), and so at least forty by 400. Any children he had must have been born by ca. 405.

SEVEN

LITERARY SOURCES OF *DE PROVIDENTIA*

I. INTRODUCTION

Thus far we have been mainly concerned with the historical facts behind *De providentia*. This is an attitude that would have astonished Synesius. He would have been distressed to know that posterity treated his masterpiece as a quarry for facts. Facts he took for granted—assuming them all too well known to his audience. His main personal contribution was the literary form into which he cast his idiosyncratic mixture of facts, half-truths, and outright lies; the philosophical basis he tried to ground it in; and the wide variety of sources he neatly adapted. It is understandable that modern historians, starved for a narrative account of Arcadian politics, should have tried so hard to extract what nuggets they could from Synesius's tale. His fiction was an irritation, to be stripped away and discarded. But such strip-mining loses too much in the process. Synesius wanted to philosophize, to edify, above all to interpret the events of his day. Let us pay him the compliment of devoting a little space to what *he* thought made his book worth reading.

Rhetorical textbooks offer little guidance to Synesius's work, although they provide keys to much other secular literature of his age. *De providentia* is too original a work. We shall have to cast our net wider and examine the large body of literature on which Synesius drew at first hand.[1] He drew variously on this living tradition, creating a new fusion of diverse elements that suited his ends. The moral and historical allegories of political oratory are the closest parallels to the overall form of his fiction and will have suggested both techniques and specific conceits; his praise of Osiris and denigration of Typhos have obvious affinities with panegyric and invective; his philosophizing draws on Neoplatonic traditions; but it is the Egyptian myth, and above all its apocalyptic dimension, that makes *De providentia* unique.

II. EGYPTIAN SOURCES

Greek ambivalence about Egypt stretches back to the classical period.[2] The manifest antiquity of the country and its monuments inspired general reverence and willingness to regard its priests as repositories of the wise traditions of an ideal civilization. Popular belief fathered Egyptian travels and education on the earliest and the most important bards and sages: Diodorus's list, for example, begins with Orpheus, Musaeus, Melampus, and Daedalus, runs through Homer and Lycurgus, and on to Solon, Plato, Pythagoras, Eudoxus, Democritus, and Oenopides.[3] Plato validated his story of Atlantis by claiming that Solon heard it in Egypt (*Tim.* 21C–23D). Solon finds that the Egyptians know more than the Greeks about ancient Greece; a priest explains that the Nile spares Egypt from the fires and floods that periodically destroy the rest of the world, so that while Greek memory extends childlike only to the most recent destruction, the Egyptians know the whole continuum. Herodotus praised the Egyptians as "cultivating the memory of all men, by far the best versed in stories of any men I have encountered" (2.77.1). They corroborated them against the Ionian geographers (2.10–18). Legends of the Greek sages' debt to Egypt were still current in late antiquity (e.g., Amm. Marc. 22.19–22).

At the same time, the zoomorphic gods of Egypt and their cults impressed the Greeks and Romans as the most ignorant superstition. Ac-

---

1. General cautions of this nature are formulated by Russell and Wilson 1981, xxxi–xxxiv, and E. R. Curtius, *European Literature and the Latin Middle Ages*, trans. W. Trask, Bollingen Series 36 (New York 1953), 444.

2. This section is in part adapted from Long 1987.

3. Diod. 1.96.2, with more details, 1.96–98. Other references may be found, for example, at Hdt. 1.30, 2.177; Pl. *Pol.* 290D–E; *Leg.* 747A; Arist. *Pol.* 1329c40ff.; Plut. *De Is. et Os.* 345D–E, 364C–D; on the tradition in general cf. W. K. C. Guthrie, *Orpheus and Greek Religion* (London 1935), 46.

cording to Plutarch, Xenophanes criticized the Egyptians for treating their crops as gods;[4] Plutarch himself condemned them for worshipping animals.[5] Herodotus ambivalently termed them "the most excessively (περισσῶς) pious of all men" (2.37).

Egyptian superstition became a cliché of the Greco-Roman world.[6] In later antiquity Sallustius still condemned Egyptian materialism in interpreting myth.[7] Porphyry criticized theurgy, a derivative in part of Egyptian magic, in the *Letter to Anebo*, to which Iamblichus replied in the persona of another Egyptian savant, Abammon, in *De mysteriis Aegyptiorum*. Typically, Porphyry objected that Egyptian traditions reduced everything to physical causes.[8] Iamblichus devotes his attention more to developed philosophical theurgy than to its Egyptian antecedents; what he does discuss, like Plutarch in *De Iside et Osiride*, he sanitizes by insisting on symbolic interpretation.[9]

Thus despite the superior antiquity of Egyptian lore in Greek eyes, its religion had to be redeemed by interpretation. In his opening words Synesius sounds a note of paradox: "The story is Egyptian. Egyptians are extraordinarily wise (ὁ μῦθος Αἰγύπτιος· περιττοὶ σοφίαν οἱ Αἰγύπτιοι). So perhaps this story, even though it is only a story, might hint at something more than a story because it is Egyptian" (89A). He goes out of his way to claim an ambiguous authority (περιττός wavers between its favorable and negative senses, playing on Synesius's enigmatic form and demanding interpretation to resolve the conflict).[10] Synesius undermines the ambiguity when he hints that the story may prove to be a "sacred discourse" (89B). By the end of book 2 he abandons the pose: then the

---

4. *De Is. et Os.* 379B, *De superst.* 171D–E, *Amat.* 763C–D.

5. *De Is. et Os.* 379D–E. He discusses various aspects of the phenomenon at great length in the following chapters to 382C; see the commentary of Griffiths (1970), particularly on the Egyptian revival of animal worship from about 700 B.C. for which he supplies references (554 n. 3).

6. E.g., Cic. *Tusc.* 5.27.78, *Rep.* 3.14, *Nat. d.* 1.36.101; Tac. *Hist.* 1.11; Juv. 15.1–13; in comparison Strabo is remarkably matter-of-fact about Egyptian animal worship, but even he finds it remarkable that their temples contain "no statue, or rather not one of a human shape, but of one of the unreasoning animals" (17.1.28). Isocrates in *Busiris* 24–27 goes as far as he can to find Egyptian piety praiseworthy: he notes that the animal-gods are not really divine, but their worship trains the Egyptians in obedience. A more detailed survey of the contradictory Greek and Roman attitudes to Egyptian civilization and religion may be found in J. Geffcken, *Zwei griechische Apologeten* (Leipzig and Berlin 1907), ix–xi; for a very full collection of hostile passages, see J. E. B. Mayor's commentary on Juvenal 15 (*Thirteen Satires of Juvenal*, vol. 2, 3d ed. [London and Cambridge 1881], 355–400).

7. *De diis* 4, p. 6.2–10 Nock.

8. E.g., apud Iambl. *Myst.* 268.5–6.

9. For example, at *Myst.* 250.7–12, introducing his discussions of mud, lotus, barque, and zodiac.

10. See LSJ, s.v.

story is something that men "will pore over with a craving to know what will be" (128B). But at the beginning, its Egyptianness implicitly challenges readers to unravel the mystical tease.

An additional, fundamental appeal of Egypt was as a pleasantly exotic setting. It was frequently a venue of the Hellenistic and later Greek romances, which capitalized on and perpetuated its image as a home to all sorts of fantastic adventure.[11] Synesius thus appealed to a broad and varied tradition.

The story of Typhos's murder of Osiris and dispersal of his limbs, Isis's quest for the body of her husband, and her and Horus's overthrow of Typhos was the central myth of the Isiac religion popular throughout the Hellenistic and Roman world and still well known in Christian times.[12] Synesius could expect the names alone to identify his mythic background.

In Greco-Roman antiquity, the myth was narrated most fully in Plutarch's essay *De Iside et Osiride*.[13] Plutarch was Synesius's primary source. He begins with an aetiology of the five epagomenal days of the Egyptian calendar, on which Rhea (Nut) gives birth successively to Osiris, Aroueris "the elder Horus," Typhos,[14] Isis, and Nephthys. At Osiris's birth, a prophetic voice proclaims: "The lord of all has come into the light!" At once, Osiris is king. He first civilizes the Egyptians, introducing agriculture, laws, and religion; later, he travels throughout the world bestowing the same benefits. While he is away, Isis rules Egypt. Her vigilance forestalls Typhos, but on Osiris's return Typhos forms a

---

11. The fanciful element is all the stronger if, as Tomas Hägg argues (1983, 96–101), the claim of Egyptian ancestry for the Greek romance is weak; against B. P. Reardon ("The Greek Novel," *Phoenix* 23 [1969]: 291–309). Heliodorus, pausing to explain the festival for the Nile inundation that figures in his narrative, notes, like Plutarch, that the Egyptians identified Isis with the earth and Osiris with the Nile, and echoes Herodotus in his refusal to reveal the substance concealed in their mysteries and fables: (*Ethiop.* 9.9.6–10.2; Plut. *De Is. et Os.* 363D). Griffiths (1970) cites ad loc. also Lydus *Mens.* 4.45; Porph. apud Euseb. *Praep. evang.* 3.11.51; Euseb. *Praep. evang.* 3.3.11; Hdt. 2.171.1 (as A. B. Lloyd 1987 notes ad loc., the importation of mystery into the Egyptian rites was the product of Greek syncretism of Isis with Demeter; thus Heliodorus's reference places him within the Greek rather than the authentic Egyptian tradition).

12. For references and discussions relating particularly to the Christian period, see F. Solmsen, *Isis among the Greeks and Romans* (Cambridge, Mass. 1979); A. Alföldi, *A Festival of Isis in Rome under the Christian Emperors of the IVth Century* (Budapest 1937); F. Zimmermann, *Die ägyptische Religion nach der Darstellung der Kirchenschriftseller und die ägyptischen Denkmäler* (Paderborn 1912).

13. Particularly 355D–358E, though some other details may be gleaned from the rest of the discussion. See in general J. Gwyn Griffiths's excellent edition and commentary (1970).

14. Typhon in Plutarch's text, but for clarity we use Synesius's form of the name throughout.

conspiracy with seventy-two men and the Ethiopian queen Aso. He secretly measures Osiris's body and prepares a beautiful chest to fit exactly. He tricks Osiris into getting into it; at once the conspirators nail it shut and throw it into the Nile. It washes out to sea through the Tanitic mouth. Hearing from Pans and Satyrs of Typhos's actions, Isis sets forth after the chest. Her quest contains the major aetiologies of the Isiac religion and occupies the greater part of Plutarch's narrative with its vicissitudes. When Isis finally finds Osiris's body, Typhos tears it apart and scatters it. Isis seeks out the pieces again and establishes the worship of Osiris throughout Egypt. Osiris then comes from the Underworld to help train Horus for his combat with Typhos. He asks Horus what animal he considers most helpful in battle, and is surprised when Horus chooses the horse rather than the lion. Horus explains that the lion will help one who is in need of aid, but that with a horse one can rout one's enemy and destroy him utterly. Osiris approves. Meanwhile, Typhos's side suffers many defections, including that of his concubine Thoueris. After a battle of many days, Horus defeats Typhos and binds him; Isis releases him, enraging Horus. Next Typhos charges Horus with bastardy, but Hermes (Thoth) defends him, and the gods judge him legitimate. Typhos is finally defeated in two further battles. At the end, Isis gives birth to Harpocrates, whom Osiris fathered posthumously.[15]

In outline at least, this will have been the myth with which Synesius's audience was familiar. He takes over the basic plot, though modifying it to suit his own purposes. Gradually it becomes apparent that Synesius has reversed the order of the brothers' births (90A, C). The change is not wholly gratuitous: in a travesty of philosophical argumentation Typhos's wife justifies his usurpation to the barbarian general's wife because he is the elder (110A).[16] But otherwise Synesius seems to derive no advantage from his change; and the explanation may simply be that Caesarius was older, as might be inferred in any case from the dates of his and Aurelian's careers.

Where in Plutarch an oracular voice proclaimed Osiris's kingship at his birth (*De Is. et Os.* 555E), Synesius elevates him from his probation in junior offices through the civic mechanism of the election. But he retains the divine voice too. The election's basic structure presupposes indirect divine influence, through the predominance accorded the priests and the outgoing king; it accommodates direct participation by the gods in the event of a tie at the human level (94C–95B). But now the gods put off their customary restraint. Even though the human vote would have

15. Harpocrates' lameness indicates that Osiris does not return to the full potency he enjoyed in life.

16. Cf. Pl. *Tim.* 34C.

been unanimous for Osiris in any case, the gods join in, visibly, from the very first, marking their special favor. And when the victorious Osiris is greeted by a joyous procession of all the participants, "immediately, great signs from heaven and auspicious divine voices and every minor and major omen by which the future is traced proclaimed the good tidings of the new reign to the Egyptians" (96A). Synesius amplifies by adding other omens, but the Plutarchean detail still plays its part.

For the primordial civilization provided by Plutarch's Osiris Synesius substitutes general benefaction, philosophically emphasizing encouragement of virtue and, characteristically, rhetorical education in particular (103C). Isis, for whom no contemporary counterpart could be found, has no role in *De providentia:* her interregnum, as well as her quest, is eliminated, and Synesius moves directly into Typhos's plot. Its mechanisms are based on contemporary events and invective motifs rather than on Plutarch's narrative, but the fact that he too assigns a crucial role to a woman helps integrate Synesius's departures into the fabric of the myth.

Synesius's and Plutarch's versions of Typhos's plot move in parallel steps. Synesius's Osiris surrenders to his brother voluntarily (111A), just as Plutarch's voluntarily gets into the chest (*De Is. et Os.* 356C). Each is at once confined, the one by a guard and the other in the chest. Synesius's Typhos demands Osiris's death, where Plutarch's evidently achieves it; then Synesius's Osiris is exiled from the country (111B) and Plutarch's is carried in the chest down the Nile and out the Tanitic mouth to Byblos (*De Is. et Os.* 356C, 357A). Synesius's Osiris too crosses water, to face the barbarian assembly that will determine his fate (111A).[17]

At the end of book I Synesius looks forward to the end of the myth, when Typhos is defeated by Osiris's son Horus and Osiris is posthumously vindicated. Such an ending has important implications for Synesius's contemporary polemic, which we will discuss later. Here it is enough to note that Synesius's closing words are intelligible only in light of the myth. Horus had previously figured in Synesius's narrative only in the service of a moral contrast between Osiris's wife and Typhos's (105D). Synesius never says explicitly that Horus will contend with Typhos, let alone win back his father's kingdom. These hopes can only be inferred by an audience that already knows the mythic action. Having seen some confirmation of the predictions he has received from the god, the rustic philosopher "waited, now understanding what was to happen about Osiris in the near future, as well as in the years yet to come, when Osiris's son Horus would decide to select the wolf, rather than the lion,

17. Gaïnas was in fact in Chalcedon, across the Hellespont from Constantinople, when he demanded Aurelian's exile: Socr. *HE* 6.6; Soz. *HE* 8.4.5; Zos. 5.18.

for his ally. The identity of the wolf is a sacred tale that it would be irrelevant to expound, even in the form of a myth" (115B). As in Plutarch, Horus faces a choice of animals as his ally, but here a choice between a lion and a wolf instead of the horse that was an important element in the genuine Egyptian Horus's iconography.[18] Synesius underlines this puzzling discrepancy with his emphatic mysteriousness here, and again in the introduction to his later republication of both parts of *De providentia*, where he identifies their division as coming at "the riddle of the wolf" (88A). Obviously it was a device with which he was particularly pleased. The solution to the riddle is to be found in the parallel narrative of the myth preserved for us by Diodorus: "They say that when Isis along with her son Horus was about to contend with Typhos, Osiris came from Hades to aid his child and wife, likened in appearance to a wolf" (1.88.6). The wolf represents a variant tradition of the myth, which Synesius has conflated with his major source to produce a purely literary puzzle.[19]

Synesius's original conception allowed Osiris to return to the scene as no more than a shadowy "wolf" assisting a new successor, Horus. No such successor had appeared when Aurelian unexpectedly returned from exile and into the focus of Synesius's hopes for restored tax benefits. Synesius was forced to depart from the myth radically if his story was not to "be left incomplete with the story of misfortunes" (88B). He brought Osiris back. But since Aurelian was not restored to office, the violation of the myth left him very little to say. And indeed the second half of book 2 trails off lamely into vague moralizing meditations and invocations of mystery. Synesius does give a vivid picture of the riot that precipitated the massacre and rout of the Goths, which naturally owes nothing to the myth. And in attempting as far as possible to suggest that Typhos suffered some defeat, he returns to the myth with Typhos's trial and acquittal. Since Synesius had a returned Osiris to deal with, and no Horus, the myth's question of legitimate succession to Osiris could not be made to apply. But Synesius does preserve the motif of defections of former close allies from the losing side, a verdict of the gods against Typhos, and his subsequent release by the mercy of the good party against justice.[20] Typhos's ultimate defeat and deposition (*De Is. et Os.* 358D) could be left for the vaguer anticipation of "the remaining days, the wisest witnesses" (*De providentia* 129A). Thus even in the necessarily

18. See Griffiths 1970, 345–47, and references there.

19. This position is argued at length by Long (1987), against traditional attempts to invest the wolf with historical significance and make the riddle into a practical political suggestion. Such attempts have always failed to satisfy, precisely because Synesius's political milieu did not admit of any such solution. See also below, chapter 8, section II.

20. Plut. *De Is. et Os.* 358D; defections: *De providentia* 122D–123A, gods' judgment: 123B, merciful release: 124A (by Osiris rather than by Isis); see discussion above, pp. 194–95.

more loosely integrated book 2, the myth supplied Synesius with his basic structures.

Egyptian material also informs the narrative in smaller details. For example, the father of Typhos and Osiris "was king and priest and sage. Egyptian tales say that he was also a god. For the Egyptians believe that thousands of gods were their kings one after another, before the land was ruled by men and the kings' descent was traced, Peiromis from Peiromis" (93D). This passage exactly reproduces the substance of Herodotus 2.144, reporting the priestly tradition that before human kings and high priests the gods had ruled Egypt. One of them was always supreme, and the last was Horus, the son of Osiris, who reigned after deposing Typhos. This much relates directly to Synesius's story. Just to mark his source, he adds from Herodotus's immediately preceding discussion of the high priests their descent "Peiromis from Peiromis."[21]

The *baris* (βᾶρις) in which Osiris crosses the Nile as the successful candidate in the royal election may be a similar pointer to another source, Hecataeus of Abdera. Since Hecataeus's *Aegyptiaca* is known principally through the first book of Diodorus's *Bibliotheke*,[22] the argument is necessarily indirect. The two sets of Egyptian funeral practices described by Diodorus at 1.72.4–6 and 1.92 share with Synesius's election their general structure as a ceremonial judgment on individuals by a specific segment of the society on behalf of the whole.[23] The detail that the commoners, who watch the proceedings without a vote, merely shout their approval (*De providentia* 94B–95A) seems a stronger, specific link. Diodorus's general rite (1.92) adds the further detail that once a favorable verdict has been reached, the coffin (*larnax*) is brought across a body of water in a *baris*.[24] The tribunal of the royal funeral is set merely "before the entrance to the tomb" (Diod. 1.72.4), without water being specified, but the two procedures are otherwise very similar. It looks as if the doublet reflects some confusion of Diodorus's sources.[25] *Baris* is, as

21. Herodotus's gloss "'Piromis' means in Greek *kalos k'agathos*" (2.143) had given the term particular prominence.

22. *FGrH* IIIa.264, with Murray 1970, 141–71.

23. The religious theme of posthumous judgment also influences Synesius's conception of the trial of Typhos; cf. above.

24. In Plutarch Osiris is washed down the Nile, also in a *larnax* that crosses water. It is not surprising that funerary usage should recollect Osirian myth; throughout the extensive material Griffiths has assembled (see his bibliography), both Egyptian and Greco-Roman, they are closely connected.

25. The possible implications of the doublet are unfortunately not addressed by A. Burton, *Diodorus Siculus Book I*, EPRO 39 (Leiden 1972), though she rejects the traditional view that Diodorus simply abbreviated Hecataeus.

Herodotus explains, simply the Egyptian name for a type of cargo boat,[26] with both religious and mundane uses (e.g., Hdt. 2.41.4–6; 2.179). Greek authors adopted the term, sometimes with and sometimes apparently without ethnological force.[27] But the one other boat Synesius mentions in the *De providentia*, that in which the betrayed Osiris "crosses the river" to face the barbarian assembly (111A), he designates a *holkas* rather than a *baris*. The details cluster suggestively, but they do not fall neatly into place with Diodorus as they do with Herodotus. Nowhere in his works does Synesius show similarly close verbal ties.[28] He does, however, seem to distinguish the *baris* here. The simplest hypothesis is that Hecataeus is their common source, and it is Diodorus who has blurred some more overt echo by which Synesius would have identified it.[29]

Synesius certainly advertised his use of Plutarch. In *De Iside et Osiride*, for example, Osiris's first acts as king give the benefits of civilization to the formerly wild Egyptians: "Later he traversed and civilized all the world, with very little need of arms; he attached the majority to himself by charming them with persuasion and reason, along with all song and poetry" (356A–B). In Synesius's rendering, Osiris "immediately strove to banish evils from the land, without making any use of force. Instead, he sacrificed to Persuasion and the Muses and the Graces and brought all men willingly into accord with the law" (*De providentia* 102D). "Sacrifice to the Graces" as an image for eloquence was a long-standing commonplace of the Platonic tradition;[30] similarly, Dio Chrysostom invokes "Persuasion and the Muses and Apollo" in a proemium (*Or.* 1.10). But the shared motif of persuasion by art instead of force, appearing at the same point in the plot, unmistakably points to Plutarch. At the corresponding stage of Diodorus's briefer narrative, Osiris is again a universal civilizer but in contrast collects "a great army" before setting forth.[31]

---

26. Hdt. 2.96, where he describes its construction and handling. A. B. Lloyd's commentary, *Herodotus Book II*, 3 vols., EPRO 43 (Leiden 1975–87), ad loc. offers extensive Egyptological and nautical detail, with further references. Cf. also Griffiths 1970, 339–40, ad *De Is. et Os.* 358A, which says that Isis used a *baris* made of papyrus to sail through the marshes looking for the pieces of Osiris's body.

27. E.g., Aesch. *Supp.* 836, 873; *Pers.* 553 (apparently the earliest: Lloyd ad Hdt. 2.60); cf. the references in LSJ, s.v.

28. Crawford (1901, 528) could find only two echoes of Diodorus, neither in *De providentia*, neither from the Egyptian book, and both questionable in any case; A. Hauck, *Welche griechischen Autoren der klassichen Zeit kennt und benützt Synesius von Cyrene?* (Mecklenburg 1911) did not include Diodorus.

29. Alternatively, of course, Synesius could have taken his Hecataean details from a different compilation now lost.

30. E.g. Eunap. *VS* 458.3; D.L. 4.6; Plut. *Con. praec.* 141F.

31. Murray (1970) follows Jacoby in considering Diodorus to have taken 1.17.1–20.6 from a source other than Hecataeus. These details would not be unsuitable for Hecataeus,

These reminiscences were for Synesius not merely ornamental. They were also meant to be conspicuous tokens identifying his sources and authenticating his work as a whole. It is a familiar technique of the novelist to mix fact with fiction in such a way that the authentic details will lend conviction to the balance of the tale. The fact that Synesius draws authentic information from sources besides Plutarch gives him license to "correct" Plutarch in other details as well. Alert readers were meant to recognize the technical elegance with which he reformulated his information.[32] "Peiromis from Peiromis" stands intact, a bright jewel from a foreign setting; but no less conspicuous is the refinement of Plutarch's naturalistic narrative in Osiris's sacrifice "to Persuasion and the Muses and the Graces."

Other Egyptian material is woven in more subtly, as for example in the royal election. The culturally authentic detail from which Synesius builds this fantastic legitimation of his Osiris's rule gives it a surprisingly plausible appearance.[33] The arrangement of voters embodies an outline of the Egyptian social hierarchy given by Herodotus and Diodorus:[34] the first citizens were the priests, just below them the warriors, and then other people. The hill on which they are ranked matches the social divisions perfectly (94C). Egypt does in fact possess many stepped contours of this type, produced naturally by erosion.[35] One hill perfectly fitting Synesius's description, right down to the "nipple" at its summit, is located near Thebes, above the Valley of the Kings.[36] Anyone who had traveled in Egypt might well be reminded of such a remarkable feature. The social hierarchy is implicit again in Plutarch's remark that the kings of Egypt were created from among the priests or the warriors and that a warrior so appointed straightaway became a priest as well.[37] It may have been this remark that inspired Synesius to make the brothers' father a

---

however, since they assimilate the god to the model of Alexander. Synesius's restriction of Osiris's activity to "Egypt" is not a significant departure.

32. It is, of course, another question how many of Synesius's original readers fully appreciated the work in its own terms. Hardly bureaucrats like Aurelian himself, but perhaps such as Anastasius, Marcian, Nicander, Pylaemenes, Theotimus, and Troïlus, Synesius's literary friends briefly evoked in chapter 2, section I.

33. Its details might be recognized as dramatic coloring, but somehow under their cloak the central claim has crept into belief unchallenged: e.g., citing Synesius simply, Bury (1923) 1958, 132: "[Gaïnas] failed to secure the appointment of Typhos. The post was given to Aurelian, and this was a triumph for the anti-German party."

34. Hdt. 2.164–68; Diod. 1.73–74.

35. F. El-Baz, *Smithsonian* 12.1 (April 1981): 116–22, particularly photographs on pp. 118 and 120.

36. See, for example, the photograph on pp. 8–9 of I. E. S. Edwards, *Tutankhamun: His Tomb and Its Treasures* (New York 1976).

37. *De Is. et Os.* 354B, based in turn on Pl. *Plt.* 290E; see Griffiths 1965, 156–57.

priest as well as king and sage (93D); it also gave an Egyptian basis for Osiris's initiation into kingship. Synesius takes care to ascribe military skill to Osiris in his youth, but even so he required a further stage in his spiritual education.[38]

At other points, Synesius legitimates his tale by inventing aetiologies for authentic Egyptiana. The taboo days of the Egyptians were generally familiar: Xenocrates wrote about them, Plutarch notes that the birthday of Typhos was among them, and Augustine refers to them simply as *dies Aegyptiaci*.[39] The Egyptians' mournful rituals were also common knowledge.[40] Synesius connects the two usages with the "exile of Osiris" of his own story and names it picturesquely "the Taboo Days of Holy Tears" (111A). It makes a plausible festival not expressly attested in authentic tradition. The images that "those to whom it is permitted" see moving on these days may owe some of their obscurity to a textual corruption;[41] but they suggest the Egyptian processions of cult statues or the oracles that the statues might give by moving.[42] But these were all public events, to which the suggestion of a restricted audience is alien. This further development derives from Neoplatonic theurgy, with the practice of divination by dedicating and animating statues of the gods.[43] Naturally the specifics were known only to initiates.[44] These rites were believed to have their roots in Egyptian magic,[45] but in Synesius's elevated context a suggestion of philosophy claims priority. Synesius's con-

---

38. Military skill: 91D–92A; Synesius drops the military element (also tied to panegyric, through a common background of kingship theory) in his later characterization of Osiris, as befitted Aurelian's civilian career.

39. Xenocrates is referred to by Plutarch in *De Is. et Os.* 361B, Typhos in 356A; August. *Expos. Gal.* 35 = *PL* 35.2130; cf. *CIL* I.374, 411–12; Marin. *V.Procl.* 19, p. 16 Boissonade; schol. in Luc. *Tim.* 43, p. 117.14 Rabe; see further A. Bouché-Leclercq, *L'astrologie grecque* (Paris 1899), 485–86; H. Webster, *The Rest Days* (1916), 295–97; L. Thorndike, *A History of Magic and Experimental Science*, vol. 1 (New York 1923; reprint, 1943), 685–89 (principally on their continued attestation in medieval texts, but with general discussion too); F. Boll, C. Bezold, and W. Gundel, *Sternglaube und Sterndeutung*, 4th ed. (Leipzig 1931), 184, 186–87.

40. E.g., Hdt. 2.85, 171; Diod. 1.83.5; Plut. *De Is. et Os.* 366E; Firm.Mat. *Err.prof.rel.* 8.3; Orph. *Argon.* 32; August. *De civ.d.* 6.10; Arn. *Adv.nat.* 1.36.

41. See Cameron, Long, Sherry 1988, 59–60.

42. Processions of cult statues: e.g., Hdt. 2.63; Apul. *Met.* 11. On the oracles the statues might give: Luc. *Syr.d.* 36; for further background see *A Saite Oracle Papyrus from Thebes*, ed. R. A. Parker (Providence 1962), particularly chap. 6 (by J. Cerny).

43. Attested principally by Proclus, e.g., *In Tim.* 1.51.25, 3.6.12, 3.155.18 (Festugière compares the Hermetic *Asclepius* 24, p. 326.9ff. Nock-Festugière), presumably drawing in some degree on the *Telestica* and *Chaldaean Oracles* of Julianus; certainly the practice was known earlier, for example, to the emperor Julian's mentor Maximus of Ephesus, whom Eunapius credits with making a statue of Hecate laugh and the torches in her hands light spontaneously (*VS* 475). See E. R. Dodds, *The Greeks and the Irrational* (Berkeley 1951), app. 2.

44. As Proclus remarks, *In Tim.* 1.273.11.

45. Euseb. *Praep.evang.* 10.4.4—hardly an unprejudiced witness.

nection of mystery with the "sufferings of Osiris" may also recall Herodotus 2.174. Herodotus identifies the enactment of these "sufferings"
with the "mysteries" of the Egyptians, but since they are mysteries, he
refuses to discuss them further. If slight at a verbal level, the echo is certainly apposite. The "Days of Holy Tears" are an even subtler web of
allusions than the royal election.

Synesius reuses from *De regno* his interpretation of the Egyptian biform figures of Hermes and Sphinx as icons of the ruler's proper combination of power and mind;[46] again, and fully within the repertory of
Greek philosophical devices, common images are invested with a convenient significance.

More casually deployed but more immediately tendentious allusions include the "holy animal" like whom Osiris feels a philosopher
ought to be free from mundane duties in order to dedicate himself to
god (104A–B). Greek authors were virtually obsessed with Egyptian animal worship;[47] Synesius takes the philosophically proper position that
the animals are "holy" for the sake of the god.[48] The obvious implication
of this expression of piety is confirmed when Synesius describes Osiris's
benefactions to the "rustic philosopher," his own self-portrait, in terms
of release from public service ($\mu\grave{\eta}\ \lambda\epsilon\iota\tau\upsilon\rho\gamma\epsilon\hat{\iota}\nu$, 113B). The honor Osiris
pays learned men generally (103B–C) makes the same suggestion more
positively. Similarly, Hecataeus's Osiris honors Hermes, the inventor of
language and expression (Diod. 1.15.9–16.2), out of similarly self-inter-
ested motives: Hecataeus too wanted favor from his patron, Ptolemy.[49]

There are two groups Synesius carefully excludes from even watching the royal election, swineherds and foreign mercenaries (94A). He
claims that both made up Typhos's party, but only the foreigners actually figure in the narrative. Swineherds nowhere reappear. It is simply
the fact of their exclusion that is grounded in tradition. According to
Herodotus, so unclean do the Egyptians consider the pig that swineherds, even native Egyptians, are alone barred from entering temples.[50]

46. *De providentia* 101B–C, nearly identical with *De regno* 7B–C.

47. E.g., Hdt. 2.65–76; Isoc. *Bus.* 26; Diod. 1.21.10, 1.83–90; Strabo 17.1.27; Plut. *De Is. et Os.* 379D–382C (for a thorough treatment, see T. Hopfner, *Der Tierkult der alten Ägypter*, Denkschriften Wien 57.2 [1913]). Herodotus uses the term $\dot{\iota}\rho\grave{\alpha}\ \zeta\hat{\omega}\alpha$, but a specific allusion need not be inferred.

48. Cf. Plut. *De Is. et Os.* 382A; Sallust. *De diis* 4, p. 6.6–8 Nock, with p. xlviii.

49. For Synesius's use of this theme, see above, chapter 3, section II; for Hecataeus, Murray 1970, 161–62.

50. $\dot{\upsilon}\dot{\iota}\ \sigma\upsilon\beta\hat{\omega}\tau\alpha\iota\ \dot{\epsilon}\acute{o}\nu\tau\epsilon\varsigma\ A\dot{\iota}\gamma\acute{\upsilon}\pi\tau\iota\upsilon\iota\ \dot{\epsilon}\gamma\gamma\epsilon\nu\acute{\epsilon}\epsilon\varsigma\ \dot{\epsilon}\varsigma\ \dot{\iota}\rho\grave{o}\nu\ \upsilon\dot{\upsilon}\delta\grave{\epsilon}\nu\ \tau\hat{\omega}\nu\ \dot{\epsilon}\nu\ A\dot{\iota}\gamma\acute{\upsilon}\pi\tau\psi\ \dot{\epsilon}\sigma\acute{\epsilon}\rho\chi\upsilon\nu\tau\alpha\iota\ \mu\upsilon\hat{\upsilon}\nu\upsilon\iota\ \pi\acute{\alpha}\nu\tau\omega\nu$, Hdt. 2.47.1; they also cannot intermarry with other ranks of Egyptians (2.47.2), an element Synesius perhaps picks up in extending his exclusion of foreigners also to men of foreign extraction ($\alpha\dot{\upsilon}\tau\grave{o}\varsigma\ \mathring{\eta}\ \gamma\acute{\epsilon}\nu\upsilon\varsigma\ \dot{\alpha}\lambda\lambda\acute{o}\phi\upsilon\lambda\upsilon\varsigma$).

Synesius's source is clear; and no less clear the fact that he introduces the swineherds solely to contaminate the foreigners. Thus he transfers another age's prejudice to his own, for his own ends.

Finally, the tokens the rustic philosopher recognizes "engraved on obelisks and sacred precincts" (114C) are of course the hieroglyphic writing everywhere conspicuous on Egyptian walls and stelae. The obelisk of Theodosius in the hippodrome of Constantinople would have kept this image present even for the least cultivated of Synesius's audience.[51] But the engravings had meaning too: they are perennially the form for recording ancient Egyptian knowledge. Herodotus provides a banal example in the pyramid inscription he was told recorded the quantity of radishes, onions, and garlic consumed by the laborers who built it.[52] Diodorus reports that only the priestly caste possessed knowledge of the hieroglyphic script, passing it down from father to son (3.3.5). Plutarch frequently discusses hieroglyphics, treating them as metaphorical ideograms.[53] Ammianus more correctly notes that they were partly alphabetical but also could stand for single words or whole thoughts (17.4.10); he characterizes them as "marked by the ancient authority of primeval wisdom" (17.4.8). Socrates records a hot interpretative controversy between Christians and pagans over crosslike hieroglyphs discovered when the Serapeum was torn down in 391 (*HE* 5.17). And within the specifically Egyptian tradition of the Hermetica, instructions to inscribe a revelation on temple stelae were given as the culminating step of its reception.[54] It is no coincidence that Synesius refers to the "sacred writings" just as his character in the tale receives a revelation from a god. But the more specific influence of this branch of Egyptian tradition on *De providentia* will be discussed separately in section VI below.

III. DIO CHRYSOSTOM

In his essay *Dion; or, On Living by His Example*, Synesius extols Dio for uniting philosophical seriousness with rhetorical beauty. Since he aspired after the same combination, and indeed wrote the *Dion* to defend it against critics (cf. *Ep.* 154), notice is given to look for reflections of Dio

51. See G. Bruns, *Der Obelisk und seine Basis auf dem Hippodrom zu Konstantinopel*, Istanbuler Forschungen 7 (1935).

52. 2.125.6; for discussion of the fraud and fantasy in Herodotus's interpreter's report, see Lloyd ad loc. (1987, 69–71).

53. *De Is. et Os.* 354E and F, 355B, 363F, 371E; cf. Griffiths 1970 ad loc.

54. E.g., N.H.C. 6.6.61–62.15; cf. Iambl. *Myst.* 267.13–268.2; and further discussion in Fowden 1986, 29–31, 35, 99.

in Synesius's writings. The search is fertile. In 1900 R. Asmus produced an exhaustive list of parallels.[55] Most relevant for *De providentia* is Dio's version of the Choice of Heracles in his first oration on kingship.[56]

In Dio's story, Zeus implants good impulses in his son Heracles and guides his actions through oracles. Finally, perceiving Heracles' desire to rule for the good of others, but mistrusting the admixture of mortality in his nature, Zeus sends Hermes to Thebes, where Heracles is being raised. Hermes takes him to a twin mountain whose peaks are called Royal and Tyrannical. On the one lives Basileia, who is radiantly beautiful, stately, and serene, attended by Justice, Good Order, Peace, and Law; on the other, Tyrannis, who is gaudy and unstable, attended by Cruelty, Outrage, Lawlessness, Faction, and Flattery. Their realms correspond, Basileia's being beautiful, fertile, and peaceful, and Tyrannis's a junk heap of expensive spoils, smeared with blood. Hermes tells Heracles that it is with Tyrannis most men are in love, but Heracles despises her and prefers Basileia. Zeus is pleased and grants him kingship over all mankind. Heracles goes on to overthrow any tyranny he encounters but to honor and protect any kingship. In stressing in his prologue to this tale that *naturally* Heracles led an army when he set about his civilizing mission (*Or.* 1.63), Dio makes plain the equation of his hero with his addressee, the soldier-emperor Trajan. Accordingly, the tale calls Trajan to be a just ruler over the semiautonomous cities of the High Empire: not only to prefer good order to excessive riches himself, but also to regulate the governments under him without taking them over, supporting the good and only interfering with the bad.

Moral allegory was a long-standing device, particularly in Cynic diatribe. Another famous example is Dio's Libyan myth, on the destructive force of lust (*Or.* 5). Any such story takes on political overtones in the appropriate context.[57] An example formally closer to Dio's Choice of Heracles is Julian's anonymous but obviously autobiographical myth in his oration to the Cynic Heracleios.[58] Here again Hermes leads a young future ruler to revelation by a mountain, but the youth is Julian, and he

55. Asmus 1900, 85–151. *Dion* was written some years after *De providentia: Ep.* 154 tells Hypatia that it and *De insomniis* were produced "this year," τῆτες (p. 271.7 G) but describes *De dono* as πάλαι γενόμενον ἐν τῷ καιρῷ τῆς πρεσβείας (p. 277.2–3 G). But Dio was no fresh enthusiasm. *De regno*, particularly, recalls him often: see Asmus, 91–104, and the pages in Lacombrade 1951b listed in his index under "Dion de Pruse (Chrysostome)"; and cf. Asmus, 104–7, on *De dono*.

56. *Or.* 1.59–84; Nicolosi 1959, 93–98. Not all of Nicolosi's parallels are convincing, and he missed some interesting parallels between *De providentia* and Dio's Choice of Heracles, as well as all parallels with Dio outside of this myth.

57. E.g., Dio Chrys. *Or.* 4.73–75 explicitly places "the Libyan myth" (apparently that of *Or.* 5) within the moral education Alexander must have to make him fit for kingship.

58. *Or.* 7.227C–234D; cf. R. Asmus, *Julian und Dion Chrysostomos* (1895).

sees justice and injustice contrasted in the realm of the gods and that of his cousin Constantius. His choice is not between principles, but between the contemplative and the active life. The gods constrain him to take the latter. Julian was moved to this composition, he says, in response to a myth that Heracleios had used in a discourse before him, "an ancient story you fitted to other circumstances" (227A). Though Julian disparages this lack of originality, it is clear that adaptation of existing stories conventionally belonged to such allegorizing. The familiarity of the model reinforced the claims of the new version.[59] Julian's autobiographical myth is a case in point: the established framework of Hermes' revelation grounds the spectacular claim that he himself rules by the design and under the protection of gods against whom his dynastic predecessors have sinned. His own model Dio too had adapted by recasting Prodicus's Choice of Heracles in political terms.[60]

Dio presents his version as an oracle given to him by an old woman he met while wandering in exile in the Peloponnese. He introduces it into his speech as a modest alternative to

> giving an account of (εἴποιμ᾽ ἂν τὸν λόγον) Zeus and the nature of the universe, since it is too much for the present time and requires more exact demonstrations. . . . But if you would like to hear a story, or rather a holy and healthful discourse told in the form of a story (εἰ δ᾽ ἄρα μῦθον ἐθέλοις τινὰ ἀκοῦσαι, μᾶλλον δὲ ἱερὸν καὶ ὑγιῆ λόγον σχήματι μύθου λεγόμενον), perhaps one that I once heard an old woman of Elis[61] telling about Heracles will not seem inapposite, both now and when later you consider it by yourself.[62]

It is this passage, with a nod at the Platonic distinction between *mythos* and *logos*,[63] that Synesius reproduces in the opening of book 1:

> The story (μῦθος) is Egyptian. Egyptians are extraordinarily wise. So perhaps this story, even though it is only a story, might hint at something more than a story[64] because it is Egyptian. If it is less a story than a sacred discourse (μηδὲ μῦθος, ἀλλὰ λόγος ἐστὶν ἱερός), all the more should it be written down.[65]

59. Synesius played with a related notion in claiming that his allegory, set in the distant past, predicted the future because of the unity and cyclic motion of the cosmos (127A–128B). He was using recent history to underpin the fiction, but the fictional setting laid claim to antiquity.

60. Xen. *Mem.* 2.1.21–34.

61. Von Arnim brackets "or Arcadia."

62. *Or.* 1.48–49.

63. Compare particularly Pl. *Grg.* 523A: "Hear then a very fair discourse (μάλα καλοῦ λόγου), which you will account as a story (μῦθον), I think, but I as a discourse (λόγον)."

64. τάχ᾽ ἂν οὖν ὅδε, καὶ μῦθος ὤν, μύθου τι πλέον αἰνίττοιτο. Asmus compared *Or.* 5.22, τυχὸν οὖν ὁ μῦθος αἰνίττεται.

65. 89A–B.

He returns to Dio again at the end of book 1 (115B) with the riddle of the wolf: [66]

> The identity of the wolf is a sacred tale (ἱερὸς λόγος), which it would be irreverent to expound even in the guise of a myth (ἐν μύθου σχήματι).

The last phrase, closing Synesius's original version of his tale, echoes Dio even more closely than the proem. Stories are entertaining. They offer scope for invention and the development of various themes, as Synesius indicates in his preface (88B). But fiction only has value if it conveys some serious message; its other features merely serve to make the vehicle attractive. Moreover, the *logoi* enfolded in the myths of both model and new creation are pointed historical allegories. The reference to one such encoded myth cued Synesius's audience to expect similar manipulations.

The religious overtones of the inner message are stressed by Dio's prophetess when she introduces her *mythos* by contrasting the "words and clevernesses of men" with "the inspiration and speech that come from the gods" (*Or.* 1.57). Synesius returns to the idea of revelation at the end of book 1 when the god prophesies Typhos's fall, and again at the end of book 2 when he says a prophet must not reveal too much too soon. But his introduction, like Dio's, simply claims authority for the tale in conventional language; the ambiguous quality of its Egyptianness complicates this authority.

Within the tale itself, the setting for the election of Osiris and Typhos (94B–96A) strongly recalls Dio's twin mountains of Basileia and Tyrannis (*Or.* 1.66–82). Dio's mountains are encircled by a river whereas Synesius's are divided by the Nile, and he places his mountains at Thebes whereas Hermes leads Heracles away from his childhood home of Thebes; but all the same features are incorporated. [67] Dio does not develop the implications of Tyrannical Mountain being "named after Typhos" (*Or.* 1.67), and Synesius does not allude to it, though he no doubt expected informed readers to remember. He also uses the mountains differently as settings for a moral choice: his "holy" mountain, on the Egyptian side, is the site of the voting (94C). The arrangement of the electors symbolizes the good order of the kingdom just as Basileia's court does on Dio's Royal Mountain, but Synesius arranges the electors according to Egyptian traditions. [68] Synesius's second mountain is merely

66. αἴνιγμα, picking up αἰνίττοιτο in the proem.
67. Dio presumably meant Boeotian rather than Egyptian Thebes, but the name is the same, and he does not specify.
68. See above, p. 262.

the place where the candidates await the results. Typhos, however, cannot bear to wait, and swims across the river to try to bribe the electors. His passage, "swept along by the river, swimming and floundering helplessly, a laughable sight" (95D), recalls the path to Tyrannical Mountain, "narrow, crooked, and arduous, so that most of those who attempt it perish over the cliffs and in the river below, I think since they go against justice" (*Or.* 1.67). The danger and twisting of the route itself in both cases are combined with the injustice of the attempt to travel it, and are colorfully depicted. Osiris in contrast waits properly and on being elected is carried over the river in a ferry and joyfully received, just as "the approach to Royal Mountain is secure and flat, so that one might enter by it without risk or misstep driving a chariot, if passage had been given to him by the greatest of the gods" (*Or.* 1.67). Here the easy routes reflect the legitimacy of the aspirants to just rule.

When Osiris is elected, the gods and his father together initiate him into kingship (96A). They both warn him against Typhos and explain the philosophical underpinnings of the tale as a whole. At the end, Osiris's father departs "by the same route as the gods" (102D), thus completing his identification with them (cf. 93D). His divinity and attention to the characters and training of his sons correspond to Zeus's guidance of Heracles (*Or.* 1.64–65). Dio's Zeus provides the essential impulse of his plot: his anxiety that Heracles might fall to the temptations of mortal nature makes him send Hermes to test him. Synesius diffuses the motif. He has two sons to test and postpones the reward for passing, actual kingship, by subordinating it to the election. That carefully articulated structure leaves the father's judgment paramount, but Synesius also wanted to inject implications about public opinion. As Asmus saw, Zeus's oracular signs to Heracles become public omens marking Osiris's election.[69] Paternal guidance takes the form first of testing Osiris and Typhos in minor offices (92A, 93D) and then of the long direct speech. The first incorporates an additional reference to Dio's first oration, outside the myth, for Synesius says Typhos's maladministration "shamed (ἤσχυνεν) both himself and the man who chose him." Dio observes that a king who fails to imitate Zeus "dishonors (ἀτιμάσῃ) the one who entrusted or gave" him office and lastingly proves his own unfitness (*Or.* 1.46). The wicked ruler bears the blame, but his elector bears some responsibility too. The second form in which Synesius casts the theme of paternal guidance allows him to weave a long philosophical exposition

---

69. Asmus 1900, 108; *De providentia* 96A. In the different context, it is questionable whether the commonplace notion of divination by signs really constitutes a specific reference. See also above, pp. 257–58.

into the fabric of his tale. Dio's model underwent a complex refraction to provide Synesius with a number of structural advantages.

One graphic detail with a broad history, which may nevertheless point to Dio specifically, is the snore or snort. Like the cordax, it is among the depraved entertainments Synesius ascribes to Typhos: he liked to "snore loudly even while awake, and delighted in hearing others do the same; he thought it an admirable piece of music. Commendations and honors were accorded to anyone who prolonged the wanton sound and rounded it out the more" (92B–C). To this remarkable vice Dio devoted his Tarsian oration (*Or.* 33), stressing its immoral connotations and lengthily comparing it to music.[70]

The linking of virtue and plainness, depreciatingly called "rusticity" (ἀγροικία), may also owe something to Dio's Euboean discourse (*Or.* 7), which Synesius defends as serious and philosophical (*Dion* 38C). It is also the prominent quality of the Peloponnesians Dio met in his exile and praises in *Or.* 1.51. Synesius adopts from Dio here his own self-portrait in *De providentia*, a philosopher (113A) kept away from his home (114B), who receives an oracle declaring that his tribulations will last a surprisingly short time (114C).[71]

Synesius also combines an image from Dio's Choice of Heracles with a separate passage when the rustic philosopher rebukes Typhos for not living up to his brother's model: he "restrained his hands (κατεῖχε τὼ χεῖρε) . . . but from his face one could picture what was going on in his mind: one form of passion succeeded another, and within moments he turned every possible color (πάγχρως ἐγίνετο)" (114B). Alexander reddens in anger at the raillery of the Cynic philosopher Diogenes but restrains himself (κατέσχε δ᾽ ἑαυτόν, *Or.* 4.18). But Alexander is too positive a figure to provide all the allusive resonance for Typhos here. Tyrannis shows his emotional fluctuation in the same way: "she turned all sorts of colors (χρώματα δὲ παντοδαπὰ ἠφίει) in fear and distress and distrust and anger."[72]

Dio's first oration also supplied Synesius with the useful character of the Dorian prophetess. Her prophecy of deliverance is spoken by the god who gives the rustic philosopher the "key to the time" (114C) with plain references to recent events. But since, unlike Dio, Synesius was not employing *post eventum* prophecy, the god's predictions did not come true as straightforwardly. Synesius was obliged to write a sequel

70. C. Bonner (*Harv.Theol.Rev.* 35 [1942]) collected further references from the second to the seventh centuries without exhausting its occurrences; see p. 343 n. 42.

71. Cf. Dio Chrys. *Or.* 1.55.

72. *Or.* 1.81, echoing Pl. *Lys.* 222B.

that forced events and his tale into closer resemblance. Naturally he focused on the most dramatic event closest to his claims, the initial rout of the Goths. Intriguingly, he reactivated the figure of Dio's prophetess. The riot begins when a Scythian tries to cut down an old beggarwoman who sits by the city gate where he had hoped to escape quietly (117C–118C). Synesius describes her as "a poor woman, quite elderly," just as Dio's prophetess is "rather advanced in years," gray-haired, and quite a part of the poor countryside (*Or.* 1.52–53). Dio casually remarked that she spoke Dorian (*Or.* 1.54); Synesius more indirectly noted that the beggarwoman held a *kothon*, which (as Athenaeus explains) is a type of Laconian drinking cup.[73] The beggarwoman is less closely in touch with the divine will than the prophetess, for she makes the same despairing assumptions about the Scythians' power and intentions that Synesius decries in the preface to book 2,[74] but she does prophesy at a lesser level. She paraphrases Synesius's *De regno* in her indictment of barbarian ingratitude,[75] concluding: "Do you suppose the gods don't punish ingratitude against benefactors?[76] For they exist and they will come, even if only when Thebes is no more!" (118B). Of course the gods' intervention is realized in the massacre itself, as Synesius had promised (117C); it is more immediately realized in her rescue from the Scythians' sword by a godlike figure who appears out of nowhere to take his blow (118C). Despite these modifications, Dio's prophetess survives recognizably.

IV. PANEGYRIC AND INVECTIVE

The discourses of a sophist like Dio praised, advised, criticized, and entertained his audiences variously, according to the needs and inspiration of the occasion. By late antiquity, circumstances became more formalized. Panegyric, or more properly, encomium, had an official role to play on virtually every occasion. Handbooks like those ascribed to Menander guided speakers with elaborately subdivided categories of praise, and detailed suggestions for each. Speakers used them avidly.[77] Corre-

73. Ath. 483C–484C; though the bulk of the literary sources he cites refer only to its use by soldiers and travelers.

74. 116D–117C; cf. pp. 286–87.

75. Cf. *De regno* 23A–B and 25C–D, particularly in the reuse of ἱκέτης/ἱκετεία, πολιτείας ἀξιοῦν, γερῶν μεταδιδόναι.

76. This is our interpretation of a difficulty in the text here; see Cameron, Long, Sherry 1988, 60–61.

77. E.g., *P.Berol.* 21849: Maehler 1974, 305–11; for general discussion, Russell and Wilson 1981, xi–xlvi.

sponding functions of blame were served by panegyric's darker twin, invective. Both varieties tended to be highly occasional, losing much of their interest once their immediate purpose had been met; relatively few of the ubiquitous examples survive. But their ubiquity had two important positive consequences. First, it will have driven more ambitious authors to employ a wide variety of techniques developing and ornamenting the basic themes, just to keep them from getting dull. Second, it will have made these speeches broad conduits of literary themes and devices among the genres.[78]

De providentia is molded by these genres most obviously in Synesius's portrayals of Osiris and Typhos. Osiris, predictably, possesses all the qualifications of the ideal philosopher-king evoked by generations of speakers,[79] most recently by Synesius himself in *De regno*. True kingship is defined in the soul, and Osiris's is heavenly. "Divine destiny" sends it down "to administer the earthly lot." Already in babyhood Osiris revealed his nature in his love for the primordia of philosophy. As a boy he was a precocious student, but becomingly modest and deferential.[80] He used his position with his father to win benefits for the Egyptians (89B–90C).[81] Not only the virtues themselves but also their biographical presentation imitate panegyric's approach to the subject's mature achievements through his ancestry, birth, and upbringing. Each stage promises future greatness as it illustrates the development of character.[82]

78. Claudian's *In Rufinum* is one case, much discussed, where a self-titled invective combines the standard rhetorical structures with other literary traditions: cf. L. B. Struthers, "The Rhetorical Structure of the Encomia of Claudius Claudian," *HSCP* 30 (1919): 49–87; H. L. Levy, "Claudian's *In Rufinum* and the Rhetorical Ψόγος," *TAPA* 77 (1946): 57–65; Cameron 1970a, 83–84; W. Barr, "Claudian's *in Rufinum*: An Invective?" *Pap. Liverpool Latin Sem.* 2 (1979): 179–90.

79. Convenient and representative are L. K. Born's synthetic sketch, "The Perfect Prince according to the Latin Panegyrists," *AJP* 55 (1934): 20–35; and synopses of individual authors from Isocrates to Augustine in the introduction to his translation of Erasmus, *The Education of a Christian Prince* (New York 1936), 44–93.

80. Both the ideals and the details through which they are elaborated belong to broad traditions, but it may be worth noting that Libanius evokes a similar complex for Julian in his *Epitaphios logos*, using some of the same techniques. Note particularly the enumeration of his family ties to emperors that comments on his decorous behavior as a student (*Or.* 18.11) and his blush at the need to speak (*Or.* 18.30). On the other hand, Libanius demonstrates Julian's aptitude by comparison with his fellow students and from his enthusiasm for Libanius's own speeches (*Or.* 18.12–15).

81. Panegyrists often praise the benevolent intercession of imperial women and children, suggesting the ruler's *philanthropia* in the absence of true power: e.g., Julian of Eusebia (*Or.* 3, passim), Themistius of Flacilla and Arcadius (*Or.* 19.231a); cf. Amm. Marc. 14.1.8 of Constantina, a counterexample.

82. Compare the synthesis of T. C. Burgess, "Epideictic Literature," *U. Chicago Stud. Class. Philol.* 3 (1902): 89–261, here 122–26. Ancient biography shared this emphasis on the subject's deeds as revealing character and his youth as presaging full maturity: see Leo 1901, 184–92.

Synesius continues with Osiris's junior career, in which the promise is made more specific: "While still a youth Osiris shared in the generalship with the men appointed to that office: the law did not permit arms to someone so young, but he ruled their will as if he were their mind, and used the generals as his hands" (91D–92A). Claudian similarly applauds Honorius as having "fought" Arbogast and Eugenius by his consular auspices,[83] or claims that he wanted to fight, but Theodosius did not permit him.[84] The authors ascribe martial prowess to their subjects in circumstances that preclude all chance of their actually displaying it.

Synesius says that Osiris's and Typhos's junior careers illustrate "the opposition of their principles."[85] In their instructions rhetoricians regularly associate principles and character (*ethos*) with the subdivision of upbringing "pursuits" (*epitedeumata*): "the pursuits encompass the imprint of the character";[86] "pursuits indicate the character and principle of men."[87] Thus in terms of panegyric structure, Synesius separates the junior tenures from the main subject of deeds (*praxeis*). Within the narrative, they are explicitly a period of testing (92A); they also continue Synesius's expository framework in accordance with the divisions and emphases of the basic panegyric scheme.

The very last stage of Osiris's upbringing is his initiation by the gods and his father into the mysteries of kingship (96A–102D). The gods summarize the implications of Typhos's character as his youthful tastes and pursuits have revealed it, and explicitly warn Osiris to remove him from the country. When Osiris protests that the gods' goodness and power frees him from apprehension, his father steps in to explain the metaphysical system within which Osiris must work. Such fatherly advice is a useful device in panegyric literature. It affords the speaker a persona implicitly sympathetic to the recipient, mitigating criticism. According to Claudian, for example, Roma rejoices in Honorius as her *alumnus* (*In Eutr.* 1.385); Justitia demands back her student Mallius Theodorus (*Theod.* 138–39); Theodosius, the great warrior-emperor, in-

---

83. *III Cons.Hon.* 88–89: "pugnastis uterque: tu fatis genitorque manu."

84. *III Cons.Hon.* 73–87, *IV Cons.Hon.* 320–95.

85. τὸ ἀντίξουν τῶν προαιρέσεων, 91D. In this context "principles" translates the idea more clearly than the conventional "choice"; see further note ad loc., p. 342.

86. τὰ γὰρ ἐπιτηδεύματα ἤθους ἔμφασιν περιέχει, Men. Rh. 372.4–5, on the *basilikos logos*.

87. ἐπιτηδεύματα γάρ ἐστιν ἔνδειξις τοῦ ἤθους καὶ τῆς προαιρέσεως τῶν ἀνδρῶν, Men. Rh. 384.20–21, on the praise of a city in the *epibaterios logos*. The further specification "separately from competitive actions" distinguishes a different indicator of moral qualities. For the same emphasis in the definition of *epitedeumata*, cf. Doxopater in Walz, *Rhet.Gr.* 2.431.32–33; for a simpler definition as "career" but still in the context of moral qualities and personal choice, Hermog. *Prog.* 38.8–10 Rabe; Doxopater in Walz, *Rhet.Gr.* 2.429.31ff.

structs the child Augustus Honorius on how to be a good ruler (*IV Cons. Hon.* 213f.); and the same Theodosius, as the last ruler of a unified empire and Stilicho's sponsor, urges Arcadius to reconcile with the West, while his father, the elder Theodosius, as a great general, inspires Honorius to attack Gildo (*Bell. Gild.* 215f.). Osiris's father represents the philosophical principles of good government even more directly than the historical Theodosii embody military ideals. The only criticism in Osiris's father's speech concerns the problem of eliminating irredeemable evil, namely, Typhos. Synesius's plot required the exhortation to fail on this point; he arranges the scene so that even this error reveals Osiris's benevolence and faith in the gods.

When the narrative advances to deeds, Osiris's kingship and Typhos's plot, the brothers are opposed more dynamically than in the earlier juxtaposed descriptions. As king, Osiris fulfills all promise shown hitherto, and Synesius evokes all the traditional encomiastic ideals.[88] "He immediately strove to banish evils from the land" through goodwill not force. Citizens willingly obey him, since he is identified with law. The gods reward his goodness with natural prosperity, which he passes on to his people. He successfully trains his citizens to love virtue, particularly through "all education, both intellectual and rhetorical." His only thought for money is that his citizens enjoy a sufficiency of it. Wherever cities are ruined or in danger of ruin, he restores and strengthens them; he also founds new ones. His benevolence extends even to the private interests of individuals. His only flaw is that he trusts too easily that his own example of goodness will redeem the wicked. Except for the last, which pointedly foretells Typhos's successful plot,[89] all the themes are entirely conventional.

Treachery forestalls the rousing paean in which a simple panegyric would have ended, but Aurelian's return allowed Synesius to resume it in book 2. Rather, in book 1 he subordinated panegyric of Aurelian/ Osiris, whom he praises throughout, to the controlling structure of his myth; in book 2 he makes panegyric the dominant constructive principle in order to restore coherence to his story. Osiris's arrival concludes the narrative action. Briefly but splendidly, Synesius proclaims the "holy return, the garlanded populace joining the gods in bringing him back and crossing over the whole promontory to escort the returning party; nightlong festivals, torch-lit processions, distributions of gifts, the eponymous year" (123D–124A). *Adventus* always attracted panegyric description, not only because its pageantry riveted the exquisite late antique

88. 102D–104C, variously reprised at 105A, 105D–106A, 106D, 108A.
89. Cf. Greg.Naz. *Or.* 4.41 on Alexander and Porus, with reference to Constantius's failure to shame Julian into a just regard by honoring him.

visual sensibility, as emperors well knew how to exploit,[90] but also because it choreographed a popular response that redounded to the arriver's credit.[91] Synesius takes full advantage of this device. He goes on
to claim that Osiris's reign rivaled in felicity the primordial reign of Justice (124C–125B). Such a "full comparison," putting the subject's deeds
in proper perspective,[92] could hardly have a more exalted correlate. A
metaphysical epilogue rounds off book 2, just as a discussion of the origins of souls served as the proem of book 1.

Invective corresponds to panegyric in its structure, the same divisions organizing vituperation rather than praise. Full-blown invectives
can hardly have been as common in real life as in the textbooks, but the
few we have are inevitably more entertaining than the hosts of panegyrics. Evil takes more varied and interesting forms than good: Claudian's two invectives put all his panegyrics in the shade, and Synesius's
villains are predictably more vivid creations than his heroes.

Typhos is presented in parallel with Osiris and displays all the qualities of Plato's unphilosophical man, the tyrant.[93] His soul bubbles up
from the murky spring. He rejects all wisdom and delights in licentious,
anarchic, and preferably harmful behavior. He practices so many vices
that they contradict one another. He makes friends only so as to have
allies in hatred of the good. As with Osiris, Synesius illustrates these
childhood attitudes with miniature pictures: Osiris blushes when need
arises for him to speak (90B); Typhos glories in bodily strength "by tearing off doors and pelting people with globs of dirt" (91A–B).

The last detail illustrates the greater vividness permitted by the de-
lineation of evil. We expect maladministration and corruption in public
office, marking the last stage in Typhos's preliminary training (92A–93C),
but we could not have predicted the ensuing catalogue of disgusting but
inconsequential behavior. Synesius mocks his victim by diminishing
him, as Claudian does to Eutropius.[94] Synesius asserts that Typhos's er-

90. For but one famous example, Constantius's entry into Rome in 357, Amm. Marc.
16.10; cf. R. MacMullen, "Some Pictures in Ammianus Marcellinus," *AB* 46 (1964): 435–55.

91. E.g., *Pan.Lat.* 2[12].37, 3[11].6–7, 5[8].8, 11[3].11; cf. S. G. MacCormack, *Art and
Ceremony in Late Antiquity* (Berkeley 1981), 17–89. Synesius also uses *adventus* after Osiris's
election (96A); for angels joining the procession, cf. Greg.Naz. *Or.* 5.16, of Constantius's
funeral procession.

92. *teleiotate synkrisis*, Men. Rh. 376.31–377.9.

93. Just as Synesius had defined the tyrant in *De regno* (6A), not only does Typhos
wallow in luxury and exploit his subjects, but at the same time he maliciously enjoys their
misery for its own sake: "His enjoyment in doing evil was enhanced by the thought that
with the tears of men he was wiping away the disrepute of his indolence at home" (92D).

94. "Rufinus he had portrayed as a primeval force, a power of darkness. Eutropius is
merely disgusting, a joke—and a bad joke" (Cameron 1970a, 133; cf. 258–59).

ratic fancy occasionally saves his victim, for he becomes unaccountably distracted into bizarre irrelevancies and loses sight of the business at hand. At other times he falls asleep abruptly and threatens to topple off his judicial seat. His instability recalls the frenzy of Plato's tyrannical soul, equally prey to every momentary impulse. He hates every sensible or competent person, directly violating the royal virtue of friendship.[95]

When defeated by his brother in the royal election, Typhos slips into suicidal and then spineless depression (104C–105A, 106D–107B), to be rescued by Synesius's most interesting creation, a wife who "drives out passion with passion" (107C), replacing defeated ambition with sexual excess. Typhos's wife represents a fascinating complex of invective techniques. Caesarius's wife was not wholly unknown in Constantinopolitan society, for Sozomen records her friendship with the Macedonian deaconess Eusebia;[96] but there is no indication that she played any such role in the politics of 400. Nor does she resemble the passive Nephthys, Typhos's wife in the myth. The Ethiopian queen Aso provides faint mythical authority for a female conspirator, but Plutarch never indicates what she does. Typhos's wife in Synesius sets the whole conspiracy in motion.

She contrasts pointedly with Osiris's wife, a woman so perfectly modest that her very existence can be deduced only from the rare appearance of Osiris's son.[97] Typhos's wife adorns herself and frequents the theater and marketplace, avid both to see and, even worse, to be seen. That she is "her own hairdresser" is a social slur that in turn bears its own implications of debased morality.[98] Theodora's theatrical career afforded Procopius leverage on the same sensibilities.[99] He presents her performances as but a sideline of her enthusiastic whoredom (*Anecd.* 9.10–28); Typhos's wife also "assembled whorish women and their male hangers-on."

95. Synesius dilates on friendship in *De regno*, especially 11B–12B, with particular regard to his actual audience and their interests (see chapter 4, section VI); but it was an established theme in kingship literature, including panegyric, e.g., Dio Chrys. *Or.* 1.30–35, 3.86–132 (echoed by Synesius in *De regno*); *Pan. Lat.* 2[12].15–17.

96. *HE* 9.2: near their tombs Pulcheria disinterred the relics of the Forty Martyrs.

97. Synesius seldom uses names or pronouns, but he names Osiris twice in successive sentence beginnings when describing his unnamed wife: clearly she is mentioned solely to demonstrate the chaste modesty of Osiris's home life. Osiris's and Typhos's wives are contrasted at 105A–D, and the character of Typhos's wife is developed in the subsequent narrative.

98. Hairdressing is ranked with pastry cooking by the censorious Julian, both contemptible professions: *Caes.* 335B.

99. Her act and the disgust it inspired: Procop. *Anecd.* 9.20–26. On his treatment of Theodora generally, see now Averil Cameron, *Procopius and the Sixth Century* (Berkeley 1985), 67–83.

Their vileness stains the husbands who are blind to it:[100] "half of [Typhos's] misfortune was the scandal of the person for whose sake he had coveted the supreme office and with whom he intended to share his power." She parodies the recommended tactic by which an empress may be praised under the rubric of her husband's temperance (σωφροσύνη): "If the queen is in great repute and honor, you will say something at an appropriate moment here: 'The woman he admired and loved, he has made a partner of his own kingship, and he does not even know if other women exist.'"[101] As the plot develops, Typhos is entirely eclipsed by his wife, his infatuation (105B) becoming emasculated dependency.

Wives wheedling their husbands into atrocities are a common invective device. The men are both evil for the acts they commit and negligible for being henpecked. They lose even the credit of a malign initiative. Once again the tactic is one of denigration by diminution. Libanius discredits Cynegius's attacks on pagan temples by calling him "a slave to his wife, obliging her in everything and thinking she is everything."[102] In Claudian, Bellona, disguised as Tribigild's wife, goads him into revolt by railing at him for his docility and lack of manhood.[103] Typhos's wife's rhetoric outdoes even Bellona's. She displaces Typhos entirely, as Synesius transcends the typical invective structure. Typhos's wife persuades the stupid, timid wife of the barbarian leader that Osiris is planning to purge his armies of barbarians. Synesius himself had recommended this very course in *De regno*, but his description of Osiris makes plain that he would never take it, even though he lose his kingdom (104C). Typhos's wife drives her point home with superb pathos, crying over "these fine children, these beautiful babies!" and chucking them under the chins where she has just envisaged Osiris's sword threatening. Her final argument is a masterpiece of antinomian sophistry: the idea that convention shackles those who will not fight, but "it is the strong man who is free, unless habit scares him from his intention" can almost claim the nobility of Platonic ancestry, in the *Gorgias*. Her argument that the barbarians

---

100. This is the force of Procopius's juxtaposing Theodora's history with Justinian's love (*Anecd.* 9.29–30; cf. 1.15–20, of Antonina's affair with Theodosius and Belisarius's willingness to be deceived).

101. Men. Rh. 376.9–13. Cf. Dio Chrys. *Or.* 3.122: "He has accounted his wife not merely the partner of his bed and pleasures, but the fellow worker of his counsel and deeds and the whole of his life."

102. *Or.* 30.46, with P. Petit, *Byzantion* 21 (1951): 295f.; cf. *HA Quadr.Tyr.* 12.3.

103. *In Eutr.* 2.174–229; the motif here is displaced onto a secondary invective victim, Claudian's primary purpose being to claim that Eutropius could not handle the crisis he himself had provoked in Tribigild's revolt. Elsewhere Claudian gloatingly pictures Alaric's wife wailing at losing the "jeweled necklaces of Ausonian matrons for her proud neck and Romans as her slave girls" that she had demanded (*Bell. Get.* 623–34).

would revolutionize nothing by promoting Typhos because as the elder son of the same father as Osiris he has the greater right to rule, travesties an argument from the *Timaeus* (34C): god must have made the soul before the body, because it is improper for the younger to rule the elder. Synesius uses every device to make Typhos's wife most dangerously subversive in every way.

Demons intervene with notable frequency in late antique history. They conveniently emblematize the unspeakable evil that seemed to inspire certain disturbances. Used in an abstract context, they may diffuse responsibility: for example, in the anonymous *Peri politikes epistemes* civil wars are seen to arise spontaneously, as if some wicked demon threw down the Apple of Discord.[104] But when the demons are attached to specific human agents, they brand them with superhuman malevolence. No further reason for their actions need be sought; evil motivates and feeds itself. A perfect illustration is Claudian's invective against Rufinus. Megaera nursed him and now finds that he has excelled her in wickedness, indeed concentrated the wickedness of all Hell combined. The infernal council sends him forth to wreck the good order of the world. He piles sin on sin insatiably, insanely, from greed to perjury to murder to betrayal of the empire. He embraces his own destruction provided he can pull down the world with him. When at last the world is saved by his murder, he is judged too wicked even for Dis and must be driven beyond Styx, beyond Erebus, below Tartarus and even Chaos,[105] to the ultimate depth of all. Synesius as bishop calls his adversary Andronicus a locust, a scourge, a murderer, then an agent of "the Tempter," and finally, repeatedly, a demon himself.[106] The letter begins with an abstract discussion of the problem of divine retribution through evil, concluding that the avenging agent, either demon or human, is nonetheless hateful to God because he acts solely to gratify his own evil impulse (p. 54.16–21G). More succinctly, Pacatus calls Marcellinus, brother and general of Magnus Maximus, a "Megaera of civil war" in describing his final battle with Theodosius.[107]

---

104. 5.104: Mazzucchi plausibly emends ἐνῆκε for the palimpsest's ενηκαι, for which Mai had read ἐνῇ καί; which still would leave both apple and demon involved. Compare the demonic involvement to which Libanius before Theodosius ascribes the Riot of the Statues: *Or.* 19.29, 30, 34.

105. Claud. *In Ruf.* 2.525: Birt's *ipsumque Chaos* or Levy's *imumque* give the most forceful and apposite sense; the MSS offer *nostrumque, vestrumque, meritumque, dirumque.*

106. *Ep.* 57 = 41G: τὴν ἀκρίδα, p. 55.16; τῇ πηγῇ, p. 56.1; τὸν παλαμναῖον τῆς χώρας Ἀνδρόνικον, p. 56.9–10; διὰ τούτου μέτεισιν ὁ πειράζων, pp. 59.16–18, 60.4–6, 61.1–2.

107. *Pan. Lat.* 2[12].35.1.

Much more elaborate is the following passage of Themistius:

> Only too true (it seems) is the old story, inspired by ancient philosophy, that at certain fixed times pure and divine powers walk the earth for men's benefit, coming down from heaven, not clad in mist as Hesiod puts it,[108] but wearing bodies like ours and assuming a mode of life inferior to their nature in order to commune with us; at others, frenzied and portentous creatures, nurslings of Cocytus and the Erinyes, things born to harm and bewitch and deceive mankind, lovers of dirges and wailing, never having their fill of lamentation, feeding on tears, charged with attacking the world in the form of earthquakes and plagues and floods whenever it is prosperous.[109]

Here we have a striking anticipation in miniature of Synesius's pairing of Osiris and Typhos as divine hero and nursling of demons, respectively. As so often, Themistius does not identify the objects of his vague descriptions, but from the context contemporaries would naturally have inferred that he had the emperor Valens and the usurper Procopius in mind. Like Synesius, Themistius explicitly grounds his rhetoric in philosophy so as to suggest spiritual, metaphysical sources for what is no more than panegyric and invective.[110] Like both Typhos and Claudian's Rufinus, Procopius is said to have been put on earth by demons to ruin the prosperity brought to the world by the writer's hero. Later in the speech (100B), Themistius calls Procopius an "avenging spirit" (ἀλά-στωρ), as he had earlier the usurper Magnentius (ἀλάστωρ βάρβαρος καὶ παλαμναῖος).[111]

When the gods initiate Osiris into the mysteries of kingship, they warn him that "Typhos too has patrons, a powerful mass of malicious demons, whose kin he is, and from whose ranks he has been brought to birth, so that they can use him as an instrument of evil against men, their wicked plans proceeding nicely. They conceived, gestated, delivered, and raised in the proper fashion their great future help: Typhos" (96C–D). Origin, upbringing, interest, and end all identify Typhos with the demons. He is everything Claudian claims for Rufinus in the Hell council and Megaera's speech, with all the same implications. Osiris and

---

108. At *Op.* 124, 253.

109. *Or.* 7, 90C–D; the translation of the first half is adapted from A. D. Nock, *Essays on Religion and the Ancient World*, vol. 2 (Oxford 1972), 937 n. 31.

110. Themistius would (of course) have said exactly the same if Procopius had won, merely reversing the identifications. "Treason doth never prosper: what's the reason? For if it prosper, none dare call it treason."

111. *Or.* 7.100B; *Or.* 3.43A.

the gods face off against Typhos and the demons. Again, panegyric and invective show themselves perfect antitheses.

As the gods foretell, Osiris's success goads the demons to revolution: "For they could not bear to watch their own cause falling ignominiously apart." Again, the malevolent psychology the demons represent exactly corresponds to *In Rufinum*, where Allecto's jealousy impels the plot.[112] "The demons," Synesius explains, "glued themselves to men of their ilk (συγγενέσιν ἀνθρώποις) and used them as their instruments" (108A).

Demonization merges with wifely instigation when the wife is demonic. Claudian's Bellona disguised as Tribigild's wife recalls Vergil's Allecto;[113] and instilling destructive passion through her embrace (*Eutr.* 2.188), she recalls Cupid disguised as Iulus before Dido.[114] According to Ammianus, Gallus's wife inflamed his innate savagery, a "Megaera in human guise" (14.1.2). The pleas of merely human wives derive their invective force from their essential feebleness as grounds for the actions they inspire. Demons are distinguished by their potency. Procopius, who variously demonizes both Theodora and Justinian, argues that only demons could have so devastated mankind.[115] Such power might seem inconsistent with petticoat domination. But in fact susceptibility to demonic influence indicates a demonic nature already prone to evil,[116] which may be seen both in the weakness of its surrender or in the force of its rage. Procopius identifies Justinian as the Ruler of Demons,[117] while asserting that Theodora dominated him, in part compelling him through demons.[118] Synesius both magnifies and emasculates Typhos. Immediately upon Osiris's exile, shortly before drawing his final picture of Typhos's wife holding her brothel court and commanding Typhos's favor for new paramours, he again identifies Typhos as the demons' "faithful servant, whom they had long since brought to birth and finally to tyranny," and credits him with "feasting them on every kind of misfortune" (111C). Similarly, the tribunal of gods sentences Typhos after

112. Claud. *In Ruf.* 1.25–67. Gregory similarly charges that Julian rebelled against Constantius in jealous resentment over the spread of Christianity and was aided by demons (*Or.* 4.45, 47).

113. *Aen.* 7.323–474.

114. *Aen.* 1.695–722.

115. Procop. *Anecd.* 12.15–17, 18.1, 18.36–37; the disasters he records in the remainder of book 18 serve as evidence in support.

116. *De providentia* 108A reflects a general rule. Similarly too, panegyrists stigmatize rather than absolve usurpers when they ascribe their actions to madness: e.g., *Pan. Lat.* 2[12].30.1 and C. E. V. Nixon, *Pacatus* (Liverpool 1987) ad loc.

117. τῶν δαιμόνων ἄρχων, *Anecd.* 12.32, 30.34.

118. *Anecd.* 22.28–32. Compare Synesius's image of the soul fortifying itself against the demons' attacks in *De providentia* 100D.

his death to punishment by the Furies in Cocytus, "that finally he be a damned soul, a demon in Tartarus, a monster in the company of Titans and Giants" (123B). Again he is the demon, here again parallel to Claudian's Rufinus (*In Ruf.* 2.521–27). Yet the one incentive Typhos offers to the plotters is rejected (110C–D). His wife alone effects his coup (110B; cf. 112D). Ostensibly contradictory tactics nevertheless cohere and denigrate Typhos from either perspective.

By the time Synesius wrote book 2, Gaïnas had ceased to threaten Constantinople, and Synesius felt free to include the barbarian soldiers in his mockery and reproach (117A–B, D; 118D). He keeps his invective focused principally on Typhos, however, who keeps treacherously trying to call them back (122A–B). He also continues to exploit his "hollow" office by extorting taxes "more strictly and more unscrupulously" than ever. At last, Synesius claims, he seeks the last resort of the desperate tyrant, that of destroying his state to save himself. Sozomen reports a parallel charge against Rufinus, that, wishing to usurp the throne, he had invited the Huns to come ravage the East.[119] In Claudian's version, Rufinus has not even that goal but invites the barbarians in order to destroy the world with himself (*In Ruf.* 2.7–85). The verse "When I am dead, let the earth be enveloped in fire" had long been proverbial.[120] Synesius varies the conclusion to sow misleading seeds of expectation for Osiris's return: even if Typhos's "darling Scythians" fail him, "at any rate he was glad to think that he would not live to see Osiris return to his country and to office."[121]

V. NEOPLATONIC THEMES

The subtitle *On Providence* (περὶ προνοίας) might seem to suggest a serious philosophical investigation in a long and distinguished tradition, running from Chrysippus down to Synesius's own contemporary Hierocles of Alexandria.[122] It is of course nothing of the sort. While Synesius promises to examine "philosophical issues hitherto undecided," in fact all he does is decorate his story with philosophical rhetoric, making his Neoplatonism subserve his literary and political ends.

A central preoccupation is the metaphysical dualism of good and

119. τυραννεῖν βούλεται, Soz. *HE* 8.1.2.

120. *TGF* Adesp. F513; Suet. *Ner.* 38.1; Dio 58.23; cf. Cic. *Fin.* 3.19; Sen. *Clem.* 2.2.2.

121. τυχόντα καθόδου καὶ γενόμενον ἐν τοῖς πράγμασιν, 122B.

122. On Neoplatonism and Synesius specifically, see Vollenweider 1985a; the analysis of *De providentia* in Bregman 1982, 66–74, sticks narrowly to the question of whether or not Synesius is trying to accommodate Christianity in the work. Helpful general surveys are Dillon 1977 and Wallis 1972. On philosophical investigations of providence, see Amand 1945.

evil. When Synesius considers the kinship of good and evil people, his explanations rely on the different origins of individual souls. In book 1 he says that good souls come from a luminous heavenly spring, and evil ones bubble up from a murky spring rooted below the earth.[123] Synesius describes the baser region with a tag from Empedocles that is also quoted variously by Julian, Hierocles, Proclus, and John the Lydian:[124] presumably they each drew on a common earlier source, perhaps Iamblichus. Synesius explains that true kinship depends on the soul, not the body. Racially and geographically disparate people may be genuinely related in this way, and "those whom we call brothers are in no way akin in the relationship of their souls" (89C). Panegyric proclaimed the importance of birth and upbringing, but Synesius's metaphysics denies it.

In book 2 he takes a fundamentally different approach to the problem. He claims that extreme characters, "not just slightly better or worse than the norm, but enormously so, virtue unmixed with evil or evil unmixed with virtue ($\mathring{\eta}$ βελτίων $\mathring{\eta}$ χείρων . . . ἀρετή . . . κακία)," seem actually to generate their opposites nearby (125D). He goes on to propose in the voice of Philosophy, and to defend in his own, a mechanism by which this is exactly the case. Philosophy suggests that "on the threshold of Zeus" stand two jars containing good and evil seeds. These two jars are a Homeric image frequently evoked, in both philosophical and sophistic contexts.[125] Synesius incorporates the Neoplatonic metaphor *spermata*. The seeds are usually mixed in roughly equal proportion and fused to compose an ordinary human character; but when only one type of seed is used for one soul, the next must restore equilibrium. This conception is made more peculiar by Synesius's unargued assumption that good and evil must balance out within each family, and positively bizarre when he declares that "it follows logically, in the manner of one geometrical corollary emerging from another, that utterly wicked children are the elder sons in their generation" (126D). It is explicable only as precious invective, for Typhos was the elder brother. Synesius sup-

123. The spring is a common Neoplatonic metaphor (e.g., Sleeman and Pollet 1980, s.v. πηγή), as is the imagery that distinguishes the levels closer to the transcendent One from the farther reaches of matter.

124. "Envy is there, and Rancor and the tribes of the other Calamities/roam through the darkness in the field of Delusion" (89D). Empedocles frag. 121.2, 4 Diels-Kranz[7] (1954, 360); Hierocl. *Ad c. aur.* 24; Procl. *In Rep.* 2.157.24 Kroll, *In Crat.*, p. 103 Boissonade; Jul. *Or.* 7.226B; Syn. *Ep.* 147, p. 258.10 G; Lydus *Mens.* 4.159, p. 176.24 Wuensch.

125. *Il.* 24.527–28 (good and bad experiences in life); Pl. *Rep.* 379D (general, disapproves the image); Plut. *De aud. poet.* 24A–B (life, disapproving), *De Is. et Os.* 369C (life, disapproving); Dio Chrys. *Or.* 64.340 (life, approving); Max.Tyr. 34.3, p. 394 Hobein (life, approving); Jul. *Or.* 3.114C (reciprocal and wholly generous love, approving); Syn. *De providentia* 126A (components of soul, approving), *De insomniis* 140B (life, approving), *Hymn* 1.663–78 (life, approving; cf. Terzaghi's notes ad loc., 1939, 155–57).

ports the basic proposition with horticultural analogies, perhaps led by the thought of "seeds": the fig tree saves all its sweetness for its fruits, and bitter plants should be planted with sweet ones to draw the bad matter from the soil.

Ultimately this argument is less dualistic than that of book 1. While distinguishing good and evil at one level, it admits as the norm souls that combine elements of both. Synesius uses moral language, but since in broader Neoplatonic terms good is produced by reason and evil by its failure, his picture parallels the conventional view that the individual is a compound of reasoning and irrational parts.[126] Even the unmixed souls are produced by a single pourer and maintain overall symmetry in the world. Implicitly, of course, good and evil oppose one another, but Synesius does not emphasize as he does in book 1 that the more matter-bound souls are hostile to the more heavenly.[127]

A related and deeper problem Synesius addresses is how divine Providence operates in the world. His second view of the generation of souls imposes no purpose on the souls themselves. They merely contribute sums to an even accounting of good and evil elements. But in book 1 Synesius says that the luminous spring "is sent down [from heaven] to administer the earthly lot" (89C). It, or rather the soul flowing from it, is required to keep itself undefiled by matter, so that it will be able to return after performing its task.

The narrative tacitly identifies Osiris as a heavenly soul meeting this generalized description from the introduction. The antipodal position the gods initiating Osiris specify for Typhos, the spawn and agent of malevolent demons (96C–D), defines Osiris's role as its opposite; the initiation itself details Osiris's instructions for his task. Osiris's father outlines the cosmic system (97B–102D). He highlights from the standard Neoplatonic hierarchy of divinity the ranks that figure in the narrative. The encosmic gods divide their activity between contemplation of the highest good and administration of the inferior regions of the cosmos.[128] Naturally, they prefer the former, the more unitary and divine activity.

126. H. J. Blumenthal, *Plotinus' Psychology* (The Hague 1971), 20–30, argues that Plotinus does not truly admit Platonic tripartition of the soul but views spiritedness and desire as different affects of the vegetative soul.

127. The murky spring "springs out from the caverns of the earth as if it could somehow violate the divine law" (εἴ πη τὸν θεῖον νόμον βιάσαιτο, 89C); the gods reiterate "the opposition earthly souls necessarily hold against celestial" (96B), as well as their more specific warnings against Typhos.

128. Since by definition it is only the encosmic gods who can act within the material cosmos, all gods described as doing so must belong to this class. Synesius hereafter dispenses with the otiose specification.

They impart a first motion to the material world and return to contemplation. The motion is perpetuated as far as possible through good souls that the gods send down into the world: "This is a divine and magnificent Providence, that through one man the gods are often able to care for thousands. From this point on they must be engaged in their own affairs" (99B).

Other orders flesh out this skeleton, as Synesius hints.[129] They descend in a succession of ranks like a chain, through which, link by link, the care of the hypercosmic gods pervades and holds the whole together: "The beings, as they descend, weaken until they err and falsify their rank, at which point even the existence of the beings ceases" (ἀλλ' ἀσθενεῖ κατιόντα τὰ ὄντα, μέχρι πλημμελήσει καὶ παραχαράξει τὴν τάξιν, ἐν ᾧ καὶ τὸ εἶναι τῶν ὄντων παύεται, 97D–98A). Where existence leaves off, begins the material world of becoming. Synesius does not explicitly use this Platonic commonplace but implies it and makes plain that he uses τὸ εἶναι in the technical sense here when he immediately distinguishes "matters down here" (τὰ τῇδε) that work analogously.[130] Synesius likens the material world to the Aristotelian image of a marionette. His point is that it cannot move itself but sustains an external impulse for a while before running down; the image also implies the emphasis of his models, on the transmission of an impulse on one part so that it engenders movement throughout the whole.[131] Thus providential care extends through both worlds, with the souls the gods send down as their agents linking the two. Synesius integrates the concept of Providence into the Neoplatonic hierarchy of existence.[132]

It is now Osiris who is the gods' agent on earth, "performing a sort of public service for the cosmos" (99C; cf. 102A). The metaphor of *leitourgia* again recalls the mission of the luminous souls (89C). Care for the world taken by superior souls follows the sense of the classical term more closely than the service every soul undergoing incarnation performs to nature, as Synesius describes at De insomniis 139C, where he apparently echoes Porphyry.[133] Through these good souls Providence

129. For the fully articulated system of Proclus, Saffrey and Westerink helpfully provide diagrams (*Proclus: Théologie platonicienne*, vol. 1 [Paris 1968], lxv–lxxv).

130. Cf. 98B: "The lowest rank of beings (τῶν ὄντων) . . . seeps away and does not await true being (τὸ εἶναι) but mimics it with becoming (τῷ γίνεσθαι)."

131. Arist. *Gen.an.* 734b, 741b (αὐτόματα θαύματα); [Arist.] *Mund.* 398b (οἱ νευροσπάσται, as Synesius: τὰ νευρόσπαστα ὄργανα, *De providentia* 98B). Plato also uses the image of a puppet (θαῦμα θεῖον . . . παίγνιον, *Leg.* 644D–645B), but to describe conflicting, hence independent, impulses in human behavior.

132. Vollenweider (1985, 168–69) sees this as Synesius's most original contribution to the problem of Providence.

133. Porph. *Abst.* 4.18; without the verbal echo, also Syn. *Hymn* 1.573–77: cf. Smith 1974, 36–38.

equips humanity to fend off evil from itself (102B). A vivid simile punches Osiris's father's final warnings about Typhos: "Providence is not like the mother of a newborn infant, who must take pains to shoo away insects that might annoy her child, for it is still imperfect and unable to help itself. Rather, Providence is like that mother who, once she has raised and equipped her child, bids it use what it has, and keep evil away from itself" (102C).

Evil arises because "the demons are connate (συγγενῶν) with the nature of this world and have as their lot a destructive essence (ἀφανιστικὴν οὐσίαν)" (98B). That is, the weakness native to the world because of its distance from the "primal region" (97D–98A) has also to cope with an actively hostile force. The demons do not merely represent a further degeneration from the gods, for they are distinguished from the confused elements of the perishable world; they oppose the gods in a dualistic cosmos.

Such dualism was controversial among the later Platonists. Plutarch was one of its few proponents, and *De Iside et Osiride*, Synesius's major source for the myth underlying *De providentia*, is the work in which he most strongly identifies the forces of evil with demons.[134] The Chaldaean Oracles also present a doctrine of evil demons. H. Lewy supposes that Synesius's entire account of the demons' assault on a soul depends primarily on the Oracles, but his notes amply document parallels in Porphyry and later Neoplatonists.[135] But Synesius alludes to them specifically in the striking image of the demons as the "offshoots" of matter, which it stirs up to war against the soul.[136] Of course, demons were evil in Judeo-Christian thought and proliferated in the popular imagination as well,[137] but (though himself a Christian) Synesius shows no interest in these traditions.

Osiris easily fulfills the positive side of his mission. Unfortunately, he lacks the necessary severity to rid Egypt of his wicked brother. As the gods warn, this mildness proves his downfall. Typhos does indeed over-

---

134. Dillon 1977, 218; elsewhere Plutarch is more apt to view demons neutrally, as intermediate between gods and men in nature and capable of either good or evil interaction, e.g., *De def.or*, 416C–421E, esp. 418F–419A. The survey of *De Is. et Os.* 361A–C makes plain that he does not deny the possibility of good demons; but he emphasizes arguments for the existence of evil demons. See further Griffiths 1970, 20–28; G. Soury, *La démonologie de Plutarque* (Paris 1942).

135. Lewy (1956) 1978, 305–9. Synesius loosely refers to both singular (100A) and plural (100B) irrational part(s) of the soul, so that the absence of clear Platonic tripartition is no criterion for Chaldaean influence (cf. Lewy, 307 n. 182); in any case, tripartition was contested within the Platonic tradition by Plotinus (Blumenthal 1971, 20–30).

136. ὅταν εἰς πόλεμον ψυχῆς ὕλη κινήσῃ τὰ οἰκεῖα βλαστήματα, 99D; cf. κακῆς ὕλης βλαστήματα, *Chald.Or.* 88 Des Places; Syn. *Hymn* 5.51–55.

137. See, for example, MacMullen 1968, 81–96.

throw him and begins to "feast [the demons] on every kind of misfortune" (111C). At the end of book 1 (114D–115A) a god appears to Synesius's double within the tale and delivers a twin prophecy:

> "When," he said, "those who are now in power attempt to tamper with our religious rituals as well, then expect the Giants"—by this he meant the aliens—"to be driven out, themselves their own avenging Furies. But if any element of their faction should remain, if it should not be altogether destroyed, if Typhos himself should remain in his tyrant's palace, even so do not despair of the gods. This shall be another token for you. When with water and fire we purify the air about the earth, now defiled by the exhalation of the godless, then even upon those who remain shall justice come. Expect immediately a better dispensation upon Typhos's removal. For we drive out this sort of monster with fiery missiles and thunderbolts."

Two goals are promised, the removal first of the aliens and then of Typhos. The first will bring itself about, in the classic pattern of *ate* established in Greek tragedy since the fifth century B.C. The second seems to promise direct divine intervention, but in fact it is somewhat vaguer. At the conclusion of the book, the rustic philosopher looks forward to the action of Osiris's son Horus (115B). That is, he expects the gods to send a second good soul as their agent, who will make his own choices and repair the failure of Osiris: Horus's vengeance for his father is built into the myth. The intervention the gods postpone until "even those who use their minds and perceptions least might distinguish the better from the worse and pursue the former and turn aside from the latter" (112B) is assumed to take the identical form it had in Osiris. The only action the gods actually promise is meteorological—literally above the region of the earth. In its essential function, Providence still relies on human beings to resolve their affairs for themselves. It operates by the same mechanism throughout book 1.

But in real life Providence did not send a Horus figure to Constantinople. Synesius did not find a way to carry through his original conception of Providence. Instead, he saw barbarian soldiers expelled by "naked, unarmed, disheartened men who had not even a prayer of victory" (117A). In book 2 (116A, D) he shifts his ground and proclaims the rout and massacre a demonstration of an opposite type of Providence, in which everything depends on direct divine intervention:

> After this, the gods' attention began to be evident, since evil was everywhere, and belief in Providence had by now faded from the minds of men, their impious suspicions supported by the evidence of what they saw. . . . When our plans succeed, God seems superfluous and lays claim to a victory that is the result of preparation. But if no one inter-

venes to produce the result, and the invisible alone is the cause of victory, we have an unimpeachable refutation of those who do not believe that the gods care for mankind. This is precisely what happened.

Socrates too ascribes Gaïnas's fall to Providence. He mentions in passing the comet of the spring of 400 but focuses on two incidents.[138] First, when he claims Gaïnas had been planning to burn the palace: "Then indeed it appeared very clearly, how God was exercising Providence over the city. For a multitude of angels appeared to the plotters in the shape of massive soldiers. The barbarians, taking them to be in fact a large, brave army, were struck with fear and departed" (*HE* 6.6.18–19). Gaïnas at first refuses to believe his men's report, but the angels continue to appear. Eventually persuaded, he retreats from the city taking his barbarians and their concealed weapons with him and precipitating the riot and massacre. When the barbarians have retreated toward Thrace and are trying to cross the Chersonnese, "then again a marvelous work of the Providence of God was manifested" in the form of a contrary wind that wrecked the barbarians but smoothed the way of the Roman army attacking them (*HE* 6.6.31–33).

This line of interpretation may well have been suggested by official propaganda: a fragment of Eunapius records disapprovingly some panels placed in the hippodrome by the prefect "Perses," depicting "the hand of God driving off the barbarians" (see above, p. 218). To Eunapius's disgust, the representation clearly takes the victory away from human agency and assigns it to God alone. Set in a conspicuous public place by the prefect, the panels were obviously meant to promulgate the view of events the government preferred. And this verdict corresponds precisely to Synesius's view of the massacre. Synesius had his own reasons for presenting the massacre as a case of divine intervention, which came at least in part from the impossibility of assigning a favorable role in the expulsion to his hero or a new Horus. But it is interesting to note that the court took the same approach in commemorating the massacre, to diffuse remaining tensions by absolving the citizens and soldiers.

Providence is conceived quite differently in the two books. In book 1 Synesius carefully works out a system in which, despite some loose language in a conclusion meant to be emotionally stirring, the divine region remains decently separate from the earthly. The gap is bridged only by a few good souls, who "both are and are not of this place but are sent down from elsewhere" (98C). In book 2 Corybantes assault the Scythian

---

138. He assumes but does not stress the providential aspect of the omen, for him presaging the danger Constantinople faced (*HE* 6.6.15); cf. *De providentia* 114D–115A and p. 168 above.

general (116B).[139] "The gods, with difficulty, gradually brought [the Egyptians] to trust in events and, their courage restored, to choose to save themselves" (117C). "Someone, either a god or like a god," appears out of nowhere to save the old beggarwoman's life (118C). The gods and elders convene a joint synod to discuss what should be done about Typhos (122D). The gods' infusion of morale into the Egyptians is different from, but not necessarily irreconcilable with, the distant and mediated beneficence exerted in book 1; but Synesius's express declaration (116D) is supported by enough patent intervention that there can be no doubt but that they are freely meddling in human events.

The two books may be reconciled with reference to an emergency clause left in Osiris's father's exposition. The gods normally descend only at the regular intervals "when the harmony they established is growing slack and old" (102A). Then they come joyfully, as a "public service to the nature of the cosmos," to tune it up again and restore the motion they had previously imparted. But "when the harmony is ruined and broken through the weakness of its inheritors, when this world can be saved in no other way," they will act to preserve it. In book 2 they wait until the horrors of Typhos's rule purify every opinion of favor toward him before calling the synod (122D). But the synod takes no practical action. The manifest intervention of the massacre had already taken place without preconditions. Opinion is similarly unanimous at the election, and Synesius emphasizes the gods' miraculous presence (95B): the inauguration of a new luminous soul into temporal power apparently belongs to the gods' regular schedule. But no new soul appears in book 2. In short, the attempt to reconcile the positions is not satisfactory.

Synesius's circumstances had changed between the writing of the two books. When he was finishing book 1, the expulsion of the Goths had not affected Caesarius's rule, and he could still hope that Caesarius would soon fall and that his successor would renew Aurelian's policies. By the time he wrote book 2, he could see that despite Aurelian's return Caesarius was more entrenched than ever. To salvage his story and give the appearance of a significant political change, he drastically changes his philosophical position.

The third Neoplatonic problem of *De providentia* was introduced in order to support an essentially frivolous literary conceit. Synesius claims that he is presenting a story of tremendous antiquity. Recognizing elements of genuinely ancient myth in his allegory of contemporary politics, his audience could confirm from its own knowledge that he accu-

---

139. πανικοὶ θόρυβοι afflicting the troops may also suggest attacks by Pan.

rately represented the past; of course, the authentic details were meant to carry the inauthentic residual along with them into credence. Synesius now addresses literary plausibility from the opposite direction: "The same things very often happen in different places and times, and as they age men become spectators of the things they heard of as boys, either from books or from their grandfathers" (127A–B). This proposition is resolved by reference to the interconnectedness of the cosmos, a principle underlying his analogy of the material world to a marionette at 98B. Since its parts are all connected, they will act upon one another. Therefore, "we may logically identify the blessed body that moves in a circle as the cause of the things of the world" (127C). That which enjoys motion of its own will impart it to inert matter. A similar phrase at *De dono* 310D identifies the blessed body as the heavens. Long traditions of cosmological speculation come into question, along with their myriad implications. One classic expression of the revolving cosmos is the same passage of Plato's *Phaedrus* from which Synesius borrowed the image "the back of heaven," the source of luminous souls:[140] Plato uses it to describe where good souls stand who have escaped the circle of the earth and are carried around its revolutions viewing the heavens. Synesius invokes the internal sympathy of the cosmos in *De insomniis* to argue the validity of divination (132B). His present concern with the interconnected, revolving system is "that when the same movements recur, the effects recur along with the causes, and that lives on earth now are the same as those of old, and so are births, upbringings, intellects, and fortunes" (127D). The "appointed times" at which the gods are said in book 1 to come to restore the motion of the earth (101D) already suggests some notion of temporal cycles. Synesius does not wrestle with detailed implications of recurrence, as did more analytical authors,[141] but avoids precision. He introduces the problem with the claim that incidents recur from within the memory of three generations; now he speaks of "ancient history (παμπάλαιον ἱστορίαν) come to life again" over a period of several months (128A). Both "simple" and "complex" illustrations recur. Apparently the complexity of the heavens (cf. *De dono* 313B–C) allows for a level of variation, even when the fundamental structure of events repeats. Men must "pore over" (συγκύψουσιν) the Egyptian tales and make uncertain guesses at what the correspondences portend.[142] "History and myth do not entirely agree with one another." But the particulars of recent events authorize their reflections in the story: for example,

140. Pl. *Phdr.* 247C; Syn. *De providentia* 89C.

141. For a survey, see R. Sorabji, *Time, Creation and the Continuum* (London 1983), 182–90.

142. εἰκάσει δὲ ἄλλος ἄλλο, 128A.

the audience will have no difficulty in recognizing "the younger brother" (90A) as Osiris, because Aurelian was Caesarius's younger brother in reality. The more precise the contemporary details, the more accurate the story appears—and that appearance of accuracy is extended to the image of the past as well if reality and narrative are identified. By this means Synesius suggests that the personalities, attitudes, and interpretations within the narrative reflect current reality as well. The doctrine of recurrence encourages the audience to accept his direction in contemporary opinion. The story is validated in contradictory ways both by authentic Egyptiana and by authentic contemporary details, and it is claimed to be predictive. The literary device rolls with enough subtlety to exert its influence on the casual reader, but it will not sustain rational analysis: Synesius is burning his myth at both ends. He overtly claims foreshadowing but attempts tacit exhortation.

VI. ORACLES AND APOCALYPSE

The Chaldaean Oracles were not the only occult writings that Synesius read and exploited in his own work. We have already seen that Hypatia's father, Theon, wrote "commentaries on the books of Hermes Trismegistus and Orpheus." [143] Given Theon's astronomical interests, we may probably assume that these were astrological Hermetica rather than the better-known philosophical corpus. [144] If Theon commented on Hermetic writings we can hardly doubt that Hypatia and, through her, Synesius had some knowledge of them. It is true that Synesius nowhere directly quotes them, but with the exception of Iamblichus's De mysteriis, written under the pseudonym of an Egyptian priest, in general "the Neoplatonists paid little attention to the Hermetica." [145] They were not after all of much philosophical interest, [146] and they could not compete as inspired books with the Chaldaean Oracles. But at Dion 51B Synesius

143. Malalas, p. 343B = p. 186 Aus.

144. So Nock in Nock and Festugière 1945–54, IV.148, no. 2; Fowden 1986, 178. On the other hand, according to Festugière (1950, 4), "ce devaient être des logoi philosophiques (car on ne peut guère songer à des ouvrages d'astrologie) et il est important de noter que, dès le IVe siècle, ceux-ci servaient de 'textbook' dans les écoles." On astrological Hermetica (not yet published as a corpus) see Festugière 1950, 89f.; they are widely quoted by astrological writers (e.g., Firmicus Maternus, Paul of Alexandria, the Anonymus of 379) before or within the lifetime of Theon.

145. W. Scott, Hermetica, vol. 1 (1924), 95–96.

146. "Few leading intellectuals, either Christian or pagan, took the philosophical Hermetica seriously as doctrinal statements. . . . Even Iamblichus treats the Hermetica as important not so much for their own sake as because they were part of the Egyptian foundations of theurgy" (Fowden 1986, 200–201).

gives a list of four sages: Amous (presumably Amoun, the founder of Nitrian monasticism),[147] Antony (the first hermit), Zoroaster, and Hermes.[148] Writers of the age often associated Zoroaster with Hermes Trismegistus,[149] and there can be no doubt that this is the Hermes to whom Synesius here alludes. Paradoxically enough, it was the Christians who paid most attention to the Hermetica in late fourth- and early fifth-century Alexandria. Not doubting that Trismegistus, like Orpheus and the Sibyl, was a genuine prophet who lived many centuries before Christ, men like Didymus the Blind,[150] who died in 398, and above all Cyril, patriarch of Alexandria from 412 to 444,[151] eagerly exploited oracles and prophecies that they interpreted as foretelling Christianity.[152] This attitude continued to prevail after their rediscovery in the Renaissance. It was because they were still being exploited by Cardinal Baronio as pagan foreshadowings of divine revelation that the Protestant Casaubon sought to demolish their credentials.[153] Among secular (not necessarily pagan) writers of Synesius's day the astrologer Paul of Alexandria might be mentioned.[154] In such an atmosphere, and given his own enthusiasm for both philosophy and Egyptiana, it would be surprising if Synesius had not shared this interest.

Above all, his thoughts are sure to have turned to the Hermetica when searching for Egyptian color for a myth set in the age of Osiris.[155]

---

147. See the discussion in Treu 1958, 78–79, 90–91. Fowden (1986, 179; cf. 32 n. 115) identifies Ammon with the apocryphal king Ammon who appears as interlocutor in a number of Hermetic dialogues (cf. Nock and Festugière 1945–54 on *Corpus Hermeticum* 16, II.228).

148. Hermes regularly appears in such lists of sages in late antique writers: for a selection, see Fowden 1986, 28. The conjunction of these four names seems less surprising after the discovery of the Nag Hammadi texts, which have revealed both Zoroastrian and Hermetic texts in a library that evidently belonged to a distant disciple of Amoun and Antony.

149. J. Bidez and F. Cumont, *Les mages hellénisés: Zoroastre, Ostanès et Hystaspe d'après la tradition grecque* (Paris 1938), II.34–35, 86, 243. See too Fowden 1986, 202–3. A passage of Psellus links Zoroaster and "Ammous the Egyptian" (Bidez-Cumont, II.140). If Synesius were really the author of the commentary on Ps.-Democritus discussed above, we might have expected him to name Ostanes here rather than Zoroaster: cf. Bidez-Cumont, I.202.

150. Fowden 1986, 179–80; the testimonia are quoted *in extenso* by W. Scott and A. S. Ferguson, *Hermetica* (Oxford 1924–36), IV.168–76.

151. Fowden 1986, 180–82; Scott-Ferguson, IV.191–227.

152. Among Latin writers, both Lactantius (R. M. Ogilvie, *The Library of Lactantius* [Oxford 1978], 33–36; Fowden 1986, 209–10) and Augustine (Fowden, 209–10) interpreted the prophecy in the *Perfect Discourse* as predicting the victory of Christianity.

153. As well brought out by Grafton 1983, 78–93.

154. W. Gundel, *RE* 18.4 (1949): 2376, on the late fourth-century date; on Hermetic influence, Festugière 1950, 105, 112.

155. Vollenweider (1985a, 168) briefly suggests some Hermetic influence on *De providentia*, but he is more concerned with Synesius's philosophical sources and does not con-

After all, Hermes did play a part in the drama of Osiris.[156] The typical
Hermetic dialogue consists of Hermes communicating arcane wisdom to
his son Tat or Asclepius or King Ammon. In another series, known as
the *Kore kosmou,* Isis instructs her son Horus, and we have a fragment
from what was presumably another series in which, as in Synesius, it is
Osiris himself who is instructed, by "the great Agathodaimon."[157] The
subject matter is normally the nature of the universe, the soul, or the
gods, and there is frequent emphasis on the need for secrecy and silence.[158] In a passage of the *Kore kosmou* reminiscent of Synesius's account of Osiris's benefits to mankind, Isis describes to Horus how God
"bestowed on the earth for a little time your great father Osiris and the
great goddess Isis" and how they "filled human life with that which is
divine . . . consecrated temples and instituted sacrifices . . . and gave to
mortal men the boons of food and shelter."[159] A fascinating chapter by
Festugière quotes scores of examples from occult writings of this motif
of the sage instructing the king, who is often also his son.[160]

The same motif can also be found in less arcane genres: for example,
in panegyric Claudian portrays Theodosius lecturing Honorius on the
duties of kingship.[161] The traditional motifs of Greek kingship literature
appear with many and striking similarities in this speech and in Synesius's *De regno* and are stitched more subtly into the narrative fabric of
De providentia. But Synesius had no reason to repeat a discussion of the
practical aspects of rulership.[162] The military motifs, in particular, would
have been inappropriate for the real-life civilian counterpart of his

sider the apocalyptic tradition. Fowden (*CP* 80 [1985]: 284) briefly suggests Hermetic influences for *Hymn* 9 (1).

156. Hermes' part is somewhat understated by Plutarch: see Boylan 1922, 11–48.

157. Frag. 31 Scott = IV.137–38 Nock-Festugière (from Cyril *Adv. Jul., PG* 76.588A).
On Agathodaimon, who plays a large role in the magic papyri and other occult writings,
see Ganschinietz, *RE* Suppl. 3 (1918): 37–59; Festugière in Nock and Festugière 1945–54, I,
p. 135 n. 75, and III, clxvf.; W. Fauth, *Kl.Pauly* 1:121–22. There are also alchemical tracts
that purport to be the instructions Isis gave Horus before he set out to depose Typhos:
Berthelot and Ruelle 1888, 28f., 33f.

158. Festugière 1950, 354.

159. Stob. *Exc.* 23.64–65, I.490–92 Scott. Civilization (generally featuring agriculture,
religion, and law) as the gift of the gods was a Greek commonplace, well represented in
Greek Egyptiana too: compare, for example, Plut. *De Is. et Os.* 356A–B and Diod. 1.17.1f.,
where, as in Synesius, the benefactions are reported in narrative.

160. Festugière 1950, 324–54. To this dossier may now be added the new Hermetic
dialogue found at Nag Hammadi, apparently called *The Ogdoad Reveals the Ennead* (cod.
VI.6). The ps.-Synesian alchemical tract too might loosely be described as a Hermetic dialogue, since it quotes Hermes and communicates the skills of the craft to a disciple.

161. *IV Cons.Hon.* 320–52.

162. He does repeat the motifs concerning statues of Hermes and the Sphinx (101C;
cf. *De regno* 7B–C) but focuses on their mystical significance.

Osiris. Moreover, he wanted at some point to set forth the philosophical underpinning of his tale, the operation of divine Providence. What better place than artistically incorporated as a speech of one of his characters, especially from the old king to the new at the moment of their transition, Osiris's initiation, incorporating warnings that Osiris later ignores to his cost? The setting nicely corresponds to the Hermetic pattern Festugière calls the *traditio mystica*. Like Horus in the *Kore kosmou*,[163] Synesius's Osiris is given secret information about the nature of kingly souls and the role of gods and demons respectively in human affairs.

Hermetic treatises too share the designation Synesius applies to his work, a "sacred tale."[164] Generally reminiscent of the Egyptian Hermes himself is the uncertainty whether the old king is man or god, and the portrayal of him as above all things a sage. More specifically, in *Kore kosmou* 6 Isis describes how, having passed his arcane wisdom on to his son Tat,[165] Hermes ascended to the stars to attend on the gods, just as the old king does in *De providentia* 102D.[166] We have already shown that Synesius drew on other traditions that also contain these elements, but their coincidence here also fits in with more profoundly significant Hermetic details.

In general we may be sure that it was not so much the doctrines of the Hermetica that attracted Synesius as the Egyptian setting. But there is one particular Hermetic text that had a deeper influence on *De providentia*: the prophecy of doom and destruction for Egypt in sections 24–26 of the *Perfect Discourse*, of which we have only fragments in the original Greek but a complete, if rather free, Latin translation known as *Asclepius* and now an earlier and more accurate version of sections 21–29 in Coptic.[167]

But it makes little sense to discuss this prophecy without first con-

163. Stob. *Exc.* 24 (I.495f. Scott = IV.52f. Nock-Festugière).

164. Fowden 1986, 158, and pp. 267–68 above.

165. I.459 Scott = IV.2 Nock-Festugière.

166. Fowden characterizes Hermes as "a mortal who receives revelations from the divine world and eventually himself achieves immortality . . . but remains among men in order to unveil to them the secrets of the divine world" (1986, 28; for a more detailed account, see Festugière in Nock and Festugière 1945–54, III.cxxxviff.). On the ambiguous status of the Egyptian kings generally, cf. Hdt. 2.144; Diod. 1.90.3; Plut. *De Is. et Os.* 354B; Pl. *Plt.* 290D–E; Griffiths 1965, 156f. Divinization is also a goal of Chaldaean theurgy. Unlike the Hermetic revelations, the arcana revealed to Osiris in *De providentia* have to do with his management of human affairs as the gods' agent on earth, according to a Neoplatonic scheme of Providence.

167. For the Latin text and Greek fragments, Nock and Festugière 1945–54, II.259–401 (Scott's willful transpositions and alterations render his text virtually unusable); for the Coptic translation, J.-P. Mahé, *Hermès en Haute-Egypte*, vol. 2 (Quebec 1982), with elaborate introduction and commentary.

sidering an earlier text that inspired it and perhaps Synesius too, the so-called Oracle of the Potter. This curious prophecy, itself inspired by the earlier Oracle of the Lamb and ultimately the Twelfth Dynasty Oracle of Neferty,[168] purports to have been given to Pharaoh Amenophis but is evidently Ptolemaic since what it prophesies is the departure of the Greeks from Egypt and the restoration of the old capital of Memphis.[169] It has a number of points in common with *De providentia:* the Greeks are described as foreigners, they are followers of Typhos, and they have interfered with the religion of the Egyptians. The Potter prophesies every sort of destruction for Egypt until Isis installs a new king, that is to say, Horus, under whom all will be well again. While the Egyptian author looks forward to the day when the Greeks will be gone, like Synesius, he is not clear how it will happen. Indeed by the second and third centuries A.D., the date of all extant versions of the Potter's Oracle, the idea of a native king who would drive out the Romans was inconceivable. By then, as Ludwig Koenen put it, "readers must have understood the oracle in apocalyptic terms."

The prophecy in the *Perfect Discourse,* probably of the third century,[170] is clearly in the same tradition,[171] with one or two differences of emphasis. Hermes foretells a time of great tribulations, once again caused by foreign invaders. The term used in the Latin version is *alienigenae,* but the Coptic reveals what must have stood in the Greek original, ἀλλόφυλοι,[172] the same word Synesius uses in 94A and 108B. The em-

168. On the Oracle of the Lamb, see most recently J. G. Griffiths, in *Apocalypticism,* ed. J. Assmann (1983), 285–87; L. Koenen, *Codex Manichaicus Coloniensis,* ed. L. Cirillo and A. Roselli (Cosenza 1986), 315–17. On the Jewish apocalyptic from Egypt, see J. J. Collins, *The Sibylline Oracles of Egyptian Judaism* (Missoula, Mont. 1974). On the Twelfth Dynasty Oracle, see J. B. Pritchard, *Ancient Near Eastern Texts,* 3d ed. (Princeton 1969), 444–46; Assmann, *Apocalypticism,* 357–61 ("Vorbild für alle späteren politischen Chaosbeschreibungen bis hin zum Töpferorakel"); Koenen 1986, 314–15.

169. All three papyri of the Oracle are edited together by L. Koenen in *ZPE* 2 (1968): 178–209, with later corrections and additions in *ZPE* 3 (1968): 137; 13 (1974): 313–19; 54 (1984): 9–13; see too J. G. Griffiths and J. Assmann in *Apocalypticism* (1983), 287–90 and 362–64; and Koenen in *Cod.Man.Col.,* 317f.; the fullest recent discussion, stressing both its Egyptian roots and its influence on the *Perfect Discourse,* is F. Dunand in *L'apocalyptique* (Paris 1977), 41–67.

170. This very passage is quoted by Lactantius, as underlined by Fowden 1986, 38–39. It follows that the reference to proscription of the old cults cannot (as usually supposed) allude to the antipagan legislation of Theodosius (so rightly Fowden). Scott (1924, 1:66–76) argued that the writer was alluding to the brief Palmyrene occupation of Egypt in 268–73, on which see further n. 192 below.

171. As underlined in the various discussions cited by Fowden 1986, 38; see especially Dunand 1977, 57–60; and Koenen 1986, 318.

172. Mahé 1982, 173, 1.21. At Mahé, p. 177.28, where the Latin has *alienus,* the Coptic again gives ἀλλόφυλος.

phasis falls much more strongly on religion: the piety of the Egyptians will have been in vain; the invaders will proscribe and persecute their faith. There is no mention of Typhos;[173] instead it is some "evil angels" (like Synesius's demons) who will occupy Egypt once the old gods have gone.[174] The invaders are identified as "Scythian or Indian or someone of that sort, that is to say, from the neighborhood of Barbary."[175] Once again, the prophet's purpose is eschatological. This is the "old age of the world"; when all the destruction is over, out of his great goodness God "will restore the world to its former beauty."

The reason no one has perceived the relevance of these earlier apocalyptic prophecies to Synesius before is because no one has perceived that *De providentia* is itself cast in the form of an apocalypse. And this is because no one has taken seriously enough Synesius's explicit statement that the original conception of the work extended only to book 1. In its original form *De providentia* closed on the climax of an apocalyptic prophecy.

At 114C a god appears to the rustic stranger and tells him that "not years but months make up the allotted time during which the scepters of Egypt will lift up the claws of the wild beasts and hold down the crests of the sacred birds." The philosopher recognizes this as a prophecy "engraved on obelisks and sacred precincts" (a traditional device for claiming authority for prophecies and magical spells),[176] and the god "gives him a key to the time." Then follows the sequence of *post eventum* prophecies of the Gothic massacre already examined. The portentous, riddling language skillfully imitates the style of apocalyptic.

It would in any case be a reasonable assumption that Synesius was familiar with the main themes of apocalypse. But there is in addition a curious allusion in the letter he wrote his brother just before leaving Cyrene on his visit to Athens: "Many people here, both priests and lay-

173. The Potter's standard term is Τυφώνιοι, which (in the sense "evil") seems not to be attested elsewhere—except in the Hermetic S.E. 25.8. Festugière's useful note ad loc. (Nock and Festugière 1945–54, IV.77, n. 23) misses this, the only parallel.

174. "Evil angels": *nocentes angeli* in the Latin; the text is badly damaged in the Coptic, but what traces there are support ἄγγελοι.

175. "inhabitabit Aegyptum Scythes aut Indus aut aliquis talis, id est vicina barbaria." On the final phrase, missing in the Coptic, see further n. 192.

176. For example, King Amenophis had the Oracle of the Potter inscribed ἐν ἱεροῖς ταμείοις (P² 52, ed. Koenen 1968a, 208; cf. P¹ 33 and 40), obviously so that men would be able to recognize, as Synesius's rustic philosopher professes to recognize, when it was finally fulfilled. Cf. Iambl. *Myst*. 268.1–2; *Kore kosmou* 66 (Nock-Festugière IV.21), with Festugière 1950, 319–24; to which we may now add *The Ogdoad Reveals the Ennead*, in which Hermes tells Tat to engrave their dialogue in hieroglyphics on turquoise stelae in his temple at Thebes (*The Nag Hammadi Library*, ed. J. M. Robinson [1981], 286; cf. Fowden 1986, 35; 66 n. 84).

men, are concocting various visions (ὀνείρους), which they call apocalypses (ἀποκαλύψεις); it looks as if they will bring me trouble in earnest
unless I go to Athens as soon as possible" (*Ep.* 54 = 56G).[177] He does not
say what this "trouble" is (most probably the threat that he will be
offered the bishopric of Ptolemais),[178] but evidently friends both lay and
ecclesiastical have been presenting him with plans for the future that he
finds frightening. All that is relevant here is the way he represents this
as "dreams, which they call apocalypses." This is not a casual analogy;
most apocalypses take the form of dreams or visions. Moreover, this
seems to be the only known metaphorical use of the term and the only
occurrence outside explicit references to specific Jewish or Christian
apocalypses. As Jerome put it, "the word itself . . . is restricted to the
scriptures and not used by any secular Greek writer."[179]

De providentia 96A suggests knowledge of the *Testament of Solomon*, a
mildly apocalyptic work that is at the same time a veritable textbook of
magic and demonology.[180] At 114C the god starts straight off with wild
beasts' claws, unmistakably evoking the brazen claws of the fourth and
most terrifying beast in the Book of Daniel.[181] The "fiery missiles and
thunderbolts" of 115A resemble the natural cataclysms of apocalyptic
more closely than the comet of April 400 to which they actually refer.[182]
And while standard invective tactics compare Goths to Giants (114D),[183]
giants are also standard denizens of apocalyptic.[184] It is also characteristic of the genre that the prophet announces how long it will be before his
prophecy is fulfilled. In contrast to the Lamb's 900 years, Synesius's god
reassuringly promises that Typhos will fall before the year is out.

Like a typical apocalypse, the entire final section of book 1 is presented in the form of a revelation to the narrator by a god, concluding, as
apocalypses often do, with a riddle: all will be well when Horus allies
himself with the wolf instead of the lion. Modern scholars have ex-

177. See further appendix 3.
178. So Liebeschuetz 1985b, 149.
179. "verbum quoque ipsum ἀποκαλύψεως, id est revelationis, proprie scripturarum
est et a nullo sapientium saeculi apud Graecos usurpatum," *Ad Galatas* i.1 (*PL* 26.347C);
cf. A. Momigliano, *Ottavo contributo* (Rome 1987), 212.
180. Cameron, Long, Sherry 1988, 55–56; on apocalyptic elements in the *Test. Sol.*,
see C. C. McCown, *The Testament of Solomon* (Leipzig 1922), 49–50; for a history of the *Testament*'s development and circulation, see E. Schürer, *History of the Jewish People in the Age of
Jesus Christ*, rev. G. Vermes, F. Millar, and M. Goodman, vol. 3.1 (1986), 372–79.
181. Dan. 7.7 and 19.
182. For meteorological predictions (comets, thunderbolts, etc.) see J. H. Charlesworth, *Old Testament Pseudepigrapha*, vol. 1 (1983), 293 (Enoch), and 345–46 (Sib.Or. 2).
183. So, for example, Claudian during these same years: Cameron 1970a, 468.
184. Charlesworth 1983, 106 n. i (4 Esra, Gospel of Eve, 2 Enoch).

pended much ingenuity in the attempt to decipher this riddle. It should by now be clear that Synesius's purpose was to present his readers with an enigma that they could *not* solve. In the Egyptian context, it went without saying that every apocalyptic deliverer was identified as Horus.

By the mere fact of setting his myth in the remote past, Synesius automatically created the potential for apocalyptic prophecy. It was, after all, standard apocalyptic technique for the writer to retroject *post eventum* prophecies from contemporary events into a much earlier dramatic date. Even before the final chapter of book 1 unnamed gods warn Osiris of his brother's evil intentions; the prophecy was clearly destined to be fulfilled before the book is finished. Indeed, much of the structure and technique of book 1 conforms closely to an apocalypse.

Of course, since Synesius made no secret of the fact that he was the author, no contemporary reader was likely to be deceived into believing that the prophecies he incorporates were genuinely written in the age of Osiris, covering events of about A.D. 400. Synesius's purpose was political rather than apocalyptic: he wanted to suggest that Typhos's regime would soon collapse, in the near rather than the remote future. At the time he wrote there had already been encouraging signs, most notably the massacre, but naturally he did not know when and how the final moment would come. He skillfully erected a series of apocalyptic revelations, all but the last stage already fulfilled in fact.

It is not surprising that he should also have adapted specific motifs from two such familiar specimens of the Egyptian tradition as the Oracle of the Potter and the Hermetic prophecy in the *Perfect Discourse*.[185] Hermes prophesies troubles that spring from the destruction and persecution of Egyptian religion. This emphasis, already present in the Potter,[186] is matched exactly by Synesius's emphasis on the attempt of his own foreigners, the Goths, to pervert the religion of the Egyptians. This is the very first "sign" the god gives the rustic stranger: "When those who are now in power attempt to tamper with our religious rituals as well, then expect the Giants"—by this he meant the aliens—"soon to be driven out, themselves their own avenging Furies (ποινηλατουμένους ὑφ᾽ ἑαυτῶν)." In the best apocalyptic style Synesius disguises the Goths as Giants and refers to their coming fate in riddling terms. They fit the Oracle of the

---

185. It is open to question how many of his listeners and readers in Constantinople picked up these allusions.

186. And also in the Jewish oracle adapted from the Potter's Oracle, *Corp. Pap. Jud.* III.520, where Koenen's restorations on the basis of the Potter (*Gnomon* 40 [1968]: 256) are confirmed by a new version on an unpublished Oxyrhynchus papyrus (information from Koenen).

Potter better than the actual circumstances of the Gothic massacre: "They will destroy themselves, for they are followers of Typhos." [187] After receiving the prophecy, the rustic philosopher "pondered how these things could happen, but it seemed beyond his powers to understand" (115B). He is at once enlightened: "Not long after there arose a false piece of religious observance . . . something ancient law bars from the cities, shutting the impiety outside the gates" (115B). Of course this false observance refers to Gaïnas's request for an Arian church, which was turned down and did not play any direct part in the events that led to the massacre. But Synesius nonetheless brilliantly exploits this providentially "impious" act of his foreigners to shape his narrative in conformity with the apocalyptic tradition.

There may be one more example of this apocalyptic shaping. The Hermetic prophecy suggests that the impious foreigners might be Scythians. Synesius's foreigners are also Scythians. There is a puzzle here that has not so far attracted attention. Like Hermes, Synesius uses the imprecise ἀλλόφυλοι for his first two references (94A, 108B), but thereafter he regularly calls them "Scythians." [188] Given his political purpose, it was inevitable that he should introduce Goths into the tale of Typhos and Osiris in one guise or another. "Scythian" was the standard archaizing equivalent for Goths in the high style of the age;[189] Synesius used the term himself in De regno (22C, 23D). But its currency made it no less anachronistic than "Goth" in the Egyptian setting of the myth. We might have expected an appropriately Egyptianizing disguise. Since Plutarch mentions Queen Aso of the Ethiopians among Typhos's band of conspirators,[190] why not Ethiopians? The more so since Ethiopians were often cast in this very role—for example, in the third and fifth Sibylline Oracles. Ethiopia is identified with Gog and Magog in the third Sibylline, a choice probably determined "by the traditional enmity of Egypt and Ethiopia." [191]

But Synesius does not disguise his Goths with an Egyptianizing

187. P² 28 and P³ 50, ed. Koenen 1968a, 204–5. Since the Potter can no longer hold out the promise of a native deliverer, he feebly concludes with the assertion that the Greeks will bring about their own downfall, presumably by internal conflicts. Obviously Synesius cannot hold out any comparable promise, though the opening chapter of book 2 does make much of the alleged panic of the Goths before the massacre.

188. E.g., 108D, 109D, 110C, 117D, 118B–D, 119D, 120B, 122B, in both books.

189. It is the invariable term in Themistius and Zosimus, for example, two writers who have occasion to refer often to Goths. See Wolfram 1988, 28; cf. 11.

190. De Is. et Os. 356B, 366C.

191. J. J. Collins, The Sibylline Oracles of Egyptian Judaism (Missoula, Mont. 1974), 79–80: their "geographical remoteness . . . made them particularly apt for the role of eschatological enemies who would come from the ends of the earth."

name; alone of his dramatis personae they are simply introduced from history into the myth. We can hardly assume mere inadvertence. Nor can it have been anxiety that his readers would miss the point, since the key is supplied early on at 108B, where the "general of the foreigners" who "had a house in the royal city" was away, "waging an unsuccessful war against a rebellious band of their own people." With so precise an allusion to Gaïnas, the identification of the "foreigners" was clearly established.

Why was Synesius so reluctant to fit his Goths to his Egyptian context? The answer is perhaps to be found in the Hermetic prophecy. Its suggestion that the invading foreigners might be Scythians legitimated the ethnic for Synesius's own purposes. We may never know why the unknown author of the Oracle picked this name;[192] at the time it must have seemed an improbable prediction that Scythians would conquer Egypt. And yet this is precisely what happened in A.D. 400, at least as transposed into Synesius's allegory. Thus the fashionable literary style for Goths was transformed into an elegant apocalyptic double entendre, hinting at Armageddon.

Book 1 of *De providentia* is an ambitious and sophisticated piece of work. Synesius indirectly signals its artistry in the preface, when he marks its original limits. The cobbling on of book 2 has obscured the craftsmanship and coherence of the whole. For example, it would be

---

192. In less exotic sources, Scythians number among the peoples conquered by Sesostris (Hdt. 2.103, 110). According to Nock and Festugière (1945–54, II.380, n. 209), "l'association 'Indiens-Scythes' paraît être devenue une banalité littéraire, cf. Horat. *Carm. saecul.* 55: *jam Scythae responsa petunt superbi / nuper et Indi; Od.* 4.14.40: *Te Cantaber non ante domabilis / Medusque et Indus, te profugus Scythes / miratur"* (so too Mahé 1982, 233). But can two passages of Horace really explain a prose oracle written two centuries later in Egypt? If Scott (1924, 1:65–76) was right in his suggestion that the oracle was inspired by the Palmyrene invasion of Egypt in 268–73, it may be suggested that Scythia is in fact what the Greeks called Indo-Scythia, on the Indus Delta (Ptolemy 7.1.55 and 62), also known as just Scythia (*Periplus Maris Erythraei* 38, with B. Fabricius, *Periplus des Erythräischen Meeres* [1883], 149; cf. W. W. Tarn, *The Greeks in Bactria and India*, 2d ed. [1950], 232–33; L. Casson, *The Periplus Maris Erythraei* [Princeton 1989], 186, with map on p. 225). Though far beyond the normal horizons of the Greco-Roman world, this Scythia was familiar to the Palmyrenes (J. Starcky, *Inventaire des inscriptions de Palmyre*, vol. 10, *L'Agora* [Damascus 1949], 59, no. 96; *SEG* vii.156, with Matthews 1984, 166). It is tantalizing that the phrase *id est vicina barbaria* is missing from the Coptic. If we could be sure that it stood in the Greek original, it could be argued that *Barbaria* was being used in the specialized, but well-documented, sense of "the coastal areas of the Arabian Sea and Gulf" (G. W. Bowersock in *Bahrain through the Ages: The Archaeology*, ed. Shaikha Haya Ali Al Khalifa and M. Rice [1986], 404, citing *Periplus* 5, 7, 12; and especially Steph. Byz., s.v. βάρβαρος· ἔστι δὲ χώρα παρὰ τὸν Ἀράβιον κόλπον βαρβαρία, ἀφ' οὗ καὶ Βαρβαρικὸν πέλαγος). It could then be held that the Oracle was designating Palmyra obliquely (in the manner of oracles), through the farthest outreaches of its empire.

easy to assume that the subtitle *On Providence* referred to the obvious divine intervention alleged in the massacre and trial of book 2. But in fact Providence is a far more important concept in book 1. Indeed it is central to the book, underpinning every stage of the narrative, from the descent of Osiris as the gods' agent for the care of the material world to their attempt to warn him against the destructive powers of matter embodied in Typhos to the rustic philosopher's expectation of Horus, who will come to repair Osiris's failure and renew his mission. This carefully developed system reconciles the transcendentalism of the Neoplatonic divine hierarchy with affirmation of the forces that hold the whole together, even to the farthest reaches of matter. It also skillfully exploits the data of the myth in terms that can reasonably be applied to contemporary politics. The whole is decked out with Egyptian coloring that lends it a harmonious and authentic tone; and it is framed in an apocalyptic structure that epitomizes both Egyptian traditions and political expectations. Echoes of the political oratory of Dio Chrysostom point the relevance of the allegory to contemporary affairs.

Book 2 in contrast banalizes Providence or at any rate introduces problems into the philosophical system so carefully elaborated in book 1. It also violates the myth and the apocalyptic expectations it naturally aroused. Those same circumstances that at the end of book 1 Synesius had found merely promising, he now was obliged to proclaim the ultimate vindication, the direct result of divine intervention. He had to fall back on the framework of panegyric, glossing over Osiris's failure with fulsome appeals to the impenetrability of mystery.

EIGHT

BARBARIANS AND POLITICS

I. GREEKS AND ROMANS

> *Perhaps this story, even though it is only a story,*
> *might hint at something more.*
> (*De providentia* 88B)

Dagron has suggested a profounder motive behind Synesius's choice of a myth of two brothers opposed in every way. *De providentia* is for him not only a straightforward roman à clef of the events of 400, but also a much more ambitious allegory of the division of the Roman Empire, Osiris representing the East and Typhos the West.

Dagron focused on the issue of language. For centuries, Greek and Latin had coexisted in the Roman Empire with clearly delimited roles: as he put it, "le latin est la langue du pouvoir . . . le grec est la langue de la culture."[1] This distinction and the equilibrium he saw it as maintaining were upset by the shift of political gravity to the East under Diocletian and Constantine, consolidated under Theodosius; particularly decisive was the rapid growth of Constantinople, a Greek city that became a genuine political capital. In its ambit, the *provinciae orientales* turned into the *pars orientalis*. Ambitious Greeks learned Latin and flocked into the imperial bureaucracy. Greek intellectuals were hostile to such tenden-

---

1. "Aux origines de la civilisation byzantine: Langue de culture et langue d'état," *Revue historique* 241 (1969): 23–56, at p. 25.

cies, as indeed they were to Constantinople itself. The conflict of culture
and power in a unified realm Dagron saw epitomized in Julian, philhellene but also "most Roman of emperors."[2]

This situation (he claims) was profoundly changed by the effective
division of the empire following the death of Theodosius in 395. Gone
was "the fiction of a single empire ruled by a pair of emperors and a
double capital."[3] In the East, Dagron saw political crisis accompanied by
a cultural upheaval, the "Nationalist crisis." This upheaval (he believes)
stands reflected in Synesius's *De regno* and *De providentia*.

According to Dagron, in *De regno* the political presuppositions are
entirely traditional: Greek cities appeal to a Roman emperor, who is responsible for administration and defense. In *De providentia*, however, he
saw a "Hellenic" interpretation of the division of the empire. The problem posed is the succession to a good king whose death precipitates a
crisis. He leaves behind him two sons of very different character. The
two brothers symbolize the two halves (*partes*) of the empire, Typhos as
the elder representing the West, and Osiris the East. Hereditary succession would have given Typhos the throne; which is to say that historical
continuity would have given seniority to the West. But instead the decision between them was made on the basis of their natural qualities, with
the result that the younger brother Osiris was chosen: that is to say, the
Eastern court declared itself the sole legatee of the entire Roman Empire.

This bold hypothesis calls forth reservations at many different levels.
In the first place, Dagron goes far beyond the text of *De regno* in reading
into it signs of the reciprocal "contract" between Greek cities and Roman emperor put forward in Aelius Aristeides' *Roman Oration*.[4] The
speech gives Synesius's mission as the delivery of crown gold (2C), but
crown gold had long ceased to be a distinctively Greek tribute.[5] Synesius
calls Cyrene not merely "a Greek city," but one "of ancient and lofty
name, in countless songs of the wise men of old" (2C–D): his emphasis
is on its venerability. He does not connect the intellectualism of his approach to his city's ethnicity.[6] Nor is ethnicity an element in the relationship he draws between the cities and the ruler; simply, they are dependent, and he is their protector.[7] "Pas de doute que le roi soit 'latin,'"

---

2. Dagron 1969, 29. This position rests ultimately on his interpretation of Julian's *Letter to Themistius:* see Dagron 1968, 60–74. The many issues raised in this connection deserve to be discussed but would take us far from the present subject.

3. Dagron 1969, 29.

4. Cf. Dagron 1969, 25.

5. In fact, as early as Augustus's triple triumph in 29 B.C.: see Millar 1977, 141.

6. Appeal through claims of philosophy was Synesius's personal favorite tactic; see
pp. 89–91 above.

7. 27A–D, pace Dagron.

indeed; but the fact that Synesius uses exempla from both recent and remote Roman history in no way cuts him or his city off from Roman traditions.[8] Conversely, Arcadius is expected to learn from Greek exempla too.[9] More positive evidence is that in context of the one ethnic distinction Synesius does make, that with the barbarians, he uses "Romans" and the first person plural interchangeably. The most clear and concise single example is the cry "*We* must recover the spirits of *Romans*" (ἀνακτητέον ἡμῖν τὰ Ῥωμαίων φρονήματα, 23B). More extended cases are to be found throughout the antibarbarian section.[10] Synesius fully includes himself and his city in the Roman Empire. The cities may have peculiar problems, because they are dependent on a central authority, but in national affairs their concerns and fates are the same as its own.

Next, as to Dagron's interpretation of *De providentia*, it is more than doubtful whether contemporaries would have recognized anything so dramatic and permanent as a *partitio imperii* in 395. It is easy to multiply social, cultural, religious, and military grounds for an eventual rift between East and West, but the process neither began nor ended in 395.[11]

8. Dagron 1969, 30; he cited 16A (court luxury), 17D–19B ("Carinus" and more recent emperors), and 24A–B (Spartacus and Crixus).

9. E.g., 20B–D (Agesilaus, Epaminondas). In discussing the term αὐτοκράτωρ at 19B–D, Synesius both compares and distinguishes constitutional features of democratic Athens and republican Rome; the governments were independent at the time under discussion, but both traditions inform present attitudes. Dagron slights the Greek exempla, indeed only acknowledges them implicitly in saying that Synesius chose Roman exempla "de préférence." Roman exempla have obvious relevance for addressing a Roman emperor.

10. "Return to *us* the king as public servant of the polity. For indeed *we* are amidst affairs such that ease can no longer advance or even step forward, for all stand on the edge of a razor, and there is need of God and king as regards affairs, to forestall the fate, already long aborning, of the *Romans'* realm" (21B); "*We* shall persuade" everyone to serve against the Scythians (22D); "The *Romans'* strength [ought] to be native; . . . how is it endurable that *with us* the masculine element is foreign?" (22D–23A); "Is the situation similar with *us*? Are *we* rearing, in every way more spectacularly, the preliminaries of the extraordinary? With *us* the initiators of strife are neither two men nor dishonored, but armies that are great and bloody and kin of *our* slaves, who have become leaders of the *Romans* by evil fate, and furnished generals in great repute among themselves and among *us*, 'by *our* weakness'; . . . *we* [Terzaghi notes that the MSS read ἡμῖν, which previous editors emended to ὑμῖν, unwarrantably] must demolish their stronghold" (24B–C); "Finding softer, not the *Romans'* weapons, but their manners. . . . [Synesius describes Theodosius's benefactions to the Goths, including "sharing *Roman* land"] But the barbarian does not understand virtue. Beginning then, up to now, they laugh at *us*, knowing both what they deserved from *us* and what they were thought to deserve" (25C–D).

11. Even Demougeot only argued that 395 was a key stage in the inevitable movement "de l'unité à la division de l'empire romain," not an overnight turning point. And even so it has generally been felt that she overargued the case: W. E. Kaegi, *Byzantium and the Decline of Rome* (Princeton 1968); against the constitutional arguments of Palanque (1944, 47–64 and 280–98) that influenced Demougeot, see Cameron in *CLRE* 13–16.

The year 395 has become canonical in the modern historical tradition simply because no emperor unified East and West again after that date. But when Synesius wrote *De providentia* it was neither obvious nor inevitable that no one ever would. The notion of the Eastern court claiming seniority on the tenuous grounds Dagron suggests makes neither political nor constitutional sense.[12] Arcadius was already acknowledged to be senior Augustus by virtue of his earlier proclamation. Nor did the East dispute the automatic reversion of this title to Honorius when Arcadius died in 408; Eastern laws duly place Honorius's name before that of Theodosius II.

It is a serious error to suppose that the empire was "divided" in any significantly new sense on Theodosius's death in January 395. It had been divided between himself and the dynasty of Valentinian during most of his reign, just as it had been divided between Valens and Valentinian before that. It was only during the last three months of his life that Theodosius had reigned over a unified empire.[13] It is true that the fifth century saw the rapid growth of the idea that Constantinople was Rome's successor; not in virtue of superior merit, however, but to fill the vacuum left by the undoubted decline of the West in the half-century after 395.[14] Rome itself had long ceased to be the political capital of the West, even before the sack of Alaric. Though Milan and then Ravenna succeeded to its practical suzerainty as homes of the Western court, neither so constellated a body of traditions that it could begin to rival Rome's domination in thought. And Constantinople's eventual eclipse of Ravenna had nothing to do with the political ambitions of Arcadius and his ministers in A.D. 400.

Third, it may be doubted whether Dagron's vision of the moral superiority of literary Hellenism justifying predominance in practical affairs would have found an audience at the Eastern court. He cited all the well-known texts of Libanius, Themistius, Eunapius, and Palladas that show contempt for Constantinople or for Greeks who aspired to become Roman functionaries, owing their careers to knowledge of the law or shorthand rather than the traditional literary culture.[15] Synesius himself may have shared this attitude, but the "best men" for whom he wrote his allegory were precisely such functionaries. Indeed Libanius singles out for special mention, among the parvenus who had risen thus from the

12. "Aux liens historiques (entre les deux *partes*) on préfère les affinités politiques ou morales (la fidélité de l'Orient à l'hellénisme)" (Dagron 1969, 31).

13. On the question of whether contemporaries would have seen a definitive partition, see above, p. 3.

14. See Cameron, *Constantinople: Birth of a New Rome* (forthcoming).

15. Dagron 1969, 28.

humblest origins to the senate of Constantinople, none other than Aurelian's father, Taurus the notary, and Philip the sausage maker's son, the grandfather of the future regent Anthemius.[16] By both origin and profession, men like Aurelian were more bureaucrats than aristocrats.

Fourth, the most curious part of Dagron's interpretation is its final stage. His view of the development of the plot is that for a while Osiris governs like a true Hellene, cultivating education and philosophy. But as a consequence he neglects the army. Profiting from the weakness of too ideal a state, Typhos usurps power with the aid of the barbarians. Osiris eventually is restored, and revises his political priorities in the light of Typhos's usurpation, "adapting them to the responsibilities of power."[17] Unfortunately, this elegant resolution of the conflict between Greek and Roman is a chimera. If the allegory is supposed to apply to the *partes*, no such jockeying and adjustment can anywhere be adduced. If to the ministers, it becomes relevant that Aurelian was not in fact restored to power on his return.[18] Though Synesius does his best to correct this unwelcome fact in the fiction of his myth, his readers of course knew what had really happened. At either level, it is far from clear what in practical terms Dagron's "adaptation" might involve. In any event, Synesius does not present Osiris acting any differently after his return. He offers only vague talk decked out in trite golden age imagery about how Osiris restored the prosperity of the Egyptians that Typhos had ruined (124C–125B). And since it comes *before* the admission that "the gods did not at once place everything in his hands" (125C), even this must describe blessings anticipated rather than achieved. It is in any case unlikely in the extreme that a thoroughgoing Hellene like Synesius would have written a work to celebrate the Romanization of a Greek ideal.

Dagron's claim that Synesius draws the contrast between Osiris and Typhos throughout in terms of Greek and Roman is farfetched in itself and unconvincing in detail. For example, while it is true that Typhos is represented as contemptuous of culture and education, Synesius praises Osiris's culture much less enthusiastically than interpreters usually suppose. The character study of Osiris in *De providentia* 90A–C, 91D–92A,

---

16. *Or.* 42.24.

17. "Synésios évoque la nécessité où est l'hellénisme de s'ouvrir à des domaines qui lui étaient jusque-là étrangers: l'armée, l'administration. . . . Il n'y a plus dès lors de fondement à la division traditionelle entre culture grecque et pouvoir romain; le pouvoir reste d'expression latine et la culture d'expression grecque, mais ils sont réunis" (Dagron 1969, 32–33).

18. As established above, chapter 5, section VI.

and 102D–104C may be construed as panegyric of Aurelian,[19] and the rules and techniques of the genre are well enough understood to illuminate clearly the text between the lines.

As a child Osiris was a keen student; but it is his keenness, not his attainments, that is praised ("eager to learn all his first elements all at once," 90A). This corresponds exactly to the rules laid down by Menander for the section on upbringing: "Then you must speak of his love of learning, his quickness, his enthusiasm for study, his easy grasp of what is taught him. If he excels in literature, philosophy, and knowledge of letters, you must praise this. If it was in the practice of war and arms, you must admire this."[20] Since Synesius does *not* in fact go on to praise Osiris for his learning or even for his eloquence, that touchstone of literary culture in late antiquity, contemporaries would have drawn only one conclusion: Aurelian had none to speak of.[21] Moreover, the fact that he is praised for entering public office while still a youth (91D–92A) strongly suggests that he did not pursue the advanced studies in rhetoric and philosophy that were indispensable for anyone with real cultural pretensions.[22] At 102D Synesius ascribes to him the clichéd "sacrifice to Persuasion, the Muses, and the Graces," but only as an explanation of how he could govern effectively without force. Synesius directly goes on to praise his administrative abilities and his encouragement of education. In the section on the "rustic philosopher," Osiris is praised as a "discerning judge of literature" (113C); the context makes it clear that Synesius has in mind only Aurelian's appreciation of his own work. If Aurelian had really shared Synesius's enthusiasm for literature and philosophy, Synesius would have said so much more clearly. As it is, the most he could claim even in his fiction was that Osiris/Aurelian lived up to the traditional role of patron of letters.[23] No Greek panegyrist could have claimed less for his honorand, and Themistius, to quote only one example, claimed much more for so unpromising a subject as the almost illiterate soldier-emperor Valens. It is only modern readers, unfamiliar with the conventions of the genre, who have exaggerated the signifi-

19. Which is not to say that it bears any relation to the truth. Individual actions ascribed to Osiris in the course of the fable are in a quite different category.

20. Men. Rh. 371, p. 83.14f. Russell and Wilson.

21. For example, Claudian manages to say something along these lines about even the dull Honorius: "quam docta facultas / ingenii linguaeque modus!" *IV Cons.Hon.* 515–16. Cf. I. Sevcenko, "A Late Antique Epigram," *Synthronon*, Bibliothèque des cahiers archéologique 2 (1968): 29–41.

22. A. Mueller, "Studentenleben im IV. Jahrhundert n. Chr.," *Philologus* 69 (1910): 292f.

23. Cf. F. Millar, *The Emperor in the Roman World* (London 1977), 491–506.

cance of something contemporaries would have recognized as very faint praise indeed.

Nor would the allegation that Typhos despised culture have identified him in contemporary eyes as a Roman.[24] In fact Synesius speaks of Typhos's cultural interests only in 90C–91C, where, as with Aurelian, it is his application *as a child* that is at issue ("when he saw his brother going to school"). It is obviously pure invention: Synesius cannot have known which of the brothers in real life was the better student. More significantly, he never claims that the adult Typhos despised culture. Nor is it really Hellenic culture that is at issue in *De providentia*, whether admired by Osiris or despised by Typhos. This distinction between Egyptian and foreign wisdom implies in contemporary terms the distinction between secular and Christian culture. Aurelian is praised for his Christian, as much as for his secular, learning, and Typhos is damned for his contempt of both.[25] All in all, there seems no reason why contemporary readers should have perceived Aurelian in any sense as a Hellene.

No better founded is Dagron's claim that Osiris "accède à la royauté par la voie noble, le présidence du sénat," while Typhos "devient usurpateur après avoir appartenu à l'administration du fisc."[26] The truth is that in real life the careers of Aurelian and Caesarius were virtually identical: both were *magister officiorum*, praetorian prefect, consul, and patrician; and of course both were appointed to all those offices by the

24. "Accusation traditionelle des 'vieux romains' contre les 'graeculi'" (Dagron 1969, 31)—but not since before the age of Cicero! During the imperial age the stock of Greek literary and philosophical culture rose steadily until for a period in the second and third centuries it bid fair to eclipse Latin as the language of culture even among Latin speakers. In real life Caesarius was a native Greek speaker who at one point kept up a house in Antioch and was on good terms with Libanius (Lib. *Or.* 21, esp. 33; *PLRE* I.171). If he was not a Themistius whose career was built on his culture, neither was Aurelian. But it is equally obvious that Caesarius owed his precocious career in the imperial service, not to the study of Latin or the law, but, like Aurelian, to the wealth and influence of his father. This is the obvious explanation of the fact that both brothers enjoyed accelerated careers; it is clear that neither worked his way up from shorthand writer or clerk.

25. Similarly, if perhaps fortuitously (Synesius does not press the allusion), Plutarch in the proem to *De Iside et Osiride* describes Typhos as "hostile to [Isis, whose name he has just connected with τὸ εἰδέναι] and puffed up because of ignorance and deceit, and tearing apart and expunging the sacred word (καὶ διασπῶν καὶ ἀφανίζων τὸν ἱερὸν λόγον), which the goddess collects and composes and transmits to initiates" (351F). As Griffiths notes (1970, 260), these actions are exactly what Typhos does to Osiris; emendation to τὸν ἱερὸν νεκρόν (J. G. Griffiths, *CR* 6 [1956]: 103), however, does not suit the relative clause, and the context already implies intellectualizing allegorization strongly enough for the equation to be understood.

26. Dagron 1974, 205; cf. 1969, 32.

emperor, as in Synesius's story by their father. The only major post Aurelian held that his brother did not is the prefecture of the city, described by Synesius in the words πολιαρχήσας καὶ βουλῆς ἄρξας (92A).[27] His purpose may indeed have been to suggest that Aurelian enjoyed the support of the senate, though contemporaries would naturally have known that the city prefect was an imperial appointee. They would also have remembered that Aurelian won the office as a supporter of Rufinus. The city prefecture was no more "Hellenic" than any of the posts held by Typhos. Synesius singles out Typhos's financial post and provincial governorship for special mention not because they were "Roman,"[28] but simply because they lent themselves so obviously to the accusation of embezzlement and extortion. His main purpose was to draw a moral, not a cultural, distinction between the two brothers. Dagron further claimed that "ce qui est fondamental dans le *Récit égyptien*, et ce par quoi l'oeuvre traduit le mieux la lutte politique de 399–400, c'est que le roi légitime est confirmé par le sénat, tandis que l'usurpateur est nommé par l'armée."[29] But even in Synesius's own terms it is Osiris who is actually elected by the army ("The soldiers vote by raising their hands," 94D). Dagron glossed the straightforward "soldiers" as "aristocratie hellénisée."[30] It had been many centuries since any Greek aristocracy saw itself as a warrior elite. It is true that Synesius alleges, quite falsely, that Typhos was supported by swineherds and barbarians, "une foule grossière . . . non hellénisée," but that does not make them or him Roman.

Dagron characterizes Typhos's sexual orgies as "très romaines." But although the modern European tradition likes to associate orgies with Roman decadence, contemporaries did not at all view it so. No one who has even glanced at the rich material assembled in book 12 of Athenaeus's *Deipnosophistai* could believe that the Romans invented the orgy.[31] The Roman who developed it to an art form was that most philhellene of emperors Nero; his more exotic sex partners all bore conspicuously Greek names (Phoebus, Sporus, Pythagoras), and his more spectacular sexual escapades were staged in Greece.[32] Roman moralists regarded such be-

27. The second phrase should not be construed as a separate office such as *princeps senatus;* it is merely part of Synesius's characterization of the office of city prefect, who was the senate's representative in its dealings with the emperor. In the same way, he uses two phrases to represent *magister officiorum.* Cf. A. Chastagnol, *La préfecture urbaine à Rome sous le Bas-Empire* (Paris 1960), 69–72.

28. On the identification of these two posts, see p. 181 n. 130 above.

29. Dagron 1974, 205.

30. Dagron 1969, 32.

31. See too Burgo Partridge, *A History of Orgies* (London 1964), 9–37.

32. M. T. Griffin, *Nero: The End of a Dynasty* (London 1984), 169, 180.

havior as characteristic of *Greek* corruption and decadence.[33] The chastity of Osiris's wife that is held up in honorable contrast to that of Typhos's (105D) was intended to evoke Christian, as much as Hellenic, ideals.

The whole house of cards collapses. There is no such imperial allegory in *De providentia*. In fact not the least interesting aspect of *De providentia* is that Synesius's allegory has no place for the part played by the West in the crisis of 399–400. We know, in most detail from Claudian, that successive Eastern ministers of the age continued to live in fear that Stilicho would march East and establish his "regency" over Arcadius by force. Eutropius went so far as to proclaim Stilicho a *hostis publicus*, probably in 397. Aurelian too must have taken a hostile line in 399 if Stilicho refused to acknowledge his consulate in January 400. Claudian refers to Aurelian's government as *iners atque impia turba*. A fragment of Eunapius shows Fravitta reproaching Count John for attempting to undermine the concord of the brothers Augusti.[34] Another fragment gives a vivid picture of the man in the street trying to make sense of the conflicting rumors:

> During the time of Eutropius the eunuch it was impossible to include in a history an accurate account of events in the West. . . . Any travelers[35] or soldiers with access to political information told the story as they saw fit, biased by friendship or hostility or a desire to please someone. And if you brought together three or four of them with conflicting versions as witnesses, there would be a furious argument, a pitched battle proceeding from passionate and heated interjections like the following: "Where did you get this from?" "Where did Stilicho see you?" "Would you have seen the eunuch?" so that it was quite a task to sort out the tangle.[36]

It is not too much to say that the Eastern and Western courts were in a more or less permanent state of cold war between 395 and Stilicho's

---

33. This is not to say that there were no differences between Greek and Roman orgies, notably in the role of food and women. At Greek symposia, "women were present only for the purposes of entertainment and sexual pleasure: the hetaira, the dancer and the flute girl" (Oswyn Murray, *JRS* 75 [1985]: 40). Romans allowed their wives to attend, which inevitably complicated matters (Murray, 48–49). Since Typhos's wife attended his orgies, to that extent they might be classified as Roman rather than Greek, but it is hard to believe that Synesius, who had no knowledge of Latin literature, was aware of this distinction.

34. 85M, quoted in full above, p. 246.

35. The text is uncertain here. Blockley reads πραττόμενοι with Boissevain for the MS πλαττόμενοι and translates "officials," but there seems no parallel for such a usage. With considerable hesitation we adopt Niebuhr's πλανώμενοι.

36. Frag. 74M = 66.2B; the translation is modified from Blockley's.

death in 408, with a slight temporary thaw during 401–3.[37] One later letter to his brother shows Synesius at least curious about news from the
West,[38] but *De providentia* is concerned exclusively with the struggle for
power in the East.

This is not in itself surprising. In the West Stilicho ruled without
rival in the name of Honorius, whom he soon took the extra precaution
of making his son-in-law. He controlled the army as well as the court. In
the East, however, there was a constant struggle for power, both among
individual civilian ministers and between civil and military authorities.
Gaïnas's military coup in 400 brought about a major internal crisis, and it
is understandable that Synesius should have concentrated on it. Even
so, there must have been a constant fear that Stilicho would take this
opportunity of intervening in Eastern affairs. In late 399 his propagandist Claudian had gone so far as to suggest that only Stilicho could save
the East from the ravages of Tribigild. But Synesius completely ignored
this dimension of the crisis.

In this respect *De regno*, which Dagron contrasted with *De providentia*, shows exactly the same limitations. Claudian's panegyrics on the
third and fourth consulates of Honorius, delivered at Milan in January
396 and 398, make frequent reference to the East and to Honorius's
brother and colleague Arcadius. Synesius writes as if there were only
one emperor and one court, in Constantinople.[39]

Under the circumstances, there is little enough to suggest to the
reader that *De providentia*, which already contains one sort of political
allegory, might also contain another on a subject in which Synesius nowhere else shows any interest.[40] It might be added that any contemporary tempted to interpret the death of the old king and the struggle between his two sons in terms of the imperial crisis after Theodosius
would naturally have thought first of Arcadius and Honorius rather than
East and West. And most would have abandoned this line the moment
they discovered that it was the younger son (Honorius) who won the
election and the older (Arcadius) who was the villain of the tale. There
are only so many balls that even the most sophisticated political alle-
gorist can keep in the air at once.

37. See pp. 246–50.
38. *Ep.* 109 *fin.*: "Tell me what I ought to think of the mysterious rumor that has come
from the West." In *Ep.* 120, referring to recent news ἐκ τῆς ἠπείρου, a few MSS offer τῆς
ἑτέρας ἠπείρου, which might be interpreted as a reference to the West. But Garzya, like
most earlier editors, prints the majority text and interprets ἠπείρου as "coast."
39. *Ep.* 48 (= 50G) and 102 both refer to Constantinople as τὴν ἔχουσαν τὸν βασιλέα
πόλιν, as though there were no other city that enjoyed this honor.
40. "Dobbiamo subito dichiarare che da tutti i suoi scritti non traspare mai il prob-
lema dei rapporti fra Roma e Costantinopoli" (Bettini 1938, 40).

II. POLITICAL EXPLOITATION OF THE MYTH

The philosophical and religious terms in which Synesius tells his tale suggest that the truths of philosophy and morality are the primary aims of his book. The preface states that he has investigated "many philosophical issues hitherto undecided," described lives that are "examples of vice and virtue," and "elaborated and embroidered the work throughout with a view to its utility" (88B). Most important of all, he claims that his tale justifies a thesis about divine Providence.

It was the events of the spring and summer of 400 that inspired Synesius to these far-reaching conclusions. But it was the conclusions, not the events, that were important to him. The events were known to all. He was not writing a history. Modern historians prepared to translate any piece of narrative into the events of A.D. 400 must pause and duly weigh the essential nature of their source. We cannot simply transfer to Caesarius Typhos's every word and act. Nor can we take the speech of Typhos's wife, whose dramatic context presents it as a tissue of skillful lies (108C), out of that context, and represent it as a report that reached Gaïnas's ears in the spring of 400.[41] It is instructive to contrast the very different emphasis of a literary study: R. Helm classified Synesius's book first and foremost as a work of fiction with a moral purpose.[42]

What was the advantage of casting his pamphlet in this form? It was not that he needed allegory to license imagination and invention. Claudian's poems well illustrate how thoroughly contemporary events can be transformed without mythical disguise. The main advantage is that the myth chosen predetermines what sort of behavior will be expected of the real-life models. To give a simple example, once the author has begun to depict the rivalry of two men in terms of, say, Hare and Tortoise, then there are certain elements both in their characterization and the development of his plot that he can take for granted. However well the Hare character seems to be doing at a given moment, we know that he cannot win. However black things look for Tortoise, we know that he will win in the end. A skillful writer will be able to play with or against these expectations in a variety of ways.

What about the real-life struggle between Aurelian and Caesarius did Synesius see reflected in the myth of Osiris and Typhos? At a simple level, there is the opposition between good and evil. A Typhos cannot be capable of a single decent thought or action. So whereas we might

41. "On racontait au chef" (Demougeot 1951, 246 n. 57).
42. *Der antike Roman* (Berlin 1948), 22; the rest of his treatment is disappointing, consisting of little more than a lengthy plot summary.

question whether a former prefect and consul like Caesarius would see the destruction of Constantinople as his best way of recovering the prefecture, we are not at all surprised that Typhos should act with irrational violence to gain his ends. More important are the expectations that the myth creates. Synesius's original plan extended only to book 1. While he wrote, Caesarius was all-powerful and Aurelian far away in exile, and Synesius so represented Typhos and Osiris at the close of book 1. But the myth guarantees that Typhos will be overthrown in turn. Synesius's representation transfers this expectation to Caesarius.

But a further element beyond the ultimate victory of good over evil is more important still. In the myth Typhos kills Osiris. Osiris never becomes king of Egypt again. He becomes ruler and judge of the Underworld. It is Osiris's son Horus who finally deposes Typhos and becomes king in his stead. Synesius points to this aspect when he closes book 1, looking forward to "the years yet to come, when Osiris's son Horus would decide to select the wolf rather than the lion as his ally" (115B).

It was because he did not fully appreciate this feature of book 1 that Barnes mistakenly detected "signs of retouching," additions Synesius made to book 1 when he composed book 2.[43] He had in mind anticipatory passages like 112A and 115A–B that prophesy the reversal of barbarian fortunes. That is to say, he assumed that Synesius added them to an original work written when there was no light at all at the end of the tunnel. But why make such an assumption? Without the expulsion, what would have been left for the god to prophesy? Since Synesius did continue the story in a second book, it would have been much simpler for him to place all the new material there.

The explanation is that Synesius wrote book 1 *after* 12 July 400. Hence the unmistakable allusion to the massacre at 115A: "It was beyond human prediction that a vast armed force . . . would be defeated with no force to resist it." The massacre of the Goths did not immediately end Gaïnas's regime or Aurelian's exile, but it was an encouraging sign. At this moment Synesius had the idea of casting his story in the form of a myth where good triumphs only after many tribulations, and of cutting the tale short in the midst of the tribulations. It is worth emphasizing how pointed, not to say eccentric, it must have seemed to end the story of Osiris with the victory of Typhos: like ending the story of Oedipus with his wedding to Jocasta, or the Gospel story with the Crucifixion. It cannot have been accidental. It was deliberately calculated to make the reader look forward with the philosopher in the tale to Horus's triumph

43. Barnes 1986a, 95.

in the next generation. The pointers to a brighter future to which Barnes draws attention are not isolated additions, but integral and indeed climactic parts of Synesius's original plan for reformulating the myth of Osiris.

In order to create this optimistic aura, Synesius stopped his Egyptian narrative just before the massacre but alluded under the guise of prophecies to it and its two harbingers, the comet and Gaïnas's request for an Arian church (114D–115B). The natural implication is that since these three "prophecies" have all come true, the further prophecies that the Goths will be driven out and Typhos's regime will last "months, not years" will also be fulfilled. Synesius says as much quite openly in the preface: "Since the events foretold by the gods appeared to be coming to pass, they [the returned exiles] wanted the tale to go on to their better fortunes" (88B).

A more puzzling example is what Synesius himself refers to as "the riddle of the wolf" (88A).[44] Generations of scholars have taken for granted that there is a political solution to the riddle, with the animals standing for real-life equivalents in the world of A.D. 400. The favorite hypothesis is that the lion stands for the Goths and the wolf for the Huns.[45] It is unlikely enough that Synesius, a philosopher from a provincial backwater whose patron was in exile from Constantinople, was in any position to offer a suggestion that might be taken seriously. Moreover, the political interpretations of the riddle offered require chronological or psychological impossibilities: either Synesius devised the riddle after the death of Gaïnas, which he cannot have done, or he wrote with genuine prescience of its surprising agent, or he made a totally uncharacteristic exception to his judgment on barbarian allies at the same moment he warned against any such alliance. In fact the wolf in the riddle is purely literary. It is the form in which, in one variant of the myth, Osiris returned from the dead to aid Horus against Typhos.[46] If anything, the wolf represents a return to Aurelian's policies by some successor Horus. The lion, in Plutarch's version of the myth, is a force too strong in its own right to be entirely trustworthy. Horus says that it "was helpful to one who needed assistance, but a horse routed the enemy in flight and utterly destroyed him" (*De Is. et Os.* 358C). The difference is that the rider remains in control of the horse and uses it for his own purposes. There is no bridle to guarantee that the lion, once having helped "one who needed assistance," may not turn and maul him next. In this sense,

44. See the detailed analysis by J. Long (1987).

45. Originally proposed by Grützmacher (1913, 58) and argued for by Lacombrade (1946).

46. Diod. 1.88.6.

the lion in Synesius represents not only Gaïnas's Goths, who were currently demonstrating the danger, but any barbarian force used by the Romans. How universally he held this opinion is demonstrated in his account of the massacre in book 2, by his reuse of material from *De regno* directed against Alaric. For what solution he expects, Synesius looks to a Horus, who will one day overthrow Typhos and restore peace and honor.[47] He is promised by the myth; and he will be, in reality, whoever turns out to fulfill this role.

The political realities of Constantinople demanded that Synesius choose, of all myths representing the struggle between good and evil, one where good does not triumph till the next generation. For his composition, the fact that Osiris's son rather than Osiris himself takes revenge on Typhos is the crucial element of the myth. It might be added that, frequently as this particular myth is used in Greek and early Christian literature, it is normally the struggle between Typhos and Horus that symbolizes the struggle between good and evil. Naturally enough: Horus, not Osiris, defeated Typhos. It is therefore Horus, not Osiris, who symbolizes good triumphant.

This original purpose of Synesius has to some extent been obscured by book 2. At the time he finished book 1, on any reasonable forecast Aurelian was politically as dead as his mythical counterpart. The past few years had seen the ruin of a succession of contenders for power at the Eastern court. Rufinus and Eutropius were killed; others like Tatianus, Timasius, and Abundantius exiled; it made little difference, since the exiles never returned. No one could have foreseen that Aurelian would return, if not to power, at any rate to his estates and past honors. When he did, Synesius was obliged to resurrect Osiris, at the cost of violating the myth and destroying the subtlety of book 1. But although Osiris was back in Thebes, he was not Horus and did not do what only Horus could. Typhos remained in power, however hard Synesius tries to suggest that his regime was tottering and that it was only because of Osiris's "clemency" that he was not condemned and executed. Once more Synesius looks to the future for hope: the gods have allowed Typhos to continue in office so that men will come to appreciate good the

---

47. In a letter written to Aurelian at some later date (*Ep.* 31), Synesius referred to Aurelian's own son as "the new Taurus, the good hope of the Romans." The letter begins with an obvious allusion to the flattery he had already administered to Aurelian in *De providentia*, and, now complimenting him as a father, he suggests that young Taurus (later a most distinguished man: consul, prefect, and patrician) might prove the very Horus figure he had conjured. But such succession could not literally fit the Roman context. It is a flattering literary allusion, not a serious suggestion.

more after knowing evil (122D). The concluding quotation from Pindar looks forward to "the remaining days as the wisest witnesses."

It was because he did not appreciate this tentative anticipation that Liebeschuetz claimed to find additions to book 2, advancing arguments similar to those of Barnes for book 1. He supposed that 124C was added after Aurelian's eventual restoration to the prefecture in 414.[48] But, quite apart from the fact that Synesius was probably dead by 412, Liebeschuetz misunderstands Synesius's method and purpose.

In the first place, the hypothesis of interpolation implies an earlier version that either lacked this section or originally contained something different. Liebeschuetz was led to his hypothesis by the apparent conflict between references to restoration and excuses for delay within the same chapter (124A–125C). But the alleged reference to restoration in 124C cannot be neatly disengaged from the context of delay. The entire second half of book 2 is devoted to vague talk about Osiris's popularity and Typhos's imminent fall, with copious metaphysical obfuscation concerning holy mysteries not to be revealed. Even its excessive length suggests an overburdened attempt to gloss over and make the best of the unwelcome reality that Aurelian was out of power. If Synesius had wanted to add a reference to Aurelian's eventual restoration, he would have done better to delete or rewrite the whole second half of the book. It is pervaded with increasingly wan excuses, and the book concludes by counseling patience yet again: "It makes no sense for a man who will soon receive his just deserts to distress himself" (129B). One sentence alluding to Aurelian's restoration does nothing to redeem the many pages that continue to imply the opposite.

For all its philosophical trimmings, *De providentia* is a piece of journalism: not reportage, but a partisan broadside with a very short effective life span. Journalism of the hour cannot be brought up-to-date by inserting one sentence. All Synesius did, when at some later date republishing the two parts together, was to add a brief preface containing two pieces of information for future readers: a clue to the identity of Typhos and Osiris, and the fact that book 1 was originally an independent work.[49]

Güldenpenning claimed that the reference to Aurelian "becoming more glorious as he grew older" (124C) has to imply the passage of a

48. Liebeschuetz 1983, 40. This suggestion was in fact first made by Sievers (1870, 368) and firmly embraced by Güldenpenning (1885, 219 n. 4).

49. The clue to the identity of Typhos and Osiris was the name of their father; even this would hardly have sufficed after a few years, especially since Synesius spent the rest of his days far from court.

decade or so.[50] But Synesius's myth cannot be translated so simplistically into contemporary terms. Aurelian was back in Constantinople, but not in office. He must therefore be portrayed as the sage elder statesman, not king, on the excuse that "a king's ears are often deceived" (125C). There is no reference in book 2 to anything that happened later than Aurelian's return. Indeed, with that one exception, the narrative stops with the massacre. It is only too obvious that Synesius wrote book 2 in some haste and embarrassment immediately after Aurelian's return, when Gaïnas was gone but Caesarius was still in power and in other respects there was little more cause for optimism than when he wrote book 1.

III. CAESARIUS AND THE EXCULPATION OF GAÏNAS

Synesius's apparently precise sequence of events for Typhos's coup misrepresents the reality of Gaïnas's coup in at least four major respects. On the identifications of Typhos as Caesarius and Osiris as Aurelian that Synesius obviously expected and encouraged his readers to make, his myth (1) ascribes to Caesarius the initiative in Gaïnas's dealings with him, (2) exaggerates and antedates these dealings, (3) suppresses Aurelian's dealings with Gaïnas, and, most important of all, (4) entirely suppresses the role of Eutropius in the political intrigues of the age.

Indeed, if the struggle for power between the two brothers really went back, as Synesius explicitly claims, before Aurelian's appointment to the prefecture in the summer of 399, then the main obstacle to the ambitions of both men was not yet Gaïnas, but Eutropius. It was only on Eutropius's fall that the praetorian prefecture, robbed of much of its power by Eutropius's palace government, became once more the supreme magistracy of state, the "kingship of Egypt" in Synesius's myth. So paradoxically the myth presupposes and yet systematically ignores Eutropius.

It is instructive to observe how skillfully Synesius contrives to gloss over the omission of what might have seemed an unavoidable element in his story, the previous occupant of the throne for which Osiris and Typhos were in such keen competition. In the first part of book 1 he gives a long account of Osiris's preparation for the kingship and the advice of

50. A man represented elsewhere "in der Blüte seiner Jahre . . . konnte unmöglich schon 'Greis' genannt werden, das paßt nur auf die Jahre 415 und 416" (Güldenpenning 1885, 219 n. 4).

the old king, his father. At 96A Osiris is initiated into the kingship by his father, who then "departed, taking the same road as the gods" (102D), much as in Claudian's description Theodosius ascends to heaven, leaving behind Arcadius and Honorius as twin masters of the Roman world (*III Cons. Hon.* 162f.). So too Synesius implies that Osiris is succeeding to the throne on his father's death. That does not quite fit the myth, but is perfectly logical:[51] if two princes are competing for a throne, it follows that the previous king, their father, must either have just died or be on the point of death.

Most scholars have assumed that Aurelian's father, Taurus, really did live till 399,[52] by a remarkable coincidence dying just before his son became praetorian prefect. The truth is that he had been dead for more than thirty years, as proved by the inscription on the statue erected to his memory in the forum of Trajan during the joint reign of Valentinian and Valens, that is to say, between 364 and 367.[53] Even if he had still been alive in 399, it would have been almost forty years since he had held the office he was supposed to be passing on to his son: Taurus had held his prefecture in 355–61. Moreover, he had been praetorian prefect of Italy, not the East. And in any case, it was of course the emperor, not Taurus, who appointed his sons to the offices alluded to by Synesius.

The old king is a purely symbolic figure, the incarnation of the best of the Greco-Roman tradition of government. By presenting Osiris as the *spiritual* heir of such a father's wisdom and experience, Synesius is able to gloss over both the identity of Aurelian's real-life predecessor and the circumstances of the succession. The omission is clearly deliberate,

51. Succession to the throne is a crucial element of native Egyptian traditions, but it is the succession of each new pharaoh as Horus incarnate to a predecessor who is assimilated to Osiris (Griffiths 1980). How Osiris came to rule is not at issue. Greek versions assimilate Hesiodic theogonies to fill in this vacancy, but still essentially take for granted Osiris's right to rule.

52. Demougeot 1951, 236f.; *PLRE* I.880 ("still alive in the East in the 390s"); von Haehling 1978, 294 ("um 390 lebte er im Osten").

53. The text as preserved reads: Jadque constantia aeq(ue) probato v.c. Tauro comiti ordinis primi, quaestori sacri palatii, patricia dignitate praef(ecto) praet(orio) per Italiam atq(ue) Africam, D.N. Valentinianus et Valens victores ac triumphatores semper Augusti statuam sub auro quam adprobante amplissimo senatu iamdudum meruerat ad perpetuam laudabilis viri memoriam reddi iusserunt (*Ann. Epigr.* 1934, 159, omitting the *viri*; correctly, R. Paribeni, *Not.d.scavi* 11 [1933]: 492, pl. xv; and *PLRE* I.879). Taurus was exiled by Julian (Amm. Marc. 22.3.4), at which time his statue in the forum of Trajan was presumably removed. It was replaced by Valentinian and Valens, evidently after Taurus's death (Vogler 1979, 128, rightly refers to a "dédicace posthume"). On any hypothesis it is odd that there is no reference to Taurus's consulate of 361. Even if he had been stripped of his consulate by Julian (for which there is no evidence), it was not removed from official lists retroactively (*CLRE* 257).

because it was in effect to Eutropius's power that Aurelian succeeded—
and with the aid of none other than Gaïnas.

At 108B Synesius introduces "the commander of the foreign troops,"
away on an unsuccessful campaign, evidently Gaïnas's campaign against
Tribigild in 399. In his absence Typhos's wife warns Gaïnas's wife that
Osiris "is preparing an accusation of treachery against him, charging
that it is a prearranged war he is fighting, with the barbarians dividing
their troops but sharing a common purpose" (108C). There can be no
doubt that it is to the allegation of collusion between Gaïnas and Tribigild that Synesius is alluding. But it is also clear from the detailed narrative of Zosimus that this collusion, or at any rate Gaïnas's refusal to
engage Tribigild, took place *before* Eutropius's fall.[54] Indeed it was by
threatening that he could not defeat Tribigild or come to terms with him
so long as Eutropius remained in power that Gaïnas prevailed upon Arcadius to depose him. It was now that Aurelian stepped in to fill the vacuum behind Arcadius's throne. It was not Caesarius but Aurelian who
was the first beneficiary of Gaïnas's intervention. Furthermore, a specific illustration of collaboration between Aurelian and Gaïnas can be
adduced.

However unsuccessful Eutropius's policies were judged to be, the
exile in Cyprus to which Arcadius originally condemned him should
have been sufficient, especially since he had been guaranteed safe conduct after taking asylum in a church. But according to Zosimus (5.18),

> at Gaïnas's urgent pressure upon Arcadius to have the man killed, the
> emperor's ministers made a mockery of the oath that they had tendered
> Eutropius when he was dragged out of the church. They recalled him
> from Cyprus; then, as if they had sworn only that they would not kill
> him while he was in Constantinople, they dispatched him to Chalcedon
> and there had him murdered.

Philostorgius names "Aurelian the prefect" as president of the tribunal
that condemned Eutropius to death at a suburb called Panteichion, a few
miles down the Asiatic coast from Chalcedon.[55] Here is Aurelian playing
the unworthy role of Gaïnas's executioner. No doubt the alliance did not
last long, but once it had broken down, naturally Synesius preferred not
to mention it. Instead he retrojects to the moment of Eutropius's fall the
allegation that Typhos had the support of barbarians to succeed to the
"throne"; indeed he claims they were his only support.

54. As established above, chapter 6, section II.
55. *HE* 11.6.

Synesius's claim that it was Typhos who took the initiative in his dealings with the barbarian general has never troubled those who believe implicitly in warring pro- and antibarbarian factions. According to Demougeot, "Synesius, dont le témoignage est le plus sûr et qu'il faut suivre de préférence à tout autre, raconte que l'initiative du complot vint de Caesarius et que ce dernier dut recourir à la ruse pour entraîner le chef des mercenaires." [56] But unlike his younger brother Aurelian, Caesarius had already held both the praetorian prefecture and the consulate and had previously served Theodosius with distinction as *magister officiorum*. He was already a distinguished elder statesman. Even granting that he wanted another spell in the prefecture, he could scarcely improve his position by plotting with a disgruntled barbarian. For if there was a struggle for power between civilians at Arcadius's court, there was a much more serious struggle for power between court and generals. None of the civilian leaders can have wanted to become the puppet of an Eastern Stilicho. Had Caesarius taken the risk of using Gaïnas to regain the prefecture, he could not be sure that Gaïnas would not end up controlling him. After all, he had destroyed all three of Caesarius's predecessors when they refused to meet his demands. [57] Why should Caesarius have thought that he, a civilian like them, could control Gaïnas any longer or better than Rufinus, Eutropius, and Aurelian?

In any case, the details of Synesius's scenario do not fit the circumstances of A.D. 400. According to Synesius, Typhos's wife stirs up the barbarians against Osiris from jealousy of his power. This represents a double displacement of responsibility for the coup: from Gaïnas onto Typhos/Caesarius and thence onto Typhos's wife, whose energy and competence demean her husband. She initiates the plot by telling the barbarian general's wife that Osiris is planning to dismiss her husband and rid the army of barbarians. Her speech, though rhetorically arresting, is far from being a statement of pro- and antibarbarian ideologies, for from context it is clear that she is lying about Osiris and that she is manipulating the unwitting and (Synesius claims) reluctant barbarians in order to win the kingship for her husband. It hardly needs to be said that nothing of the sort happened in 400. Gaïnas was no innocent tricked into rebelling against Aurelian by a civilian. He had already done almost exactly

56. Demougeot 1951, 249.
57. It is usually assumed that Gaïnas's role in the killing of Rufinus was undertaken solely in Stilicho's interests (Demougeot 1951, 154–57). It is in fact more than doubtful whether Gaïnas was at any time Stilicho's creature (Cameron 1970a, 146–48), and it seems most likely that before executing his plan he attempted to extract a command from Eutropius.

the same thing the previous year when he forced Arcadius to depose Eutropius in the summer of 399. Nor did any civilian inspire him on either occasion.

Why was Synesius so anxious to exculpate Gaïnas at Caesarius's expense? A recent study by Rita Lizzi has argued that Synesius's thoughts about barbarians "matured" between *De regno* and *De providentia:*[58] on closer study he came to realize that barbarians were in themselves a neutral force, who could be of service to the state if correctly handled. It is true that book 1 of *De providentia* is less openly hostile toward barbarians than *De regno*. But what Lizzi overlooked is that book 2 treats them as savages once more; indeed, the old beggarwoman's speech at 118A–B paraphrases *De regno* 23A–B and 25C. There is no mystery here—and certainly no change of heart by Synesius. It is all a matter of placing each book in its context.

Synesius wrote *De regno* a full year before Tribigild's rebellion, when Gaïnas was an unemployed *comes rei militaris* with no prospects, and Alaric was far away in Illyricum. It was therefore safe for Synesius to say what he thought about barbarians. Book 2 of *De providentia* he wrote after Gaïnas had withdrawn to Thrace,[59] when the immediate crisis was over and he could once more say what he thought. Book 1, however, he wrote in the immediate aftermath of the massacre of 12 July, when the crisis was still far from over. Gaïnas was encamped outside the city with the greater part of his army intact. He might easily decide on vengeance. It was at this moment that Synesius formulated the plan of his work. Gaïnas was still too much of a threat to be the villain of the piece, so Synesius cast the new prefect Caesarius in that role. Personal motives may have played some part; Caesarius apparently reduced or delayed the tax remissions Synesius had won for Cyrene from Aurelian.[60] In addition, Caesarius had supported Gaïnas's demand for an Arian church inside

58. Lizzi 1981, 60–62.

59. 122A refers to embassies sent to Gaïnas when he had already "withdrawn a great distance from Thebes," clearly alluding to Chrysostom's embassy to Thrace (Theod. *HE* 5.33.1).

60. 112C, 114B; since Synesius three times elsewhere claims to have secured great benefits for Cyrene (*Hymn* 1.496f., *Ep.* 154 *fin.*, *De insomniis* 148D), it does not look as if Caesarius can have actually revoked Aurelian's concessions. In general it is probably safe to disregard the accusations of wholesale misgovernment Synesius levels against Typhos, partly because they are all traditional clichés, but perhaps more because he had been in office only three months when Synesius wrote. There had hardly been time for him to undo all Aurelian's work, as Synesius claims he did (112B). On the older interpretation and chronology, it could have been argued that Aurelian undid his brother's work in turn when reappointed to the prefecture, but on the new chronology this option is no longer open. Synesius left Constantinople shortly after Aurelian's return in the fall of 400, with Caesarius still prefect. *Ep.* 129 shows him setting out on another voyage to Constantinople the following year (Garzya's date of 403 presupposes the old departure date of 402), but being

the city walls (115B). The circles in which Synesius moved, shocked at what they saw as Caesarius's collaboration with Gaïnas, were no doubt urging Arcadius to appoint someone more loyal to deal with the crisis. In the event, of course, with the able support of Fravitta, Caesarius was able to retrieve the situation triumphantly. But at the time he wrote book 1, Synesius seems to have been convinced that Caesarius would soon fall from power. This is made clear by 114C. In the course of listing the "prophecies" that are supposed to foretell the downfall of Typhos and his barbarians, Synesius adds: "If Typhos himself should remain in his tyrant's palace, even so do not despair of the gods." This is the first time Synesius sounds the note that becomes so insistent in book 2: it is only a matter of time before Typhos falls. In book 2 his conviction seems increasingly to fail, but there is no reason to doubt that when writing book 1 Synesius genuinely believed that Caesarius could not hold on to the prefecture much longer. This conviction is the cornerstone of *De providentia*.

It explains, for example, why Osiris does not himself take any action against the barbarians. Not only does he not put into effect the anti-barbarian measures proclaimed in *De regno*; he is apparently taken quite unawares by the barbarian coup. This is the less surprising because, the way Synesius sets the scene in *De providentia*, it is not the barbarians who are the danger, but Typhos, secretly plotting behind Osiris's back. One of the strangest passages in book 1 is 108C–D, where it is Typhos's wife who accuses Osiris of planning to rid the state of barbarians. After *De regno*, this is just what we should expect any hero of Synesius to do, ruthlessly and proudly, but in the context we are bound to interpret the accusation as a malicious calumny along with the rest of her self-seeking lies. Indeed there is a clear indication in the text. At 108B Typhos's wife "adds horror on horror" in her attempt to win over the wife of the barbarian general, "announcing supposed secret plots (βουλεύματα δῆθεν) against them." The particle δῆθεν unmistakably suggests "that the words used are untrue."[61] This is a common classical usage that survives through Byzantine into modern Greek, but it may be worth citing one

---

foiled by unfavorable winds. What the purpose of this visit was and whether it was ever completed we do not know.

61. J. D. Denniston, *The Greek Particles*, 2d ed. (Oxford 1954), 264–66; cf. too J. Enoch Powell, *A Lexicon to Herodotus* (Cambridge 1938), 85: "implying falsity of speech or thought." Powell cites (among other examples) Hdt. 7.211.3, φεύγεσκον δῆθεν, "they pretended to flee." The particle always follows the word it qualifies (Denniston, 266). This is a usage particularly common in Herodotus, a favorite of Synesius (Crawford 1901, 531f.). As may be seen from the careful analysis in W. Fritz, *Die Briefe des Bischofs Synesios von Kyrene: Ein Beitrag zur Geschichte des Attizismus im IV. und V. Jahrhundert* (Leipzig 1898), 168–73, Synesius exploits a rich selection of classical particle combinations.

illustration from a contemporary writer, Philostorgius: Τριγίβιλδος [sic], ὡς δῆθεν τὸν Γαϊνᾶν διαφυγών, "Tribigild, *pretending* to flee Gaïnas."[62] Why does Synesius handle this central issue so paradoxically?

The solution lies in his anxiety not to offend Gaïnas. There is some truth in the words of Typhos's wife. If Gaïnas had been imprudent enough to walk back into Constantinople in April 400 without a bodyguard, Aurelian almost certainly would have "taken away his command."[63] That is why Gaïnas made his preemptive strike. That much but no more is true of the barbarian coup in Synesius's allegory. The barbarian deposes Osiris to protect himself; the difference is that, according to *De providentia*, his belief is mistaken. He has been taken in by the lies of Typhos's wife. Synesius was writing in the fear that Gaïnas would reassert his control of Constantinople. If that happened, his allegory purported to show that Gaïnas had acted under a misapprehension. Aurelian had never wished him any harm; that was all the doing of his crafty brother. In *De providentia* Synesius performs the remarkable feat of writing an account of the coup of 400 that exculpates both Aurelian and Gaïnas; all the blame is put on the shoulders of a man who was not even in office when it took place!

There are other passages that bear out this interpretation. For example, at 111A Synesius claims that Typhos wanted Osiris "put to death as soon and as violently as possible," while the barbarians, "although they believed they had been wronged, were indignant at this and respected his virtue." According to Zosimus (5.18.9), in complete contrast, Gaïnas threatened the hostages with drawn sword before agreeing to settle for exile. The picturesque detail of the sword may be an embellishment to enhance the picture of the ruthless barbarian, but Chrysostom's *Homilia cum Saturninus et Aurelianus acti essent in exilium* confirms the danger in which the hostages at one stage stood. Yet according to Synesius, the barbarians not only refused to execute Osiris but were "embarrassed" even to exile him and "decided that it should not be exile but *retirement* (μετάστασις)!"

It should be remembered that it was Gaïnas who had insisted on the execution of Eutropius.[64] It was also Typhos, Synesius alleges, who sug-

---

62. *HE* 11.8 (p. 138.22 Bidez-Winkelmann; cf. pp. 16.25, 52.14). Cf. Hdt. 7.211.3, just cited.

63. "Osiris has decided to bring him back with all the compulsion and trickery he can manage. As soon as he is away from his troops, he will take away his command and cruelly destroy him and you and your children" (108C).

64. Zos. 5.18.2. Compare too the evidently ironic frag. 75.6 (= 67.10 Blockley) of Eunapius: "But when Gaïnas had destroyed the enemy (for he waged an extremely vigorous campaign against the eunuch, so very noble a man was he)."

gested that the barbarians sack "Thebes," a suggestion that, once more, the barbarians repudiated (110C). For their leader "said he marched against Osiris not as a volunteer but under a compulsion that Osiris himself had created" (110D).

Coming from Synesius of all people, this astonishing apology for a barbarian unanimously condemned in the rest of our tradition is the clearest possible proof that he was writing while Gaïnas was still alive and still a threat. In book 2, by contrast, written when Gaïnas evidently no longer threatened Constantinople, we are assured that the barbarians were planning "utterly to destroy Egyptian society and govern it in Scythian fashion" (121B). So much for the boldness with which Synesius has so often been credited.

Such audacious manipulation of the facts must appear all the more piquant when it is borne in mind that Synesius had chosen the wrong side. It should now be clear why book 2, written after Gaïnas had withdrawn to Thrace, is such an evasive and unsatisfactory work. Still clearer, Synesius had nothing to gain by adding to his book in later years. So disastrously misconceived a work could not possibly be brought up to date. Before long Gaïnas was killed, and far from being replaced by Aurelian Caesarius went from strength to strength. It was in wholly different circumstances that Aurelian was eventually recalled to the prefecture in 414.

IV. ANTI-GERMANISM IN ACTION

Racial prejudice is always at least latent in any society with a sizable minority of a different ethnic origin. And the problem is always worse when, as with the Goths in the Roman world, there is a religious, as well as a racial, difference. The question is, Was anti-Germanism a *political* issue in East Roman society? Simplistic answers have held the field hitherto. With barbarian rebellions on every side, it will surprise no one that there was an antibarbarian party. The question is, Was there a *pro*-barbarian party?

The thesis of an antibarbarian party committed to "de-Germanize" the army was inferred from Synesius's *De regno* and *De providentia*. We have now seen that, read properly, neither work supports the idea. But what of the evidence outside Synesius? Seeck and Demougeot set forth most clearly as an explanation of various events in 399–401 the hypothesis that once in power in 399 Aurelian ruthlessly put antibarbarian policies into effect and purged the army of Gothic soldiers and generals alike. For example, Seeck claimed that it was because of this new policy that Tribigild broke off negotiations with Arcadius and Gaïnas joined him in open rebellion. It was also because Aurelian dismissed him from the command in Illyricum that Alaric resumed the life of a freebooter and turned to Italy; Aurelian thus bears indirect responsibility for the sack of Rome. Closer inspection will show that these are highly dubious connections. To begin with Gaïnas and Tribigild, did the advent of Aurelian in August 399 really affect the behavior of the two Gothic commanders in Phrygia?

We have already seen reason to doubt whether, as Zosimus alleges, Gaïnas and Tribigild planned their rebellion in advance. Indeed, there was no one rebellion in which both collaborated. First came Tribigild's rebellion, which Gaïnas exploited to his own ends; and nearly a year later the coup of April 400 at Chalcedon, in which Tribigild played no part. A number of intermediate stages may be distinguished. We should not imagine that Gaïnas had the coup at Chalcedon in mind when he left Constantinople on Tribigild's trail the year before. A review of the successive stages suggests less a preconcerted plan than a series of *ad hoc* responses, each more drastic than the last. Even after Chalcedon, Gaïnas still seems to have had no clear plan of campaign; whence the rapid disintegration of his position.

Gaïnas's first move, not taken till after Leo's defeat, was to tell Arcadius that he was not strong enough to inflict a military defeat on Tribigild and that the only solution was to give way to his demands. Chief among these demands was the surrender of Eutropius, who he claimed was responsible for the entire situation.[65] The best that can be said for Gaïnas's conduct at this stage is that after the destruction of his colleague's army he may have been genuinely dubious about committing his own Gothic troops against Tribigild's Goths.[66] But even so, it was not for Gaïnas in such a situation to tell the emperor to surrender his chief minister to the enemy. Tribigild might in fact have been satisfied with the Roman command he had asked for before rebelling. But at no point do we hear what Tribigild's own terms were; Gaïnas claimed to speak for him. There can be little doubt that Gaïnas was using Tribigild to satisfy both his own ambition and his long-standing grudge against Eutropius.[67]

Arcadius responded by dismissing Eutropius from office and send-

65. Zos. 5.17.5.

66. So, for example, Albert 1984, 121f.

67. According to Zosimus, he felt that he had not been "considered worthy of the appropriate rank" (5.13.1) and was especially disgruntled by the twin honors Eutropius had recently acquired, the consulate and patriciate (5.17.4).

ing him to exile in Cyprus. This was not enough for Gaïnas. He wrote again, insisting that Tribigild would not be satisfied till Eutropius was "got rid of."[68] Once more Arcadius complied; Eutropius was recalled from Cyprus and executed. Again, there seems no reason to doubt this account. Book 2 of Claudian's *In Eutropium*, together with its long "stop press" preface, confirms that Eutropius's fall did indeed happen in two stages: first, exile to Cyprus and, then, recall and execution.[69]

For the next stage of the story it may be helpful to quote Zosimus 5.18.4 entire:

> Although it was obvious to everyone that Gaïnas was now moving toward revolution, he thought he was undetected; having Tribigild under his thumb because of his superiority in power and rank, he made a truce with the emperor and exchanged oaths on behalf of Tribigild. He then returned through Phrygia and Lydia, followed by Tribigild.

Unfortunately Zosimus does not date this encounter, but it must by now have been fairly late in the year. The reference to oaths suggests that Gaïnas and Arcadius met face-to-face; and if Gaïnas concluded a truce on behalf of Tribigild, the implication is that he was present and Tribigild not. It is interesting to note that however "obvious" it may have seemed after the event that Gaïnas and Tribigild were in collusion at the time, Gaïnas himself was still behaving—and being treated by the imperial government—as an independent agent.

Aurelian must now have been in power for at least a month, and there is no suggestion that Gaïnas was reacting drastically to a drastic new antibarbarian policy. On the contrary, he came to Constantinople to announce that the trouble with Tribigild was over. Zosimus shows that in retrospect at least he was thought to be lying, but there seems no reason to doubt that at this stage Gaïnas hoped that with Eutropius finally out of the way both he and Tribigild would receive the rank and honor they deserved. So both Tribigild's revolt and Gaïnas's prevarication antedate Aurelian's prefecture. Not only did Aurelian not provoke the two Goths to revolt. The first month of his prefecture saw a temporary solution to the grievances of both. Not only did he not immediately take a firm antibarbarian stand. He began, as we have seen, by collaborating with Gaïnas, superintending the treacherous execution of Eutropius.

68. Zos. 5.18.1.

69. Zosimus also twice mentions Eutropius's asylum, confirmed not only by Claudian but by the homily Chrysostom delivered while the unfortunate eunuch was cowering behind the altar. Zosimus's further claim that Eutropius was executed at Chalcedon so as not to violate the oath given him in church is also borne out in part by Philostorgius's statement that the execution took place at Panteichion, a suburb of Chalcedon (*HE* 11.6).

The next stage was Gaïnas's return in April, when he demanded the surrender of Aurelian, Saturninus, and John. Unfortunately Zosimus gives no explanation for this demand, but we may surely infer that Aurelian did not keep some agreement made with Gaïnas at the earlier meeting. It is of course open to believers in the nationalist program to infer that it was during this interval that Aurelian finally proclaimed it.[70] Yet is it conceivable that he did so at a moment when all three Eastern *magistri militum* were Goths and one of them suspected of collusion with a Gothic rebel?[71] Whether or not Aurelian agreed with Synesius about the desirability of a national army, there were obviously serious practical problems in eliminating the current system. Seeck conceded that Aurelian chose an "unhappy moment" to make his announcement, but saw him as a fanatic whose intransigence provoked the rebellions of both Gaïnas and Alaric.

The weakest element in this highly influential characterization of Aurelian is that not even Synesius so portrays him. Osiris is presented throughout as a *weak* ruler: well-meaning and noble, but culpably weak. When Demougeot claimed that Aurelian "attempted to rid himself of Gaïnas with a prosecution for high treason,"[72] citing the speech of Typhos's wife in *De providentia* 109A, she entirely ignored the fact that these are the words of a character who is patently represented as lying. Even so, she suppressed the one element in the context that made the suggestion, however false, at any rate not absurd: namely that Osiris's plan was *secret*. It is only because the secret was betrayed to him by Typhos's wife that Gaïnas *anticipated* Osiris's move by rebellion. So the only source directly contradicts what it is alleged to prove: that Gaïnas rebelled in response to the new anti-German policy.

Aurelian's crime was not some new policy toward Gaïnas, but precisely his reversion to the old. This explains why Gaïnas reacted in April 400 exactly as he had done in July 399. It was the continuation of Eutropius's policy toward Gaïnas that brought about Aurelian's fall. Zosimus does not tell us Arcadius's side of the truce with Gaïnas, but we may surely infer that Gaïnas was concerned then with the same issues that concerned him after the deposition of Aurelian.

For all the talk in our sources about Gaïnas's outrageous demands,

---

70. "Proclaimed" is Seeck's own word ("verkündigte," 1913, 318). At the very least one would expect such a potentially explosive scheme to be put into effect secretly over a long period—which, significantly enough, is just what Synesius's fiction envisages (108D–109A).

71. The three: Alaric, Fravitta, and Gaïnas.

72. Demougeot 1951, 246.

the only two that can be identified are, first, an Arian church in Constantinople and, second, the consulate. When arguing against the Arian church, Chrysostom is represented by Theodoret as begging Gaïnas to be satisfied with his wealth and honors, remarking specifically: "You have been deemed worthy of the consular robe" (τῆς ὑπατικῆς ἠξιώθης στολῆς).[73] According to a recent interpretation, Gaïnas was "granted the status of an ex-consul."[74] But there is no other evidence for the conferment of honorary consular status before the reign of Zeno.[75] In any case, why should Gaïnas have settled for anything less than the real thing? Why should he not have aspired to the ordinary consulate? Most of the great Theodosian marshals, three of them barbarians, had been so honored: Saturninus (cos. 383), Richomeres (384), Bauto (385), Timasius and Promotus (389), Abundantius (393), and (in 400) Stilicho. Zosimus draws particular attention to Gaïnas's indignation at Eutropius's consulate, and we may imagine how he felt when he learned that the Eastern consul for 400 was to be not himself but Eutropius's successor Aurelian. If we may press the chronological context in Theodoret,[76] within a week or so of the coup Gaïnas was already consul designate for 401. This was surely a request that Aurelian's successor, the new and more realistic prefect Caesarius, finally prevailed upon Arcadius to grant.

Arcadius considered the other request seriously, but after consulting Chrysostom he finally turned it down.[77] It is significant of Gaïnas's aims that even at this stage he accepted refusal and submitted to the indignity of attending a church outside the city walls. Here too Caesarius may have supported Gaïnas's request. In book 2 Synesius accuses Typhos of being "Scythian" in his religion (121B), but in book 1 he employs the tactic (analyzed in section III, above) of transferring responsibility from Gaïnas to Typhos. There he claims that Typhos tried to introduce a false temple into the city, "not in his own person, for fear of the people of Egypt, but through the barbarians" (115B). That is to say, Synesius claims, preposterously enough, that it was really Caesarius who wanted the Arian church, but to protect himself he tried to use Gaïnas to achieve his own ends. It will be noted that in effect Synesius unwittingly concedes that there was no direct evidence to associate Caesarius with the

73. As quoted by Theodoret (*HE* 5.32.6).

74. *PLRE* I.380.

75. *CLRE*, pp. 9–10.

76. Theodoret evidently did considerable research for the lost five-book *Life of Chrysostom* summarized by Photius (Cod. 273, p. 507b Bekker); see too above, p. 98, for unique firsthand source material on Chrysostom cited by Theodoret. Baur (1959, 1:xxix–xxx) unnecessarily belittles Theodoret's value for the study of Chrysostom.

77. Theod. *HE* 5.32.

incident at all. It is almost inconceivable that a man who had enjoyed a distinguished career under Theodosius should actually have been an Arian. But a man whose father had been an Arian might at any rate be tolerant.[78] A law addressed to Caesarius as prefect and probably to be assigned to December 395 allows the extremist Arian sect of the Eunomians the right to make wills,[79] a right taken away from them by his intolerant predecessor Rufinus earlier the same year.[80] Not too much should be made of this one law since another, dated to April 396, orders that those responsible for the "crime of the Eunomians," whose "madness induced them to such false doctrine, shall be tracked down and expelled as exiles from the municipalities."[81] But it was enough for a bigot like Synesius to tar Caesarius with the same brush as his "darling Goths" (122B).

Seeck's influential thesis of a "victory of anti-Germanism" following Gaïnas's defeat is entirely dependent on the assumption (now shown to be false) that Aurelian was restored to the prefecture on Gaïnas's fall and carried out the rest of his reforms over a period of several years (401–5). If there were independent evidence that the prefect who collaborated with the Goths had been disgraced, if the Gothic general had soon been executed and the nationalist patriot restored to office, there might have been some basis for such speculations. But Caesarius was no more of a collaborator than Aurelian, and he was not disgraced or deposed; Aurelian was no more of a patriot than Caesarius, and he was not restored; and Fravitta remained the ranking Roman *magister militum* for several years. Indeed Fravitta's consulate in 401 must have been construed, as it was surely intended, as an eirenicon to the Gothic community of the Eastern empire, a sign that not all Goths were rebels and traitors: those who served the state could still rise to the pinnacle of fame.

This brings us to Alaric. We have seen that up till the sudden outbreak of Tribigild's rebellion, the main barbarian threat within the Eastern empire had been Alaric. He had plundered the Balkans for three

78. Taurus was Constantius's representative at the Council of Ariminum: Seeck 1894, 444; *PLRE* I.879–80; T. D. Barnes, *Entretiens . . . Fondation Hardt* 34 (1989): 313–14.

79. *Cod. Theod.* 16.5.27; 24 June (MSS), when Rufinus was still alive; 25 December (Seeck 1919, 287).

80. *Cod. Theod.* 16.5.23.

81. *Cod. Theod.* 16.5.31; cf. 32; 28, addressed to an Aurelian who was proconsul of Asia on 3 September 395, lays down sanctions for all heretics "who deviate in even a minor point of doctrine from the path of the Catholic faith." If both date and office are correct, this cannot be the famous Aurelian, who could not have been proconsul of Asia after already holding the higher post of city prefect.

years, laid siege to Constantinople, and indirectly been the ruin of both
Rufinus and Eutropius. It looks as though it was at one time feared that
he might assist Tribigild, since Eutropius's original plan was to send Leo
against Tribigild himself, at the time in Phrygia, and Gaïnas "to meet the
enemy in Thrace and the Hellespont if he found them disturbing those
regions."[82] Tribigild might have marched down to the Hellespont,[83] but
it is also the place Alaric would have crossed if he had wished to do so.[84]

Unfortunately, though so loquacious about Tribigild, Zosimus tells
us nothing at all about the activities of Alaric between 396 and 402. And
though he gives an account of Stilicho's expedition of 396 that forms a
useful corrective to Claudian,[85] he dated it to 395, having confused it
with the earlier expedition during the lifetime of Rufinus.[86] It is from
Claudian, not Zosimus, that we learn the key to Synesius's antibarbarian
tirade in De regno: Eutropius's appointment of Alaric to the Roman command in Illyricum.[87] This presumably kept him quiet for a while, though
in 398 the "skirmishings" mentioned by Synesius seemed to some to
augur a renewal of hostilities. But they never came. The real puzzle of
400–401 is that Alaric suddenly decided to leave Illyricum and invade
Italy, arriving there on 18 November 401.[88]

On the traditional interpretation, this has never seemed much of a
problem. According to Seeck,[89] in the summer of 399 the new prefect
Aurelian at once dismissed Alaric from his command and withdrew his
subsidies, whereupon Alaric began to devastate Illyricum again. Within
a year he had bled Illyricum white and so turned to the West. Yet is it
credible that Aurelian would have wantonly provoked aggression from
Alaric when he was already faced with the problem of Gaïnas and Tribigild in Asia? For Seeck he was a fanatic, but we have shown that there is

82. Zos. 5.14.1.
83. At 5.14.3 Zosimus alleges that Gaïnas had planned to meet up with Tribigild at
the Hellespont, so that they could take over all of Asia; but that is surely no more than an
inference—and a very improbable inference—from Gaïnas's location there.
84. So Ridley 1982 ad loc., but there seems no justification for his further inference
that Gaïnas was already "distrusted by Eutropius." After all, serious as Gaïnas's subsequent collusion with Tribigild proved to be, collusion with Alaric would have been even
more disastrous. If Eutropius had the slightest reason to suspect Gaïnas of harboring treasonable designs, he would never have appointed him in the first place.
85. Cameron 1970a, 86f., 169f.
86. Cameron (1970a, 474–77) shows that "the telescoping of the two campaigns was
already present in Eunapius." See too forthcoming article of Cameron on date 396.
87. According to Zosimus, it was a Roman command that Alaric really wanted,
"being angry [in 395/96] that he did not command an army but had only the barbarians
Theodosius had given him when he helped to put down the tyrant Eugenius" (5.5.4).
88. Chron.Min. I.299.
89. Seeck 1913, 318 and 328.

no support for this view even in Synesius. As for the renewed devastation of Illyricum, the only source cited surely refers to Alaric's return to
the East in 403, after his failure to break into Italy.[90] Faced with the withdrawal of his subsidies, we should expect Alaric to have brought direct
pressure to bear on Arcadius, desperately vulnerable during most of
399–400 because of Tribigild's rebellion and Gaïnas's coup. The invasion
of Italy was not just a campaign: the Goths took their women and children and booty with them.[91] There must have been some major reason
for such a mass emigration. Mazzarino remarked casually that "the antibarbarian party purged Illyricum of barbarians."[92] But it is difficult to believe the Eastern government capable of such a feat in 400–401, and it is
certainly remarkable that such a victory should not have been recorded.
At a time when imperial victories were not as common or decisive as in
happier days, more was made of every success.[93] The local chronicle of
Constantinople that is partially preserved in the *Paschal Chronicle* and the
Chronicle of Marcellinus routinely records the announcement of imperial
victories at Constantinople,[94] and we might expect to have found some
mention of a victory over Alaric here if not in the erratic Zosimus.

The end of 400 saw the arrival of a new factor on the scene, one
whose significance has perhaps been underestimated: Uldin the Hun. A
week or two after the massacre Gaïnas withdrew to Thrace, but, finding
it hard to provision his troops there,[95] he decided to make for the Chersonnese and cross the Hellespont into Asia. Not having any ships, he
improvised rafts from freshly cut trees. But Fravitta had ships with
bronze prows and easily cut Gaïnas's force to pieces. Gaïnas himself,
who had remained in the Chersonnese, withdrew into Thrace again,
where Fravitta (as we have seen) did not pursue him. Gaïnas first killed
his remaining Roman troops, whose loyalty he suspected,[96] and then

90. *Collectio Avellana* 38.

91. Claudian describes how the Romans captured Gothic women, and the plunder of
Greece after Pollentia: *Bell.Get.* 84–85, 615–26; *VI Cons.Hon.* 130, 243–45, 282, 297.

92. Mazzarino 1942, 68.

93. See McCormick 1986, 59–60 ("There appears to be a correlation between severe
and widely perceived blows to imperial prestige and intensification in the rhythm of imperial victory celebrations"). But his statistical argument is misleading, since he makes insufficient allowance for the different nature of the sources from the late fourth century on:
the chronicles list victory announcements that might not have been mentioned at all in
earlier sources.

94. *CLRE* 54–56; McCormick 1986, 56f.

95. "He found the cities defended by walls and guarded by their magistrates and inhabitants: as a result of previous attacks, they were not only prepared for war, but ready to
fight with all their strength" (Zos. 5.19.6). It is optimistic to attribute this, with Demougeot
(1951, 259), to the implementation of Aurelian's national program.

96. Zos. 5.21.6.

"crossed the Danube with his barbarians, intending to return to his native land and there spend the rest of his days." This is most unlikely. We may compare the case of the Frankish *magister militum* Silvanus falsely accused of treason in 355: after considering rejoining the Franks beyond the frontier he decided that they would "either kill him or betray him for a bribe."[97] A Romanized barbarian could not return to the old life. Gaïnas had the additional disadvantage of not coming from a Gothic royal house. He had deserted from the Gothic army after Adrianople and enlisted in the Roman army as a common soldier.[98] Paradoxically, here was a barbarian leader whose authority was limited to the Roman world.

Did he then actually cross the Danube, and was it there that he was killed by Uldin? So it has usually been supposed in modern times. But as Gibbon observed long ago, "the narrative of Zosimus . . . must be corrected by the testimony of Socrates and Sozomen, that he was killed in Thrace; and by the precise and authentic dates of the . . . Paschal Chronicle."[99] According to the *Paschal Chronicle,* the battle with Fravitta took place on 23 December 400, and Gaïnas's pickled head arrived at Constantinople on 3 January 401. The interval is far too short for the several encounters Gaïnas is said to have had with Uldin and the trip from wherever the final battle took place to Constantinople,[100] though one of the dates may be wrong.[101] But Socrates and Sozomen both place Gaïnas's death in Thrace, even if they do make the blunder of saying that he was killed by a Roman army. And according to Philostorgius, perhaps present in Constantinople at the time and writing ca. 430, it was after retiring to "upper Thrace" that "some Huns soon after attacked and killed him."[102] Even if Gaïnas briefly crossed the Danube to evade pursuit and recruit reinforcements, he will surely have crossed back again when Uldin began his pursuit. It is likely enough that the final battle took place in Thrace.

So it may be that 401 saw a major Hunnic incursion into Thrace.

97. Amm. Marc. 15.5.16.
98. Soz. *HE* 8.4.1.
99. *Decline and Fall,* ed. Bury (1909), 3:394 n. 39.
100. This is true even if we accept Maenchen-Helfen's ingenious suggestion (1973, 59) that the final battle took place near Novae, "the place on the Danube nearest the capital, connected with it by a first-rate road."
101. It is possible that 23 December could be the date of the battle with Uldin rather than Fravitta, which might have fallen much earlier (December would be rather late in the year for an experienced commander to try crossing the Hellespont on rafts). The usually more reliable Marcellinus places Gaïnas's death in February. For both texts, Mommsen, *Chron. Min.* II.66.
102. *HE* 11.8, p. 139.17–18 Bidez-Winkelmann.

Zosimus goes on to describe how Uldin received a reward for Gaïnas's head and concluded a treaty with Arcadius. No terms are mentioned, but the Huns presumably offered to fight as federates on the usual terms. The obvious guess is that they offered to fight the Goths in Illyricum. Since it was to escape the Huns that the Goths had made their fateful crossing of the Danube in 376, this cannot have been welcome news to Alaric. If it was now that the Eastern government withdrew Alaric's subsidies, he might well have felt that this was an opportune moment to move on to fresh pastures.

A contemporary document makes an interesting link between the fall of Gaïnas and Alaric's departure for the West. It is a homily falsely ascribed to Chrysostom that was delivered at the tomb of St. Thomas on his festal day, that is to say, as Tillemont saw, at Edessa on 22 August.[103] The homily is an attack on Arianism, which the preacher associated particularly with barbarians, that is to say, Goths. St. Thomas is represented as reproaching Arius for taking holy plunder from the hands of a barbarian and for despoiling the apostles. "Fall with your own allies," he cries. "I have cast down one of your citadels; I have freed Thrace of your tyranny."[104] Thomas promises that he will soon chase him from the rest of the world; soon he will free the West from Arius's folly. "Blessed Thomas, as you have freed Thrace, so may you free the West. I shall hear that the bandit has been destroyed like the tyrant before him." The only explanation that fits all these clues, as again Tillemont saw, is that the tyrant is Gaïnas, the bandit Alaric,[105] and the year 402.[106] The preacher clearly seems to think of Alaric as having been driven from Thrace rather than leaving it of his own accord.

His talk of freeing the West as Thrace had been freed is particularly hard to reconcile with the popular modern notion that it was with the blessing of the Eastern government that Alaric was sent off to be a thorn

103. PG 59.497–500, with Montfaucon's introduction; cf. too J. A. De Aldama, *Repertorium pseudochrysostomianum* (Paris 1965), 193, no. 517. The sarcophagus of Thomas had been brought to Edessa on 22 August 394: H. Delehaye, *Les origines du culte des martyrs*, 2d ed. (Brussels 1933), 59 and 212–13.

104. PG 59.500.

105. Tillemont knew that Gaïnas is not said to have stolen any holy vessels, but made the unhappy conjecture that Arcadius had been forced to give him vessels from the Holy Apostles in Constantinople. This is most improbable. It must have been Alaric's men who robbed churches during his three years of plundering. It is clear even from Orosius's apologetic (*Hist. adv. pag.* 7.39) that the Goths plundered the churches of Rome in 410.

106. Alaric is still thought of as a threat to the West, suggesting that the preacher was speaking before he returned to Illyricum in 403, driven out of Italy by Stilicho. Demougeot (1951, 269 n. 194) strangely thought that the bandit was Stilicho (who was not even an Arian) and that the homily reflected the propaganda of the "antibarbarians" that Stilicho would soon fall from power.

in Stilicho's side.[107] There is in fact a decisive argument against this hypothesis. In 401 Stilicho recognized the Eastern consul for the first time since 398, and in 402 Honorius publicly signaled the restoration of concord between East and West by taking the consulate jointly with his brother. It is not till the end of 403 that relations began to deteriorate again, with a series of formal protests from Honorius that Arcadius ignored and the nonrecognition of the Eastern consul for 404. It would be impossible to explain this temporary thaw in the cold war if there had been the slightest suspicion that Alaric had been paid or encouraged to invade the West.[108]

Whatever the reasons for Alaric's departure, the Eastern government surely took the credit for it. And the head of the Eastern government at this time was undoubtedly Caesarius. There was no need of antibarbarian fanatics to take what steps were required to save the East from Gaïnas and Alaric. Indeed it may have been a providential intervention by the Huns that helped speed Alaric on his way, as it had previously cut off Gaïnas's escape. There is no reason to believe that Caesarius was any more of a friend to the Goths than his brother was. He was just a shrewder politician. It is not that there were no antibarbarians. But since there were no pro-barbarians, it makes little sense to talk of an antibarbarian party. The East may well have cut down so far as possible on the use of federates in the years to come, but by enrolling barbarians individually in the regular army rather than building up a genuinely national army. And there is certainly no evidence that there was a barbarian purge. The massacre was a response to the tyranny of Gaïnas rather than the expression of a deep hatred of all Goths. Many Goths, both Catholic and Arian, survived the massacre. There was a thriving community of Arian Goths in fifth-century Constantinople, whose theological differences with a splinter group known as the Psathyrians were reconciled by the consul Plinta in 419.[109]

V. CONCLUSIONS

Predictably enough, the antibarbarian straitjacket was never a comfortable fit. Inevitably, the founding members of the coalition (apart from Synesius himself) had to be Aurelian, John, Saturninus, and Eu-

---

107. E.g., Demougeot 1951, 269; Grumel 1951, 39; Stein 1959, 248 ("Le gouvernement oriental . . . avait ainsi le double avantage de se débarasser de Barbares dangereux et du même coup de tenir, grâce à eux, Stilicon en échec").

108. As rightly emphasized by W. N. Bayless, *Classical Journal* 72 (1976): 65–67.

109. E. A. Thompson, *The Visigoths in the Time of Ulfila* (Oxford 1966), 135–38.

doxia. But Saturninus, as Holum has already remarked, "had earlier been an architect of the Theodosian Gothic settlement in 382, whence the barbarian 'problem' took its roots."[110] And Eudoxia was the daughter of a Frankish general.[111] Of course, it is always possible to argue that Saturninus came to repent the Theodosian policies he had been obliged to execute, and that to gloss over her own German origins Eudoxia did her best to be more Roman than the Romans. But there is no evidence at all that even John and Aurelian were antibarbarians, much less fanatics.[112] Not one of Arcadius's ministers pursued a consistently antibarbarian policy.

Hardly more convincing than this "anti-German coalition" is Dagron's thesis that it was a "senatorial party" that took over from Eutropius: "Ce qui est certain, en revanche, c'est que toutes les analyses politiques de cette époque tiennent le plus grand compte de l'existence d'un sénat à Constantinople et de la personnalité de ce sénat."[113] But it is not easy at any time to identify the Constantinopolitan senate as a separate body with esprit de corps and policies of its own distinct from those of the court.[114] And of Aurelian's two identifiable associates, John was clearly a court favorite, in 400 perhaps not yet even a member of the senate. And Saturninus had been a professional soldier all his active life (from ca. 350 to at least 383). As perhaps the oldest surviving Eastern consul, he could no doubt be described as a prominent senator, but his continuing importance was undoubtedly due to his abilities as a courtier. He is described by Zosimus as a flatterer, "adept at pandering to the whims and schemes of imperial favorites."[115] So far was he from being a staunch senatorial champion that he even curried favor with Eutropius, betraying his former colleague Timasius.[116] It was not on ideological grounds that Gaïnas singled out Saturninus as one of his victims in April 400, but because he saw him as a creature of Eutropius, a turncoat against his class. As for Caesarius and Aurelian, while they were certainly prominent members of the Byzantine senate, at the same time they were men who, like their father before them, had spent all their lives in the imperial service. It is not obvious that such men represented senatorial traditions as distinct from those of the imperial bureaucracy.

110. Holum 1982, 68 n. 80.
111. It was for this reason that Güldenpenning (1885, 97) put her in the pro-German camp; more hesitantly, Bury 1889, 79.
112. "Nationalistes farouches," in Demougeot's favorite formulation (1951, 265).
113. Dagron 1974, 204.
114. Cameron 1978, 276.
115. Zos. 5.9.3.
116. Zos. 5.9.3.

Moreover, they were rivals. And their rivalry stemmed from the fact that each had attached himself to a different court favorite.

The even less plausible recent appeal to a party of "traditionalists" or "Hellenists" has been discussed in chapter 3. There is no identifiable correlation between classical tastes in literature and philosophy and either religious or political views.

Byzantine politics are not to be explained in terms of these anachronistic party labels. All political rivalry was overshadowed and conditioned by the paramount need to gain and maintain influence with the emperor. We must accept the obvious explanation of the infighting at court ca. 400: the inevitable struggle for power behind the throne of a weak emperor. In 399 the issue was not so much hostility toward Goths in general as the very real threat from one particular Goth: Gaïnas. The ascendancy at which Gaïnas aimed would have threatened the independence of all the civilian rivals for the power behind Arcadius's throne. Eutropius made use of Gaïnas to rid himself of Rufinus and was then unwise enough not to fulfill his part of the bargain. The ambitious Eudoxia wanted Eutropius out of the palace for her own reasons. There is no need to fabricate an ideological basis for Aurelian's ambition—and certainly no evidence on which to do so. It was the combined efforts of Eudoxia, Gaïnas, and Aurelian, each with different aims, that brought Eutropius down. There is no new anti-Germanism evident in Aurelian's policies once he was prefect. Indeed in the only areas where we might have looked for it, that is to say, in his dealings with Gaïnas and Stilicho, he pursued exactly the same policies as Eutropius. He even repeated Eutropius's fatal mistake of underestimating Gaïnas's ambition and determination.

We do not need to credit Caesarius, waiting in the wings, with a probarbarian ideology. If he supported Gaïnas's perfectly reasonable demand for an Arian church, he showed himself more of a traditionalist than his brother. Synesius describes Typhos as "overturning ancestral laws" in championing the barbarian's demand (115B), the Hellene unexpectedly here showing himself a prophet of the new intolerance of his age. In fact it was less than twenty years since Theodosius had forbidden Arians to worship within the city walls.[117] If Caesarius negotiated with Gaïnas in the immediate aftermath of the massacre, as Synesius alleges, this was hardly "to invite him back, as though no irreparable damage had been done" (121B), but to implore him not to take the terrible revenge all must have been fearing. It was, after all, the Goths who were

117. *Cod.Theod.* 16.5.6 (381), 12 (383), 13 (384); cf. Socr. *HE* 5.20.

the injured party, with thousands of civilians butchered in the streets, and women and children burned alive in their own church. So long as it was prudent, Caesarius negotiated; once the situation permitted, he declared Gaïnas a public enemy and saw to the rapid mobilization of Fravitta's army.[118] Despite Synesius's repeated allegations of plotting and collusion with the Goths, within a year of taking office Caesarius had achieved a more satisfactory solution of the Gothic problem than any of his predecessors.

The reluctance of Eutropius and Aurelian after him to give Gaïnas what he wanted is surely to be interpreted less in terms of racial prejudice than as just one aspect of a (largely successful) attempt to keep the generals subordinate to the civil authorities. Eutropius, a palace eunuch with no independent power base, was naturally anxious to protect himself against all rivals. But he was most concerned about the military. It is no coincidence that there had been no more military consuls since Theodosius's death. Eutropius had actually treated Gaïnas better than he had treated such Roman generals as Abundantius and Timasius. Gaïnas he refused to promote, but Abundantius and Timasius he accused of treason and exiled. Yet however personal his motives, perhaps the main achievement of Eutropius's much-maligned administration was, at the critical moment, to have prevented a military takeover of the government by an Eastern Stilicho, whether barbarian or Roman.

Caesarius relaxed the unwise confrontational policy toward Stilicho pursued by his three predecessors without making any real concessions. His chief general Fravitta was a man of barbarian birth, but thoroughly Romanized, loyal, and above all successful. It was thanks to Eutropius, Caesarius, and their longer-lived successor Anthemius that power at the Eastern court continued to remain firmly in civilian hands, despite the incapacity of Arcadius and the minority of Theodosius II. This is a phenomenon of greater importance and more lasting significance than the transient, if terrifying, wave of anti-Germanism that racked Constantinople on 12 July 400.

118. It was the praetorian prefect who supervised conscription and acted as quartermaster general for the army: R. Grosse, *Römische Militärgeschichte* (Berlin 1920), 158–60.

• NINE •

TRANSLATION OF *DE PROVIDENTIA: EGYPTIANS; OR, ON PROVIDENCE* *

Preface[1]

88A   This is a story about[2] the sons of Taurus[3] and the first part, as far as the riddle of the wolf, was recited[4] while the wicked brother

---

*The page numbers of Petau's edition constitute the most generally useful system of reference to Synesius's text, since the editions of both Migne and Terzaghi include them; other systems of reference are less universal. Accordingly, we have used the Petau numbers throughout our argument and have placed them in the margin of our translation.

1. προθεωρία: Viljamaa (1968, 71–72) distinguishes the drier *protheoria*, announcing the writer's subject and approach, from *prolalia* and *dialexis*, in which *captatio benevolentiae* was a more important element. Synesius's preface introduces books 1 and 2 united. A preface to book 2 would have been placed immediately before it (cf. Cameron 1970b, 77–78); section 2.1 (116B–117C) serves as a proem to book 2 (see ad loc.). The two books may not have been published together till after Synesius's return home, when a clearer hint at the identity of the protagonists ("the sons of Taurus"; see note below) had become necessary. (Allegorical riddling was a game of Synesius's correspondence, e.g., *Ep.* 142.) By explaining the work's genesis, the preface also apologizes for its formal awkwardness: book 1 is artistically unified and complete by itself, and though book 2 continues the tale, it goes beyond the data and implications of the myth.

2. Not "in the days of" (so Fitzgerald, Nicolosi, Casini; an odd locution in any case since "the days of the sons of Taurus" were Synesius's own as well), which would require genitive rather than dative with ἐπί, as Krabinger (1835) points out ad loc.; "auf die Söhne des Taurus" correctly Grützmacher (1913, 56).

3. Cos. 361; *PLRE* I.879. On the identification of his sons Aurelian and Caesarius, see chapter 5; there was a third brother, Armonius, who was killed ca. 391/92 (Joh. Ant. frag. 187; *PLRE* I.108).

4. Despite 113D it is doubtful how widely so outspoken a tract was disseminated at the time.

88B   was exercising the power he had won in the rebellion.[5] The second
was added after the return of the best men, who asked that the
book not be left incomplete with the story of their misfortunes.
Since the events foretold by the god[6] seemed to be coming to pass,
they wanted the tale to go on to their better fortunes. And so,
while events had begun to shape the tyrant's downfall,[7] the story
followed along. It is especially remarkable for its comprehensive
treatment of many themes. Several philosophical issues hitherto
undecided[8] found a place for consideration in the story, and each
one was closely investigated. Lives were described, to be examples
of vice and virtue; the work also contains a history of current
events, and the story has been fashioned and elaborated throughout with a view to utility.

Book I

89A   I. The story is Egyptian. Egyptians are extraordinarily wise. So
perhaps this story, even though it is only a story, might hint at something more than a story because it is Egyptian. If it is less a story
89B   than a sacred discourse, all the more should it be written down.[9]
          Osiris and Typhos[10] were brothers, born of the same seed. But

    5. That is to say, Gaïnas's coup of April 400.
    6. At 114C–115A.
    7. πραττομένης οὖν ἤδη τῆς τυραννικῆς καθαρέσεως. The present participle is highly
tendentious, as are equally misleading claims from 121B on (καὶ τὰ ἄλλα ἡ τυραννὶς
ἄψυχος ἦν, etc.). In fact Caesarius remained in power till long after the publication of both
books of *De providentia*. Synesius's *suggestio falsi* has misled most translators, who imply
that Typhos was actually deposed or was on the point of deposition at this time (e.g.,
Fitzgerald, "already in progress"; Nicolosi, "mentre avveniva"). He is a "tyrant" in both
late antique senses of the word, a usurper and an abuser of the power he holds (cf. Lampe,
s.v.). Clauss (1980, 133–34) errs in trying to identify Osiris's kingship (with implications
for Typhos's tyranny) as a formal regency or the consulate.
    8. I.e., the heavenly rather than corporeal origin of the soul, allegedly proven by the
existence of blood brothers with opposite characters, and the operation of divine Providence, allegedly proven by Typhos's (allegedly impending) downfall. There is a strong
general Neoplatonic influence on Synesius's thought, and he recalls various Neoplatonic
and other philosophers at many points, especially Porphyry and Plato himself, yet there is
no single (extant) philosophical text that could be described as a "source." It seems natural
to suppose that much of what he writes reflects Hypatia's teaching.
    9. This proem echoes Dio Chrysostom's introduction to his allegory of Heracles at
Or. 1.49 (εἰ δ' ἄρα μῦθον ἐθέλοις τινὰ ἀκοῦσαι, μᾶλλον δὲ ἱερὸν καὶ ὑγιῆ λόγον σχήματι
μύθου λεγόμενον, etc.). Synesius repeats the claim that his fable will be a guide to men's
future at 128A–B. He draws his plot principally from Plutarch's *De Iside et Osiride*, for
which see the excellent commentary of J. Gwyn Griffiths (1970).
    10. To judge from the unanimity of the MSS, Synesius spells Τυφώς, though his
major source Plutarch wrote Τυφῶν (*De Is. et Os.* 351F, 354A, 358A, etc.). On the variant
forms of the name in Greek literature, see M. L. West on Hesiod *Theog.* 306. The currency
of the form ending in -ν facilitated identification with the giant.

the kinship between souls and bodies is not one and the same. For it is not appropriate that souls be engendered by the same earthly parents, but that they should flow from a single spring.[11] The nature of the cosmos provides two, one luminous and the other murky. The murky spring bubbles up from the ground, since it is 89C rooted somewhere below. It springs out from the caverns of the earth as if it could somehow violate the divine law. But the luminous spring arises from the back of heaven;[12] it is sent down in order to administer the earthly lot. Upon coming down it is ordered to take special care in case, while organizing and arranging the disarranged and disordered, it become infected itself by its proximity to ugliness and disorder. There is a law of Themis laying down that if a soul communes with the farthest edge of being and yet guards its nature and survives undefiled, it will flow back again by the 89D same road and pour back into its own spring,[13] just as nature also compels souls that have somehow started out from the other region to settle at the lairs from which they sprang:

> Envy is there, and Rancor and the tribes of the other Calamities
> roam through the darkness in the field of Delusion.[14]

II. Among souls, these are "the noble and the ignoble";[15] it might happen that a Libyan and a Parthian are related in this way and that those whom we call brothers are in no way akin in the 90A relationship of their souls. The two Egyptian children appeared right from their births to be such a pair. They demonstrated it clearly as they matured.[16] The younger[17] was engendered and nur-

---

11. πηγή is a common Platonic metaphor for the origin of souls: e.g., Proclus *In Rep.* 2, p. 212.12 Kroll.

12. Image from Pl. *Phdr.* 247C.

13. E.g., Plotinus 1.6.7 on the descent of the soul, a commonplace of later Neoplatonism.

14. Empedocles frag. 121.2, 4 Diels-Kranz[7] (1954, I.6:360). Hierocles and Proclus quote from the same verses in a similar context (see Diels-Kranz, 360), as do Julian (*Or.* 7 [226B]) and Joh. Lydus (*Mens.* 4.159, p. 176.24 Wuensch), both omitted by Diels-Kranz. Synesius quotes the last line alone in *Ep.* 147 (p. 258.10 G); Garzya assumed that he took the line from Julian, but Julian quotes only the one line, and the present passage shows that Synesius knew more. Julian, Hierocles, Synesius, and Proclus must all be drawing from a common source.

15. εὐγένειαι καὶ δυσγένειαι, Pl. *Rep.* 608D.

16. Synesius departs from the myth to develop the characters of Osiris and Typhos, philosophical and immoderate respectively; the technique has affinities with contemporary panegyric and invective.

17. Osiris, as becomes apparent. In the myth (Plut. *De Is. et Os.* 355E–F, reflecting authentic Egyptian traditions: see Griffiths 1970, 296–307; inexplicitly, also Diod. 1.13.4), Osiris is the elder, born on the first epagomenal day, and Typhos only on the third. Sy-

tured by divine destiny, and in infancy he was fond of listening and fond of fable, for fable is a child's philosophy book.[18]

As he grew older, he loved an education that ever reached beyond his years. He gave full attention to his father, and he wanted to devour every point of each man's field of knowledge. He was eager to learn all his first elements all at once, like a puppy dog[19]—

90B   as of course is the way with natures that promise great things: they chafe and start up before their time, since they have already dedicated themselves to some cherished goal. And yet long before adolescence he was more sedate than a well-bred elder: he would listen decorously and whenever the need arose to speak, whether to ask a question on a point of the discussion or on some other matter, everyone noticed that he would hesitate and blush.[20] And he would make way and give up his seat for the Egyptian elders[21]—and this though he was the son of the man who held the supreme office![22]

90C   He also treated other children with respect. Consideration for people was very much a part of his nature. Even at that age it would have been difficult to find an Egyptian for whom the lad had not obtained from his father some favor or other.

The elder brother, Typhos, was, in a word, a complete boor. He wholeheartedly despised all wisdom,[23] both Egyptian wisdom and such foreign wisdom as the king was having his son Osiris taught.[24] Typhos ridiculed such stuff as being trivial and mind-

90D   enslaving. When he saw his brother going to school and living a

---

nesius could so casually diverge from the myth only on the basis of contemporary reality. The chronology of the brothers' careers supports the inference.

18. Plato approves the traditional use of fable in the first stages of a child's education (*Rep.* 377A); Aristotle remarks that it reflects the same wonder at the world that is the start of philosophy (*Metaph.* 982b18f.). Cf. Synesius *Ep.* 105, p. 188.17f. G; *Dion* 45B.

19. Many details of this section, including the comparison to a puppy dog and the reference to blushing, are taken from Xenophon's *Cyropaedia* (1.4.4); cf. too Pl. *Rep.* 539B.

20. Libanius's biography of Julian combines the same motifs of learning and modest blushing in discourse (*Or.* 18.30).

21. Cf. Hdt. 2.80; Achilles Tatius 8.17.5.

22. Libanius similarly emphasizes how decorously Julian behaved as a student by enumerating his relationships to emperors (*Or.* 18.11). It is notable that Synesius first identifies Typhos's and Osiris's father in terms as applicable to a Roman official—specifically, the praetorian prefect—as to an Egyptian king. Cf. *Ep.* 31 to Aurelian, in which Synesius refers to the benefits ὧν ἐπὶ τῆς μεγάλης ἀρχῆς ἅπασιν ἔθνεσιν αἴτιος γέγονας; in 123C he refers to Osiris as obtaining the μεγάλη ἀρχή. The portrait of the philosopher-king that follows is not meant to depict the real-life Taurus.

23. The emphasis on literary culture is in full harmony with Synesius's views expressed elsewhere, especially in the *Dion*. It is also a note that he played loudly in all his solicitations of patronage at this period: cf. *De dono* 309B–C, *De regno* 7B–C, 15B.

24. The distinction between native and "foreign" wisdom seems curious in the Egyptian context; teachers are specified only for "foreign." There can be little doubt that Syne-

well-mannered and modest life, he thought it cowardice if no one saw him punch or kick anyone or cheat in a race, although he was nimble and lean, and the body that clad him was a light burden for his soul. In addition, Osiris never even once gulped his drink or so roared with laughter[25] that it convulsed his whole body, as Typhos did constantly. He believed that a man lived up to his freedom only

91A by doing whatever he wanted in every situation he encountered. In his nature, Typhos did not resemble his kin or for that matter any other man in any way. To put it neatly, he was not even much like himself but was in every way a thing of evil.[26] At one moment, he would appear to be a sluggish and "useless burden of the earth,"[27] only rising from sleep long enough to glut himself and stock up with other necessities for his return to sleep; at other times, neglecting even nature's modest requirements, he would leap about gracelessly and bother both young and old. He admired bodily

91B strength as the most perfect good and employed it badly by tearing off doors and pelting people with globs of dirt.[28] And if anyone was hurt or if he could inflict any other damage, he took pride in this as if it proved his valor. Also, he would swell to ill-timed passion and be most violently inclined to engage in sex. Envy against his brother smouldered[29] within him. He also hated the Egyptians because the populace admired Osiris both in speech and song:[30] at home and at the common temples[31] all men everywhere prayed for all good things for him from the gods. This was Typhos's character and manner. He formed a gang of senseless children for the sole pur-

91C pose (it not being in him to love anyone from the heart) of having partisans who did not share Osiris's views. It was an easy thing for anyone to buy Typhos's favor and procure from him anything a child might want: just whisper abuse against Osiris.

sius is alluding to the contemporary Christian distinction between Christian and "external" culture (ἡ θύραθεν παιδεία), namely, pagan learning: see chapter 2, section IV.

25. ἐξεκάγχασεν, Xen. *Symp.* 1.16.

26. For the commonplace of self-contradiction in viciousness as vice's ultimate point, cf. 92C–D, 105C, 107C below; *De regno* 10D–11B (set within an exposition, 9D–11B, that suggests that this chaotic personality has its antecedents in Plato's contrast of the philosophical and tyrannical man, *Rep.* 8–9); Claud. *Bell. Gild.* 1.162–63.

27. *Il.* 18.104.

28. Cf. Xen. *Cyr.* 83.27; Men. *Dysk.* 83, 365.

29. ὑπετύφετο, a pun on "Typhos"; cf. Plut. *De Is. et Os.* 351E.

30. The same is said of Cyrus at Xen. *Cyr.* 1.4.25; with contemporary reference also to prose and verse panegyrics; cf. 113B below.

31. Cf. Hdt. 2.47: (in contrast to Greek practice) Egyptian temples were open to all with the one exception of swineherds; notably, so were Christian churches. Cf. John Chrysostom's reply to Gaïnas's request for an Arian church, "Every church is open to you" (Theod. *HE* 5.32).

And so from childhood their different natures assured the difference of their lives.

III. When roads fork, they part gradually at first and grow ever farther apart as they advance, until they reach the point of their 91D farthest divergence. One can see the same pattern in the young: a slight tendency to differ sets them far apart as they grow older.[32] With these two, it was no slight tendency. They took off in opposite directions at once, the one taking perfect virtue as his share, the other perfect vice. As they grew up, so too the opposition between their principles[33] grew along with them. More conspicuous still, their deeds were evidence of their different stamping.[34] While still a youth Osiris shared in the generalship with the men appointed to that office: the law did not permit arms to someone so 92A young, but he ruled their will as if he were their mind, and used the generals as his hands.[35] And as his nature grew, like a plant, he brought forth fruit of ever greater perfection. When he became commander of the guards, in charge of royal audiences, city prefect, and leader of the senate, each office he laid down more ennobled than when he took it over.[36]

But Typhos, when appointed treasury official (their father had decided to test the nature of his sons in lesser positions), shamed both himself and the man who chose him by being convicted of embezzlement, of venality, and of capriciousness in his administration.[37] Next he was transferred to another type of office, in the hope that he might live up to it, but he acted more disgracefully 92B still. And that province of the good kingdom over which he presided had one unspeakably bad year.[38] He went on to govern

32. For progressively developing differences, cf. Arist. *Cael.* 271b *init.* The image of dividing roads as a moral choice comes ultimately from Prodicus's Choice of Heracles (Xen. *Mem.* 2.1.21–34); it is especially common in Hermetic writings: Nock 1972, 27.

33. προαίρεσις, an Aristotelian term (*Eth. Nic.* 1111b4ff., 1139a31ff.) conventionally rendered "choice." For its use in this broader sense, cf. Syn. *Ep.* 140 (p. 245.7 G), 96 (p. 164.6 G), 95 (p. 160.9 G), 26 (p. 43.2 G), 31 (p. 46.5 G), 32 (= 45 G, p. 84.1); *Dion* 35B, 35C, 37C, 38B; Epict. 2.10; Runia (1976, 59) defines it as "the fundamental ethical principle underlying action."

34. The metaphor is Platonic (*Rep.* 377B, *Tht.* 194C).

35. Osiris's military aspect is appropriate to an Egyptian prince or an emperor (cf. the program enjoined in the *De regno*); a Roman civil official at this date of course would not have been involved with military posts at all. Notably, Synesius does not carry through Osiris's military skill into his actual reign.

36. On the careers of Aurelian and Caesarius, see chapter 5, section V. Only two offices are indicated here: master of offices and city prefect.

37. Phrase borrowed from Aeschin. 2.164.

38. The reference may be to the proconsulate of Achaea or Asia, the sort of prestigious post to which a young man of good family might aspire. Appointments to the proconsulate of Africa (for which there is more evidence) continued to be made for one year in

others, and lamentation pursued them too. Such was Typhos in his public life.

In private, he was a cordax dancer,[39] and he rounded up all the most indecent Egyptians, foreigners too—anyone who was ready to say or hear,[40] to do or suffer anything at all, so that his dining room would be a "doing room" of debauchery of every description.[41] Typhos himself would snore[42] loudly even while awake, and delighted in hearing others do the same; he thought it an admi-
92C   rable piece of music. Commendations and honors were accorded to anyone who prolonged the wanton sound and rounded it out the more. One member of this band, by far the boldest, blushed at absolutely nothing. As he shrank from nothing shameless, he hit upon many of the top prizes; in particular, offices were conferred upon him as a reward for a shameful impudence.[43] Such was Typhos at home.[44]

IV. Whenever he took his seat ostensibly to conduct public

the first instance, often renewed for further periods of one year: Barnes 1983, 256f.; 1985, 144–53, 273–74. Fewer incumbents are known for Asia and Achaea, though for Asia between 394–97 see Barnes 1983, 260–61; for Achaea, E. Groag, *Die Reichsbeamten von Achaia in spätrömischer Zeit*, Diss. Pannon. 1.14 (1946), 44. At 111D Synesius refers to provincial governorships in general as annual offices.

39. The cordax was a notoriously obscene dance: e.g., Ar. *Nub.* 540, 555; Theophr. *Char.* 6.3. In Syn. *Ep.* 32 (= 45 G, p. 85.15) it is a characteristic item of behavior to be feared in a particularly ruffianly slave Synesius is sending his brother.

40. Or perhaps "be called."

41. We render ἐργαστήριον "doing room" to bring out Synesius's play on words, a figure of which he was particularly fond (cf. the "auction hall for lawsuits," 112C). More simply "factory," especially one employing slaves; the word may also be a class slur like κομμώτρια in 105B.

42. ἔρρεγκε, in Greek used for both the (properly) involuntary noise "snore" and the voluntary "snort." There can be little doubt that Synesius is inspired by *Or.* 33 of his idol Dio Chrysostom, an extraordinary attack on the people of Tarsus for making just this noise, a "harsh, disgusting sound produced by violent inhalation or exhalation through the nose," according to C. Bonner, "A Tarsian Peculiarity," *Harv.Theol.Rev.* 35 (1942): 2; cf. C. P. Jones, *The Roman World of Dio Chrysostom* (Cambridge, Mass. 1978), 73–74; G. Highet, *Classical Papers* (New York 1983), 95 n. 53. Dio goes so far as to claim that it is the sort of sound one expects to hear in a brothel (*Or.* 33.36). Bonner collects various other examples from the second to the seventh century (though omitting both Synesius's and Ammianus's account of the Roman *plebs:* "turpi sono fragosis naribus introrsum reducto spiritu concrepantes," Amm. Marc. 14.6.25), all cases where ῥέγκω or a similar word is used of a sound clearly felt to be utterly disgusting. According to Sophronius, a young man was deservedly struck blind for making such a noise in the shrine of Saints Cyrus and John (*Mir. SS. Cyr. et Ioh.* 31 (N. Fernandez Marcos, *Los Thaumata de Sofronio: Contribucion al estudio de la Incubatio Cristiana* [Madrid 1975], 306).

43. Synesius seems to imply that some actual member of Caesarius's administration won his office in this way; unfortunately, it cannot be determined whom he is libeling.

44. Remarkably enough, Bury (1889, 80–81) quotes all of this in his text, concluding with the observation that "Typhos was the leading spirit of a sort of society for the promotion of indecency."

business,[45] he would clearly demonstrate that evil is a thing of
92D every description. (In fact, evil is at variance with virtue and with
itself, and both opposites are portions of it.) Dolt that he was,
he would suddenly go wild and, howling harsher than an Epirot
dog,[46] ruin a private citizen, a house, or a whole city. His delight in
doing evil was enhanced by the thought that with the tears of men
93A he was wiping away the disrepute of his indolence at home.[47] There
was one advantage in his badness: often when he was in the very
act of doing something terrible or issuing a perverse judgment, he
would lapse into strange suspicions so that he seemed possessed,
carrying on about "the shadow in Delphi."[48] In the meantime, his
potential victim would escape, and no further word of him was
brought up. Or else lethargy and drowsiness would grip Typhos
for a while so that his mind was not on its business. Even when he
had collected himself, his memory of recent events had already
93B evaporated. Then he would quibble with his subordinates about
how many grains of wheat a peck contained and how many gills
were in a firkin, and so display an excessive and absurd shrewd-
ness. More than once sleep too snatched a man from calamity, because it fell on Typhos at just the right moment—it would have
shoved him off his armchair onto his head had not an attendant
dropped his lamp and propped him up. In this way a night-long
orgy of tragedy would often turn into comedy. Typhos would not
conduct business in the day at all, since his nature was averse to
sun and light and suited to darkness. He was well aware that
93C everyone with even the tiniest bit of sense indicted him for the
most consummate ignorance. Yet he would not blame himself for
his absurdity. Rather, because of it he was the common enemy of
all intelligent people, as if they were doing wrong because they
knew how to administer justice, while he was innocent of state-
craft, but ingenious in craftiness.[49] Folly and desperation were

45. The literature of the age always refers to governors in their official capacity as
sitting on their judicial seat: Robert 1948, passim.

46. Terzaghi supposes that the "Epirot dog" comes from an otherwise unattested
proverb; but it is in fact merely a disguised reference to the Molossian hounds so often to
be found in Roman poetry (e.g., Verg. *G.* 3.405; Lucr. 5.1063; Hor. *Sat.* 2.6.114).

47. So Terzaghi's text. But greater emphasis would be given if a second μεῖζον had
suffered haplography: "The greater the evil, the more he rejoiced, as if with the tears
of men" etc.

48. The reference is to Dem. 5.25, πρὸς πάντας περὶ τῆς ἐν Δελφοῖς σκιᾶς νυνὶ
πολεμῆσαι, a variation of the proverb περὶ ὄνου σκιᾶς (μάχεσθαι); for which see, s.v.
ὄνος, *RE* 6.1.646; cf. also Ar. *Vesp.* 191; Pl. *Phdr.* 260C7.

49. A double *figura etymologica*: ἄπορος/ποριμώτατος, βουλεῦσαι/ἐπιβουλεῦσαι.

united in him, those mutually reinforcing banes of the soul—no evils greater than these two and more apt to destroy the race of men exist now or ever will arise in nature.[50]

93D   V. Their father saw and was aware of each of these things, and he took thought for the Egyptians. For he was king and priest and sage.[51] Egyptian tales say that he was also a god.[52] For the Egyptians believe that thousands of gods were their kings one after another, before the land was ruled by men and the kings were traced in their descent, Peiromis from Peiromis.[53]

At last the divine laws translated him to the ranks of the greater gods.[54] The day appointed arrived. A public announcement had
94A been made long in advance, and now a brotherhood of priests[55] from every city of Egypt gathered together with the native soldiery. These men were there under the compulsion of the law. As for the other parts of the citizen body, they were allowed to be absent, but none was barred from being present to watch the voting, though not to vote themselves. But swineherds were not allowed even to watch,[56] nor any foreigner or man of foreign extraction[57] who

50. Merely emphatic; cf. *De insomniis* 155D.

51. Cf. Plut. *De Is. et Os.* 354B.

52. For this uncertainty about the status of the old king, even whether he is alive or dead, see pp. 81, 316–18.

53. Hdt. 2.143–44, of priestly succession; Synesius standardizes Herodotus's Ionic form of the name.

54. The apotheosis of the old king removes him from the throne so that the action can begin in earnest, while yet permitting him an active role in the election and initiation of his successor through the next six chapters. Thus Synesius never says in so many words that he dies; but in any case this philosopher-king is an imaginary stock character, not any image of Aurelian's real father, Taurus, dead by 367. It is not clear that Neoplatonic doctrine countenanced actual apotheosis; but in the fable's mythologizing language, it represents the king's attainment of perfect knowledge (cf. Syn. *Ep.* 142, p. 248.14–15 G, φιλοσοφίᾳ χρώμενος εἰς τὸ θεῖον ποδηγετούσῃ). There seems no connection with the report at Diod. 1.90.3 (and thus of Synesius's source Hecataeus; see F. Jacoby, *FGrH* IIIa) that the Egyptians honored their living kings as gods (for euhemeristic reasons); still less with the actual deification after death that ancient Egyptian kings enjoyed (through their identification with Osiris; see Griffiths 1980, a revised and expanded version of his *The Origins of Osiris*, Münchner Ägyptologische Studien 9; see also Griffiths 1960). Synesius's device is rather in the Greco-Roman rhetorical tradition: compare the speech of the living Theodosius to Honorius in Claud. *IV Cons. Hon.* 214–418; more general training of his son in *III Cons. Hon.* 7–89, and similar language of his death, 106–7; see also MacCormack 1981, 139–41.

55. As Terzaghi observes, Synesius evokes Herodotus by the use of an Ionic form.

56. Cf. Hdt. 2.47.

57. Many of the Goths who deserted to the Roman side after Adrianople must by now have had sons of military age, perhaps by Roman mothers, whom Synesius also wishes to exclude. This criterion would also have banned Eudoxia, daughter of the Frankish general Bauto. Synesius's position is thus far more extreme than mere disapproval of barbarian federates.

fought for the Egyptians as a mercenary.[58] These groups were forbidden to be present.

It was for this reason that the elder son had far less support:
94B Typhos's faction consisted of swineherds and foreigners. They
were a senseless and numerous category, but one that yielded to
custom, and neither put their disfranchisement to the test nor even
complained at it. They accepted it as the penalty imposed by law,
and in any case natural for their birth.[59]

VI. The Egyptians choose their kings in the following fashion.[60]
There is a holy mountain beside the great city of Thebes, and another mountain opposite;[61] the Nile flows between them. Of the
mountains, the one on the far side is in Libya. It is the law that the
candidates[62] for the kingship dwell on it for the period of preparation,[63] so as to see nothing of the election.

94C   The holy mountain is in Egypt. There is a tent on the peak for
the king,[64] and beside him all the priests who are wise in the great
wisdom.[65] The arrangement continues for all the elite, allotting the
places according to the dignity of their priesthoods. They form a

58. The Egyptian context permitted a clear distinction between natives and foreigners, enabling Synesius to dismiss barbarians in Roman legions as mere mercenaries.

59. Cf. 118A–B and note (πολιτεία).

60. Nothing in the Egyptian traditions could have suggested to Synesius that the
Egyptians elected their kings, nor does the election in any way correspond to the appointment of a praetorian prefect by the emperor. It is rather a vivid dramatization asserting that
Typhos/Caesarius was popular only with the vilest elements of the society, whereas Osiris/
Aurelian was esteemed by all the better groups, right up to the gods themselves. Details
from Egyptian traditions do serve to authenticate the fantasy; see above and Long 1987,
103–15. Similar graphical expressions of social strata are also to be seen in imperial art of
the period: see L'Orange 1985, passim.

61. A photograph that perfectly fits Synesius's description of the "holy mountain,"
even to the nipple on the peak, may be found in Edwards 1976, 8–9; the mountain is, however, not on the "Egyptian" side of the Nile, but above the Valley of the Kings. Nor can two
mountains be said to face one another across the Nile anywhere near Thebes. Synesius
rearranges the topography considerably, but it is unnecessary to suppose with Fitzgerald
that he invented, without having seen or at least heard of it, so remarkable a feature by
pure coincidence so much resembling what is actually in the area. The use to which the
mountains are put is very different, but their duplication might have been influenced by
the mountains of Kingship and Tyranny in Dio Chrys. Or. 1.66–67, ἡ μὲν βασίλειος ἄκρα,
ἱερὰ Διὸς βασίλεως, ἡδὲ ἑτέρα τυραννική, Τυφῶνος ἐπώνυμος (Dio does not develop the
reference to Typhon).

62. ὑπόψηφος in the sense of "candidate for election," otherwise Christian: Socr. HE
4.29.2, 5.5.6; Soz. HE 6.23.1. In Synesius's day, none but bishops were elected.

63. For Jews and Christians, παρασκευή had long been the term for the "day of
preparation" for the Sabbath, but in other contexts it also retained its more general sense
(see Lampe, s.v.). Its associations as a religious technical term could only be very tenuous
here. Synesius explains the Jewish usage in Ep. 4 (= 5 G) to his brother.

64. The outgoing one.

65. Similar construction at Pl. Ap. 20D, of a different sort of wisdom.

single first circle around the king as its heart. The soldiers come next as a second circle surrounding this one.[66] They too stand around the peak, which is another mountain upon the mountain slopes and stands up just like a nipple,[67] displaying the king in full view even

94D for the most distant bystanders. All those permitted to be present at the spectacle stand around the nipple on the lower slopes of the mountain. They merely shout their approval at whatever they see, and the others actually decide the election.[68]

Once homage has been paid to the king, those whose duty it is cause the whole assembly[69] to rise, since the divinity is present and joins with them in the deliberations over the election. The name of one candidate for the kingship is proclaimed, and the soldiers vote by raising their hands. But those who carry the sacred images, and the temple acolytes and the interpreters of the oracles cast ballots.

95A They are fewer in number but have by far the most power. For the interpreter's ballot is worth a hundred hands, and the image bearer's twenty, and the acolyte has the power of ten hands. Then the name of the other royal candidate is proclaimed, and the hands and ballots on him are taken. If the tally is nearly equal, the king's vote will make a clear majority for one side or the other. If he gives his vote to the losing candidate, he puts them on a level. Then they must set aside the vote and turn to the gods, waiting for a longer time and performing the sacred rites more minutely. At last, not

95B through screens, nor yet by any of the usual signs, the gods them-selves proclaim the king,[70] and the populace hears the proclama-tion handed down from the gods.

The ceremony turned out this way or that, as it chanced on each occasion. But in the case of Typhos and Osiris, the gods were visible from the very first without any action by the priests, draw-ing up the ranks themselves, each marshaling his own initiates; and it was obvious to all on whose side they were. And yet, even if they had not been there, every hand, every ballot, was waiting for

95C the name of the younger of the royal youths.[71] But great things are prefigured here by the corresponding greatness of their omens.

66. Similarly at *De regno* 12B Synesius terms soldiers the emperor's δεύτεροι φίλοι.
67. Pace LSJ, s.v. "breast."
68. Cf. Diod. 1.72.5.
69. κωμαστήριον, "gathering of κωμασταί" (*Sammelbuch* 5051), those who carried sa-cred images in processions: e.g., *P.Oxy.* 519 (2d cent.), 1265 (4th cent.). Terzaghi is unduly impressed by the fact that these terms do not appear in literature before Synesius.
70. αὐτόν is puzzling; perhaps αὐτοί.
71. I.e., Osiris. Spontaneous unanimous election is a common encomiastic motif: e.g., Aug. *Res gestae* 34.1; Tac. *Hist.* 1.45; Pacatus *Pan.Lat.* 2[12].31.2.

And the mark of divinity appears on events destined to surpass the ordinary,[72] whether for better or worse.

VII. Osiris remained in the place where he had originally crossed over, as he was supposed to. But Typhos was chafing with anxiety to know the result of the vote and in the end could not restrain himself from an attempt to corrupt the balloting. And so,
95D taking no account of himself or of the royal laws, hurling himself into the river, swept along by the current, swimming and floundering helplessly, a laughable sight, he landed on the other side of the river. He thought no one had noticed him, except for those he approached and promised money. But everyone knew, and they loathed him and his plan. Yet they decided not to rebuke a deranged character.

In fact, it turned out to be the worst thing he could have done: in his own presence, in his own hearing, he stood condemned by every judgment, voted against by every hand. The gods put their curse upon him as well.

But Osiris, who had not troubled himself at all, arrived when
96A he was sent for, with the gods, priests—everybody, in fact—advancing to meet him beside the riverbank with holy garlands and holy flutes, where the ferry[73] which was taking the new king from the Libyan side had to land.[74] Immediately, great signs from heaven, and auspicious divine voices and every minor and major omen by which the future is traced, proclaimed the good tidings of the new reign to the Egyptians.[75] The demons of the worse faction[76] were not likely to acquiesce in this or tolerate the good fortune of

72. It would be strange for Synesius to have used παρά two times within four words, with different cases and senses, especially since ἐπισημαίνομαι takes a bare dative; we therefore delete the first παρά.

73. βᾶρις was the Egyptian name for a type of native cargo boat: Hdt. 2.96, describing its construction and handling. A. B. Lloyd's commentary (1975–87) ad loc. offers extensive Egyptological and nautical detail of its use in both religious and mundane contexts. Greek authors adopted the term, sometimes with and sometimes apparently without ethnological force (e.g., Aesch. Supp. 836, 873; Pers. 553; cf. references in LSJ, s.v.). In the present context, however, where Synesius appears to borrow other elements of the funeral practices described by Diodorus Siculus at 1.72.4–6 and 1.92, it may be a more significant echo (probably of Hecataeus of Abdera as their common source, for Synesius does not appear to adapt Diodorus's text directly anywhere in his works; only two feeble possibilities are canvassed by W. S. Crawford, Synesius the Hellene [London 1901], 528). In De providentia 111A Synesius also mentions a ὁλκάς.

74. Such scenes of adventus were a commonplace of late antique life; see MacCormack 1972, 721–52. A similar procession greets Osiris's return from exile at 123D–124A.

75. Cf. Plut. De Is. et Os. 355E.

76. Demons are associated with Typhos in the gods' warnings to Osiris (97A); they enter the actual narrative in 107D–108B.

mankind; they resolved to attack and cause it to fester.[77] A plot too was indicated.

VIII. When the gods and his father had conducted him
96B through the royal initiation, possessed of clear knowledge, they gave him clear foreknowledge of countless good things. Above all, they told him to get rid of his brother, so that he should not bring everything into confusion. Typhos had been born to bring ill fortune to the Egyptians and to his father's hearth. Osiris must prevent him from seeing or hearing of the health and prosperity[78] of Egypt that his own kingship would bring about. For Typhos's nature could endure nothing good. And they imparted to him knowledge of the double essence of souls and the opposition earthly souls necessarily hold against celestial.

They told him to prevent these consequences and, undaunted
96C by what men call kinship, to cut off Typhos's hostile nature from the good and divine series.[79] They told him all the things that he himself and the Egyptians and their neighbors and all their territory would suffer if he showed weakness. For the evil did not lack power, and everyday precautions would not suffice to obstruct and
96D blunt[80] attacks both open and covert. Typhos too had patrons, a powerful mass of malicious demons,[81] whose kin he was and from

77. Reading οἰδανεῖν (fut.); see Cameron, Long, Sherry 1988, 55–56. The collocation of the verb and ἐπίβουλος, of demons attacking human happiness, seems to echo *Test. Sol.* 5.7 (see McCown 1922, 23*).

78. εὐημερία and εὐετερία are peculiarly Aristotelian terms, as Terzaghi notes, citing *Eth. Nic.* 1098b26, 1099b7.

79. Synesius's dualism echoes the patterns of early Pythagoreanism with its "series" (συστοιχίαι) of opposites. See Diels, *Vorsokr.*, vol. 3 (reprint, 1954), 415.

80. Homeric metaphor: *Il.* 13.562.

81. The original Platonic conception of demons was simply intermediate supernatural beings between gods on the one hand and heroes and men on the other (e.g., *Symp.* 202D–203A; *Rep.* 392A, 427B; cf. Des Places 1969, 113–17). The belief of later Platonists in demons, good as well as evil, is most fully described in Porph. *Abst.* 2.37–43 (text with commentary in J. Bidez and F. Cumont, *Les mages hellénisés*, vol. 2 [1938], 275–84; cf. F. Cumont, *Les religions orientales*, 4th ed. [1929], 142, 280–81; Lewy [1956] 1978, 497–508; for surveys, MacMullen 1968, 90–93 and notes; C. Zintzen, *RLAC* 9 [1976]: 644–68). But none goes as far as Synesius in presenting them as exclusively evil (Vollenweider 1985a, 178–79); indeed some Neoplatonists actually denied the existence of evil demons (notably Sallustius; see Nock's edition, pp. lxxviii–ix). Synesius's demonology is of a piece with his thoroughgoing dualism, but we should make some allowance for the fact that his plot required evil to triumph over good, at least temporarily. It is also of relevance that he took the myth from a source in which dualism is more marked than in the generality of Middle Platonism: for a synthetic discussion see J. Dillon, *The Middle Platonists* (London 1977), 199–225; see also Griffiths 1970, 482–86, for a discussion of Plutarch's reference to Plato *Leg.* 896Df. as authority for the dualism of good and evil world-souls (*De Is. et Os.* 370F). Synesius also bears the influence of such works as the Hermetica and the

whose ranks he had been brought to birth, so that they could use
him as an instrument of evil against men, their wicked plans proceeding nicely.[82] And they conceived, gestated, delivered, and
raised in the proper fashion their great future help: Typhos. They
thought that one thing was still lacking in their bid to win everything, that they invest him with the might that ruling brings. Then
97A he would be a perfect child of perfect parents, willing and able to
do great evils.[83]

"You they loathe," said one of the gods, "as bringing profit to
men and loss to themselves; for the disasters of the nations are entertainment for base demons."[84] Recognizing Osiris's natural mildness,[85] they warned him again and again to escort his brother out of
the country, expelling[86] the pollution to some distant part of the
earth.[87] In the end, they were forced to tell him that he would hold
out against his brother for a while; but eventually he would yield
unawares and betray himself and all men, in the fine name of
97B brotherly love winning what was in fact the greatest of disasters.

"But if you will graciously assist me," said he, "I shall not fear
my brother if he remains, and I shall be free from the wrath of the
demons. For it is easy for you, if you are willing, to remedy anything I overlook."

IX. "You misunderstand the situation, my son," said his father
in reply. "The divine region in the universe is reserved for other
beings; it acts for the most part in accordance with the primal
power it possesses, and it is filled with noetic beauty.[88] In that place

Chaldaean Oracles (Lewy [1956] 1978, 259–309), to which he alludes at 99D. Lewy characterizes *De providentia* 97B–101B as "probably the most vivid extant account of demonic
temptation given by a Platonist" (305).

82. "Proceeding nicely" translates ὁδῷ βαδίζοντες, an expression not unique to Plutarch (e.g., Lib. *Decl.* 9.1.10.3; [Bas.] *Const.* 31.1376.13), but of which he was fond: *Lyc.*
92.1.8; *Ages.* 13.1.1; *De gen.* 595F; *Comm.not.* 2059A; *De Is. et Os.* 371C (see Griffiths ad loc.,
who renders "in good order"; there of activities that the demonic Typhos obstructs).

83. The independent parallel of the evil demons' creation of Rufinus in Claudian's
invective is striking (*In Ruf.* 1.86ff.). They have a common ancestry in a tradition now
mostly lost.

84. Terzaghi connects this passage with 107D, where the "base demons" suggest to
Typhos and his band of dissolute revelers that they effect a coup.

85. Synesius constantly emphasizes Osiris's mild, not to say weak, disposition; this
portrait is hard to reconcile with the popular modern conviction that he was a fanatic.

86. Reading ἐλᾶν; see Cameron, Long, Sherry 1988, 56.

87. Metaphorical use of ἀποδιοπομπεῖσθαι, "to escort [purificatory holy fleece] out
of the country" (literally, of a scapegoating ritual); cf. Pl. *Cra.* 396E; *Leg.* 2.877E, 900B (explained in a gloss); *De regno* 3B.

88. The Plotinian expression τὸ νοητικὸν κάλλος designates that beauty perceived by
mind rather than the senses; cf. Plotinus 1.6, 5.8.

there is another race of gods, the hypercosmic,[89] which holds together all beings down to the very last. In itself it is unswerving
97C and unrelenting toward matter.[90] This race is the blessed object of
contemplation of those who are gods in the natural world,[91] but to
look upon its source is still more blessed. In its isolation it is over-
flowing with goodness, as it overflows with itself. It is good for the
other gods to direct their eyes toward the divinity there. But they
also have charge of the regions of the cosmos, for the activity of
goodness is not single or uniform. As far as it is possible, they
97D lower their contemplative activity to what they administer. Therefore, the pure element in them is arrayed just beneath that primal
essence. They themselves order those closest to them, and the succession of ranks descends one after another to the farthest levels of
existence. All things enjoy the care of the first rank through these
intermediaries. Of course, there is no equality among them, for
then the chain could not exist. Beings, as they descend, weaken
98A until they err and falsify their rank, at which point even the existence of the beings ceases.[92]

"Something like this occurs in matters down here. That which
inherently errs is allotted the farthest and most perishable element

89. The distinction between the transcendent hypercosmic gods and the encosmic
gods, providentially involved in this world, is a commonplace of later Platonism. The distinction, together with many subdivisions in both categories, the "succession of ranks" to
which Synesius alludes a few sentences later, was already worked out in some detail as
early as Sallustius in the mid–fourth century: "Of the gods some are mundane (ἐγκόσμιοι),
some supramundane (ὑπερκόσμιοι). By mundane I mean the gods who make the universe. Of the supramundane some make the essences of the gods, some the intelligence,
some the souls: they are therefore divided into three orders, all of which may be found in
treatises on these matters. Of the mundane some cause the universe to exist, others ani-
mate it, others harmonize it out of its varied components, others guard it when so harmonized" (*De diis* 6, trans. Nock, pp. 11–13). It may go back to Iamblichus (J. Dillon in *ANRW*
II.36.2 [1988]: 899). For a more allusively described hierarchy, see Syn. *Hymn* 1.278–93:
πᾶσά σε μέλπει γενεὰ μακάρων (οἳ περὶ κόσμον, οἳ κατὰ κόσμον, οἳ ζωναῖοι οἵ τ᾽ ἄζωνοι
κόσμου μοίρας ἐφέπουσι σοφοὶ ἀμφιβατῆρες, οἱ περὶ κλεινοὺς οἰηκοφόρους, οὓς ἀγ-
γελικὰ προχέει σειρά) τό τε κυδῆεν γένος ἡρώων ἔργα τὰ θνητῶν. For the yet more elaborate hierarchy of Proclus, see H. D. Saffrey and L. G. Westerink, *Proclus: Théologie platonicienne*, vol. 1 (Paris 1968), lxv–lxxv, with diagrams.
90. That is to say, it has nothing to do with matter: the hypercosmic gods are entirely
dedicated to contemplation of the ultimate verities. Cf. *De insomniis* 133B.
91. τοῖς μὲν φύσει θεοῖς, an odd expression, but the reference must be to the
ἐγκόσμιοι θεοί, who are concerned with the world and (albeit reluctantly) man. Other passages where φύσις is used in this sense: ἡ τοῦ κόσμου φύσις at 89B6 and 102A5, τῆς ἐν
γενέσει φύσεως at 98A3, and τῆς τῇδε φύσεως at 98B4.
92. ἐν ᾧ καὶ τὸ εἶναι τῶν ὄντων παύεται. Synesius uses τὸ εἶναι in the conventional
Neoplatonic technical sense that distinguishes the world of true Being from the material
world of Becoming, as is made plain by his immediate distinction of "matters down here"
from it, and of "true being" from mimicry with "becoming" below.

of the nature that is subject to generation, and of the lot that appertains to bodies.[93] Heaven, however, is allotted the primal and most imperishable element and is assigned a corresponding type of soul. And what they are there," he said, indicating the gods, "the demon[94] is here, among these turbid elements—a capricious and rash nature and, because his distance from that place above is so great, one that does not perceive the orderliness of divine things.

98B   "As it is the lowest rank of beings, it is not sufficient for its own salvation. It seeps away and does not await true being but mimics it with becoming. And since the demons are connate with the nature of this world[95] and have as their lot a destructive essence, it is necessary for the divine element to turn its attention here and impart a first motion that existence here follows successfully for as long as the impulse lasts.[96] Similarly, marionettes continue to move even though the force that imparted the source of motion to the mechanism

98C has stopped, but do not move perpetually, for their motion does not come from within—only while the power given them retains its strength and is not slackened by its progressive separation from its own generation.[97] Understand, my dear Osiris, that in the

93. "The . . . most perishable element . . . of the lot that appertains to bodies" echoes in part Plutarch's physical allegorization of Typhos: "[Typhos is] of the element that appertains to bodies, the perishable element" (*De Is. et Os.* 371B).

94. Although Synesius normally writes of demons in the plural, there is nothing in the present context to warrant taking this singular demon as the "lord of the demons" (so Vollenweider 1985a, 180).

95. συγγενῶν ὄντων τῆς τῇδε φύσεως, with which compare γηγενεῖς ὄντας at 99C and δαίμοσιν οἳ γᾶς ἀπὸ κευθμώνων ἀναπαλλόμεναι at *Hymn* 1.623–25; cf. δαίμονα γαίας, 1.247; δαίμων ὕλας, 1.90, 1.542, 2.258.

96. 99B refers to "appointed times" when the gods come down to earth and "impart motion" to it; 102A describes how this motion eventually runs down and the gods return to "rekindle" it, again (unless required earlier by human weakness) at "appointed times." The conception is inspired ultimately by the myth of Plato's *Politicus*:

There is an era in which the god himself assists the universe on its way and helps in its rotation. There is also an era in which he releases his control. . . . When it must travel on without him, things go well enough in the years immediately after he abandons control, but as time goes on and forgetfulness sets in, the ancient condition of discord also begins to assert its sway. At last, as the cosmic era draws to its close. . . at that very moment, the god looks upon it again, he who first set it in order. Beholding it in its troubles . . . he takes control of the helm once more. (269C–273D; trans. J. B. Skemp)

97. Cf. [Arist.] *Mund.* 398b, where the analogy is of the transmission of motion from one part to another, following the divine impulse (cf. Arist. *Gen.an.* 734b, 741b), rather than the degeneration of motion. Both Synesius and *De mundo* use the term δύναμις for the Aristotelian ἐνέργεια (Plotinus speaks of the One as ἡ δύναμις πάντων, e.g., *Enn.* 5.1.7.10; cf. *Metaph.* 1072a25ff.). Fitzgerald (note ad loc.) and Lacombrade (1951a, 29) are perhaps unnecessarily skeptical about Synesius's knowledge of Aristotle: Hypatia is said to have taught his works, and in *De regno* Synesius speaks in the same breath of "Aristotle and Plato, my mentors" (8A).

same way, the good and the divine both are and are not of this place but are sent down from elsewhere. Because of this, good souls may be found here, though only with difficulty; and whenever the divine overseers do this, they do what belongs to their province and not to that of the primal life. To these gods belongs a
98D second kind of blessedness, the simple enjoyment of the first order. That is a more blessed thing than the ordering of inferior beings, for the one means turning away from this world, but the other, turning toward it.

"Surely you have viewed the rite[98] in which there are two pairs of eyes: the bottom pair must close whenever the top pair is open, and when the top pair closes, the bottom pair opens correspondingly. Consider this a riddle of contemplation and action. The in-
99A termediate gods perform each alternately, while the more perfect gods are more often occupied with the better activity. They associate with the worse only as much as is necessary. This is the work of the gods, who do what is necessary for the cosmos, though that is not their principal good work.[99] Men too at times look after household affairs of more or less importance and at other times pursue philosophy; but it is when they do the latter that they are more divine.[100]

X. "'Mark my meaning'[101] from this. Do not demand that the gods attend on you, for they have contemplation and the first
99B regions of the cosmos as their principal occupation. They are in heaven, far away. Do not suppose that it is easy for them to descend or that they stay forever. They come down at appointed

98. Fitzgerald translates τελετήν "statue," and the context may in fact suggest an (unparalleled) sense "effigy." John Finamore, for whose suggestions on this passage we are most grateful, compares Iambl. *Myst.* 7.2 on the Egyptian symbology of mud, lotus, and boat. These, however, are images from life, not a manufactured figure that performs in a certain way; and Finamore knows of no other reference to such a statue or cult image in the writings of Iamblichus or Proclus. Nor can we find other references to such a rite. Its principle seems straightforward enough. Perhaps Synesius is investing something as simple as a child's game with mystic significance. See Courcelle 1963, 137–41, on the most famous such case, Augustine's *tolle, lege.* We accordingly translate in the attested sense "rite."

99. That is to say, not even the encosmic gods can be counted on to attend constantly to the affairs of men. Once they have paid one of their periodic visits (described in the next paragraph), man must fend with the demons as best he can on his own.

100. Synesius refers similarly elsewhere to the common Neoplatonic distinction between contemplation and action: "When the mind is not occupied with the matters of this world, it is occupied with the divine. For there are two parts of philosophy, contemplation and action," *Ep.* 103 (p. 178.4ff. G); cf. *Ep.* 57 (= 41 G, p. 66.4ff.); *Ep.* 101 and 151 to Pylaemenes urge him to cast off the agora's sullying influence on the temple of his mind. Cf. Plotinus 1.6.6, 3.6.5, 4.4.3.

101. σύνες ὅ τοι λέγω, Pind. frag. 105.1, perhaps via Pl. *Meno* 76D.

times to impart, like engineers, the beginning of good motion in a government.[102] This occurs whenever they create harmony in a kingdom by bringing down into it souls akin to them. This is a divine and magnificent Providence,[103] that through one man the gods are often able to care for thousands. From this point on they must 99C be engaged in their own affairs. And you, cut off as you are amidst aliens, must remember whence you come,[104] and also that this is a sort of public service you are performing for the cosmos.[105] Try to raise yourself up, not draw the gods down. Take every precaution for yourself, just as if you were living in a camp in enemy territory, a divine soul among demons, who, because they are earthborn, are likely to grow angry and attack anyone who observes alien laws within their borders. You must be content to be vigilant night and 99D day, with this one concern: to strive not to be overpowered, one man against many, a foreigner among natives.[106]

"There is also in this world a holy race of heroes[107] who care for men. They are able to help in small things and in the pursuit of the higher good.[108] They live here like a hero who resides in this world though foreign to it, so that its affairs may not be abandoned without some share in a better nature.[109] These heroes lend assistance where they have power. But when matter stirs up its own off-

102. Cf. *Ep.* 57 (= 41 G, p. 67.14ff.), where Synesius takes this model of behavior for himself as bishop. Runia (1976, 53) notes that "specific divine intervention [is] a repugnant idea to a pagan Neoplatonist," referring to Wallis 1972, 121. But Synesius's exposition here makes plain that he takes for granted that it is the *intermediate* gods who intervene; which is Neoplatonic orthodoxy, e.g., Jul. *H.Helios.*

103. The same phrase is used at *De regno* 29D, of a king sending out governors, analogously to God's use of Nature (imitation of God/Providence more generally, *De regno* 8B); and again at *Ep.* 73 (p. 131.23 G), requesting Troïlus to convey to Anthemius a plea for a better governor for Libya.

104. Cf. Plotinus 5.1.1ff. on the soul's forgetfulness of its origin; Osiris is enlightened, in contrast.

105. More precise use of the metaphor of *leitourgia* than *De insomniis* 139C, which seems to echo Porph. *Abst.* 4.18; cf. Smith 1974, 36–38.

106. Contemporary reality influences Synesius's choice of language, importing a suggestion of alien mercenaries into his philosophical exposition. It produces a striking paradox, for in real life, of course, Aurelian was the native and the soldiers foreigners.

107. On the place of the heroes in the hierarchy of being, between gods and humans, see Euseb. *Praep.evang.* 4.5 (quoting from the "theology" of the Hellenes); Iambl. *Myst.* 2.1; Proclus *In Crat.*, p. 68.16–69.3; p. 75.25–76.4 Pasquali. The philosopher Asclepius refers to his teacher Ammonius as a ἥρως (*In metaph.*, p.92.29 Hayduck). On the general Neoplatonic belief that the souls of the great are of superhuman origin, Lewy (1956) 1978, 224–25.

108. Same use of πρεσβύτερον at *De dono* 310D.

109. Several times in the *De providentia* Synesius makes use of this remarkable figure of thought: he begins to explain his subject with an analogy, but the analogue turns out to be virtually identical with the subject itself. A sort of mental implosion results.

shoots[110] to war against the soul, there is little resistance on this side
in the absence of the gods. For each thing is strong in its own prov-
100A ince. The demons' first hope will be to make this one their own.

"This is how they will attack. It is not possible that any creature
on the earth should lack some portion of irrationality in his soul.[111]
This irrational part the majority brandish in front of them; the wise
man keeps it sheathed. But of necessity all men have it. The demons
work through this element that is kindred to them to betray and
attack the living creature. What happens is just like a siege. Consider what happens to coals under a torch, quickly kindled because
of their natural predisposition to fire. In the same way, the nature
100B of a demon, which is passionate, or rather, passion itself,[112] living
and moving, draws near to a soul and arouses the passion in it and
leads its potential into action. It accomplishes everything through
proximity. Each passion becomes like the passion that stirred it up.
Thus the demons ignite lust, anger, and all their sibling evils, dealing with souls through the parts of the soul that are related to
themselves. These parts naturally perceive their presence and are
agitated and strengthened by it in their rebellion against mind, until they either take possession of the whole soul or despair of their
purpose. This is the greatest of contests.

100C   "There is no opportunity, trick, or place that the demons neglect in their attack. They make their assault from just that place
where one would never expect it. Everywhere there are traps,
everywhere devices, everything stirs up the war from within, until
the demons either take control or abandon the fight. But the gods
are spectators on high of these noble contests, in which you shall
win the crown. May the same be true of your second contest.[113]

110. βλαστήματα, echoing κακῆς ὕλης βλαστήματα in *Chald.Or.* 88 Des Places (cf.
Lewy [1956] 1978, 263 n. 14; 268–69). There is a similar passage in *Hymn* 5 (51–55), again
linking demons and heroes: νεάτας καὶ μέχρις ὕλας, ἵνα δαιμόνων ὅμιλον φύσις ἰζάνοισα
τίκτει πολύθρουν καὶ πολυμήταν· ὅθεν ἥρως, etc.

111. According to orthodox Platonic teaching (e.g., *Rep.* 435Aff.) the soul has a rational and two irrational elements (λογιστικόν, θυμοειδές, ἐπιθυμητικόν). Plotinus, however, blurred and "the Chaldaeans ignore" the Platonic tripartition (H. J. Blumenthal,
Plotinus's Psychology [The Hague 1971], 20–30; Lewy [1956] 1978, 307 n. 182). Synesius here
implies only one irrational element (τινα . . . μοῖραν ψυχῆς ἄλογον . . . ταυτήν); on the
other hand, 100B refers to the demons entering through those *parts* (μέρη) of the soul that
are related to them.

112. This identification of demons with the passions derives from Porphyry, as
quoted by Proclus in *In Tim.* 1.171.19f.: ὑλικοὺς δὲ τρόπους ἀποκαλεῖ τοὺς δαίμονας . . .
εἶναι δὲ τούτους ὑλικὰς δυνάμεις, ἠθοποιοὺς τῆς ψυχῆς. That is to say, Porphyry treated
demons as "personifications of the passions" (Lewy [1956] 1978, 502; cf. 306).

113. The next paragraphs suggest that Osiris's first victory is the moral one within
himself (which receives its recognition in his election); the second contest will be Typhos's
coup, which of course Osiris loses.

"But there is reason to fear that you may win in the one and lose in the other. For whenever the divine portion of the soul does not follow in the train of the worse portion but repeatedly beats it 100D back and turns toward itself, it is natural that in time even that divine portion will grow hardened so as to withstand the enemy's charges, roofed over[114] so as to become impervious to the influxes of the demons. In this way, then, the creature actually becomes a unified and divine whole. And it is a heavenly plant upon the earth[115] that does not accept any alien graft and produce its fruit; even that it transforms into its own nature.

"When the demons have despaired of this attempt, then with all their energies they fight the second contest, to excise and eliminate the plant utterly from the earth, since there is no way it can 101A belong to them. They are ashamed of the defeat if some alien should go about triumphant in their lands, a trophy of victory real and visible. Such a man harms them, not just in himself alone, but also by leading others to revolt against their dominion. When excellence becomes the goal, the inferior must perish. For these reasons, the demons plot to destroy both citizen and ruler, anyone at all who rebels against the laws of matter. But now, since you are king, you can protect yourself more easily than any citizen.[116] For when attempts from within have failed, they attack from without, 101B using war and faction and everything else that harms the body,[117] things to which a provident king is least likely to fall victim.[118] When might and wisdom are united they are invincible; when they are separated from each other, strength is foolish and prudence weak, and they are easily conquered.[119]

114. Accepting Petau's emendation στεγανωθεῖσαν.

115. The phrase is adapted from Pl. *Tim.* 90A, of the best of the three parts of the human soul.

116. The text as it stands offers a plain optative, ῥᾷον ἅπαντος ἰδιώτου φυλάττοιο ("May you protect yourself more easily than any citizen!"). As such, the wish has little point, and since Osiris's father goes on to explain why a good king should be able to protect himself, it seems better to assume that a potential optative has suffered corruption. ἄν could very easily have dropped out between ῥᾷον and ἅπαντος. We so translate.

117. Lacombrade (1951a, 114 n. 17) claims much too close a relationship between this passage and *Leg.* 906A, where Plato merely says that men face an eternal moral combat, in which the gods are their allies. Terzaghi somewhat more relevantly compares *Rep.* 560C, where at least the moral struggle is described in terms of "faction and counter-faction and fighting within a man, against himself." Synesius, however, here distinguishes "war and faction" from the internal struggle, specifying that they harm the body.

118. At *De regno* 27D, Synesius states that such external pressures find the good (i.e., philosophic) king invulnerable.

119. From this sentence through the explanations of Hermes and the Sphinx, a close paraphrase of *De regno* 7B–C. Cf. also *De dono* 309B–C.

XI. "Surely you have admired how ingeniously our fathers devised their holy images. Consider Hermes: we Egyptians make the 101C form of the divinity twofold, setting a youth beside an elder, because we think that if any of us is to supervise well, he must be both wise and brave, since the one quality achieves nothing without the other.[120] This is why the Sphinx stands in our temple precincts:[121] she is the holy symbol of the union of two good qualities, a beast in might and a human in prudence. Might that lacks rational leadership tends to be capricious, mixing up everything and confounding affairs; and intelligence is useless for action if it has no hands to serve it.

101D   "It is only with difficulty that virtue and fortune join together. They meet only for great ends, as in fact they have in you. So trouble the gods no more, since you can preserve yourself from within if you are willing. It is not good for them to be continually away from their provinces and to become attached to alien, inferior places—if, indeed, it is not actually impious to make inadequate use of the resources sown within us for keeping earthly affairs in order according to the arrangement bestowed upon this world. This is what men are doing if they force the gods to return before the appointed times to take charge of the affairs of this world. 102A Rather, when the harmony they established is growing slack and old,[122] they come back again to tighten it and to rekindle the flame,

120. Such a biform image of Hermes is not in fact known for Egypt; it has always puzzled commentators, starting at least with a second hand in a thirteenth-century manuscript, quoted by Krabinger ad loc. (1825, 179–81; 1835, 225–27). There might be some connection with the Cabiri, an older-younger pair of divinities who are themselves sometimes connected with Hermes (B. Hemberg, *Die Kabiren* [Uppsala 1950]) and sometimes with the Dioscuri; Krabinger's scholiast adduces Polydeuces here. But a more attractive possibility is the pair of Hermeses mentioned in the Hermetic *Asclepius* (37), another old puzzle recently explained by Garth Fowden, who suggests that it was the younger (Trismegistus) who was thought to have translated into Greek the works of his grandfather, the original Thoth-Hermes (1986, 29–31).

121. At *De Is. et Os.* 354B Plutarch says that the Egyptians place sphinxes before their temples as a mark of "the riddling wisdom their theology holds"; similarly Clem.Al. *Strom.* 5.5. Griffiths (1980) notes that for the Egyptians the sphinx bore no suggestion of mystery or enigma; the association is entirely Greek.

122. Vollenweider (1985a, 168) derives "growing old" from *senectus mundi* at *Asclepius* 26 (Nock-Festugière II.329.24). That Synesius knew this work (in its Greek original) there can be little doubt (chapter 7, section VI), but the reference there is eschatological: old age is accompanied by catastrophes of every sort until finally god steps in and restores the world. In Synesius the gods "joyfully" rekindle the "aging" harmony, which is contrasted in the next sentence with the extreme condition "when the harmony is ruined and broken through the weakness of its inheritors." Then the debility of the world gives occasion to some particular destructive force, such as that represented by Typhos. But such a force is superadded to the ordinary old age described here, at which the world arrives naturally at regular intervals.

as it were, when it has grown cold. This they do joyfully, for they are performing a sort of public service for the nature of the cosmos. Otherwise, they will come only when the harmony is ruined and broken through the weakness of its inheritors, when this world can be saved in no other way. Consequently, a god is not roused by any trivial occurrence or every single error about this or that. He is truly a wonder, that one man for whose sake a member of the blessed

102B race comes down here! But whenever the whole order and its great affairs are destroyed, then the gods must pay a visit to impart the beginning of a new ordering. Therefore let men not complain when their troubles are their own fault, nor let them accuse the gods of not providing for them. Providence requires men to make their own contributions too.

"It is not surprising that there are evils in the region of evils. Rather, it is remarkable if there is anything else here as well. Such a thing is an alien dwelling in a foreign land.[123] It is the gift of Providence, which permits us, if we are not idle but make use of what

102C she gives us, to be happy in all things in all ways. Providence is not like the mother of a newborn infant, who must take pains to shoo away insects that might annoy her child, for it is still imperfect and unable to help itself. Rather, Providence is like that mother who, once she has raised and equipped her child, bids it use what it has, and keep evil away from itself. Study this wisdom always, and reckon it of infinite value for men to know. For they will believe in Providence and take thought for themselves, becoming both pious

102D and attentive. And they will not think that respect for god and the practice of virtue conflict with each other.

"Farewell. Be prudent[124] and stop your brother. Prevent the destiny that hangs over you and the Egyptians. It can be done. But if you are weak and give in, you will find yourself awaiting the gods when it is too late."

XII. So he concluded and left by the same route as the gods.[125]

---

123. μέτοικον recalls the hero-metics of 99D, ἀλλότριον the description of Osiris at 99C. These references, and that to λειτουργία just above (102A), all reinforce the implicit identification of Osiris/Aurelian as the gift of Providence, a native of a higher realm administering this below.

124. The term used, σωφρονεῖν, is the epitome of Socratic virtue and thus makes a fitting climax for Osiris's father's exhortation. Cf. *Ep.* 140 (p. 245.12, 246.9 G) for a similar motif.

125. Cf. the similar conclusion to the deceased Theodosius's speech to Stilicho at *Claud. IV Cons. Hon.* 162–77: "Nec plura locutus / sicut erat liquido signavit tramite nubes / ingrediturque globum Lunae." (The imagery of souls among the stars is a commonplace with no real pagan associations: see the Christian examples at Cameron 1970a,

Osiris was left behind, a prodigy beyond the deserts of this world.[126] He immediately strove to banish evils from the land, without making any use of force. Instead, he sacrificed to Persuasion and the Muses and the Graces, and he brought all men willingly into accord with the law.[127] And when the gods, from reverence for the 103A king, furnished in generous abundance all the gifts that air and sea and land hold, he passed on these advantages to his people. He himself abandoned all leisure and assumed every labor, taking as his lot little sleep and many cares; he pursued without relaxing the relaxation of all.[128] Accordingly, man by man, household by household, family by family, city by city, province by province, he filled 103B all men with goods both internal and external. He encouraged a zeal for virtue, directing every lesson and every profession to be practiced for the sake of this one goal. He established rewards for those who were best at governing and at making their subjects like themselves. All that is honored must flourish, and all that is neglected must perish.

There also grew in him a passion for all education both intellectual and rhetorical.[129] Men who excelled in such areas were no

209 and notes.) The translation to heaven of Osiris's and Typhos's father is now definitely achieved: he does not reappear in the tale.

126. Recalling 99C.

127. Precious reworking of Plut. *De Is. et Os.* 356A–B: "Later he traversed and civilized all the world, with very little need of arms; for the most part, he attached them to himself by charming them with persuasion and reason [πειθοῖ . . . καὶ λόγῳ: Griffiths takes as hendiadys, "persuasive speech"] along with all song and poetry." On the passage as a whole compare Diod. 1.13.5–17.2 (there, however, Osiris gathers a large army before setting out to civilize the world: the Egyptian deity follows the path of Alexander the Great! A similar accommodation of myth to addressee, in this case Trajan, may be found in Dio Chrysostom's insistence in *Or.* 1.63 that another world-civilizer, Heracles, of course had an army). As an image for eloquence, "sacrifice to the Graces" was a commonplace of the Platonic oral tradition: cf. Eunap. *VS* 458.3; D. L. 4.6; Plut. *Con. praec.* 141F. Dio Chrysostom similarly invokes "Persuasion and the Muses and Apollo" in a proemium (*Or.* 1.10). This passage should not be used as the basis for drawing a picture of Aurelian as a patron of the arts (Bury, Zakrzewski, Demougeot, Holum); though on the other hand, there is no need to question the passion of Synesius's commitment to Hellenism in the cultural sense.

128. The selfless industry of the ideal king goes back, for example, to Xenophon (*Cyr.* 1.6.8). The key terms (leisure vs. labor, sleep vs. cares) are repeated in countless panegyrics of the imperial age; Dio *Or.* 1.13, 21, is representative. In the civil sphere (notably, not the military) Osiris generally lives up to the ideal Synesius proposed in *De regno*, with frequent verbal echoes (e.g., *De regno* 5C: no leisure, little sleep, many worries); conversely, Typhos and his wife exemplify tyrannical behavior as *De regno* describes it (e.g., the justice/auction hall, 30C/112D; his pleasure in the suffering of his subjects is a defining characteristic of the tyrant, 6A).

129. Cf. Diod. 1.15.9–16.2: Osiris particularly honors Hermes as the inventor of τὰ μουσικά and ἑρμήνεια; Hecataeus's interest in such honors paralleled Synesius's. Libanius

longer to be seen among the common herd. Instead, they shone
with the honors the king gave them for showing that rhetoric[130] is
the servant of prudence because the mind advances when it is
103C clothed in words. Whether it is dressed well or less well will reveal,
as clothes the man, if it is decent or indecent.[131] Osiris thought it
right to honor even elementary education, for he thought that education was the source of virtue. Truly at this time above all others
was piety in vogue among the Egyptians. These are the goods of
the soul, and the Egyptians abounded in them during Osiris's
reign.[132] The land seemed to be a school of virtue,[133] with the chil-
103D dren looking to only one man, the leader, doing only what they
saw and saying only what they heard.

About money he himself cared not at all but made every effort
that there should be enough for all. He would never accept a gift,
but he delighted in giving.[134] He released cities from taxation[135] and
gave freely to those in need. What had fallen he raised up, and
what was in danger of falling he restored to health. One city he
raised to greatness; another he adorned and beautified. Where
there was no city, he founded one.[136] A deserted city he repopu-
lated. Individuals too inevitably benefited from the general pros-
104A perity. Osiris did not shrink from lowering his gaze to ordinary
folk, so that during his reign no man was to be seen weeping. Nor

has similarly interested praise for Julian, with added religious concerns (*Or.* 18.154–61).
Imperial patronage of education was commonplace throughout the empire: see Millar
1977, 491–506.

130. τέχνη here must bear the specific sense.

131. The analogy of style and clothing is a commonplace: e.g., Sen. *Ep.* 114.4ff.,
Maecenas's *solutae tunicae.*

132. Though he begins with ἀρετή and ends with εὐσέβεια, the body of Synesius's
discussion rather surprisingly identifies both with literary culture. Many cultivated Christians might well accept the importance of a classical literary education, but it is undoubtedly eccentric of Synesius actually to equate it with piety. Aurelian must not be assumed to
have shared this extreme position. For Synesius's estimation of παιδεία generally, see
chapter 2, section VI; cf. *Dion,* passim; *Ep.* 137: "The masses think that uprightness of life
does not exist for the end of wisdom but stands by itself and is itself the perfection of
man. . . . In this view they are mistaken. . . . To live according to reason is the end of
man"; *De regno* 31C: "Love Philosophy and real education," for the two necessarily complement each other.

133. The *locus classicus* is Thuc. 2.41.1 (Pericles' funeral oration).

134. ἀδωρότατός τε ὢν καὶ φιλοδωρότατος; typically, a commonplace of ideal kingship turned into epigram (less elegantly, e.g., Dio Chrys. *Or.* 1.23).

135. *De regno* has much to say about the virtue of remitting the taxes of cities, particularly Synesius's own (esp. 27D).

136. A motif of traditional panegyric with no necessary *comparandum* in Aurelian.
Kings and emperors often founded cities (cf. Diod. 1.15.1–2, Osiris's foundation of
Thebes), but it seems inconceivable that a praetorian prefect would have.

did Osiris fail to know who needed what and what was preventing
this man or that from being happy. One man craved his due honor,
so he gave it to him. If another man so devoted himself to his books
that he had no time to make a living, he gave him his meals in the
Prytaneum.[137] Still another cared nothing for the honors of men; although his income supported him comfortably enough, perhaps
104B he felt unworthy of office.[138] Osiris knew his feelings and excused
him from public service. Osiris was not distressed; rather, he distressed the recipient, by giving before being asked. Osiris, with his
reverence for wisdom, thought it right for such a man to be independent and free to dedicate himself to god like a sacred animal.[139]

In a word, no man was deprived of his due reward unless he
deserved ill. To him Osiris did not give his due. He made it his ambition to conquer even the most shameless man with mild words
and good actions; in this way he thought he would win over his
brother and his comrades, using his own abundance of virtue to
alter their natures. In this one judgment he was mistaken. Malice is
104C not assuaged by virtue; it is inflamed. For if it is natural to cling to
the good, nevertheless as much as the good increases, the grief
caused by it grows also. This is what his brother suffered under the
rule of Osiris, and deeply did he groan.

XIII. No sooner had Osiris taken over the sovereignty than
Typhos nearly killed himself by cracking his wicked head on the
ground and smashing it against columns. For days at a time, glut-
ton though he was, he took no food, and despite his fondness for
wine he refused drink. Longing for sleep, he continued without it.
104D He was hard-pressed by insomnia when he tried to conjure it
away.[140] He tried shutting his eyes to free his mind from stinging
memories, but memory struggles hard against the man who wants

---

137. The honor of sitesis for the state's benefactors is a commonplace: e.g., Dem.
23.130; Dio Chrys. *Or.* 7.60; perhaps uppermost in Synesius's mind, however, Pl. *Ap.* 36D.

138. Note how explicitly Synesius links wealth with the qualification for public office.
The alleged feeling of unworthiness masks a less modest annoyance at the burden that
office imposed on the local magnate; as A. H. M. Jones has argued (1964a, 749), it was
largely a matter of the time his duties consumed. Synesius hints at the problem in the next
sentences; more generally, 125C; *De insomniis* 148C; *Hymn* 3 (= 1 Terzaghi).429–504;
Ep. 100; cf. Dam. *V.Isid.* 187.5–6 Zintzen, πολιτεύεσθαι . . . ἀναγκαζόμενος . . . οὐδεμίαν
εἶχε σχολὴν πρὸς φιλοσοφίαν.

139. Like the "rustic philosopher" of 113Aff., this man seems to represent Synesius's
own hopes. The "sacred animal" conforms with authentic Egyptiana: animals sacred to
various gods, such as the Apis bull (on which see Amm. Marc. 22.14.6–8), were kept and
were prominently entombed within temple precincts (e.g., *P. Teb.* 5; *P. Oxy.* 1188). Synesius uses a similar image of his own life before the bishopric in *Ep.* 57 (= 41 G, p. 58).

140. ἀποδιοπομπεῖσθαι: cf. 97A.

to lay it to rest. When he did close his eyes, the recollection of his ills remained with him, and when, if ever, sleep did come to him, a dream would make him still more wretched. Before his eyes he would see the mountain, the ballots, the hands, every last one for his brother. Gladly would he awaken then in disgust at that painful

105A sight, and for a long time his ears would ring with the echo of the cheering crowd.

Nor could he bear to keep quiet in the distress of his soul. He had only to sneak out of the house for his misfortunes to continue to dog him. Osiris was in the words, actions, and poems of everyone: "How good-looking the new king is!" "He speaks so wisely!" "High-minded yet not boastful; mild yet not lowly!" [141]

Then Typhos would creep back home again and shut himself in. He and his wife had no reason for living. She was another ap-

105B palling abomination. [142] She tarted herself up [143] and never got her fill of the theater [144] and marketplace, pleased to suppose that she was

141. It is interesting that Synesius presents humility, $\tau\alpha\pi\epsilon\iota\nu\acute{o}\tau\eta\varsigma$, as undesirable when in Christian values it had already become a more positive virtue (Lampe, s.v. $\tau\alpha\pi\epsilon\iota-\nu\acute{o}\varsigma$ 7; note particularly the self-depreciatory formula $\acute{\eta}$ $\acute{\eta}\mu\tilde{\omega}\nu$ $\tau\alpha\pi\epsilon\iota\nu\acute{o}\tau\eta\varsigma$). For a useful discussion of the role of empresses as exemplars of humility, see Holum 1982, 25–27, 57–58, 187–88.

142. In the character and role of Typhos's wife Synesius departs entirely from Plutarch's myth. There (*De Is. et Os.* 356B–C), Typhos forms a conspiracy with seventy-two men and the Ethiopian queen Aso; having secretly measured Osiris's body, Typhos makes a chest to fit and tricks Osiris into climbing into it, at which point the conspirators seal him in and hurl it into the Nile to be carried out to sea. Plutarch never indicates Aso's role in the conspiracy, though he does exploit her connection with Ethiopia in a physical allegorization (366C–D). Synesius doubles her in the figures of Typhos's and the Scythian general's wives and makes them lead the plot (108Bff., esp. 113B). Her character bears no resemblance to the passive Nephthys, Typhos's wife of the myth; she rather embodies the antithesis to Osiris's ideally decorous domestic life. Synesius never names these women or the general (or for that matter the old king), presumably because they have no precise correspondents in the myth. Typhos himself, though introduced as the epitome of wickedness, is remarkably inactive in arranging his coup. For this deflection of responsibility from Gaïnas to Caesarius (and wife), see chapter 8, section III (cf. too 110C–D, 111A–B); the ascription of the initiative to his wife is even more discreditable to Caesarius (cf. 107C, 112D; and for further examples of the technique, chapter 7, section III). Naturally, these intimate scenes of intrigue are entirely invented. It is hardly necessary to add that there is no evidence that Caesarius's wife played any such role.

143. Bury ([1923] 1958, 1:128) notes that Caesarius's wife "was her own tirewoman, a reproach which seems to mean that she was inordinately attentive to the details of her toilet." More tellingly, Synesius suggests a class distinction that she basely violates: a $\kappa o\mu-\mu\acute{\omega}\tau\rho\iota\alpha$ would normally be a slave. At *Caes.* 335B, Julian links $\kappa o\mu\mu\acute{\omega}\tau\rho\iota\alpha$ with pastry cook as lowly and contemptible professions.

144. Cf. Chrys. *Hom. in Eutr.* 1 on the vice of theater attendance; Claud. *In Eutr.* 2.86–87, 338–41, 354–64; and more generally, C. Baur, *John Chrysostom and His Time*, vol. 1, trans. M. Gonzaga, 2d ed. (1959), 235–48; and the references in Cameron 1976a, 224 n. 6.

turning every head. Her husband's fall from the kingship[145] distressed her even more, because she had been planning to prostitute the government on a larger scale and to squander its authority in luxury.[146] Middle-aged though he was, Typhos fell for her like a teenager in love for the first time. Half of his misfortune was
105C the scandal of the person for whose sake he had coveted the supreme office and with whom he had intended to share his power. Even in her personal life she was a most conspicuous creature, ambitious to distinguish herself in the most contradictory ways. She was more feminine than women[147] in discovering yet another luxury, in adding to her beauty, and in surrendering to her nature. She was more reckless than men in applying herself to a scheme and in daring an enterprise—a meddlesome and manipulative fe-
105D male. On top of everything else, she had assembled whorish women and their male hangers-on,[148] to enjoy their unanimity[149] and use them according to her natural propensities at home or elsewhere.

As for Osiris, only the sight of his child reminded men that there were women's quarters in his home. Indeed his child Horus was seen rarely; for the sole virtue of a wife, Osiris thought, was not to leave the courtyard either in person or in name.[150] Consequently, her rise to the summit of good fortune did not disturb this sensible woman's established routine, unless by making her even more retiring because of her greater rank. Osiris himself took no

145. Synesius lets it slip (despite the conflict with his elaborate fantasy of the royal election) that Typhos had already been king; which on the equation of the kingship with the praetorian prefecture means that Caesarius had already been praetorian prefect. The comparative in the next clause then implies "a larger scale" than Typhos/Caesarius's wife had managed during his first tenure.

146. The same phrase is used at *De regno* 6A of the typical behavior of a tyrant.

147. Superlative for comparative; cf. Kühner-Gerth (hereafter K-G) 2.1.22. The masculine/feminine contrast is a commonplace: e.g., *De regno* 10B, *Ep.* 140 (p. 245.10 G), 146 (p. 256.6, 9 G); *Cod. Theod.* 9.14.3.2 ("pro infirmitate sexus minus ausuras"); Claud. *Carm. min.* 17.18 ("sexu debiliore").

148. πελάτης most commonly means "client" in the Roman sense, "a dependent"; but it is also used, for example, of Ixion, of a man who "approaches" a woman sexually, so possibly of a whore's "client" in the modern sense.

149. Literally, "to have them all like-minded": a travesty of the ideal unanimity of a good king's court; cf. 106D; *De regno* 29C.

150. Characteristically, Synesius gives a more extreme, epigrammatic formulation to a traditional view; e.g., Thuc. 2.45.2; Xen. *Oec.* 7.5ff.; Men. frag. 546 Körte (= 592 Gomme-Sandbach). Holum (1982) discusses the stress laid by contemporary rhetoric on the ταπεινότης of the necessarily conspicuous imperial women, finding in it a strategy to accommodate them to the ideal; for much literature on the life of women at Constantinople in this period, see Elizabeth A. Clark, *Jerome, Chrysostom, and Friends,* Studies in Women and Religion 2 (New York and Toronto 1979).

106A pleasure from his good fortune on this score. Rather, he knew that
even without it he would have been no less fortunate: if he wishes
to be good, each man controls such things for himself. We can see
that those who live virtuously, both private citizens and public officials, are happy in the same way. Each and every life is material for
virtue.

Just as we see on the stage,[151] a tragic actor who has trained his
voice well can play the roles of Creon or Telephus equally well;
purple robes will in no way differ from rags as far as concerns the
volume and beauty of his delivery, or his ability to captivate the
106B theater with the ring of his song.[152] But he will portray both the
handmaid and the lady with the same artistry, and the director of
the drama will demand that he play his part properly whichever
mask he wears. Thus god and fortune provide us, as if with masks,
with lives in the great drama of the cosmos;[153] one life is neither better nor worse that another, and each must use his own as he is able.
The serious man is able to live his life well everywhere, whether
106C playing the part of the pauper or the prince. It makes no difference
whatever what the mask is. The actor who avoided one mask but
chose another would be ridiculous! For example, if he shines in the
old woman's role, he wins awards and public acclamation, while if
he turns in a feeble performance as the king, he is hooted and hissed
off the stage, possibly even pelted with stones. No life is our own
possession; rather, we are costumed on the outside with the lives
of others. Both the better and the worse of us do and show what is
experienced within ourselves, players in a real-life drama. Just like
106D costumes, lives may be put on and taken off.

XIV. Now Osiris, since he had been taught what was his own
province and what was not, understood that the soul is the measure of happiness. He tried to harmonize his own opinions and
those of the members of his household so that, citizens and officials, they might not be intimidated by external forces. But Typhos
and his wife (who lived by their sensations, without sense) were

151. It is doubtful whether classical drama was still performed in Synesius's day;
surely not on the basis of χορηγία liturgy. In light of the material collected in the next note,
probably a purely literary reference. Synesius implies the classical convention whereby a
male actor played female parts.

152. A commonplace of popular philosophy, the comparison of actors in rags or
purple robes appears to go back to Epictetus: Stob. *Flor.* 3, p. 211.11 Meineke (frag. 11,
p. 412.7 Schenkl); see O. Hense, *Teletis reliquiae,* 2d ed. (Tübingen 1909), cxff.; compare too
the related development in Dio Chrys. *Or.* 38.39–40.

153. Another implosive comparison; cf. p. 354 n. 109.

reckless lovers of fortune. They reckoned as their own what was not, and they were filled with vanity,[154] expecting the kingdom would be theirs. When it did not come their way, they began to de-
107A spair of themselves and to think that life was insupportable. It is worth emphasizing again and again that it is the hallmark of boorishness in men not to await life patiently like a course of a meal, brought round for us to help ourselves, but instead to snatch surreptitiously out of turn. Even if he gets away with it, someone like this will be laughed at as an unmannerly guest and will be despised by the host because he churlishly disturbs the arrangements on his own account. And if he fails, he will cry like a child and cling to the
107B dish that has passed him by and gone on to his neighbor.[155] Everything of this sort was happening to Typhos: the gods had come to hate him. He himself was lamenting, and the situation had become a public joke. Even when he took to his bed for many months[156] and was likely to die any day, it aroused no pity. Those of a more manly bent were moved to anger and those of a milder to ridicule. The affair became proverbial, so that anyone who was pale might be asked, "Has something good happened to your brother?"[157]
107C He might have killed himself, and rightly too, so much was he given up to evil. But now his abominable wife, all too much a woman even in this crisis, rescued herself and her husband. Managing him with ease as always, she stopped his tears by keeping him busy with herself, driving out passion with passion[158] and barricading his grief with pleasures. In this way he renewed the struggle, yielding in turn to the most contradictory evils. He would groan at one moment and swell with passion at the next. Then in-
107D deed licentious boys slipped into his house in even greater numbers; there were revels and carousals so he might kill time in their company and assuage the gloom of his soul.[159] They devised other

154. A similar phrase at *Ep.* 143 (p. 250.15 G), of people who falsely pride themselves on philosophic knowledge that is really only superficial.

155. Or perhaps "and make a spectacle of himself when the dish has passed him by and gone on to his neighbor." Julian (*Or.* 2.69C), echoing Pl. *Rep.* 354B, more flatteringly applies the same image to himself, for trying to include too much all at once in his speech.

156. This is such a specific allegation, without any tendentious implication, that it must be true. If so, then Jones's solution to the problem of the sequence of prefects allows Aurelian far too short a tenure: see chapter 5, section IV.

157. For a similar witticism, see Macrob. *Sat.* 2.2.8.

158. A proverbial expression going back to Arist. *Eth. Nic.* 1154a27; cf. *Rh.* 1418a13; here with a more playful application than in the later *Ep.* 57 (= 41 G, 62.3–4) and 79 (143.17–18 G).

159. Pl. *Alc. min.* 150E; used also at *De regno* 15B of Arcadius's dissolute pastimes.

things too, so that he had as little free time as possible to recall the good fortune of Osiris. They made swimming pools and islands in the pools and on the islands artificial hot baths. There they could strip among the women and leap on one another without restraint.[160]

XV. While they were occupied in this way, evil demons prompted Typhos and his wife to attempt a coup.[161] The demons showed them the way, and now openly helped them manage their 108A other affairs, dancing constant attendance upon them. For they could not bear to watch their own cause falling ignominiously apart: prudence practiced, piety increasing, injustice driven away, concord established, and all good things coming into flower. As for weeping, only the word was left to the Egyptians. All was auspicious; all was in order. Law was the soul of the state, like a single organism's, and it moved accordingly, its members harmonizing with the whole.

Maddened by these things, the demons glued themselves to 108B men of their ilk and used them as their instruments. It was in two boudoirs that the evil was concocted.[162] The general of the foreign troops[163] had his home in the royal city.[164] He and his troops appeared to be fighting for the Egyptians. They were currently conducting a campaign of sorts, unsuccessfully, against a contingent

160. We have preferred the reading of A, γυναιξὶ καὶ, to the vulgate, which produces the mysterious "There they could strip *for one another* among the women and mount [sc. them?] without restraint." The verb ἐπιθορνύομαι is normally used of animal copulation. There were many private baths in Constantinople (Janin 1964, 216–24), many of them heated, and all often described by poets of the sixth century (e.g., *Anth. Pal.* 9.606–40; sex and baths connected, esp. 620, 626, 627). The idea that hot baths were immoral goes back at least to classical Athens, e.g., Ar. *Nub.* 1043–54. Bury solemnly chronicles Typhos's swimming pool orgies as the consolations of his political disappointment. Rather, the series of increasingly remote and artificial pleasances dramatizes again Typhos's unmanly retreat from action and replaces his lethargy with even less wholesome activity.

161. Demonizing the instigators of disruption is a useful rhetorical technique: cf. *Ep.* 57 (= 41 G); Claud. *In Ruf.* 1, passim; Lib. *Or.* 19.29, 30, 34; anon. *Peri politikes epistemes* 5.104 (Mazzucchi [Milan 1982], 33.20 = A. Mai, *Script. vet. nov. coll.* [Rome 1827], 2:597); the advantage was that no serious motive need be considered. In the present case, Synesius wishes to suggest that the initiative for the plot did not come from the barbarians. They are drawn in later.

162. Another displacement of responsibility, now with demeaning overtones of emasculation, which is directed against Caesarius, not Gaïnas (cf. below 112D). For the associations of the women's quarters, cf. Dio Chrys. *Or.* 2.6 on the tyranny of Sarandapallus.

163. For Gaïnas's barbarian retinue see chapter 4, section III.

164. "The royal city" is a very common periphrasis for Constantinople. Many references from church council *acta* are collected in the topographical index of *ACO* 4.3.3 (1984) 89ff.; cf. Fenster 1968; Dölger 1964, 70–115.

of their own people[165] that had rebelled,[166] and some Egyptian villages had been faring badly. The demons had devised this for the purpose of their drama.

108C   Typhos's wife, a knavishly subtle creature, visited the wife of the general day and night. She had no difficulty in winning over the ignorant and barbarous old woman to the belief that she was concerned about her and foresaw evil befalling them if things turned out according to Osiris's plans. For he was, she claimed, accusing the general of treason on the grounds that he was fighting a collusive war, the barbarians pursuing a common policy with their armies divided.[167]

"Osiris has decided," she would say, "to bring him back with all the compulsion and trickery he can manage.[168] As soon as he is away from his troops, he will take away his command and cruelly destroy him and you and your children.[169] These fine children, these beautiful babies—he has decided to cut their throats before 108D they grow up!" With these words she would burst into tears, chucking them under their chins and pretending goodwill by her compassion. The old Scythian[170] woman immediately began to wail, thinking that she was about to see these frightful things before her very eyes and suffer them herself.

Then Typhos's wife would add another horror, and horror on horror every day, announcing supposed[171] secret plans against them: the Scythian race was to be completely eliminated from the country, and Osiris was daily working toward this end, infiltrating

---

165. We read αὐτῶν (or ἑαυτῶν; cf. 108D, 111A) for αὑτῶν of previous editions: see Cameron, Long, Sherry 1988, 59.

166. I.e., the revolt of Tribigild, another Goth, who was commander of barbarian federates in Phrygia. This is one of the most precise references to the events of 400 in book 1.

167. Contemporaries certainly believed that Gaïnas and Tribigild had planned from the start the rebellion that culminated in Gaïnas's coup, and many moderns have followed them (e.g., Paschoud 1986, 124f.). It is very doubtful whether this was so: see chapter 6, section II. Synesius is not, as usually assumed, a contemporary source here, since he did not write till at least a year after the outbreak of Tribigild's rebellion.

168. ἁπάσῃ βίᾳ καὶ μηχανῇ, a variation on a common antithetical topos of injustice: e.g., Pl. *Rep.* 344A: [τυραννίς] οὐ κατὰ σμικρὸν τἀλλότρια καὶ λάθρᾳ καὶ βίᾳ ἀφαίρεται; 345A: ἀδικεῖν ἢ τῷ λανθάνειν ἢ τῷ διαμάχεσθαι; Amm. Marc. 30.1.18: "ut per vim ei vel clam vita adimeretur."

169. Gaïnas's children are mentioned by Theodoret (*HE* 5.32) as present with Gaïnas in Thrace later on.

170. This is the first time the Goths are referred to as Scythians, a barbarian tribe described by Herodotus in a famous digression, 4.46–82. It was a standard reference for the Goths by Synesius's day (Maenchen-Helfen 1973, 5–9); he uses it also at *De regno* 22C and 23D among other places.

171. This note is unmistakably suggested by the particle δῆθεν (cf. Denniston 1954, 264–66): see p. 321 n. 61 and chapter 8, section III more generally.

the military rolls[172] and making other provisions so that the Egyptians might be independent. The barbarians they would either kill
109A or drive out.[173] This would be easiest if he made their general a private citizen by formal dispatch and brought legal proceedings against him. He thought that once he had managed this, the others would present no difficulty.

"At this very moment," she says, "Typhos is at home in tears. He has your affairs at heart, and his policies have always favored barbarians. It was on your account that we fell short of the kingdom too, since you did not stand by Typhos at the accession.[174] If you had, you would now be allowed to insult the Egyptians, own
109B their possessions, and treat your masters as slaves. But you did not help us then, and now we are powerless to come to your aid. It is a misfortune for us now that disasters are threatening our friends."

In this way Typhos's wife outmaneuvered the old woman and utterly terrified her, as if there were no escape. She then laid on her next scheme, to lead the barbarian back from her panic. The woman had already learned to follow her lead, and now she gradually strengthened her and filled her again with hope.

"It is a bold plan," she said, "and requires uncommon daring if we are not to be under Osiris's rule and live or die as he deter-
109C mines." At first she spoke of insurrection in obscure riddles, then she hinted at it, and finally she revealed the plan. Bit by bit she accustomed her to the proposal and the adventure, until finally she had made the timid creature bold, showing her that Osiris's power would come to nothing if only they were willing.

"For custom," she said, "habituation to rank, and ancient and ancestral usages make willing slaves of the lazy. But the revolutionary puts the weak to the test. It is the strong man who is free, un-
109D less habit scares him from his intention. Let us not suffer that while you are armed and Osiris does nothing but pray to the gods, re-

---

172. I.e., with nonbarbarians. The expression nicely exaggerates the barbarian dominance in the army. Compare Amm. Marc. 31.16.8, remarking that in 378 the Thracian units all had Roman commanders, "quod his temporibus raro contigit."

173. This was the program recommended by Synesius himself in the *De regno*. Though the policy is universally attributed to Aurelian by modern scholars, it is significant that Synesius himself does *not* directly attribute it to Osiris, leaving it to the allegations of Typhos's wife. Indeed, he saw its neglect as a major factor in Aurelian's downfall (cf. 96C–97B).

174. Synesius's scenario for the royal election did not allow barbarians the vote (94A), so this reproach underlines Typhos's wife's duplicity. At most, she suggests a campaign of intimidation.

ceive delegations, judge lawsuits, or pursue some other peaceful activity.[175] But if we make common cause, with us supplying the nobility and you the forces, Osiris will never again cause trouble to any of the Scythians. The Egyptians will not think that you are debasing anything great or disturbing Egyptian affairs or changing the constitution, but only administering and managing things alto-

110A gether better; for you will be securing the rule for Typhos, who has the same father as Osiris and is older and has a greater right to rule Egypt.[176] To begin with, the Egyptians are not likely to unite against you, since there would be no great change in their ancestral government. The appearance of rule will be ours, but the advantage will be yours; you can then feast on all Egypt as if it were handed to you on a platter. Only promise that you will persuade your husband."

"And you," said the barbarian, "will join me in persuading him."[177]

And so they did. When it was announced that the general was

110B riding up, a surreptitious vanguard discreetly dropped word of Osiris's plot, proclaiming it more clearly with their pretense of secrecy than if they had cried aloud what they imagined they were hiding. Obscure letters enjoining safety threw things into confusion. Already someone said, openly, that they must save themselves from Osiris's ambush, then another said it more conspicuously, then another and yet another repeated these things. All these men belonged to Typhos's party and were the women's fellow conspirators.[178]

As the finishing touch to all this, the women, the authors of the

175. Conventional duties of the emperor in peacetime; Millar 1977, chap. 5. Diodorus also records similar activities for Egyptian kings (1.70); for their basis in Hellenistic political philosophy, see further O. Murray, *JEA* 56 (1970): 141–71.

176. A delightfully sophistic argument, seeking to justify Typhos's revolution with the claim that he is not a revolutionary at all but merely wishes to substitute the rule of one brother for another. Possibly her argument is to be seen as a travesty of Pl. *Tim.* 34C, where it is asserted that god must have made the soul before the body, because it is improper for the younger to rule the elder.

177. We follow Fitzgerald in assigning this sentence to the barbarian, against Terzaghi's punctuation. It is hard to believe that καὶ σύγε refers to the same person as σύ in the previous sentence. The fact that Synesius added ἔφη here perhaps supports the argument; and paragraphi dividing one speaker from another in dramatic texts and philosophic dialogues drop out of manuscripts with notorious ease.

178. A remarkable example of the implosive metaphor (p. 354 n. 109) being lived out: the conspirators, who are part of the actual army, draw their general into the plot by metaphorical military tactics.

110C drama, held a meeting, and Typhos himself, leaving town as if on
some other business, conferred with the general secretly.[179] He
made a compact about the kingship and persuaded the general to
go ahead with the deed at once. If necessary,[180] he was even to
destroy the royal city along with Osiris. He actually made such a
concession as this, on the grounds that the rest of Egypt would
suffice for him. "What's more," he concluded, "your soldiers can
make themselves rich by enslaving a prosperous city, the common home of Egypt's illustrious men, and by plundering their
possessions."

And so the excellent Typhos pledged the city away, hating it
because of the goodwill its inhabitants had shown toward Osiris.
But the Scythian for his part refused. For he held in high esteem
110D the sacred council and the decent citizens and the prerogatives of
the city. He said that he marched against Osiris not as a volunteer
but under a compulsion that Osiris himself had created. And if he
succeeded in overcoming him, with the city safe and the countryside unravaged, he said, he would reckon it a gain that no greater
evil proved necessary.[181]

XVI. Our story refuses to dwell on the sufferings of Osiris; it is
111A not in its nature to persevere obstinately in a painful tale. But the
inauspicious[182] Days of Holy Tears have been observed from that

179. Evidently Gaïnas had not yet returned to the city; presumably this meeting took
place at the camp, although the specification that the general's home was in the city (108B)
implies that his wife and Typhos's met there, and the metaphorical level of the military
language in the intervening paragraph obviates assuming a change of scene. It is interesting to note that Caesarius's wife must often have been in and out of the city visiting her
friend Eusebia (cf. Soz. HE 9.2), whereas Caesarius himself might have aroused suspicions
by openly visiting the camp at such a moment. But, of course, Synesius may simply have
invented this visit.

180. We take καί adverbially; see Cameron, Long, Sherry 1988, 59.

181. This extraordinary apologia for a barbarian unanimously condemned in the rest
of the tradition (written after his death) is a clear indication that Synesius wrote book 1
before his defeat; Lizzi (1981) claims that Synesius had genuinely moved away from his
rabid antibarbarianism of the De regno, but she ignores the fact that Synesius gleefully reverts to this earlier attitude in book 2, as soon as Gaïnas was no longer a live threat. Among
other things, it seems to prove that Gaïnas did *not* occupy Constantinople by force.

182. ἀποφράδες: of *dies nefasti;* cf. Sallustius *De diis* 18 (p. 34.5 Nock); Luc. *Pseudol.* 1,
8, 12; Luc. *Tim.* 43, with schol., p. 117.14 Rabe; Marin. *V.Procl.* 19, p. 16 Boissonade (specifically ἀπ. of the Egyptians); August. *Ep.Gal.* 35 (*PL* 35.2130) refers to "days called Egyptian," on which building and like activities may not be begun, which seems to correspond
to the "Egyptian" ἀποφράδες of Marinus. For a general account, Anastos 1948, 246–47.
Synesius also uses ἀποφράδες nontechnically, of the three years he spent at Constantinople (*De insomniis* 148C).

time until the present, and those to whom it is permitted have beheld their images moving.[183]

This much is fitting for everyone to hear. For his country, for its laws, for its temples,[184] Osiris delivered himself into the hands of men who were prepared to destroy everything if they could not take him. He crossed the river in a barge.[185] He was immediately put under guard wherever he went. The barbarians held an assembly to decide what should be done to him, and Typhos demanded
111B that he be put to death as soon and as violently as possible. But the barbarians, although they believed they had been wronged, were indignant at this and respected his virtue.[186] They were for impos-

183. The immediate context does not provide a referent for "their"; there may be some textual corruption. If so, it is insoluble, and may obscure the key element in the reference. On the face of it, Synesius refers to a current festival, for which he supplies an aetiology. Since the tale itself is a fiction, this claim need not be taken too seriously. The festival is described as if it were Egyptian, and suits the dolorousness of Egyptian rituals that was notorious among Greeks (e.g., Hdt. 2.85, 171; Diod. 1.83.5; Plut. *De Is. et Os.* 366E; Firm. Mat. *Err. prof. rel.* 8.3; Orph. *Argon.* 32; August. *De civ. d.* 6.10; Arn. *Adv. nat.* 1.36). Synesius could have known from Lucian, for example, that Egyptian cult statues gave oracles by moving (*Syr. d.* 36). But that took place in public processions (see *A Saite Oracle Papyrus from Thebes,* ed. R. A. Parker [Providence 1962], esp. chap. 6, by J. Cerny), which would seem to be excluded by the reference "to whom it is permitted." That detail better suits a Greek mystery cult (or something considered in that light: for example, *De regno* 16B uses the same phrase of the possibility of seeing the emperor). The most reasonable suggestion is the practice in later Neoplatonic theurgy of divination by dedication and animation of statues (E. R. Dodds, *The Greeks and the Irrational* [Berkeley 1951], app. 2, particularly 291–95 and notes). A Christian reference might also be considered: a sorrowful festival at this time of year (April/May) might suggest Good Friday—though the expectation of resurrection three days later is much too optimistic for Aurelian at this juncture: the most Synesius could suggest at the conclusion of book 1 was eventual vindication. It is worth observing that references to works or items surviving "to the present day" are a common trick of fraudulent works claiming a measure of authenticity, e.g., the *Historia Augusta,* where the alleged survivals almost never are; see Syme 1968, 98–99; 1971, 263–80; 1976, 311ff. (= 1983, 98–108).

184. There is a similar collocation in *Ep.* 113 to Evoptius, of Synesius's labors in the defense of the Pentapolis. There is no reason to believe that "temples" has a partisan religious reference in this context.

185. ὁλκάς: see note at 96A. The meeting with Gaïnas did in fact take place in Chalcedon, on the other side of the Hellespont, which Synesius transforms into the Nile but otherwise preserves the correspondence with events of 400.

186. Synesius spectacularly transfers blame from the barbarians to Typhos/Caesarius. Zosimus (5.18.9), on the other hand, pictures Gaïnas actually resting his sword across the hostages' necks before agreeing to pardon them. Chrysostom claims that he interceded for the lives of Aurelian and Saturninus (*PG* 52.413). The general shape of the plot here (Osiris's voluntary surrender to his brother, confinement, facing the threat of death, and removal from the country) parallels that of Plutarch at Osiris's imprisonment and death in the chest, which floats down the Nile and out the Tanitic mouth (*De Is. et Os.* 356C, 357A).

ing exile. But they were embarrassed even at this and decided that it should be not an exile but a "retirement."[187] They allowed Osiris to keep his wealth and property, although Typhos had offered it to them. They touched none of it, any more than they would touch the sacred objects.[188]

Osiris was dispatched under divine and semidivine escort[189] so that he would be away at the times fated. Divine law did not permit that the worse elements should prevail in Egypt or that everything

111C should quickly lapse into disorder and sorrow while a holy soul was living there. The demons responsible began by uniting against Osiris so that these things might happen. Typhos, their faithful servant, whom they had long since brought to birth and finally to tyranny, was feasting them on every kind of misfortune.[190] The taxes on the cities were at once multiplied. Nonexistent obligations were "discovered"; others long buried were dug up.[191] River-

111D dwellers were assigned to service inland; boats were requisitioned from landsmen so that no one might have time to enjoy human pleasures.[192]

These were the most public abuses, but another was commoner still. Typhos sent out venal men to be his lieutenants and governors for the provinces. He publicly auctioned off cities.[193] Indeed, though their contracts ran for a single year,[194] even the youngest lessors of this or that governorship expected to amass the

187. μετάστασις, a penalty less than exile, cf. Pl. *Epin.* 8 (356E) of deportation.

188. It might be reasonable in an Egyptian context to expect barbarians to sack temples, but in Constantinople in 400 it is significant that the barbarians were Christians, if heretics. On just this ground were Orosius and Augustine to play down the significance of Alaric's sack of Rome. But for a puzzling reference to Arians "despoiling the apostles" in a homily of 402, see chapter 8, section IV.

189. Literally, "under the escort of god and beneficent heroes." In general, the *De providentia* presupposes a plurality of gods (91B, 93D, 95A, 95D, etc.), of whom Synesius sometimes refers to an individual (e.g., 88B, 102A, 114Bff. [see note ad loc.], 118C). The remaining singular references are generalizing, as here. Synesius's usage of ὁ θεός in the letters is similar (see Runia 1976, 256); and in the unquestionably Christian eighth hymn Synesius twice uses θεοί in the plural (the stars are νυχίων θεῶν, 48; Aion is the "steward of the gods (θεοῖς)," 71). Nor did even pagan Neoplatonists absolutely identify a plurality of gods with the supreme God.

190. Synesius uses the same metaphor of feasting at 97A and 110A.

191. Cf. Amm. Marc. 26.6.17, *sepulta negotia:* possibly reflecting a common source in Eunapius.

192. The charge has an obviously Egyptian flavor, but no clear contemporary reference. Possibly some Alexandrian client of Synesius's.

193. Sale of offices was an extremely trite charge of political invective: e.g., Claud. *In Ruf.* 1.180, *In Eutr.* 1.196–209; Eunap. frag. 87 (= 72.1 and 2 Blockley); Zos. 4.28.3, 5.1.2; Procop. *Anecd.* 22.7–9; on *suffragium* and its abuses generally, see Jones 1964a, 390–96.

194. For the duration of provincial governorships, see above, p. 342 n. 38.

wherewithal for a licentious old age. This is just one of the things
that happened under Typhos's rule.[195] For cash down, he would
112A write up an agreement as to the term of office. Formerly, a man
would be relieved of office at a charge of malfeasance, another rewarded for his virtue by a senior post, a larger province, and pro-
longation of his term. But from this time on, everyone everywhere
was continually lamenting, each with a personal woe to tell. Community by community, council by council, they were bludgeoned
by every sort of evil, so that a single voice, the echo of a common
lament, rose from Egypt to heaven.

112B   The gods pitied the race and were preparing to defend it. But
they decided not to do so until virtue and vice were still more
manifestly contrasted. Thus even those who used their minds and
perceptions least might distinguish the better from the worse and
pursue the former and turn aside from the latter.[196]

XVII. Typhos now undertook to excise the reign of Osiris completely from the memory of man. Among many routes to this goal,
112C his particular favorites were to have cases that had been settled at
law reopened. He would require that the man who had been convicted now be the winner. He also enacted new measures with regard to earlier embassies: anyone who had been favored by the divine voice of Osiris was now to be an enemy; he, his city, and his
people were forced to live in misery.[197]

In an impossible situation, two stratagems against Typhos
were available. First, one could give money to his wife. She held
court quite openly, like a brothel,[198] and used her whorish atten-
dants as pimps for her body and her business, transforming what
the Egyptians used to call a hall of justice into an auction hall for

195. It will be remembered that at the time of writing Typhos had been in office for
barely three months.

196. A frail justification for Caesarius's long tenure in power.

197. Synesius obviously has in mind his own embassy (cf. *De insomniis* 148C–D,
Hymn 1.431), implying that Caesarius revoked benefits Aurelian had conferred. The reference to reopening settled lawsuits may be entirely general, but perhaps Caesarius had also
reversed some judgment involving Cyrene or Synesius, or someone whose sympathy he
hoped to win. Synesius's charge need not imply any actual abuse by Caesarius: *Cod. Theod.*
11.30.16 (1 August 331) had formally established the praetorian prefect's as the court of
final appeal.

198. Krabinger (1835, 292–93) shows that ἐπὶ τέγους here means "in a whorehouse":
cf. Syn. *Calv.* 85B; Clem. Al. *Paid.* 3.21.2, 3.74.4; Xen. Eph., ἐπὶ οἰκήματος, 5.5.4; προ-
στησομένην τέγους, 5.7.3; and add Chrysostom, ἐπὶ τέγους, *Ad Theod.* (SC 117; Paris
1967), 14; ἐπὶ τ., *Les cohab. suspectes*, ed. J. Dumortier (Paris 1955), 1.41; πρὸ τέγους, *On
Vainglory* 2.42, p. 72.2 A.-M. Malingrey (SC 188; Paris 1972) (Laistner 1951, 79, rightly rejects the suggestion that the rich man in 4f. is actually Eutropius).

112D lawsuits.[199] Whoever had intercourse with her[200] found Typhos gracious—he was tame and submissive toward the women's quarters,
especially since he was grateful for their having obtained his throne
for him. This was one path out of trouble for those who found Typhos hostile. The other was to approach one of his abominable crew
of eating companions. They were called "great" and "blessed,"[201]
wretched, false little men[202] that they were. One had to go to these
people and let drop some deliciously contrived piece of abuse
against Osiris. Those who did this were the people least concerned
with virtue, the ones who were not ashamed to profit from any
113A source whatever. Thereupon their fortunes changed as quickly
as their opinions. The story weaseled its way up to the tyrant's palace and was paraded at dinner. Typhos always returned favor for
favor.[203] One man after another did this and profited from it, though
they knew they were hated by the gods and by decent men. Most
people just tried to endure.

XVIII. There was a certain man, dignified, but nurtured by philosophy in a rather rustic manner and unacquainted with the ways
of the city.[204] And this man, like all of mankind, had met with in-
113B numerable benefits from Osiris. He himself was not obliged to per-

199. An echo of *De regno* 30C, the practice of a ruler whose injustice stems from avarice. Synesius was fond of this type of figure: e.g., 92B above; *Ep.* 32 (= 45 G, 84.2, 85.2),
παιδοτρίβην . . . πορνότριβα; 57 (= 41 G, 60.23), [Andronicus] τὴν στοὰν τὴν βασιλέων,
τὸ πάλαι κριτήριον, ἀποδείξας βασανιστήριον.

200. The double meaning is clearly present in the Greek.

201. The terms probably do not have any more particular significance than that
people fawned on Caesarius's friends. Μέγας and its compounds were used very commonly in honorific address. As Runia (1976, 323) notes, Synesius is one of relatively few
authors to use μακάριος and related forms of the living (curiously, not the classicistic ὦ
μακάριε); usually of the dead (Dineen 1929, 81–83, 94).

202. ἀνθρώπια; the diminutive also at *Ep.* 110 (196.13–14 G), of a favorite of Gratian
who was ugly but of good character.

203. A topos of *gratiarum actiones*, e.g., Auson. 1.1; Synesius slyly puts Caesarius in
the subservient position.

204. The philosopher represents Synesius himself within the tale (cf. 114B), on the
model of Dio Chrysostom's self-portrait within *Or.* 1: wandering in exile (50), he arrives in
the Peloponnese and stays away from cities, preferring "herdsmen and hunters, men of
noble and straightforward characters" (νομεῦσι καὶ κυνηγέταις, γενναίοις τε καὶ ἁπλοῖς
ἤθεσιν, 51); there he receives a prophecy of relief and his allegorical fable of Heracles from
an inspired priestess (53ff.). Synesius's emphasis on his rusticity is more than the commonplace apology for one's style (e.g., *Calv.* 67A; Corippus *Ioh.* pr. 28; see T. Janson, *Latin
Prose Prefaces*, 130–36; E. R. Curtius, *European Literature and the Latin Middle Ages*, 83,
410–12) or a provincial's genuine self-consciousness in the capital: it transfers to himself
the virtues Dio claimed for the Peloponnesians (note that Synesius describes the full flush
of his παρρησία as particular "rusticity," 113C–D). ἐμβριθής might punningly add
a touch of humor if Synesius happened to be portly; perhaps better "weighty" for
"dignified."

form public service, and his country's obligations had been made
less burdensome.[205] Hundreds upon thousands were then writing poems and speeches, panegyrics on Osiris, returning favor for
favor.

This man was as grateful as they—even more so, being better
endowed. For he wrote both poems and speeches and sang to the
lyre in the Dorian mode, which he considered the only one able to
allow for depth of character and diction.[206] He did not expose his
work to the public, but if there was an audience that could appreci-
113C ate manly discourse and would not tolerate titillation and would
take to heart what they heard, he would entrust his work to them.[207]
He knew that Osiris was a discerning judge of literature, especially
of this sort, and could tell the ephemeral from the enduring. Yet he
rejected the idea of addressing Osiris on the subject of himself, because he considered words an unequal recompense for deeds and
was ashamed lest he acquire a reputation for flattery because of the
rusticity of his background.[208]

But when Typhos had seized Egypt by force and was ruling as
113D a tyrant, this man acted the rustic even more than before. It was
then that he published, then that he revealed his compositions,
horrifying every listener. He considered it impious not to be perfectly candid in his hatred of those who had done outrageous
things to his benefactor. In speech and in writing, he called down
the direst curses on Typhos. Previously guilty of silence, he became a great talker both at home and in public. Osiris was everywhere in his discourse, and everywhere he met people he sang the
praises of Osiris. He inflicted his tales even on those who would

205. This is the apparent sense of the text as it stands, but a plain dative αὐτῷ that
will not construe may signal some deeper corruption. See Cameron, Long, Sherry 1988, 60.

206. Synesius casts his self-portrait in the image of Plato's Laches, who at 188D identifies the Dorian mode as "the one Hellenic harmony," which marks a man whose deeds
bear out his words about virtue. (D. Roochnik in forthcoming work will explore this element of Laches' character.) Plato's contrast of λόγοι and ἔργα in this speech is echoed by
Synesius's ἤθους καὶ λέξεως. Synesius did in fact pride himself on writing Doric verse
(*Hymn* 7.1, 9.5). Possibly this allusion also suggests that some of these works had begun to
circulate at Constantinople.

207. Cf. *De regno* 1C–2A, where also Synesius describes his speech as "manly." This
passage specifically implies that that work was aimed at a select audience.

208. Repudiation of flattery is a panegyric commonplace (e.g., Dio Chrys. *Or.* 3.2;
Them. *Or.* 15; with an accuracy uncharacteristic of the topos, the *De regno* prologue). Synesius holds himself above Typhos's crowd of servile flatterers and fits his behavior to the
pattern of philosophic παρρησία (on which see R. MacMullen, *Enemies of the Roman Order*
[1966], chap. 2), claiming a virtue for his failure to show gratitude to Aurelian before the
exile. The fact that he needed to do so argues against the usual assumption that he was a
committed member of Aurelian's party before the coup.

not bear them. He paid no attention to older men and friends who
114A admonished him. Fear did not shake him from his impetuosity; he
was like a man raving with an unrestrained madness. He did not
stop until he stood as close as possible to Typhos himself, at a time
when distinguished men from all the world were gathered around
him, and gave a long speech in praise of his brother. He urged him
to strive after the virtue so closely related to him.[209] Typhos flared
114B up and was visibly infuriated, though out of shame before the
gathering he restrained himself, compelled to be reasonable. But
from his face one could picture what was going on in his mind: one
form of passion succeeded another, and within moments he turned
every possible color.[210]

From then on he became more hateful and behaved worse. He
had already obliterated the good works of Osiris's reign, but now
he was committing crimes of his own in addition, harassing the
cities on whose behalf the rustic philosopher had spoken, and con-
triving a personal hardship for the man himself so that he might
never return home, forced to remain in the city lamenting and
watching men who hated him enjoy their success.[211]

114C   Amidst these circumstances, a god[212] appeared to the stranger
in full epiphany and gave him new strength, bidding him endure.
For he said that not years but months made up the allotted time[213]

209. It is impossible to translate adequately the double meaning of προσήκουσαν,
both "related to" Typhos, i.e., his brother's, and "befitting" his kingly state.

210. A reference to Dio Chrys. *Or.* 1.81, where Tyranny's expression is said to turn
"all sorts of colors" from her unsteady emotions; Dio's phrase in turn echoes Pl. *Lysis* 222B,
where Hippothales' face turns all sorts of colors "from pleasure." Compare further Lib.
Or. 33.12.

211. Though Synesius purports to be reporting fresh outrages, he also repeats the
charge relating to his own embassy. There seems no reason why Caesarius should have
wanted to retain so obnoxious a character at court; Synesius himself felt obliged to remain
in hopes of restoring his tax exemption. In *De insomniis* 148C–D he says that dream-divina-
tion helped him to escape plots directed against him while he was serving as ambassador,
which may or may not be connected with the "hardship" here described.

212. On Synesius's own system, apparently an individual god of the intermediate
class, who himself refers to "the gods." Grützmacher (1913, 51) connects this manifesta-
tion with Synesius's claims for dream warnings, *De insomniis* 148C–D. But the god is not
issuing private warnings against the personal hazards alluded to in *De insomniis.* He delivers an apocalyptic prophecy for the whole Egyptian people. The prophecy reflects a long
Egyptian tradition (see above, chapter 7, section VI), and this unidentified god is merely a
device for working it into Synesius's plot.

213. The interval before the restoration of better times is normally far longer (900
years in the case of the Oracle of the Lamb). This short interval, as well as corresponding
with what Synesius hoped would be the facts, in addition provides a further parallel with
the prophecy Dio Chrysostom represents himself as receiving from the Peloponnesian
priestess at *Or.* 1.55 (cf. p. 374 n. 204). It is often inferred from this passage that the real-life

during which the scepters of Egypt would lift up the claws of the wild beasts[214] and hold down the crests of the sacred birds.[215] This is an ineffable token. The stranger recognized it as the writing engraved on obelisks and sacred precincts.[216] The god interpreted for him the meaning of the hieroglyph and gave him the key to the 114D time.[217] "When," he said, "those who are now in power attempt to tamper with our religious rituals as well,[218] then expect the Giants"[219]—by this he meant the aliens—"soon to be driven out, themselves their own avenging Furies.[220] But if any element of their faction should remain, if it should not be altogether destroyed, if Typhos himself should remain in his tyrant's palace, even so do not despair of the gods. This shall be another token for you. When with water and fire we purify the air about the earth, now defiled by the exhalation of the godless,[221] then even upon those who re-

counterpart to Typhos can only have held his prefecture for "months, not years," but Typhos was still in office when Synesius wrote. It is an optimistic *prediction*, not a statement.

214. The claws evoke the brazen claws of the fourth and most terrifying beast in Daniel (7.7 and 19). The wild beasts are of course Typhos and the barbarians.

215. Presumably the sacred hawks of the Egyptians; according to D'Arcy Thompson, archaeologists have found "no less than twenty-six species of diurnal rapacious birds . . . in a collection of over a thousand Egyptian bird-mummies" (*A Glossary of Greek Birds*, 2d ed. [Oxford 1936], 118). The lowering of their heads symbolizes the humiliation of the Egyptian monarchy. Krabinger (1835, 305) improbably suggested that the crest of the hoopoe was meant, on the grounds that the hoopoe was legendary for its filial piety (Thompson, 99) and might therefore symbolize Osiris, humiliated by his exile.

216. More than casual Egyptian coloring. This is a traditional device giving authority to the prophecy: see Fowden 1986, 35 and 66 n. 84.

217. Synesius specifies hieroglyphs in part for obvious historical reasons, in part because by his day it was believed that even for the ancient Egyptians they were "ineffable symbols" (for a contemporary illustration, see Socr. *HE* 5.17). The fifth-century treatise of Horapollon, himself from Upper Egypt, "combines correct notions of the meanings of many hieroglyphic signs with the most grotesque allegorical reasons for those meanings" (A. Gardiner, *Egyptian Grammar*, 3d ed. [1957], 11). For more details, Fowden 1986, 63–65.

218. A transparent reference to Gaïnas's attempt to obtain an Arian church within the walls of Constantinople, thwarted by John Chrysostom (Theod. *HE* 5.32).

219. For Giants as an apocalyptic symbol, see J. H. Charlesworth, *Old Testament Pseudepigrapha*, vol. 1 (1983), 106 (4 Esra; Gospel of Eve; 2 Enoch). Even in less specialized contexts battles with barbarians might be compared to the Gigantomachies of Greek myth: for example, Goths in Claudian (Cameron 1970a, 468).

220. Another detail taken from the apocalyptic tradition: the Oracle of the Potter prophesies that the invaders will kill themselves (chapter 7, section VI).

221. The defiling of the air need not have any contemporary meteorological reference; it is another datum of the apocalyptic tradition: "fructus terrae conrumpentur nec fecunda tellus erit et aër ipse maesto torpore languescet" (*Asclepius* 25, Nock-Festugière II.329.22–23), whence Lactantius: "aër enim vitiabitur et corruptus ac pestilens fiet" (*Div.inst*. 7.16.6); and though the text is damaged, it is clear that the various versions of the Oracle of the Potter said something very similar (Koenen 1968a, 200–202; Nock-Festugière II.382, n. 219). On the other hand, the gods' purifying of the air "with water and fire"

115A main shall justice come. Expect immediately a better dispensation upon Typhos's removal.[222] For we drive out this sort of monster with fiery missiles and thunderbolts."

Then the stranger felt that what he had long felt harsh seemed to augur well, and he no longer grieved at his compulsory detention, since through it he was to be an eyewitness to the visitation of the gods. For it was beyond human prediction that a vast armed force—the barbarians had the legal right to carry weapons in peacetime[223]—be defeated with no force to resist them. He pondered how these things could happen, but it seemed beyond his powers to understand.

115B   But not long thereafter there arose a false piece of religious observance, a counterfeit ritual like a counterfeit coin: something ancient law bars from the cities, shutting the impiety outside the gates, beyond the walls.[224] When Typhos tried—not personally, for fear of the populace of Egypt, but through the barbarians—to introduce this innovation and grant a temple in the city, dissolving the ancestral laws, the stranger immediately realized that this was what the god had predicted. "Perhaps then," he thought, "I shall also see what is to follow." And he waited, now understanding what was to happen about Osiris in the near future, as well as in

(presumably the same as the "missiles and thunderbolts" of the next sentence) is to be the second sign after the tampering with religion. It should therefore be a real and conspicuous heavenly phenomenon, something that Synesius's audience would instantly identify. The obvious candidate is the conspicuous comet of March–May 400 (see p. 168). Vollenweider (1985a, 166) rashly added the earthquakes and other "Naturerschütterungen" listed by Claud. *In Eutr.* 2.24–45 and Philostorg. *HE* 11.7. But Claudian's portents are imaginary, and if the quake happened at all, it was not till after the publication of both books of *De providentia*. It was the quake in the autumn of 400 that encouraged Synesius to leap on the nearest boat home (Cameron 1987, 351–54).

222. Though Synesius alludes above to Caesarius's continuation in power even after the expulsion of the Goths, it is notable that he still expects that he will fall soon; not altogether unreasonably, on the assumption that they had been his support, provided that Synesius finished book 1 very shortly after the expulsion. In a few months, when he came to write book 2 and the Goths had fallen back from the city and Caesarius nevertheless still was not deposed, a more elaborate apology became necessary.

223. On the importance of this curiously anachronistic allusion to the Roman ban on civilians bearing arms, see chapter 6, section I.

224. The "ancient law" referred to was in fact Theodosius's, as Theodoret indicates (*HE* 5.32): he says that Arcadius was willing to grant Gaïnas this concession, but Chrysostom persuaded him not to yield by calling upon his filial duty. It was only in his myth that Synesius could claim that heresy had always been against the law; in fact this was an innovation of his own day. Holum (1982, 86 n. 30) oddly cites this passage in illustration of Aurelian's religious views; for Synesius's own hostility to heresy, see chapter 2, section IV.

the years yet to come, when Osiris's son Horus would decide to select the wolf rather than the lion for his ally. The identity of the wolf is a sacred tale that it would be irreverent to expound, even in the form of a myth.[225]

Book II[226]

116B   I. After this, the gods' attention began to be evident, since evil was everywhere, and belief in Providence had by now faded from the minds of men, their impious suspicions supported by the evidence of what they saw. The barbarians were using the city as a camp,[227] and no human remedy was anywhere to be found. The general suffered from terrors in the night—Corybantes, I think, assaulted him—and outbreaks of panic[228] seized the army by day.[229]

116C This recurrent alarm rendered them witless and unable to control their thoughts. They wandered around alone or together, all of

225. ἐν μύθου σχήματι, a phrase borrowed from the same passage in echo of which Synesius first began his tale (Dio Chrys. *Or.* 1.49; 89A and note). The "riddle of the wolf" alludes to the next stage of his myth, Horus's defeat of Typhos (cf. Plut. *De Is. et Os.* 358C). The wolf is grafted onto Horus's choice between two animal allies for his contest from a variant tradition that Synesius probably knew from Hecataeus of Abdera but that is preserved for us at Diod. 1.88.6. For more details, see Long 1987. It is notable that "the years yet to come" looks to the distant future for the vindication of Osiris's cause. Even the partisan Synesius does not suggest the possibility that Osiris himself will return. It would (of course) have ruined the myth if he had! It is Horus, not Osiris, who eventually destroys Typhos, and it is the victory of Horus to which Synesius here looks forward. This is the first time we encounter the motif, so overworked in book 2, of Synesius's alleged inability to tell some detail of his story because it would be "irreverent."

226. Book 2 shows signs of being a much quicker and less careful composition than book 1. Roughness of construction is particularly apparent in the first chapter. Synesius starts a narrative of the Gothic occupation but almost immediately turns aside into a moralizing summary anticipating the action to come, which he then summarizes more concretely, stressing the theme just brought out: a proem, with one false start.

227. Curiously, στρατόπεδον or *castra* was the standard term for the imperial court (e.g., Syn. *Ep.* 110 [p. 196.3G]; Amm. Marc. 14.5.9, 16.8.15; Jul. *Ep.* 46, 74.2, 76.1, 129; Soz. *HE* 4.16.20; Constantine apud Athanasius *Contra Arian.* 70.2, 86; Lydus *Mag.* 2.30; Chrysostom, *PG* 63.472). But the term reverts to its basic sense in a different context.

228. At Plut. *De Is. et Os.* 356D, "panic" is etymologized from the behavior of Pans and Satyrs on hearing of the death of Osiris.

229. A mysterious anxiety that afflicted Gaïnas before the massacre is well documented: see chapter 6, section I. Synesius exploits this anxiety extravagantly, without at all explaining its origin (a fear of reprisals from the civilian population; justified, in the event). Synesius does not deny the Goths' nervousness but ascribes it to divine inspiration so as not to complicate his claim that the Egyptians/Constantinopolitans were helpless before the barbarians and owed their salvation not to ill-provoked violence against Gothic civilians, but to divine Providence. This marks a new conception of Providence from that developed in book 1: see next paragraph and notes.

them like men possessed. At one moment they would test the draw of their swords[230] as though already eager to do battle, and at the next piteously beg to be spared. Or they would leap up, now apparently in flight, now in pursuit, as if some opposition had hidden itself in the city. But there was not a weapon in the place nor anyone to use it,[231] and the populace was an easy prey delivered up by Typhos.

116D   It is as clear as day that even those who are well prepared are in need of God if their preparations are not to be in vain. Victory has no other source. In judging, imprudently, that the better prepared are likely to win, one robs the higher cause of its due. When our plans succeed, God seems superfluous and lays claim to a victory that is the result of preparation.[232] But if no one intervenes to produce the result, and the invisible alone is the cause of victory,

117A   we have an unimpeachable refutation of those who do not believe that the gods care for mankind.[233] This is precisely what happened.

Brave, victorious, armed men, whose work and play alike were all training for war and the battle line, whose cavalry went about the marketplace in ranks, moving in squadrons to the sound of the trumpet—if any of them needed a shopkeeper or a shoemaker or someone to polish his sword, all the rest stood guard over his need, so that the phalanx would not be broken even in the streets—these are the soldiers who fled in rout from naked, unarmed, disheartened men who had not even a prayer of victory. They withdrew

117B   from the city at a signal, stealing away with their children, their wives, and their most valued possessions—as if they could not quite openly have enslaved the Egyptians' wives as well![234]

When the populace saw them packing up, they did not yet

230. ξιφουλκία, a rare, Plutarchean word (*Cam.* 29; *Arist.* 18; *Pomp.* 69) also used by Synesius at *De regno* 23C–D, in connection with barbarian contempt for the toga as being impractical for drawing a sword.

231. On this tendentious assertion see chapter 6, section I.

232. For the text, see Cameron, Long, Sherry 1988, 60.

233. In book 1 Synesius carefully defines Providence as the action of the gods periodically sending down individual good souls as the agents of their care for mankind (Osiris, who fails, and the anticipated Horus, who presumably will not). He now redefines Providence in a sense more like the modern conventional usage, as direct divine intervention, through which an unarmed and demoralized populace, without planning or organization, turned on and defeated an occupying army.

234. Once again, Synesius does not explain why the barbarians were trying to leave the city secretly instead of enslaving the natives, as he claims was their intention. The reference to wives, children, and possessions makes it plain that Gothic civilians, not soldiers, are in question. Similarly, Sozomen says that the exiting Goths had weapons concealed "in women's coaches." See chapter 6, section I.

understand what was happening but despaired for themselves all the more. Some locked themselves up at home to wait there for the fire. Others, choosing the sword instead, purchased a lighter instrument of death, not for any enterprise, but so they might offer themselves to the slaughter when it came. Still others were trying

117C to sail away, their minds set on islands and villages and foreign cities; any place now seemed safer than great Thebes, where the palaces of the Egyptians stood. How the gods, with difficulty, gradually brought them to trust in events and, their courage restored, to choose to save themselves is a tale that will strike the hearer as utterly incredible.

II. A poor woman, quite elderly,[235] had her business next to one of the side gates, not a lucrative trade, but one of need. She held

117D out her hands in the hope someone would give her an obol.[236] She had come to her mendicant's seat very early in the morning—the necessities of life are good at cheating nature of sleep—and she sat there doing what one might expect, sending the early risers to their work with blessings, proclaiming the glad tidings of the day, praying, and proclaiming that god was propitious.

When she saw in the distance what the Scythians were doing, since it was fully daylight and they kept on running in and out like burglars, all packing their goods and carrying them away, she concluded with horror that this was the last day Thebes would see:

118A they must be doing this so that the city would no longer contain anything of theirs as security. As soon as they had moved camp, they would strike the first blow without fear that they might share in the consequences, as would have happened if criminals and victims had been living together.

She knocked over her beggar's cup[237] and cried out, with many

---

235. γυνὴ πένης, μάλα πρεσβῦτις; she bears a certain resemblance to the prophetess of Dio (*Or.* 1.53; cf. note on 113A). Structurally, Synesius had assigned the role she plays in Dio's oration to the god in book 1 (114Cff.), but he was still free to reuse her character, taking advantage anew of its associations. Bury ([1923] 1958, 133) incautiously invests her with historical reality: "It happened that a beggar-woman was standing at one of the western gates."

236. Synesius intended the "obol" to be an antiquarian touch; but in fact the use of coins was introduced into Egypt only by the Macedonians. When Lacombrade makes Synesius refer to "aurei" in *Ep.* 129 (1978b, 566–67) the anachronism is his and not Synesius's, who writes νομίσματα correctly.

237. κώθων, which, as Athenaeus explains, is a type of Laconian drinking cup (483C–484C). Synesius was a Dorian chauvinist on his own account (cf. 113B and note; *Ep.* 57 = 41 G, p. 63.15); moreover, Dio specifies that his Peloponnesian prophetess spoke a Dorian dialect (*Or.* 1.54). It was presumably for its ethnic origins, and for the authority that they would lend her words, that Synesius chose his cup; somewhat recondite, since

a lament and appeal to the gods: "When you were wanderers
exiled from your own land, Egypt received you as suppliants. But
118B she treated you more generously than suppliants deserve, for she
even honored you with political rights[238] and shared privileges
with you,[239] and, to top it all, gave you authority in our affairs, so
that there are already some Egyptians who act like Scythians;[240] the
affectation actually benefits them. Your ways are more esteemed
than our own! But what is this? Why are you moving camp? Why
are you packing up and going away? Do you suppose the gods
don't punish ingratitude against benefactors?[241] For they exist and
they will come, even if only when Thebes is no more."

Saying this, she threw herself face down on the ground. A
Scythian sprang upon her, cutlass drawn to chop off the head of
118C the wretched creature who, he surmised,[242] was reviling them and
had made their night's work public. He had thought they were still
acting in secret: none of the people who had noticed had been courageous enough to confront them. She would have fallen before
his steel, but someone appeared, either a god or like a god—he
appeared, at any rate, as a man[243]—who rose up in indignation,
turned the Scythian toward himself and met his onslaught, got in
118D the first blow, lifted him up, and threw him to the ground. Another
Scythian was upon him and quickly met the same fate. A shout

the bulk of the literary sources Athenaeus cites refer only to the κώθων's use in military
contexts.

238. At 94A Synesius denies to barbarians and swineherds a vote in the Egyptian reg-
nal elections. Presumably πολιτεία here bears a limited sense, though in view of the complete rupture of the myth represented by Osiris's return, Synesius cannot be said to have
worried greatly about consistency between the two parts. In real life, of course, Goths like
Gaïnas and Fravitta who earned commands in the Roman army undoubtedly possessed all
the rights of Roman citizens.

239. Where Dio's prophetess told him the myth with which he was to instruct the
emperor on good kingship, Synesius's old lady now paraphrases his own De regno. Compare particularly De regno 25C–D (note the reuse of ἱκέτης/ἱκετεία, πολιτείας ἀξιοῦν,
γερῶν μεταδιδόναι) and 23A–B.

240. Synesius is probably thinking of the adoption of barbarian dress and hairstyle, a
well-documented affectation that, in the West at least, inspired legislation attempting to
ban it: Cod.Theod. 14.10.2 (tentatively dated by Mommsen to 7 April 397; by Seeck 1919, 77,
to 399), 3 (6 June 399), 4 (12 December 416); cf. De regno 23C; Claud. In Ruf. 2.82–85, IV
Cons. Hon. 466, Bell.Get. 481; Chrys. Hom.act.apost. 37 (PG 60.267); Rut. Namat. Red. 2.49.

241. For the text, see Cameron, Long, Sherry 1988, 60–61.

242. His difficulty in understanding her language underlines the soldier's foreignness.

243. There is a marked epic flavor to this whole passage. Compare Socrates' vision of
angels defending the palace, and his recommendation that "those who want to learn more
precisely about that war [of the Roman army against Gaïnas] should turn to the Gaïnias of
Eusebius Scholasticus, who was at that time a pupil of Troïlus the sophist; and having been
an eyewitness of the war, related the events of it in an epic of four books; and since the
events were recent, he was greatly admired for the poem" (HE 6.6).

rose up from the spot, and men rushed to help. On the one side were the barbarians who were on the point of leaving or else just outside the gate when the crisis overtook them. They let go their pack mules and started back to help their own as quickly as possible. On the other side was a great mass of Egyptians. One fell wounded. Another killed a Scythian before another Scythian killed him in turn. Men were killing and being killed constantly on both sides.

119A For the Egyptians, everything that came to hand was a weapon in time of need. They stripped the dead for swords to use or took them from the living. They outnumbered the aliens, some of whom had encamped as far as possible from the city to minimize their fear; god had threatened them with ambush, groundlessly,[244] so that they would abandon the city whose center was in their hands. The remainder, the smaller part,[245] were still in the city, busy with their furnishings so that nothing would be left behind. As it was, a force many times greater engaged the smaller, any who happened to be around the gates and others as they arrived to leave.

119B The shouting became louder, and at that point the attention of the gods became manifest. The entire city, large as it was, had now perceived the uproar, and news of it reached even the aliens' camp. Each side had long feared attack from the other. Every citizen now thought that this was Egypt's day appointed, when they were fated to wipe away the shame the barbarians caused them.

119C They resolved to die in action and to win honor in the grave, for not even a god could have offered a credible guarantee against death. They all forced their way through to the disturbance, where every one of them wished to be, thinking that he would gain by courting danger while there were still witnesses left to see him.[246]

The barbarians had tried to conceal their departure. When they realized that they were detected, they ignored those who were left behind, something like a fifth part of the army.[247] Fearing only for

244. Returning to the theme of barbarian anxiety, Synesius gives a sensible explanation for their behavior (which the event bore out), only to reject it at once in favor of divine Providence.

245. We have preferred the reading of C, τοῦ πλήθους ἀνὰ τὴν πόλιν. See further Cameron, Long, Sherry 1988, 61.

246. That is, while they could at least inspire others by a noble attempt, if not succeed.

247. Zosimus reports that 7,000 of the Goths took refuge in a Catholic church (5.19.4). It is tempting to combine the figures (whence the traditional estimate that Gaïnas had 35,000 men: Albert 1984, 131). But it is impossible to determine how accurate either might be. It seems unlikely that the church would be large enough to hold 7,000 refugees, as Bury ([1923] 1958, 134) remarks. Nor is it clear whether Synesius's estimate refers to

119D themselves, in case the enemy came out after them, they fled and took their position a little distance away. They were grateful that the majority had been saved, when they might have risked the entire force.

Some of the people they left behind were still in their houses. The gods had long filled them with foreboding; they suspected that the Scythians were to suffer some fatal ill at the hands of the Egyptians. They concluded that those who were leaving were being pursued as fugitives and that their camp would soon be ransacked. They supposed that it would be to their advantage to stay right where they were if they laid down their arms and presented them-

120A selves as suppliants. It might appear that they had been left behind all alone because they had done no harm to Egyptian concerns, whereas the others had quit the city in fear of just punishment for what they had done.

Only those who happened to be by the gates, in the middle of the terrible scene, knew the truth: the Egyptians had no strong organized force, no spearman, no spear; no javelin thrower, no javelin. They based their decision on present circumstances. They resolved to seize the gates, if they could, and call in their comrades, whose fear had been groundless,[248] for then the entire city could[249] be plundered like a bird's nest. A mighty battle was joined; the

120B Egyptians triumphed and sang a song of victory. This too inspired fear in the barbarians, both inside the city and out. Each group thought that the Egyptians raised the song in triumph over the other, so that both broke into lamentation. The victors had not barred all the doors of all the gates (no small task in Thebes, which Greek poetry hails as the "hundred-gated"[250]) before one of the combatants from the struggle around the gates ran out from the middle of the fighting to report what was happening and promise the city to the Scythians. They were there at once, but to no avail.

120C In one moment they praised and blamed their fortune. For a while, they were overjoyed at the fact that they had escaped the net, but

Gothic soldiers only, civilians being uncounted; to Gothic soldiers and civilians as a fraction of the total Gothic population in the city; or to Gothic soldiers and civilians counted together but reckoned in terms of the number of the army. Liebeschuetz's cautious "numerous" (1986c) is the best estimate that can be reached.

248. I.e., the four-fifths of the "army" that had fled the city in groundless fear of ambush, presumably still close enough to be called back.

249. ἄν appears to have dropped from the text. See Cameron, Long, Sherry 1988, 62.

250. *Il.* 9.383. Constantinople too was a walled city with many gates, though when Synesius was there not yet the Theodosian wall and gates that still stand.

then they decided to break through the wall and reoccupy the city. How irresistible a thing is the wisdom of god! No weapon is mighty nor mind ingenious unless god stands by it! And so it is that before now men have waged war against themselves. It seems to me an excellent observation that man is god's plaything, and with his affairs god ever jests and gambles.[251] I think Homer was the first of 120D the Greeks to understand this, when he made up the contest and set the prizes for every sort of competition at the funeral of Patroclus. In every instance the more likely winners fall short. Teucer gets second prize after an insignificant archer, "the best man drives last his single-hoofed horses,"[252] the young man is defeated on the running track by his elder, and Ajax loses the contest in heavy armor—yet Homer himself proclaims that Ajax was far the best 121A of all those who mustered at Troy, except for Achilles. But skill, Homer is saying, and practice and youth and natural superiority are all small matters compared to the divine.

III. The Egyptians, when they had gloriously won the gates and put the city wall between themselves and the enemy, turned against those who had been left behind. They bombarded them with missiles, beat them, and stabbed them, whether alone or in groups. Any who seized some fortified position they smoked out[253] like wasps, along with their priests and temples,[254] to the indignant

251. As Terzaghi points out, the passage evokes Heraclitus frag. 52 Diels-Kranz and perhaps Plato *Leg.* 803C. Although this strange formulation of divine Providence seems closer to the spirit of Homer than to that of Platonism, it recalls as well the Neoplatonists' concern with the demiurge's children, the creators of the sublunar world (*Tim.* 69C).

252. *Il.* 23.536.

253. ἔτυφον, a pun on "Typhos."

254. Apparently an understated reference to the burning of the (Catholic) church of the Goths in Constantinople. According to R. Janin (1969, 80) there is no information on the location of this church. He was evidently unaware of the title of Chrysostom's one extant sermon delivered there, stating that it was "the church beside the church of Paul" (*PG* 63.499). Unfortunately, it is not clear where the church of Paul was (Janin, 394–95). Zosimus states that the Gothic church was "near the palace" (5.19.4). According to the *Paschal Chronicle* (*Chron. Min.* II.66) "many Goths" were killed in the Λαιμομακέλλιον, which (despite the puzzling difference in form) is presumably to be identified with what later sources call the Leomakellion (connected with the emperor Leo by the patriographers). Janin places it at Heptascalon (1964, 379–80) on the basis of a text that can no longer be verified (*Cod. Koutloumous* 109, as quoted by Gedeon). The so-called *Dispositio topographica* (Preger, *Script.orig.Cpol.*, 2:297, no. 139) places it in the area of the church of the Holy Apostles. The story in Cedrenos 2.612–13 = Skylitzes 481 Thurn implies that it was west of the praetorium. Tzetzes *Ep.* 58 (85–86 Leone) associates it with the shop of a perfumer, but according to regulations laid down in the Book of the Prefect 10 (p. 30 Freshfield), the perfumers had their stalls near the palace gate. "None of this adds up" (letter from Cyril Mango, 21 June 1987). In any case, it is not certain that the Gothic church was near the Laimo- (or Leo-) makellion. The image of the wasps skillfully shifts sympathy

121B protest of Typhos. He had become Scythian[255] even in his religious beliefs.[256] He demanded that they negotiate with the barbarians, and was again working to admit the enemy army,[257] claiming that no irreparable damage had been done. The people[258] had no leaders but commanded themselves; with the aid of the gods every man was himself both general and soldier, captain and comrade-in-arms. What may not occur when a god wills it and imparts to men the impulse to save themselves by every device? They still did not yield the gates to Typhos, and in general his tyranny was as good as dead, since the force that sustained it had been driven from the city.[259]

121C   The people held their first meeting in the presence of the great priest.[260] The holy fire was kindled,[261] and there were prayers of

away from the victims (as Grützmacher 1913, 54, notes). So does the false implication, through the immediately following reference to "Scythianizing beliefs," that they were Arians. The ecclesiastical historians record this embarrassing incident without comment, but Zosimus reports (and we may well believe him) that "devout Christians considered this a grave defilement" (5.19.5). Yet further proof of how far Synesius's account is from being a simple "eyewitness report."

255. In view of the fairly extensive imperial legislation against Gothic fashions (see note on 118B) it seems unlikely that, as Terzaghi suggests, Synesius actually coined the term σκυθίζειν.

256. For Caesarius's Arian sympathies, see pp. 327–28.

257. Grützmacher (1913, 55) seems to identify this attempt with John Chrysostom's embassy to Gaïnas in Thrace (Theod. *HE* 5.33), but the barbarians cannot have gotten that far yet (he makes a second attempt when they have "withdrawn a great distance from Thebes," 122A). This must be some earlier negotiation. Synesius's feeling that any such attempt was rank treachery was not universal.

258. ὁ δῆμος might possibly be a gloss.

259. From now on Synesius consistently and falsely suggests that though still in office Typhos/Caesarius completely lacked influence.

260. There has been much debate about which historical character Synesius's "great priest" represents, the main candidates being Arcadius and John Chrysostom. He is better seen as an imaginary, composite character. Synesius's equation of the praetorian prefect with the king of Egypt left no room for a superior civil office, once the old king was out of the way. See chapter 5, section VII, for a full discussion. Neither the patriarch nor the emperor would have held public meetings to convict the praetorian prefect, as a simple equation would imply. These meetings merely embody what Synesius claims was popular opinion. The importance of the great priest to the narrative is that a popular appeal might be addressed to him. The appeal itself is Synesius's own wishful thinking; there is no evidence that Caesarius suffered any unpopularity in connection with Gaïnas.

261. It has been suggested that "the holy fire" refers to the eucharist, which hardly seems likely (Crawford 1901, 520–21). McCormick (1986, 109 n. 126) regards the scene as a Christianized form of victory celebration, but we cannot join him in following Lacombrade (1951a, 105, 109) to identify the great priest as Arcadius. The scene is evocative but vague. The premise of his "prophetic myth" makes Synesius particularly fond of antique references obscurely suggesting contemporary counterparts; here perhaps Ar. *Vesp.* 860–62 might be compared.

thanksgiving for what had been achieved and of supplication for what was going to come. They demanded Osiris, seeing no other salvation for their affairs. The priest promised that he would return if the gods granted it, as well as those who had been exiled with him for sharing his policies.[262] Typhos they resolved to string along[263] for a while.

121D Typhos did not at once suffer what he deserved, which was that he be made a sacrificial offering for the war, as the man most responsible that the Egyptians were so long the Scythians' slaves. Since Justice, who is wise and knows how to husband her opportunities, kept deferring his case, he thought he would escape the gods' punishment altogether. Still maintaining his hollow tyranny, he began to extort taxes more strictly and more unscrupulously.[264] He was already gathering up a second round of contributions even

122A from his underlings, now threatening that he would do some prodigious evil while he could, now again humbly begging pity, "so," he would say, "that I may not be expelled from the tyranny." He was, in fact, so utterly infatuated and arrogant[265] as to hope to get around the priest with flattery and bribes—a man to whom putting money before ancestral customs was anathema.[266] Even when the aliens had completely abandoned their position and withdrawn a great distance from Thebes, Typhos invited them back again with

122B envoys and pleas and gifts.[267] His every act and stratagem proclaimed clearly that he was going to pledge Egyptian affairs to the barbarians again. He himself apparently had no anxiety about his darling Scythians; or at any rate he was glad to think that he would not live to see Osiris return to his country and to office.

Barbarian hostility toward the country was now directed not at modifying Egyptian society, as formerly, but at destroying it utterly and governing in Scythian fashion.[268] To put it briefly, what was

262. Synesius's one indication that there were other exiles; most other sources mention Saturninus, but only Zosimus names John (5.18.8).

263. βουκολεῖν, "beguile," "cheat." The implication that the people had any choice in the matter is of course absurd.

264. If true, an indication that Caesarius's authority, despite Synesius's assertions, was just as strong as ever.

265. τὸν νοῦν ἐτετύφωτο, another pun on "Typhos." In this context of tyranny and empty show, perhaps also an allusion to *De regno* 20A (kingship, unlike tyranny, is ἀτύφον, for it partakes of divinity and God is not a showman).

266. τῶν πατρίων suggests the νόμος ἀρχαῖος that bans "impiety" (Arianism) from the city (115B); but perhaps more literal and nationalistic. Cf. 115B.

267. Cf. Theod. *HE* 5.33: the "great distance from Thebes" would suit John Chrysostom's embassy to Thrace.

268. In book 1 Synesius made the barbarians high-mindedly reject this offer of Ty-

now happening embodied the worst elements of the twin evils,
122C war and faction. Faction's part was its concessions and betrayals
from within, which are no part of war, and war's part was the fact
that the risk belonged to all in common; since the factions, thinking
to save the common lot, sought to transfer sovereignty from those
who had it to the other side. In the present situation both worse
elements from both evils prevailed. There were no Egyptians left
who did not think that the tyrant thought thoughts and did deeds
that were reprehensible; even the wholly reprobate were being
122D chastened by fear. It was this for which the gods had resolved to
wait, so that no smoldering ember[269] of the opposite faction might
be nursed secretly in the government, with specious if not just pre-
texts for evil.[270]

At long last a synod of gods and elders convened to discuss
Typhos,[271] and matters long debated by individuals were brought
into the open. Women who were bilingual interpreted from barbarian into Egyptian and from Egyptian into barbarian for the benefit
of women who did not understand one another's views.[272] Eu-

---

phos and his wife; he now implies that it had been their intention all along. Apparently
Gaïnas no longer seemed to threaten the city, so Synesius now felt free to blame him.

269. *Od.* 5.488–90 is the *locus classicus* for the banking of coals to preserve a fire.

270. This is the development for which the gods had been waiting in book 1 (112B;
the moralist has to deny the possibility that on longer acquaintance people might actually
prefer evil), but now their remedy is to bring back Osiris, whereas in book 1 it was to send
a Horus to succeed where Osiris had failed (115B). Formerly they had refused to intervene
on behalf of a single mortal, as Osiris's father explains, preferring to send down good souls
individually to succor all mankind (97Bff.). In effect, Synesius reverses his picture of the
operation of Providence, after the fact, to suit present political conditions.

271. The synod balances the election of part 1. Both represent (supposed) popular
opinion, but whereas the election fictionalizes the imperial appointment, the synod refers
to no real event and even in the fiction has no effect.

272. The fact that the translators and audience are women is puzzling. They may be
meant to balance artistically the coup's inception "in two boudoirs," or the jury of elders,
who are presumably male. They expand the tableau like a tragic chorus, suggesting avid
interest in the community; possibly Synesius's point is that dissatisfaction with Typhos is
so widespread that even women turn out for the trial. They may bear an emotive charge as
well, though the passage stresses merely the exchange of information: compare *Ep.* 67
(= 66 G, p. 106.11ff.), where the emotional reaction of the women of the town to their lack
of a bishop, over and above that of the men, touches even Synesius and his party. It is
notable here that Synesius reveals there were still Goths left unslaughtered for whom to
translate. Herodotus refers to the class of Egyptian interpreters (2.154). By this period professional *interpretes diversarum gentium* were on the staff of the *magister officiorum* (R. Helm,
in *Antike Diplomatie*, ed. E. Olshausen and H. Biller, Wege der Forschung 462 [Darmstadt
1979], 321–408, cites numerous testimonia on p. 407 n. 343). And John Chrysostom is reported to have used interpreters in his attempts to convert Goths from Arianism (Theod.
HE 5.30; further on interpreters in the Church, see MacMullen 1966, 364 n. 44, for numerous references; and Holl 1908, 252f.).

nuchs[273] were there too and clerks,[274] all from the group Typhos and
123A his wife had set against Osiris.[275] These people had just produced
the most damaging evidence that Typhos had surrendered key
positions and all but arranged the siege himself[276] so that the holy
city might be gripped by a reign of terror. And he was, they said,
all eagerness for the Scythians to cross to the other side of the river
as well[277] so that there should be no half-measure in the ruination of
Egyptian affairs and everything might be utterly destroyed, with
no time to summon Osiris.[278] When all this had come out, the human jury unanimously sentenced Typhos to be put under arrest,
123B and voted for a second trial to determine his penalty or fine. The
gods for their part commended the members of the jury for giving
an adequate sentence.[279] They themselves voted, when Typhos
should have departed life, to hand him over to the Furies to be in
Cocytus, and that finally he be a damned soul, a demon in Tartarus,[280] a monster in the company of Titans and Giants. He was

273. ἀνδρόγυνοι: Fitzgerald translates "effeminates," Nicolosi, "ermafroditi," but the
gloss preserved in the *deteriores* ("eunuchs") is surely correct. The palace eunuchs whom
Typhos/Caesarius is accused of having enlisted were privy to ugly secrets, which they now
disclose. See generally K. Hopkins, *Conquerors and Slaves* (Cambridge 1978), 172–96; Peter
Guyot, *Eunuchen als Sklaven und Freigelassene in der griechisch-römischen Antike* (Stuttgart
1980).

274. ἀπογραφεῖς is traditionally interpreted as "informers" here, but it could have
this sense only on the basis of what they do next in the narrative, and so could hardly serve
to designate them beforehand. Petau conjectures ὑπογραφεῖς, a term John the Lydian
states was the equivalent of *scriba* (*Mag.* 2.30; cf. Lib. *Or.* 2.44,58 of notaries; similarly, Syn.
Ep. 133 [p. 230.14 G] of a private secretary; the term ἀπογραφεύς is not attested). Neither
word is attested as a technical term of the bureaucratic hierarchy but would presumably
denote lower-ranking officials, who might still have access to information.

275. Plutarch records that just before Typhos's defeat "many," including "his concubine Thoueris" "changed over to Horus's side" (*De Is. et Os.* 358C). Synesius exploits an
opportune pattern in the myth to prop up his own wishful thinking.

276. Since the "siege" of July 400 was a freak accident, the implied transference of
this accusation to Caesarius is naturally preposterous.

277. As there is no previous indication that the barbarians of the myth were on the
other side of the Nile, this can only refer to Goths crossing the Bosporus from Chalcedon.

278. Literally, "seek after Osiris"; Synesius's wording is prompted by the focus of the
myth in Plutarch on the search of Isis for Osiris, and his information that this was reflected
in Egyptian ritual. Nothing in book 2 really fits the myth, least of all Osiris's return, but
Synesius incorporates such suggestions of it as he can, to lend some coherence to the work
as a whole. He does use vocabulary proper to the recall of exiles in the prologue and in
124A below.

279. Curiously, for all they had done was to postpone the sentencing.

280. There may be a suggestion of damnation of his soul as a heretic; hardly of excommunication, since Typhos was to be dead by the time it would be applied. Note that
Synesius is still waiting for Typhos/Caesarius's death; he was still in power at the time of
writing. Interestingly enough, Synesius himself later on was one of the first bishops to use
excommunication as a political measure, against the governor Andronicus (*Ep.* 57, 58 =

not ever to see Elysium, not even in a dream, much less lift up his
123C head to glimpse the holy light that is the object of contemplation of
good souls and the blessed gods.

IV. This is the story of Typhos. It may all be told—for what
story of earthly nature could be holy and ineffable? But the affairs
of Osiris are a sacred tale, of divine inspiration, so that it is dangerous to risk a narrative.[281] But his birth and upbringing, his primary
and higher education, his high offices, his election to the supreme
123D office on the vote of gods and godly men, his rule, the growth
of the conspiracy against him, how far it succeeded, and where
it fell short[282]—these things should be proclaimed to all, as they
have been.[283]

It might be added that to a man who is blessed in all things
even exile may not be without profit. During that time he was
initiated into the most perfect rites and mysteries of the gods
above. Letting go the reins of government, he lifted up his mind to
contemplation.[284]

124A   Let his holy return be told also,[285] the garlanded populace joining the gods in bringing him back and crossing over the whole
promontory to escort the returning party; night-long festivals,
torch-lit processions, distributions of gifts, the eponymous year,[286]

41, 42 G); for the process, see J. Bingham, *The Antiquities of the Christian Church* ([1708–22]
1875), 887f.

281. From now on Synesius consistently veils his own reluctance to reveal Aurelian's
failure to be restored to office in terms of fear to disclose holy mysteries.

282. Literally, "how it did not succeed in all respects." It should be noted that Synesius does not dare to claim that Typhos's alleged plot failed outright. It was implausible enough to claim any reversal, since Caesarius was still in office. The alleged failure
amounted to no more than Gaïnas's defeat and Osiris's return, neither of which is there
any evidence Caesarius opposed.

283. Synesius's own table of contents for the two books so far, corresponding to the
divisions of formal panegyric.

284. It is possible that the disappointed exile devoted more of his time to prayer, but
the enthusiasm for mysteries is characteristic of Synesius. His purpose in any case is to
lend respectability to Aurelian's period of removal. It is typical of the panegyrist to make a
virtue of necessity; Pacatus similarly makes Theodosius's enforced retirement from public
life a georgic idyll in old-Roman style (*Pan. Lat.* 2[12].9). On Synesius, Aurelian, and the
mysteries, see chapter 3, section I.

285. Synesius has prepared for the possibility of Osiris's return in the narrative, but
strikingly he states neither its cause nor its consequences. He implies that Osiris is summoned back by an adoring population disgusted with Typhos, but according to Zosimus
the exiles either escaped their jailors or bribed their way out. Zosimus concludes: "Whatever the manner of their escape, they unexpectedly returned to Constantinople" (5.23.1).

286. ἐπώνυμος ἀρχή or ἐπονυμία is a standard periphrasis for the consulate (e.g.,
Them. *Or.* 5, 64D; 71B; 16, 200A; 205C; 33, 367C; 34, 8 p. 218.16 Downey-Norman), so this
will be a reference to Aurelian's consular year; see chapter 5, section IV.

and the second sparing of his hostile brother, for whom he interceded with an enraged populace, praying to the gods for his salvation. In this last matter he behaved with more clemency than justice.

V. We may venture to say this much about Osiris; let holy silence cloak the rest.[287] So says one who touches on holy discourse
cautiously. It would take a rash mind and tongue to attempt what
124B lies beyond; let it remain in holy silence, undisturbed by writing,
lest someone "cast his eye on things not permitted."[288] Both he
who reveals and he who sees arouse the anger of the divine, and
Boeotian tales pull to pieces those who intrude and look upon the
rites of Dionysus.[289] Obscurity is majesty for initiations. Therefore
are the mysteries entrusted to night, and grottoes dug that may not
be trodden. These are the times and places that know how to conceal the divine and the ineffable.[290] Perhaps this is the one thing
124C that we may and do say, cloaking the inviolable as we are able: the
glory of Osiris's youth increased with his years,[291] and the gods
granted him the reward of overseeing the state[292] with a higher

287. Synesius had originally called his tale a "holy discourse" to enhance its authority (89A); he now takes advantage of this "holiness" to avoid saying any more about
Osiris. Much of the rest of the work is devoted to further pseudoreligious rationalization.
Cf. O. Casel, *De philosophorum Graecorum silentio mystico* (1919) and O. Perler "Arkandisziplin," *RAC* 1 (1950): 667–76; Anastos 1948, 274–76. The truth is that since Aurelian
had not been restored to office, there was nothing more to say. The farther Synesius might
carry the story, the more obvious it would become. He can hardly have expected his readers to take all this seriously, but it is another matter to claim with Liebeschuetz (1983) that
his reticence is "patently humorous."

288. Terzaghi unnecessarily separates οἷς from Synesius's quotation (source unknown).

289. E.g., Eur. *Bacch.*

290. Terzaghi suggests that Synesius adopted ἀρρητουργία from Clement (*Protr.*
15.1), but in view of the concentration of technical terms from the mysteries in this passage, it seems likelier that they all came from a common source or body of sources in the
pagan tradition, where they were used favorably. Synesius uses similar language of philosophy in letters to Herculian, e.g., *Ep.* 137, 143; cf. *Ep.* 151 (Pylaemenes), 154 (Hypatia). He
was later to speak in the same way of the resurrection of Christ as a mystery not to be
discussed with the unilluminated masses: *Ep.* 105 (p. 188.7ff. G, ἀπόρρητον); cf., however,
Ep. 13 (p. 33.13–14 G, μυστήριον) and *Ep.* 57 (= 41 G, p. 58.9–13, ἀρρήτους τελετάς, μυστήριον), in Christian contexts without such overt implications of exclusivity (with exclusivity implied ironically, *Ep.* 44 to Joannes, on which Fitzgerald cites Basil, *PG* 31.568A,
"mysteries").

291. On the basis of this passage and 125C, Liebeschuetz (1983) argues that Synesius
describes Aurelian's actual return to the prefecture in 414, when he was indeed an old
man. But Synesius himself probably died in 412. The reference to old age is admittedly
puzzling. Presumably, since he cannot claim his restoration to office, Synesius is trying to
make Aurelian into an elder statesman, a senior voice of wisdom speaking quietly but au-
thoritatively behind Arcadius's throne: see chapter 5, section VI.

292. Synesius uses the dative with ἐπιστατῆσαι for its more general sense "be set
over" (e.g., Pl. *Grg.* 465D, of the soul over the body), rather than the genitive, more specifically "be in charge of" (LSJ, s.v.). Even with the genitive, the term is applied to any of

title,[293] to show that he was above the injuries inflicted by men. And the prosperity that he had given to the Egyptians and found extinguished during Typhos's supremacy he restored and actually increased. It surpassed its earlier felicity, which now seemed to have been but a prelude of the good fortune yet to come, no more than a promise once talked of by the poets of the Greeks, how 124D the virgin who is now among the stars, whom we call Justice, I think—[294]

> The story runs
> that earth was once her home,
> that she mixed in human throngs and never shunned
> society of man or woman of the olden times
> but sat among them, immortal though she was.

She dwelled under the same roof with men.

> As yet they knew not baleful strife
> nor parted interests' bitter feud nor battle.
125A Thus they lived, far from the dangerous sea,
> and no ships brought their food from foreign lands,
> but oxen and the plough and throned Justice
> yielded thousandfold to all their needs, with distribution due.
> These things were when earth still fed the golden race.

So long as[295] men made no use of the sea, he says, they were golden 125B and enjoyed the intercourse of the gods. But when ships came into the service of commercial life, Justice departed so far from the earth that she is scarcely to be seen on a clear night. Even now when we do see her she stretches forth to us an ear of corn, not a rudder. Perhaps she might descend now, and will again converse with us in person, if farming were encouraged and sailing discouraged.[296]

---

several offices. Since Synesius so conspicuously uses this much vaguer expression rather than his usual equivalent for the prefecture, namely, the kingship of Egypt, this passage cannot be held to prove that Aurelian was restored to the prefecture.

293. Apparently Aurelian's patriciate (chapter 5, section VI, above); he would then have received that honor somewhat earlier than otherwise attested.

294. Aratus *Phaen.* 101–4, 108–14. The omitted 105–7 include her name. We adapt slightly the translation of E. Poste (1880).

295. Krabinger's Atticizing correction of the text (followed by Terzaghi) is unnecessary; the sense is unaffected. See further Cameron, Long, Sherry 1988, 62–63.

296. Whatever Synesius may genuinely have thought about agriculture and commerce in Cyrene, he is here the prisoner of his Hesiodic/Aratean commonplace. At Lib. *Or.* 18.284 and Amm. Marc. 22.10.6 and 25.4.19 the return of Justice, without the opposition of agriculture and commerce, is applied to Julian, whom Ammianus says applied this tag to his own reign.

No other age has closer approached the tales that poets of old sang about Justice than Osiris's most glorious kingship.

125C   But if the gods, having brought him back from his "retirement," [297] did not immediately place everything in his hands at the same time, [298] let us make no more of it than this: the nature of the body politic does not admit of wholesale change for the better as it does for the worse. [299] Evil is an instinctive thing, but virtue is attained with toil. [300] Someone must intervene to clear the way; the divine must proceed in a leisurely and orderly fashion. It was necessary that Osiris, before being deprived of leisure, [301] see and hear many things. A king's ears are often deceived. [302]

125D   VI. But we must take care not to divulge any of the ineffable mysteries. May the divine be propitious.

Now that we have learned the fortunes of one brother long ago and one in our own day, a fascinating question confronts us. Why is it that whenever a nature arises that is not just slightly better or worse than the norm, but enormously so—virtue unmixed with evil or evil unmixed with virtue—its undiluted opposite also springs up somewhere nearby? Widely divergent offspring proceed from one home, and the root for the two shoots is single. [303]

Therefore, let us ask Philosophy what she will identify as the
126A cause of this paradoxical situation. Perhaps she will borrow something from Poetry and answer, "Mortals,

297. μετάστασις, the same term Synesius used at 111B.

298. Synesius's way of conceding that Aurelian was not restored to office. Pace Liebeschuetz, this passage does not imply that Synesius knew that Aurelian was eventually reappointed (see above, n. 291). The concluding note Synesius sounds for the tale, looking to "the remaining days," looks to the future as much as the "riddle of the wolf" that concludes book 1.

299. Synesius proposes two contradictory justifications for Osiris's not being restored to office: (1) Typhos is allowed to continue in office until everyone is fully convinced of the undesirability of evil, and then the gods will intervene; and (2) a preliminary cleansing of the state must be done before the godlike Osiris will deign to resume the kingship. The problem is that Typhos's rule covers the latter period also.

300. The concept can be traced back to Hes. *Op.* 287ff.

301. Synesius in *Ep.* 100 contrasts σχολή with political action. Compare, for example, *Ep.* 11 and 57 (= 41 Garzya, who cites ad loc. Pl. *Tht.* 172D, παρέστη σχολή), of the leisure of contemplation against the bishop's mundane duties (the press of duties is well emphasized by Liebeschuetz 1986b), or Claud. *Theod.*, where the incredible indolence of *Carm.min.* 21 is suddenly represented as scholarly otium in the best tradition (on which more generally, see Matthews 1975, 1–12).

302. At *De regno* 27B, ambassador Synesius says that it is only through embassies that the king can have full knowledge of his realm.

303. This image dramatically contradicts Synesius's derivation of good and evil souls from diametrically opposed springs (book 1, 89B). A similar point about the proximity of extremes is made by Themistius (*Or.* 22.267C, vol. 2:55.22 Downey-Norman).

on the threshold of Zeus are set two jars
of gifts such as he grants, one of evil, the other of good.[304]

He usually pours and mixes in an equal or nearly equal amount
from each jar, producing a symmetry in accordance with nature,[305]
since at the beginning the generations of man have equal quantities
of seed from both jars, and the good and bad seeds are united by
reason of the nature they share.[306] But whenever he pours exclusively from one or the other portion, and a father is entirely blessed
or cursed in the elder of his children, the entirety of what is left in
126B the jars goes to a future child. The god who is doing the pouring
will make up the deficiency, since the two jars must be drained
equally. Whenever a god somehow exhausts one portion on the
first child, the remainder will be unmixed."[307]

If she were to say these things, she would persuade us, since
we observe likewise that the sweetest part of the fig tree is the fruit,
but the leaves, bark, root, and trunk are all very bitter. It would
seem that the nature of the tree consumes all the inferior matter it
possesses in its inedible parts, but lets its best matter remain pure
126C in its fruit. Accordingly the sons of farmers (let us be content with
humble illustrations to help us do more to convey the truth) in
accordance with nature, perhaps instinctively, plant bad-smelling
plants beside good-smelling ones, and sweet ones beside bitter
ones. Through their affinity with it, the bitter plants draw to themselves all the bad matter the earth holds matted within it, leaving

---

304. *Il.* 24.527–28. Plato (*Rep.* 379D) reproaches this passage for implying that the
god causes evil as well as good; he is followed by Plutarch (*De aud. poet.* 24A–B; *De Is. et
Os.* 369C). Sophists also quote the passage freely, often without criticism, e.g., Dio Chrys.
Or. 64.340; Max.Tyr. 34.3 (p. 394 Hobein); Syn. *De insomniis* 140B, *Hymn* 1.663–78 (Terzaghi ad loc. adduces among other passages *De providentia* 89B, but in fact the two springs
represent a different kind of dualism: they have to do with the type of soul, not its experience, and the springs do not mix). It is clear that Synesius belongs to the rhetorical rather
than the philosophical tradition, especially since he here flagrantly contradicts his earlier
dualism. His implication that the net good and bad must be equal within every family is
highly idiosyncratic.

305. Cf. 127A, ὅπερ ἐν μὲν τοῖς κατὰ φύσιν ἔχουσιν . . . συμπεπλεγμένας ἔχει καὶ
δίδωσιν. Synesius refers to Nature undisturbed the normal, even blend of good and evil in
souls. A purely good soul can be produced by special divine intervention, however, ne-
cessitating a purely evil soul as a preliminary by-product, in order to preserve the overall
balance.

306. Cf. the similar use of κοινός in *Ep.* 8 (p. 29.5–6G). We transpose the clauses ἢ
καὶ τὴν ἀρχήν . . . καὶ ἓν ἄμφω . . . φύσεως to follow συμμέτρως here, so that Synesius's
argument will follow logically. See further Cameron, Long, Sherry 1988, 63–64.

307. Cf. 91C.

126D distilled in the better roots only the better sap and smell. This is how they purify a garden.[308]

VII. It follows logically, in the manner of one geometrical corollary emerging from another,[309] that utterly wicked children are the elder sons in their generation.[310] And this purifies the seeds in a family whenever a god prepares a birth of immaculate and pure virtue. Thus it comes about that the thing that is seemingly most 127A one's own is actually the most alien of all. This will not happen to those who follow nature, half bad and half good, but rather to those who disdain the natural condition and are distributed in its separate parts, which nature keeps united. It would be miraculous if it did not happen to such people.

This is enough on that point. But another problem arises that requires another discussion. The same things very often happen in different places and times,[311] and as they age men become spec-127B tators of the things they heard of as boys, either from books or from their grandfathers: this seems very strange to me. And if it is not to remain a puzzle, we should seek an explanation. Let us find and expound its proper cause—although that may be no small or simple problem.

Let us suppose that the cosmos is a single whole composed of its parts. We shall then think of it as flowing and breathing as one, for thus might it preserve its oneness.[312] And we shall assume that

308. Rotating crops is advantageous, of course, and certain plants do grow well in company with one another; but Synesius obviously speaks as a philosopher, not as a gardener. His information comes from Plut. *Quaest. conv.* 5.9, 684B.

309. Synesius was fond of such plays on the language of geometry, doubtless with some thought of Hypatia: cf. *Ep.* 93 (to Hesychius, p.155.11–12 G), 131 (to Pylaemenes, p. 225.1–3 G).

310. A remarkable deduction, evidently based on the fact that Aurelian was a younger son (though Synesius himself was an older brother!). Synesius probably just ignored Caesarius's and Aurelian's other brother Armonius: he had been dead for nearly a decade and may have been the middle or youngest in any case. ἐν τοῖς γένεσι, the same phrase as in 126B/A above (transposed passage), evidently refers to individual families. The point seems necessary to Synesius's context but does not otherwise figure in his expression.

311. Fitzgerald (1930, 434–36) reads this passage too narrowly as alluding to Plato's doctrine of recurrent cataclysm and divine intervention in the world, though certainly his version of the idea of cycles of time exerted great influence on the later traditions (see in general Sorabji 1983, 182–90); here his periodic destruction is absent. Synesius introduces the question particularly to hint again that his myth has its counterpart in recent history.

312. Terzaghi cites *De insomniis* 132B, where Synesius claims that the possibility of oracles is implied by the sympathy of the universe (cf. Pl. *Tim.* 40A, and more generally 20Cff., 33–34).

its parts do not lack sympathy for one another, for how may they be one if they are not joined together by nature? Accordingly, the parts will act upon one another and be acted upon by one another. 127C Some will only act, and others will only be acted upon. Proceeding to our second problem with this assumption, we may logically identify the blessed body that moves in a circle as the cause of the things of this world.[313] For both are parts of the cosmos, and they have some effect on one another. If there is generation in the realm about us, the cause of generation is in the realm above us. It is from this source that the seeds of events arrive here. If anyone should 127D propose on the basis of astronomy that the proofs, some simple and others complex, recur with the circuits of the stars and spheres, he would be following the lore of Egypt as well as Greece,[314] supremely wise in both, combining intelligence with knowledge. Such a man would know that when the same movements recur, the effects recur along with the causes, and that lives on earth now are the same as those of old, and so are births, upbringings, intellects, 128A and fortunes.[315] Therefore, we should not be surprised to see ancient history come to life again. Indeed, we have seen it, since events that happened in the past and have been happening for a period of several months[316] agree exactly with the revelations of this story. The forms hidden in matter accord with the mysteries of the fable. What they may be is not yet for me to reveal. Different people will have different guesses, and if the myth's clarion call sounds around their ears, men will pore over Egyptian tales with a 128B craving to know what will be, and draw the parallel to present events from the allegory. But history and myth do not entirely agree with one another.[317] Let men know that it is no act of piety to attempt to unearth what should be buried for the present,

for the gods keep life hidden from man.[318]

313. Cf. *De dono* 310D (τὸ μακάριον οὐρανοῦ σῶμα): astronomy is propaideutic of philosophy because the cosmos imitates mind.

314. Egyptian claims to the origins of astronomical science are well attested in the Greek tradition: e.g., Diod. 1.9.6, 1.50.1–2 (beyond the section believed to have been taken from Hecataeus of Abdera; see Jacoby, *FGrH* 264), 1.81.6, 5.57.2–4; Griffiths refers also to Pease on Cic. *Div.* 1.2.

315. Again, the biographical schedule of panegyric; cf. 123C–D.

316. We translate as "happen" Synesius's ἀνθέω compounds. Other translators follow him more literally, but "blossom" seems to have no particular force in this context.

317. Synesius's own admission that the wishful thinking of his myth does not invariably correspond with the unwelcome facts of A.D. 400. He also avoids the philosophical difficulties that a rigorous doctrine of recurrence presents.

318. Hes. *Op.* 42. As with Philosophy's Homeric tag above (126A), Synesius takes his

VIII. Pythagoras of Samos says that the wise man is simply a spectator of things that are and things that come to be, for the wise man enters the cosmos[319] as though it were a holy contest,[320] in order to watch what happens. Hence let us reason out what sort of

128C spectator the man in this position should be. Do we need to state the obvious, that it is the man who waits in his place[321] for things to emerge from the curtain one by one in order? But if anyone should force his way onto the stage and brazenly look in[322] as though he had a right to inspect all the jumble of stage equipment through

128D the proscenium, the judges of the competition alert their guards against him. Even if he got away with it, he would understand nothing clearly, scarcely even making out the confused and indistinguishable images. Indeed, it is the custom of the theater for some things to be stated in a prologue:[323] someone must come forward and explain to the audience what they are about to see. This man causes no offense. He serves the producer and gets his information from him, not by prying or by disturbing things better left undisturbed.[324] Moreover, once he has learned his part he must keep silent before rushing to make it public. Custom does not always permit even the actors to know the time of their competi-

129A tion—instead they must wait for the signal for them to go on. So too let him with whom god shares life's stage equipment, which nature holds in reserve, keep silent out of respect for the honor— even more so, perhaps, than those who did not hear it. We guess at what we do not know, but the farther a guess is pushed, the more uncertain it becomes and the more controversy it generates. But

---

quotation and its interpretation (actually again a misinterpretation: Hesiod meant by βίος "livelihood") from a secondary source, now Plutarch (frag. 178, ed. F. H. Sandbach, Loeb vol. 15, p. 324).

319. παραγγείλαι: cf. *Calv.* 70C (p. 204.3–6T), ὁ δὲ ἄρτι παραγγείλας εἰς φαλα-κρούς, as the recipient of a divine summons to an equivalent of initiation.

320. Cf. 100B–101B, the "greatest contest" and the "second contest" of Osiris, of which the gods will be θεαταὶ ἄνωθεν, and (closer in sense) *Ep.* 101 (p. 171.5–7G), where Synesius says that an environment uncongenial to philosophy is his own ἀγώνισμα καὶ βάσανος.

321. As Osiris awaits the results of the royal election (95C; cf. 94B). The message here is that Aurelian must wait patiently for his restoration.

322. Literally, "as the saying goes, look dog-eyed into it." The verb κυνοφθαλμίζομαι is otherwise known only from *Com. adesp.* 1058 (a one-word fragment); whether Synesius has the term from comedy or not, it derives ultimately from the Iliadic κυνῶπις (3.180, 18.396), an expression for shamelessness.

323. See Viljamaa 1968, 68–92; Cameron 1970b, 119–29.

324. For the proverb see *Anth.Pal.* 9.685 and the other passages quoted in the Budé edition ad loc.

knowledge of truth is precise; precise too its telling.[325] This too will be concealed by the wise man, since it has been given to him on 129B trust by god. Men hate babblers. If god does not think a man worthy of initiation, he should not push himself forward, nor should he spy. Men hate busybodies; it makes no sense for a man who will soon receive a fair portion to become upset.[326] It is only a short time before men are allotted their deserts, and things end up being seen and heard by all:

> The remaining days
> are the wisest witnesses.[327]

325. Cf. Amm. Marc. 14.10.13, "veritatis enim absoluta semper ratio est simplex," on which Rolfe cites Cic. *Fin.* 5.14.38.

326. The Greek of these concluding sentences is extremely vague, but the Pindaric tag makes it plain that Synesius is thinking of the information he withholds, in justification of his failure to complete his story.

327. Pind. *Ol.* 1.33–34. As with his allusion to Horus at the end of book 1, Synesius urges his audience to await patiently Osiris/Aurelian's eventual vindication—demonstrating, against Liebeschuetz 1983, 40, that he wrote before Aurelian's return to office in 414.

AURELIAN AND PULCHERIA

Little attention seems to have been paid to the circumstances in which Pulcheria came to power. It was hardly inevitable that she should take charge so completely of the affairs of a brother only two years younger than herself. How did she first persuade his ministers to take her seriously? Modern accounts have advanced little, it seems, beyond the hagiography of Ada B. Teetgen: "it was felt that Pulcheria possessed not only the right of kinship to the emperor, but the qualifications of a well-trained mind and a balanced judgement to claim for her an office whose demand for loyalty she could best meet."[1] But who felt this, and when? Stein reports without comment that the regency "passa à sa soeur aînée Pulcheria."[2] Holum, too, after referring to her grandmother Flaccilla's fairly routine coronation as a "dramatic innovation," reports Pulcheria's without surprise or comment.[3]

That Pulcheria was the ablest and strongest of Arcadius's children goes without saying. But even so it was a major break with recent precedent for an emperor's sister to be proclaimed Augusta. The last case of an emperor's sister so honored was perhaps Ulpia Marciana, the elderly sister of Trajan.[4] Not only was

1. *The Life and Times of the Empress Pulcheria* (London 1907), 73; Teetgen referred to her subject throughout as "St. Pulcheria."

2. Stein 1959, 275.

3. Holum 1982, 31;96–97.

4. *PIR* III[1] U.584; cf. E. J. Bickerman, "Diva Augusta Marciana," *AJP* 95 (1974): 362f. Constantina, the elder sister of Constantius II and wife successively of Hannibalianus and the Caesar Gallus, is said to have been given the rank by her father Constantine (*PLRE* I.222), but numismatic corroboration is lacking: for doubts, Holum 1982, 31 n. 90. It would

Pulcheria not an imperial consort; not only was she not the mother of a future
emperor; she was only fifteen years old.

There is obviously some connection between the emergence of Pulcheria
and the end of Anthemius's long tenure of the praetorian prefecture (July 405–
April 414). According to Socrates, Anthemius "was considered and indeed was
the most prudent man of his time, who seldom did anything without consulta-
tion; he took the advice of many of his friends when decisions had to be taken."[5]
We may well believe that part of the reason Anthemius contrived to stay in
power so long was his ability to secure the cooperation of his peers as well as the
favor of the young emperor and his sister. But the moment he was gone, the
usual rivalry for the power behind the throne is bound to have broken out once
more. We have no Synesius to describe it for us this time, but evidence does
exist.

It has hitherto been assumed that Aurelian directly succeeded Anthemius.
In fact Anthemius is last attested in office on 18 April 414, and Aurelian not till
30 December. There is room for a brief tenure between them, and another prefect, Monaxius, is indeed attested in office on 10 May. On 30 November he appears as urban prefect. According to Seeck,[6] who assumed that either Anthemius or Aurelian was praetorian prefect on these two dates, Monaxius was
actually urban prefect. But we now know that he was wrong. Monaxius held
three prefectures.[7] Two can be identified with certainty: he was urban prefect in
408–9 and PPO in 416–20. And the third must have been another praetorian
prefecture, because there survives a dedication at Perinthus in which he describes himself as *prae(fectus) praet(orio) II.*[8] So it was the praetorian prefecture
he held in 414,[9] an unusually short tenure after the unusually long tenure of
Anthemius.

Anthemius had been out of office for more than two months by the time
Pulcheria was proclaimed Augusta. The regency was not an office that could be
straightforwardly transferred from, say, Anthemius to Pulcheria. There was no
such thing as a formal regency in Roman constitutional law.[10] Theodosius had
been crowned Augustus in 402, and in theory he was entitled to rule in his own
right from that moment. Arcadius may well have commended him to Anthemius
on his deathbed,[11] but this will have been a purely informal arrangement, not
linked to his office as prefect and not transferable. There will have been others

be curious for Constantius not to have corrected the anomaly if Constantina really possessed a rank denied to his own wife.

    5. *HE* 7.1.
    6. Seeck 1919, 114.41, followed by von Haehling 1978, 129.
    7. Callinicus, *Vita Hypatii* 21.11 (cf. p. 186 and n. 150).
    8. *CIL* III.14207[5].
    9. So *PLRE* II.765, though without explanation or comment.
    10. Mommsen, *Hermes* 38 (1903): 101f. (= *Ges. Schr.* 4:516f).
    11. As Theodosius I commended Arcadius and Honorius to Stilicho, according to
Stilicho: Cameron 1970a, 39f. Significantly enough, the Eastern court refused to acknowledge the validity of this alleged deathbed commission.

who influenced the young emperor in any case: the chamberlain Antiochus, for example.[12]

When Arcadius died, Theodosius was only seven, clearly in need of guidance. When Anthemius left office, he was thirteen; Anthemius's successor was not likely to be able to exercise the same influence. It was natural that the young emperor should turn increasingly to his now fifteen-year-old sister, evidently ambitious and experienced beyond her years. Such informal influence was traditional for imperial women; for example, Constantius II's wife Eusebia, reputed to exercise great power[13] but never honored with the title Augusta. Eudoxia had not been content with this role, and Pulcheria was determined to follow in her mother's footsteps. But she had to act quickly. In the ordinary way, she could expect to be married off before long.[14] Suitors at least she could discourage by taking a public vow of virginity,[15] but in order to give herself a permanent *locus standi* at court, she needed rank.

The status of Augusta was ill defined.[16] On a strict definition, Augustae were not members of the imperial college, since their names did not appear in the headings to imperial laws.[17] But their names and images appeared on the coinage, and (by ca. 400 at least) they were entitled to their own household, or rather bedchamber (*cubiculum*), with a staff and treasury of their own.[18] The mere fact that they could dispense sums beyond the reach of private citizens must have encouraged obedience.[19] But the revival of the title in the Theodosian

12. Holum's speculations about Antiochus are very uncertain, as also his conviction that we know exactly when Pulcheria displaced him (1982, 94). A glance at his entry in PLRE II.101–2 will show that there are other versions, all of them late.

13. *PLRE* I.300–301.

14. The legal minimum age for marriage remained fourteen for men and twelve for women.

15. It is not clear why Holum wants to date this vow as much as two years before her proclamation (Holum and Vikan 1979, 128; Holum 1982, 93–95), except to associate it with an alleged attempt by Anthemius to marry her to a kinsman. Nothing in Sozomen, *HE* 9.1 (the only source), warrants separating it from her proclamation, which he does not mention. This entire chapter of Sozomen is a timeless panegyric of Pulcheria's regency; in such a context, it may be doubted whether his remark that she was "not yet fifteen" when she made her vow even justifies dating it before her 15th birthday (19 January 414). The proclamation is dated to 4 July 414 (*Chron.Min.* II.71).

16. S. Maslev, "Die staatsrechtliche Stellung der byzantinischen Kaiserinnen," *Byzantinoslavica* 27 (1966): 308–43, hardly lives up to its title. Unsystematic and superficial, it lurches wildly from the first to the fourteenth century and back again, taking no account of changing historical contexts. More specifically, nothing is said of the importance and innovations of the early fifth century, and Augusta is treated as no more than a literary variation for *basilissa, despoina,* or *basilis.* For the period he covers, see T. D. Barnes, *The New Empire of Diocletian and Constantine* (Cambridge, Mass. 1982), 9.

17. Ulpian's statement that "princeps legibus solutus est: Augusta autem licet legibus soluta non est, principes eadem illi privilegia tribuunt, quae ipsi habent," was quoted by Justinian (*Dig.* I.3.31) and again (in Greek) in *Basilica* 2.6.1.

18. See *N.D., Or.* 17.8, with Jones, 1964a, 349–50. Texts of the early empire refer to the title as no more than a *cognomen:* Bickerman, *AJP* 95 (1974): 369.

19. The Augusta Helena, mother of Constantine, disposed of huge sums in largess as well as on her churches in the Holy Land: E. D. Hunt, *Holy Land Pilgrimage in the Later*

house after a half-century's abeyance also introduced something new. As we learn from Honorius's indignant letter of protest when Eudoxia was proclaimed, her images were circulated around all the provinces for *adoratio*. It was "unprecedented," he complained, "provoking disapproval throughout the world." [20] This was the practice followed when a new Augustus was proclaimed. [21] We may in fact doubt whether the innovation began with Eudoxia, since a number of inscribed bases from statues to Flaccilla Augusta have been found in the eastern provinces. [22] And we may surely assume that it was also followed for Pulcheria's proclamation. Theodosius's purpose in establishing the practice was presumably no more than glorification of the dynasty. [23] But the greater public prominence thereby accorded an Augusta could the more easily be parlayed into real power by the wife—or sister—of a weak emperor.

Anthemius's successor in the prefecture found a changing situation in the palace. The brevity of Monaxius's tenure suggests that he did not succeed in reconciling all interests. It may be that he underestimated Pulcheria. At all events, when Aurelian succeeded him in December, his first recorded act as prefect was to dedicate golden busts of Pulcheria, Honorius, and Theodosius in the Senate house. [24] The local chronicle of Constantinople that is partially preserved for us in the sixth- and seventh-century versions of Marcellinus and the *Paschal Chronicle* recorded only a very limited selection of items: [25] military victories, natural phenomena (earthquakes, fires, and the like), and major events concerning the imperial house (births, deaths, and coronations). To merit inclusion, Aurelian's gold busts in 414 must have been perceived as falling in this category.

Here was a man anxious to win the favor of the new rising star in the imperial firmament. Whether or not the Senate had played a part in the original proclamation, it was essential that Pulcheria's ambition should be taken seriously by the governing class. For in the last analysis no empress wielded more actual power than either the emperor or his appointed officials allowed. Without the cooperation of men like Aurelian, Pulcheria would not be able to act in her own right rather than through her brother in the traditional way.

We have already seen that Aurelian almost certainly played a role in the pre-

Roman Empire (Oxford 1982), 37f. But when Eusebius describes how she recalled exiles and released prisoners (*Vita Constantini* 3.44), we may doubt whether such actions were based on any specific powers. Who would dare refuse the Augusta?

20. *Epistulae imperatorum pontificum aliorum . . . Collectio Avellana, CSEL* 35, ed. O. Guenther (Vienna 1895), no. 38.1.

21. H. Kruse, *Studien zur offiziellen Geltung des Kaiserbildes im römischen Reiche* (Paderborn 1934), 23–32; S. G. MacCormack, *Art and Ceremony in Late Antiquity* (Berkeley 1981), 67–70.

22. Holum 1982, 34–35.

23. Certainly not to encourage the "imperial dominion of women," as alleged by Holum (1982, 3), though he may well have intended that imperial women should play a more prominent role in the religious life of the capital, a role Holum's book well illustrates.

24. *Chron. Pasch.* p. 571.17f. (= *Chron. Min.* II.71).

25. On which see the brief characterization and bibliography by Cameron in *CLRE* 53–57.

mature proclamation of Eudoxia on 9 January 400.[26] At all events, we can hardly doubt that it was with her aid that he won the prefecture in 399, and it was certainly with Pulcheria's support that he returned to the prefecture in 414. That makes two occasions on which Aurelian won himself a prefecture by courting an empress. We may also recall that it was by courting the infamous Rufinus that he won his urban prefecture. Here was a consummate schemer, a man who knew exactly how to charm the most varied patrons.

It has been assumed that the initiative in the aggressive new religious policy so apparent in the legislation of 415 was Pulcheria's. We might perhaps now wonder whether the sexagenarian who had been persecuting heretics since before her birth was really doing no more than carrying out the orders of his sixteen-year-old sovereign. With his own attempt to import the relics of Stephen now dated to the same period, Aurelian stands forth as just the sort of contemporary Christian we might expect the new Augusta to choose as her first minister.

26. Pp. 170–73 above.

· APPENDIX II ·

CHRYSOSTOM'S MOVEMENTS
IN 400–402

Two points stated summarily above presuppose a chronology for Chrysostom's movements in 400–402 that has yet to be established.

First, according to C. Baur and, more recently, Père M. Aubineau and W. Liebeschuetz,[1] it was in the first quarter of 401 that Chrysostom paid his protracted visit to Ephesus to settle the simony suit between Eusebius of Valentinopolis and Antoninus of Ephesus,[2] at a time when, on our chronology, he was completing his homilies on Acts at Constantinople. The sermon he delivered on his return home begins with a tantalizingly imprecise allusion to the duration of his absence. Historians have hitherto relied on the Latin translation in *PG* 52.421, apparently unaware that in 1961 A. Wenger published the original Greek text from a MS in Moscow.[3] Unfortunately, the Greek contains the same ambiguity as the Latin:

> After leaving his people for 40 days, Moses found them making idols and stirring up sedition. I, however, having been away, not 40 days but 50 and 100 and more (ἀλλὰ καὶ πεντήκοντα καὶ ἑκατὸν καὶ πλείους =

1. Baur 1960, 145, 155 n. 13; Aubineau 1983, 13; Liebeschuetz, *Nottingham Medieval Studies* 29 (1985): 5.

2. The whole sordid business is described at length by Palladius, *Dialogus de vita S.Iohannis Chrysostomi* 47–53, pp. 84–93 Coleman-Norton; briefly, above, pp. 169–70.

3. "L'homélie de saint Jean Chrysostome à son retour d'Asie," *REB* 19 (1961): 110–23, in addition republishing the (perhaps fifth-century) Latin version from an earlier and better MS.

sed et quinquaginta et centum et amplius), have found you rejoicing and philosophizing and persevering in the fear of God.

Is he saying that he has been away for 150 days?[4] Or is he just counting upwards from his biblical exemplum: "40, 50, 100, even more"?[5] If he means 150, that would make more than 5 months. Even 100 days would add up to well over 3, and if we add in the "more," perhaps nearer 4. He goes on to regret not celebrating Easter at Constantinople, implying that he did not miss it by much. In 401 Easter fell on 14 April. Five months back from mid-April 401 takes us to mid-November 400.

But is it likely that Chrysostom would have set out on such a long journey with the war against Gaïnas undecided? His services had been called upon more than once already as an intermediary Gaïnas apparently trusted, and might be again at any time. It was the threat from Gaïnas that had led him to put off going in April, and the danger had by no means passed.

Indeed, is there even enough time to squash all the events Palladius describes between April and November 400? To enumerate: his own wait of nearly 2 months at Hypaipa,[6] after leaving Constantinople no earlier than April; followed by 40 days in the summer heat; followed by another 30 days (a good 5 months if we add in travel to and from Constantinople); the report of Antoninus's death at Constantinople; and an unspecified period of delay and debate before Chrysostom finally decided to go himself. There is barely enough time (assuming 100 days) to squeeze them between April 400 and January 401, quite apart from the improbability of a departure by sea that late in the year.

More important, Palladius twice emphatically states that the suit lasted 2 years (pp. 89.23, 91.3), and the first passage clearly refers to the opening of the synod of Ephesus when Chrysostom was present. Since Palladius dates the beginning of the suit to the thirteenth indiction (September 399–September 400), just before Gaïnas's coup, that places it in April 400. If Chrysostom was back in Constantinople by the end of April 401, that would make barely 1 year. It must be Easter 402 (6 April) that he just missed on his return, which would place his departure, 100+ days earlier, in December 401.[7] That would be late enough to

---

4. So Seeck 1913, 577 n. 18 ("mehr als 150 Tage").

5. So Père Aubineau: "J'avais d'abord pensé que Jean opposait 40 jours et 'plus de 150,' mais la progression de la seconde partie, marquée par les trois 'et,' indique les étapes (50 et 100) pour arriver à une centaine bien arrondie" (1983, 13 n. 15).

6. G. Albert, *Historia* 29 (1980): 507.

7. This would also explain why Palladius was already waiting at Apamea to meet Chrysostom (p. 89.5). On the Baur/Liebeschuetz chronology he would not have had time to do anything but leave Constantinople together with Chrysostom. So already Coleman-Norton: "Palladius probably spent the winter at Helenopolis" (p. xvii), though he must be mistaken to date their rendezvous "early in 401." That would have taken Chrysostom back to Constantinople in plenty of time for Easter 402—but caused him to miss Easter 401. On the other hand Seeck (1913, 577), with "Ende 401 oder Anfang 402," puts his departure a little too late. The sermon quoted above implies that he just missed Easter.

suit Palladius's reference to winter (p. 88.24), well outside the limits of what was considered the safe sailing season.[8]

So in all probability Chrysostom did not leave Constantinople till December 401.[9] It follows that he could after all have delivered his homilies on Acts in unbroken sequence from late summer/early autumn 400 into the early months of 401.

Second, the quarrel with Severian of Gabala. According to Socrates and Sozomen, it was while Chrysostom was away in Asia that Severian began to cause trouble in the Constantinopolitan church. Chrysostom was jealous of stories that reached him during his absence of Severian's intrigues and oratorical successes, and their relationship rapidly deteriorated on his return. It was Severian's quarrel with Chrysostom's trusted deacon Sarapion that led to their final breach. Chrysostom ordered Severian to leave Constantinople and return to the obscure see he had abandoned for so long. Severian left but went no farther than Chalcedon, counting on Eudoxia's intervention. She at once used all her wiles on Chrysostom and secured the restoration of her favorite. Chrysostom delivered a sermon extant only in Latin, *De recipiendo Severiano* (*PG* 52.423–26), and Severian replied with the extant sermon *De pace* quoted in chapter 5.[10]

According to Père Aubineau, for whom Chrysostom returned from Asia in April 401, it was "dès l'été ou au début de l'automne 401" that Chrysostom sent Severian packing. On this chronology, the two sermons will have fallen in autumn 401. But on the alternative chronology here suggested, they would have to be dated to autumn 402 instead.

Nothing in the accounts of Socrates and Sozomen opposes the later date. Socrates, whose chronology can usually be pinned down by the fact that he "gives consular dates for virtually every year of his narrative,"[11] becomes very vague during this period. His account of Gaïnas's rebellion in *HE* 6.6 dates the war by the consuls of 400 and then refers to Fravitta's consulate of 401, correctly dating the birth of the future Theodosius II to 10 April of that year. But he then omits the consuls of both 402 and 403, giving no firm date till the consuls of 404 in 6.18. The story of Chrysostom and Severian is told in 6.11. Both preceding and following chapters concern the intrigues of Theophilus of Alexandria, but nothing that can be pinned down to a particular year.

8. The regular sailing season ran from 27 May to 14 September, but the outside limits were 10 March to 10 November: L. Casson, *Ships and Seamanship in the Ancient World* (Princeton 1971), 270. Having spent all his life in two of the greatest commercial cities of the empire, Chrysostom was well aware of the dangers of winter sailing. In fact, Rougé (1952, 319–20) cites a series of texts from Chrysostom on the subject. But he misses Palladius, p. 88.24, cited above, n. 2.

9. Baur attempts to support his chronology by referring to Palladius's statement that the bishops Chrysostom had deposed at Ephesus "four years before" were reinstated after his exile in 404 (p. 91.9), but we have no reason to believe that they were reinstated immediately after his exile.

10. See pp. 181–82, 248.

11. Cameron, *CLRE* 89.

In fact, either 401 or 402 would fit Socrates' account. Since there appears to be no other evidence that bears directly on the issue, the argument from Chrysostom's movements must be held decisive. Severian's *De pace* was delivered in autumn 402.

We have seen that in this sermon Severian alludes to a representation of the brother emperors embraced by an allegorical figure of Concord (p. 17 Papadopulos-Kerameus). Of course, this is a traditional motif, but it had presumably been conspicuous by its absence during the successive administrations of Rufinus, Eutropius, and Aurelian, a period of virtual cold war between East and West. Severian did not come to Constantinople till ca. 398/99.[12] The numerous poems Claudian wrote during these years all stress concord as an ideal that was constantly frustrated. For example, by Rufinus: "geminas inter discordia partes/hoc auctore fuit" (*In Eutr.* 2.540–41); by Eutropius: "geminam quid dividis aulam/conarisque pios odiis committere fratres" (ibid. 1.281–82); and by Gildo: "in fratres medio discordia Mauro/nascitur" (*Bell. Gild.* 236–37). Severian too claims that Concord shines forth as Discord flees: ἐπέλαμψεν ἡ ὁμόνοια καὶ ἔφυγεν ἡ διαφωνία.[13] This flight of Discord was surely not shown in the picture or relief Severian describes. It is a detail he supplied from his own experience of the political background in Constantinople. The renewed propagation of the motif of brotherly concord between East and West can be dated to the joint consulate of Arcadius and Honorius in 402, represented in precisely those terms on the sculptures of the base of Arcadius. It was the new policy of Caesarius. This passage of Severian surely points to 402 rather than 401.

12. Aubineau 1983, 12.

13. The only MS gives the last word as διγόνια, which (though not marked as such by Papadopulos-Kerameus) is meaningless and must be corrupt. The early Latin version ascribed to Peter Chrysologus (*PL* 52.598–99; *PG* 52.425–28) gives what is obviously the general sense required: "fugiat discordia, resplendescente concordia." It looks as if the scribe carelessly repeated the last two syllables of ὁμόνοια. Since Severian elsewhere uses συμφωνία of the concord of the brother emperors (above, pp. 181–82, 248), the obvious correction is διαφωνία. The period placed by Papadopulos-Kerameus after the καὶ should also be omitted.

SYNESIUS'S VISIT TO ATHENS

In one of the best known of his letters (*Ep.* 136), Synesius wrote to his brother from Athens, lamenting its sad decline:

> May the accursed ship captain who brought me here perish! Athens no longer has anything sublime except the country's famous names. Just as in the case of a victim burnt in the sacrificial fire, there remains nothing but the skin to help us to reconstruct a creature that was once alive, so ever since philosophy left these precincts, there is nothing for the tourist to admire except the Academy, the Lyceum, and, by Zeus, the Painted Stoa that has given its name to the philosophy of Chrysippus— though it is not painted any more. The proconsul has taken away the panels into which Polygnotus of Thasos poured his skill. Today Egypt has received and cherishes the fruitful wisdom of Hypatia. Athens was formerly the home of wise men: today the beekeepers alone bring it honor. Such is the case with that pair of Plutarchean *sophists* who draw the young to their lecture room, not by the fame of their eloquence, but by pots of honey from Hymettus.

It is usually assumed that Synesius visited Athens sometime between 395 and 400. The detailed recent study of Roques argues for August 399, on the way to the embassy in Constantinople.[1] If so, then (as Alison Frantz has put it) "he must have seen Athens at its lowest ebb since the Herulian invasions [267]." For in 396, like much of the rest of Greece, Athens was overrun by Alaric and his marauding Goths. Archaeology has confirmed that he penetrated "at least as far

---

1. Roques 1989, 87–103—in fact, with his usual preposterous precision, "vers le 18 août" (102).

as the Agora, where he destroyed a number of buildings."[2] If Synesius had arrived in Athens soon after this disaster, we might have expected him to mention it, even though it is the intellectual rather than the material decline of Athens that his letter is concerned with.[3] In fact there are good reasons for preferring a much later date.

The key is provided by the letter he sent his brother before leaving Cyrene, complaining about some terrifying prospect (described as an "apocalypse") held before him by his fellow citizens, "priests and laymen alike" (*Ep.* 54 = 56G) This letter is usually and doubtless correctly linked to another (*Ep.* 94 = 95G), in which Synesius writes of leaving his property at a time of barbarian invasions in difficult personal circumstances. It also mentions divisive public debate about an embassy to Constantinople. This embassy has hitherto been assumed to be the well-known one that took Synesius on his three-year exile, and it was on this basis that Roques dated the Athenian trip to 399 (397 on our chronology), en route to Constantinople. But Liebeschuetz has recently proposed an entirely different and more persuasive interpretation of *Ep.* 94: the trouble Synesius was fleeing is the prospect of being consecrated bishop, and it is another, later embassy.[4] This would give us 410, a date supported by the reference to barbarians occupying his house. This would explain why the terrifying prospect to which he alludes in *Ep.* 54 was being put to him by laymen as well as priests. In the context, it is the mention of laymen that is more emphatic. Clearly something involving the Church, something so alarming that Synesius left town to avoid facing up to it. What can this have been in 397? How can it be reconciled with his embassy of that year? Embassies were regular events, called forth at least once every five years to present the emperor with his quinquennial crown gold.[5] We should expect a prominent curial like Synesius to mention more than one embassy in a correspondence that covers some fifteen years. The only weakness in Liebeschuetz's case is that he was unable to pin down the occasion of this second embassy, noting only that it would have been rather late for the "accession" of Theodosius II in 408. But that would not have been commemorated in this way.[6]

2. Alison Frantz, *The Athenian Agora XXIV: Late Antiquity: A.D. 267–700* (Princeton 1988), 51–56. According to Zosimus (5.6.1–2), Athena and Achilles appeared on the ramparts, and Alaric abandoned his siege, sent heralds, was entertained in the city, and departed "bearing gifts." We can hardly doubt that he used the extortion tactics he later used while besieging Rome, threatening to sack the entire city if not paid off. Zosimus swallowed the face-saving Athenian version of his departure—the more willingly because it seemed to demonstrate the power of the old gods.

3. The references to tourist sites are not the responses to autopsy they might seem. Synesius had already described how the proconsul stole the panels from the Painted Stoa in a letter to his brother shortly before leaving Cyrene (*Ep.* 54 = 56 G); evidently it was a story he had heard at home. And though he implies that he has visited the Academy and Lyceum, there were no buildings left on the sites; in Synesius's day, Plato's successors taught in private houses (the house of Plutarch and Proclus can perhaps be identified: Frantz 1988, 42–44).

4. Liebeschuetz 1985b, 146–54.

5. See chapter 3, section III.

6. See p. 92 for the modern fallacy of counting imperial anniversaries from "accession" rather than *dies imperii*.

The occasion was undoubtedly Theodosius's *decennalia* in 411.[7] The final link in the chain is *Ep*. 96 to Olympius (quoted above, p. 23), one of a group of letters in which Synesius confides to friends his doubts about becoming bishop: if he is not able to reconcile his episcopal duties with his convictions and way of life, he will "make straight for glorious Greece." Hitherto it has been assumed that by Greece Synesius here meant the Hellas of the spirit rather than the Roman province of Achaea. But perhaps it was after all in Achaea that he spent those six months of soul-searching away from home before he accepted the bishopric.[8] Perhaps he really meant that he would live in Greece if things did not work out.

On this reconstruction, it will have been in 410 that Synesius sailed to Athens, not as a student but as bishop-elect. The "pair of Plutarcheans" must be Plutarch son of Nestorius (d.431/34), the Athenian who reestablished Athens as the center of philosophical study in the early decades of the fifth century,[9] and his disciple and successor Syrianus; in which case it might be added that 410 squares much better with the career of Syrianus than 394 or 399.[10]

7. Marcellinus, s.a., with R. Burgess, *Num. Chron.* 148 (1988): 86.

8. Liebeschuetz 1985b, 149–50; it tells us something of the complexity of the man that he went to Athens to consider becoming a bishop.

9. *PLRE* I.708; see too Saffrey and Westerink 1968, xxvif.

10. *PLRE* II.1051.

BIBLIOGRAPHY

References in the notes are normally given in the form: Albert 1980, 504; Liebeschuetz 1986a, 190.

Albert, Gerhard. 1979. Stilicho und der Hunnenfeldzug des Eutropius. *Chiron* 9:621–45.

———. 1980. Zur Chronologie der Empörung des Gaïnas im Jahre 400 N.Chr. *Historia* 29:504–8.

———. 1984. *Goten in Konstantinopel*. Studien zur Geschichte und Kultur des Altertums, n.s. 1, vol. 2. Paderborn.

Alföldi, A. 1937. *A Festival of Isis in Rome under the Christian Emperors of the IVth Century*. Budapest.

Allen, Pauline. 1981. *Evagrius Scholasticus the Church Historian*. Louvain.

Amand, D. 1945. *Fatalisme et liberté dans l'antiquité grecque*. Louvain.

Anastos, M. V. 1948. Pletho's Calendar and Liturgy. *Dumbarton Oaks Papers* 4:183–305.

Asmus, R. 1895. *Julian und Dion Chrysostomos*. Tauberbischofsheim.

———. 1900. Synesius und Dio Chrysostomus. *Byzantinische Zeitschrift* 9: 85–151.

———. 1907. Hypatia in Tradition und Dichtung. *Studien zur Vergleichenden Literaturgeschichte* 7:11–44.

———. 1911. *Das Leben des Philosophen Isidoros von Damaskios aus Damaskos*. Leipzig.

Aubineau, M. 1983. *Un traité inédit de Christologie de Sévérien de Gabala: In centurionem et contra Manichaeos et Apollinaristas*. Cahiers d'orientalisme 5. Geneva.

Aujoulat, Noël. 1986. *Le Néoplatonisme alexandrin: Hieroclès d'Alexandrie.* Philosophia antiqua 45. Leiden.

Bagnall, Roger S., Alan Cameron, Seth R. Schwartz, and Klaas A. Worp. 1987. *Consuls of the Later Roman Empire.* Atlanta (cited as *CLRE*).

Baldwin, Barry. 1976. 'Perses': A Mysterious Prefect in Eunapius. *Byzantion* 46:5–8.

Banchich, Thomas M. 1984. The Date of Eunapius' *Vitae Sophistarum. Greek, Roman and Byzantine Studies* 25:183–92.

Barnes, T. D. 1975a. Constans and Gratian in Rome. *Harvard Studies in Classical Philology* 79:325–33.

――――. 1975b. *Patricii* under Valentinian III. *Phoenix* 29:155–70.

――――. 1975c. The Embassy of Athenagoras. *Journal of Theological Studies* 26:111–14.

――――. 1978. Claudian and the *Notitia Dignitatum. Phoenix* 32:81–82.

――――. 1982. *The New Empire of Diocletian and Constantine.* Cambridge, Mass.

――――. 1983. Late Roman Prosopography: Between Theodosius and Justinian. *Phoenix* 37:248–70.

――――. 1985. Proconsuls of Africa, 337–392. *Phoenix* 39:144–53.

――――. 1986a. Synesius in Constantinople. *Greek, Roman and Byzantine Studies* 27:93–112.

――――. 1986b. When Did Synesius Become Bishop of Ptolemais? *Greek, Roman and Byzantine Studies* 27:325–29.

――――. 1989. Christians and Pagans in the Reign of Constantius. In *L'église et l'empire au IVᵉ siècle,* edited by Albrecht Dihle, 301–43. Entretiens sur l'antiquité—Fondation Hardt 34.

Barr, William. 1979. Claudian's *in Rufinum:* An Invective? *Papers of the Liverpool Latin Seminar* 2:179–90.

Bauer, A., and J. Strzygowski. 1905. *Eine Alexandrinische Weltchronik.* Denkschrift der k. Akad. der Wissenschaft in Wien, Phil.-hist. Kl. 51.2.

Baur, Chrysostomus. Vol. 1, 1959; vol. 2, 1960. *John Chrysostom and His Time.* Translated by M. Gonzaga. 2 vols. Westminster, Md.

Bayless, William N. 1976a. The Visigothic Invasion of Italy in 401. *Classical Journal* 72:65–67.

――――. 1976b. Anti-Germanism in the Age of Stilicho. *Byzantine Studies/Etudes byzantines* 3.2:70–76.

――――. 1977. Synesius of Cyrene: A Study of the Role of the Bishop in Temporal Affairs. *Byzantine Studies/Etudes byzantines* 4.2:147–56.

Becatti, G. 1960. *La colonna coclide istoriata: Problemi storici, iconographici, stilistici.* Rome.

Beck, H. G. 1966. *Senat und Volk von Konstantinopel.* Sitzungsberichte München.

Berthelot, M., and C.-E. Ruelle. 1888. *Collection des anciens alchimistes grecs.* Vol. 2. Paris.

Bettini, G. 1938. *L'attività pubblica di Sinesio.* Udine.

Bickerman, E. J. 1974. Diva Augusta Marciana. *American Journal of Philology* 95:362–76.

Bidez, J., and F. Cumont, eds. 1938. *Les mages hellénisés: Zoroastre, Ostanès et Hystaspe d'après la tradition grecque.* Paris.

Bingham, Joseph. [1708–22] 1875. *The Antiquities of the Christian Church.* 10 vols. London. (Reprint 2 vols. London.)

Blockley, R. C. 1980. The Ending of Eunapius' History. *Antichthon* 14:170–76.

———. Vol. 1, 1981; Vol. 2, 1983. *The Fragmentary Classicising Historians of the Later Roman Empire: Eunapius, Olympiodorus, Priscus and Malchus.* 2 vols. Liverpool.

———. 1984. On the Ordering of the Fragments of Malchus' History. *Liverpool Classical Monthly* 9:152–53.

Boll, F., C. Bezold, and W. Gundel. 1931. *Sternglaube und Sterndeutung.* 4th ed. Leipzig.

Bonner, Campbell. 1942. A Tarsian Peculiarity. *Harvard Theological Review* 35:1–11.

Bonsdorff, Max von. 1922. *Zur Predigttätigkeit des Johannes Chrysostomus.* Helsinki.

Born, L. K. 1934. The Perfect Prince according to the Latin Panegyrists. *American Journal of Philology* 55:20–35.

———. 1936. *The Education of a Christian Prince.* New York.

Bouché-Leclercq, A. 1879. *Histoire de la divination dans l'antiquité.* Vol. 1. Paris.

———. 1899. *L'astrologie grecque.* Paris.

Bowersock, G. W. 1969. *Greek Sophists in the Roman Empire.* Oxford.

———. 1986. Tylos and Tyre: Bahrain in the Graeco-Roman World. In *Bahrain through the Ages: The Archaeology,* edited by Shaikha Haya Ali Al Khalifa and M. Rice, 399–406. London.

———. 1990. *Hellenism in Late Antiquity.* Ann Arbor.

Boyce, A. A. 1965. *Festal and Dated Coins of the Roman Empire: Four Notes.* American Numismatic Society Numismatic Notes and Monographs 153. New York.

Boylan, P. 1922. *Thoth: The Hermes of Egypt.* London.

Bregman, Jay. 1974. Synesius of Cyrene: Early Life and Conversion to Philosophy. *California Studies in Classical Antiquity* 7:55–88.

———. 1982. *Synesius of Cyrene: Philosopher-Bishop.* Berkeley.

Brilliant, Richard. 1984. *Visual Narratives.* Ithaca, N.Y.

Brisson, L., M.-O. Goulet-Cazé, R. Goulet, and D. O'Brien. 1982. *Porphyre: La vie de Plotin.* Vol. 1. Paris.

Brown, Peter. 1988. *The Body and Society.* New York.

Bruns, G. 1935. *Der Obelisk und seine Basis auf dem Hippodrom zu Konstantinopel.* Istanbuler Forschungen 7.

Brunt, P. A. 1966. The Roman Mob. *Past and Present* 35:3–27.

———. 1980. On Historical Fragments and Epitomes. *Classical Quarterly* 30:477–94.

———. 1990. *Roman Imperial Themes.* Oxford.

Bulmer-Thomas, Ivor. 1971. Eutocius of Ascalon. *Dictionary of Scientific Biography* 4:488–91.

Burgess, Richard. 1988. Quinquennial Vota and Imperial Consulship, 337–511. *Numismatic Chronicle* 148:77–96.

Burton, A. 1972. *Diodorus Siculus Book I.* Etudes préliminaires aux religions orientales 39. Leiden.

Bury, J. B. 1889. *A History of the Later Roman Empire from Arcadius to Irene.* London.

———. [1923] 1958. *History of the Later Roman Empire from the Death of Theodosius I to the Death of Justinian.* 2 vols. Reprint. New York.

Cameron, Alan. 1965a. Palladas and Christian Polemic. *Journal of Roman Studies* 55:17–30 (= Cameron 1985b, chap. 4).

———. 1965b. Wandering Poets: A Literary Movement in Byzantine Egypt. *Historia* 14:470–509.

———. 1968a. Theodosius the Great and the Regency of Stilicho. *Harvard Studies in Classical Philology* 73:247–80.

———. 1968b. Notes on Claudian's Invectives. *Classical Quarterly* 18:387–411.

———. 1969. The Last Days of the Academy at Athens. *Proceedings of the Cambridge Philological Society,* n.s. 15:7–29 (= Cameron 1985b, chap. 13).

———. 1970a. *Claudian: Poetry and Propaganda at the Court of Honorius.* Oxford.

———. 1970b. *Pap.Ant.* iii.115 and the Iambic Prologue in Late Greek Poetry. *Classical Quarterly* 20:119–29.

———. 1973. *Porphyrius the Charioteer.* Oxford.

———. 1976a. *Circus Factions: Blues and Greens at Rome and Byzantium.* Oxford.

———. 1976b. The Authenticity of the Letters of St. Nilus of Ancyra. *Greek, Roman and Byzantine Studies* 17:181–96.

———. 1976c. Theodorus *triseparchos. Greek, Roman and Byzantine Studies* 17:269–86.

———. 1977. Some Prefects Called Julian. *Byzantion* 47:42–64.

———. 1978. The House of Anastasius. *Greek, Roman and Byzantine Studies* 19:259–76.

———. 1979. The Date of the Anonymous *de Rebus Bellicis.* In *Aspects of the De Rebus Bellicis: Papers Presented to Prof. E. A. Thompson,* edited by M. W. C. Hassall and R. I. Ireland, 1–10. British Archaeological Reports: International Series 63 (= Cameron 1985b, chap. 9).

———. 1982. The Empress and the Poet: Paganism and Politics at the Court of Theodosius II. *Yale Classical Studies* 27:217–89.

———. 1985a. Polyonomy in the Roman Aristocracy: The Case of Petronius Probus. *Journal of Roman Studies* 75:164–82.

———. 1985b. *Literature and Society in the Early Byzantine World.* London.

———. 1987. Earthquake 400. *Chiron* 17:332–50.

———. 1988a. A Misidentified Homily of Chrysostom. *Nottingham Medieval Studies* 32:34–48.

———. 1988b. Flavius: A Nicety of Protocol. *Latomus* 47:26–33.

————. 1990. Isidore of Miletus and Hypatia: On the Editing of Mathematical Texts. *Greek, Roman and Byzantine Studies* 31:103–27.

————. 1992. Review of Roques 1987 and 1989. *Journal of Roman Archaeology* 5: 419–30.

————. Forthcoming. *Constantinople: Birth of a New Rome.*

Cameron, Alan, Jacqueline Long, and Lee Sherry. 1988. Textual Notes on Synesius' *de Providentia. Byzantion* 58:54–64.

Cameron, Averil. 1975. The Empress Sophia. *Byzantion* 45:5–21.

————. 1976. *Fl. Cresconius Corippus: In laudem Iustini Augusti minoris libri IV.* London.

————. 1985. *Procopius and the Sixth Century.* Berkeley.

Capelle, W. 1924. Erdbebenforschung. *Realencyclopädie der classischen Altertumswissenschaft,* Suppl. 4:344–74.

Carile, A. 1981. Giovanni di Nikius, cronista bizantino-copto del vii secolo. *Felix Ravenna* 4, ser. 1:103–55.

Carson, R. A. G. 1981. *Principal Coins of the Romans.* London.

Casel, O. 1919. *De philosophorum Graecorum silentio mystico.* Giessen.

Casson, Lionel. 1952. Bishop Synesius' Voyage to Cyrene. *American Neptune* 12:294–96.

————. 1971. *Ships and Seamanship in the Ancient World.* Princeton.

————. 1989. *The Periplus Maris Erythraei.* Princeton.

Charlesworth, J. H. 1983. *Old Testament Pseudepigrapha.* Vol. 1. New York.

Chastagnol, André. 1960. *La préfecture urbaine à Rome sous le Bas-Empire.* Paris.

————. 1962. *Les Fastes de la Préfecture de Rome au Bas-Empire.* Etudes prosopographiques. Vol. 2. Paris.

————. 1968. Les préfets du prétoire de Constantin. *Revue des études anciennes* 70:321–52.

————. 1987. *L'Africa romana: Atti del III convegno di studio, Sassari, 13–15 dicembre 1985,* edited by A. Mastino, 263–73. Sassari.

Chestnut, G. 1977. *The First Christian Histories.* Paris.

Chitty, Susan. 1975. *The Beast and the Monk: A Life of Charles Kingsley.* New York.

Chuvin, Pierre. 1990. *A Chronicle of the Last Pagans.* Translated by B. A. Archer. Cambridge, Mass.

Clark, Elizabeth A. 1979. *Jerome, Chrysostom and Friends.* Studies in Women and Religion 2. New York and Toronto.

————. 1982. Claims on the Bones of Saint Stephen: The Partisans of Melania and Eudocia. *Church History* 51:141–56.

————. 1986. *Ascetic Piety and Women's Faith.* Lewiston.

Clausen, E. T. 1831. *De Synesio philosopho Libyae Pentapoleos metropolita.* Copenhagen.

Clauss, M. 1980. *Der magister officiorum in der Spätantike.* Munich.

Clover, F. M. 1979. Count Gaïnas and Count Sebastian. *American Journal of Ancient History* 4:65–76.

Collins, J. J. 1974. *The Sibylline Oracles of Egyptian Judaism.* Missoula, Mont.

Coster, C. H. 1940–41. Synesius, a *curialis* of the Time of the Emperor Arcadius. *Byzantion* 15:10–38 (= Coster 1968, 145–82).

———. 1960. Christianity and the Invasions: Synesius of Cyrene. *Classical Journal* 55:290–312 (= Coster 1968, 218–68).

———. 1968. *Late Roman Studies.* Cambridge, Mass.

Courcelle, P. 1963. L'admonition par jeu d'enfants dans l'antiquité paienne. In *Les Confessions de Saint Augustin dans la tradition littéraire,* 137–41. Paris.

Cracco Ruggini, Lellia. 1972. *Simboli di battaglia ideologica nel tardo ellenismo.* Pisa.

Crawford, W. S. 1901. *Synesius the Hellene.* London.

Croke, Brian. 1981. Two Early Byzantine Earthquakes and Their Liturgical Commemoration. *Byzantion* 51:122–47.

———. 1983. The Context and Date of Priscus Fragment 6. *Classical Philology* 78:297–308.

Cumont, F. 1929. *Les religions orientales.* 4th ed.

Curtius, E. R. 1953. *European Literature and the Latin Middle Ages.* Translated by W. Trask. Bollingen Series 36. New York.

Dagron, G. 1968. *L'empire romain d'orient au IVᵉ siècle et les traditions politiques de l'hellénisme: Le témoignage de Thémistios.* Travaux et mémoires 3. Paris.

———. 1969. Aux origines de la civilisation byzantine: Langue de culture et langue d'état. *Revue historique* 241:23–56.

———. 1970. Les moines et la ville: Le monachisme à Constantinople jusqu'au concile de Chalcédoine (451). *Travaux et mémoires* 4:229–76.

———. 1974. *Naissance d'une capitale: Constantinople et ses institutions de 330 à 451.* Paris.

———. 1981. Quand la terre tremble. . . . *Travaux et mémoires* 8:87–103.

Datema, C. 1970. *Asterius of Amasea: Homilies I–XIV.* Leiden.

De Aldama, J. A. 1965. *Repertorium pseudochrysostomianum.* Paris.

de Blois, Lukas. 1986. The *Eis Basilea* of Ps.-Aelius Aristeides. *Greek, Roman and Byzantine Studies* 27:279–88.

Delehaye, H. 1933. *Les origines du culte des martyrs.* 2d ed. Brussels.

Delmaire, Roland. 1989. *Les reponsables des finances impériales au Bas-Empire romain (IVᵉ–VIᵉ siècles).* Collection Latomus 203. Brussels.

Demandt, A. 1970. Magister Militum. *Realencyclopädie der classischen Altertumswissenschaft,* Suppl. 12:553–790.

Demougeot, Emilienne. 1950. Le préfet Rufin et les barbares. In *Mélanges Grégoire* 2: 185f. Brussels.

———. 1951. *De l'unité à la division de l'empire romain, 395–410: Essai sur le gouvernement impérial.* Paris.

———. 1974. Modalités d'établissement des fédérés barbares de Gratien et de Théodose. In *Mélanges d'histoire ancienne offerts à William Seston,* 143–60. Paris.

———. 1979. *La formation de l'Europe et les invasions barbares.* Vol. 2.1. Paris.

Denniston, J. D. 1954. *The Greek Particles.* 2d ed. Oxford.

de Ste. Croix, G. E. M. 1981. *The Class Struggle in the Ancient Greek World.* Ithaca, N.Y.

Des Places, E. 1969. *La religion grecque*. Paris.

———. 1971. *Oracles Chaldaïques*. Paris.

Dillon, John. 1977. *The Middle Platonists*. London.

———. 1988. Iamblichus of Chalcis. *Aufstieg und Niedergang der römischen Welt* II.36.2:862–909.

Dineen, L. 1929. *Titles of Address in Christian Greek Epistolography to 527 A.D.* Washington, D.C.

Dodds. E. R. 1951. *The Greeks and the Irrational*. Berkeley.

Dölger, F. J. 1911. *Sphragis, eine altchristliche Taufbezeichnung in ihren Beziehung zur profanen und religiösen Kultur des Altertums*. Paderborn.

———. 1964. Rom in der Gedankenwelt der Byzantiner. In *Byzanz und die europäische Staatenwelt*, 70–115. Darmstadt.

Döpp, Siegmar. 1978. Claudian's Invective against Eutropius as a Contemporary Historical Document. *Würzburger Jahrbücher für die Altertumswissenschaft*, n.s. 4:187–96.

———. 1980. *Zeitgeschichte in Dichtungen Claudians*. Hermes Einzelschriften 43. Wiesbaden.

Downey, G. 1955a. Education and the Public Problems as Seen by Themistius. *Transactions of the American Philological Association* 86:291–307.

———. 1955b. Earthquakes at Constantinople and Vicinity, A.D. 342–1454. *Speculum* 30:596–600.

Drew-Bear, Thomas. 1972. Some Greek Words. *Glotta* 50:61–96 and 182–228.

———. 1977. A Fourth-century Latin Soldier's Epitaph at Nakolea. *Harvard Studies in Classical Philology* 81:257–74.

Drew-Bear, Thomas, and Werner Eck. 1976. Kaiser-, Militär-und Steinbruch Inschriften aus Phrygien. *Chiron* 6:289–318.

Dudley, D. R. 1937. *A History of Cynicism*. London.

Dunand, F. 1977. *L'apocalyptique*. Paris.

Edwards, I. E. S. 1976. *Tutankhamun: His Tomb and Its Treasures*. New York.

Enβlin, W. 1930. Zum Heermeisteramt des spätrömischen Reiches. *Klio* 23:306–25.

———. 1953. *Die Religionspolitik des Kaisers Theodosius d.Gr.* Sitz. Munich.

———. 1954. Praefectus Praetorio. *Realencyclopädie der classischen Altertumswissenschaft* 22.2:2391–502.

Errington, Malcolm. 1983. Malchos von Philadelpheia, Kaiser Zenon und die zwei Theodoriche. *Museum Helveticum* 40:82–110.

Évrard, E. 1977. A quel titre Hypatie enseigna-t-elle la philosophie? *Revue des études grecques* 90:69–74.

Fabricius, B. 1883. *Periplus des Erythräischen Meeres*.

Feissel, Denis. 1983. *Receuil des inscriptions chrétiennes de Macédoine du IIIᵉ au VIᵉ siècle*. Paris.

———, with G. Dagron. 1985. Inscriptions inédites du musée d'Antioche. *Travaux et mémoires* 9:421–61.

———. 1991. Praefatio Chartarum Publicarum: L'intitulé des actes de la Préfecture du Prétoire du IVᵉ au VIᵉ siècle. *Travaux et mémoires* 11:437–64.

Fenster, E. 1968. *Laudes Constantinopolitanae.* Diss., Munich.

Fernandez Marcos, N. 1975. *Los Thaumata de Sofronio: Contribucion al estudio de la Incubatio Cristiana.* Madrid.

Festugière, A. J. 1945. Sur les hymnes de Synésios. *Revue des études grecques* 58:268–77.

———. 1950. *La révélation d'Hermès trismégiste I: L'astrologie et les sciences occultes.* Paris.

———. 1959. *Antioche païenne et chrétienne: Libanius, Chrysostome et les moines de Syrie.* Paris.

Fitzgerald, Augustine. 1926. *The Letters of Synesius of Cyrene.* London.

———. 1930. *The Essays and Hymns of Synesius of Cyrene.* 2 vols. London.

Fowden, Garth. 1978. Bishops and Temples in the Eastern Roman Empire, A.D. 320–435. *Journal of Theological Studies* 29:53–78.

———. 1985. Review of Bregman 1982. *Classical Philology* 80:281–85.

———. 1986. *The Egyptian Hermes: A Historical Approach to the Late Pagan Mind.* Cambridge.

———. 1987. Pagan Versions of the Rain Miracle of A.D. 172. *Historia* 36:83–95.

———. 1990. The Athenian Agora and the Progress of Christianity. Review of Frantz 1988. *Journal of Roman Archaeology* 3:494–501.

Fowler, D. H. 1987. *The Mathematics of Plato's Academy.* Oxford.

Frank, R. I. 1969. *Scholae Palatinae: The Palace Guards of the Later Roman Empire.* American Academy in Rome Papers and Monographs 23. Rome.

Frantz, Alison. 1988. *The Athenian Agora XXIV: Late Antiquity: A.D. 267–700.* Princeton.

Fraser, P. M. 1972. *Ptolemaic Alexandria.* Oxford.

Frend, W. H. C. 1985. *The Donatist Church.* 3d ed. Oxford.

Fritz, W. 1898. *Die Briefe des Bischofs Synesius von Kyrene: Ein Beitrag zur Geschichte des Attizismus im IV. und V. Jahrhundert.* Leipzig.

Garzya, Antonio. 1973. Synesius' Dion als Zeugnis des Kampfes um die Bildung im 4. Jh. n. Chr. *Jahrb. Österr. Byz. Gesell.* 22:1–14.

———. 1974. *Storia e interpretazione di testi bizantini.* London.

———. 1978. Problèmes textuels dans la correspondance de Synésios. *Byzantine Studies/Etudes byzantines* 5.1–2:125–36.

———. 1979. *Synesii Cyrenensis epistolae.* Rome.

———. 1986. I germani nelle letteratura greca tardoantica. In *Byzance: Hommage à André N. Stratos* 2:425–44. Athens.

———. 1989. *Opere di Sinesio di Cirene.* Classici greci: Aurori della tarda antichità e dell'età bizantina. Turin.

Gibbon, E. 1909. *The Decline and Fall of the Roman Empire,* edited by J. B. Bury. London.

Gluschanin, Eugenij P. 1989. Die Politik Theodosius' I. und die Hintergründe des sogenannten Antigermanismus im oströmischen Reich. *Historia* 38:224–49.

Goodchild, R. G. 1971. *Kyrene und Apollonia.* Zurich.

———. 1976. *Libyan Studies.* London.

Goulet-Cazé, M.-O. 1990. Le cynisme à l'époque impériale. *Aufstieg und Niedergang der römischen Welt* II.36.4:2720–833.

Grabar, A. 1936. *L'empereur dans l'art byzantin*. Strasbourg.

Grafton, A. 1983. Protestant versus Prophet: Isaac Casaubon on Hermes Trismegistus. *Journal of the Warburg and Courtauld Institutes* 46:78–93.

Grégoire, Henri. 1907. *L'Eparchos Romes*: À propos d'un poids-étalon byzantin. *Bulletin de correspondance hellénique* 31:321–27.

Griffin, M. T. 1984. *Nero: The End of a Dynasty*. London.

Griffiths, J. Gwyn. 1956. Plutarch, *Moralia* 351F. *Classical Review*, n.s. 6:103.

———. 1960. *The Conflict of Horus and Seth*. Liverpool.

———. 1965. Plato on Priests and Kings in Egypt. *Classical Review*, n.s. 15:156–57.

———. 1970. *Plutarch's de Iside et Osiride*. Cardiff.

———. 1980. *The Origins of Osiris and His Cult*. Numen Suppl. 40. Leiden.

Grigg, Robert. 1977. *Symphonian Aeido tes Basileias*: An Image of Imperial Harmony on the Base of the Column of Arcadius. *Art Bulletin* 59:469–82.

Groag, E. 1946. *Die Reichsbeamten von Achaia in spätrömischer Zeit*. Dissertationes Pannonicae 1.14.

Grosse, R. 1920. *Römische Militärgeschichte*. Berlin.

Grube, G. M. A. 1965. *The Greek and Roman Critics*. London.

Grumel, V. 1951. L'Illyricum de la mort de Valentinien Ier (375) à la mort de Stilicon (408). *Revue des études byzantines* 9:5–46.

———. 1958. *La chronologie*. Traité d'études byzantines 1. Paris.

Grützmacher, G. 1913. *Synesios von Kyrene: Ein Charakterbild aus dem Untergang des Hellenentums*. Leipzig.

Güldenpenning, A. 1885. *Geschichte des oströmischen Reiches unter den Kaisern Arkadios und Theodosios II*. Halle. Reprint, Amsterdam, 1965.

Gundel, W. 1922. Kometen. *Realencyclopädie der classischen Altertumswissenschaft* 11:1143–93.

Guyot, Peter. 1980. *Eunuchen als Sklaven und Freigelassene in der griechisch-römischen Antike*. Stuttgarter Beiträge zur Geschichte und Politik 14. Stuttgart.

Hadot, Ilsetraut. 1978. *Le problème du Néoplatonisme alexandrin: Hieroclès et Simplicius*. Paris.

Hadot, Pierre. 1971. *Marius Victorinus: Recherches sur sa vie et ses oeuvres*. Paris.

Hägg, Tomas. 1983. *The Novel in Antiquity*. Berkeley.

Harvey, Susan Ashbrook. 1990. *Asceticism and Society in Crisis: John of Ephesus and the Lives of the Eastern Saints*. Berkeley.

Hauck, A. 1911. *Welche griechischen Autoren der klassischen Zeit kennt und benützt Synesius von Cyrene?* Mecklenburg.

Heath, T. 1926. *The Thirteen Books of Euclid's Elements*. Vol. 1. 2d ed. London.

Heather, Peter J. 1988. The anti-Scythian Tirade of Synesius' *de Regno*. *Phoenix* 42:152–72.

Heiberg, J. L. 1880. Über Eutokios. *Jahrbücher für classische Philologie*, Suppl. 11:363–71.

————. 1882. *Literargeschichtliche Studien über Euclid*. Leipzig.

Helm, R. 1932. Untersuchungen über den auswärtigen diplomatischen Verkehr des römischen Reiches im Zeitalter der Spätantike. *Archiv für Urkundenforschung* 12:375–436 (= Olshausen, E., and H. Biller, eds. 1979. *Antike Diplomatie*. Wege der Forschung 462:321–408. Darmstadt).

————. 1948. *Der antike Roman*. Berlin.

Hemberg, B. 1950. *Die Kabiren*. Uppsala.

Hense, O. 1909. *Teletis reliquiae*. 2d ed. Tübingen.

Hermann, A. 1962. Erdbeben. *Reallexikon für Antike und Christentum* 5:1070–113.

Hermelin, Ingebord. 1934. *Zu den Briefen des Bischofs Synesios*. Uppsala.

Heussi, K. 1917. *Untersuchungen zu Nilus dem Asketen*. Leipzig.

Highet, Gilbert. 1983. Mutilations in the Text of Dio Chrysostom. In *Classical Papers*, edited by Robert J. Ball, 74–99. New York.

Ho Peng Yoke. 1962. Ancient and Medieval Observations of Comets and Novae in Chinese Sources. In *Vistas in Astronomy* 5, edited by A. Beer, 127–225. New York.

————. 1966. *The Astronomical Chapters of the Chin Shu*. Paris and The Hague.

Hoffmann, Dietrich. 1969. *Das spätrömische Bewegungsheer*. Epigraphische Studien 7.1–2, vol. 1. Düsseldorf.

————. 1970. Ibid. Vol. 2.

Höistad, R. 1948. *Cynic Hero and Cynic King*. Uppsala.

Holl, K. 1908. Das Fortleben der Volkssprachen in Kleinasien in nachchristlicher Zeit. *Hermes* 43:240–54.

Holum, Kenneth. 1977. Pulcheria's Crusade A.D. 421–22 and the Ideology of Imperial Victory. *Greek, Roman and Byzantine Studies* 18:153–72.

————. 1982. *Theodosian Empresses*. Berkeley.

Holum, Kenneth, and Gary Vikan. 1979. The Trier Ivory, *Adventus* Ceremonial, and the Relics of St. Stephen. *Dumbarton Oaks Papers* 33:113–33.

Homes Dudden, F. 1935. *The Life and Times of St. Ambrose*. Vol. 1. Oxford.

Honoré, Tony. 1986. The Making of the Theodosian Code. *Zeitschrift des Savigny-Stiftung für Rechtsgeschichte* 103:133–222.

Hopfner, T. 1913. *Der Tierkult der alten Ägypter*. Denkschriften Wien 57.2.

Hopkins, Keith. 1978. The Political Power of Eunuchs. In *Conquerers and Slaves*, 172–96. Cambridge.

Hunger, Herbert. 1978. *Die hochsprachliche profane Literatur der Byzantiner*. 2 vols. Handbuch der Altertumswissenschaft 12. Byzantinisches Handbuch 5. Munich.

Hunt, E. D. 1982. *Holy Land Pilgrimage in the Later Roman Empire, A.D. 312–450*. Oxford.

Jackson, H. M. 1978. *Zosimus of Panopolis on the Letter Omega*. Missoula, Mont.

Janin, R. 1964. *Constantinople byzantine*. 2d ed. Paris.

————. 1969. *Les églises et les monastères: La géographie ecclésiastique de l'empire byzantin*. Vol. 1, *Le siège de Constantinople et le patriarchat oecuménique*. Vol. 3. 2d ed. Paris.

Janson, Tore. 1964. *Latin Prose Prefaces: Studies in Literary Conventions.* Stud.Lat. Stockholmiensia 13. Stockholm.

Jeep, Ludwig. 1885. Quellenforschungen zu den griechischen Kirchenhistorikern. *Jahrbücher für classische Philologie,* Suppl. 14:53–178.

Jones, A. H. M. [1960] 1968. *Studies in Roman Government and Law.* New York.

———. 1964a. *The Later Roman Empire, 284–602: A Social, Economic and Administrative Survey.* 3 vols. Oxford.

———. 1964b. Collegiate Prefectures. *Journal of Roman Studies* 54:78–89 (= Jones 1974, 375–95).

———. 1971. *Cities of the Eastern Roman Provinces.* 2d ed. Oxford.

———. 1974. *The Roman Economy.* Oxford.

Jones, A. H. M., J. R. Martindale, and J. Morris. 1971–80. *Prosopography of the Later Roman Empire.* 2 vols. Cambridge (cited as *PLRE*).

Jones, C. P. 1978. *The Roman World of Dio Chrysostom.* Cambridge, Mass.

Jones, T. B. 1978. *In the Twilight of Antiquity.* Minneapolis.

Jüthner, J. 1923. *Hellenen und Barbaren.* Leipzig.

Kaegi, W. E. 1968. *Byzantium and the Decline of Rome.* Princeton.

Karlsson, G. 1962. *Idéologie et cérémonial dans l'épistolographie byzantine.* Uppsala.

Kennedy, George. 1980. *Classical Rhetoric and Its Christian and Secular Tradition from Ancient to Modern Times.* Chapel Hill, N.C.

———. 1983. *Greek Rhetoric under Christian Emperors.* Princeton.

Kent, J. P. C. 1978. *Roman Coins.* New York.

Keydell, R. 1956. Zu den Hymnen des Synesios. *Hermes* 93:151–62.

———. 1957. Palladas und das Christentum. *Byzantinische Zeitschrift* 50:1–3.

King, N. Q. 1960. *The Emperor Theodosius and the Establishment of Christianity.* Philadelphia.

Klauser, T. 1944. Aurum coronarium. *Röm.Mitt.* 59:129–53 (= Klauser 1974. *Gesammelte Arbeiten.* Jahrbuch für Antike und Christentum Ergänzungsband 3:292–309).

Knorr, Wilbur R. 1985. Review of Sesiano 1982. *American Mathematical Monthly* 92:150–54.

———. 1989. *Textual Studies in Ancient and Medieval Geometry.* Boston.

Kobusch, T. 1976. *Studien zur Philosophie des Hierokles von Alexandrien: Untersuchungen zum christlichen Neuplatonismus.* Munich.

Koenen, Ludwig. 1968a. Die Prophezeiungen des 'Töpfers.' *Zeitschrift für Papyrologie und Epigraphik* 2:178–209.

———. 1968b. Ibid. *ZPE* 3:137.

———. 1974. Ibid. *ZPE* 13:313–19.

———. 1984. Ibid. *ZPE* 54:9–13.

———. 1986. *Codex Manichaicus Coloniensis.* Edited by L. Cirillo and A. Roselli, 315–17. Cosenza.

Kopp, H. 1869. *Beiträge zur Geschichte der Chemie.* Braunschweig.

Krabinger, J. G. 1825. *Synesius des Kyrenäers Rede an den Selbstherrscher Arkadios oder über das Königthum.* Munich.

———. 1835. *Synesius des Kyrenaeers Ägyptische Erzählungen über die Vorsehung.* Sulzbach.

Kramer, Edna E. 1972. Hypatia. *Dictionary of Scientific Biography* 6:615–16.

Kruse, H. 1934. *Studien zur offiziellen Geltung des Kaiserbildes im römischen Reiche.* Paderborn.

Lacombrade, Ch. 1946. "Synésios et l'énigme du loup." *Revue des études anciennes* 48:260–66.

———. 1949. Notes sur aurum coronarium. *Revue des études anciennes* 51:54–59.

———. 1951a. *Synésios de Cyrène: Hellène et chrétien.* Paris.

———. 1951b. *Le discours sur la royauté de Synésios de Cyrène à l'empereur Arcadios.* Paris.

———. 1956. Sur deux vers controversés de Synésius, *Hymnos hebdomos. Revue des études grecques* 69:67–72.

———. 1961. Perspectives nouvelles sur les hymnes de Synésios. *Revue des études grecques* 74:439–49.

———. 1978a. *Synésios de Cyrène.* Vol. 1, *Hymnes.* Paris.

———. 1978b. Encore la Lettre IV de Synésios et sa nouvelle lune. *Revue des études grecques* 91:564–67.

Laistner, M. L. W. 1951. *Christianity and Pagan Culture in the Later Roman Empire.* Ithaca, N.Y.

Lane Fox, R. 1987. *Pagans and Christians.* New York.

Lemerle, P. 1971. *Le premier humanisme byzantin.* Paris.

Leo, F. 1901. *Die griechisch-römische Biographie.* Leipzig.

Lepelley, Claude. 1979. *Les cités de l'Afrique romaine au Bas-Empire.* Vol. 1. Paris.

Leroy, F. J. 1967. *L'homilétique de Proclus de Constantinople.* Studi e testi 247. Vatican City.

Levy, Harry L. 1935. *The Invective In Rufinum of Claudius Claudianus.* New York.

———. 1946. Claudian's in Rufinum and the Rhetorical ψόγος. *Transactions of the American Philological Association* 77:57–65.

Lewy, H. [1956] 1978 (with addenda and indices). *Chaldaean Oracles and Theurgy: Mysticism, Magic and Platonism in the Later Roman Empire.* [Cairo] Paris.

Liebeschuetz, W. 1972. *Antioch: City and Imperial Administration in the Later Roman Empire.* Oxford.

———. 1983. The Date of Synesius' *de providentia. Actes du VIIᵉ Congrès de la Fédération internationale d'études classiques* 2:39–46. Budapest.

———. 1984a. Friends and Enemies of John Chrysostom. In *Maistor: Classical, Byzantine and Renaissance Studies for Robert Browning,* edited by Ann Moffat, 85–111. Canberra.

———. 1984b. Review of Bregman 1982. *Journal of Hellenic Studies* 104:222–23.

———. 1985a. The Fall of John Chrysostom. *Nottingham Medieval Studies* 29:1–31.

———. 1985b. Synesius and Municipal Politics of Cyrenaica in the Fifth Century A.D. *Byzantion* 55:146–64.

———. 1986a. Review of Albert 1984. *Classical Review* 36:158–59.

————. 1986b. Why Did Synesius Become Bishop of Ptolemais? *Byzantion* 56: 180–95.

————. 1986c. Generals, Federates and Bucelarii in Roman Armies around A.D. 400. In *The Defence of the Roman and Byzantine East*, edited by P. Freeman and D. Kennedy. British Archeological Reports International Series 297: 463–74. Oxford.

————. 1987. The Identity of Typhos in Synesius' *de Providentia. Latomus* 46: 419–31.

————. 1990. *Barbarians and Bishops: Army, Church, and State in the Age of Arcadius and Chrysostom.* Oxford.

Lippold, Adolf. 1972. Theodosius II. *Realencyclopädie der classischen Altertumswissenschaft,* Suppl. 13:961–1044.

————. 1980. *Theodosius der Große und seine Zeit.* 2d ed. Munich.

Lizzi, Rita. 1981. Significato filosofico e politico dell' antibarbarismo sinesiano: Il *de regno* e il *de providentia. Rendiconti dell'accademia di archeologia, lettere e belle arti di Napoli* 56:49–62.

————. 1987. *Il potere episcopale nell' Oriente Romano: Rappresentazione ideologica e realtà politica (IV–V sec. d.C.).* Urbino.

Lloyd, A. B. 1975–87. *Herodotus Book II.* 3 vols. Etudes préliminaires aux religions orientales 43. Leiden.

Lloyd, G. E. R. 1979. *Magic, Reason and Experience.* Cambridge.

Long, Jacqueline. 1987. The Wolf and the Lion: Synesius' Egyptian Sources. *Greek, Roman and Byzantine Studies* 28:103–15.

————. 1988. A New Solidus of Julian Caesar. *American Numismatic Society Museum Notes* 33:111–18.

————. 1991. Review of Roques 1989. *Classical Philology* 86:357–64.

L'Orange, H.-P. Reprint, 1985. *The Roman Empire: Art Forms and Civic Life.* New York.

Maas, P. 1906. Review of *Codex Theodosianus cum constitutionibus Sirmondianis et leges novellae,* by Th. Mommsen and P. M. Meyer. *Göttingische gelehrte Anzeigen* 8:641–62 (= Maas 1973, 608–28).

————. 1913. Verschiedenes II: Hesychios, Vater des Synesius von Kyrene. *Philologus* 72:450–51 (= Maas 1973, 175–76).

————. 1973. *Kleine Schriften.* Munich.

MacCormack, Sabine. 1972. Change and Continuity in Late Antiquity: The Ceremony of *Adventus. Historia* 21:721–52.

————. 1981. *Art and Ceremony in Late Antiquity.* Berkeley.

MacMullen, Ramsay. 1964. Some Pictures in Ammianus Marcellinus. *Art Bulletin* 46:435–55.

————. 1966. *Enemies of the Roman Order: Treason, Unrest and Alienation in the Empire.* Cambridge, Mass.

————. 1968. Constantine and the Miraculous. *Greek, Roman and Byzantine Studies* 9:81–96.

————. 1984. *Christianizing the Roman Empire.* New Haven.

Maehler, H. 1974. Menander Rhetor and Alexander Claudius in a Papyrus Letter. *Greek, Roman and Byzantine Studies* 15:305–11.

Maenchen-Helfen, Otto. 1973. *The World of the Huns: Studies in Their History and Culture.* Edited by Max Knight. Berkeley.

Mahé, J.-P. 1982. *Hermès en Haute-Egypte.* Vol. 2. Quebec.

Malcus, Bengt. 1967. Die Proconsuln von Asien von Diokletian bis Theodosius II. *Opuscula Atheniensia* 7:91–159.

Malingrey, Anne-Marie. 1961. *Philosophia.* Etudes et commentaires 40. Paris.

Mango, Cyril. 1972. *The Art of the Byzantine Empire: 312–1453.* Englewood Cliffs, N.J.

———. 1975. *Byzantine Architecture.* New York.

Mango, Cyril, and Ihor Sevcenko. 1961. Remains of the Church of St. Polyeuktos at Constantinople. *Dumbarton Oaks Papers* 15:243–47.

Marrou, H.-I. 1952. La 'conversion' de Synésios. *Revue des études grecques* 65:474–84.

———. 1963. Synesius of Cyrene and Alexandrian Neoplatonism. In *The Conflict between Paganism and Christianity in the Fourth Century,* edited by A. Momigliano, 126–50. Oxford.

———. 1965. *Histoire de l'éducation dans l'antiquité.* 6th ed. Paris.

Maslev, S. 1966. Die staatsrechtliche Stellung der byzantinischen Kaiserinnen. *Byzantinoslavica* 27:308–43.

Mason, H. J. 1974. *Greek Terms for Roman Institutions.* Toronto.

Matthews, J. F. 1966. Review of Pavan 1964. *Journal of Roman Studies* 56:245–46.

———. 1974. Review of Jones, Martindale, and Morris 1971. *Classical Review* 24:97–106.

———. 1975. *Western Aristocracies and Imperial Court: A.D. 364–425.* Oxford.

———. 1984. The Tax Law of Palmyra: Evidence for Economic History in a City of the Roman East. *Journal of Roman Studies* 74:157–80.

Mayor, J. E. B. 1881. *Thirteen Satires of Juvenal.* Vol. 2. 3d ed. London and Cambridge.

Mazzarino, S. 1942. *Stilicone: La crisi imperiale dopo Teodosio.* Studi pubblicati dal R. istituto italiano per la storia antica 3. Rome.

———. 1966. *End of the Ancient World.* London.

McCormick, Michael. 1986. *Eternal Victory: Triumphal Rulership in Late Antiquity, Byzantium, and the Early Medieval West.* Cambridge.

McCown, C. C. 1922. *The Testament of Solomon.* Leipzig.

Millar, Fergus. 1977. *The Emperor in the Roman World.* London.

Mitsakis, K. 1967. *The Language of Romanos the Melodist.* Byzantinisches Archiv 11. Munich.

Mogenet, J., and Anne Tihon. 1981. Le 'Grand Commentaire' aux *Tables Faciles* de Théon d'Alexandrie et le *Vat.Gr.* 190. *L'antiquité classique* 50:526–34.

———. 1985. *Le 'Grand Commentaire' de Théon d'Alexandrie aux Tables Faciles de Ptolémée.* Vol. 1. Studi e testi 315. Rome.

Moles, J. L. 1978. The Career and Conversion of Dio Chrysostom. *Journal of Hellenic Studies* 98:79–100.

Momigliano, A. 1951. Review of *Libertas as a Political Idea at Rome during the Late Republic and Early Principate*, by Ch. Wirzubski. *Journal of Roman Studies* 41:146–53 (= Momigliano 1975. *Quinto contributo*. 2 vols. Storia e letteratura 135 and 136:958–75. Rome.)

———. 1963. *The Conflict between Paganism and Christianity in the Fourth Century.* Oxford.

———. 1987. *Ottavo contributo alla storia degli studi classici e del mondo antico.* Rome.

Mommsen, T. 1903. Stilicho und Alarich. *Hermes* 38:101–15 (= Mommsen 1906. *Gesammelte Schriften* 4:516–30. Berlin).

———. 1910. Die diocletianische Reichspräfektur. *Gesammelte Schriften* 6:284–302. Berlin.

———. 1887–88. *Römisches Staatsrecht.* 3 vols. 3d ed. Leipzig.

Moore, H. 1921. *The Dialogue of Palladius.* London.

Moulard, A. 1949. *Saint Jean Chrysostome: Sa vie, son oeuvre.* Paris.

Mueller, A. 1910. Studentenleben im IV. Jahrhundert n. Chr. *Philologus* 69:292–317.

Murray, Oswyn. 1970. Hecataeus of Abdera and Pharaonic Kingship. *Journal of Egyptian Archaeology* 56:141–71.

———. 1985. Symposium and Genre in the Poetry of Horace. *Journal of Roman Studies* 75:39–50.

Musurillo, H. A. 1954. *The Acts of the Pagan Martyrs.* Oxford.

Nau, F. 1906. *Revue de l'orient chrétien* 11:199f.

Neugebauer, Otto. 1949. The Early History of the Astrolabe: Studies in Ancient Astronomy IX. *Isis* 40:240–56 (= Neugebauer 1983. *Astronomy and History: Selected Essays*, 278–94. New York).

———. 1975. *A History of Ancient Mathematical Astronomy.* Studies in the History of Mathematics and Physical Sciences 1. 3 vols. New York.

Nicolosi, Salvatore. 1959. *Il "de providentia" di Sinesio di Cirene.* Padua.

Nock, A. D. 1972. *Essays on Religion and the Ancient World.* 2 vols. Oxford.

Nock, A. D., and A. J. Festugière. 1945–54. *Corpus Hermeticum.* 4 vols. Paris.

Ogilvie, R. M. 1978. *The Library of Lactantius.* Oxford.

Ommeslaeghe, F. van. 1979. Jean Chrysostome et Eudoxie. *Analecta Bollandiana* 97:131–59.

Pack, Roger. 1952. A Romantic Narrative in Eunapius. *Transactions of the American Philological Association* 83:198–204.

Page, Denys. 1981. *Further Greek Epigrams.* Cambridge.

Palanque, J.-R. 1933. *Essai sur la préfecture du prétoire du Bas-Empire.* Paris.

———. 1944. Collégialité et partages dans l'empire romain aux IVe et Ve siècles. *Revue des études anciennes* 46:47–64 and 280–98.

Pando, J. C. 1940. *The Life and Times of Synesius of Cyrene as Revealed in His Works.* Washington, D.C.

Parker, R. A. 1962. *A Saite Oracle Papyrus from Thebes.* Providence.

Paschoud, F. 1971. *Zosime: Histoire nouvelle.* Vol. 1. Paris.

———. 1976. *Cinq études zur Zosime.* Paris.

———. 1979. *Zosime: Histoire nouvelle*. Vol. 2.1–2.

———. 1985a. Zosime et la fin de l'ouvrage historique d'Eunape. *Orpheus: Rivista di umanità classica e cristiana*, n.s. 6:44–61.

———. 1985b. Eunapiana. *Bonner Historia-Augusta-Colloquium 1982/83*, 239–303. Bonn.

———. 1986. *Zosime: Histoire nouvelle*. Vol. 3.1.

Pavan, M. 1964. *La politica gotica di Teodosio nella pubblicista del suo tempo*. Rome.

Pearce, J. W. E. 1953. *Roman Imperial Coinage*. Vol. 9. London.

Peeters, P. 1941. La vie géorgienne de Saint Porphyre de Gaza. *Analecta Bollandiana* 59:65–216.

Penella, Robert J. 1984. When Was Hypatia Born? *Historia* 33:126–28.

———. 1990. *Greek Philosophers and Sophists in the Fourth Century A.D.: Studies in Eunapius of Sardis*. Liverpool.

Perler, O. 1950. Arkandisziplin. *Reallexikon für Antike und Christentum* 1:667–76.

Perry, B. 1952. *Aesopica*. Urbana, Ill.

Petit, P. 1951. Sur la date du 'Pro Templis' de Libanius. *Byzantion* 21:295–310.

———. 1956. Recherches sur la publication et la diffusion des discours de Libanius. *Historia* 5:479–509 (= G. Fatouros and T. Krischer, eds. 1983. *Libanios*. Wege der Forschung 621:84–128. Darmstadt).

Piganiol, André. 1972. *L'empire chrétien*. 2d ed. Paris.

Powell, J. Enoch. 1938. *A Lexicon to Herodotus*. Cambridge.

Praechter, K. 1912. Christlich-neuplatonische Beziehungen. *Byzantinische Zeitschrift* 21:1–27.

Pritchard, J. B. 1969. *Ancient Near Eastern Texts*. 3d ed. Princeton.

Quasten, J. 1960. *Patrology*. Vol. 3. Utrecht.

Ramsay, W. M. 1890. *The Historical Geography of Asia Minor*. London.

Reynolds, Joyce. 1959. Four Inscriptions from Roman Cyrene. *Journal of Roman Studies* 49:95–101.

———. 1960. The Christian Inscriptions of Cyrenaica. *Journal of Theological Studies* 11:284–94.

———. 1978. Hadrian, Antoninus Pius and the Cyrenaican Cities. *Journal of Roman Studies* 68:111–21.

Ridley, Ronald T. 1982. *Zosimus: New History*. Byzantina Australiensia 2. Canberra.

Rist, J. M. 1965. Hypatia. *Phoenix* 19:214–25.

Robert, Louis. 1948. Epigrammes du Bas-Empire. *Hellenica* 4. Paris.

Robinson, J. M. 1981. *The Nag Hammadi Library in English*. 2d ed. San Francisco.

Rome, A. 1936. *Commentaires de Pappus et de Théon d'Alexandrie sur l'Almageste*. Vol. 2. Studi e testi 72. Rome.

———. 1943. Ibid. Vol. 3. Studi e testi 106. Rome.

Roques, Denis. 1977. La lettre 4 de Synésios de Cyrène. *Revue des études grecques* 90:263–95.

———. 1982. Synésios, évêque et philosophe. *Revue des études grecques* 95:461–67.

————. 1987. *Synésios de Cyrène et la Cyrénaïque du Bas-Empire.* Etudes d'anti-quités africaines. Paris.

————. 1989. *Etudes sur la correspondance de Synésios de Cyrène.* Collection Latomus 205. Brussels.

Rougé, J. 1952. La navigation hivernale sous l'empire romain. *Revue des études anciennes* 54:316–25.

————. 1966. L'Histoire Auguste et l'Isaurie au IVᵉ siècle. *Revue des études anciennes* 68:282–315.

Ruether, R. R. 1969. *Gregory of Nazianzus: Rhetor and Philosopher.* Oxford.

Runia, David T. 1976. Studies in the Letters of Synesius. Diss., Melbourne.

————. 1979. Another Wandering Poet. *Historia* 28:254–56.

Russell, D. A., and N. G. Wilson. 1981. *Menander Rhetor.* Oxford.

Sabatier, J. 1862. *Description générale des monnaies byzantines.* Paris.

Saffrey, H. D., and L. G. Westerink. 1968. *Proclus: Théologie platonicienne.* Vol. 1. Paris.

Schürer, E. 1973–86. *History of the Jewish People in the Age of Jesus Christ.* Revised by G. Vermes, F. Millar, and M. Goodman. 3 vols. Edinburgh.

Schwartz, J. 1966. La fin du Sérapéum d'Alexandrie. In *Essays in Honor of C. Bradford Welles.* American Studies in Papyrology 1:97–111. New Haven.

Scott, Walter. 1924–36. *Hermetica.* 4 vols. Oxford.

Seeck, Otto. 1894. Studien zu Synesios. *Philologus* 52:442–83.

————. 1906. *Briefe des Libanius zeitlich geordnet.* Leipzig.

————. 1913. *Geschichte des Untergangs der antiken Welt.* Vol. 5. Berlin.

————. 1914. Die Reichspräfektur des vierten Jhdts. *Rheinisches Museum* 69:1–39.

————. 1919. *Die Regesten der Kaiser und Päpste für die Jahre 311–476 n. Chr.* Stuttgart.

Sesiano, J. 1982. *Books IV to VII of Diophantus's* Arithmetica *in the Arabic Translation Attributed to Qusta ibn Luqa.* Sources in the History of Mathematics and Physical Sciences 3. New York.

Shanzer, Danuta. 1985. Merely a Cynic Gesture? *Rivista di filologia* 113:61–66.

Sievers, G. R. 1870. *Studien zur Geschichte der römischen Kaiser.* Berlin.

Simon, M. 1986. *Verus Israel.* Translated by H. McKeating. Oxford.

Smith, Andrew. 1974. *Porphyry's Place in the Neoplatonic Tradition.* The Hague.

Snee, Rochelle. 1985. Valens' Recall of the Nicene Exiles and Anti-Arian Propaganda. *Greek, Roman and Byzantine Studies* 26:395–419.

Solmsen, F. 1979. *Isis among the Greeks and Romans.* Cambridge, Mass.

Sorlin-Dorigny, A. 1876. Inscriptions céramiques byzantines. *Revue archéologique,* n.s. 32:82–95.

Soury, G. 1942. *La démonologie de Plutarque.* Paris.

Spawforth, A. J., and Susan Walker. 1985. The World of the Panhellenion. *Journal of Roman Studies* 75:78–104.

————. 1986. Ibid. *JRS* 76:88–105.

Stein, E. 1934. Review of Palanque 1933. *Byzantion* 9:327–53.

———. 1949. *Histoire du Bas-Empire*. Ed. française, J.-R. Palanque. Vol. 2. Paris.

———. 1959. Ibid. Vol. 1.

Straub, J. 1943. Die Wirkung der Niederlage bei Adrianopel auf die Diskussion über das Germanenproblem in der spätrömischen Litteratur. *Philologus* 95:255–86.

Stroheker, K. F. 1970. Princeps clausus. *Bonner Historia-Augusta-Colloquium 1968/69*. Antiquitas 4.7:273–83. Bonn.

Struthers, L. B. 1919. The Rhetorical Structure of the Encomia of Claudius Claudian. *Harvard Studies in Classical Philology* 30:49–87.

Syme, R. 1968. *Ammianus and the Historia Augusta*. Oxford.

———. 1971. *Emperors and Biography*. Oxford.

———. 1976. Bogus Authors. *Bonner Historia-Augusta-Colloquium 1972/74*, 311–21. Bonn (= Syme 1983. *Historia Augusta Papers*, 98–108. Oxford).

Tannery, Paul. 1895. *Diophanti Alexandrini opera*. Vol. 2. Leipzig.

———. 1912. *Mémoires scientifiques*. Vol. 2. Paris.

Tarn, W. W. 1950. *The Greeks in Bactria and India*. 2d ed. Cambridge.

Teetgen, Ada B. 1907. *The Life and Times of the Empress Pulcheria*. London.

Terzaghi, Nicolaus. 1939. *Synesii Cyrenensis hymni*. Rome.

———. 1944. *Synesii Cyrenensis opuscula*. Rome.

Theiler, Willy. 1942. *Die Chaldäischen Orakel und die Hymnen des Synesios*. Schriften der Königsberger Gelehrten Gesellschaft 18.1. Halle.

———. 1953. Review of Lacombrade 1951. *Gnomon* 25:195–97.

Thompson, E. A. 1982. *Romans and Barbarians*. Wisconsin Studies in Classics. Madison, Wis.

Thorndike, L. [1923] 1943. *A History of Magic and Experimental Science*. Vol. 1. New York.

Tihon, Anne. 1985. Théon d'Alexandrie et les Tables Faciles de Ptolémée. *Archives internationales d'histoire des sciences* 35:106–23.

Tinnefeld, Franz. 1975. Synesios von Kyrene: Philosophie der Freude und Leidensbewältigung. *Studien zur Literatur der Spätantike*, edited by C. Gnilka and W. Schetter. Antiquitas 1.23:139–79. Bonn.

Toomer, G. J. 1976. Theon of Alexandria. *Dictionary of Scientific Biography* 13:321–25.

———. 1984. *Ptolemy's Almagest*. London.

———. 1990. *Apollonius, Conics Books V to VII: The Arabic Translation of the Lost Greek Original in the Version of the Banu Musa*. Vol. 1. New York.

Treu, K. 1958. *Synesios von Kyrene: Ein Kommentar zu seinem "Dion."* Texte und Untersuchungen 71. Berlin.

Vanderlinden, S. 1946. Revelatio Sancti Stephani. *Revue des études byzantines* 4:178–217.

Vandersleyen, C. 1962. *Chronologie des préfets d'Egypte de 284 à 395*. Brussels.

Vellay, Ch. 1904. *Etudes sur les Hymnes de Synésius de Cyrène*. Grenoble.

Vikan, Gary, and John Nesbitt. 1980. *Security in Byzantium: Locking, Sealing, Weighing*. Dumbarton Oaks Publications 2.

Viljamaa, Toivo. 1968. *Studies in Greek Encomiastic Poetry of the Early Byzantine*

Period. Commentationes humanarum litterarum Societas scientiarum Fennica 42.

Vogler, Ch. 1979. *Constance II et l'administration impériale*. Strasbourg.

Volbach, W. F. 1976. *Elfenbeinarbeiten der Spätantike und des frühen Mittelalters*. 3d ed. Mainz.

Volkman, R. 1869. *Synesius von Cyrene: Eine biographische Charakteristik aus der letzen Zeiten des untergehenden Hellenismus*. Berlin.

Vollenweider, S. 1985a. *Neuplatonische und christliche Theologie bei Synesios von Kyrene*. Forschung zur Kirchen- und Dogmengeschichte 35. Göttingen.

———. 1985b. Synesios von Kyrene über das Bischofsamt. *Studia patristica* 18:233–37.

von Haehling, R. 1978. *Die Religionzugehörigheit der hohen Amtsträger des Römischen Reiches seit Constantins I. Alleinherrschaft bis zum Ende der Theodosianischen Dynastie (324 bis 450 bzw. 455 n. Chr.)*. Antiquitas 3.23. Bonn.

Waithe, Mary Ellen. 1987. *A History of Women Philosophers*. Vol. 1, *Ancient Women Philosophers, 600 B.C.–500 A.D.* Dordrecht.

Walden, J. W. H. 1909. *The Universities of Ancient Greece*. New York.

Wallis, R. T. 1972. *Neoplatonism*. London.

Ward-Perkins, J. B. 1972. Recent Work and Problems in Libya. *Actas del VIII Congreso Internacional de Arqueologia Cristiana, Barcelona, 4–11 Octubre 1969* 1:232–33. Barcelona and Rome.

Webster, G. 1985. *The Roman Imperial Army*. 3d ed. Totowa, N.J.

Wenger, A. 1952. Notes inédites sur les empereurs Théodose I, Arcadius, Théodose II, Léon I. *Revue des études byzantines* 10:47–59.

———. 1961. L'homélie de saint Jean Chrysostome à son retour d'Asie. *Revue des études byzantines* 19:110–23.

Westerink, L. G. 1962. *Anonymous Prolegomena to Platonic Philosophy*. Amsterdam.

———. 1976. *The Greek Commentaries on Plato's Phaedo*. Amsterdam.

Weyman, C. 1894. Omonoia. *Hermes* 29:626–27.

Wilamowitz-Moellendorff, U. von. 1907. Die Hymnen des Proclos und Synesios. *Sitzungsberichte der königlich preussischen Akademie der Wissenschaften* 14:272–95.

Wilson, N. G. 1983. *Scholars of Byzantium*. London.

Wolfram, Herwig. 1988. *History of the Goths*. Translated by Thomas J. Dunlap. Rev. ed. Berkeley.

Wolska-Conus, W. 1989. Stéphanos d'Athènes et Stéphanos d'Alexandrie: Essai d'identification et de biographie. *Revue des études byzantines* 47:5–89.

Wortley, John. 1980. The Trier Ivory Reconsidered. *Greek, Roman and Byzantine Studies* 21:381–94.

Young, Frances M. 1983. *From Nicaea to Chalcedon*. Philadelphia.

Zakrzewski, Kazimierz. 1931. *Le parti théodosien et son antithèse*. Eos Suppl. 18. Lvov.

Ziegler, K. 1934. Theon 15. *Realencyclopädie der classischen Altertumswissenschaft* 5.A.2:2075–80.

Zimmermann, F. 1912. *Die ägyptische Religion nach der Darstellung der Kirchen-schriftseller und die ägyptischen Denkmäler.* Paderborn.

Zintzen, C. 1967. *Damascii vitae Isidori reliquiae.* Hildesheim.

————. 1976. Geister (Dämonen): Hellenistische und kaiserzeitliche Philosophie. *Reallexikon für Antike und Christentum* 9:640–68.

INDEX

Adventus, literary motif, 248, 258, 274–75, 348, 390

Aeschines: allusion in *De prov.*, 342

Alaric: career, 2, 4, 7, 112–13, 116–19, 121, 203, 328–33; in *De reg.*, 111–13, 116–21; Roman view of Gaïnas patterned on, 202–3, 205

Albert, Gerhard: on Gaïnas, 203; on *De reg.*, 108–9

Alchemy, text ascribed to Synesius, 52–54

Alexandria: Neoplatonism at, 49–52, 55–56, 58; local politics and murder of Hypatia, 59–62

Allegory, literary, especially in *De prov.*, 35–37, 80–82, 143–45, 266–70, 301–10, 311–16

Andronicus, governor of Pentapolis attacked by Synesius as bishop, 24, 278

Anthemius: career, 109 and n. 11, 400; political allegiances, 82–83, 185; Synesius's approaches to, 68, 89

Anth.Plan. 73 and career of Aurelian, 184–86

Antibarbarianism: as political policy, 9–10, 72, 171–72, 183, 236–52, 323–33; in *De reg.*, 109–26, 136–37; in *De prov.* 10, 117, 122–24, 206, 209–10, 213, 264–65. *See also* Aurelian; Nationalist party, supposed

Antoninus, Neoplatonist teaching at Alexandria, 51–52

Apocalypse, form of *De prov.* 1, 290–99

Apollonius, mathematical commentary by Hypatia, 48–49

Aratus, *Phaenomena:* quoted in *De prov.*, 392

Arcadius: weak emperor, 3–9; column of, 238, 247–48; in *De reg.*, 92–93, 127, 131, 138–39; possible identification in *De prov.*, 191–92

—ministers: power and rivalries, 4–10, 225, 319, 333–36; attacked in *De reg.*, 125–26, 131, 136. *See also* individual ministers

Arianism: associated with Goths, 98–100; accusation in *De prov.*, 36, 38, 79, 327–28, 335. *See also* Heresy

Aristotle: allusions in *De prov.*, 284, 349, 352

Army, Roman: Eastern mobile forces, 1–2; of Gaïnas, 201–11; of Fravitta, 224–26

Asterius of Amasea, Homily against the Kalends, 168

Astrolabe: Synesius's understanding of, 54, 55, 84 and n. 67

Athens: Neoplatonism at, 50, 56–58, 409; Synesius's visit to, 409–11

Augusta: conventions surrounding proclamations of, 170–73, 399–402

Aurelian: career, 8; appointed praetorian prefect August 399, 126; date and significance of consulate, 164–68; deposed and exiled April 400, 8, 161–75; return from exile, 233–36; patriciate, 189; second praetorian prefecture not on return from exile but in 414–16, 182–90
—supposed leader of supposed nationalist party, 9–10, 72, 333–34; barbarian policy, 121–26, 321–22, 323–33; policy toward Stilicho, 250
—political relationships: with Anthemius, 185; with Caesarius, 124, 181–82; with Eudoxia, 79, 171–72; with Eutropius, 181; with Gaïnas, 318, 335; with John Chrysostom, 171–72, 234; with Pulcheria, 77–79, 399–403; with Rufinus, 79, 180–81; with Senate of Constantinople, 334
—supposed Hellenism, 71–72, 76–77, 80–82, 83–84, 305–7; zealous Christianity: founded church of St. Stephen and secured relics of Isaac, 72–75; possibly baptized during exile, 75–77; religious policies during prefecture of 414–16, 77–79
—relations with Synesius, 71–72, 80, 126, 127, 184, 190, 235–36; represented as Osiris in De prov., 75–77, 80–82, 122–24, 149, 305–7, 314–15, 326. See also Synesius, De prov., Osiris
Aurum coronarium: and Synesius, 91–93, 302
Ausonius: shared praetorian prefecture with son Hesperius, 150

Barnes, T. D.: on Aurelian's consulate, 168; on Synesius's embassy, 92; on De reg., 107–8; on possible revisions in De prov., 1, 312–13
Bonsdorff, Max von: on John Chrysostom, Homilies on Acts, 95–101
Bregman, Jay: on Synesius's personal religion, 14, 20, 27–28, 28–35
Bury, J. B.: on Aurelian's consulate, 164

Caesarius: career, 6–9, 177–79; reappointed praetorian prefect April 400, 177–82; patriciate, 189; remained prefect till 403, 191–97
—supposed leader of supposed pro-barbarian party, 9, 72; relations with Gaïnas, 318–21; actions after massacre of Goths in June 400, 223–24, 231–33, 335–36; probable hero of Eusebius Scholasticus, Gaïnias, 83; barbarian policy, 333, 335–36; religious policy, 38, 320–21, 327–28; policy toward Stilicho, 250
—relations with Aurelian, 124, 181–82; relations with Rufinus, 180–81; relations with Senate of Constantinople, 334
—and Synesius's embassy, 320 and n. 60; represented as Typhos in De prov., 149, 177–82; degree of cultivation, 307; blamed for coup of Gaïnas in De prov., 122–23, 213, 316–23; Typhos's wife and Caesarius's wife, 276. See also Synesius, De prov., Typhos
Callinicus, praepositus sacri cubiculi of Justinian, 108
Chaldaean Oracles: Neoplatonists' interest in, 50–51; Synesius's interest in, 29, 32–33, 50, 52, 285; allusion in De prov., 354–55
Claudian: generic relationship of IV Cons. Hon. with Synesius, De reg., 81, 137–38; invective technique in In Ruf., 231, 278, 279–80; Stilichonian views of Eastern politics in In Eutr., 4, 6, 108, 116, 227–29; panegyric technique in quasi-paternal speeches, 273–74
Clearchus, urban prefect of Constantinople in 400–402, 221–22
Codex Theodosianus: dates of laws, 149–59, 175–77, 183, 184
Comet, visible at Constantinople March–May 400, 168–69
Constantinople: supposed Gothic occupation of, 207–11, 216–17; massacre of Goths in, 199–223; commemoration in of Fravitta's victory, 237–39, 247–48
—churches in, 72–75, 78, 98, 217, 327–28, 385 n. 254; comet visible at, 168–69; earthquakes at, 10, 92, 93–102; prefects of, 221–22; and Rome, 220–21, 301–2, 304; senate of, 307–8, 334–35; society, 71–84
Consulate: Aurelian's, 164–68; Fravitta's, 237, 328; Gaïnas's nomination to, 327; recognition of between courts, 164–67, 246–47
Count(s), unnamed, in Synesius's letters, 86–89

Cynic philosophy: supposed of Hypatia, 41–44; rhetorical stance, 130–31, 135

Cyrene: religion, 14–15; and Synesius's embassy, 13, 140–42, 320 and n. 60

Cyril, patriarch of Alexandria: murder of Hypatia, 59–62

Dagron, Gilbert: on political allegory in De prov., 301–10; on senatorial politics of Constantinople, 307–8, 334–35

Damascius: unfavorable picture of Hypatia, 41–44, 56–58

Demons: in historiography, 278; in invective, 278–81; in philosophical or religious contexts, 32, 285; in De prov., 279–81, 283, 286, 348–50 and n. 81, 354–56. See also Gods

Demosthenes: allusion in De prov., 344

Demougeot, Emilienne: on Aurelian, 185, 323–24, 326; on Fravitta, 224; on massacre of Goths, 199–200

Dio Chrysostom: Synesius's views on, 62–63, 135; influence on De reg., 135; influence on De prov., 265–71, 338, 343 and n. 42, 376, 379, 381

Diodorus: Egyptian cultural information in De prov., 260–61, 262, 347

Diogenes, cousin of Synesius, 89–90

Diophantus: mathematical commentary by Hypatia, 48

Dioscurius, nephew of Synesius, 18

Dualism of good and evil: in De prov., 281–83, 285

Earthquake: and date of Synesius's embassy, 10, 92, 93–102

Egypt: Greco-Roman conceptions of, exploited in De prov., 254–65

Empedocles: quoted in De prov., 282, 339

Empire, Roman: administration of, 1–9, 246; armies of, 1–2, 201–11, 224–26; barbarian policy of, 9–10, 72, 112–19, 121–26, 171–72, 183, 227–28, 231–33, 236–52, 319, 321–22, 323–36. See also Antibarbarianism; Arcadius, ministers; and individual ministers

—division and unity of: cultural, 301–3, 304–7, 308–9; political, 1, 3–4, 165–67, 246–50, 301–10, 332–33, 408

Eriulph: Goth killed by Fravitta, 251–52

Eudoxia: role in Constantinopolitan politics, 6, 8, 333–35; proclaimed Augusta January 400, 170–73, 247; relations with Aurelian, Saturninus, and John, 79, 171–72, 235; feud with John Chrysostom, 171–72, 234, 407

Eunapius: frag. 74M = 66.2B on Western information, 309; on revolt of Tribigild, 229–30; frag. 78M = 68B on Perses, 218–23, 287; frags. 82, 83, 85, 86, 87M on Fravitta, 239–52; VS on contemporary philosophers, 50–51

Eunuchs, themes associated with, 107–9, 119–20, 138–39, 228

Eusebius Scholasticus, Gaïnias: 83, 200–201

Eutocius of Ascalon, mathematical commentaries, 46–47, 48–49

Eutropius: role in politics of Arcadius's court, 6–7, 153, 181, 336; barbarian policies, 7–8, 72, 112, 115–16, 118–19, 227–28, 329; deposition, exile, and death, 8, 109, 162–63, 318, 324–25, 335

—Western court's positions on, 166, 227–28; attacked in De reg., 107–9, 116–21, 125, 131–32, 138–39; political role suppressed in De prov., 316–18

Eutychian, praetorian prefect and possible Typhos in De prov., 6–9, 149–50, 154, 155–61, 175–77, 196–97

Evagrius: biographical notice on Synesius, 34, 39–40

Evoptius, brother of Synesius, 17, 18, 21; letters of Synesius to, 20–22, 56–58, 295–96, 409–11

Eyewitness, reliability of, 1, 199–201, 206–7, 212, 214

Festugière, A. J.: on religion in Synesius's hymns, 28–31

"Foreign wisdom": 35–37, 307. See also Hellenism

Fravitta: career, 112, 116, 224–26, 245; campaign against Gaïnas and rewards, 8, 83, 224–26, 237–39, 328; execution, 236–52

Fravitta, patriarch of Constantinople, 252

Gaïnas: enters Roman service, 112, 114; promoted to magister militum on Tribigild's revolt, 5, 117, 118, 203–5, 329; alleged collusion with Tribigild, 117, 226–31, 318; overthrows Eutropius, 7–8, 109, 117–19, 162–63, 318, 324–25; coup of 400, 8, 38, 161–75, 201–11, 319–20, 322, 326–28; decay of coup ending in massacre of

Gaïnas (*continued*)
  Goths, 211–17; withdrawal from
    Constantinople and war against Fra-
    vitta, 8, 203–7, 223–24 and n. 115,
    231–32, 330; killed by Uldin and
    Huns, 9, 233, 331
—in balance of power at Arcadius's
    court, 335–36; degree of Romaniza-
    tion, 117, 201–7; relations with John
    Chrysostom, 100, 173–75, 235, 327,
    406; Nilus of Ancyra's letters to, 98,
    117
—possible target of *De reg.*, 109–10,
    116–19; exculpated for coup in *De
    prov.*, 122–24, 316–23. *See also* Syne-
    sius, *De prov.*, Scythian general and
    wife
Gods, in *De prov.*, 145; Osiris's father
    identified with, 260; in election of
    Osiris, 257–58; initiate Osiris into
    kingship, 269, 273–74, 279–80, 292–
    93; Providence of, 283–88, 300;
    images, 264; "Taboo Days of Holy
    Tears," 263–64; one prophesies to
    rustic stranger, 196, 258–59, 271, 286,
    295–98; in riot and massacre, 214–16,
    286–88, 300; in trial of Typhos, 193–
    95, 259. *See also* Demons
Goths: in Roman Empire, settlement and
    army service, 1–2, 109–21, 206–7; as
    slaves, 111; supposed occupation of
    Constantinople, 207–11, 216–17;
    massacre in Constantinople, 8, 96–
    98, 199–223. *See also* Alaric; Fravitta;
    Gaïnas; Tribigild
—popularized leather clothing, 99,
    382 n. 240; religion, 98, 99–100, 217;
    called "Scythians," 116, 298–99
—attitude of John Chrysostom, 96–99; in
    De reg., 109–21, 207; in *De prov.*,
    206–7, 209–17, 227, 264–65, 297–99,
    313–14, 316–23, 326, 335–36
Gregory Nazianzen, on Julian's Hellen-
    ism, 66–67
Greuthungi. *See* Goths; Tribigild
Güldenpenning, A.: on anti-Germanism,
    9; on chronology of *De prov.*, 315–16

Heather, Peter: on *De reg.*, 112
Hecataeus of Abdera: possible allusion in
    De prov., 260–61
Hellenism: Aurelian's supposed, 36,
    71–72, 76–77, 79–83, 304–5; gener-

ally, 66–69, 82–83, 304–5; supposed
    political force, 71–72, 79–83, 304–5,
    335; Synesius's, 36, 39, 62–69, 71–72,
    79–83, 304
Hercules, Choice of: in political allego-
    ries, 266–70
Herculian, letters of Synesius to, 26–27,
    86–91
Heresy, legislation against: of Theodo-
    sius I, 2–3, 38, 335; of Arcadius, 328;
    of Theodosius II, 78. *See also* Arianism
Hermetica: general interest in, 52, 290–
    91; influence on Synesius, 52, 264,
    290–99, 357 n. 120
Herodotus: Egyptian cultural informa-
    tion in *De prov.*, 260, 262, 264–65, 345
Herrenianus, *vicarius*: arrested and fined
    Hierax, 245–46
Hesiod: quoted in *De prov.*, 396
Hesperius: shared praetorian prefecture
    with father Ausonius, 150
Hesychius, father of Synesius, 16–17
Hesychius, eldest son of Synesius, 16, 17
Hesychius, school friend of Synesius, 16
Hierax: brought about death of Fravitta,
    239, 242–46
Hierocles, Neoplatonist teaching in Alex-
    andria, 49–50, 51–52
Homer, allusions by Synesius: *Ep.* 142,
    88; *De dono* and *De reg.*, 90; *De prov.*,
    282, 341, 385, 394
Honorius: weak rule, 3–4; relations with
    Arcadius, 238, 246–50
Hormisdas: possible urban prefect of
    Constantinople, 222
Horus: as initiate in Hermetica, 292; and
    trial of Typhos in myth, 194–95; role
    anticipated in *De prov.*, 258–59, 286,
    312–14
Hosius, *magister officiorum*: ally of Eu-
    tropius, 6–8, 108–9; possible target of
    De reg., 108–9
Hostis publicus, Gaïnas declared, 223–24
    and n. 115, 232
Huns: killed Gaïnas, 9, 233, 330–32; and
    Gothic migration in 400–401, 330–32;
    possible allusion in *De prov.*, 313–14
Hypatia: taught Synesius, 13, 40, 49–59;
    interest in Chaldaean Oracles, 50;
    supposed Cynic teaching, 41–44; in-
    terest in Hermetica, 290; interest in
    literature, 68; mathematical works,
    44–49; interest in music, 42–43; in

Neoplatonic tradition, 49–58; religion, 58–61; murder, 59–62

Illustrate: precedence and titulature, 77, 116
Isaac, Syrian monk at Constantinople, 72–75
Ision, friend of Synesius, 87–88

Jews: reference in John Chrysostom, Hom.Acts, 99; activities against, 62, 78
John Chrysostom: confirms earthquake of 400, 94–101; relations with Goths, 96–99, 100, 169–70, 173–75, 235, 327, 405–8; enmity of Eudoxia and her circle, 73, 171–72, 234–35; Homily on the Exile of Saturninus and Aurelian, 99, 173–75, 179–80; possible identification as Great Priest in De prov., 191–92
—ps.–Chrysostom, Homily to St. Thomas against Arians: refers to Alaric, 332
John, comes: exiled by Gaïnas, 8, 171; friendship with Eudoxia and hostility to John Chrysostom, 171–72, 234–35, 240–41; role in death of Fravitta, 240, 246, 249–50
John of Nikiu, Chronicle: on Hypatia, 40–41, 59–60
Jones, A. H. M.: on collegiate prefectures, 149–60; on identity of Typhos, 161, 175–78
Jones, C. P.: on Synesius and Dio Chrysostom, 62–63
Julian: and Hellenism, 66–67; panegyric technique, 81–82

Lacombrade, Ch.: on Synesius's Hymns, 18, 29
Leo: campaign against Tribigild, 7, 203, 227–29, 329
Letters: transmission of in antiquity, 27, 79
Libanius: on Caesarius, 178–79; on Constantius, 82; on Hellenism, 67; limited publication of speeches, 132–33
Liburna, in Fravitta's victory and its commemoration, 238
Libyarchy, in Synesius's family, 16–17
Liebeschuetz, W.: on Aurelian's consulate, 164–66; on Gaïnas, 161–64,

203–7; on Synesius's attitude to the bishopric, 23–24, 410–11; on Synesius's father, 16; on possible revisions in De prov. 2, 188 and n. 155, 315
Lizzi, Rita: on Synesius's attitude to barbarians, 320
Lysis the Pythagorean: allusion in Synesius, Ep. 143, 27

Magister militum: precedence of, 116. See also Alaric; Fravitta; Gaïnas; Stilicho
Magister officiorum: powers of, 6. See also Hosius
Marcellinus, Chronicle: dates of earthquakes, 92, 101–2
Marcian, patron of a literary salon in Constantinople, 79–80, 90
Marcus Diaconus, Vita Porph., 155
Marrou, H.-I.: on Synesius's personal religion, 20–21
Mazzarino, S.: on Aurelian, 185–86
Menander Rhetor: prescripts for speeches, 128–29
Monaxius, praetorian prefect in 414, 197, 400, 402
Mystery, language and theme of: in Hermetica, 292–93; in De prov., 75–76, 186–90, 263–64, 292–93, 315, 391, 393, 396–98
Myth of Typhos and Osiris: adaptation in De prov., 143–45, 256–60, 311–16

Nationalist party, supposed: supposed partisans and aims, 9–10, 72, 79–84; supposed success of, 236–52, 321–23, 323–33; De reg. supposed manifesto of, 109–21, 121–26, 137. See also Anti-barbarianism; Aurelian
Neoplatonism: at Alexandria, 49–52, 55–56, 58; at Athens, 50, 56–58, 409; supposed ideology of supposed nationalists, 10, 72; influence on Synesius's Hymns, 19, 29; supposed reference in De dono, 85; references in De prov., 81, 263, 281–90, 350–58
Nicander, friend of Synesius, 68, 83
Nilus of Ancyra, Letters, 76–77, 98, 117

Olympius, letters of Synesius to, 23–24, 87–89, 411
Orestes, prefect of Egypt: and Hypatia, 59–62

Osiris: relevance of Egyptian myth for
    De prov., 124, 179–80, 181–82, 196,
    256–60, 261, 311–16. *See also* Au-
    relian; Synesius, *De prov.*, Osiris

Pacatus: rhetorical techniques, 138, 278
Paeonius: identity and role in Synesius's
    embassy, 84–91, 134
Paganism: Aurelian's supposed, 36–37,
    71–79; Hypatia's, 58, 59–62, 68; Syn-
    esius's supposed, 19–39, 39–40, 68;
    pagan terms used with Christian ref-
    erence, 28–35, 75–77
Palladius, *Dial.Vit.Ioh.Chrys.*, 155–56,
    169–70
"Panhellenion": identity and signifi-
    cance, 71–84, 90
P.Vindob.lat. 31: and career of Eutychian,
    159–60
Parrhesia: traditional license of philoso-
    pher before ruler, 129–32, 270
Paschoud, François: on Zosimus, 240–41
Patriciate: significance of, 189
Patronage: mechanics of, 84–91, 127–32,
    134–42, 264
Pentapolis. *See* Cyrene
Peri basileias: thematic genre, 129, 137–38
Perses, urban prefect, 218–23, 287
Philostorgius, 201
Philostratus: on Dio Chrysostom, 62–63;
    on "simulated argument," 139
Photius: biographical notice on Synesius,
    39–40
Pindar: quoted in *De prov.*, 189, 353, 398
Plato: allusions in *De reg.*, 99, 350, 365;
    allusions in *De prov.*, 267, 339, 342,
    350, 356, 361, 365, 369, 375
Pliny: panegyric technique, 138
Plotinus: allusion in *De prov.*, 350
Plutarch: *De Is. et Os.* and Synesius, *De
    prov.*, 194–95, 256–63, 285, 351–52,
    359; other works and Synesius, *De
    prov.*, 350, 380
Praepositus sacri cubiculi: duties, 108
Praetorian prefect: power of, 5, 8, 316–
    18; possibility of collegiate prefecture,
    149–61; titulature (also urban pre-
    fects), 152–56, 186
—prefects of the East, tables: as attested
    in laws of 395–405, 156–58; recon-
    structed *fasti* for 395–415, 197
Probarbarian party, supposed. *See* Cae-
    sarius; Antibarbarianism; Nationalist
    party, supposed

Procopius, *Anecdota*: invective tech-
    niques, 276–77, 280
Prophecy: literary device, 110–12, 290,
    297–98, 312–15
Providence: models of, in *De prov.*,
    283–88, 300
Pulcheria: administration, 246; relations
    with Aurelian, 77–79, 399–403
Pylaemenes, friend of Synesius, 68, 83,
    90; Syn. *Ep.* 61 to, 80, 183, 235–36

Recurrence of events, cyclical, doctrine
    in *De prov.*, 288–90
Regency, possibility, 3–4, 154, 250,
    400–401
Rhetoric, formal genres: *homilia*, 129;
    presbeutikos logos, 129; *stephanotikos
    logos*, 128; panegyric and invective,
    influence on *De prov.*, 271–81, 305–7
—techniques: allegations of treachery,
    281; allegations about wives, 276–78,
    280–81; alleged popular opinion, 144,
    193–95, 236, 257–58, 269, 274–75,
    290; demonization, 278–81; philo-
    sophical slogans, 89–91, 119–20, 138,
    279; quasi-paternal speeches, 140,
    273–74; religious accusations, 36, 38,
    79, 327–28, 335; "simulated argu-
    ment," 139–40
Riddle of wolf and lion in *De prov.* 1,
    258–59, 268, 296–97, 313–14, 378–79
Rome: as name for Constantinople,
    218–21; status as capital, 304
Roques, Denis: on Synesius's life, 13 n. 1;
    on Synesius's religion, 14–15
Rufinus, praetorian prefect of Arcadius:
    career, 5, 180; barbarian policy, 72; re-
    ligious policy, 79; relations with Au-
    relian and Caesarius, 79, 180–81; in
    Claudian's invective, 278–80
Rusticity: as mark of virtue, 270

Saturninus: role in church and court poli-
    tics of Constantinople, 8, 72, 75,
    171–72, 234, 334; possible identity of
    Paeonius, 85–86
Scholae: involvement in riot and massacre
    of Goths, 208, 212–17; recruitment of,
    207
Scythians: late antique literary appella-
    tion for Goths, 116, 298–99
Secret operations: in alleged collusion of
    Gaïnas and Tribigild, 230
Seeck, Otto: on Aurelian and anti-

Germanism, 9, 183–86, 323–33; on collegiate prefectures, 149–60; on Synesius's embassy, 9, 10, 92–96

Senate: traditionally nominated Augustae, 172–73; of Constantinople, supposed political faction, 307–8, 334

Serapeum, destruction of, 53 and n. 191, 62

Severian of Gabala: concord as theme of homilies, 181–82, 248–49, 407–8

Shanzer, Danuta: on Hypatia, 42–43

Sievers, G. R.: on Aurelian, 76; on Synesius's embassy, 92

Simplicius, *magister militum*: 83–84, 85, 88, 116

Snort: object of disgust, 270

Socrates, *HE*: on Hypatia, 40–41, 43, 59–60; on Gaïnas, 199–201, 287; chronology, 407

Sophists, Synesius's attitude toward, 56–58, 62–66, 90

Souls, origins of, in *De prov.*, 282–83, 283–86, 287

Stein, E.: on council of gods and elders in *De prov.*, 193

Stephen, Saint: church built and dedicated to by Aurelian, 72–75, 78

Stilicho, *magister militum* of Honorius: relations with Eastern government, 3–4, 118, 165–67, 227–28, 246–50

Synesius: birth, 13 and n. 1, 17; family, 13–19; studies with Hypatia, 13, 40, 49–59; embassy to Constantinople, 9–10, 13, 91–102, 126, 133, 134–42, 320 and n. 60; baptism, 28–35; marriage, 18–19, 35; elected bishop, 19–26, 409–11; activities as bishop, 24–26, 38–39, 79, 278; death, 20, 188 and n. 155

—Christianity, 14–17, 19–39, 69, 79; erudition, attitude toward, 56–58, 62–66, 89–91, 135; Hellenism, 36, 39, 62–69, 71–72, 79–83, 304; Neoplatonism, scientific and occult interests, 19, 26–27, 29, 32, 49–59, 81, 85, 263, 281–90, 350–58

—nationalism, 9–10, 72, 109–21, 136–37, 301–10, 313–14, 320–23; relations with Aurelian, 71–72, 80, 126, 127, 184, 190; as witness of events in Constantinople in 398–400, 1, 9–11, 199–201, 206–7, 212, 214

—*De dono*, 84–91. *See also* Astrolabe; Paeonius

—*De reg.*: summary, 103–6; antibarbarianism in, 9, 10, 109–21, 121–26, 136–37, 303 and n. 10; Arcadius in, 119–20, 127, 131; Arcadius's ministers in, 107–9, 119–20, 131–32, 134, 136, 138–39; date, 10, 107–9, 126; literary allusions in, 90, 99; literary form, 81, 103, 130–31, 134–35, 137–38; publication, 127–33; religious stance of, 37; rhetorical exploitation of philosophy in, 90–91, 119–20, 130–31, 138, 140–42; and Synesius's embassy, 131–33, 134–42, 302–3; echoes of, in *De prov.*, 117, 320, 356–57, 382, 387

—*De prov.*: summary, 145–49; translation, 337–98

——beggarwoman, 214–15, 271, 381–82

——great priest, 191–92, 386–87

——Horus, 258–59, 276, 286, 312–14, 363, 378

——old king, 81, 262–63, 269, 273–74, 283, 293, 316–18, 345, 349–58

——Osiris: origins and childhood virtues, 272, 338–42; junior career, 178, 273, 342; election, 257–58, 262, 264–65, 268–69, 308, 345–49; initiation, 262–63, 269–70, 273–74, 283–85, 292–93, 349–58; kingship, 91, 261, 272, 274, 306, 359–61; is deposed and exiled, 75–77, 370–72; is recalled and intercedes for Typhos, 194, 274–75, 387, 390–91. *See also* Aurelian; Osiris

——Osiris's wife, 276 and n. 97, 363

——prophetic god, 196, 270, 286, 295–98, 376–79

——riot and massacre, 143, 199–217, 259, 286–88, 312–13, 380–86

——rustic philosopher: limited publication, 133, 374–75; speaks before Typhos, 125, 130, 135, 270, 375–76; receives prophecy, 196, 258–59, 265, 270, 286, 295–98, 376–79

——Scythian general and wife, 117, 122–24, 206–7, 209–17, 227, 232, 316–23, 366–72. *See also* Gaïnas

——Typhos: origins and childhood vices, 275, 338–42; junior career, 177–79, 275–76, 342–45; in election, 269, 346, 348; depression and orgies, 276, 308–9, 361–66; plot against Osiris, 258, 316–23, 366–72; tyranny, 161–62, 270, 275, 372–76; trial, 144, 191–96, 239–40, 259, 387–90. *See also* Caesarius; Eutychian; Typhos

Synesius, *De prov.* (*continued*)
——Typhos's wife: characterization of, 276–77, 280, 362–66, 373–74; her lies effect coup, 122–23, 227, 277–78, 281, 318–22, 326, 366–70
——date, 10, 312–16
——political history: allegorized, 9, 35–37, 80–82, 143–45, 266–70, 301–10, 311–16; antibarbarianism, 10, 117, 122–24, 206, 209–10, 213, 264–65; facts reflected, 122–23, 125, 154, 160–61, 167, 169, 175, 186–90, 192–93, 195–96, 209–10, 214–16, 235, 239–40; facts distorted, 123–24, 191–96, 206–7, 210–13, 227, 232–33, 236, 316–23; popular opinion alleged, 144, 193–95, 236, 257–58, 269, 274–75, 290
——mystery-language in, 75–76, 186–90, 263–64, 292–93, 315, 391, 393, 396–98; philosophy in, 81, 263, 281–90, 339, 350–58, 364, 380, 393–98; religion in, 35–37, 75–77, 79, 320–21, 327–28
——artistry of, 143–45, 253–54, 299–300; Aeschin., allusion, 342; Arat., quoted, 392; *Chald.Or.*, allusion, 354–55; Dem., allusion, 344; D.Chr., influence, 265–71, 338, 343 and n. 42, 376, 379, 381; Diod., information used, 260–61, 262, 347; Egyptiana, sources and exploitation, 254–65; Emped., quoted, 282, 339; Hecat.Abd., possible use, 260–61; Hermetica, influence, 290–99, 357 n. 120, 376–78; Hdt., use, 260, 262, 264–65; Hes., quoted, 396; Hom., allusions, 282, 341, 385, 394; panegyric and invective, influence, 271–81; Pind., quoted, 189, 353, 398; Plat., allusions, 267, 339, 342, 350, 356, 361, 365, 369, 375; Plotin., allusion, 350; Plut., influence, 194–95, 256–63, 285, 350, 351–52, 359, 380; Test.Sol., allusion, 296, 349
—*De insomn.*, 91 n. 88, 129; *Calv.Enc.*, 63; *Dion.* 62–69, 265, 290–91; lost book on hunting, 63
—Hymns: religious development in, 19, 28–29; Hymn 1 and religion, 29–35; Hymn 7 and family, 16–19
—letters: concerning Athens (*Ep.* 54, 136 to Evoptius), 56–58, 295–96, 409–11; concerning Aurelian (*Ep.* 31, 34, 48 to

Aurelian; *Ep.* 61 to Pylaemenes), 80, 183, 190, 235–36; on bishopric (*Ep.* 11 to elders of Ptolemais; *Ep.* 66, 67 to Theophilus; *Ep.* 96 to Olympius; *Ep.* 105 to Evoptius), 20–26, 411; on literary culture (*Ep.* 154 to Hypatia), 62–66; mentioning Panhellenion (*Ep.* 101 to Pylaemenes), 79–80; on patronage (*Ep.* 98, 99 to Olympius; *Ep.* 142, 144, 146 to Herculian; *Ep.* 26, 73, 101, 118, 119, 131 to misc. addressees), 86–91; on philosophical mysteries (*Ep.* 143 to Herculian), 26–27
—Nachleben, 37–38, 52–54

Taurus, father of Aurelian and Caesarius, 81, 317 and n. 53
Taurus, son of Aurelian, 185, 314 n. 47
Tervingi. *See* Goths; Alaric; Fravitta; Gaïnas; Tribigild
Terzaghi, Nicolaus: on Synesius's Hymns, 28
Testament of Solomon: allusion in *De prov.*, 296, 349
Theaetetus Scholasticus, *Anth.Plan.* 33, 108
Themistius: on Hellenism, 67; rhetorical techniques, 2, 81–82, 91, 132–33, 139–40, 279
Theodosius I: barbarian policy, 1–2, 112–15; religious policy, 1, 2–3, 38, 335; death, consequences, 1, 5; assigned Caesarius to investigate Antiochene Riot of the Statues, 178–79
Theodosius II: CONCORDIA AVGVSTORVM coinage, 248; religious legislation, 78
Theon, father of Hypatia: mathematical works, 44–48, 55; occult interests, 52, 290; possibility Synesius studied with, 54–55
Theophilus, patriarch of Alexandria: destroyed Serapeum, 53 and n. 191, 61–62; relations with Synesius, 19, 24–26, 35
Theotimus, poet client of Synesius, 68, 83, 87, 89
Thucydides: *locus classicus* for conceit in *De prov.*, 360
Trial: political, 193, 194; of Typhos in *De prov.*, 144, 191–96, 239–40, 259
Tribigild: enters Roman service, 112, 114–15; relations with Eutropius, 115–16, 118–19; revolt, 7–8, 111–21,

227–30; and Gaïnas, 117, 163–64, 226–31, 318, 324–25

Troïlus of Side, sophist, 82–84, 89–90

Typhos: relevance of Egyptian myth for *De prov.*, 124, 179–80, 181–82, 192–96, 256–60, 311–16, 318–23. *See also* Caesarius; Eutychian; Synesius, *De prov.*, Typhos

Uldin, Hun chieftain, 233, 330–33. *See also* Huns

Unfulfilled intentions, alleged of Gaïnas, 201–3, 210, 215–16, 229–30

Urban prefect: of Constantinople in 399–401, 218–22; of Rome in 399–402, 218; titulature, 155–56, 186, 220–21

von Haehling, R.: on Aurelian, 183–84

Weapons: bans on carrying, 211, 212–17

Wilamowitz-Moellendorff, U. von: on Synesius, Hymn 1, 29–30

Xenophon, *Cyr.*: allusions in *De prov.*, 340, 341

Zakrzewski, Kazimierz: on anti-Germanism, 9–10, 72; on Paeonius, 85

Zosimus: on collusion of Gaïnas and Tribigild, 162–64, 229–30; on Gaïnas's forces, 205–6, 208–9; on return of exiles, 234–36; evidence concerning death of Fravitta, 240–41

Designer: Barbara Jellow
Compositor: G&S Typesetters
Text: 10/13 Palatino
Display: Palatino
Printer: Braun-Brumfield, Inc.
Binder: Braun-Brumfield, Inc.